MIGRANT CITY

Panikos Panayi was born in London to Greek Cypriot immigrants and grew up in the multicultural city developir~~g~~ ~~1960~~ ~~1970~~ A leading authority on the history of migratio at De Montfort University.

Further praise for *Migrant City*:

'For anyone interested in the evolution of the capital this is an interesting and rewarding book. You can be familiar with the facts of everyday life in a cosmopolitan, multicultural city but still be surprised and enriched by Panayi's scholarly analysis.' James Evans, *Spectator*

'Admirably thorough ... Anyone curious about the impact of migration on the history and culture of London could do worse than read the chapter on food in this exhaustive history.' Andrew Holgate, *Sunday Times*

'*Migrant City* is a big-hearted book, brilliantly researched and accessibly written ... Panayi has given us the history of how London has pretty much always been open to the world. Long may it remain so.' Jerry White, *Literary Review*

'A love letter to the UK's capital and its history of immigration ... Complex yet hopeful, Panayi's history helps Londoners understand who they are.' Maya Goodfellow, *Prospect*

'Immigrants from near and far are the lifeblood of any great city, none more than London. This is a masterly and invaluable history of a neglected topic.' Simon Jenkins, author of *A Short History of London*

'An eclectic integration of interviews, personal stories, case-studies and historical analyses, *Migrant City: A New History of London* tells a powerful story about London's reliance on immigration. Its potency comes from its incontrovertibility; without immigration, London would not exist as we know it. Panayi bravely confronts the lazy and often arbitrary distinction between immigrant and native to boldly showcase what it really means to be a Londoner in the modern world.' David Lammy, MP for Tottenham and campaigner for the Windrush generation

'The history of London book I've been waiting a London lifetime for – Panayi delivers modern and ancient truths about this city through a personal, heartfelt style that beats from the page. In these divisive times, this is an urgent and necessary history of our capital city.' Sabrina Mahfouz, contributor to *The Good Immigrant*

'This book convincingly argues that, more than in any other city in Europe, let alone the world, migrants have shaped the destiny of London.' Francis Ghiles, *Esglobal*

'[A] compendious and illuminating survey of London ... *Migrant City* shines above all as a sprawling treasure house of immigrant trajectories framed by an unusually firm grasp of the capital's economic realities.' Boyd Tonkin, *The Arts Desk*

'In an atmosphere of closed doors and tightened borders, *Migrant City* is timely, focusing on the immigrants who have brought cultural richness to London over the centuries.' *Financial Times*

'Said to be the first history of London to show how immigrants have built, shaped and made a great success of the capital city, *Migrant City* by Panikos Panayi is a fascinating and revealing book.' John Singleton, *Methodist Recorder*

'An impressive and detailed overview of the arrival and settlement of immigrants in London over the centuries. ... It should be on the bookshelf of all those seeking to understand how London has become one of the world's leading global cities.' Anne J. Kerschen, *History*

'Detailed and well-referenced ... a valuable resource.' Jad Adams, *Who Do You Think You Are?*

'*Migrant City* is a fantastic text, combining breadth with depth and broad trends with personal stories. It will be useful to a range of scholars and students, not just those studying immigration, but to economic, urban, and social historians. Whether seeking demographic data, analysis of pivotal events, or the personal stories of everyday Londoners, *Migrant City* will, for years to come, remain a defining text on London's immigration history.' Jack Crangle, *Twentieth Century British History*

PANIKOS PANAYI

MIGRANT CITY

A NEW HISTORY OF
LONDON

YALE UNIVERSITY PRESS
NEW HAVEN AND LONDON

For information about this and other Yale University Press publications, please contact:
U.S. Office: sales.press@yale.edu   yalebooks.com
Europe Office: sales@yaleup.co.uk   yalebooks.co.uk

Set in Adobe Garamond Pro by IDSUK (DataConnection) Ltd
Printed in Great Britain by Clays Ltd, Elcograf S.p.A

Library of Congress Control Number: 2019954652

ISBN 978-0-300-21097-2 (hbk)
ISBN 978-0-300-26472-2 (pbk)

A catalogue record for this book is available from the British Library.

10 9 8 7 6 5 4 3 2

This book is dedicated to four Londoners: Avtar Singh Deogan; Surjeet Kaur Deogan; Chrystalla Panayi; and Nestoras Panayi.

CONTENTS

PLATES AND TABLES

PLATES

TABLES

ABBREVIATIONS

BI	Bishopsgate Institute
BT	Board of Trade
BUF	British Union of Fascists
CO	Colonial Office
CPWB	Constructing Post-War Britain
DO	Dominions Office and Commonwealth Relations Office
ECHP	Eastside Community History Project
FCO	Foreign and Commonwealth Office
GDA	Greek Diaspora Archive
HO	Home Office
IRA	Irish Republican Army
IRB	Irish Republican Brotherhood
JML	Jewish Museum London
KCL	King's College London
LAB	Ministry of Labour
MEPO	Metropolitan Police
MLOHC	Museum of London Oral History Collection
NA	National Archives
NRPF	No Resource to Public Funds
PCOM	Prisoners and Prison Staff
P/RAM	Personal Papers of Edith Ramsey
THLHA	Tower Hamlets Local History Archive

ACKNOWLEDGEMENTS

While this book may have emerged over many decades of thinking (essentially since the summer of 1967) and writing (since my 1985 undergraduate dissertation supervised by Roland Quinault at the Polytechnic of North London on 'The Plight of the German Community in Britain Following the Outbreak of the First World War'), I would like to thank the British Academy for providing me with a Small Grant which allowed me to complete my research by financing visits from Leicester to London during the 2016–17 academic year. I was therefore able to make use of the Bishopsgate Institute, the Black Cultural Archives, the British Library, the British Library of Political and Economic Science, the Guildhall Library, the Jewish Museum London, the London Metropolitan Archives, the National Archives, and Tower Hamlets Local History Archive. I would also like to thank Judith Garfield, who allowed me to use interviews from the Eastside Community Heritage Project, which she directs. I am grateful to the Faculty of Arts, Design and Humanities at De Montfort University, which granted me a semester free of teaching at the end of 2018 to complete the writing of this book. I would like to express special gratitude to Deborah Cartmell, the then faculty head of research and, especially, to Elizabeth Tingle, my head of school, who strongly supported this project. De Montfort University also allowed me to employ a 'frontrunner', a student research assistant in the form of the multi-talented Tabitha Bolam, who found many sources for me and travelled to various London repositories, while the project remained otherwise dormant. I am extremely grateful to Tabitha. I would also like to thank Gavin Schaffer of the University of Birmingham who wrote my British Academy reference. My colleague in history, Matt Taylor, head of the subject research committee at De Montfort,

ACKNOWLEDGEMENTS

offered support in many ways including lending me some of his football books and helping me to formulate my ideas when considering the chapter on sport. I would like to thank Matt and my colleague Dave Dee, who lent me many Jewish memoirs and other volumes. Dave also assured me that my book was evolving well during numerous lunch discussions in the staff common room at De Montfort. Having worked with Dave from his early days as an under-graduate through to the supervision of his PhD, it feels very satisfying to receive helpful advice from a former student. At Yale University Press, Marika Lysandrou and Heather McCallum offered outstanding support and I am especially grateful to Heather for commissioning this volume. I also thank my copy-editor Richard Mason. For permission to use pictorial material I am grateful to the following: Age Fotostock; Alamy; Getty; Paul Halliday; Historic England; the London Metropolitan Archives; London Metropolitan University; and the National Portrait Gallery.

The book is dedicated to four Londoners, my parents-in-law and my parents whose lives reflect those of millions of other foreigners who have made their home in the world's capital. Avtar Singh Deogan, born in Kasumo in Kenya, initially arrived in 1961 but joined the RAF and did not finally settle in London until 1966. He initially worked as a printer but then sold a variety of products from the end of the 1970s. Surjeet Kaur Deogan, a trained nurse in Kenya, reluctantly moved to join the rest of her siblings in Southall in 1970 and spent the rest of her working life employed in various west London hospitals, as well as bringing up two daughters, Mundeep, my wife, and Simrit. Nestoras Panayi arrived in 1958 and, after some temporary jobs and a spell living in Leman Street, secured employment as a pastry cook in the Lyons Corner House on Tottenham Court Road, the trade which his uncle, Halepi, had taught him in his eponymous, pioneering patisserie in Nicosia. In the Lyons Corner House my father met my late uncles Panayiotos Kourdoullou and Demetrios Louca, who introduced him to my mother. Nestoras then spent the rest of his working life in the employ of two Greek Cypriot firms, T. Pittas and Barnaby. My mother, Chrystalla Louca, arrived in Camden Town in 1960 to join her brother and sister Anna initially lodging with her uncle Charlie who had arrived in the interwar years. As well as bringing up three children (Myllia, Rodothea and Panikos), Chrystalla laboured long hours at home, paid by the piece, working for Greek Cypriot employers in the rag trade.

PROLOGUE

I became conscious in the summer of 1967. Before then I had no need to understand the world around me in the cocoon in which my Greek Cypriot immigrant parents raised me in various parts of north London, latterly at 61 Uplands Road in Hornsey (or Crouch End as my father always insisted). Only scraps of memory survive before that summer. But two events occurred in rapid succession which brought my analytical brain to life.

First, I travelled to Cyprus with my parents and my sister, Myllia, for the first time. I can recall this trip in remarkable detail, almost like a nineteenth-century imperial travel writer. I remember the journey, which, at that stage, involved changing from a jet aeroplane to a propeller craft in Athens for Nicosia airport. We spent much of the holiday with my maternal grandparents in their whitewashed, three-roomed house in the village of Lympia. The most exciting aspects of this existence for a young boy from Crouch End growing up in the key metropolis of the swinging sixties lay in the absence of running water, which meant queuing up at a well with earthenware jugs, and a lack of electricity, which necessitated the use of candles. When we next visited Cyprus in 1971 I felt disappointment at the fact that running water and electricity had arrived in Lympia. Most exciting of all, when we opened the back door of my grandfather's house, hundreds of chickens and turkeys came running towards us. When we visited my auntie Maria's, she even kept rabbits which lived in burrows in her front yard, one of which would serve as our supper.

We went to Cyrus for the wedding of my uncle Argyros to his young fiancée Aphrodite. He lived with my paternal grandparents in Mitseron and would move to his newly constructed house in nearby Arediou with his new bride. I remember the wedding day vividly, especially the shaving ritual with a cut-throat razor accompanied by a fiddler but also a note of alarm, a bad omen, that the goat slaughtered for the wedding was pregnant. During the wedding ceremony I had wandered off with one of my cousins, Savva, and came close to an accident on the main road that connects Arediou to Nicosia.

The pure joy of my first long summer in Europe came crashing down to earth a few weeks after we returned home because of the second major event of 1967: my first day at school. Many children find this event traumatic because of separation from their mother. For me, an additional disadvantage came from the fact that I did not speak any English and found myself in an alien environment, screaming my head off, which annoyed the teachers and dinner ladies who tried to calm me down, including Miss Sharpe, who, not surprisingly, became irritated. My early days at school did not improve quickly. I found myself with a number of others in a dunce class for people who could not speak English. While I made some friends, I quickly realized that I needed to stop crying (that was the instruction from my mother and teachers) in order to make it into the mainstream. This served as just one of my worries in my early days at school. When I reached the playground, dropped off by my mother, the school bully awaited me. I guess we would describe him as a racist, because the fact that I could not speak English seemed to add to the violence against me which included hair pulling, punching in the stomach and kicking. This became a daily ritual. I am not sure how long it lasted but I accepted it as part of the new world away from my parents. It ceased suddenly when one day, my father, an early-rising pastrycook, decided to go in to work slightly later and dropped me off at school. The bully experienced the same treatment as me and disappeared from my life forever.

Things would improve gradually. The transition from Greek Cypriot dialect-speaking immigrant to Londoner would take a year or two to complete. The process involved an early white English friend, Ray (or Rain in my developing English), together with Robert Burton, another white English child. Most importantly, I found a translator in the form of Laggi Efthimiou, who played a central role in my integration. By the age of seven I could read and write like the rest of my classmates. The fact that I discovered that my father spoke and understood good English helped me further as I started speaking to him in the imperial language even though he has always replied in his mother tongue.

My first schools, St Mary's Infant and St Mary's Junior, represented microcosms of London in the late 1960s and early 1970s. While aware of the fact that the children in my classes came from different ethnic backgrounds and that they were not the same colour as me in some cases, friendship simply operated on the basis of those I liked, as it seemed to do for all of my class-mates. Despite my early traumas, I became a popular member of my year group. My friends included the West Indian Carl Anderson, Noel Barratt, Andrew Hodge, Desmond McCleod (who I think was adopted by a white mother) and Eddie Malcolm (whose brother Joseph was in the same year as my sister), the mixed-race Mandy Mattis, the Sri Lankan Christopher Ludwick, Erol Songancilor (with a Turkish or Turkish Cypriot father and an English mother, who told me I was a good dancer when I went to her son's birthday party, a compliment I have never received since), together with the Greek Cypriot Mylitsa Charalambous, the Italian (or Spanish) Sylvia Pereino, and a series of white English (or perhaps in some cases Welsh) kids including Anne Evans, David Spencer and Denise Treveleyan. My early school years also involved two Indian teachers who wore saris. This early experience of diversity formed the way I think and orientate myself to the extent that, as an adult, I have found countless situations in which a lack of diversity makes me feel uncomfortable, which I initially realized when I moved to my first academic position at Keele University in 1989–90, working in an all white male history department (although one of the white males, Colin Richmond, had a profound influence on me by telling me to be myself) and an almost all white city so that on one occasion, while walking home, a child called me 'Paki'. When I took up my permanent post in Leicester in 1990 I felt more at home in a city with a significant Indian and West Indian community, although not as diverse as London.

Returning to my childhood, another key turning point in my life happened in 1972, when I went to my first Chelsea match, after pestering my father for years. This established my identity as a Londoner and, just as importantly, in that year, I read my first Enid Blyton book, which revealed to me the power of the written word. By that time, some of the West Indian boys in my class had become conscious of the consequences of their difference and I think they even accused one of my teachers, Mr Emmett, a veteran of the Second World War, of racism. By the end of my junior school racialized terms such as 'honky' and 'sambo' had entered the playground largely as a result of the broadcast of the racial situation comedy *Love Thy Neighbour*. My secondary education took place at Stationers' Company's School, an even more diverse environment, where the white British constituted the minority unlike in St Mary's – where I seem to remember an English majority. By the time we left this inner-city school we had become fully conscious of the meanings of racism. Perhaps the most remarkable fact about my secondary education in a failing school, which would cease to exist a few years after I left, is that while 270 boys began my year group, only 5 left with A levels.

The narrative that follows, while based upon decades of scholarly research, evolves from my experience and history as a native-born Londoner. The book tells the story of the role of migrants and their offspring in the evolution of one of the world's great capitals. I have made use of interviews, memoirs, autobiographies and biographies as much as possible, although this has proved easier in some chapters, such as those on 'Fighters and Footballers' (Chapter 10) and musicians (Chapter 11), in comparison with 'Ghetto and Suburb' (Chapter 2) or 'Cheap Labour' (Chapter 3), because those at the bottom end of the social scale tend not to write about their experiences. The book integrates numerous personal stories into the history of London in an attempt to demonstrate that immigrants constitute real Londoners in the same way as the white British do. While the writing focuses upon the former, who have arrived from all over the world, it argues that the lives of immigrants mirror those of natives, especially as, over time, the children of immigrants become natives themselves. The volume focuses especially upon the nineteenth and twentieth centuries, although it goes back further where necessary and many of the chapters also take into consideration the twenty-first century. While it tries to tackle as many groups as possible, the book focuses upon the most numerous, long-lasting and impactful groups in London's history: the Irish; the different streams of Jews who have migrated to the city; West Indians and Africans; South Asians, especially Punjabis, Gujaratis, Bangladeshis and Pakistanis; Cypriots; Germans; Italians; and East Europeans, especially Poles. It focuses upon the first and second generations and also deals with short- and long-term residents. While the book deals with London as a whole, according to the time period covered, those areas which have most experience with immigrants, especially the East End, receive the most attention.

The book serves as a case study for the importance of migration in the modern world. However, the heart of Empire, the largest city in the world for most of the nineteenth and twentieth centuries, has a series of features which make it unique. First, with the exception of Rome and not on such a significant scale, London has experienced migration for longer than any other city: indeed, a migrant (invader) group in the form of the Romans established it. Second, taking a national perspective, London has counted more than half of most communities which have settled in Britain (in some cases considerably more) including, for example, nineteenth-century Germans and twentieth-century Cypriots. For Jewish and black settlers London served as the heart of these communities. Third, London became incredibly diverse by the end of the twentieth century. While a series of groups including the Irish, Jews, Germans and Africans had a long history of settlement in the metropolis, the early post-war years meant that immigrants began to originate from beyond Europe in large numbers (hundreds of thousands), especially from the Empire and Commonwealth, for the first time. By the beginning of the twenty-first century, London could count immigrants from every part of the world.

Immigration has played a central role in the evolution of London because, from the eighteenth century, linked with the development of Empire, it became the most important city in the world, whether in terms of political power (the heart of Empire or the seat of the first democracy attracting people of all political persuasions), finance, commerce, demography or culture, high and low. While it may have reached its peak in the late nineteenth and early twentieth centuries any decline since that time remains relative, overtaken, or perhaps equalled, by cities such as Tokyo and New York. If the last two centuries have seen a type of globalization never previously experienced in world history, the city which has played the leading role for the longest period of time in this process has been London, politically, commercially, financially and culturally. For this reason, London has acted as a magnet for people from all over the world.

This book does not simply tell the same old story about the exploitation and persecution of migrants or the way in which London provides opportunities for social mobility allowing people to rise from rags to riches (although both of these issues receive detailed attention). Instead, it argues that the relationship between migration and the evolution of London only becomes fully comprehensible by accepting that migrants have impacted upon all sectors of the economy, society and culture. While the majority of immigrants have entered the lower echelons of the labour market, London has also acted as a key centre for global elites, especially bankers but also, for example, musicians and, in recent decades, footballers. Migrants have played a role in all sectors of the economy, whether builders, waiters, factory workers, shopkeepers, bankers, footballers or musicians.

The book investigates the impact of immigration upon specific aspects of London life, each covered within the individual chapters. Collectively, they demonstrate how the history of modern London and the history of immigration into the city have become the same. Without the arrival and impact of international settlers, the history of this urban space would have taken a completely different trajectory. In short: no immigration, no London. Or certainly not as it has evolved in terms of cultural diversity and wealth.

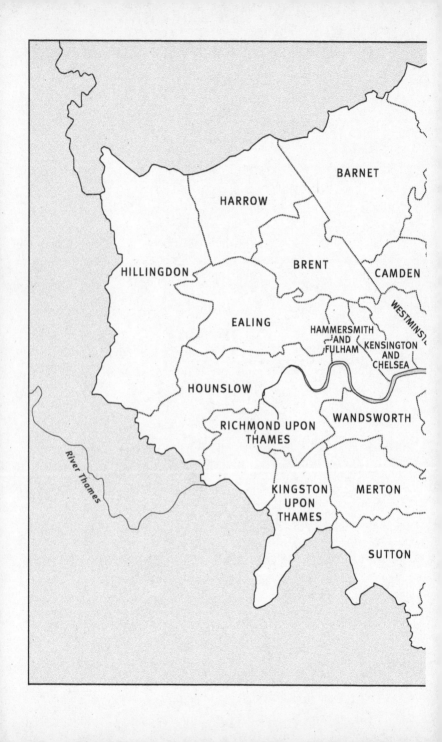

1

THE UNIQUENESS OF LONDON

No one knows exactly what London is, where it begins or ends, or how many people inhabit it. It is a city, a county, a postal district, and it is ever spreading, growing, and changing its form.[1]

The cosmopolitan character of London is generally known but perhaps indifferently realized. Statistics are sometimes presented showing how large an army of strangers is in occupation, and of what curiously mixed contingents it consists. But it is hard to clothe such figures with the interest that would bring about their proper appreciation. And the wonderful, mobile, shifting mass is a marvel, from so many points of view, that curiosity is easily satiated without considering details. The great metropolitan hive may fitly be called a 'City of Nations'.[2]

At the beginning of the twenty-first century a new age of migration[3] appears to have emerged in which, against a backlash from nativist sentiment in much of the developed world, migrants have become increasingly visible and targeted. This new age of migration appears linked to a new era of globalization in which not only people but also goods and services seem more mobile than at any time in human history. The apparently increasingly mobile age has meant that advanced Western states have become *de facto* multicultural[4] in the sense that people with migrant backgrounds have become visible in the labour market, especially its lower echelons, but also in the evolution of residential ethnic concentrations, especially in larger cities. At the centre of twenty-first-century globalization lie major international metropolises with mixed-up populations, playing leading roles in the global marketplace. Such centres include New York, Frankfurt, London and Tokyo, although the last of these has experienced relatively little immigration compared with the other three.[5] These new global cities not only contain diverse populations, they also have the characteristics of a hierarchical division of labour linked with neo-liberal economics, which has given rise not simply to an era of unprecedented growth (despite the 2008 financial crash) but also increasing inequalities compared with the period of the 'post-war consensus' covering the four decades after the end of the Second World War when Britain, for example, would experience the most egalitarian era in its history. These new global cities, epitomized by London, therefore appear to share several characteristics, above all: the internationalization of their economy through the entry of firms from other parts of the world; the increasing ethnic diversity of their workforce and population; and, as a consequence of the first two, increasing inequality.[6]

Such assumptions lack historical perspective, viewing the late twentieth and early twenty-first centuries in particular against the background of the relative equality of the post-war consensus years; failing to take account of the history of globalization, which has impacted upon everyday life since the European 'discovery' of the Americas; as well as ignoring the role of local, national, continental and international migration in the evolution of many of the major metropolises which exist in the world today over decades if not centuries.

While London has much in common with many of the other global cities which exist today, it has, purely from the point of view of migration, five characteristics that help to make it unique. First, it has a history of immigration dating back at least two millennia, linked to the fact that migrants, in the form of invading Romans, founded the city. Within the British context, whereas some urban locations may have attracted immigrants for shorter periods of time, which may have lasted for centuries, the migration history of London stretches over two millennia, mirroring its history as a city. Two of the most significant communities in the city's entire history, the Jews and the Irish, have resided there continuously on a significant scale, replenishing themselves regularly for close to a thousand years.[7] Second, it has become 'super-diverse' in recent years due to the range of countries from which the population of the British capital has originated as well as the range of languages spoken and religious pluralism,[8] although, once again, we need to beware of the contemporaneity of such developments because of the longevity of migration to London linked with its long history as a global metropolis. Perhaps 'cosmopolitan'[9] sums up its long-term history of attracting people from beyond British shores, as well as emphasizing its international nature. A third unique characteristic, within the British context, lies in the fact that, for much of its history, especially the last two centuries, London has served as home to at least half, and often more, of most of the migrant groups which have settled in Britain. Fourth, as the city and its population have increased together with the number of immigrants, the concentration of foreigners has moved away from the East End heartland where migrants settled for much of the nineteenth century (and continue to do so)[10] to encompass the entire capital of Britain.[11] Fifth, migrants to London do not simply fit into neat theories of labour migration acting as a surplus labour supply, carrying out the work which natives refuse to undertake and therefore undermining the living standards of people born in the capital because of their readiness to accept less pay.[12] Migrants into London have played this role throughout its recent history, and not simply since 2000[13] or since 1945, but over the course of the last two centuries. However, London's foreign population has never simply carried out work which those higher up on the social scale have shunned. Migrants have found employment throughout the economic spectrum from the banking and mercantile elites who played a central role in its medieval and early modern history and who have remained a central characteristic of London life almost throughout its history.[14] At the same time, the global capital became a city of opportunity for many of those who moved towards it, as the growth of migrant shops and shopkeepers since the end of the nineteenth century indicates.[15] Migration has shaped the evolution of the global metropolis both because of the sheer numbers of foreigners who have moved to London but also because they have engaged in occupations on all parts of the social spectrum, from Irish navvies in the nineteenth century to Russian billionaires in the twenty-first century, and in all areas of the city's economy and culture ranging from Georg Friedrich Handel to Thierry Henry.

THE DEVELOPMENT OF THE GLOBAL CITY

Any understanding of the importance of London as a magnet for migration needs to appreciate its international importance since its development as a city within the Roman Empire and, more importantly, since the rise of the concept of globalization which, in the modern era, became inextricably linked with the expansion of the British Empire. London did not assume its international position as a result of the 'liberation' of markets at the end of the twentieth century, because this status had emerged over centuries.

Before the arrival of the Romans the area now covered by London 'was occupied . . . by only a scattered rural population in units no larger than a small village, gaining its living mainly by mixed farming, supplemented to some extent by fishing'.[16] Londinium emerged as a Roman city in the first century AD. What concerns us here is its international importance, which seems questionable at this stage although 'it became the largest city in Britain and the fifth most populous Roman centre north of the Alps, with some 30,000 inhabitants by the year 250, and even more in the next century, the halcyon days of Roman London'.[17] Its national and international importance from Roman times onwards lay in the fact that 'it stands in a superb position: ideal for communication both with the rest of the country and with the Continent'.[18] London became central in the Roman road system.[19]

At this stage of its history London maintained national and north European importance, although it remained a relatively minor outpost in the Empire. Its status as the biggest city in Britain, but with relatively limited importance beyond, did not change for over a millennium after the withdrawal of the Romans in the early fifth century as Saxons, Vikings and Normans took control of the city. However, it became an increasingly important centre of international trade as merchants from all over Europe entered the city from the Norman period onwards.[20] The arrival of Christianity and the establishment of the first St Paul's Church at the beginning of the seventh century also indicate the internationalization of London.[21]

The development of London into a global capital from the early modern period and, more especially, during the nineteenth century, remains inextricably linked with its status as the heart of Empire so that by 1900 it, rather than Paris, had become the capital of the world.[22] Roy Porter dates its status as 'the world's greatest city' from 1570 to 1986, from the opening of the Royal Exchange until the closure of the Greater London Council,[23] although, since the publication of his social history of the capital in the early 1990s, it has gone a long way to regaining this status.

London's position as the heart of a vast commercial and political network determined the fact that it became the largest city in the world, which, despite the importance of immigration in recent history, especially after 1945, largely occurred because of population movement within Britain (although we would have to include the Irish within this equation). While London in 1550 retained its status as the dominant city in England, which it had held since the Roman Empire, it remained largely on the periphery of Europe, away from the wealth and culture of the continent in which the English language remained irrelevant.[24] However, two centuries later, as a result of the economic and mercantile transformation driven by both English and foreign merchants[25] helping to develop a global empire, 'the Union Flag flew from Canada to India, and from Gibraltar to Tahiti'. Not only did London hold the status of imperial capital, it had become Europe's 'greatest port, its financial and banking centre and its largest city, inhabited by about 675,000 people'. London had also expanded physically beyond the old City as far as the West End, Westminster, Marylebone, Hoxton, Islington and Southwark. In this first age of globalization London traded goods from all over the world ranging from tea to slaves,[26] which resulted in the development of the first significant black population in the capital. By 1800 London housed 900,000 people. From the late seventeenth century the population had increased as a result of migration towards London from all over England, as well as Ireland and Scotland, together with, on a much smaller scale, the arrival of refugees from the wars of religion following the Protestant Reformation on the continent, as well as a growth in the birth rate and a fall in the death rate.[27]

These trends would continue during the eighteenth century when London further developed into a 'great emporium'[28] and, as part of the globalization process, also evolved into the largest shipbuilder and largest shipowner in the world,[29] which, in consequence, also meant that the areas covered by docks expanded. This emporium and the ships and docks associated with it meant that a growing merchant class imported a vast quantity and variety of goods from all over the world.[30] Despite the population increase, for most of the eighteenth century burials continued to exceed baptisms, a situation which did not reverse consistently until the 1790s. Most population growth continued as a result of migration from other parts of England, but the eighteenth century also witnessed a notable increase in the number of foreigners with the development of visible Irish, Jewish and black communities, as well as the arrival of other continental European groups, especially Germans.[31]

The status of London as the world's greatest city in terms of both size of population and economic power continued into the nineteenth and early twentieth centuries when it would reach its zenith. *The Million-Peopled City*[32] which emerged in the early nineteenth century created almost a new civilization described by numerous contemporaries epitomized by Charles Dickens but incorporating countless others, who focused especially upon the diversity of people who lived in this great urban settlement. John Garwood revealed one half of the 'million-peopled city' to the other half. While the volume he wrote partly consisted of middle-class gawping at and disapproval of poverty with a focus on 'criminal and destitute juveniles', it also dealt with Greenwich and Chelsea pensioners, cab drivers, omnibus men and, above all, the Irish.[33] Similar classic works on Victorian London included John Thompson and Adolphe Smith's *Street Life in London*, which covered a broader array of people and themes including sellers of shellfish, nomads and street doctors.[34] Perhaps the most famous of these panoramas of the Victorian metropolis consisted of Henry Mayhew's writing for the *Morning Chronicle*,[35] focusing upon the poor in the middle of the nineteenth century, Charles Booth's scientific account of London in the late nineteenth century[36] and, above all, because of the breadth of subjects it covers, including a large array of migrant communities, the three volumes edited by George R. Sims appearing at the beginning of the twentieth century as *Living London*. This also moves away from the focus on poverty driving Mayhew and Booth, to incorporate a vast array of aspects of the capital's life, including the ethnic diversity of its population.[37]

This Victorian Babylon,[38] the heart of Empire, continued the growth which had begun from the seventeenth century and which intensified during the nineteenth, reaching a zenith on the eve of the First World War. Despite the economic transformation of much of Britain and Europe from the end of the eighteenth century, 'the metropolis was the greatest centre of industrial production in Britain and Europe, before, during and after the industrial revolution'.[39] Even in the middle of the nineteenth century its residents found employment in a wide variety of occupations, with manufacturing accounting for just 33.48 per cent, followed by domestic service with 22.42 per cent, indicating the inequality which existed but also the importance of this sector in Victorian Britain, followed by 'dealing' at 11.91 per cent. Statistics from the 1851 census also pointed to the importance of building and general labour.[40] London also constituted the heart of the world financial system as well as the trading centre of the country and the world beyond, building on its status as an emporium from the eighteenth century and evolving into an entrepot, meaning a further development of the docklands.[41] The city expanded both demographically and geographically. The 958,863 inhabitants of 1801 had increased to 6,586,000 by 1901, 'a fifth of the inhabitants of England and Wales' largely because of international migration, with over 80 per cent of those arriving between 1841 and 1891 originating in Great Britain, 7 per cent from Ireland and 10 per cent from other parts of the world, overwhelmingly Europe;[42] although the period from the late eighteenth until the middle of the nineteenth century also resulted in a fall in London's death rate which now resembled the rest of the country, due to some improvement in cleanliness and some growth in living standards.[43] Nevertheless, the London slum evolved in the metropolis to house the population growth, both in reality and in middle-class fears,[44] as many of the newcomers found homes in the urban sprawl which occurred, swallowing an increasingly large section of the surrounding countryside. Some of the areas devoured by the expansion such as St Pancras had greater populations than some of the major provincial cities including Bradford, Bristol or even Leeds.[45] The growth of the first four decades of the century 'was broadly bourgeois in tone, making its biggest push in the north and west'. The middle of the century meant 'amazing hypergrowth', which involved both the middle and working classes 'pushing in every direction at once in a frantic land-rush, with railways the engine of change'. Finally, the 1880s and 1890s meant continued growth mostly in the east and especially involving 'the lower-middle and artisan classes'.[46]

By 1900 the heart of Britain and its Empire had reached a mature status emerging from the chaotic growth which had characterized the nineteenth century. The essays in the volume by George R. Sims do not concentrate on the dangers of outcast London,[47] focusing instead, as the subtitle suggests, upon *Its Play, Its Humour and Its Pathos, Its Sights and Its Scenes*,[48] while Ford Madox Ford's simultaneously published survey also moves away from the concern with poverty which characterized Victorian writers.[49] The mature imperial metropolis gained validation from the grandiose reconstruction of Westminster to reflect its rule over 400 million people and its international economic and cultural importance. By this time imperial elites, conceptualizing their nascent nationalist ideas, were flocking to London, as goods and people passed through the capital in ever increasing numbers.[50]

Following the early twentieth-century zenith, London experienced a decline, reflecting the Empire over which it ruled, but this decline remained relative in comparison with national or imperial decay. The city continued to grow in both geographic and demographic terms, reaching a peak population of 8,615,000 in 1939.[51] The space covered by the capital doubled between 1919 and 1939, stretching 'from Cheshunt in the north to Banstead in the south, and from Uxbridge in the west to Dartford in the east'.[52] A unified transport system helped the growth of the suburbs and the evolution of the semi-detached home, while the capital continued to experience economic expansion despite the instability of the interwar economy, in both the manufacturing and the service sectors,[53] although the latter had already accounted for a significant proportion of employment during the nineteenth century in view of the capital's importance in commerce and banking.[54] Britain remained 'the greatest maritime nation' with London 'their greatest port, the greatest in the world, New York perhaps excepted'.[55] This economic success, however, should not obscure the reality of urban poverty which characterized parts of inner London at this time.[56] By the 1930s the capital, especially Soho, had also become important in cosmopolitan avant-garde popular culture including dancing and jazz.[57] The interwar years also witnessed the development of a unified London government as the London County Council, established in 1889, reached maturity.[58] The growth of the city became increasingly planned, especially with regard to the emergence of the suburbs and the green belt, consolidated in the passage of the Town and Country Planning Act of 1947 and the development of the Greater London Plan, which meant that the sprawling city of the nineteenth century became far more controlled.[59]

Post-war recovery from the Blitz meant a gradual rebuilding of the areas in the City and the East End destroyed by German bombers, as well as a continuing relative decline, again not quite as dramatic as that which afflicted the country and more especially the disappearing Empire. One of the most obvious indicators of London's decline consisted of the reduction in population. Although it still totalled just over 8 million in 1951, it had fallen to just below 7 million by 1993[60] largely because white Londoners moved to other parts of the south-east[61] at the same time as people migrated towards the capital from parts of the world beyond Europe which had previously sent a trickle. In the first few decades after the end of the Second World War, London witnessed a decline in manufacturing that had sustained growth in the interwar years, while the docks virtually disappeared with the growth of Tilbury on the Thames estuary, which took over the transhipment that had characterized the eastern half of the capital.[62] In 1991 'London had endured two decades of sluggish growth', even 'lagging behind the national average'[63] in contrast to most of the previous four centuries.

Since that time London has risen to the type of global pre-eminence which characterized the city when it served as the heart of Empire. This was largely driven by the 1986 'Big Bang' in financial services, meaning that it consolidated its position as a global financial capital with the number of foreign banks operating in the city increasing from the 500 in 1991,[64] indicating that it had never lost its pre-eminent financial position. London's economy has seen growth rates which exceed those of similar global cities, driven by the financial sector.[65] The clearest indication of the continuing global importance of London lies in the fact that the population decline which had characterized the early post-war years significantly reversed, so that in 2015 it counted more residents than at any time in its history, surpassing the peak 8.6 million of 1939 and reaching 8.8 million by the summer of 2017, with some projections suggesting that it would rise to 11 million by the middle of the century.[66] Much of the population growth from the 1990s onward occurred as a result of immigration, building on the fact that while the white working classes may have increasingly moved to the suburbs in the second half of the twentieth century, immigrants had increasingly taken their place. While critics of globalization point to the fact that London has become an ever more unequal city in terms of wealth distribution in recent decades,[67] this situation differs little from that which existed for much of its history.

This potted history of global London has revealed its long-held status as a leading international centre in the following ways: population size; political power in the sense that it controlled much of the world from the eighteenth to the twentieth centuries; economic pre-eminence in a variety of sectors but especially finance; and cultural capital. These factors have meant that it has attracted migrants from all over the world during the past two millennia.

MIGRATION SINCE THE ROMANS

While migration from beyond British shores may have taken place to the area now covered by London before the arrival of the Romans,[68] any history of the city focused upon immigration must begin with the fact that European migrants in the form of the Romans founded the settlement, making it a city of immigrants from its inception. It 'is generally agreed that there was no city in the area before the arrival of the Romans',[69] even though some small settlements may have existed in locations now covered by the capital.[70] 'London is a Roman town. It was deliberately founded by the Roman government for a specific purpose, on a site chosen by the government for that purpose.' It 'was built in the midst of a dark untamed forest, in a region hitherto uninhabited'.[71] The city acted as the administrative capital but would also emerge as the leading commercial centre of England.[72]

Our concern lies with the population of the new city which originated from continental Europe. The invasion of Britain for the purpose of settlement through Kent involved 40,000 men in AD 43,[73] although these did not simply live in London. The population may have peaked to around 50,000 during the Roman Empire.[74] Roman Londoners appear to have consisted of a variety of Europeans because of the multi-ethnic nature of the Empire. Those within the ruling classes consisted of a minority of Italians and would have included citizens from Gaul, Spain and even North Africa. Merchants and financiers appear to have originated in the eastern half of the Empire from as far away as Greece. Small tradesmen and craftsmen, mostly free men, also had a variety of origins. Soldiers would also have settled from all over the Roman territories, possibly even from North Africa. Slaves, on the other hand, would have consisted mainly of Britons.[75] The destruction of London by Boudicca in AD 60, eliminating both Roman settlers and native Britons, points to the revenge of the natives, but the quick rebuilding of the city[76] meant a rebirth of the first multicultural version of London, the template for others to follow in which migrants played a role in all layers of society and the economy.

Roman London fell into decline at the same time as the rest of the Empire and came under Anglo-Saxon rule during the fifth and sixth centuries, although the ethnic diversity of the imperial centuries disappeared. In fact, this multiculturalism may have facilitated the entry of German tribes because mercenaries from these lands may have rebelled, taken control and opened the south of Britain to their kinsmen from the continent.[77] Although London had fallen from its former glory, the period from the sixth to the ninth centuries resulted in a resurgence of trade and, consequently, the arrival of some foreign merchants.[78] By the tenth and eleventh centuries the history of London, like the rest of England, became a struggle between Saxons, Danes and Normans, with the last of these taking control by the end the eleventh century. Clearly, this period witnessed a diversification of the population of London, even if it might not have had quite the multicultural character of the height of the Roman city.[79]

From the Norman Conquest those who moved to London essentially change from invaders to immigrants as controls over the entry of foreign populations into England develop. One of the most visible communities in early medieval London consisted of the Jews, essentially an offshoot of the community of Normandy and more especially Rouen. The Jewish population of England expanded at the end of the eleventh century because of an influx of refugees from the continent fleeing pogroms at the time of the First Crusade. Further streams followed from Spain, Italy and even Russia.[80] The best-known occupation of Jews in the Middle Ages consisted of moneylending, as Gentiles could not involve themselves in usury under canonical law. This meant that London Jewry as a whole in the twelfth century became wealthy compared with the rest of the city's population.[81] But Jews also worked as clerks, doctors, merchants, goldsmiths, soldiers, fishmongers, cheesemongers and vintners.[82] Just before the expulsion of Jews from England in 1290 the 'great majority' lived 'either in a state of abject poverty or bordering on that condition', depending heavily upon service to their co-religionists.[83] The main Jewish settlement in medieval London emerged in what would become Old Jewry, while another developed closer to the Tower.[84] Here the Jews developed a sense of community, forced upon them, whether they liked it or not, by endemic antisemitism.[85] At least one synagogue emerged during the twelfth and thirteenth centuries.[86] Marriages usually took place between Jews.[87] Medieval London Jewry reached a high point during the reign of Henry II between 1154 and 1189, but strong hostility to Jews arose near the end of his reign, resulting in a serious riot on 3–4 September 1189 leading to the deaths of some members of the community,[88] although London Jewry would survive and even flourish into the thirteenth century.[89] However, it would come under attack again in 1236 and, more seriously, in 1262 and 1264.[90] This indicated increasing antisemitism in late thirteenth-century England which culminated in the Jewish expulsion of 1290, meaning the disappearance of legally practising Jews from the capital until the seventeenth century.[91] By the early medieval period, they had played a central role in the financing of the city and the monarchy.

German merchants from Bremen, Cologne, Hamburg and Lübeck also moved to London from the eleventh century. They would eventually join together in 1281 to establish the Hanseatic Kontor (or Steelyard), on the banks of the Thames, the main English base of the Hanseatic League, a transnational organization which controlled much of the trade of medieval Europe. Like the Jewish community, the fate of this group fluctuated according to the prevailing economic and political circumstances and by 1598 its members faced expulsion and the confiscation of their property by Queen Elizabeth, although they would have it returned in 1605, by which time the Hanseatic League entered a period of terminal decline. This change of fortune for the Hansa symbolized a rise of hostility towards them as the English-based Merchant Adventurers received support from the monarchy.[92]

Other Europeans also traded in London during the medieval period because the policy of the monarchy generally remained positive towards them, which meant that they made an important contribution to English trade.[93] Some of the most important foreigners in London during this period came from northern Italy, especially Venice, Milan, Florence and Genoa, playing a role in the export of wool but also importing luxury Italian goods. They may only have numbered 100 people but they had developed outstanding networking and business skills, operating either as individuals or as firms. Most importantly, Italians became central to the development of banking and money-lending in London following the expulsion of the Jews in 1290.[94]

The sixteenth and seventeenth centuries witnessed an increase in the diversity of London because of the presence of several distinct groups.[95] Economic migrants in the form of merchants and craftsmen worked in specific occupations not staffed by natives, which facilitated a skills transfer.[96] Italian craftsmen, scholars, miners, artists and industrialists moved to Britain during this era so that the Italian church in London had a membership of about 150 in 1568. A variety of foreign merchants, in addition to the Hansa, also retained a presence in Britain during the sixteenth and seventeenth centuries, trading in a range of products. Hostility towards such groups never remained far below the surface and exploded most famously in the xenophobic London riots of 1517 known as 'Evil May Day'.[97]

Refugees fleeing the Counter-Reformation in France, Germany and the Low Countries also crossed the Channel from the 1540s, with Calvinist congregations emerging in London by 1550. The largest and most important centred on the Austin Friars Church in the capital where Germans, French, Walloons and Flemings worshipped separately. The accession of the Catholic Queen Mary to the throne in 1553 forced them to leave the country but they would return in larger numbers following Elizabeth's accession in 1558, especially French and Walloon speakers fleeing the suppression of the Dutch Revolt and French Protestant Huguenots who moved to Britain in significant numbers following the St Bartholomew's Day Massacre in 1572. A French church with a membership of over 1,500 emerged from the late 1560s to the 1580s, while the Austin Friars Church, which had become Dutch, counted 1,850 members in 1583 and still carried out forty-two baptisms as late as 1680. The refugees experienced xenophobia as riots broke out in London in 1586, 1593, 1595 and 1599.[98] Over 50,000 Huguenots moved to Britain following the revocation of the Edict of Nantes by Louis XIV,[99] settling mainly in London and working especially in textiles, particularly silk weaving in east London. The Huguenots developed a rich religious life. They initially received a positive response in the capital but subsequently endured hostility both because of their perceived economic threat and cultural distinctiveness, facing identification with Louis XIV and his foreign policy, from which they had fled.[100]

Late seventeenth- and eighteenth-century London witnessed the influx of four groups which would remain ever present in the capital and would play a large role in its ethnic diversity. The smallest group consisted of people of African origin, mostly slaves, stemming from the capital's central role in the development of the transatlantic slave trade. The majority of the 10,000 to 15,000 Africans in Britain at this time lived in London. Most remained slaves who worked as servants, valets and butlers for the upper classes. Free black people, meanwhile, worked in a variety of occupations including road sweeping, fruit vending and street entertainment, while some tried to survive through begging. Males predominated amongst the black population. Enslaved women usually acted as maids, while freed ones found employment in laundry work, sewing and prostitution. By the end of the eighteenth century a sufficient number of free black people allowed the development of a community in London which had completely assimilated by the early nineteenth century through intermarriage despite endemic racism.[101]

The Irish community also developed in London during the course of the eighteenth century, building upon foundations dating back to the early Middle Ages.[102] The majority found employment at the lower end of the social scale, a situation that would continue into the nineteenth century and beyond, which meant that many lived in 'colonies', especially in St Giles, although others emerged, for example in Whitechapel, Poplar and Southwark.[103] The endemic anti-Catholicism culminated in the Gordon Riots of 1760.[104] Nevertheless, in addition to the poor labouring Irish, a middle-class community, attracted by the global city, also emerged, including lawyers, businessmen, merchants and bankers,[105] again part of a long-term process bringing Irish elites to London.

Similar to the Irish, the Jewish community remained central to London life following readmission in 1656 and also counted a range of groups throughout the social spectrum. An additional element to their diversity came from the fact that they originated from different parts of the continent in the form of Sephardic Jews from Spain and Portugal, who initially predominated, while by the eighteenth century increasing numbers of Ashkenazi believers arrived in London from northern and central Europe, and from the Netherlands through to Russia by the nineteenth century. Major London synagogues established by the 1720s included the Bevis Marks (Sephardic) and the Great and Hambro (Ashkenazi), while smaller congregations also evolved. Benevolent organizations and schools had also developed, meaning that, by the beginning of the nineteenth century, the foundation stones of the established Ashkenazi and Sephardic communities were firmly in place.[106]

By the end of the eighteenth century a fourth migrant population had emerged in London in the form of the Germans. Like their Irish and Jewish contemporaries, they represented a variety of social and occupational groups but remained focused in various forms of labour towards the lower end of the social and economic ladder and would remain ever present in the capital, despite the attempts to eliminate them during the First World War. By the early nineteenth century, they had established six Lutheran and one Roman Catholic church in London. These acted as the main form of community cohesion and organization.[107]

There was a significant increase in migrant settlement in London during the nineteenth century because the city lay at the centre of globalization,[108] which directly impacted upon migration. Population growth meant that people moved away from the land towards cities within their own nation states or empires and beyond. As the nineteenth century progressed, demographic change created increasingly diverse global cities – whether London, Paris or New York – because of the pulling power of their economies.[109] Whereas migration over shorter distances had characterized much of the early modern period, the nineteenth century developed into an age of international and intercontinental migration. This was facilitated not simply by global economic growth involving interlinked economies, which resulted in increasing ease of movement for people, goods and services, but also, at its very centre, ease of transportation due to the development of the steamship. Journey times were reduced and travel was made safer, which meant that people could move over much longer distances, whether from Europe to North America[110] or from one part of the British Empire to another.[111] As the largest port in the world, London lay at the centre of the transatlantic and global passage of peoples, especially during the early part of the nineteenth century when many of those crossing the Atlantic had to change ships in London. This process continued and would enable the growth in London of European groupings such as Germans and Jews, who sometimes decided to stay in the capital or other English cities rather than sail all the way to the United States.[112] The importance of London as a transport hub also led to the development of communities of sailors, especially in the East End, perhaps most famously lascars, a collective term of the time used to describe settlers originating from a vast area stretching from the Middle East to China,[113] although the term has come to refer primarily to those from British India.[114] European sailors also settled in London.[115] These structural enabling factors in the form of population growth, the economic and political pulling power of London, and the role of the imperial capital as the centre of global trade, only provide part of the explanation for the evolution of migrant communities. The migration history of London consists of millions of individual stories involving a decision to move. While some pioneer settlers from a variety of communities may have had a high level of motivation, in reality migrant communities in London both during the nineteenth century and beyond evolved as a result of the development of networks which could bring people from the same area to the capital.[116]

The Irish became the largest group in nineteenth-century London, as contemporary writers recognized. Henry Mayhew described the 'Irish street-sellers' as 'both a numerous and peculiar class of people'.[117] John Garwood's 'million-peopled city' included 200,000 Irish described in paternalistic, racist and, above all, anti-Catholic language, with a focus upon their religious habits, their drunkenness,[118] and the fact that they lived in some of the poorest parts of the capital including 'St. Giles's, Fields-lane, Westminster, parts of Marylebone, Drury-lane, Seven Dials, East Smithfield, Wapping, Ratcliff, the Mint in Southwark, and the crowded lanes and courts between Houndsditch and the new street in Whitechapel', as well as in suburban areas such as 'West Ham,

Deptford, Poplar, Plaistow, Kensington, Hammersmith, Fulham, Chelsea, Camberwell, and Greenwich'. But, 'wherever in London . . . a "Rookery" exists, we may be assured that it is inhabited by Irish'.[119] More objective accounts of the Irish in London included that by F. A. Fahy and D. J. O'Donoghue which appears to consist of articles from the *Dublin Evening Telegraph*.[120] This pointed to the fact that in 1851, the peak year of Irish in the Victorian capital, following the mass emigration as a result of the Famine, the 108,548 Irish constituted one out of every twenty-two Londoners. This proportion would decline as the century progressed,[121] during which time the Irish in the capital had become a mature migrant community with their own organizations, revolving around the Roman Catholic Church and also including a small middle class.[122]

As the Irish became an increasingly integrated group and as anti-Catholicism declined, the Jewish community, especially in the form of refugees from Tsarist oppression, concentrated overwhelmingly in the East End, became the focus of an obsessive antisemitic drive.[123] While the newcomers consolidated the Jewish East End, which would survive into the post-Second World War period,[124] London also acted as home to the increasingly integrated Jewish community which had arrived following readmission, as well as other middle-class newcomers. The result was that a distinct Jewish elite had emerged by the late Victorian period, which resented their poor working-class brethren who toiled especially in the manufacture of clothing and footwear.[125]

The other significant European groups who settled in nineteenth-century London consisted of Germans, Italians and French people. The Germans lived throughout the capital, focused especially upon the East End and the West End (between Euston Road and Goodge Street) but also living in the suburbs by the end of the century, including Sydenham, where wealthier Germans settled. During the nineteenth century and before the First World War, Germans found employment throughout the social scale, from prostitutes to merchant bankers, and developed a rich ethnicity revolving especially around religion and politics.[126] Italians, meanwhile, a more working-class community, labouring especially as street musicians and hawkers of various goods, were concentrated in Clerkenwell.[127] The French in London included political exiles fleeing persecution from the various revolutionary outbreaks after 1789, cooks, and by the early twentieth century, individuals employed in a wide variety of occupations.[128] Other European groups which emerged in nineteenth-century London included a wealthy Greek community[129] and Polish political exiles.[130]

The nineteenth and early twentieth centuries also witnessed an increase in settlers from beyond Europe to London. While they have attracted attention from historians since the end of the twentieth century and also caught the eye of contemporaries, they amounted to small numbers, significantly below the tens of thousands of Jews, Italians, Germans and French people, and the hundreds of thousands of Irish men and women. London acted as a magnet for educated elites, culminating in the Pan-African Conference of 1900 which attracted both Africans and African Americans,[131] although the heart of Empire, along with other university cities, especially Oxford, also attracted leading Indian intellectuals.[132] But the Indian population of London included individuals from across the social and economic spectrum.[133] By the beginning of the twentieth century, contemporary commentators had become concerned with the presence of the Chinese in the capital, especially in Limehouse, despite their census total of just 247.[134]

Britain witnessed relatively little migration during the interwar years, which meant that no significant new communities emerged in London. The eastern European Jews who had settled in the East End during the late nineteenth century experienced social mobility which meant that they moved towards East and North London suburbs,[135] while refugees from the Nazis settled in areas of northwest London such as St John's Wood.[136] Irish migrants also moved to London from the 1920s as part of a wave that would last into the second half of the twentieth century.[137] The German communities destroyed by the Germanophobia of the First World War witnessed a rebirth.[138] Both the French and Italian communities also became a feature of London life, employed in a variety of occupations with the evolution of distinct settlement patterns, building upon Victorian foundations.[139] Neither the Italian nor the German communities remained immune from the political changes which took place in their homelands as fascism and Nazism developed within them.[140] Some increase also occurred in the numbers of migrants from beyond Europe, including political leaders, although it is important to note that Indians, Africans and West Indians still settled in the capital in small numbers with little local community development in the way which would occur after 1934.[141] The Chinese remained visible in Limehouse, attracting orientalist narratives[142] and those with epicurean palates in search of the Chinese food which began to take off not just in Limehouse but also elsewhere in London by the 1920s and 1930s.[143] Journalists, social commentators and other writers became increasingly conscious of the cosmopolitan nature of

London's culture by the 1930s, especially in terms of music, dancing, food and other 'nights out', focusing especially upon Soho, which had become home to a diverse population (particularly waiters) originating especially from continental Europe.[144]

Wartime London witnessed an influx of political refugees from the continent so that the capital reached one of the most important points in its history of offering exile to those fleeing persecution in Europe, this time from the Nazis. Joining those Jews and left-wing political refugees who had already escaped Germany before 1945 came a whole series of other groupings from a range of countries invaded by Germany, including Poland, France and Belgium.[145] The war also meant an increase in the presence of the West Indian population in Britain (Table 1).[146]

The nature of migration to London and to Britain as a whole changed significantly in the second half of the twentieth century in a variety of ways. While a black and an Asian presence in Britain may have existed for centuries or even millennia,[147] the increase in numbers of these two streams had a transformative impact which they had not had before this time. Prior to 1945 the overwhelming majority of foreign settlers consisted of Europeans, who had helped to shape the evolution of London in numerous ways. However, while a significant proportion of the new arrivals who settled in the capital after 1945 may have arrived from beyond Europe, and especially from former British colonies, a large percentage still originated in Europe. In fact, for much of the post-war period the most

Table 1: Number and Percentage in Each Ethnic Group, London in 2001

Ethnic Group	Total	Percentage
White British	4,287,861	59.8
White Irish	220,488	3.1
Other White	594,854	8.3
Mixed	226,111	3.2
Asian/Asian British	886,693	12.1
Black/Black British	782,849	10.9
Chinese/Other Ethnic Group	193,235	2.7
Total	7,172,091	100.0

Source: Greater London Authority, *The World in a City: An Analysis of the 2001 Census Results* (London, 2005), p. 18.

important country of origin remained Ireland, which was overtaken, by the end of the twentieth century, by India. By this time over 179 countries each contributed more than 200 people to the total population of London of 7,172,091, pointing to the fact that more immigrants moved to London in the second half of the twentieth century than all previous new arrivals put together during the city's entire previous history. According to the 2001 census 1,980,478 residents of London had birthplaces outside Great Britain, totalling 27.6 per cent of the entire population of the capital. By this time the United Kingdom census had started using the concept of ethnicity as a way in which people identified themselves and which would therefore include the second and subsequent generations, meaning a white British percentage of just 59.8 per cent of the total. The rest of London's population consisted of a variety of ethnic groups, divided in a rather crude way, as Table 1 demonstrates, including those who counted themselves as originating from 'other white' backgrounds. The 2001 census represents something of a turning point in the post-war history of London, before the increase in movement that took place as a result of the expansion of the European Union in 2004 which included the accession of Poland.[148] Table 2 indicates the top ten states which sent most migrants to London in 2001.

Before moving forwards to consider the changes of the early twenty-first century, it is important to move backwards. Even as late as 1951 only 'one in

Table 2: Top Ten States of Origin of the London Population in 2001

Rank	Country of Birth	Number	Percentage of London's Population
1	India	172,162	2.4
2	Republic of Ireland	157,285	2.2
3	Bangladesh	84,565	1.2
4	Jamaica	80,319	1.1
5	Nigeria	68,907	1.0
6	Pakistan	66,658	0.9
7	Kenya	66,311	0.9
8	Sri Lanka	49,932	0.7
9	Ghana	46,513	0.6
10	Cyprus	45,888	0.6

Source: Greater London Authority, *The World in a City: An Analysis of the 2001 Census Results* (London, 2005), p. 72.

twenty Londoners was born outside the UK'.[149] At this stage the most significant migrant groups would have consisted of those which had characterized the recent history of London in the form of the Irish[150] and Jews,[151] although by this time West Indian migration had begun to take off, leading to a string of ultimately objective academic publications; these, however, carried titles such as *The Coloured Quarter* and *Dark Strangers*, reflecting wider societal fears about black immigration, which focused initially upon the East End, then Notting Hill and, increasingly, South London.[152] A series of European groups also developed in the capital in this period, including the Cypriots, mostly Greek Orthodox together with Turks,[153] Poles,[154] Armenians[155] and Maltese,[156] while Italian life developed still further.[157]

Despite the introduction of the Commonwealth Immigrants Act of 1962, which, as its name suggests, aimed at restricting the arrival of people from parts of the dying and reconstituted British Empire, the decades that followed resulted in a significant increase in the numbers of migrants settling both in London and in the country as a whole. In fact, while the early post-war settlement of Greek Cypriots and West Indians had focused heavily upon London, the South Asians arriving directly from Pakistan and India, as well as via East Africa, did not only settle in the capital, moving especially towards the north and the Midlands.[158] The 2001 census pointed to the presence of 2,027,000 people of South Asian ethnicity in the country, of whom 886,693 lived in London, meaning that 43.7 per cent of this group resided in the capital.[159] South Asians settled throughout the capital, changing from a primarily East End phenomenon, which had especially characterized the nineteenth and early twentieth centuries, to one that impacted upon the whole of London. While those of Pakistani and Bangladeshi origin focused mainly in the east of the city, those from India have settled primarily in the west of the capital, especially in an arc stretching from Hounslow towards Wembley and further inward towards Ealing. By the late twentieth century, London had become a patchwork of neighbourhoods.[160] In 2001, 45 per cent of ethnic minorities in Britain resided in London.[161]

The following decade resulted in a significant increase in the migrant population of London, reflected in the country as a whole, as well as a significant growth in the population of the capital as a result of the influx. The one in twenty Londoners born outside the United Kingdom in 1951 had increased to one in five by 1991 and grew further to more than one in three by 2011. 'In just the decade 2001–11, the non-UK population increased by 1 million.'[162] In numerical terms 2,998,000 out of 8,173,941 Londoners in 2011 had birth-places outside the United Kingdom, although this figure excludes the second generation. By this time less than half of the capital's population described themselves as White English/Scottish/Welsh/Northern Irish/British.[163] A major reason for the increase which occurred after 2001 was the accession of ten new countries to the European Union in 2004 (Cyprus, the Czech Republic, Estonia, Hungary, Latvia, Lithuania, Malta, Poland, Slovakia and Slovenia), whose residents became entitled to free movement to Britain and London; this was in contrast to several other major European states, including Germany, which introduced a moratorium on migration to prevent movement from these states.[164] Nevertheless, significant immigration also occurred from other EU countries which were already members before 2004, including France, as well as from other parts of the world. The top ten countries of origin changed after 2001, as Table 3 indicates, with Poland counting the second-largest number of migrants, although India, Pakistan and Kenya retained their original positions. In fact, the numbers of people born in South Asia had increased. At the same time, increasing numbers of middle-class and elite migrants settled in the capital to work in service industries, as indicated by the numbers of French, Australasians and Americans, although all these groups have a long history of settlement in the

Table 3: Top Ten States of Origin of the London Population in 2011

Rank	Country of Birth	Number	Percentage of London's Population
1	India	262,000	3.2
2	Poland	158,000	1.9
3	Caribbean	144,000	1.8
4	Republic of Ireland	130,000	1.6
5	Pakistan	112,000	1.4
6	Australasia	83,000	1.0
7	France	67,000	0.8
8	Somalia	65,000	0.8
10	Kenya	64,000	0.8
10	USA	64,000	0.8

Source: Greater London Authority, *Londoners Born Overseas, Their Age and Year of Arrival* (London, 2013), p. 7.

capital.[165] By the early twentieth century, communities of Latin Americans also became visible.[166] By this time Londoners spoke over 300 languages.[167]

Clearly, London has acted as a magnet for global migration for millennia, with a significant increase occurring in numbers in recent decades. The explanation for its pulling power lies primarily in its economic attractions which have remained constant. It has always housed elites, from the Hansa and the Lombards to contemporary bankers, because of its importance as a commercial and banking centre. Its reputation as a location 'where money lies on the street'[168] has meant that all social classes gravitated towards the global capital, with hundreds of thousands living in poverty. At the same time, we also need to re-emphasize the political importance of London, which attracted refugees from the continent continuing to fight their causes, from Karl Marx through Italian and Polish nationalists to pan-Africanists and elites who moved from different parts of the Empire to London to prepare for independence struggles.[169] Since 1945 London has attracted a wider range of refugees encompassing not simply elites but others from lower down the social scale, a process that began with the settlement of Russian Jews in the East End of London in the late nineteenth century but which continued into the post-war period with the arrival of groups such as Ugandan Asians, Ghanaians and Somalis, despite the introduction of increasingly restrictive immigration and asylum laws.[170] At the same time, the role of London as a cultural capital has helped to attract numerous musicians, whether in the classical tradition or, from the middle of the nineteenth century onwards, practitioners of more popular forms including Victorian Italian organ grinders and twentieth-century American jazz practitioners. From the 1960s distinctly black British styles of music have also emerged from second-generation Africans and West Indians.[171]

This points to the importance of networks when considering migration to London or anywhere else in the world. The economic, political and cultural significance of London may act as underlying pull factors, but each individual makes a choice about settling. While popular media routinely use aquatic metaphors, especially floods, when describing movement towards Britain and elsewhere, more sophisticated analyses have focused upon 'networks' or 'interpersonal ties that connect migrants, former migrants and non-migrants in origin and destination areas through bonds of kinship, friendship, and shared community origin'.[172] In the case of London, occupational connections have played a leading role. 'Migrant networks tend to decrease the economic, social and psychological costs of migration' partly because people have already made the journey to the country of destination and can therefore provide the links, help and information necessary to make the move.[173] Such 'cross-community networks' involve 'co-operation across distance and across boundaries of language and culture' and 'facilitate the movement of migrants from one place to another'.[174] Networks can last for centuries.

A few examples illustrate the importance of networks in the migration history of London. The nineteenth-century German population encompassed political, regional and occupational groupings.[175] Most Italian immigrants in Victorian and Edwardian London originated in four areas: the Como, Parma, Lucca and Liri valleys in central and northern Italy. The largest number migrated from 'the Appenine region south of Parma, at the juncture of Emilia, Liguria and Tuscany', within which 'it was from the twin valleys of the rivers Taro (Valtaro, or Valditaro) and Ceno (Valceno) that the largest number of people came, especially from the former'.[176] More recently, South Asians have originated from distinct areas. For example, Bangladeshis who settled in East London came primarily from Sylhet. Their movement developed from the fact that many Sylhetis served on board British ships and landed in British ports from the end of the eighteenth century, a tradition which continued into the middle of the twentieth. During the 1950s and 1960s, especially before the passage of the Commonwealth Immigrants Act of 1962, increasing numbers of male Sylhetis moved to Britain, particularly East London, followed by their families during the 1970s.[177] Similarly, the evolution of the Gujarati community in London depended upon network migration.[178] Polish migration after 2004 has built upon links with Poles who settled during and immediately after the Second World War.[179]

THE CONSTANT MAGNET

This survey of the history of migration to London might also appear to apply to other parts of Britain. Most of the groups outlined above did not simply settle in the capital, but also moved to cities throughout the country, whether Hanseatic merchants, Jews, the Irish or Germans. But clear differences exist. The first consists of the continuity of settlement. While a significant Jewish community has always existed in London, the history of provincial Jewry has no other continuous focus. Medieval Jews settled in Bristol, Cambridge, Exeter, Gloucester, Lincoln, Oxford and York,[180] but even the rise of provincial Jewry from the eighteenth century[181] did not revive some of these communities. Similarly, the centres of the Hanseatic League in England in the high Middle Ages, such as Ipswich, Yarmouth, Hull and York, have not constituted major areas of migrant settlement in recent centuries. Outside London the major Jewish communities of the nineteenth and twentieth centuries emerged in the big industrial cities of Manchester,[182] Leeds[183] and Glasgow.[184] At the same time, the nineteenth-century Irish settled in major cities such as Liverpool[185] and Newcastle upon Tyne,[186] which have not become locations of post-war migration on anything like the same scale as London. This is not to deny a continuity of migrant settlement in these big British cities, especially Liverpool, which witnessed black settlement because of its role in the slave trade.[187] Clearly London is different because it has *always* acted as the main area of settlement for most migrant groups who have made their way to Britain. No break exists in this history. This is essentially due to the centrality of London in the economic, political and cultural history of Britain. While the Industrial Revolution gave birth to new urban centres, important medieval and early modern towns such as York, Norwich or Bristol did not experience significant growth. London, on the other hand, expanded at the same time as the great industrial cities mushroomed during the nineteenth century.[188]

In terms of the continuity of migration, London would also appear fairly unique when making global comparisons. Clearly, great American cities such as New York[189] or Chicago[190] have evolved as a result of migration over the last two centuries, while German urban concentrations such as Berlin or Frankfurt have had similar multicultural histories since the Second World War.[191] But none of these four examples can compare with the British capital in terms of the longevity of migration, dating back millennia. Perhaps the only European settlements which have similar experiences are the imperial capitals of Rome[192] and Paris,[193] which have a comparable long-term history to London.

DIVERSITY, SUPERDIVERSITY AND COSMOPOLITANISM

London has become a supreme example of diversity, leading to the development of the concept of diversity because of the range of migrant groups and languages spoken in the capital by the beginning of the twenty-first century. This idea partly works on the assumption of individual groups leading separate lives, with a necessary level of interaction. However, the concept of cosmopolitanism or multiculture in which interaction does not simply revolve around daily economic interaction, but also involves friendships and relationships developed from ethnically diverse schools, has also emerged.

Diversity and superdiversity appear closely linked to the second half of the twentieth century and, more especially, the twenty-first century in the case of superdiversity. However, diversity, if not superdiversity, has deep historical roots, at least amongst the elites in banking and trade in the city of London. By the end of the seventeenth century the rebirth of the Jewish community added a further layer to the levels of difference which existed, with the native population displaying both positive and negative attitudes. Although the percentage of foreigners amongst London's population remained lower than in the late twentieth and twenty-first centuries, it may have totalled as much as 12.5 per cent. The variety of Europeans who lived in the capital both interacted with the majority community by, for instance, entering the guilds, and developed a distinct identity primarily by establishing their own places of worship[194] which have remained a central feature of London life since the seventeenth century. Two nineteenth-century publications concerned with religious diversity in London and perhaps pointing to the origins of the acceptance of difference in contemporary Britain included not simply the wide range of different Protestant sects in Britain, but also a variety of practices with continental European origins. J. Ewing Ritchie, for example, opened his account with an introductory chapter 'On Heresy and Orthodoxy', which concluded, however, that: 'It is well when people come to think that there may be something purer, higher, holier, than unreasoning uniformity of opinion.'[195] His description of the diversity of religious life in London begins with chapters on 'The Jews', 'The Reformed Jews', 'The Greek Church' and 'The Roman Catholics', which, however, include condescending and racist language.[196] The reverend C. Maurice Davis, in his description of *Unorthodox London*, also described religious diversity, which included both British groups and those with continental origins, using language more acceptable in the early twenty-first century.[197] In 1904 the encyclopaedic study of *Religious Life in London*, led by Richard Mudie-Smith, listed what appears to be every place of worship in the capital, including numerous locations established by immigrants. Mudie-Smith and his contributors used a social scientific methodology when carrying out their research and writing up their work.[198]

Mudie-Smith's edited book appeared at the same time as the three volumes put together by George R. Sims. Perhaps a secular parallel to Mudie-Smith's book, this edited collection contains essays on a vast variety of aspects of London life from 'Marrying London' to 'Bar and Saloon London' but including essays on 'Russia in East London', 'Oriental London', 'Italy in London', 'Cosmopolitan London', 'Jewish London', 'American London', 'German London' and 'Some Foreign Places of Worship in London'. Although impressionistic rather than scientific, these essays use a generally non-judgemental tone viewing migrant groups as central to London life.[199] While Sims and his contributors followed the work of the journalist Henry Mayhew and the social scientist Charles Booth, as well as other Victorian writers, in recognizing migrants as an element of London life,[200] the publication of the volumes edited by Mudie-Smith and Sims in the first few years of the twentieth century suggested a new departure in the acceptance of cultural and religious difference as part of London life.

Fifty years later a group calling itself 'The School's Committee of the Council of Citizens of East London', which emerged from a desire to prevent the rebirth of fascist activity led by Oswald Mosley in the area,[201] issued two thoroughly researched publications on the history of religion and migrant settlement in East London. The former covered the Church of England, Roman Catholicism, the Free Churches, Judaism and Islam.[202] A pamphlet entitled 'How We Came Here' passionately argued the case for the history of migration in the formation of East London and concluded with a call for 'diversity in unity' as the way forward.[203]

At the start of the twenty-first century a series of articles in the *Guardian* focusing upon the range of migrant groups, religions and races in the capital argued that London had become 'the most diverse city ever',[204] in which everything had become available.[205] The acceptance and celebration of superdiversity by the leading organ of liberal opinion in Britain followed decades of government policies which had outlawed ethnic and racial discrimination from the 1960s and which increasingly celebrated ethnic difference by the beginning of the twenty-first century, driven forward by the fact that ethnic minorities rejected a traditional concept of Britishness focusing upon the ethnic majority. While superdiversity may appear to have dangers because different communities seem to live their own lives in a transnational world in which they reluctantly communicate with fellow Londoners, everyday interaction at all levels including work, shopping and relationships means that a new London identity has emerged in which difference has become the norm, although a reading of Sims or the publications of the School's Committee of the Council of Citizens of East London points to the fact that diversity, if not superdiversity, has determined London's history. Such a situation has given rise to a cosmopolitanism that may have characterized Soho and the West End from the late nineteenth century but which now exists throughout London despite the development of areas that may appear to resemble ghettoes. While some ethnic groups may be concentrated in specific areas of the capital, ethnic mixing or cosmopolitanism and the acceptance of these facts of London life act as the lubricant which keeps the capital running.[206]

The millennia of migration to the capital have ensured that cosmopolitanism has formed a key aspect of London life. While ethnic enclaves may have acted as characteristics of migrant settlement since the Norman invasion, so has ethnic intermixing whether through the development of relationships between individuals, especially during the last two centuries, or by the economic and cultural impact of the new arrivals. This impact does not simply work through the newcomers transforming practices in particular areas of London life, although this may happen, especially in specific geographical locations, and in specific fields, such as religion. In many cases, such as food and music, a process of cultural transfer occurs whereby elements from the lives and practices of the migrants interact with the norms of London society to produce a new form.[207] Examples would be reggae, which emerged from Jamaican migrants in London from the 1960s,[208] or fish and chips, in which a Jewish food (fried fish) combined with the developing taste for fried potatoes in the middle of the nineteenth century to evolve into fish and chips.[209]

Multiculture or cosmopolitanism has therefore characterized the evolution of London since the arrival of the Romans who founded this city of immigrants. Successive waves of newcomers have had a profound impact upon its cultural, religious, social, political and economic development. Many newcomers have remained distinct from wider London society (although this distinctiveness forms a fundamental aspect of London life) while others have helped its cosmopolitan evolution. Even when first generations have remained separate, their descendants have become absorbed into, and determined, the nature of London's history.

2

GHETTO AND SUBURB

Clannishness, tradition, a sort of historical fear of separation from their co-religionists, their obligation to observe peculiar ritual ordinances, added to the promptings and difficulties which tend to keep men of the same tongue and habits together in a strange land – all these things act as an inducement, almost as a spell, which brings the Jewish immigrants into the already crammed and congested areas of the East End, where their brethren are aggregated and segregated. And the native folk cannot assimilate this element, for intermarriage with Gentiles is forbidden by the precepts of the Jewish faith and is opposed to the Hebrew ideal.[1]

I am writing this in the afternoon of a typical London day. I deposit my daughter at school with her Mexican classroom assistant . . . I return to let a Sikh furniture upholsterer into my house . . . Saying hallo to my Brazilian cleaning lady, I make for the local Italian café for breakfast, and then on to the British Library where two African women and a Cypriot check my pass, and where a variety of excellent and helpful library clerks man the Issue and Return desk. Today they consist of two West Indians, an Italian, several different African nationalities as well as white English. A Malaysian cuts my hair.

Then I have lunch at the Travellers' Club where my meal is brought to me by a friendly Bulgarian, my wine by a Frenchwoman and my coffee by an Egyptian. I go home on a Tube train driven by a Trinidadian, buy my copy of the evening paper from a Pakistani corner shop, pick up my dry cleaning from the Irish family who run Paradise Dry Cleaning, Park Way and buy my bottle of hooch from the Irish man and woman who run the local off-licence. I pop into the local bookshop, run by refugees from Hitler's Vienna and their son, say hello to some neighbours – one Zimbabwean, another American married to a Greek – and I go home.[2]

The visibility of migrants in London often became associated with concentration in what contemporary observers often essentially regarded as ghettoes – from the Irish 'rookery' in St Giles during the eighteenth century to the Jewish East End by the late Victorian period to the 'coloured quarter' immediately after the end of the Second World War, focused especially upon the East End, but increasingly moving to other parts of the capital, including South London, especially around Brixton. By the beginning of the twenty-first century the ethnic concentrations which had characterized the history of London became a feature of the entire metropolis, as a patchwork of ethnic concentrations developed. This apparent universalization of settlement based upon ethnic lines reflected the increasing numbers of migrants moving to London, as well as the growing diversification of these newcomers.

Ethnic concentration seems the easiest way of understanding the migrant settlement in London, perpetuated by contemporary observers racializing and exoticizing new arrivals. Ghettoization, to the extent that it exists, offers just one way of understanding the living patterns of migrant populations in London. The ghetto remains a temporary phenomenon, at least for the ethnic group which settles within it, as social mobility means that migrants and their offspring usually move to more prosperous parts of London, epitomized by the East European Jews who initially settled around Whitechapel at the end of the nineteenth century but would gradually, by the middle of the twentieth, form concentrations in a variety of suburban areas.

The East End has remained a classic transitory zone and has acted as home to centuries of migrants from the Huguenots through to Irish, Germans, Jews, Africans and Bangladeshis. But it has not served as home to all newcomers, as demonstrated during the nineteenth century by the example of Italians, concentrated mostly upon Clerkenwell, and Germans, who lived in small communities in a variety of parts of London, including the East End. Settlement patterns largely find explanation in the economic status of migrants and the pull of already established populations. Poor East European Jews moved towards the least prosperous parts of London, attracted by the existing Jewish community which had evolved during the course of the nineteenth century. On the other hand, the wealthier migrants who have characterized London life have settled in more attractive areas of the capital, whether German merchants and bankers moving to nineteenth-century Sydenham, or Russians settling in late twentieth-century Kensington.

The Jewish East End provides the closest example to a ghetto in the modern history of London because of the level of ethnic concentration. While people from the same part of the world live in close proximity throughout the capital in the twenty-first century, mixed-residence patterns have increasingly become the norm, providing a good indication of the existence of cosmopolitanism, with roots not simply in Soho but also in the East End, as one migrant group replaces another.

THE HOMELESS MIGRANT

Ghettoization, suburbanization and cosmopolitanism reflect the settlement of migrants in London, but so does homelessness, displaying patterns of life in the capital which characterize all ethnic groups, both majorities and minorities, partly explained by the movement of migrants, whether internal or international, who fall on hard times. During the nineteenth century such homeless people constituted part of the Victorian underworld,[3] victims, but also opportunists, in the rapidly expanding metropolis.

Beggars constituted one group of the Victorian underworld and included foreigners, as identified by Henry Mayhew whose mid-nineteenth-century account of London labour and the London poor identified not simply a generic group of 'foreign beggars', but also, more specifically, a 'French beggar', 'destitute Poles', 'hindoo beggars' and 'negro beggars'.[4] Many of the Poles were refugees who had fallen on hard times and who, according to Mayhew, made a living through swindling and deception. He gave the example of 'one fellow' whose 'real name is lost among his numerous aliases', who eventually 'became the scourge and terror of hotel-keepers, and went from tavern to tavern living on every luxury and, when asked for money', he decamped and left 'nothing but portmanteaus filled with straw and bricks'.[5] One of the 'hindoo beggars' with the name of Joaleeka, lived in 'Charles Street, Drury Lane'.[6] The Irish street-sellers interviewed by Mayhew lived in 'two kinds' of houses: 'clean and dirty'.[7] Mayhew's nuanced and well-researched account resisted the temptation to stigmatize all Irish people in London with the concept of squalor, which had become the norm from the eighteenth century.[8]

The London City missionary Joseph Salter, concerned with 'Asiatics' in London for whom he helped to construct a 'Strangers Home' in the docklands, identified homeless people who had made their way to London, above all lascars, paying attention to their living conditions, homelessness and the evils to which they fell prey, including drunkenness and opium smoking. He asserted that 'Westminster has always had its contingent of Asiatic mendicants'.[9] Meanwhile, 'the dark stranger' could also 'be found' in Shadwell. 'Within a short distance of the Houses of Parliament some twenty Asiatic vagrants are residing.'[10] In the immediate aftermath of the Second World War the type of shifting population identified by Salter, composed of people from all over the world, still existed in the East End. The 'Indians' consisted mainly of Bengalis, mostly illiterate, but some Sikhs also lived here, often residing in overcrowded housing, although some Indians started buying houses and renting them out to West Indians. One report from 1950 claimed that the Indians 'live in a show of outward oriental splendour, and inward oriental squalor'.[11] The 'daily average floating population, not including casual visitors', stood at 298 at one stage during the course of the Second World War, including 150 'Negro American soldiers stationed outside London but spending their leave periods in the area'.[12]

If we move back to the nineteenth century we discover that a range of European groups experienced poverty both in the East End and elsewhere in London. The Germans, for example, included people who had made their way to the imperial capital and found difficulty in obtaining employment. Others faced straitened circumstances as a result of an economic downturn accentuated by the Victorian 'Great Depression' from the 1870s to the 1890s[13] or a deterioration of their own trade, while the aged formed a section of the destitute before the arrival of state pensions. During the 1850s refugees from both Germany and other European states faced difficult times after fleeing from the failed 1848 revolutions. Some of these turned to begging while others ended up in debtors' prisons. Some came from middle-class and even upper-class backgrounds.[14] Similarly, an account from the 1880s claimed that 'among the numerous homeless Germans in London there are always to be found persons of culture and education, who have seen better days and now could be thankful to be sure of a bed, a crust and a cup of tea'. The reason for this situation lay in the fact that: 'Competition is so fierce in all departments of labour, in all branches of business, that there are constantly many thousands of natives, as well as foreigners who can find no opportunity of utilising their stalwart arms or acquired skill.'[15] Several charities emerged in London to assist the German poor and working classes, including the Society of Friends of Foreigners in Distress and the German Society of Benevolence. These may have jointly assisted about 6,000 people during the 1880s, a significant percentage of whom consisted of the aged.[16]

Italians in Victorian London had also established charities to look after their poor, especially in the form of the Italian Benevolent Society. One group of poor Italians who attracted the attention of British public opinion, especially charities and particularly the Charity Organization Society, consisted of street musicians, partly because of the noise they made but also due to the fact that children played much of the music under the control of *padrones*. These were men who controlled the activities of the children they brought with them from Italy – usually with the knowledge of the parents – to work on the streets of the capital, leading to claims of exploitation and abuse.[17]

The established Jewish community of Victorian London had opened charities to assist its poor, largely in the form of newly arrived migrants, partly as a means of social control but also because wealthier established Anglo-Jewry did not want newcomers to undermine their position by causing a rise in anti-semitism.[18] One account from the middle of the nineteenth century claimed that 'The immigrants come over in a wretched state. They have no knowledge of our language, and are generally without a trade. In a few days, or at the most in a few weeks, their scanty means are all spent and they have no resource but to appeal to the tender mercies of their own countrymen.'[19]

The most important Jewish charity consisted of the Board of Guardians but, as immigration increased during the second half of the nineteenth century following expulsion from Eastern Europe, this body had to deal with large numbers of paupers, leading to the establishment of a six-month residency period before individuals could receive assistance.[20] New organizations therefore came into existence to assist the newcomers, perhaps most importantly the Poor Jews Temporary Shelter, which helped over 1,000 people by the end of the 1880s, although the Board of Guardians assisted between 11,000 and 14,000 people in the second half of the 1880s, a figure which had increased to almost 23,000 by 1904. Apart from helping newly arrived migrants, the Poor Jews Temporary Shelter also acted as something of a clearing centre as shipping companies contacted it with the aim of transporting the Jewish poor to the United States.[21] Those who stayed in Britain would find jobs in the East End sweated industries of shoe and cap-making and tailoring, the first step on the path to social mobility, which would take them from temporary accommodation to the ghetto and gradual suburbanization, a process which could take generations. In 1882 the Anglo-Jewish establishment newspaper, the *Jewish Chronicle*, described 23.6 per cent of London Jewry as paupers.[22] Not all migrants and their descendants experienced a smooth transition to the suburbs. Max Cohen, for example, experienced poverty and homelessness as he looked for work in London during the interwar depression.[23]

Immediately after the end of the Second World War one of the most famous instances of migrants living in temporary accommodation, if not poverty, consisted of the West Indians who arrived on the *Empire Windrush* in June 1948. About half of the 417 passengers spent time in the Clapham Deep Shelter, which was reopened for them. This acted as a 'clearing house' from where the newcomers would subsequently move to more suitable accommodation. Although the Ministry of Labour initially intended to house the new arrivals for just seventy-two hours, some would remain for three weeks.[24] Those who spent time in the shelter included W. George Brown, who remembered his experience with mixed feelings. He recalled the 'admission price' of 'one shilling and sixpence per night' and 'tea and cakes . . . being served at a small counter', which caused a rush as those 'who did not partake in the rush went without'. The experience in the shelter, together with negative racist press headlines which greeted the *Windrush* arrivals, led to 'frustration, loneliness, sadness, regret and similar emotions'. However, Brown quickly managed to secure a room nearby at 44 Orlando Road.[25]

As the twentieth century progressed refugees faced some of the greatest difficulties in securing housing, partly because of the fact that they arrived without any planning, fleeing from war or persecution, combined with a lukewarm reception from local and central government and a negative reaction from a hostile press.[26] This repeats the experiences of the Jewish exiles fleeing from the Russian Tsars in the late nineteenth and early twentieth centuries, who were forced into short-term accommodation such the Poor Jews Temporary Shelter. This type of temporary residence continued to play a role in the housing of refugees in the immediate aftermath of the First World War due to the combination of a hostile press, backed up by established Jewish opinion, and a national government intent on pushing any arrivals to Britain towards the United States, and leading to the establishment of the Atlantic Park Hotel as a temporary hostel in Southampton.[27] The restrictive asylum policies which had characterized the 1920s eased during the 1930s, meaning that tens of thousands of Jewish refugees from Nazism entered Britain, as fleeing children, domestic servants or middle-class adults. A significant percentage settled in London, although the first residence usually acted as a stepping stone in a process of social mobility or the re-establishment of social status in the early post-war period.[28] In the immediate aftermath of the Second World War refugees from Eastern Europe fleeing regime change in Poland and the Baltic states in particular arrived to progress through the type of temporary accommodation which had characterized refugee settlement since the end of the nineteenth century.[29] The next significant influx of refugees that attracted hostile public attention[30] occurred in 1972 in the form of Ugandan Asians. They too faced a hostile public opinion, and initially settled in temporary accommodation with the help of the Uganda Resettlement Board, which aimed to disperse them throughout the country and away from areas regarded as having a heavy migrant population. Like their German Jewish predecessors, they experienced social mobility, or, perhaps more accurately, the re-establishment of their social status, in the decades after their arrival.[31] One of the newcomers, Keshavji Mandalia, initially stayed with his brother-in-law in a rented house in Enfield ('three bedroom house, so one bedroom use me, and two bedroom use my brother's whole family'), but would quickly purchase a house in Manor Park.[32] In 1974, two years after the arrival of the Ugandan Asians, refugees from another former British colony proceeded to the United Kingdom following the Turkish invasion of Cyprus, leading many of them to find temporary accommodation in Haringey with support from the local council, the Greater London Council and central government.[33]

The dispersal policy which had emerged by the 1970s (especially away from London) had become government policy, although this did not prevent some refugees, who found it increasingly difficult to secure asylum except under specific schemes aimed at particular groups, settling in London. By the beginning of the twenty-first century Newham in East London acted as home to a variety of groups, who moved into the borough in mostly cheaper rented accommodation.[34] The increasingly restrictive asylum legislation which emerged by the end of the twentieth century, however, also meant that those who had moved to the capital and had not secured asylum sometimes disappeared and became 'ghosts', outside any form of state entitlement and assistance, meaning that they experienced destitution.[35] In fact, failed asylum seekers constitute one section of over half a million undocumented migrants who may be living in London.[36] Some of these end up living on the streets and have become known as NRPFs ('no recourse to public funds'). By 2013 over 50 per cent of 'rough sleepers' in London did not consist of UK nationals and 40 per cent of these did not originate in the European Union. Accommodation options for NRPFs remained limited and included night shelters and the use of houses provided by religious groups, charities and housing associations.[37] Take the example of Samir, an Iraqi Kurdish poet who arrived in London in 1999 and applied for asylum, but whose financial support ceased in April 2006:

> Samir is homeless. He has no money for transport and has to walk from place to place in London. With no address, he has no access to medical treatment for his psychological problems. Food and other necessities are provided by Kurdish friends but he feels weakened by his situation and upset when they help him . . .
>
> He believes he would be killed if he returns to Iraq because of his poems, the website he has created, and the political activities he has continued in the UK.[38]

London contains migrants from all over the world struggling for survival, living throughout the capital in a vast array of makeshift or overcrowded accommodation or on the streets.[39]

It seems difficult to imagine how these ghosts at the bottom of the London housing market, who would face deportation if they came back to life again, could ever experience the type of social mobility which characterized the lives of Russian Jewish émigrés who moved to the East End in the late nineteenth century, the refugees from Nazism, or those who fled from Idi Amin's Uganda. They have more in common with those Germans who moved to London in the Victorian period and who survived with the support of German charities or, in some cases, simply disappeared from view to die on the streets of the metropolis.

THE GHETTO

Many of those who have eventually lived in good-quality London accommodation initially resided in the ghetto, as the classic example of the East End Jews in the late nineteenth and early twentieth centuries indicates. As the quote at the start of this chapter by William Evans-Gordon – who campaigned for the 1905 Aliens Act – indicates, racists and antisemites[40] paint a negative picture of ethnic concentrations repeated throughout the history of London, as well as the history of xenophobia and racism. In the case of London, as well as other major European cities, the origin of this concept lies in restrictions on the settlement patterns of medieval Jews who lived in ghettoes sometimes surrounded by walls. In thirteenth-century London, the ethnic concentration remained looser so that, although Jews were focused in the four London parishes of St Olave, St Laurence, St Stephen and St Martin Pomary, others resided in another five, while those in the four main parishes lived 'side by side' with Christians.[41] Although the concept of an East End ghetto has become linked with the period 1840–1939[42] and more especially 1880–1939, Jews had begun settling in the eastern half of the city of London since their readmission in 1656, with the nineteenth-century newcomers expanding these areas further eastwards.[43]

The East End areas which became the centre of Jewish life by 1900 had acted as home to a previous group of European refugees, the Huguenots.[44] The nineteenth century also witnessed the arrival of Irish, Germans and Chinese in the area beyond the Tower of London. While the Chinese may have resided close to the docks, the Irish and Germans lived in areas further north, either side of Whitechapel in which Jewish migrants would become concentrated by 1900. In 1901 the London borough of Stepney, which incorporated the East End, housed 54,310 of the 135,377 aliens living in the imperial capital and served as the focus for the largest communities of, amongst other minorities, Russian and Polish Jews, Scandinavians, Dutch, Germans, Austrians and Hungarians.[45] The interwar years proved a high point for the Jewish East End, even though it had begun to break down.[46] In the post-war period a variety of migrants have settled in the area, especially West Indians and Africans (in the 1940s),[47] as well as Bangladeshis[48] and Maltese,[49] for example.

Associated with the poorest of migrants, a transitory zone, the East End has attracted the gaze of sociologists, racists and former Jewish residents with a sense of nostalgia. The area evolved as a result of the settlement of migrant labour from other parts of Britain as well as the arrival of foreign migrants and refugees, especially as this part of the capital grew with the development of the docks and imperial trade.[50] Its proximity to the city meant that not simply Jews moved to the East End from their original London areas of settlement, but also Germans, who like their Jewish counterparts had originally resided in the eastern half of the city when their community began to develop during the course of the eighteenth century, especially around newly established churches.[51] This closeness to the City of London offers one explanation for the development of the East End as an area of migrant settlement, at least for German and Jews. As the City expanded eastward during the nineteenth century, its already established migrant populations in the eastern half moved with it. At the same time, the proximity to the London docks also helps in an understanding of the East End as an area of migrant settlement. The early Chinese and Indian communities here, which emerged close to the Thames in Limehouse and Ratcliffe Highway respectively, developed as a result of sailors from these groups who came to land.[52] A third reason for the evolution of the East End as an area of migrant settlement lies in its poverty in comparison with most other areas of London, which has meant that it has attracted settlers looking for cheap accommodation and working in migrant trades which entail exploitation or sweating.[53] Finally, the reputation of the East End as an area of immigrant settlement led to the further influx of people from the same group, who would feel comfortable living amongst those who practised the same religion and ate the same food. Thus the Jewish community developed in this way during the course of the nineteenth century[54] while Bangladeshi settlement following the Second World War traces its roots back to the nineteenth-century pioneers.[55] In this way the migrants felt transplanted rather than uprooted,[56] as the presence of people who spoke the same tongue and held the same beliefs eased the trauma of migration. This is a classic example of migrant networks in action, which applies not simply to Jews, Bangladeshis and other groups settling in the East End, but to the evolution of migrant concentrations in other parts of London (as well as other urban settlements) throughout its history.

The Jewish East End, which evolved between Aldgate and Bromley-by-Bow and north and south of Whitechapel,[57] presents one of the best examples of an ethnic concentration in the history of modern London, especially because of the amount of attention it has attracted. By the beginning of the twentieth century the area had come to symbolize everything wrong with mass migration in the eyes of racists, including overcrowding, sweating, filth and clannishness. In addition, partly because of its proximity to the centre of power in Westminster, the area acted as the springboard for the introduction of the seminal piece of legislation to control immigration in modern Britain – the Aliens Act of 1905.[58] As well as Evans-Gordon, numerous other observers came to similar conclusions about the area. C. Russell and H. S. Lewis in their study of *The Jew in London*, with a map of Jewish concentration, aimed to study *Racial Character and Present-Day Conditions* and began by commenting, in a chapter entitled 'The Jewish Question in the East End', on 'the peculiar "solidarity" which holds the Jewish race together', despite its attempt to adapt to its local environment, wherever its members settled.[59] Russell and Lewis reduced the 'Jewish question' to three elements: the 'general social question' or the extent to which Jews and Gentiles mixed; the 'industrial question' or the impact of 'economic conditions in maintaining or diminishing' the 'isolation' and 'unpopularity of the Jewish race'; and the 'religious question' or 'How far is the "separateness" of the Jewish community due to the tribal and exclusive character of Judaism?'[60] Such accusations became commonplace with the spread of antisemitism throughout Europe in the late nineteenth century.[61] As well as appearing in the local and national press, similarly racist articles, with an element of exoticization, also surfaced in periodical publications of the time. A piece by George A. Wade on 'Israel in London' or 'How the Hebrew Lives in Whitechapel' made a variety of negative assertions, as indicated by the following: 'To stroll down Middlesex Street on any ordinary day is to invite death from suffocation or poisoning. The fetid smells, the nauseous odours from dirty shops, fried-fish establishments, meat-shops, and unclean houses, are not easily to be described.'[62] Meanwhile, James Strang, in a stereotype-laden article on 'The Jewish Colony in London', began by describing the men as either 'with very hooked nose, long beard, and a certain air of reverend gravity' or 'sallow complexioned, not so prominent of nose nor so profuse of beard, voluble and without response'.[63]

These pieces simply form the tip of the antisemitic iceberg which engulfed the East End Jewish community. At the same time, social scientists focused upon this group, pioneered by Charles Booth in his *Life and Labour of the People in London*. Booth could not really ignore the community in view of their significance when he carried out his research during the 1880s and 1890s.

Although he and his research team, especially Beatrice Potter, used a rational methodology and provided a detailed analysis of the working, living and religious conditions of the community, largely devoid of the type of language used by Lewis and Russell, the survey did not remain free of assumptions about the Jewish community.[64] The less thoroughly researched study by Walter Besant, which details a variety of migrant groups in East London, partly based on Booth's findings, also holds some assumptions about the Jews without employing blatant antisemitism.[65] The *New Survey of London Life and Labour* published during the 1930s could again not ignore the Jewish population of East London as the community continued to exist, although on this occasion the writer of this section of the survey was actually the Jewish Henrietta Adler, who wrote the piece without making assumptions about Jewish behaviour, focusing upon the residential, domestic, social and religious life of the community in the East End.[66] A more impressionistic account, *The Real East End*, similar to Besant's, with antisemitic undertones, appeared at about the same time as Adler's, describing 'special restaurants, about a score of synagogues', and labelling Brick Lane the 'main street of the Ghetto . . . It contains everything for the daily needs of the Jew, and there is scarcely a shop, a house, or a stall that is not Jewish'.[67]

Some Jewish East Enders romanticized the area after they had moved to more salubrious parts of London. Israel Zangwill, the son of East European Jewish immigrants,[68] pioneered this approach, especially in his *Children of the Ghetto*, a fictional depiction of Jewish life in Victorian London.[69] He made particular use of food as a symbol of Judaism, writing, for instance, that 'Fried fish binds Anglo-Jewry more than all the lip-professions of unity.'[70] However, the book also revealed the reality of poverty and sweating in this locality,[71] as did autobiographies and memoirs which appeared after the First World War. These accounts came from the children of immigrants who had become professional writers and focused upon a series of themes. First came their own provenance, with precise descriptions of their places of birth in Eastern Europe, the journey to London and the place of settlement. The mathematics professor Selig Brodetsky recalled that his father 'was born in a small Ukrainian village, Golovanensk', and his mother in 'the Ukrainian town of Olviopol', his own birthplace.[72] His father moved to London first and he followed with his mother in August 1893, involving a journey which 'took a whole month'. They initially resided in 'just one room in a small turning off Brick Lane'. After the birth of two more sisters they 'still lived in crowded conditions, moving from one part of Whitechapel to another'.[73] Ralph Finn remembered similar poor housing conditions during his childhood in Broughton Buildings in Goolden Street in Aldgate where he lived at the start of the twentieth century with his mother, grandparents, three sisters and three brothers in two flats. 'Downstairs in the basement, there were rats. Not just mice, but rats. And bugs. Upstairs in the show rooms there were just bugs. Legions of them'.[74] Broughton Buildings also served as 'a hotbed of hotbeds' used by prostitutes.[75] Despite focusing upon the negative aspects of the East End, which, in some cases, also included working in a sweatshop, as in the case of Willy Goldman, who, however, recalled his experiences in a humorous way by ridiculing his employers,[76] many of these children of the ghetto looked back with nostalgia at their childhood. They would focus upon community, with both Jews and non-Jews;[77] education, especially as many of the writers went on to successful careers grounded in their schooling, which often included attendance at the Jews Free School, and supported by encouraging parents;[78] and food, which played the same symbolic role for these children of the ghetto as it did in Zangwill's novel. Harry Blacker, who grew up in Gibraltar Walk in Bethnal Green, remembered:

> Native-owned delicatessens were a veritable cornucopia of tasty titbits. Pickled herring beringed with onions, sour cream, soft cheese, black and green olives, dutch cucumbers, sauerkraut, sweet cabbage and appetite-whetting smoked salmon cut paper-thin and sold by the ounce . . .
>
> Almost without exception, every home in the quarter ate its daily quota of rolls (with or without poppy-seeds), platzels (with or without onion) and countless rings of crisp crunchy bagels.[79]

Religion loomed large over all of the activities of the Jewish community of East London. Russian Jews established their own synagogues to continue the religious practices they had developed in their homeland, distinct from the Judaism which had emerged amongst established Anglo-Jewry since readmission in the seventeenth century,[80] although Jewish youths had a variety of attitudes towards their faith.[81]

The Jewish East End reflects life in other London ghettoes, including those which used the same location that have included the Irish, Germans, Chinese, black people and Bangladeshis. Irish settlement by the eighteenth century included Wapping, Whitechapel, Poplar and, by the beginning of the twentieth century, Limehouse. Those who lived here found employment especially in the docks and street trades. In 1848, just after the mass emigration following the Irish Famine, an average of 2.7 people slept in each bed in St George's in the east of London. St George's became the area where the poorest and most unskilled Irish migrants would settle and where those who arrived tended to remain. Whereas Roman Catholicism played a significant role in their lives in the earlier nineteenth century, this had declined in importance by the beginning of the twentieth.[82]

Poorer Germans also became concentrated in the East End during the course of the nineteenth century, especially in Whitechapel, St George's in the east and Mile End. Both English and German visitors commented upon the poverty of the Germans in the middle of the nineteenth century, although, as census statistics indicate, the number of Germans living here had declined by the beginning of the twentieth century. This was due to demolition work following metropolitan improvements, the arrival of Jews, and the decline of sugar refining, which was the main reason for the original development of the German community here at the end of the eighteenth century.[83] Nevertheless, an article on the German community in London published in *Living London* could still, in 1903, describe Leman Street as the 'High Street of German London in the east'.[84] Many of those Germans who had lived here during the nineteenth century moved further eastward, outside the area usually described as the East End, towards Hackney, Stratford, West Ham and Silvertown.[85]

By the beginning of the twentieth century a small Chinese community had also become established in the East End, more especially Limehouse, originally emerging from the presence of seafarers, although the range of employment had diversified by the outbreak of the First World War. This small group received significant attention because of the level of their difference and the prevalence of an orientalist discourse. This focused upon the question of inter-ethnic marriages between Chinese men and English women, and their mixed-race children, the question of opium smoking, the threat of cheap Chinese labour, and an imported orientalist discourse from South Africa, while more general views of Limehouse focused upon the mixture of races who lived in the area. However, this orientalism also had a slightly more positive exotic aspect to it, partly encapsulated in the attraction of Chinese women, as well as the flavour of Chinese food. The numbers of Chinese living in the East End remained minuscule, standing at seventy in 1881 and reaching just 167 by 1931 when the size of the Chinese community in the capital totalled just 1,194, although the number of Chinese businesses in Limehouse had reached twenty-four by 1930.[86]

At the end of the Second World War, Africans, West Indians and Bangladeshis arrived in the East End, although their history of settlement in this area dates back to the nineteenth century. While black settlement remained somewhat transitory, the Bangladeshi community would resemble its Jewish predecessors. The 'Coloured Quarter' constituted 'a depressed working-class neighbourhood sheltering residents of many races and nationalities' with a consequently 'cosmopolitan character'. Stepney had become 'the coloured man's district' even though just 292 African and 167 West Indian males (together with just 66 African women and 43 West Indian women) lived here in 1951.[87] This black community partly emerged from seafarers or those who found employment in manufacturing, building and catering.[88] Rather like their Chinese predecessors, the Africans and West Indians, despite their small numbers, attracted attention because of a racist discourse and because they became associated with crime and miscegenation, not just in the East End, but also in the other parts of London where they had begun to settle, especially Brixton and Notting Hill.[89]

Along with the transitory black population of Stepney, there also developed a more permanent Bangladeshi[90] community from the end of the Second World War. In 1951, 564 men and 234 women from India, Pakistan and Ceylon lived in Stepney.[91] Ten years later the figure for Pakistanis had reached 799,[92] although the most significant migration would occur during the 1960s and 1970s with an initial settlement of males followed by wives and children. By 1991 the number of people describing themselves as having Bangladeshi ethnicity (including those born in the UK) in Tower Hamlets had increased to 36,000 and then by 2011 to 81,377 (out of a total population of 254,096), making it the largest ethnic group in this diverse borough.[93] Bangladeshi settlers faced similar problems to their Jewish predecessors, including poverty, poor housing and racism.[94] But they transformed the areas where they lived, especially Spitalfields,[95] into a rich ethnic concentration with Islam becoming the prominent religion (although Judaism has not completely disappeared)[96] and the commodification of the presence of Bangladeshis in the area through the development of the idea of Banglatown as a tourist attraction with the help of local government.[97]

While the East End has the longest history of ethnic concentration in London, it does not constitute the only ghetto (as imagined by racists, social scientists and romanticists), especially in the post-war period. Poorer migrants also lived in a variety of other areas of the capital during the nineteenth century. 'Little Irelands', associated in the Victorian anti-Catholic driven popular imagination with poverty and popery, emerged not simply in the East End but elsewhere in London and, just as importantly, in urban settlements throughout the country to a greater extent than any of the other East End concentrated migrant populations.[98] The concept of the London Irish ghetto had actually emerged from the eighteenth century when one of the most important settlements developed in St Giles, 'a centre for beggars and thieves and the headquarters of street sellers and costermongers',[99] as well as in Southwark, Marylebone and Whitechapel.[100] During this period the Irish in London 'were a police problem, a sanitary problem, a poor-law problem and an industrial problem'.[101] By the Victorian period, following the emigration consequent upon the Potato Famine, in addition to the East End, the Irish settled in two other broad areas: South London, especially a continuation of the eighteenth-century Southwark settlement, and Kensington. Most Irish 'were relegated to the side streets and back alleys of their neighbourhoods'. Although they lived close to the English, 'they remained apart' to the extent, in the short run at least, that 'neither geographic nor social assimilation took place'.[102] The fact that the vast majority of the Irish worked in manual and unskilled occupations with low earning power determined their status as residents of poorer parts of London.[103] By the middle of the nineteenth century the Irish communities in London consisted of both migrants and, like the ethnic minorities which developed after the Second World War, those born in the capital.[104] By the 1890s, in addition to the East End,[105] the Irish were 'numerous' in Marylebone, North Kensington, Chelsea, Fulham and Westminster.[106] 'On the south side of the Thames, you find small colonies of our people in Camberwell, Peckham, and other centres.' By this time the largest Irish populations south of the Thames lay in Bermondsey, Rotherhithe, Deptford and, above all, Southwark.[107] The last of these, sustained by 'poverty and faith', dated back to the eighteenth century and grew in size during the nineteenth.[108]

The Italian community also became the victims of a combination of xeno-phobia, anti-Catholicism and prejudice against poverty during the Victorian period. Although Italians lived in significant numbers in six different boroughs,[109] those in Clerkenwell attracted the most attention both at the time and from local historians. Those who lived here from the 1850s until the 1870s included street musicians together with individuals working in a series of other skilled trades, but by 1895 hawkers of ice cream, potatoes and chest-nuts had become important.[110] The presence of this community led to the opening of St Peter's Church in 1863 and it retained its Italian character until the middle of the twentieth century, with the internment of aliens during the Second World War having a significant negative impact.[111] Despite the nega-tive attention which the Italian quarter had attracted in connection with organ grinding and child exploitation in the middle of the nineteenth century, it had developed a more positive image by the beginning of the twentieth – certainly in the article by Count Armfelt in *Living London* focusing upon an annual religious procession in mid-July celebrating Our Lady of Mount Carmel, but also pointing to the colour, orderliness and patriotism towards Britain of its inhabitants.[112] A less positive article on 'The Italian Colony in London' described the Italian woman as 'the patient servitor of the man'[113] while also focusing upon a dance involving 'the lowest class of Italians' and girls who 'are all English without exception and all of the lowest London type',[114] repeating concerns about interracial mixing with other groups. However, Clerkenwell during the day was 'pleasant and cheerful', which meant 'knots of laughing men, with olive-tinted skin, dark eyes and curly black hair' and 'groups of gossiping women, with quaint head-gear, big earrings, white chemisettes and brilliant shoulder-shawls; merry children, with picturesque touches of colour in their dress, and oddly foreign-looking'.[115]

The myth and reality of the ghetto survived after the Second World War as a patchwork of ethnic communities emerged throughout London. The initial arrival of West Indians led to the type of fascination and hostility which had characterized the Jewish East End during the nineteenth century. While these newcomers 'were found dispersed throughout London, they were not evenly distributed', with 'two quite noticeable clusters' emerging in the form of Brixton, Stockwell and South Lambeth in the south and Paddington, North Kensington and Shepherd's Bush and Hammersmith in the west.[116] In the early 1950s, even before these areas had developed as significant West Indian settlements, the Metropolitan Police began to focus upon them, claiming that the immigrants accentuated overcrowding, caused public health problems and moral problems, participated in anti-social behaviour, including 'stabbing affrays, frequently as a consequence of quarrels over white women', and led to a rise in unemployment.[117] At this stage only about 500 black people lived in Brixton.[118] The early arrivals who had spent time in the Clapham Deep Shelter would eventually move into more permanent accommodation,[119] whether privately rented or owner-occupied, both within the initial London areas of settlement and in the areas to which they increasingly became dispersed during the course of the 1960s.[120] Of the sociologists who examined the arrival of *Dark Strangers*, Sheila Patterson, following in the footsteps of Charles Booth, provided one of the most all-encompassing studies of the consequences of the arrival of West Indians on South London housing, pointing out that they settled in areas already suffering depreciating property values, rather than causing house prices to fall. The West Indians faced more hostility than European groups such as the Irish or Cypriots, partly because of perceived behavioural differences, although race would clearly have played a role; but, despite the presence of hostility, by 1960 some 'absorption' had begun.[121] The hostility had already reached its major post-war peak in the other significant area of West Indian settlement in Notting Hill, where the activities of Oswald Mosley's racist anti-immigration Union Movement helped to spark the rioting which took place here in August 1958. The background to the rioting was a housing shortage that became synonymous with the exploitative activities of the Jewish holocaust survivor Peter Rachman, who purchased properties *en masse*, as well as resentment at interracial relationships, which acted as the spark for the riots.[122] Although Notting Hill declined in importance as a West Indian area after the riots, Brixton would remain the symbolic home of this group during the second half of the twentieth century. Like the East End Jewish ghetto, Brixton symbolized both deprivation, which ultimately led to the Brixton riots of the early 1980s[123] accentuated by a type of police persecution which Jews never experienced, and a reconstruction of the homeland. This was encouraged both by religious activity and by the foundation of community groups,[124] but also by the way in which West Indian settlement had transformed the nature of street life in Brixton.[125]

Because of the association with violence and racism, Brixton became the most visible ghetto in post-war London. However, such spaces replicate themselves throughout the capital, whether in the case of, for example, Bangladeshi Spitalfields, or the settlement of Sikhs in Southall and other locations in West London such as Hounslow and Slough, leading to the type of nostalgia which characterized the Jewish East End symbolized by the film *Bend it Like Beckham*.[126] The London borough of Ealing, in which Southall lies, had become concerned about the concentration of Sikhs from the 1960s, to the extent that it implemented a policy of 'busing' pupils to schools in other parts of the borough. This was a short-lived policy which broke down due to resistance from anti-racist groups in particular, although it did continue on a limited scale until 1981.[127]

THE SUBURB

Ghettoization offers just one way of understanding the history of migrant settlement in the metropolis. Despite the level of concentration which occurred amongst the Jewish population in Stepney immediately before and after the First World War, 'the American ghetto model of hypersegregation is not present' in early twenty-first-century London, certainly not in the same way as black concentration in the United States,[128] despite the concerns of academics and politicians,[129] who simply repeated earlier anti-Irish and antisemitic discourse.

The concept of the ghetto partly operates on the assumption that ethnic concentrations never break down, which the example of the East End invalidates. Furthermore, even in the case of Jews, while this area may have served as a major area of concentration in London, Jews settled in a variety of other locations in Great Britain even during the nineteenth century. More importantly, suburbanization occurred during the course of the twentieth century as part of a process of social mobility in which moving away from the original area of settlement proved key. This went together with occupational change, the adoption of English as the main language of communication, the decline of religious observance and changing food patterns. Yet moving away from the original area of settlement involved more than just the immigrant generation.[130]

In 1911, 43,925 of the 63,105 Russians (overwhelmingly Jews) recorded in the census for England and Wales lived in the East End borough of Stepney, meaning that it housed up to 70 per cent of newly arrived Jews. In 1889 East London accounted for 90 per cent of the capital's Jews.[131] By the early 1930s only 60 per cent of the capital's Jewish population resided in East London.

Even within this part of the metropolis dispersal occurred away from Stepney, where just 52 per cent of Jewish families lived, towards Hackney, Bethnal Green, Stoke Newington, Shoreditch and Poplar, as well as to areas outside East London.[132] After the Second World War, as Jewish social mobility continued apace, further dispersal occurred to the outer London suburbs, especially eastwards towards Redbridge, although in the 1970s nearly 15 per cent of the population of Hackney still consisted of Jews. A concentration also emerged in the north-west of London stretching from Golders Green and Hendon towards Edgware. Significant concentration has taken take place so that in the 1980s 60 per cent of all Jews in Barnet lived in 6 of the 20 electoral wards in the borough.[133] However, by this time they had become 'middle-class ethnic minorities . . . freed from many of the financial – and perhaps even social – constraints that worked against' the original Jewish migrants who settled in the East End a century earlier. The descendants of those who migrated at the end of the nineteenth century no longer desired 'residential segregation' in the sense of 'being separated or isolated from others in the general population', despite the concentration which continued to exist.[134] A focus on the Jewish communities of Hendon and Golders Green reveals that they began to evolve from the end of the First World War as Jews moved into this area from the East End with the opening of the Northern Line.[135] Significantly, those arriving in Golders Green 'were moving to an area that had not been settled to any great extent',[136] meaning it became Jewish from its inception. It developed further during the 1930s as a result of increasing settlement from the East End, which would continue into the post-War period, and the arrival of refugees from the Nazis, who also settled in other areas of north-west London.[137] In 2001 Jews constituted 37 per cent of the population of Golders Green, making it 'the most Jewishly populous neighbourhood in the country'.[138]

While the East End Jewish ghetto may have broken down during the course of the twentieth century, clustering has taken place, although the description above ignores the decline of the Jewish population due to exogamy and falling fertility and the fact that the newly established state of Israel attracted Jews from all over the world.[139] In contrast, London remained a magnet for the Irish in the twentieth century. The Irish quarters which developed during the nineteenth century reached terminal decline by 1900,[140] even though decline 'was more apparent than real . . . because migrants again clustered together in newer parts of the city'.[141] There appears no continuity of settlement patterns between the Irish migrants of the nineteenth and twentieth centuries. Southwark and the East End no longer constituted Irish areas. Some post-war migrants moved to inner London during the 1930s and into the 1950s and beyond, in Camden, Hampstead, St Pancras, Marylebone, Hammersmith, Westminster, Kensington, Chelsea and Marylebone, continuing the Victorian precedent of settling in poorer areas to undertake manual labour. However, other twentieth-century Irish migrants settled in expanding suburbs such as Brent, especially in Kilburn and Cricklewood. The Irish have developed into one of the myriad of foreign groups which have populated London since the Second World War, although many of those who arrived in the immediate post-war years lived in poor accommodation similar to the experiences of the West Indians, partly as a result of racism and the refusal to rent to Irish families with children. The Irish have become increasingly invisible, despite their significant overall numbers in comparison with other migrant groups, not simply because of less concentrated settlement, but also because of the greater visibility of the increasing numbers of people of colour.[142]

The same statements apply to another European group with a long-term history of settlement in Britain, at least in the post-war period, in the form of Cypriots, both Greek and Turkish. Greek Cypriots have few connections with the Greek merchant elites who lived in the City from the nineteenth century,[143] although some continuity exists with the pioneer settlers who worked especially in the catering trade in Soho during the 1930s, particularly in Italian restaurants, as some of them acted as the first link in a family or village migrant network. While neither Greek nor Turkish Cypriots developed nineteenth-century-type ghettoes because of their small numbers, they did reside in ethnic concentrations, initially in inner London, and then became increasingly suburbanized. The first major post-war settlement was in Camden Town where three Greek Orthodox churches developed, including All Saints and St Andrews, although settlement also took place in other parts of inner North London in particular. These initial migrants worked in manual occupations, with women becoming seamstresses and dressmakers in particular, many of whom laboured at home. Men took a variety of jobs, including as tailors, shoemakers, waiters and bus drivers.[144] The story of the Cypriots in London resembles that of their Eastern European Jewish predecessors in that they initially settled in an inner London area near their workplace, remaining quite concentrated, and then experienced social mobility and consequent suburbanization, moving ever northwards, initially towards Haringey and then Enfield, following the 29 bus route and developing a high rate of home ownership.[145] While Soho may have initially acted as the main concentration for the Greek Cypriots during the course of the 1930s, replaced by Camden Town during the 1950s and 1960s, by the 1970s the concentration had changed to Haringey, especially around Green Lanes (part of the 29 bus route) near Haringey Stadium dog track. In some of the roads off Green Lanes over 60 per cent of residents were Cypriots. Green Lanes itself included coffee shops with names such as Famagusta Café or Larnaca Café, as well as both Greek and Turkish Cypriot greengrocers and a range of other businesses including Greek and Turkish banks. Despite the Turkish invasion of Cyprus in 1974 which resulted in the partition of the island, Greek and Turkish Cypriots lived in close proximity in London and often worked together, although socialization remained unusual, at least amongst the settlers, and intermarriage was even rarer both because of the political situation but, more especially, as a result of religious differences. By the 1970s, as well as manual occupations, Greek Cypriots displayed a high degree of self-employment, although, for the first generation, professional occupations remained rare. Immigrant women continued to work heavily in the clothing trade.[146] Turkish Cypriots had also developed a separate ethnic enclave in a part of Green Lanes towards inner London in Stoke Newington, described by one commentator as Famagusta, N16.[147] By the beginning of the twenty-first century, as the number of Cypriot migrants declined, with little migration to London after 1974, and the second generation increasingly marrying out, the visible settlements which had characterized Camden Town and Green Lanes, at least in the Greek Cypriot case, disappeared. The Turkish Cypriot areas survived but changed because of the settlement of increasing numbers of migrants from Turkey in London, so that over 200,000 Turks and Turkish Cypriots resided in the capital by 2013.[148]

Despite the survival of Brixton as the heartland of West Indian London into the 1980s, movement out of this area had begun southwards from the 1960s towards South Norwood and Addiscombe, although by the 1970s concentrations of West Indians had also developed in North London, especially around Hackney and Haringey, and north-west London, particularly Brent.[149] George Brown, who initially spent time in the Clapham Deep Shelter and then moved to nearby Orlando Road, subsequently found accommodation in Comerford

Road in Brockley when his wife arrived from Jamaica. They spent four years here and then moved to 79 Lewisham Road in January 1952, securing a mortgage despite the prejudice against lending to black people.[150]

While suburbanization as a result of intergenerational social mobility may explain the presence of some groups outside poorer areas of London, international economic elites have always made their home in wealthier parts of the metropolis. The nineteenth-century Greek banking community, for example, settled in the City, especially around Finsbury Circus during the 1820s and 1830s, but by the 1870s they had moved westwards towards Paddington, Bayswater and Notting Hill, and even established their own elite burial ground in West Norwood Cemetery. After initially worshipping in the chapel of the Russian Embassy in Welbeck Street, they moved to a room in Finsbury Circus on the first floor of the offices of Ralli Brothers, one of the leading Greek banking houses, after which they opened a church in London Wall. By the 1870s St Sophia in Bayswater had become the most important Greek Orthodox church in London.[151]

A century later further elite West End communities emerged including Russians and Arabs. The former settled especially in Kensington, partly evolving out from the Soviet and, subsequently, Russian, Embassy in Kensington Palace Gardens.[152] During the course of the 1990s immigration regulations eased for those prepared to invest at least £1 million in Britain, attracting a range of groups to London including Russians who had become rich following the selling of state assets after the collapse of communism, perhaps most famously Roman Abramovich. He moved to London in 1997 and initially rented a large apartment in Cadogan Place, near Sloane Square, before subsequently purchasing other properties in the area, as well as a country estate in West Sussex and Chelsea Football Club in 2003. By 2005 he had bought a £9.3 million property in Chester Square, followed by further purchases nearby.[153] By the 1970s 'oil-rich Arabs' had already begun buying properties in Knightsbridge and adjacent areas of London,[154] although in the decades which followed an Arab community based upon a wider range of social groups emerged in a broader area of the western half of London.[155]

LONDON'S DIVERSITY

This account of communities concentrated in particular locations provides just one interpretation of the settlement of migrants in London. For, with the growth of the capital during the nineteenth and twentieth centuries, the presence of migrants had become increasingly universal, a process which has its origins in the early modern history of London, as foreigners settled throughout the capital even at that time.[156] As we have seen, the Irish lived throughout London, both during the Victorian period and before, which meant that they also resided in close proximity to the English, as well as to other migrant communities, especially in the East End. Meanwhile, the Irish law students, lawyers, bankers and merchants who settled in eighteenth-century London did not reside in the 'rookeries' associated with their poorer brethren.[157]

Dispersal finds replication amongst other groups in Victorian London, especially Germans and Jews. The German community in the east of the city became one of many settlements which emerged. While Leman Street may have become the centre of German East London by the beginning of the twentieth century, 'the neighbourhood south of Fitzroy Square is the heart of German London in the west'. It lay 'between Great Portland Street and Regent Street on one side and Tottenham Court Road and Charing Cross Road on the other' and constituted a predominantly working-class community.[158] In fact, Germans had resided in this area from the middle of the nineteenth century and included refugees from the 1848 revolutions and the German Anti-Socialist Laws of 1878. But by the 1911 census Germans lived throughout the capital,[159] including Islington where 'there is a large settlement of small tradespeople and mechanics' while 'German merchants who go daily to the city' lived 'about Hampstead and more particularly, in the South-eastern suburbs, Camberwell and Forest Hill'.[160]

The Jewish community, meanwhile, did not simply emanate outwards from the East End of London to much of the rest of the northern half of the capital during the course of the twentieth century: suburbanization away from the City had occurred during the Victorian period as the increasingly wealthy and professionalized earlier wave of Jews moved away from the dirt and grime of the expanding metropolis to more pleasant environments further out. Like the Greek Cypriots 150 years later the early Victorian 'Jews tend to move in straight lines outwards from the City', which would help to explain their concentration in North London, rather than South London, even at this stage. The new suburbs included Bloomsbury, Bayswater, Maida Vale, Highbury, Hackney, St John's Wood and Hampstead. Jewish working-class settlements also emerged in Tottenham and Edmonton, East and West Ham and Clapham.

Suburbanization also meant the development of synagogues in the areas where Jews settled.[161] One of the most durable Jewish areas of settlement outside the City and East End consisted of the West End. While wealthier Jews lived in some parts of this district, from the end of the nineteenth century newly arrived immigrants also settled here.[162] Those working-class Jews born in the West End included Sid Spellman (9 February 1927), whose parents, Hyman and Bella Spiegleman, 'came from a town in Poland called Szydlowiec' and who may have originally settled in the East End. Spellman's parents and grand-parents had established a successful tailoring business which allowed them to move to a '17 room house' in Notting Hill.[163] However, few Jewish tailors in the West End experienced this level of success, often working long hours in a seasonal trade.[164]

Within the West End, Soho became something of a model for the evolution of post-war London in the sense that it contained a variety of groups living in close proximity from the end of the nineteenth century, meaning that it acted as a pioneer of cosmopolitanism:

> No part of the world presents in such a small area so many singular and interesting pictures of cosmopolitan life as Soho, which is the cherished home of foreign artists, dancers, musicians, singers, and other talented performers, and the sanctuary of political refugees, conspirators, deserters, and defaulters of all nations.[165]

Soho also acted as home not simply to Jewish tailors, working especially in the high-class bespoke trade in Savile Row,[166] but to tailors from other nationalities including Germans. In 1901, 24 per cent of the Soho population found employment in 'dress', which 'compared with 2 1/2 per cent elsewhere in Central London'. Just as importantly, Soho became the birthplace of the foreign restaurant in London, which played a central role in its cosmopolitan character and also meant that the area served as home to thousands of conti-nental waiters, beginning with French, Swiss and especially Germans before 1914. The latter were replaced by Italians following the internment and depor-tation of Germans during the Great War. Meanwhile Greek Cypriots, who had begun to find employment in the restaurant trade by the 1930s, actually participated in anti-Italian riots following Mussolini's declaration of war in June 1940. They would remain important in this trade after 1945, when restaurants increasingly became identified by their nationality and also when a Chinese quarter emerged in Soho.[167] The residents of the area included the Greek Cypriot Evangelou family, who lived at 57 Riding House Street and whose neighbours were 'French, Italian, and Cypriot, both Greek and Turkish, with a lot of Jewish families as well'. Helen Evangelou, the daughter of the immigrant Photis Evangelou and Vasilou Ktori, who arrived here during the 1930s, remembered that during the 1950s it 'was great growing up in such a colourful and, on the whole, friendly neighbourhood. Today we would call it "diverse", a big melting pot, but at the time I never gave it much thought.'[168]

Perhaps Soho acts as the model for the evolution of post-war London in the sense that migrants of different nationalities and, increasingly, from all over the world, live in close proximity to each other; although, as we have seen, this builds upon a pattern already established during the nineteenth century, especially in the East End, continuing into the early post-war period when this area housed a combination of Africans, West Indians, Indians (mostly from Bangladesh), Maltese, Cypriots and Mauritians, although all of these groups also settled in other parts of the capital.[169] This pattern continued in this area into the twenty-first century. Although Bangladeshis had become the most significant ethnic group here by 2011, making up 32 per cent of the population, followed by white British (31 per cent), all minority ethnic groups made up 55 per cent of the population of the area including Indians, Pakistanis, Chinese, black ethnic groups, those of mixed race and Irish.[170] Although by this time gentrification had begun to occur, meaning the arrival of new populations, both white and other ethnic groups.[171]

By the beginning of the twenty-first century Tower Hamlets had become the London borough that comprised the third-largest percentage of ethnic minorities amongst its population, with 57.1 per cent – behind Brent (70.8) and Newham (66.2). By 2001 9 out of 33 boroughs in superdiverse London comprised an ethnic minority population of over 50 per cent, while only one, Havering, had less than 10 per cent.[172] Clustering certainly occurs, following the patterns established in the early post-war years and the suburbanization patterns which followed: Asians tend to be concentrated in western and eastern boroughs, with one of the highest proportions in Harrow (counting Gujaratis in particular), where they predominated in 98 per cent of census output areas, while the highest concentration of blacks was to be found in Lewisham. Interestingly, the borough with the highest concentration of people of Irish ethnicity was Havering, pointing to the fact that this group had participated in the type of flight which characterized the white British.[173]

New communities emerged from the late twentieth century including Ghanaians in the Broadwater Farm Estate in Tottenham; Iranians in Queensway; Lebanese and Arabs in Edgware Road; Poles in Acton (although this group built upon earlier arrivals who migrated in the aftermath of the Second World War); Portuguese in Lambeth and Stockwell; Somalis in Crystal Palace, Dormers Wells, Southall, Stratford, Wapping and Wembley; Sri Lankans in a variety of areas, including Tooting, which has also become a more South Asian area also housing Indians and Pakistanis; while West Africans also live in the East End, Peckham, Stroud Green, New Cross and Woolwich and Plumstead.[174] A Latin American presence became increasingly visible by the early twenty-first century, dispersed throughout the capital but with concentrations in inner London boroughs, particularly Lambeth and Southwark (especially Bolivians, Brazilians, Colombians, Ecuadorians and Peruvians), Newham (Ecuadorians), Brent (Brazilians), Tower Hamlets (Brazilians), Barnet (Brazilians), Islington and Hackney. Shopping areas have developed in Elephant and Castle and Seven Sisters.[175] Latin Americans resemble South Asians in the sense that there may exist an umbrella ethnic identity distinguishing them from the white British, which breaks down into a more specific national or religious identity in the case of South Asians, whether Sikh, Pakistani, Indian or Sri Lankan. While these groups may concentrate in specific locations, whether Sikhs in Southall, Gujaratis in Wembley or Bangladeshis in Spitalfields, these areas do not remain unique to these individual minorities partly because social mobility means they move to new areas while the arrival of new communities means those who have left are replaced.

London appears to have become increasingly diverse not simply in terms of the overall picture of settlement throughout the capital but also on a local level. While particular ethnic groups may dominate in specific boroughs and the neighbourhoods and wards within them, some of the larger migrant communities live throughout the capital. To give just one example, Bangladeshi 'elders' who settled in London shortly after the end of the Second World War reside not simply in Tower Hamlets but also, for example, in Camden.[176] The metropolis has therefore inevitably become cosmopolitan because of the range of ethnic groups which live within it. Some minorities and, more importantly, some individuals within these communities, may choose to retain a distinctiveness and remain close to their own ethnic group. Like the Jewish East Enders at the beginning of the twentieth century, migrants continue to live and work within particular locations of the capital, although schooling and integration mean that this becomes less likely for their descendants. It seems rather simplistic to suggest that 'Bangladeshi Londoners who are born and bred in the city are less likely to appropriate' discourses of 'belonging and cosmopolitan imaginaries' than Caribbean, Indian or white residents.[177] Individuals living in London have accepted 'commonplace diversity' as part of their everyday experience, interacting with other ethnic groups to varying extents, whether while they shop or in mixed social activities.[178] Clearly, those who practise their religion usually do so with people of their own ethnic group, although this remains just one aspect of the lives of Londoners who have not abandoned God.[179] The way in which London has evolved has meant that while there may exist a dominant white British national culture, individual boroughs and districts within them count their own individual dominant cultures, where other groups may perceive themselves as minorities.[180]

London is certainly not 'sleepwalking into segregation'.[181] What appear to be ghettoes have emerged throughout London's history, but they have broken down quite rapidly as a result of social mobility and the arrival of new minorities. The classic example of the East End has revealed this over the last two centuries, but this process has become widespread in the post-war period, as the examples of Greek Cypriots and West Indians illustrate. Yet the East End also demonstrates the history of migrant diversity in London because, while Jews had evolved into the dominant group by the early twentieth century, they lived in the part of London which also became home to the Chinese, Germans, Irish, black people and South Asians. At the same time, Jews did not simply reside in the East End for they had established synagogue-based settlements throughout the capital by 1900, a process which continued into the twentieth century. Similarly, the Irish and Germans also lived throughout London, especially in 'rookeries' but also in wealthier areas.

The depopulation of London by the white majority (which also included some Irish) in the early decades of the post-war years meant that migrants from all over the world settled in the areas vacated by people moving to the home counties. This led to the creation of superdiverse London, a term which applies to the vast majority of London boroughs, although those further out tend to display a lower concentration of ethnic minorities at the beginning of the twenty-first century. While the level of diversity may have changed since 1945 and, more especially, 2004, migrants have historically settled throughout London. In recent decades the cosmopolitanism which characterized the East End and Soho has become increasingly universal throughout the capital.

3

CHEAP LABOUR

A kind-hearted German missionary was my companion, and as soon as I put my head in at the door of bakery, the nature of the manufacture in progress was at once made apparent to my senses. Just as unmeasured indulgence in sugar is nauseating to the palate, so was the reek of it palling to one's sense of smell. You could taste its clammy sweetness on the lips just as the salt of the sea may be so discovered while the ocean is yet a mile away.

It was a sort of handy outer warehouse, that to which we were first introduced – a low-roofed, dismal place with grated windows, and here and there a foggy little gas-jet burning blear-eyed against the wall. The walls were black – not painted black. As far as one might judge they were bare brick, but 'basted' unceasingly by the luscious steam that enveloped the place, they had become coated with a thick preserve of sugar and grime. The floor was black, and corrugated and hard, like a public thoroughfare after a shower and then a frost. The roof was black, and pendent from the great supporting posts and balks of timber were sooty, glistening icicles and exudings like those of the gum-tree.[1]

I had to get up before six to catch the bus down at Finsbury Park at seven. I could only gulp the bare cup of tea before going out. As soon as I got to the job, I was started off digging a trench. It was a gorgeous day and after a while I felt as light-hearted as a lark . . . Four and three-halfpence is what they are paying here and no talk of subsistence. I'll stick it for a while but that's all.[2]

My first journey was a nightmare. I was on the 134s, which ran from Potter's Bar to Pimlico, and I can remember I stood for so long fumbling with the change I didn't have a chance to go upstairs many times. I remember somebody asking me, is upstairs a free ride. I didn't have a clue where I was, where the bus was going.[3]

THE ROLE OF MIGRANT LABOURERS IN THE LONDON ECONOMY

Prominent migrants have had a profound impact on the economic and cultural life of London, often becoming celebrated because of their visibility and the contribution they have made in a particular field, whether banking, football or music. Beneath these celebrities, millions of more humble Londoners from Europe and other parts of the world have formed the backbone, skeleton and flesh and blood of the city's life. Before 1945 the white British constituted the majority of the working class in the metropolis, but migrants played a role in a series of fields. Most of these occupations have continued since the 1940s, when they have become increasingly important to the London economy as the white British have either left the capital or experienced social mobility, leaving increasing numbers of manual jobs for less educated and less well-connected new arrivals.

Migrant labourers fit into the working life of the world's capital in a series of ways. In the first place we can see them as part of a type of underclass, undertaking tasks which the white British shun. Even 'the Emerald Islander' rejected the work environment described in the sugar bakery above 'on account of its excessive hardship', meaning, according to James Greenwood, that only Germans would undertake such work.[4] This pattern also applied to a series of other occupations in nineteenth-century London including tailoring, which attracted both Jews and other migrants, as well as Germans. After the Second World War the global post-war economic boom, fuelled by the need to rebuild war-ravaged economies lasting until the middle of the 1970s, meant there was a demand for migrant labour not simply in London but in the rest of the United Kingdom as well as on the European continent. Western Europe became a net importer of population, moving away from its status as a net exporter of people during the nineteenth century.[5] Because of its size as the largest European city and the process of white flight, London became the centre of this system, as migrants arrived initially from Europe and then, when their supply dried up, from the Empire and Commonwealth, as a racist British government accepted, at least temporarily, the need to allow black and Asian people to fill labour shortages on a national scale.[6] The overwhelming majority of these new arrivals undertook manual work which the mainstream population increasingly shunned but from which they had certainly not disappeared, meaning that immigrants worked side by side with Londoners of all ethnic groups. The newcomers found employment in all sectors of the metropolitan economy, from bus drivers to nurses to unskilled factory workers producing everything from clothing to food. As the economic boom following the Second World War came to an end and unemployment returned to levels last experienced during the 1930s, post-war migrants and their offspring suffered higher rates of joblessness than the majority population for decades to come, partly as a result of racism in the labour market.[7]

The migration which was channelled towards London after 1945 points to the globalized nature of the London labour market, which has long-term origins if we consider the role of the nineteenth-century Irish and Jews and, venturing further back, the arrival of slaves from Africa and the West Indies. The increase in the number of migrants who moved to London in the twenty-first century, thereby super diversifying the city, partly occurred as a result of the deregulation of labour markets, but also because of free movement within the European Union. While some of these new arrivals have entered the bottom of the labour market, helping, for example, to fill the demand for cleaners needed for the vast office blocks which characterize London,[8] they have, like their nineteenth-century and early post-war predecessors, found employment in a vast variety of manual occupations, as well as throughout the economic scale. The decline in manufacturing industry and consequently the number of people it employs in London, from 32.4 per cent in 1961 to just 11 per cent in 1991, has also had an impact on the London labour market, as it has meant some polarization of employment, which, however, has existed throughout the history of the metropolis. The recent rapid expansion of London's banking, insurance and business services sectors, and consequent growth in the number of managerial and professional households, has 'fuelled demand for low-paid workers to service both the institutions of the new financial economy (as porters, cleaners and security staff, for example) and the professional and managerial elite themselves (as domestic cleaners, restaurant staff and nannies)'.[9] But, as we shall see, these occupational groups have always existed in significant numbers in London. The perspective that focuses on recent deregulation and polarization implies a return to a new era of Victorianism which had characterized employment in London during the nineteenth century but which changed as a result of unionization and state intervention from the later nineteenth century until the early post-war decades.

This overview of the globalized nature of the London labour market, and the role of migrants within it, needs further deconstruction. There seems no doubt that numerous people who have made their way to London from overseas would merit the description of cheap labour, but this description provides only a starting point. The cheapest labour of all consisted of slaves brought to the capital with their masters during the eighteenth century in particular, slaves who would achieve liberation but who would, in most cases, subsequently experience poverty and destitution. These link together with those migrant Londoners who made a living on the streets, including prostitutes. Foreign sojourners have also played a role in London, especially in the form of foreign sailors, whose presence became inevitable in view of the global significance of the docks. Such groups would best merit the description of outsiders and outcasts, according with the Marxist concept of the underclass. Whether in Victorian London or in the London of the twenty-first century they experience uncertain employment and living conditions. Above this stratum come the skilled and unskilled workers with more secure employment. Irish construction workers, for example, became a characteristic of London life for much of the nineteenth and twentieth centuries, often working side by side with people from a variety of ethnic groups. Foreign manufacturing workers, whether the German sugar bakers of the East End, the Jews employed in the sweated industries in the same area before the First World War, or the migrants engaged in the production of all manner of goods after 1945, played a key role in the London economy, especially in clothing, which remained a key employer of migrant labour in substandard conditions. The concept of cheap labour, associated not only with sugar bakers but, more especially, with Jewish 'sweaters', arose especially in clothing, shoe and hat and cap manufacture in the East End before 1914.

Cheap labour offers one explanation for the evolution of these concentrations of ethnic labour because, for example, the sugar bakers actually formed part of a migrant employment network, which brought Germans from Hanover in particular to work in this occupation. These networks have characterized numerous other migrant occupations in the metropolis, from German governesses to Irish builders and West Indian bus drivers.

Migrants have carried out all manner of manual and service employment in London, from prostitutes to governesses. By 2006, 33 per cent of 'the employed residents of London are either immigrants or working visitors',[10] a figure which would almost certainly exceed 50 per cent if it included the second generation. Migrants do not simply play a role in all parts of the London economy as a type of paid servant to the white British who work and live in the City and Westminster, they also drive the local economies which have emerged throughout the capital from Hounslow to Newham.[11] While foreigners may have become more important in the London economy in the early twenty-first century than at any time before, they have remained key over the last two centuries, working in unique fields of their own but also together with the white British and other ethnic groups.

THE MARGINALIZED

Just like people who moved to London from other parts of the United Kingdom to find employment at the bottom end of the economic ladder, so have migrants from all over the world. Some of these had no choice, such as the slaves who arrived from the sixteenth century. Others fell on hard times and had to undertake work which did not initially attract them, as examples from the Victorian period illustrate. The nineteenth century also provides an illustration of the role of sojourners in the form of the countless foreign sailors who became part of London life. In the twenty-first century migrants have become increasingly important because of deregulation and the emergence of the 'gig economy', with some of those working in sectors such as cleaning lacking legal status. Black slaves, the Victorian underclass, foreign sailors and the twenty-first-century deregulated migrants all have in common the fact that they remain outside mainstream London employment without regular pay, while also playing a central part in driving the metropolitan economy.

Black people began to arrive from the sixteenth century with the development of the transatlantic slave trade and by the eighteenth century between 10,000 and 15,000 may have lived in Britain. They were concentrated especially in London but also in other major slave ports such as Bristol and Liverpool.[12] West Indian and American planters brought their slaves back with them because they would not have to pay them (in contrast to white servants), and they also became a status symbol. The treatment of this group varied widely. Whereas the Jamaican manservant Francis Barber was fortunate enough to become the residual heir of Samuel Johnson, other blacks received treatment similar to what they had experienced in plantations. For example, David Lisle nearly killed his slave Jonathan Strong by hitting him on the head with a pistol.[13] The abolition of slavery in Britain by the beginning of the nineteenth century resulted in an increase in the numbers of black paupers in London. 'Some blacks swept crossings, some knitted night-caps and socks and others manufactured garden-nets for their livelihood.'[14] Others simply begged.[15]

Although black people had become a rarity in London by the Victorian period as migration from Africa largely ceased, other migrant groups helped to populate the Victorian and Edwardian underworld. Meanwhile the factory system continued to evolve, sucking in many newcomers from Europe, as the example of Germans and other Europeans indicates. One German account from 1887 claimed that 'an astonishing number of swindlers and impostors exist among the Germans of London'.[16] Some German criminals continued activities which they had begun in their homeland. They formed part of a wider criminal underclass of Europeans, who included Russian and Polish Jews, French and Italians. Between 1906 and 1913 the number of Germans who faced expulsion orders for criminal activity in London included 201 for larceny and receiving, forty-four for housebreaking and frequenting, twenty-eight for forgery and false pretences, and nineteen for 'crimes against the person'.[17]

Germans and other Victorian and Edwardian migrants also became involved in prostitution. Between 1906 and 1913, 254 Europeans (Russians and Poles, Germans, French and Italians) faced deportation for soliciting and importuning, fifty-six for brothel keeping, together with 103 for living wholly or partly on prostitution and procuring.[18] Some of the women engaged in prostitution in London in the decades before the First World War became victims of the 'white slave traffic'. This involved abduction or deception either in the homeland or following arrival in London in a period when prostitution became a worldwide network,[19] indicating the centrality of the capital in yet another globalized process. The victims included 'Lisette Schweighoffer, age 15½, native of Homburg' who 'had been abducted from her home on 15 June 1895, brought to London and here procured for immoral purposes'.[20] Some Jewish women fell into prostitution because they could not obtain any type of charitable support after arriving in London, even from Jewish organizations.[21] Many French and German prostitutes worked in the West End including

Kellner's in Leicester Square, where 'a naughty continental atmosphere was fostered'.[22] A report by the National Vigilance Association from 1904 estimated that 2,000 foreign prostitutes worked in London.[23]

A larger number of foreign sailors spent time in London, again linked to the global significance of the London port and dating back to the eighteenth century, when the East India Company started recruiting staff in India because white British equivalents fell victim to disease and could not be replaced by other Britons. The company had to find a solution and it consisted of employing Indian workers, some of whom were sailors who came ashore and, with no financial support, started begging. Although racist legislation had come into operation to prevent the hiring of Indian seamen by the end of the eighteenth century, mercantile growth during the nineteenth century had forced a reversal of this decision in 1849.[24] By the late Victorian and Edwardian periods sailors from all over the world spent time in London, including Indians, Malays, Arabs, Africans and Chinese. The London City missionary Joseph Salter, who set up a home to care for them in the East End, became concerned about the vices to which they could succumb.[25] At the end of the First World War black and other international sailors who came ashore faced rioting from demobilized troops and white seamen,[26] while black sailors subsequently faced constraints with the passage of the Special Restriction (Coloured Alien Seaman) Order of 1925.[27] Despite facing deportation and restriction, foreign sailors remained a feature of dock life in the East End during the Second World War when the numbers of black people employed increased due to labour shortages, caused by conscription, as had happened during the First World War. In the late 1940s and early 1950s the 'coloured seamen' in Stepney found employment 'in ships' engine rooms as firemen, greasers or donkeymen', in 'work that is hard, dirty and monotonous'. By this time, while on shore, they could actually receive a weekly maintenance allowance from the companies that employed them, even though this remained less than what they earned while at sea. Some took work while on shore in cafés or at the Beckton Gas Works.[28] By the early 1950s black sailors found it increasingly difficult to secure employment on British ships, which they believed originated in a racist refusal of both the ship owners and white crews. A few dozen signed on for unemployment benefit in 1951.[29] As the importance of the London docks declined after 1945, so did the numbers of foreign sailors present in the East End.

For much of the nineteenth century a key occupation for women consisted of domestic service, which relied upon people born in Great Britain.[30] One exception to this rule was the German governess, who became a feature of aristocratic and upper middle-class life to such an extent that an Association of German Governesses came into existence in 1876, helping 6,000 women to secure posts in Britain during the 1880s and 1890s. While these women may appear to have lived relatively comfortable lives, prized over their British equivalents because of their ability to teach foreign languages and music, they earned little and essentially retained second-class status, slightly above the rest of the servants with whom they lived, but not part of the family.[31] Further domestic servants arrived from Germany during the 1930s under a Ministry of Labour Scheme that allowed up to 14,000 Jewish refugees to enter the country to take up such employment. About 7,000 accepted the offer, mostly concentrated on London, despite efforts to disperse them throughout the country. Like the German governesses, they came from middle-class backgrounds and often faced humiliation as a result of the work they undertook, which generally terminated during the Second World War.[32] Labour shortages at the end of the war meant that female refugees were accepted from all over Europe as a result of government schemes aimed at filling occupations experiencing shortages, including domestic work in hospitals.[33] The post-war equivalent of the German governess was the au pair, who could originate from anywhere in the world. For example, Flora left Colombia just before her twenty-second birthday in 1974 partly in order to learn English. Although she initially enjoyed living with the family for whom she worked, she found that they 'started expecting me to be a domestic and being paid as an au pair. They started being very mean with food. If you had a shower or bath they said it was expensive and started restricting my freedom.' Consequently she left and eventually became a nurse.[34]

Au pair work has continued to attract South Americans in the more deregulated economy of the early twenty-first century, which has impacted not simply upon migrants but also native Britons and Londoners. The availability of cheap labour, often illegal, has given employers the upper hand in setting conditions and pay.[35] The need to 'make ends meet' applies to many Londoners, whether white British, migrants or the descendants of migrants,[36] in locations throughout the vast employment landscape of the capital.[37] Migrants work in all sectors of the London economy from bankers to cleaners. But those working at the bottom end of the scale tend to originate from poorer countries and sometimes have an irregular status, whereas those from wealthier countries tend to have similar occupations to native Britons and Londoners. In 2005 the lower-end jobs where migrants played a large role (over 20 per cent) included manufacturing (25 per cent), construction (21 per cent), transport and distribution (31 per cent), and hotels and catering (42 per cent).[38]

More specifically, cleaning, construction, hospitality and food-processing became some of the sectors in which foreigners played an increasingly important role. One project examining the role of migrant labour in these areas assessed people from sixty-three different countries of origin, ranging from Eastern Europe to sub-Saharan Africa. About one-third of the 429 workers surveyed 'appeared to lack the papers to work', whether they lived in London as students (real or imagined) or asylum seekers (with applications failed or pending). They had no access to the benefits system because of their status but moved to London precisely because they could find employment, which they secured through networks of their countrymen. Within their workplace they experienced 'multinationalism', like the rest of the London population, precisely because of the range of nationalities employed in the capital. But the newcomers also faced poor employment conditions, often earning the national minimum wage without the benefit of sick or holiday pay.[39]

The Yorùbá community in London work in a variety of sectors including night-time cab driving (an occupation dominated by a variety of migrants) as well as the early-morning and late-evening physically demanding job of cleaning offices, with poor job security and pay. 'The sight of them in the buses and the underground between four thirty and six o'clock in the mornings, half-awake, half-asleep, recalls the plight of the blacks in Britain in the sixteenth, seventeenth centuries and afterwards when blacks were used as domestic servants.'[40] In fact, the Yorùbá constitute just one African group involved in this type of employment, as indigenous English cleaners had essentially disappeared from offices by the end of the twentieth century.[41]

It might seem tempting to view black Africans as having a particular place at the bottom of the London labour market, but individuals from all over the world work in lower-end jobs. One such group which has emerged in London at the beginning of the twenty-first century consists of Latin Americans. This community had remained largely absent from London until this time, although some prominent figures had previously travelled to the city, including exiles, diplomats, businessmen, writers and artists, perhaps most famously of all

Simón Bolívar in 1810 as he sought the support of Britain in the independence struggle of Venezuela.[42] Significant numbers of Latin Americans did not begin to arrive until the 1970s, including refugees, especially Chileans fleeing the repression of General Pinochet, while others followed from totalitarian regimes in Uruguay and Argentina. Further refugees, together with students and those seeking work, made their way to London during the 1980s and began to form community organizations. The numbers increased from the 1980s from Colombia, Ecuador and Bolivia due to political upheaval while, after 2000, Brazilians became the largest Latin American group to seek out London, including students and professionals. By the beginning of the twenty-first century about 113,500 Latin Americans were residing in London, including 17,100 irregular migrants.[43] By this time economic motivations proved most important in sending them to the metropolis, although others made the move for educational or political reasons. Over half actually migrated via Spain and Portugal.[44] Most Bolivians stated that the economic situation in their own country 'was so dismal that leaving the country was the only way in which they could improve their life chances. In other words, London was seen as a place harbouring opportunities not available in Bolivia.'[45] Most Latin Americans entered Britain with temporary visas, although others possessed EU documents which allowed settlement in the United Kingdom. A significant percentage changed their immigration status to allow them to work in London. Although engaged in all types of employment, 55 per cent worked in 'elementary occupations' and 'personal service occupations', including 'cleaners, kitchen assistants, porters, waiters and waitresses, hotel chambermaids and security guards', as well as domestic cleaning and au pairing – in other words exactly the type of work which migrants undertake in a polarized London society. A third of Latin Americans work in domestic and office cleaning.[46] Other jobs included working as couriers and drivers, which accounted for 10 per cent of Brazilians.[47] Reflecting the experience of similar migrant groups in early twenty-first-century London, Latin Americans experienced a decline in occupational status, tended to receive pay around the national minimum wage, and sometimes had to work in more than one job to survive, with an average of thirty-eight hours per week, although this exceeded forty-eight hours in some cases.[48] Peruvians experienced a decline in 'well-being' as a result of their movement to London due to the level of state control over their immigration status, difficulties in bonding with the English, the importance of routine, loss of social status because of the nature of the work undertaken and the long hours involved.[49]

Despite the psychological problems experienced by Peruvians, the fact that most of them, like their fellow Latin Americans, possess a legal status, means that their position represents an improvement on the experiences of the undocumented from all over the world living throughout the capital often in substandard accommodation and working in all manner of occupations.[50] The metropolis also acts as the centre of illegal Chinese migration, which diverts people to work in other parts of the country.[51] Even the building of the Olympic village involved the use of some illegal migrants including a Macedonian called Constantin who lived with his wife in a house in East London shared with ten other irregular workers. When he lost his job here he found another working for a property maintenance company carrying out small repairs across the capital while his wife earned over £500 per week in cash by working six days a week as a cleaner in four houses.[52]

BUILDERS

Constantin offers one example of a trade in which migrants have played a significant role in the history of London. The Irish have proved especially important as builders although they have also found employment in a wide variety of predominantly working-class occupations not simply in London but also in the country as a whole.[53] During the nineteenth century most entered the country as unskilled labourers and worked in occupations which matched their lack of training towards the lower end of the social scale, fulfilling the role now undertaken by a range of migrants in twenty-first-century London. While they served as cheap labour the Irish did not undercut British workers precisely because of their lack of skills.[54] During the eighteenth century the London Irish 'were builders' labourers, chairmen, porters, coal-heavers, milk-sellers and street hawkers', while others worked as silk weavers.[55] They continued in similar jobs during the nineteenth century and provided a major resource for employers in the metropolis. In 1851 their most significant occupation was as 'general labourers' working in the docks and on construction projects. The major employment for Irish women consisted of domestic service.[56] One survey of occupations amongst the Irish in the East End from the 1851 census revealed that from a selection of 274 Irish-born men and 179 women the most important group consisted of 142 labourers among the men, far in excess of the next group of dock labourers (21), followed by 19 builders, while 54 of the women worked as domestics, followed by 28 dressmakers. In the building industry 'the Irish provided a strong, mobile labour force' which played a large role, for instance, in the building of the East End Tunnel between 1825 and 1843.[57] Some occupational mobility occurred during the Victorian period, even during the course of the 1850s, when the percentage of unskilled amongst the London Irish decreased from 20.25 per cent to 18.73 per cent.[58] Charles Manby Smith, using patronizing and racist language, gave the example of Terence O'Donoghue. 'When I first met Terry he was in the enviable position of a hanger-on at the underground warehouse of a small printing-office, where two or three minor monthly publications were rolled off from a machine in a cellar, the motive-power of which was supplied by a steam-engine in an adjoining factory.' Previously, 'Terry had no regular engagement; his earnings were limited to fetchings and carrying out of errands; and when he had nothing to do he had nothing to receive.' However, the 'untaught Irishman, bred in the bogs of Connaught', volunteered to 'supersede the steam-engine' when it broke down by the use of a handle to operate the machine and managed to secure a permanent job.[59]

Many of the Irish males who migrated to London in significant numbers during the twentieth century, especially in the early post-war period, continued to concentrate on the building trade. The reasons for migration away from Ireland in this period included poverty, especially in comparison with the opportunities for employment in London and elsewhere in Britain, as well as the contrast between the excitement of the big city and rural poverty in Ireland. Many emigrated in their late teens or early twenties.[60] Some Irishmen arrived in London as a result of direct recruitment from the Second World War period into the 1950s. The Civil Engineering Foundation sometimes interviewed Irishmen in their local employment exchange in Ireland and then paid for their fare. Irish women also moved to London during the war years, undergoing a medical examination in Ireland and often working as domestic servants. Other Irish people simply made their own decision to migrate and found employment in factories and on building sites.[61] Morning pick-up points developed for construction workers in Cricklewood Broadway, Kilburn High Road, Camden High Street, Elephant and Castle and Hammersmith. 'After being picked up by vans and trucks' the Irish navvies 'would be scattered to various construction sites'.[62] Together with building, the sectors which employed most Irish people were the transport, distribution and service industries. During the 1950s and 1960s Irish women especially worked part-time either in semi-skilled manual employment or in clerical work.[63] They often experienced difficult, unstable and exploitative working conditions.[64] Furthermore, the Irish also faced discrimination in the labour market. This hostility would survive until the end of the twentieth century with prejudice linked to the activities of the IRA.[65]

The Irish continued to find employment in the building industry in London into the 1960s and 1970s and played a role in the construction of the South Bank Centre and the Barbican. The main firm involved in the building of the former was Higgs and Hill, which had existed since 1874. Its Irish employees included Michael Houlihan and Jim McDonald.[66] The firms directing the construction of the Barbican between 1962 and 1982 included Robert McAlpine, which was involved in many London building projects and routinely employed Irishmen. Those who worked on this project included Michael Houlihan as well as Noel Clarke, Jim Moher, Tony McGing and Jim McDonald.[67] These individuals had contrasting working lives, which did not simply involve one or both of these projects, but also a series of others, either within London or elsewhere in Britain. Noel Clarke was born in Dublin in 1945, the son of a carpenter who first introduced him to the building trade. He first travelled to London on holiday at the age of fifteen to visit his brother in Holloway Road and secured a job in the Craven A factory in Camden Town but quickly moved to another one in Finsbury Square. He subsequently worked in Bristol and Oldbury and returned to Shepherd's Bush to work for the BBC. He married in 1965 and began working on the Barbican for John Laing.[68] Meanwhile, Michael Houlihan was born in County Kildare in 1934 and left Ireland in 'the Hungry Fifties' because 'there was no work available other than casual work and, of course' the pay was very, very poor, not enough to sustain body and soul'. He moved to London at the age of twenty-three and first worked for 'Willesden Borough Council, on the buildings', although he subsequently found a series of jobs in central London, especially as a scaffolder, as well as in other parts of Britain, eventually marrying a woman from Jersey and settling in North Kensington. He began working on the Barbican in 1966.[69] Tony McGing, born in County Mayo in 1941, moved to Wimbledon in 1961 and 'started work on the . . . Royal Marsden Hospital in Sutton' when 'somebody . . . brought me along and taught me how to do scaffolding'. He worked here for two years and moved to other jobs in London before starting to work on the Barbican. 'They were nearly all Irish there. All the crane drivers were Irish.'[70] Jim McDonald, meanwhile, born in Kilkenny in 1947, moved to London in 1967 and quickly secured a job on the South Bank project after a couple of other positions in London.[71] All of these Irish builders in London also remembered working with members of other ethnic groups including Jamaicans who specialized in 'shuttering mainly'[72] and Sikhs and Pakistanis who made 'first-class carpenters'.[73]

Migration from Ireland to London continued into the later twentieth century but some changes had taken place in the type of employment secured. The reasons for leaving Ireland included a high unemployment rate and the opportunity to secure work elsewhere, while the particular attractions of London included the fact that the migrants already knew people living there and the sense of freedom within the British capital. Reflecting changes in the London economy during the 1980s, the 'new migrants are much more likely to work in service industries such as shops, offices and in professional or management positions'. However, 44 per cent in one survey still worked in unskilled manual or skilled manual occupations.[74] While some social mobility may have taken place amongst the earlier post-war arrivals, the 1981 census revealed that the Irish counted a higher proportion of unskilled manual labourers than any other ethnic group.[75]

INDUSTRIAL FODDER

For most of the nineteenth and twentieth centuries the Irish have played the role of the main reserve of labour which has migrated to London to carry out work at the bottom end of the social scale, especially in the building trades shunned by many native Londoners. But the Irish formed just one section of the historical lower rung of the economic ladder which has worked in manufacturing, a key driver of the London economy from the Victorian period to the 1960s, frequented also, during the nineteenth century, by the Germans and, increasingly, East European Jewish migrants. As James Greenwood pointed out in the paragraph that begins this chapter, even the Irish would not undertake some tasks.

He referred to sugar baking in the East End of London, a process in which Germans specialized and which constituted the final stage in the transformation of West Indian sugar cane to refined sugar. While Greenwood may have some justification in suggesting that Germans undertook this task because all other ethnic groups shunned the work, there are also other explanations. For example, Germans, more especially Hanoverians, had become involved in this trade from the end of the eighteenth century. This meant that they continued to migrate to East London to work in this occupation until the sugar refineries disappeared in the early twentieth century as sugar beet, with a different production process, replaced cane as the main source of this sweetener.[76] The German sugar bakers, like the Irish builders, therefore demonstrated an ethnic clustering in employment which lasted for over a century. Greenwood's assertions about the position of the Germans at the bottom of the occupational ladder during the Victorian period contain some truth as they also worked in other poorly paid East End manufacturing occupations involving long hours and poor pay: skin-dyeing and dressing, tailoring and shoemaking. Women shoemakers could work up to twelve hours a day and earn just eight shillings per week.[77] A type of chain migration also existed in the employment of German tailors. One of Henry Mayhew's interviewees claimed that: 'Ven I came over here I vent to sew at one of my own countrymen, and I have mostly been working for my own countrymen ever since. Most of the Chermans I have worked for have been vot you call sweaters in dis country, because they do make a man sweat.' He claimed he earned fourteen shillings but that ten of them went towards the rent provided by his employer, an experience shared by other German tailors.[78]

By the end of the nineteenth century the ethnic group in London which had become most closely connected with the clothing and footwear trades concentrated in the East End were the East European Jews. These immigrants had a high level of concentration in these trades. In 1901 '42 per cent of all Russian and Polish males in East London, and 54 per cent of females, were engaged in the tailoring trades; a further 13 per cent of the men were employed in boot, shoe and slipper manufacture.'[79] The development of these trades in the East End had much to do with the demand for clothing due to the expansion of the population of the metropolis as a whole,[80] building upon a system which existed before the Jewish influx of the later nineteenth century (as indicated by Mayhew's German interviewee). Public opinion focused upon the role of the Jews in the development of sweating, although the link between Jews and exploitative employment practices evolved partly because their entry into London in the 1880s occurred during a time of economic recession and rising unemployment.[81]

Jews gravitated towards the 'sweated industries' for other reasons, including the existence of an endemic everyday antisemitism in late Victorian Britain. One Jewish workman claimed: 'I know many Jewish engineers, painters, brushmakers, &c., who were compelled to take to tailoring because they are Jews and foreigners. The Jew, being excluded from the means of livelihood in ordinary trades, has created industries for himself.'[82] However, a significant percentage of the new arrivals had already laboured in garment workshops in Russia. One survey of residents of the Poor Jews Temporary Shelter in selected years between 1895 and 1907 revealed that 23 per cent had worked in clothing and 9 per cent in boots and shoes, although these figures remained lower than the concentration in these industries following settlement in the East End.[83] The newcomers, often following their short spell in the Poor Jews Temporary Shelter, with little knowledge of English, moved towards an area of employment which their countrymen increasingly came to dominate, which meant they could remain in a Jewish milieu.[84]

Rather than working in large-scale factory units which developed during the industrialization process, the immigrants found employment in workshops, continuing the East European system that had also characterized the East End. The production of garments also relied on a subcontracting system, which encouraged a further depression of wages as one level of employer could simply demand cheaper products from the level underneath, and which also resulted in employing women at home.[85]

As with the concept of the ghetto, of which the sweating system formed a key element, both British writers and immigrants and their offspring played a role in propagating this concept, although with no nostalgic looking back in this case. Willy Goldman claimed: 'I began, I believe, with what must be the world's record in low wages. I got sixpence per week. The boss was a relative of a neighbour of ours and considered he was doing my people a favour in having me to work for him. Because of that I wasn't made to carry parcels to the shop.'[86] British public opinion, whether newspapers, racist writers or parliamentary inquiries, focused upon the idea that the non-unionized newcomers undermined domestic workers by labouring for longer hours in worse conditions than those which natives would accept. William Evans-Gordon claimed that 'East of Aldgate', 'sweaters workshops' had appeared in dwellings which 'quite recently were in the occupation of English working men and their families . . . No matter at what hour of the day or night one passes, the machines are heard.' The 'descendants of pharaohs brickmakers' still worked 'at two or three in the morning, after fifteen or eighteen hours of work'.[87] Parliamentary inquiries did not use such overtly antisemitic language but pointed to the evils of the sweating system, especially in smaller workshops, sometimes the lodgings of the 'sweater', where work was carried out in overcrowded, 'filthy and unsanitary conditions'.[88] On the other hand, the 'foreign Jewish immigrant is extremely thrifty, and very industrious', while 'sobriety' represented 'the chief cause of his willingness and ability to accept lower wages'.[89] Beatrice Potter's analysis of the tailoring trade in the East End examined different branches and the quality of clothes they produced and concluded that 'the lowest class of trade' dependent on a 'constant supply of destitute foreigners and of wives forced to supplement their husband's irregular earnings' represented the main problem, although the 'real "sweater" had a threefold personality' in the form of 'an ignorant consumer', a 'fraudulent' wholesaler or trader, and 'a rack-renting landlord'.[90] Newly arrived Jews therefore formed one element of this system.

The sweating system appears to have reached its height in the 1880s and 1890s, at least from the point of view of Jewish involvement.[91] As some of the extracts above indicate, not all of the newcomers experienced the worst of this system and, if they did, they often moved away from it once their status as 'greeners' had expired. The development of a trade union movement amongst the Jews working in the East End and other inner city areas, especially Leeds, also helped to alleviate the worst conditions.[92] Jewish tailors in London did not simply focus upon the East End but also lived in the West End, where they accounted for between a third and a half of Jewish employees. But the type of sweating which occurred in the East End did not occur here. 'The West End tailor handled more of the specialised high-quality work, which was natural given that the centres of upmarket trade were Savile Row and the Oxford Street stores', although many Jews here also produced women's clothing.[93]

Jews also found employment in other occupations, perhaps most significantly cabinet-makers who had already acquired their skills in Eastern Europe and would enter a trade in the East End in which firms of various sizes would play a role, including a series of Jewish establishments which emerged during the course of the nineteenth century.[94] Those employed in this trade included Sam Clarke, born in Bethnal Green in 1907, and his father, who had migrated from Russia. His father was a skilled cabinet-maker who earned 2d an hour above the union rate while, by the 1930s, Sam specialized in large bedroom suites.[95]

By this time the East End Jewish community, with a significant percentage born in London, had not only begun to disperse geographically but had also experienced occupational mobility and a movement away from the areas of employment which characterized the decades before the First World War. In 1913 nearly half of Jewish youth aged between fourteen and twenty entered tailoring but by 1930 this had declined to a quarter, partly because mechanization had decreased the demand for labour. Similarly, few Jews worked in the shoe trades and in cap-making, again due largely to mechanization. Cabinet-making, on the other hand, had increased in importance, as had cigarette-making. Jews also became furriers, engineers, hairdressers and barbers. Women moved towards clerical work.[96] A minority experienced more rapid social mobility and entered the professions,[97] a process which would continue into the post-war period when the Jewish community became the most profession-alized in London.[98] One of the most remarkable examples of social mobility before 1945 was the Ukrainian-born Selig Brodetsky who moved away from his East End roots to a Cambridge education and then a chair in mathematics at Leeds University.[99]

The migrants who settled in London after the Second World War did not quite replace their Jewish predecessors because they did not experience the same exploitation and conditions or the same level of concentration in specific occupations. Equally, post-war arrivals did not simply focus upon a small number of inner city locations, but in industrial employment throughout the whole of the metropolis.

The increase in the diversity of migrants after the Second World War meant that, while particular groups may have concentrated in specific sectors of industry in the early post-war years, when manufacturing still had a significant role to play in London, some factories employed people from a variety of ethnic origins. During the second half of the 1960s, in factories in Croydon which employed over 100 immigrants, 42.3 per cent originated in Europe including Eastern European refugees from the fallout of the Second World War, exiles from the failed 1956 Hungarian uprising, and 'economic migrants' from Western Europe, while most of the remaining 57.7 per cent came from the Commonwealth. Industry here had access to a diversity of labour ranging from Poles to Hungarians to Irish to Maltese, Cypriots, Indians, Pakistanis, Africans and West Indians.[100] Individual factories within Croydon also employed a variety of ethnic groups, although some level of concentration occurred.[101] In addition to Sheila Patterson's important study of Croydon another survey of immigrant employment in Croydon and Tower Hamlets from the same period identified Cypriots, Pakistanis and West Indians, pointing not only to the diversity but also to the ubiquity and normality of migrant employment in London by the end of the 1960s.[102] In such a situation a camaraderie developed, which could involve individuals utilizing ethnic stereotypes as illustrated in one North London factory during the 1970s.[103]

Some concentration inevitably occurred, related to the skewed geographical distribution involving particular groups focused on specific areas. While a variety of migrants may have worked in Croydon by the 1960s, West Indians became especially visible in South London from the 1950s, although they also worked in significant numbers in the other areas in which they settled: the East End and Notting Hill. In 1951, 65 per cent of West Indians and 75 per cent of West Africans in Stepney consisted of unskilled and semi-skilled labourers according to employment exchange records. The only two 'industries' which utilized significant numbers of these two groups in Stepney were building and clothing, with employers in the clothing trade made up almost entirely of Jews.[104] Meanwhile, many of those living in North Kensington during the 1950s 'were employed by municipalities or in public transport'.[105]

Most of the West Indians came from a rural background and had not therefore acquired the technical skills necessary for the British job market. The Ministry of Labour estimated that 13 per cent of the West Indians were skilled, 22 per cent semi-skilled and 65 per cent unskilled.[106] The main reason for their migration to Britain during the 1950s lay in the limited job opportunities which existed in the West Indies. By the end of the 1940s about one-quarter of Jamaica's population was jobless.[107] Despite the assertions of the Ministry of Labour, the majority of the migrants did not perceive themselves as unskilled or semi-skilled, yet over 60 per cent of them found such jobs in Britain.[108] Part of the explanation for this lay in the fact that 'the West Indian migrant tends to accept the first job offered' and, in a situation of low unemployment in Britain during the 1950s, they often switched jobs quite frequently.[109] Nevertheless, as many personal narratives demonstrate[110] and as evidenced most clearly in the Notting Hill riots of 1958, the newcomers faced racial prejudice. Many employers believed that West Indians had a different work ethic to white workers, while trade unions regarded them as a threat to their working conditions.[111] Many West Indians actually came to Great Britain as part of defined schemes directed to particular areas of employment,[112] but others would become factory fodder, along with immigrants from all over the world, as Sheila Patterson demonstrated. An earlier survey of West Indians by the same author covering 1955 to 1958 revealed that men and women worked in a range of industries in South London including food processing, light engineering, heavy industry, the sale and repair of cars, the garment trade and building and construction, again reflecting the population of London as a whole, including other immigrants.[113] By the 1970s most West Indians had experienced an upgrading in their employment status compared with the situation in their homeland, although many did not perceive this improvement, resenting the racial prejudice they had experienced which, in some cases, had also resulted in downward social mobility.[114] By this time unemployment had begun to become an issue for both West Indians and the wider population in London[115] due to the beginnings of industrial decline. This would intensify during the 1980s.[116] It meant that migrants and their offspring would experience higher unemployment rates than their ethnic majority counterparts due to a combination of factors including racial prejudice, concentration in inner city areas with some of the worst schools, and the fact that many of the first generation found it difficult to retrain due to their age,[117] leading some to establish small businesses.[118] As early as 1961 West Indian males in London endured an unemployment rate of 6 per cent compared with 3.2 per cent for men born in England.[119]

Pakistanis also faced unemployment in London and elsewhere from as early as the late 1950s[120] and together with other Asians they would experience higher rates of joblessness from the 1980s.[121] Yet South Asian migrants played a significant role in factory work following their arrival. Manual work offers just one avenue for employment amongst Asians in London, who have worked across the employment spectrum, especially as small shopkeepers.[122] Some groups, including Goans, some of whom originated in East Africa, have concentrated in clerical and managerial employment. This can be explained by their higher educational qualifications than those held, for example, by Bangladeshis and Pakistanis.[123]

Bangladeshi men 'were the most poorly qualified compared to other ethnic groups', which meant that along with African-Caribbeans they 'were more often found at lower job levels than employees in other ethnic groups'. In the early 1990s national figures demonstrated that 70 per cent of Bangladeshi men compared with 19 per cent of whites worked in semi-skilled or unskilled manual jobs.[124] In the early 1960s East and West Pakistanis who had moved to London from rural backgrounds, most of whom could not speak or write English, could only secure unskilled jobs.[125] Abdu Ali, for example, initially worked in a shoe factory in Liverpool Street gluing shoes together from 1963 to 1968. He went home for a year, during which time his factory had faced demolition, which meant that he found another job in the boiler room in the Mile End Hospital for two years but then faced redundancy.[126] During the course of the 1960s and 1970s Pakistanis or, more especially, Bangladeshis, and especially women, increasingly worked in the East End clothing industry, acting as a replacement for the Jewish community. Like their Jewish predecessors the South Asians had a greater tolerance of poorer working conditions than native-born Londoners. Also like their Jewish predecessors, in a situation which also applies to other ethnic groups in London, including Greek Cypriots, Indians and Pakistanis, homeworkers also worked for their countrymen who started up small businesses and could save on labour (by paying a cheaper rate, usually by piece) and factory costs by sending work out to the homeworkers. At the same time employers and employees often avoided paying income tax and VAT partly by making homeworkers self-employed, in anticipation of the practice which multinationals would utilize in the 'gig economy' of the twenty-first century. In this situation clothing production could continue despite the international competition from imported goods which decimated much of London's manufacturing industry.[127] Bangladeshi men also worked in this trade so that by the 1970s they provided the largest percentage of males in the clothing industry and also accounted for 20 per cent of jobs in Tower Hamlets where Bangladeshis were concentrated.[128] While women have unquestionably faced exploitation in the London rag trade, they often chose to work at home rather than in a factory environment for a variety of reasons: these included, for Bangladeshis, the Islamic need to separate men from women; the lack of command of the English language; and, perhaps most importantly, working at home allowed women to earn a living as well as carrying out their domestic responsibilities of child rearing, cooking and cleaning.[129]

While a significant percentage of Bangladeshi women chose to work at home in the rag trade, this offers just one example of South Asian manufacturing employment in London. Some Sikhs also laboured in the East End clothing industry but others, centred on Southall, worked in light manufacturing industries in both the food and other sectors, as well as finding a wide range of jobs at Heathrow Airport.[130] One South Asian woman, Raksha, born in India in 1951, started working in Heathrow in 1969 on 'tray-set, you know the meals on flights. I was not used to standing all day, so I found that hard. It was okay. But what can I say. For someone who had never worked before, it will be hard. I found it hard to touch meat, as I did not eat meat. I often used to feel sick.'[131] Saran, meanwhile, born in the Punjab in 1957, undertook a series of jobs after her arrival in London including working in a United Biscuits factory and packing food for Japan Airlines, as well as working for the Royal Mail, during which time she also gave birth to three children.

Like some other Asian women, Saran became involved in a union,[132] the most famous example of which consisted of those who worked for the Grunwick Film Processing Laboratories which lay in Dollis Hill in Willesden. In this case the majority of the strikers consisted of Asians from East Africa, especially Kenya, who moved to Britain during the course of the 1960s. Many of them had previously worked in administrative and clerical positions but, in these early days of their settlement in London, they could only secure factory and manual work. The factory owners viewed the newcomers as a form of cheap and docile labour but the workers, led by Jayaben Desai, walked out on 20 August 1976, following the dismissal of Devshi Bhudia, and gained union recognition for their cause from the Association of Professional, Executive, Clerical and Computer Staff. The dispute became a cause célèbre for the wider trade union movement, which supported the workers but, in the end, those who had faced dismissal lost their right to reinstatement after a dispute which lasted for two years.[133]

European groups also acted as fodder for small and large-scale industrial enterprises in London in the earlier post-war decades. East Europeans who moved to the country in the immediate post-war years, often recruited to work in specific industries, such as textiles, settled throughout Britain, mostly in the north and Midlands.[134] Similarly, the direct recruitment of Italians into specific industrial occupations outside London occurred during the late 1940s and early 1950s in an attempt to fill labour shortages.[135] However, by the 1960s not only did East Europeans become a feature of industrial life in London, as revealed in the case of Croydon,[136] but Italians, together with Portuguese and Spanish migrants, became heavily concentrated in London,[137] with employment across the occupational scale.[138]

One of the post-war European groups with the highest concentration in London were the Cypriots who, like their southern European counterparts, worked across the employment spectrum.[139] The jobs that Cypriots undertook 'like other migrants ... were those least attractive to the indigenous popula-tion'.[140] During the 1950s about 33 per cent of Cypriot men worked as tailors, shoemakers, mechanics, electricians, carpenters, painters and decorators, plumbers and bricklayers, with a further 15 per cent as cooks, waiters and barbers.[141] At the same time 85 per cent of Cypriot women 'were employed as dressmakers and machinists in small workshops owned by Cypriots or Jews'.[142] However, Cypriots also had a high rate of self-employment which would continue for the rest of the century.[143]

Like Jews and Bangladeshis, Cypriots therefore were concentrated particu-larly in the clothing trades, demonstrating similar patterns of work and employment and attracted to this sector for similar reasons. The preponder-ance of women in these trades was because most had learnt this skill in Cyprus in preparation for marriage and had traditionally worked in employment with little contact with men, facilitating the development of homeworking which allowed those with high productivity rates to maximize their earnings.[144] Again, like Bangladeshi women, Cypriots who worked at home could also raise children, which meant their income essentially acted as a supplement to that of their husbands who usually worked outside the home, sometimes in a dress-making or tailoring factory or workshop owned by a relative. Cypriot women also tended to have a limited command of English, especially upon arrival in Great Britain. Economic necessity meant that both men and women worked in an attempt to maximize income and prospects for their family units. A system of subcontracting which had caused concern about sweating amongst Victorian and Edwardian Jews also continued, although it was not quite as exploitative. The way the system operated involved a factory owner securing a contract with a firm which may have had a West End showroom. The Cypriot factory owner would produce the number of garments required by employing between fifteen and thirty machinists on his premises and a similar number working from home. Because of the small scale of such operations, the Cypriot entrepreneur could open a business with a fairly limited financial outlay. Conditions in the factory developed to a good standard and the employees tended not to work excessive hours, although this differed in the home, where women, who often paid no tax or national insurance as a result of their status as self-employed, could work as many hours as they liked. While a significant proportion of those employed by Cypriots were their compatriots, the facto-ries, like other industrial producers in the capital, employed a variety of ethnic groups. The children of the Cypriot migrants rarely moved into these clothing trades, having gone through the British education system and obtained some qualifications, no matter how basic in some cases. Instead, they secured work across the whole range of opportunities available in the London economy and public sector.[145] By the end of the 1970s the area around Finsbury Park (especially Fonthill Road) had become the headquarters of the Cypriot rag trade in London, counting both factories and showrooms.[146]

This type of ethnic occupational clustering became common in London. A number of those who moved into the rag trade certainly had some experience of working within it, as the example of Jewish tailors and Cypriot dressmakers indicates, but they were not specialists specifically recruited by sectors of the British state to work in particular fields of public service or imported by their countrymen already in London to work in particular occupations. The rag trade has had the function of absorbing migrants at the bottom of the linguistic and skills ladder who often had little alternative but to become involved in it, especially in the case of women who wanted to combine home work with child-rearing.

SPECIALISTS

Specialists have also moved to London since the Victorian period to work in specific occupations. In the case of waiters and other restaurant personnel, they have formed part of a European-wide network. Migrants progressed to London and elsewhere in the United Kingdom in an attempt to develop their skills with the aim of securing the best possible permanent position at the end of the process, whether in London, Paris or in a restaurant or hotel elsewhere in Britain or Europe. Germans became particularly important in this process.[147] One way of understanding the migration of Germans to Britain before 1914 consists of breaking them down into a series of specialists who included not simply sugar bakers and governesses but also butchers, bakers and barbers, imported as employees by their countrymen and progressing to set up their own businesses and to import further German migrants.[148] Germans also became particularly important as foreign correspondence clerks in London in the late Victorian period due to their knowledge of French and German, their training in Germany, their efficiency, and their readiness to accept lower pay. Many of them simply worked in London on a short-term basis in an attempt to improve their skills and knowledge with the aim, like waiters, of securing a better position once they returned to Germany. Some may even have worked as volunteers because they received funding from German mercantile unions as part of a formal apprenticeship to a merchant.[149]

The evolution of the Italian community in Victorian London resembles that of the Germans in that it consisted of a series of specialists, including waiters, ice cream sellers and musicians.[150] In addition, Italians became important in a series of other skilled occupations. These included makers and sellers of small statuettes who originated in two communes in Lucca and Toscana. They travelled throughout the world, settling initially in London from the 1840s with many subsequently moving northwards as far as Scotland, although some firms survived in London for decades. George R. Sims met an artisan in 'one of the little courts' in Clerkenwell in a 'single room that still serves him well. He is a quiet old fellow who left his native Pisa forty years ago' and specialized in making statuettes of dogs. Italians also became important as knife grinders in the Victorian capital, originating mostly from two villages in Trento, Pinzolo and Carisolo, travelling, like the figurine makers, throughout Europe and arriving in London by 1850. They parked their barrows at the back entrances of hotels and shops and offered to instantly grind all of the cutlery, surviving into the later twentieth century. Other Italians, focused upon Clerkenwell and often originating from specific villages, worked in even more specialized occupations, attracted by the reputation of London as centre of high-quality manufacture, including barometer and thermometer makers, looking-glass manufacturers, carvers and guilders, cabinet-makers and picture-frame makers. Mosaic and terrazzo workers from Friuli moved to London and Manchester from where they dispersed to work on a variety of private and public buildings. A more unskilled but again specialized occupation consisted of asphalt laying.[151]

Migrants continued to focus upon specialized occupations into the twentieth century but, by the post-war period in particular, the British government, public sector organizations and individual companies essentially began to import people to work in particular job categories. As we have seen, this process of selection had already begun in the 1930s with regard to directing middle-class German Jews to work in domestic service.[152] At the same time a system of targeted recruitment developed in the Irish Republic, partly aimed at specific areas but also driven by a desire to restrict free movement due to security concerns during wartime, although in 1947 controls on movement across the

Irish Sea disappeared.[153] Importation into specific industries intensified in the immediate aftermath of the Second World War when British government officials scoured camps for displaced persons throughout Europe looking for individuals who wished to escape the devastated continent. Interviewees from the Ministry of Labour recruited potential employees in good working health for sectors of industries that were short of workers: the National Health Service, farming, coal mining and textile production. Ultimately, most of those recruited through these schemes did not settle in London.[154]

Nevertheless, migrants have certainly played a significant role in public sector work in London, as the examples of the National Health Service and London Transport indicate. Irish nurses had travelled to London from the 1930s, as part of a more general process in which Irish women left their country to settle in Britain, escaping from poverty in their homeland.[155] Josephine, born on a small farm in Killaloe, County Clare, in 1919, initially worked in the Post Office in Monkstown near Dublin but decided to leave Ireland in 1936 in order to become a nurse in London, taking the decision herself as a pioneering lone migrant without telling her parents. Although she had cousins in Hendon they did not meet her when she arrived at Euston as planned. She had written to Hammersmith and University College Hospitals but secured a post at the Royal Marsden where she initially worked on the tuberculosis ward. She instantly disliked it and only remained in this career for eight months. She returned to Ireland temporarily but subsequently moved back to London to work for the Post Office, reflecting the experience of numerous other migrants, as well as indigenous Londoners who had a diverse career history.[156] The establishment of the National Health Service in 1948 created an urgent demand for nurses, which led to an aggressive recruitment campaign in Ireland. By the 1950s Irish nurses worked in hospitals throughout the capital, becoming deeply embedded within these institutions by the beginning of the following decade.[157] By this time nurses from the Commonwealth had also made an appearance in London, especially from the West Indies, as several life histories demonstrate. For example, Elma Sampson from Trinidad, trained as a nurse in her homeland but moved to London in the middle of the 1950s primarily to have an operation on her ear. She initially stayed with a cousin in Hayes and then worked in a series of hospitals in central and East London.[158] Ruth Barnett, from Bermuda, initially 'trained in my general at the Whittington hospital and then I went to the Plaistow maternity hospital then worked for a period and then went to Claybury hospital where I trained for psychiatric nursing'.[159] These Irish and West Indian women acted as pioneers for a hospital service which has imported people from all over the world to work throughout Britain in a wide variety of jobs, from doctors to cleaners, in an increasingly targeted national migration system aimed at specialists.[160]

Another public sector institution which employed people from Ireland, the West Indies and other parts of the world was London Transport. It was established in 1933 by the amalgamation of tram, trolleybus, bus and tube operators into the London Passenger Transport Board and covered an area of almost 2,000 square miles. Yet it faced difficulties attracting local people to work long and unsociable hours. In 1950 it opened a recruitment office in Dublin, using advertisements in local newspapers and on the radio.[161] In 1956 representatives from London Transport visited Barbados and hired fifty male conductors, twenty female conductors and seventy stationmasters. By the end of 1961 it had employed 2,112 Barbadians working throughout the metropolis. Similar direct recruitment schemes followed in Trinidad and Jamaica in 1966, while some of the descendants of the initial West Indian immigrants have also taken jobs on London Transport, as have migrants from other parts of the world. Some of those who arrived in the 1950s would spend their entire working lives in London on the buses and Underground trains. British Rail also adopted a similar pattern of direct recruitment from the West Indies, including Barbados.[162]

MIGRANTS IN THE LONDON WORKFORCE

It bears repeating that migrants have played a crucial role in the evolution of the London economy. The slaves brought back to England by their owners from the sixteenth century onwards may serve as a symbol for the millions of people who followed from all over the world. While they have not actually belonged to owners as property, countless free men and women have struggled at the lower end of the London labour ladder. The experiences and significance of the Irish builder for hundreds of years bears witness to this, as does the variety of migrant groups who have worked in the rag trade, focused especially upon the East End. Similarly, the position of the Germans at the bottom of the Victorian labour market in London, perhaps even below the Irish, supports this perspective, as does the variety of migrant groups working in a range of jobs on insecure contracts and poor pay in the early twenty-first century.

Some newcomers have worked in specific niches in the capital, as the example of the London sugar bakers would indicate. Ethnic concentration in employment also occurs higher up the social scale, as the prevalence of German foreign correspondence clerks in late Victorian Britain demonstrates. Some migrants deficient in English have preferred to work with their own countrymen in particular sectors of employment, as in the rag trade. This trade also enabled women to work at home for a variety of reasons, including their lack of English. Meanwhile, some firms or institutions have directly recruited from specific parts of the world during labour shortages, as in the example of London Transport.

This, however, offers an incomplete interpretation of the position of migrant labour in the modern and contemporary London labour market. While the rag trade or the various groups of Germans in Victorian London offer one paradigm of ethnic employment concentration, in reality migrants usually work alongside members of other ethnic groups, whether people from other parts of the world or native-born Londoners from a variety of ethnic origins, as the example of factories, buses and building sites in the immediate post-war years indicates.

Migrants may often find themselves at the bottom of the occupational ladder and may face discrimination, underlining their low status. However, newcomers and their offspring form a central part of the manual labour market in the metropolis. Just like immigrants arriving from all over the world, people born in Britain or within London itself have also had to undertake manual labour, often of a casual or seasonal nature,[163] especially before 1945. The need for reconstruction, the continued survival of London industry and the depopulation of the capital by white people opened up working opportunities for migrants from abroad after 1945. While the decline of manufacturing in London led to a rise in unemployment, which disproportionately impacted upon minority ethnic groups, the recovery of the 1990s and the early twenty-first century created an economy in which those working in poorly paid jobs at the bottom of the social and economic ladder experienced increased insecurity and a deterioration in their working conditions irrespective of their ethnicity.

Manual labour has offered just one type of working opportunity for people moving to London. Part of the uniqueness of the metropolis lies in the fact that migrants have worked up and down all rungs of the social and economic ladder, from prostitutes to merchant bankers. Although some of the people arriving in Britain did not stay in London, including the Irish navvy who worked throughout the country both before and after 1945,[164] many of the migrants described above focused upon London. At the same time, most of the narrative to date has concentrated upon the first generation of immigrants. The second and third generations usually experience social mobility both within London and beyond.[165]

4

A CITY OF HAWKERS, SHOPKEEPERS AND BUSINESSMEN

Of the Irish street-sellers, at present, it is computed that there are, including men, women and children, upwards of 10,000. Assuming the street-sellers attending the London fish and green markets to be, with their families, 30,000 in number, and 7 in every 20 of these to be Irish, we shall have rather more than the total above given. Of this large body three-fourths sell only fruit, and more especially nuts and oranges; indeed, the orange-season is called the 'Irishman's harvest'. The others deal in fish, fruit, and vegetables, but these are principally men. Some of the most wretched of the street-Irish deal in such trifles as lucifer-matches, water-cresses, &c.[1]

. . . my grandfather, having the nucleus of the workforce, without resorting to outside labour, was able to open a bakery. He was known in Poland as the Lodzer baker and he opened a small bake house at 71 Hessel Street the year before the First World War. And, erm, he built on his early success, people were thronging to his shop because it provided them with an authentic east European loaf . . . I know that my grandfather, in 1913, bought from Artofex a dough mixer that had been in use since 1909 and therefore was already second hand. And this was used right until the last day that the business folded, in 1985, Erev Pesach 1985.[2]

Data from the 2004 London Annual Business Survey (LABS) reveals that there were almost 39,000 Asian-owned businesses in London in 2004. This was about 14 per cent of all London businesses covered by the survey . . .

Asian-owned firms provide around 300,000 jobs to the London economy. This represented around 12 per cent of total employment by firms covered in the survey.[3]

ETHNIC ENTREPRENEURS

In the same way that migrants have worked in all sectors of the London economy as paid employees, whether in factories, buses or hospitals, they have also established their own businesses throughout the capital, especially as small shopkeepers selling all manner of products. While the Asian corner shop came to epitomize this process by the 1980s, those with origins in India, Pakistan, Bangladesh and Sri Lanka provide just one example of the importance of migrant businesses in the global metropolis. As the above quotes from Henry Mayhew and the Greater London Council indicate, migrant self-employment has involved enterprises on a variety of scales involving the selling of goods on the streets, on market stalls and in shops. At the same time, migrants have established businesses on a vast scale, a process which wealthy elites moving to the city may lead, but which also takes place through migrant generations as exemplified by the various Jewish communities. These three groups find themselves on different rungs of the London social ladder, from Irish at the bottom to the 'middling' Asian shopkeepers and elites at the top.

The extracts from Mayhew and the Greater London Council suggest that migrants tend to move into self-employment to a greater extent than the white British. The Irish and South Asians provide just one example of an entrepreneurial spirit in the Victorian period and the early twenty-first century respectively. To the former period we could also add Jews, Italians and Germans, and to the latter we could include virtually every migrant group living in London after 2000. The GLA report points to a self-employment rate of all ethnic groups in London of 14.9 per cent in 2001, reaching 16 per cent for Indians and 19.2 per cent for Pakistanis but only 11.7 per cent for Bangladeshis, with the figures for black Africans and black Caribbeans at less than 10 per cent. The Chinese stand at 17.7 per cent. These figures suggest that just 12.3 per cent of 'other ethnic groups' worked for themselves, while the figure for 'other white' self-employed stood at 16.7 per cent.[4] Other statistics point to a higher self-employment rate amongst those of European origin. As we have seen, both Greek and Turkish Cypriots opened their own businesses in the early post-war decades, especially in the rag trade. In 1966 a total of 19.6 per cent of Greek Cypriots were self-employed on a national scale, when the figure for the population as a whole stood at 7.1 per cent.[5] If we venture back into the late Victorian and Edwardian periods we find that Germans became especially important as hairdressers, butchers and bakers to the extent that the anti-German riots of May 1915 resulted in temporary bread shortages in some parts of London.[6]

Meanwhile, one in eight Jewish grooms married in London between 1880 and 1914 'was an entrepreneur', a figure which reaches 16.5 per cent for the period 1907–14, pointing to the fact that 'Jewish workers were at the very least twice as likely to be self-employed' as non-Jews, a pattern reflected amongst Jewish migrants on a global scale at this time.[7] At the end of the Second World War, Jews owned 11,000 of 71,675 (or 15.3 per cent) firms which existed in London, Manchester, Leeds, Glasgow, Cardiff and Newcastle. By this time members of this community owned one in six food shops in London.[8] Chinese people have demonstrated a similar level of entrepreneurship and self-employment since they became visible in London at the end of the nineteenth century, when they opened laundries and then restaurants, the latter of which became a key area of employment from the 1950s. The Chinese 'are far less likely to be employees than whites and members of other ethnic groups and two to three times more likely to be self-employed'.[9] Returning to the twenty-first century as a whole, while Chinese and South Asians may have become the most visible entrepreneurs in terms of the proportion of self-employed, reflected in their reputation for this situation in academic and public consciousness, they form the tip of the iceberg. Although black people may have a lower entrepreneurial rate, in 2004 London contained 'around 16,000 businesses owned by people of Black Caribbean and Black African descent' with an annual turnover of £10 billion and employing 100,000 people. By this time people from the Middle East owned about 2,500 businesses in London, while about 10,000 Turkish (including Turkish Cypriot) enterprises may have existed in the United Kingdom, with grocery stores becoming especially prominent. Similarly, Vietnamese businesses had also developed by this time.[10] Polish and other East European migrants have also opened their own businesses building, in some cases, on foundations laid by their predecessors who arrived in the 1940s. By 1954 about 1,000 'Polish-owned business establishments' existed in Britain as a whole, while by 1960 'the annual directory published by the Union of Polish Merchants and Industrialists in Britain listed about 2,500, three-quarters in London'.[11] On the other hand, some of the most recent of the new arrivals, concentrated in lower-end jobs, sometimes with dubious residential and work-permit status, such as Latin Americans, have not yet established businesses to any great extent.[12]

These statistics point to the fact that entrepreneurial self-employed migrants have characterized London life for centuries. Most have established small-scale enterprises but some of the above figures also include much bigger businesses with large turnovers.[13] At the same time, we should not forget the itinerant peddlers of a variety of goods who characterized London life from the eighteenth century. Some ethnic groups including Greek Cypriots, Indians, Pakistanis and Jews have a significantly higher rate of self-employment than the population of London as a whole. Other groups appear to display lower levels of entrepreneurship. As is the case with migrant employees, the patterns of self-employed migrants reflect those of the rest of London's population, even though some divergence exists, meaning that we should consider them a fundamental part of London life.

Following on from this assertion, we might divide migrant businesses into two types. In the first place, we can identify precisely those that emerge because of the size of the London consumer base, meaning that they seek out the same customers as entrepreneurs of any other ethnic groups, whether they be the Irish street-seller of Victorian London, the German baker of the Edwardian period, the migrant fish and chip shop owner, whether Jewish, Greek Cypriot or Pakistani,[14] or the Indian corner shop owner. Clearly, over the last three centuries, the nature of consumerism, the market, consumption and retailing in the capital has altered. However, the one constant is that London has always had the largest market and consumer base in the country, because its population has far exceeded any other British city, and, for much of this period, it has remained the largest city in the world. However, the nature of retailing has changed, meaning the numbers of street-sellers characterizing Georgian and Victorian London, who included Jews, Irish people and Italians, decreased by the beginning of the twentieth century as retail outlets of all sizes increasingly became sedentary.[15]

The uniqueness of London also partly lies in the number and diversity of ethnic concentrations that have emerged. These have spawned ethnic marketplaces all over the capital, beginning with the East End Jewish ghetto, which needed to provide food products according to religious dietary requirements.

This also applied to Muslim residents by the beginning of the twenty-first century. However, this religious group, a large percentage of whom originate in Bangladesh, India and Pakistan, form part of an even larger South Asian market that revolves around food (especially spices, pickles and vegetables) and female dress in particular, which operates on a national level because South Asian communities have evolved all over Britain. Out of the 2 million South Asians in Britain the 750,000 living in London, according to the 2001 census, have created a vast metropolitan and national market. Most of the businesses which have emerged have done so in the areas of South Asian concentration, whether in East London, especially Tower Hamlets, or in the west of the capital in Southall and the London boroughs of Hounslow, Harrow, Brent and Ealing.[16] While the late nineteenth- and early twentieth-century Jewish populations and the late twentieth- and early twenty-first-century Asian communities may have acted as the demand base for the most vibrant ethnic communities in London, these find replication amongst every other group of any significance which has settled in London.[17] The size of the 'ethnic market', especially for South Asians – the 750,000 living in London in 2001 exceeded the total South Asian population of virtually every other British city with the exception of Birmingham and Manchester – offers a key explanation for the success of migrant entrepreneurs, allowing these businesses to operate amongst distinct ethnic groups, as well as also facilitating the development of 'the ghetto' because food offers a key element in its survival.

Before examining the other reasons for migrant self-employment, we might also ask whether ethnic minority entrepreneurs concentrate on selling particular products. The food sector proves especially important and, as we shall see, migrants from all over the world have played a key role in the history of the restaurant in London. Clearly, the necessity for adhering to dietary restrictions, especially amongst those Jews and Muslims who chose to do so, has meant that the provision of meat and bread (for Jews) becomes a key sector in the ethnic market. However, migrants have also become heavily involved in selling products to their countrymen which have no relationship to religious restrictions, because the taste of home acts as a key way in which newcomers maintain the link with their place of origin – even if the foodways which emerge take a path that diverges from the original products of the country of origin by incorporating flavours from the new environment.[18] Nevertheless, a wide variety of migrants have established grocery stores offering provisions for the population as a whole, from the German butchers and bakers in the late Victorian and Edwardian periods to the late twentieth-century Asian corner shop owners. A central explanation for this situation is that food represents a key retail sector. This would also help to explain the fact that migrants have focused upon the retailing of clothing, another significant sector.

We can also examine the size of migrant businesses in London before further investigating the causes of entrepreneurship. A focus upon the Jewish and Irish hawkers in the eighteenth and nineteenth centuries reveals people working as individuals on the streets but often part of a wider family or ethnic network.[19] The German shopkeepers of the late Victorian period remained small in scale consisting, in most cases, of individuals and their families running their own businesses, although occasionally they constituted a small chain of a handful of shops.[20] East London Jews could open a workshop at the beginning of the twentieth century with just £1, with such workshops requiring at least two sewing machines, a pressing table and about eight or nine workers.[21] At the start of the twenty-first century 91 per cent of Asian-owned businesses in London employed 10 workers or fewer, while 48 per cent used fewer than 5.[22] While this may remain the norm, some London migrant enterprises have mushroomed into large businesses operating on a metropolitan, national or international scale, especially when they involve different generations of the same family.[23]

Apart from the peculiarities of London which have facilitated the development of migrant businesses, a series of more general factors, applying to London and elsewhere in Britain, present themselves as explanations for this phenomenon. In the first place, we need to emphasize that many of these businesses remain small in scale and often fail: those who open them often feel that they have no other options available because of the existence of racism which confines them to the bottom of the labour market. To take the most extreme example, Henry Mayhew's Irish peddlers resemble navvies or servants at the lowest end of the social scale, selling products that nobody else would, a point which also applies to the Jewish hawkers of Georgian London.[24] One explanation for the emergence of South Asian businesses focuses upon the racism which the owners have faced as well as the fact that Indians, Pakistanis and Bangladeshis suffer higher rates of unemployment than their white counterparts meaning that entrepreneurship almost becomes a necessity. Some of these Asian businessmen have high educational qualifications, which allows them to navigate the economic complexities of running a small enterprise. However, in many cases, these businesses become an 'economic dead end' offering small profit margins with a high rate of failure.[25]

However, this predominantly negative explanation for migrant entrepreneurship – that newcomers open up small businesses because they have no other avenues open to them and, even when they do, they either have small profit margins or their businesses fail – offers just one perspective. Those who establish small enterprises clearly do so with a positive frame of mind and it is worth investigating the origins of this confidence. One perspective emphasizes religion as a factor in this process, focusing especially upon Jews but also upon more recent migratory groups. In fact, this idea originated in the influence of Protestantism in the development of capitalism in Britain as it placed a greater emphasis upon individualism than Roman Catholicism.[26] Nevertheless, the idea of religion playing a role in the evolution of London businesses proves incongruous because East European Jews, Muslims originating from all over the world, Greek Orthodox Cypriots, Gujarati Hindus, German Protestants and Italian Catholics cannot all have the same religious values which drive them forward towards business success, and neither do these values differ enough from those of the majority population.[27]

These individual groups bring with them distinct assets that facilitate their move into business, which no general theory of immigrant entrepreneurship would cover.[28] Some migrants already possess business skills and experience. This would apply especially to East African Asians, who already ran their own businesses in Uganda and Kenya.[29] While Cypriots may not have had previous business experience and while many may have initially worked as employees, especially in the catering and clothing sectors,[30] they have a strong sense of individualism and a belief in property ownership, because they came from an island in which the Ottomans had abolished feudalism centuries previously, creating a society and economy in which individuals owned their own homes and self-sufficient land plots. Cypriots therefore had 'a strongly developed ideology of property possession as both a right and a goal'.[31] Some Pakistani businessmen also previously owned property and therefore established businesses shortly after arriving in London, although others initially worked in manual occupations, utilizing the skills of thrift, industriousness and self-reliance to succeed.[32] But these personal qualities would apply to all small businessmen, whatever their ethnicity or religion. In contrast, an argument for why people of African-Caribbean origin display a less entrepreneurial spirit than other migrant groups may originate in 'their history of oppression, which destroyed their self-esteem and resulted in weak family and community ties, poor individual motivation and a lack of personal resources',[33] an argument that might also apply, to some extent, to Irish migrants, especially in the nineteenth century.

Networks prove especially important in the establishment of migrant enterprises. They take a variety of forms but revolve especially around family support, particularly as many enterprises are family businesses and one could argue that the more family-oriented newcomers such as Greek Cypriots, Jews, Asians and Chinese have experienced the greatest economic success. The early Chinese laundries in the late Victorian and early Edwardian periods 'fetched over relatives to staff existing businesses' or even to establish new branches, while families usually run post-war Chinese takeaways.[34] The children of South Asian families (a fact which applies to other groups) provide 'motivation to become self-employed and to develop the business (either for financial reasons or in order to provide family employment)', as well as offering a potential supply of labour.[35] Networks also operate in other ways. For example, if they do not rely upon members of their own family to help with the running of businesses, the next potential easy labour supply consists of members of the same ethnic group, who, as we have seen, also comprise the consumer base in many cases.[36] At the same time, migrants sometimes borrow money from members of the same ethnic group. Jews who entered London in the late nineteenth and early twentieth centuries could obtain funding from the Board of Guardians from 1866.[37] In recent decades some migrants have secured money from groups of friends and relatives, partly because of the fear of rejection based on racism if approaching banks. For example, in the case of one Somali business owner in North London, 'more than 25 friends, acquaintances and relations had contributed a total of £7,000 (in the form of an interest-free loan) out of the £8,000 required to start and run a telephone call centre for the first six months of its existence'.[38]

A complexity of factors has therefore facilitated the growth of migrant small businesses in London's history, a process which has its origins in the early modern period,[39] with the Huguenots who settled in Spitalfields regarded as pioneers in this process.[40] While some migrant groups appear more entrepreneurial than others, as supported by statistics, it seems that virtually all ethnic minorities have opened small businesses, providing a means of social mobility and helping in the assimilation process.[41]

THE IRISH

As with much else in the migrant history of London the entrepreneurial activities of the Irish, together with Jews, differ from other twentieth-century arrivals because of the longevity of their presence in the capital. This means that they have operated in a variety of economic systems and have also, especially in the case of the Jews, experienced intergenerational social mobility, although this does not become so apparent in the case of the Irish.

Hawkers from Ireland sold their goods in London from the eighteenth century if not before[42] and would continue to do so into the nineteenth century, as Henry Mayhew identified in great detail, describing the 'Irish street-sellers' as 'both a numerous and peculiar class of people',[43] suggesting traces of the endemic anti-Irish prejudice which existed at this time.[44] As the extract at the beginning of this chapter indicates, Irish street-sellers comprised up to 30,000 people. Mayhew believed that their numbers had doubled in recent years,[45] connected with the increase in Britain as a whole following the Irish Potato Famine.[46] Mayhew offered a series of explanations for the significance of the Irish in street-selling. On the one hand, he suggested that 'Irish women and girls who sell fruit &c., in the streets' essentially lay at the bottom of the social and skill scale. 'They are a class not sufficiently taught to avail themselves of the ordinary resources in the humbler walks of life.' A lack of skill 'at their needles' meant that they could not even secure employment as shirt-makers, while their 'ignorance of household work (for such description of work is unknown in their cabins in many parts of Ireland), incapacitates them in a great measure for such employments as "charring", washing, and ironing, as well as from regular domestic employment'. Mayhew continued: 'Very few of these women (nor indeed of the men, though rather more of them than the women) can read, and they are mostly all wretchedly poor.' Consequently, 'there seems to remain to them but one thing to do – as indeed was said to me by one of themselves – viz., "to sell for ha'pinny the three apples which cost a farrruthing" '.[47] Mayhew distinguished street-sellers, who stood at the very bottom of London society and 'who gain a scanty maintenance, or what is rather a substitute for maintenance, by trading, or begging, or by carrying the two avocations simultaneously in the streets of London',[48] from costermongers, or those who undertook this as a regular form of employment, although only about a quarter of the Irish fitted into this category. In any case, they still struggled to make a living.[49] Mayhew examined the way in which 'the street-Irish displanted the street-Jews in the orange trade', suggesting that this came about because Jews diversified the products they sold and experienced a type of social mobility, which left this trade for the Irish from the 1820s.[50] He also examined the 'Irish "Refuse"-Sellers, between twenty and thirty in number', who purchased fruit which had essentially passed its sell-by date from the London fruit markets and then sold it on further, especially in 'pitches . . . on Saffron Hill and in Petticoat Lane'.[51]

Although the London Irish experienced some social mobility in Victorian Britain,[52] fifty years after Mayhew's investigations a periodical article on this community, which did not carry the same level of research and which used more overtly Irish stereotypes, asserted that the Irish still dominated the 'retail vegetable trade'. By the early twentieth century 'your typical coster is your London Irishman', suggesting a progression from the 1850s. However, their earnings remained uncertain, although 'the Irish coster class are a necessity to working-class London'.[53]

By the second half of the twentieth century, while the majority of the Irish in London focused on working-class occupations, a small well-educated element also migrated, especially doctors.[54] Nevertheless, the type of low-scale entrepreneurial activity associated with either their nineteenth-century prede-cessors or their contemporaries from all over the world after 1945 does not seem to have taken place to a great extent. Exceptions certainly exist, especially in the building trade, where perhaps the most famous figure was James Murphy, born in 1913 in Ohermong, near Caherciveen, County Kerry. He moved to London in the late 1930s, where he initially shovelled snow at Heathrow Airport but subsequently established a subcontracting business to supply labour from Ireland to the big construction companies, which would become one of the largest building firms in Britain. Murphy, a family firm which also involved James's brother John,[55] provides an excellent classic example of a rags to riches story found amongst other London migrant groups. Some Irish people also established their own small businesses which did not grow expo-nentially. As a child growing up in Hornsey, my mother sent me to the local grocery store owned by Mr O'Reilly in Weston Park – usually to buy a loaf of sliced white bread when we had run short, sometimes to purchase breaded ham – which had for me the added attraction of seeing the slicing machine in action. Mr and Mrs O'Reilly, whose store predominantly sold processed and tinned food, always wore white overalls. Meanwhile a television repair firm owned by three Irish brothers, situated in Tottenham Lane, visited us regularly at 61 Uplands Road in an attempt to eliminate the 'ghosts' from our screen.

Such small Irish firms no doubt existed throughout post-war London. The absence of any Irish 'quarter' in the capital comparable with either the nineteenth century or with those established by migrants from other parts of the world after 1945 has meant that the twentieth-century Irish have not opened enterprises in the same way.[56] Small businesses in London life in the latter part of the nineteenth century[57] offered a niche for groups such as the newly arrived Germans.[58] Just as importantly, and in contrast to groups such as Africans, Italians, Germans, Cypriots and, more especially South Asians and Jews, whose diet is controlled by religion, Irish food patterns closely resemble those of the ethnic majority in London, which has meant that no need has arisen for the establishment of Irish food shops to sell the products eaten in the homeland. The birth of the Irish pub in the late twentieth century did not originate in an organic fashion in the same way as the food outlets of other ethnic groups, as it essentially represented a marketing technique.[59] As Henry Mayhew and other writers recognized, usually as a racist trope, the nineteenth-century Irish, both traders and others, together with those who arrived after 1945, remained unconcerned as to the ethnic origins of the drink they consumed, although they appear to have preferred whisky to gin.[60]

THE JEWS

While Jewish migrants in London resemble the Irish because of their continuity of settlement since the middle of the seventeenth century in this case, in terms of their status as entrepreneurs they stand at the opposite end of the scale, offering the best example of a business-minded group in London's history. Rather than providing generalizations about Jewish business acumen to rationalize this state of affairs, the main overarching explanation lies in the range of activities in which Jews have become involved. Until the nineteenth century, and even into the twentieth, this community played a large role in hawking in a similar way to the Irish. A major difference from the Irish, however, lies in the level of difference from mainstream London society. While both groups may have lived in nineteenth-century ghettoes as a result of poverty and racism, the Jewish concentration also had the function of providing the services necessary for the practice of the Jewish faith, especially in the form of food, as dietary restrictions prove central to devout believers, which provided the opportunity for the opening of bakeries and butchers in particular. This community, as we have seen, also enabled the development of small-scale businesses in the East End, employing newly arrived 'greeners'. Finally, the story of James Murphy, which seems unusual in the history of the Irish community in Britain, finds replication in numerous Jewish cases, especially through generations, as the example of Tesco indicates.

Although the readmission of the Jews into England in the 1650s essentially involved the entry of commercial and banking elites, who add yet another element to Jewish entrepreneurial activity in London,[61] the increase in Jewish numbers in the early eighteenth century, mostly from the German states and Holland, but also from Spain and Portugal, consisted predominantly of people 'with few material resources or artisanal skills', who therefore began hawking a variety of goods on a small scale, reflecting the activities of the Jewish community on the continent. As in the case of the Irish peddlers, the trade required little financial outlay and those who became engaged in this occupation remained at the lower end of the social scale.[62] This occupation allowed Jews to work their own hours, avoiding trade on the sabbath, and also required a limited command of English, other than a few necessary choice phrases.[63] 'The most characteristic Jewish street trade was the buying and selling of old clothes', essentially the recycling of the cast-offs of the upper and middle classes for poorer Londoners. These Jewish old-clothes men, who may have counted in the thousands by the end of the eighteenth century, collected their wares in London squares and then bartered and sold them at Rag Fair in Rosemary Lane near Tower Hill.[64] While social mobility occurred during the course of the eighteenth century,[65] Henry Mayhew focused upon the continuing importance of Jews in hawking in Victorian London, although he asserted that they no longer had a monopoly in any branch as they did 'a few years back' because the Irish now 'undersold' them.[66] However, Mayhew identified a series of goods that Jews continued to sell, which included old clothes, even though the numbers involved had declined. Those still working in this trade generally consisted of the sons of 'a former old-clothes man, but some were cigar-makers, or pencil-makers, taking to the old-clothes business when these trades were slack'.[67] Mayhew claimed that those who became involved in this activity needed about £1 to begin, borrowed from 'a neighbour or . . . a publican', which 'he always pays back'. By this time Petticoat Lane had become an important trading point. The hawkers generally lived in the East End in rooms which 'are far from being comfortable'. About 500–600 may have operated in the capital at this time earning an average of 20 shillings per week, 'but the gains are difficult to estimate'.[68] Mayhew also suggested that 'there are about 50 adult Jews (besides old-clothes men) in the streets selling fruit, cakes, pencils, spectacles, sponge, accordions, drugs, &c.', most of whom had worked in this trade 'from their boyhood'. He further identified 'rather more than 100 Jew boys engaged principally in fruit and cake-selling in the streets', together with 50–100 occasional or casual street-sellers 'vending for the most part cocoa-nuts and grapes and confining their sales chiefly to Sundays'.[69] Few Jewish women became involved in street-selling.[70] As the century progressed London Jews increasingly moved into more secure occupations,[71] emphasizing the fact that, as in the case of the Irish, this type of employment attracted those at the sharp end of entrepreneurialism.

Jewish street traders did not disappear until the twentieth century as Middlesex Street (Petticoat Lane) remained 'the headquarters of the Jewish trader in Whitechapel',[72] although markets continued to survive all over London. They included one in Well Street in Hackney where Jack Cohen, the founder of Tesco and the son of Jewish immigrants from Poland, established his market stall in the aftermath of the First World War.[73]

The settlement of tens of thousands of Jews in the East End of London in the decades leading up to the First World War proved a significant boost for the development of Jewish entrepreneurship, especially in trades in which the East European settlers had participated before their arrival such as tailoring and furniture-making. The emergence of the small tailoring workshops, utilizing the labour of fellow migrants,[74] provides an excellent example of entrepreneurial ethnic networking. The development of a Jewish economy in both the East End and Soho also enabled the evolution of a retail trade to service the food needs of the newcomers, controlled by a series of dietary authorities,[75] precisely at the time when shops increasingly became a feature of London life. A significant number of Jewish butchers had emerged by the outbreak of the First World War. Mayhew mentioned the presence of two in

Whitechapel market in the middle of the nineteenth century, who worked with the aid of assistants.[76] One of the largest Jewish butchers at the start of the twentieth century was E. Barnett of '79, 81, & 83 Middlesex Street, Aldgate', who placed regular advertisements in the *Jewish Chronicle*. On 18 March 1921 the business offered 'SOMETHING BETTER FOR PURIM', including beef, mutton, veal, lamb, Vienna sausage, cooked tongues, smoked tongues, worsht, Warsaw worsht, breakfast sausage and cooked beef. In the same year, J. Nathan claimed to produce 'The only sausages that bear the schechita board seal', including worsht, liver sausage, garlic worsht, breakfast sausage, Viennese sausages and saveloys.[77] Jewish bakers also proliferated in the East End by the end of the nineteenth century. Like butchers, they advertised their wares in the *Jewish Chronicle*. Levy Brothers of Bishopsgate, which claimed to have existed since 1710, offered 'Passover Cakes, Finest Manufactured', with 'carriage free to any part of London'.[78] Myers and Joseph, 'Cooks and Confectioners' of Houndsditch, claimed to 'supply the best confectionery', selling 'ices, jellies, creams' and 'French and Italian pastry made to order'.[79] Meanwhile, Joseph Bonn claimed to provide a 'Gargantuan Feast of Passover Delicacies', which 'has its place on the thoughts of all bent on Passover Shopping'. The products it offered included 'Dreadnoughts, made from the finest almonds by Captain Naph-Drukker', 'motza puddings and motza kleis'.[80] Abraham Lewis opened a provision store in Soho in 1902, which would survive into the post-First World War period,[81] where the customers 'could pinch the bread and rolls for crusty freshness, caress the *schmalz*-herring for softness ... finger the soft cream cheese for a tasty lick, and, if needs be, slake their thirst with our milk at twopence per cup'.[82] In 1933 *The New Survey of London Life and Labour* asserted that 'Jews prefer brown or black bread to white, and even when they eat the latter they prefer it to be baked by Jewish bakers.'[83] The number of Jewish retail outlets declined in the post-war period linked with the fall in the number of practising Jews in the London.[84] By the 1980s the *Jewish Chronicle* regularly carried stories of food shops closing down.[85] On 24 January 1975 the paper reported that 'less than 50 per cent of the Anglo-Jewish community are today buying kosher meat and poultry, as against 90 per cent before the war'. The number of kosher butchers therefore declined from 198 in 1956 to seventy-three in 1979 and just twenty-six by 2005.[86] One baking firm which has survived into the twenty-first century is Grodzinski, established in 1888 by Harris and his wife Judith and initially baking in the ovens of 'Mr Galevitz', with the resultant rolls sold 'from a barrow in Petticoat Lane'. They subsequently opened their own establishment which would move several times, undergoing significant expansion in the middle of the twentieth century as new stores opened in the areas to which Jews migrated, including Willesden, Edgware, Belsize Park, Swiss Cottage, St John's Wood, Golders Green, Hendon, Finchley, Cricklewood and Stamford Hill. By 1988 Grodzinski, still a family business owned by the descendants of Harris and Judith, was running eighteen bakeries in London.[87]

Despite the overall decline in the number of kosher food stores, twentieth-century Jewry experienced social mobility driven by entrepreneurialism and education. *The New Survey of London Life and Labour* suggested that 'no less than 20 per cent of Jewish earners in East London are owners or managers of shops, workshops or factories'.[88] The areas where Jews remained especially important in the middle of the twentieth century included textiles, drapery and fashion, as well as furniture, building on Victorian and Edwardian origins, jewellery, the fur trade, 'largely founded by Jews – and since the Nazi regime a considerable number of Jewish refugee fur traders have helped to make London, instead of Leipzig, the centre of the European fur trade', cosmetic and toilet preparations, and the radio and electrical trade.[89] Many second-generation Jews became self-employed on a small scale, mirroring their nineteenth-century predecessors, in commercial travelling, taxi driving and hairdressing.[90] Even in the early post-war years Jews may have made up a third of taxi drivers in London.[91] On the other hand, the history of Anglo-Jewry, especially in the case of the late nineteenth-century arrivals and their descendants, often constitutes a tale of rapid economic mobility and the establishment of businesses, in which the 'escape from the ghetto' took place not simply amongst those who settled in the East End, but also in inner city areas in Leeds, Manchester, Glasgow and elsewhere.[92] Apart from Tesco, other large firms with origins in the East End included the men's clothing retailer Cecil Gee, born in Lithuania in 1903 as Sasha Goldstein,[93] while an earlier generation of Jewish immigrants from Germany, Samuel and Henry Gluckstein, established the Lyons catering empire.[94] Jewish entrepreneurship received a boost as a result of the arrival of refugees from the Nazis during the interwar years.[95] While the East End ghetto may have disappeared during the course of the twentieth century, a more middle-class area of Jewish shopping appeared in Golders Green, following the migration away from Whitechapel and its surroundings, a process which became noticeable by the 1930s and intensified further after 1945, with the area becoming the heartland of kosher retailing in London.[96] By the beginning of the twenty-first century the descendants of the immigrant Jews in Britain had a self-employment rate of over 30 per cent, higher than any other ethnic group.[97]

GERMAN FOOD SUPPLIERS

The history of London Jewry demonstrates the centrality of entrepreneurialism through generations. The German community which emerged at the end of the nineteenth century displays some similarities in the sense that a German food quarter evolved to service the needs of the migrants in East London in particular but also demonstrates one fundamental difference not simply from the Jewish community but from all migrant groups in modern London: the British state destroyed German entrepreneurialism during the First World War when it closed down all German businesses in the country as part of the Germanophobic campaign which included internment and deportation, helped by the London population which destroyed virtually every German-owned shop in the capital.[98]

The late Victorian and Edwardian period witnessed a proliferation of small London businesses owned by Germans, although other activities preceded this period including publishing and bookselling, as well as sugar baking. The former began at the end of the seventeenth century and lasted into the nineteenth.[99] The German (especially Hanoverian) sugar bakers at the bottom of the London labour market worked especially for other Germans, indicating the role of networks in the success of employers in this field. Of eighty-two East End sugar-baking firms in 1823–4 at least thirty were owned by Germans, while by 1875, by which time sugar beet increasingly replaced sugar cane and the necessity for the boiling process in London, eight out of twenty-five sugar bakers had German names.[100]

Networking also played a role in the evolution of German bakers and butchers in London in the late Victorian and Edwardian periods. Many of these small businessmen initially migrated to work as employees for their countrymen in these occupations with the long-term aim of acquiring 'sufficient knowledge and a little capital' to open up their own shops. They subsequently employed their own newly arrived countrymen who again had the aim of buying their own shops.[101] After importing German agricultural labourers, German master bakers would initially provide their new employees with food and lodging for a couple of years, after which they would move to obtain about 18 shillings per week. Subsequently, they would progress in the same way. About half of 4,000 master bakers in London in 1887 may have consisted of Germans, present in all parts of London, in the East and West End and from Tooting to Holloway and Fulham to Edgware.[102] Germans worked as both bakers and confectioners. It seems tempting to suggest that Germans introduced new breads and cakes into Britain. The Soho bakery of P. Hahn made a wide variety of breads, including 'cottage', rye, black and caraway, together with 'rows of French rolls resembling huge cigars'.[103] Germans also established themselves as butchers, becoming especially important in the sale of pork, where it proves tempting to suggest that they introduced a variety of German meats, especially sausages, at the end of the nineteenth century. Between 1881 and 1911 the census counted about 1,200 German butchers on a national basis.[104]

By 1896 foreigners, including Frenchmen and Germans, made up about 30 per cent of master hairdressers in London, with Germans proving especially important as barbers. Some moved to Britain as unskilled agricultural labourers but others had already received a full training. They included G. Schlect, who had served an apprenticeship in Münster and then worked in Mannheim, Dresden and Munich followed by employment in various Swiss towns and then Paris, eventually arriving in London in 1906. As in baking and the meat trades Germans worked both as employers and employees in the hairdressing trade, again demonstrating ethnic networking in small business.[105]

Although Germans have no dietary restrictions on their food, the entrepreneurial spirit, the close connections between the advanced trading economies of Britain and Germany, the development of German quarters in the East and West End of London and, perhaps above all, a consequent desire to preserve the taste of home, led to the development of a German food economy in London before the outbreak of the First World War. By 1913 the main thoroughfare of the German community of the West End of London, Charlotte Street, contained at least forty German names out of the 138 businesses here, including five tobacconists, three tailors, two artists and two employment agencies. Food was also well represented, including two butchers, four restaurants, one baker and three foreign provision dealers.[106] German food shops had already emerged in London by the 1860s, including John Wittich of East India

Dock Road, who sold 'German brown bread', while A. Klapper, of Whitechapel, a 'Konditorei', sold 'German tarts, cakes and pastries'.[107] Delicatessens had also appeared in London by the end of the nineteenth century. W. Bedbur, of Portland Street, sold a wide variety of products including at least seven types of sausages, 'Westfalian and Brunswick ham', 'Pommeranian goose breast', 'Hamburg smoked meat', 'Mainz Sauerkraut' and 'Saxon salt'. The firm offered free delivery to all parts of London.[108] An advertisement by Löwenbräu in the *Londoner General Anzeiger* of 3 January 1900 listed seventeen establishments in London which sold this beer. The same edition carried an advertisement by Edwin Schür of 7 Commercial Road, declaring that he produced the best wedding cakes. In the years leading up to the First World War, a series of fairly large German food companies had become established in London, including the Damm'sche Braun and Scwarzbrot-Bäckerei, based in Fitzroy Square, the heart of German West London, which distributed bread to thirty German bakers and other establishments in London.[109] Charlotte Street even seems to have had its own 'German sausage factory' by the Edwardian period.[110]

But two giants appear to have emerged in the world of London German delicatessens by 1914. The first consisted of Rühmann Brothers, situated in Tottenham Court Road, but with a café connected to it in Leicester Square. This business sold an extraordinary range of products including sausages, hams, fish and cheeses.[111] Meanwhile, H. Appenrodt described himself as the 'most distinguished German delicatessen in London' and as the 'largest importer of all types of German delicacies' and wines. The premises had a German pastry shop and 'Viennese café restaurant' connected with it. The two branches of 1900, in Coventry Street and the Strand, had increased to nine by the outbreak of the First World War, suggesting that its foods appealed to an English clientele, as the locations lay outside the German West End. By 1914 this firm also had its own 'sausage and canning factory with the newest machinery and the most modern and hygienic appliances'.[112] Although First World War Germanophobia eliminated the vast majority of Germans from Britain, together with their businesses and food,[113] Appenrodt reopened some of his establishments in the 1920s, having sold them (probably compulsorily) in 1919, but finally dispensed with them in 1936.[114] Meanwhile, Schmidt's of Charlotte Street described themselves as 'importers of foreign produce' and 'manufacturers of all kinds of continental sausages and delicacies' including 'Frankfort sausages'.[115]

ITALIANS

The smaller Italian community which emerged in London during the nineteenth century did not develop quite the vibrancy of its German equivalent, although neither did it face the type of destruction of the First World War, even though something similar, but not quite on the same scale, occurred to this group following Mussolini's declaration of war on 10 June 1940.[116] Italian food had actually become fashionable in Georgian London, leading to the opening of 'warehouses' which sold it.[117] During the nineteenth century, in addition to the itinerant trades in which Italians became involved, which meant the employment of imported labour from the homeland,[118] a small food community also evolved. In 1874 an article in the *Food Journal* entitled 'Italian Produce' described a 'foreign quarter' in central London 'filled with an Italian population . . . Macaroni, in all its forms, is naturally the first characteristic of Italian produce', while dried mushrooms sold at 4d per ounce, Lombard wine at 8d per bottle, and tomato puree at 1d per ounce. The shops also stocked olive oil and 'numerous forms of preserved fish and meats', including 'pickled tunny'.[119]

The most important culinary contribution made by Italians during the nineteenth century was the popularization of ice cream. By the 1870s 'ice cream street vendors had become a common feature in London – and they were virtually to a man, Italian', appealing especially to the working classes. By 1891 ice-cream making and selling had become the main occupation of the Italians in Clerkenwell, evolving from the previous itinerant trades in which this community had become involved.[120] One of the major figures in the development of this trade was a Swiss Italian immigrant, Carlo Gatti, selling ice cream from the 1850s.[121] Many of the migrants could not make a living for the entire year because of the seasonal nature of this trade, which meant that they often resorted to chestnut selling during the winter. By the beginning of the twentieth century some of those who had previously sold products on the streets had established their own shops which offered a variety of products, including ice cream.[122]

CYPRIOTS BEYOND CLOTHING

Despite the large percentage of Cypriots employed in the clothing trade in London after the Second World War, either as factory owners or employees of their countrymen, the ethnic clustering which took place in Camden Town, Stoke Newington and Haringey during the second half of the twentieth century enabled the development of food outlets selling products consumed in Cyprus. This occurred on a significant scale from the 1960s when fresh produce had 'been flown direct from Cyprus to Britain – such vegetables and fruit as aubergines, lemons, grapes, parsley'.[123] A description of the Turkish Cypriot Green Lanes area in Newington Green from the 1980s noted 'a row of Turkish shops and cafes' including a confectioner selling 'delicious little pistachio baklavas'. In one café 'men drink coffee, play backgammon and read the Turkish-language newspapers that are flown in daily from Frankfurt' while other shop windows contained 'all sorts of Turkish goods'.[124] Progression further northwards along Green Lanes towards Haringey revealed that this major thoroughfare became increasingly Greek Cypriot. Not simply grocers and cafés appeared but also furniture shops, opticians and driving schools,[125] reflecting developments amongst all migrant groups in post-war London. Niazi Osman established Zodiac Travel Service in Old Kent Road in 1962 but his firm attracted a largely Turkish and Turkish Cypriot custom base because Turkish Airlines used his company as one of its main London agents.[126]

Asil Nadir became the most famous and infamous Turkish Cypriot businessman in late twentieth-century London. Born in Lefka (now in the Turkish-controlled area of Cyprus) in 1941, his family moved to Famagusta in 1943 where his father İrfan had opened up a shop but left for England in 1959 as a result of the ethnic tension between Greek and Turkish Cypriots which had led to outbreaks of violence, especially against the latter. Once in London the Nadir family initially lived in Kingsland Road in Hackney where İrfan moved into the rag trade, establishing Nadir Modes, but the family quickly progressed up the property ladder to a semi-detached house in Romford. In the early 1960s Asil actually lived in Istanbul studying for an economics degree but dropped out of the course to return to London to help with his father's business. In 1965 he opened his own clothing business called Wearwell with a head office in Commercial Road. In 1968 with a turnover of £370,000 it made £10,000 profit but by 1973 these figures had increased to £4 million and £672,000 respectively, by which time the firm had opened its own shops in London and other big British cities. The company was also floated on the London Stock Exchange, while by this time Asil Nadir had started raising funds overseas. In 1980 he took over Polly Peck, indicating, once again, the importance of a variety of migrants in the economic history of modern London, as the firm had originally come into existence as a result of the efforts of Jewish immigrants from Poland, the Zelkers, in the aftermath of the First World War. The son of the founders had diversified during the 1970s by purchasing London property. After Nadir took over Polly Peck even further diversification occurred with the development of an international company with a base in Turkey and Turkish-occupied Cyprus, where the export of fruit, especially oranges, using land belonging to refugees who had fled south, became central. The fall and consequent infamy of Polly Peck came in the early 1990s when the company went bankrupt and Nadir faced accusations of fraud and theft. He fled to the north of Cyprus in 1993[127] where he remained until 2010, returning to face trial at the Old Bailey and receiving a ten-year prison sentence two years later.[128]

ASIAN BUSINESSMEN AND WOMEN

Asil Nadir essentially became part of the international bourgeoisie, despite his relatively humble background with, however, a father who had business experience. Many Asian entrepreneurs had a similar commercial heritage, although others rose from manual labour or even unemployment after arrival in Britain. The high numbers of Asian businessmen is partly explained by the size of the ethnic economy for Indians, Bangladeshis and Pakistanis. It operates not simply in the parts of London where these groups are concentrated but forms part of a larger national market revolving especially around food and women's clothing, trading directly with the countries of origin.

Together with the South Asian economies which emerged in Britain after 1945, a Chinese economy, much smaller in scale, also emerged, with origins in the small community that developed in Limehouse in the late Victorian and Edwardian periods. The two main areas of self-employment before 1914 consisted of laundries and restaurants,[129] two fields in which migrants from China specialized throughout the world, which catered for both Chinese and white people. Although only a few laundries existed in Limehouse at the beginning of the twentieth century,[130] by 1931 their numbers had reached between 500 and 800 in Britain as a whole, with those in London dispersed throughout the capital. The Chinese gravitated towards this industry because of their limited knowledge of English and discrimination in other areas, and also because it required little investment in equipment, meaning that washing essentially represented an entrepreneurial activity at the bottom of the economic ladder. Those who ran laundries had previously worked as washmen on British ships. They operated as small family units. They disappeared from London after the Second World War because they did not adapt to new technology.[131] The Chinese also became associated with opium-smoking establishments before the First World War – when the drug remained legal – frequented by both Chinese and English people.[132] The few hundred souls in Limehouse also managed to sustain grocery shops, which sold Chinese products,[133] including 'water-lilly roots, water chestnuts, canned bamboo-shoots' and lichees.[134] The largest and longest-lasting establishment appears to have been Wong's, opened before 1914,[135] 'a shop crammed to the ceiling with the delicacies of the East', lasting into the 1930s.[136] By the interwar years the Chinese community in Soho began to emerge and would become the centre of this group in the capital following the destruction of the former heart of London's Chinese community in Limehouse by German bombers during the war and the opening up of a series of restaurants in Gerrard Street during the 1960s. The Chinese who have worked long hours in these establishments socialize with their countrymen and also purchase foods familiar to them.[137]

South Asians work in a much wider variety of small-scale entrepreneurial activities than the Chinese beyond the rag trade and catering which have proved especially attractive to Bangladeshis.[138] Some of the earliest businesses concentrated on supplying Indian food. 'The first Indian grocery business started in 1928–9 in London' supplying Indian students, other businessmen and professionals, Indian officials of the high commission and some Englishmen who had probably spent time in India.[139] In 1931 there followed the Bombay Emporium in Grafton Street, while the first Bengali food shop in London's East End, Taj Stores, opened in 1936.[140] By the early 1960s, although the South Asian population of London remained relatively small, the number of South Asian businesses had increased and, at this stage, because ethnic concentrations had not yet developed on a significant scale, the family-run businesses, predominantly Gujarati and Punjabi, made home deliveries in an age of ethnic dispersal and limited car ownership.[141] By the 1980s, as the number and concentration of Asians in London had increased significantly, so had the number of Indian shops. In some parts of Ealing, for example, which incorporates Southall, Asian-owned businesses skyrocketed, totalling 899 in the five electoral wards of Dormers Wells, Glebe, Northcote, Springfield and Walpole. By this time, as diversification had taken place away from simply the provision of Indian food, the percentage of white and West Indian customers increased, with the former making up the majority. Many of these businesses opened for long hours six or seven days a week with almost half open on Sundays.[142]

Many of the Asian small businessmen in London originated in Gujarat, moved to the metropolis via East Africa, where their families may have lived for generations, and belonged to particular castes which helped their entrepreneurial drive. They included Patidars, significant landowners in the areas from where they originated. Once they moved to East Africa, especially in the early twentieth century, they concentrated in trade and white-collar occupations.[143] Nevertheless, those who migrated to Britain did not automatically move into these areas of employment, sometimes having to initially undertake manual labour.[144] This did not always happen, as in the case of a driving instructor who owned his own business in both Nairobi and South London, although, in this case, the latter failed but, in the longer term, after working for a foreign investment company, the former driving instructor became a moneylender.[145] The Patel caste has a similar history, moving to East Africa from Gujarat in the late nineteenth and early twentieth centuries and then fleeing to London and elsewhere in Britain as a result of Africanization policies during the 1960s and 1970s, initially from Kenya and then from Uganda. Upon arrival in the capital some of the businessmen and other professionals entered the retail sector especially by opening corner shops selling newspapers, confectionery and tobacco. A small minority of professionals established accountancy firms, chemists, opticians and dental surgeries. Others opened shops all over London, despite the Gujarati concentration in Wembley. While the first generation often ran shops, many of the children of the migrants moved into the professions.[146]

The South Asian owners of a small business from the 1960s took a variety of paths, whatever their religious and geographical origins, so that while some may have moved straight into shopkeeping, others worked as employees in a variety of sectors upon first arrival. One survey from the middle of the 1990s demonstrated that 71 per cent of self-employed Asians previously worked as employees, 16 per cent faced unemployment and 14 per cent came from education.[147] We can give a few more examples to illustrate the diversity of experiences. One accountant from Kampala moved to Britain with £350 and initially resided in a refugee camp. Both he and his wife then worked on factory assembly lines while also helping Indian shopkeepers with the accounts. After ten years of factory work they purchased a shop selling confectionery, tobacco and newspapers in London with the help of a loan from relatives in the United States.[148] Ajit Rai's experience differed in a variety of ways. Born in the Jalandar district of the Punjab in 1928, he remembered a childhood of poverty, leaving school in 1946 and spending time in detention because of his membership of the Communist Party in the Punjab. He remained politically active after his release and arrived in London in 1956, moving to Southall and initially working in an unskilled job in the R. Wolf Rubber factory, where 'always the vacancies were filled by the Asians' and where 'it was . . . 90 per cent Asians and 10 per cent the host country or Irish people. Irish or . . . Polish', while 'the factory was owned by Jews'. After a few months he moved to another branch of the same firm in Barking, living in Aldgate East and, shortly afterwards, secured a post with Nestle in Hayes where he 'was offered a lab job because I was a science student', which allowed him to move back to Southall. He remained here until 1959 and then worked for an engineering firm but faced dismissal, which led him to start his 'own business in early '60's in a mobile van delivering goods . . . to the members of my community in the houses in different towns'. He subsequently purchased a shop at '139 The Broadway Southall for £11,500' with a bank loan. He kept this until 1966 but sold it, went 'to a job in Uxbridge in the industrial area. But after that again I came back to the business. Since then I am still in business' – for over thirty years.[149]

Like many other Asian businessmen Ajit Rai worked in the food industry, in his case selling groceries, as part of a large and nationwide economy, which sustained a series of firms providing Indian foods and products, many of them based in London, both for people from India, Bangladesh and Pakistan, as well as other Londoners. L. G. Pathak, for example, started making samosas in his own kitchen in 1956, then bought his first shop in Drummond Street. The company subsequently moved to become a multimillion-pound business providing a wide range of products including pickles and curry pastes aimed at all ethnic groups. Ibrahim Kanamia, who migrated to Britain from Gujarat in 1972, established Kwality Ices, which produced kulfi. Raj and Shobnha Radia, meanwhile, founded Raj Foods in Park Royal in London, which has made ready meals since the 1980s as well as products such as Bombay Mix.[150] Bestways, NATCO and T. R. Sutewalla, meanwhile, mostly concentrated on the importation of goods from India and Pakistan. Sutewalla, for example, established in 1957, brought in 'rices, pulses, cereals, spices, herbs, pickles, edible oils and poppadoms'.[151]

While food may have become the most visible sign of South Asian entrepreneurialism in Britain, by the beginning of the twenty-first century people with origins in India, Bangladesh and Pakistan had become involved in all manner of small businesses, especially shops, meaning that the wholesale and retail sectors remained the key areas of self-employment for this group. The only other sectors where South Asians had become more heavily involved than the population as a whole consisted of 'hotels and restaurants' (essentially the latter) and 'transport and communications'. This probably refers to taxi firms and drivers,[152] as this group has moved into this occupation in the same way as Jews in the middle of the twentieth century, representing a low-scale and relatively low-risk type of self-employment, even though it requires an initial outlay for the vehicle purchase.[153] By the beginning of the twenty-first century South Asians had also moved into the London 'creative industries', the 'third largest sector in terms of employment' for all Londoners. Asians, who would include the second generation, have become over-represented in 'music and the performing arts, arts and antiques, designer fashion and software/computing'.[154] Designer fashion finds expression in the vibrant South Asian dress scene, linking London with the rest of the country and with South Asia.[155]

BLACK BUSINESSMEN AND WOMEN

The size and diversity of the South Asian community has enabled the development of small businesses for this group. Statistics suggest that people of African and African-Caribbean origin do not have the same level of self-employment, partly explained by the fact that a food market has not evolved on the same scale, and also the fact that African and African-Caribbean food has not transferred to the rest of the population in the same way as curry. Nevertheless, people from Africa and the Caribbean certainly have continued to eat the food of their homeland, most visible in the case of London by the products sold in Brixton market.

A few case studies of black people born both abroad and in Britain help to illustrate black entrepreneurial activity in London. Dyke and Dryden has become one of the most celebrated of these businesses, established by Len Dyke and George Dryden, both born in Jamaica. The latter had already opened a contracting business at home and initially worked as an electrician for British Rail.[156] Their first venture was a shop in West Green Road, which initially established a name 'for its records' but which would 'soon become internationally known for the widest selection of ethnic hair care and cosmetics available in the UK'.[157] This base served as the launchpad for the evolution of a network of shops throughout London, subsequently leading to the emergence of both a wholesale and a manufacturing arm of the business, as well as the development of a travel side.[158] By 1986 the firm had a sales turnover of £5 million.[159] Apart from the entrepreneurial opportunism of Dyke and Dryden, success had clearly come, as in the case of numerous other migrant businessmen, because of the demand for a specific 'ethnic product'. Other black people have moved into areas which do not have such an obvious link with Africa and the Caribbean. These include both women and men of the first and second generations. The areas where they operate have included the entire business, retailing and industry spectrum from accountancy to catering to employment agencies to floristry.[160]

MIGRANT ENTREPRENEURS AS LONDONERS

While some migrant groups may appear more entrepreneurial than others, all communities which have settled in London have become self-employed. Some, like the Jewish peddlers of the eighteenth century, superseded by the Irish during the nineteenth, have essentially remained at the bottom of the social scale, below those involved in regular manual labour, whether skilled or unskilled, selling old clothes or anything else they could secure in order to earn a living. While this type of trader disappeared from the streets of London during the course of the twentieth century, many of the small ethnic businesses which have more recently come into existence survive on small profits.

One explanation for levels of entrepreneurship amongst migrants lies in the development of ethnic economies in which food plays a major role. The size of such economies and the distance of food consumption patterns from those of the English also provides one explanation for the opportunities which arise for migrants. The largest has consisted of the South Asian economy, which perhaps offers the best explanation for the high levels of entrepreneurs from this group, which, however, remains lower than that for the Chinese, clustered especially in the Chinese restaurant business catering for the population as a whole. On the other hand, the Irish appear the least entrepreneurial group in the post-war period, perhaps because they fit more comfortably into the white working classes than any other group, facing less discrimination,[161] therefore eliminating any need to enter into self-employment to escape for such reasons. Their nine-teenth-century predecessors had no choice but to sell all manner of products on the streets. The Irish also have no real culinary distance from the mainstream London population, eliminating the need for entrepreneurialism in this sector.

Ethnic economies, however, offer just one explanation for migrant self-employment. The history of the restaurant in London provides the best example of foreigners seizing market opportunities,[162] as does, for example, the selling of ice cream by Italians in the Victorian metropolis. The same applies to Jewish and Irish hawkers and to Asian shopkeepers in the late twentieth century. As in the case of the foreign manual labourers who played a central role in the London economy, so do ethnic entrepreneurs: they remain ever present and they have played a key role in London's development. While we can distinguish and identify those who have sold goods to members of their own communities, in one way it seems pointless distinguishing between migrants and non-migrants because of the centrality of both in London's economic history. While it may appear that foreign businessmen operating on a small scale have become more prominent as the percentage of London's migrant population has increased in recent years, migrants have always played a key role in this sector of the economy, speeding up the wheels of commerce. The city of shopkeepers at the centre of the nation of shopkeepers has always consisted largely of a city of migrant hawkers, shopkeepers and entrepreneurs as the economy of London has developed from a situation where much buying and selling, especially amongst poorer groups, changed from an activity which took place on the streets, to one which increasingly took place in shops. Migrants remained a key element of this process of exchange.

5

THE INTERNATIONAL BOURGEOISIE

Looking back to that time I have often asked myself: 'From where did I get the courage to open a business in London' and after taking stock of my assets at that period, I come to a most remarkable conclusion.

I had no capital to speak of, I had no personal knowledge of the London Bourse, I had only an imperfect knowledge of the language: I had hardly any connections worth mentioning but plenty of enemies. Not real enemies of course. But many who wished to deny me the right to join the ranks of their competitors. Even those who were personally quite friendly, gave me the cold shoulder in the beginning. It was a terrible experience; it was as though I was trying to climb a wall and having already placed my hands firmly on the top, someone came from the other side to beat me off.[1]

London is regarded throughout the British empire as the fountain of the civilization with which British administrators have sought to endow the colonies; it is the Mecca of every ambitious colonial and the influence and opinions of visitors and students when they return to their native homes is out of all proportion to their numbers.[2]

THE ANATOMY OF THE INTERNATIONAL BOURGEOISIE

The sheer number and diversity of hawkers, shopkeepers and other relatively small-scale businessmen in London point to a unique aspect of its history. An examination of more established members of the middle classes points to another unique aspect in the history of London in the form of the centrality of commerce and finance, which have attracted people from all over the world, especially continental Europe and, more recently, from further afield, to the City of London. The international bourgeoisie played a major role in the history of London even before it rose to prominence as the financial capital of the world from the eighteenth century and, from Jews to Lombards to Germans to Americans, has helped to lead this development. The essence of the London international bourgeoisie does not simply lie in its income, occupation and lifestyle,[3] but also in its elite international status. These elites usually form part of a wider international network, as families such as the Rothschilds and the Speyers, for example, will demonstrate. London has formed one link in a wider chain which could also encompass cities both in other parts of Europe and beyond, especially as the British Empire extended its control to much of the world during the course of the nineteenth century in particular.

The Victorian globalization of London attracted all manner of elite individuals who moved to the world's capital for the purpose of using it as a type of entrepôt, arriving and then sailing out to ventures throughout the British-controlled Empire. In the case of Germans they included not simply businessmen but also scientists and missionaries.[4] For example, highly educated German evangelists who sailed to India in the early part of the nineteenth century often made a stopover in London, not simply for the purpose of transhipment, but also in order to gain knowledge of the Indian environment by meeting the leading figures in the British missionary societies, for whom they worked.[5]

All manner of other elites have used London as a base, especially for political purposes.[6] While nineteenth- and twentieth-century racist commentators criticized Indians, Chinese and black people living in apparent squalor in the East End of London, they often ignored the foreign students and intellectuals who moved to the capital to study, as the colleges of the University of London, along with a series of other establishments, including Edinburgh, Oxford, Cambridge and Manchester, developed into elite global institutions attracting people from all over the world by the outbreak of the First World War.[7] When Min-Chien T. Z. Tyau, a Doctor of Law from London University, described his 'seven and a half years in London', his section on the 'Chinese in England' primarily focused upon students who moved to England, above all London. In the late nineteenth century many studied 'navigation and shipbuilding', including, in 1900, 'four students . . . sent here by the Nanyang College . . .

placed under the charge of Prof. J. C. Lambert, of the Greenwich Royal Naval College'. In 1908 'a special Educational Mission was appointed with head-quarters in London to supervise the whole body of students'. By 1916, 116 of the 292 Chinese students in Britain registered with the University of London, undertaking subjects ranging from agriculture to medicine to sociology.[8] Fifteen years later 220 of the 395 Chinese students in Britain from China,[9] Hong Kong and Malaya studied in London, again in a wide range of subjects, especially medicine, law and engineering, but also 'general and preparatory education' and 'social, economic and political sciences'.[10] In order to 'cater for the needs of the ever-growing number of Chinese students', China House in Gower Street opened on 17 February 1933.[11] These pioneers act as the prede-cessors of the Chinese students who flock to Britain in the twenty-first century, paying higher fees than their British counterparts and helping to keep British universities in clover.[12] African students became visible in Britain, especially London, around 1900,[13] again acting as a corrective to those who negatively portrayed Africans because of colour and poverty. By 1950 there were 'some 1,500 colonial scholars, more than half of whom came from West and East Africa, scattered among most of the universities and training colleges in the country', who obtained scholarships together with another 2,500 who 'have little or no money' but 'deliberately choose to put up with a hard life as the only means of acquiring the higher education from which they will be able to reap immense advantages – financial as well as social and political – when they return to their homes'.[14] African students had a long history of studying in London and other British cities as the example of Zimbabweans who arrived during the 1960s and 1970s would indicate.[15] The heart of Empire played the same role for all manner of elite Indians as it did for Africans from the late nineteenth century, including princes, writers and students, even though encounters which took place between upper-class Britons and Indians often revolved around the racial hierarchy that existed.[16]

Students form just one element of the elites who have settled in London over the last two centuries. Naturalization certificates provide an indication of the diversity of the London international bourgeoisie because the fee required to become a Briton often proved prohibitive to those towards the lower end of the social scale.[17] A snapshot from the four years of 1870, 1875, 1905 and 1935 points to the diversity of the London migrant elites in terms of occupation, nationality and residence across London. A sample of eighty-four people who became Britons in 1870 includes sixteen who described themselves as merchants or general merchants, together with a wine and spirit importer, two wool brokers, a cigar importer, a hop factor, two drug merchants, a silk agent, two diamond merchants, an 'importer of foreign produce' and a watch importer. Several shopkeepers also took out naturalization certificates in this year, including: fifty-four-year-old Matheu Adolphe Oberdorffer from the German state of Württemberg, resident in Regent Street; the thirty-five-year-old Prussian Anthony Hartmann, who lived in the 'City of London', describing himself as a 'licensed victualler'; the fifty-four-year-old Frenchman Pierre Justel, 'proprietor of a laundry establishment' with an address in Portland Place; and the twenty-nine-year-old Italian, Achille Bendi, also a licensed victualler who lived in Greek Street. These four individuals fall into the category of shop-keepers, although we might assume that they ran fairly large-scale and exclusive establishments from the descriptions of their premises and their addresses. The sample also includes others who appear to come from more humble back-grounds, including a Hanoverian tailor (thirty-five-year-old Nathan Edward Wertheim, resident in Regent Street), a French bootmaker (forty-six-year-old Alexis Maillard also of Regent Street), a Prussian tailor (thirty-nine-year-old Frederick Neilde of Conduit Street), as well as three German bakers. The list I compiled includes three German bakers (one from Heße Darmstadt and two Prussians).[18] We can zoom in further on a series of other individuals who would appear to have more solid elite credentials. For example, the fifty-two-year-old 'journalist and literary man' Anthony Zabicki, originally from 'that part of Poland called Galicia in the Empire of Austria', had lived in London for eigh-teen years and in 1870 his address lay in Judd Street.[19] Thirty-five-year-old Bernhard Heymann, a 'Prussian subject . . . has resided in England upwards of twelve years his place of residence being London during which period he has been and still is in the profession of a teacher of language'.[20] A Swiss watch importer, thirty-nine-year-old Paul Milleret, had lived in Myddelton Square in Pentonville for five years with his wife and three children where he carried out his business.[21] Alexandre Vacherot, an architect born in the department of Lyon on 1 May 1826, had lived with his wife and two children in Notting Hill for six years.[22] Unusual cases include Louise de Perthius (French) and Josephine Catherine Antoni (Prussian), both described as a 'nun of the Community of Notre Dame de Lion, and engaged in teaching a young ladies' school'.[23] The nationalities of the eighty-four individuals in my sample included forty-six (i.e.

more than half) who would soon become part of the new Germany, predominantly Prussians, although by this time this state had expanded out of its historic eastern heartland to control much of the country which would soon dominate the German Empire, but reflecting the fact that Germans constituted the most significant group in London at this time. The second most important group, counting just eleven people, consisted of French people. The rest included Austrians, Italians, Swiss, Dutch, a Norwegian and Moses Afrilat, a merchant from the 'Kingdom of Morocco' residing in Finsbury Square. Two Greek merchants, George Nicholas Caravokeras and Giovanni Constantino Palojannis, originated in the 'Kingdom of Turkey'.[24]

A sample of thirty people who became Britons in 1874 reveals a similar preponderance of Germans (fourteen), together with a similar list of countries of origin to those from 1870, as well as two Russian Jews in the form of pictureframe maker Lipman Davis of Botolph Bishopsgate and Harris Goldstein, a tailor living in Spitalfields, and the Spanish wine merchant Adolfo Serafin Malvido, just twenty-one years of age, living in Hackney. The most prominent occupation consisted of seven merchants together with a manager to a merchant and a merchant's clerk. The sample again includes bakers, shopkeepers, as well as an artist and a teacher of French. Places of residence cover much of London.[25]

Another sample of thirty from 1905 includes twelve Germans but, by this time, they just outnumbered eleven Russians, probably all Jews in view of the increase in numbers of this community which had taken place at the end of the nineteenth century. These eleven did not simply consist of people involved in the East End rag trade, although they included Hyman Sadokierski, a draper from Hornsey Road, and Hermann Lefkowitz, a tailor living in Charlotte Street. Others included Solomon Nagli, a builder from Spitalfields, and Isaac Jacobs, a woodcarver from Shoreditch. Leon, Lewis, David and Charles Spiro, originally from Wloclawek, all described themselves as 'waterproof manufacturer', together with Leon Fauber, a lace importer, and Josef Getcofsky, a dentist in Holloway Road.[26]

A final sample of thirty from 1935 reveals that the Germans had almost disappeared, counting just two people in the form of Alfred August Eicher, a chemical engineer living in Wimbledon, and Mary Katherine Knornschild, a shorthand typist from Highgate. The list also includes eleven Russians, by now the largest group, who appear to consist predominantly of upwardly mobile Jews such as Reuben Bozinsky, a master tailor from Greenwich, and Nathan

Hyman, a boot and shoe dealer from Cricklewood. However, we should also mention Jankel Joseph Bialsky, a 'music composer and choir master' of Vestry Road, London N15. Those becoming naturalized in 1935 also included refugees from the Russian Revolution such as Marguerite Rastedt, a teacher from Clapham Common, 'of no nationality (but born in St Petersburg)', and Julia Kaufman, an accountant from Stoke Newington 'of no nationality but born in Balta, Ukraine'. The four sample years demonstrate the dominance of Europeans in the naturalization statistics, with the first American appearing in 1935 in the form of Arabella Josephine Pappé, a resident of Maida Vale 'of no occupation', who, however, was 'born in Birmingham and became a naturalized American'.[27]

In fact, all four sample years reveal that virtually all of those taking out naturalization consisted of Europeans. On the one hand this finds explanation in the fact that those who travelled to Britain from imperial territories would have had British citizen or subject status.[28] However, the absence of US applicants seems surprising, especially in view of the fact that an American middle-class community appears to have evolved in London by the period under consideration.[29] While, on the one hand, many of those who succeeded in gaining British citizenship may merit the description of elites, such as merchants, industrialists, teachers and artists, attracted by the global significance of the London economy in the case of the first two and the presence of a large educated middle class in the last two, upwardly mobile foreigners also tried to obtain naturalization. At the same time, some clearly working-class people also managed to secure citizenship, including, for example, Nils Laurentius Svenson, a Swedish 'donkeyman and greaser' from Limehouse who became naturalized on 24 April 1935.[30] On the other hand, despite their numbers and significance in the City of London, few bankers appear to have become British, perhaps seeing no benefit in this status because of the international nature of their activities. Yet some of the most famous financiers certainly did take out naturalization, especially Victorian and Edwardian German settlers who would consequently face persecution during the First Wold War, including Sir Edgar Speyer, Sir Ernest Cassel, Sir Felix Schuster and Baron Bruno Schröder.[31] One fact which comes through in the sample is the dispersal of those seeking naturalization throughout the capital, no matter what their social status, even though some enclaves for the international bourgeoisie developed, such as the Greeks, who initially concentrated around Finsbury Circus from the 1830s but, as the Victorian period proceeded, moved further west towards areas such as Holland Park, Westbourne Terrace and Notting Hill.[32]

Similarly, German middle-class communities had also developed by the late Victorian period, especially in south-west London.[33] While this social group amongst the Germans counted significant numbers of bankers and industrialists, German elites carried out a wide variety of occupations, a statement which applies both to those who arrived before 1914 and the refugees from Nazism. German scholars moved to take up posts throughout Britain and its Empire in the Victorian period.[34] At the same time, several Germans secured Chairs in London including Friedrich Rosen, who became founding Professor of Oriental Languages at the University of London in 1828, succeeded by another German, Theodor Goldstücker. Meanwhile, Friedrich Althaus took up the Chair of German at University College London in 1873.[35] Rather than simply focusing upon the uniqueness of London in this case, it proves just as useful to view it as one focal point in a global network which allowed scholars to secure posts around the world.[36] A focus upon the overwhelmingly middle-class Jewish refugees who escaped from Nazism before 1939 reveals that they worked in a wide variety of professions. Academics included lawyers, physicists and medical practitioners. Beyond the scholarly world the newcomers impacted upon the fine arts and theatre. Once again, we need to see movement to London as part of a wider process which helped German Jews escape persecution to other parts of the world, although, after 1938, Britain proved especially welcoming.[37]

London has clearly attracted all manner of other elites from all over the world beyond those engaged in banking, commerce and industry. The city has acted as home to educated Irish people, despite the fact that the labouring poor have always significantly outnumbered them both in reality and in the popular imagination. During the eighteenth century, for example, the metropolis housed significant numbers of both law students, studying at the Inns of Court, and some practising lawyers, who decided to remain in the British capital and would, in some cases, use it as a base to work elsewhere in the Empire.[38] One nineteenth-century account on *Ireland in London* provided a compendium of the Irish in the great institutions of the metropolis, whether Fleet Street, the Inns of Court or the City, as well as listing numerous organizations, many of which appear to be gentlemen's clubs, and political bodies, counting significant numbers of Irish. The book lists 'Irish Dramatists and Actors in London' from the time of Shakespeare, concluding with a further listing of 'Irish Literary Men in London', including those involved in journalism and political commentary.[39] For such educated Irish people London has a similar function to that which it held for colonial students in the sense that it acted as the capital to which the elite would flock, either as part of their education, in the case of the law students, or as the final destination in their career path, because of its role as the centre of British life.

Black elites in London also worked in a variety of areas during both the nineteenth and twentieth centuries. Edwardian London, for example, acted as home to black writers, musicians and clerics, despite the overt racism which existed at this time.[40] In the post-war period people of African and African-Caribbean heritage have become central to London's cultural life, as a couple of examples illustrate. Rudolph Walker, one of the most famous black actors in Britain from the 1970s, moved to the metropolis in 1960, initially working as a printer and studying drama at night school. Although he initially made his name in the now discredited situation comedy *Love Thy Neighbour* in the early 1970s, he would subsequently move into the mainstream in the long-running soap *East Enders*, as well as playing major roles on the stage.[41] Perhaps the most famous black British writer in post-war London was Ben Okri, who moved to London at the age of four from Nigeria in 1963.[42] Clearly, as we have seen with the case of the Irish, London has acted as a beacon calling writers from all over the world and playing a central role in the formation of their ideas, as well as impacting upon the evolution of modern thought.[43] This also applies to academics who have become public intellectuals, perhaps most famously Paul Gilroy, born in East London in 1956 to an English father and Guyanese mother. It seems impossible to imagine the development of his ideas on British and black identities without his London upbringing and education.[44]

EARLY MODERN INDUSTRIALISTS AND FINANCIERS

Although London has acted as a magnet to a variety of elites, its uniqueness essentially revolves around its status as the centre of international finance and commerce for centuries. Nevertheless, we need to reiterate the fact that it was always easily the most significant British city and increasingly gained significance as a European city from the late medieval period. We have already seen the importance of Germans, Italians and other foreigners in the development of medieval and early modern London.

Before their expulsion in 1290 the Jewish financial elite, who made up just one portion of London and Anglo-Jewry, had a complicated relationship with the Crown from their arrival in significant numbers with the Normans. Although initially offered royal protection and lending money to the monarch, the lives of all Jews increasingly became blighted by exorbitant taxation, which went hand in hand with an increasing antisemitism, eventually leading to expulsion from the entire kingdom in 1290.[45] Because canonical law forbade moneylending, Jews had served this role in medieval London both for the Crown and for others, protected in this occupation by the King, although Jews became involved in other employment, both elite and non-elite, meaning a sizeable Jewish poor lived in London before 1290. During the thirteenth century, however, Jews played a significant role in funding commercial activity in London, including property development because of exclusion from investing in land held on feudal tenure. Jews especially invested in the housing market in this period, although the renting out of houses by Jews ceased as a result of legislation in the City during the 1270s.[46] By this time a series of significant Jewish moneylending families had developed in the capital, including the Le Blund family, which paid over a third of tallages due to the Crown from Jews between 1221 and 1242.[47]

Although some Jews had continued to live in London after the expulsion, the decision to allow re-entry to England in 1656 partly revolved around their financial expertise aided by progressive Protestant opinion which emphasized reading the word of God in the original language, leading to the study of Hebrew at the English universities. The spread of millenarianism also favoured Jewish readmission. On the continent the efforts of the leading Jewish cleric Menasseh ben Israel, based in Amsterdam, further helped in the shift of opinion. The readmission took place following the Whitehall Conference in December 1655 involving merchants, political leaders including Oliver Cromwell, and religious figures.[48] Those who arrived in the second half of the seventeenth century, primarily Sephardic Jews, especially from Holland, France and the Iberian Peninsula, included overseas merchants, commodity brokers, individuals who dealt in jewellery, commercial clerks and physicians. Those involved in business and commercial activities formed part of a wider international Jewish trading elite, underlying the utilitarian reason for allowing their readmission despite opposition from local business interests in London.[49] The earliest of the Sephardim to settle in London included Alvaro da Costa, the 'first Jew to own landed property in England' in Totteridge. In 1680 the financier Rowland Gideon moved from Barbados to London and left his son Samson £7,900 when he died in 1720. Samson initially dealt in lottery tickets and rose to become one of the leading City financiers by the middle of the eighteenth century and one of the richest men in the country, purchasing landed property in several English counties and essentially becoming assimilated into English society.[50]

During the course of the seventeenth and eighteenth centuries, when the overwhelming majority of Anglo-Jewry lived in London, 'a small, often very wealthy and sometimes powerful elite' emerged at the same time as the Jewish community lower down the social scale, but counted relatively few people in the professions because of the existence of an official antisemitism. At the top of the Jewish social scale stood 'a relatively small handful of highly successful magnates in the City of London, typically involved in merchant banking, government finance and contracting, the Stock Exchange, insurance, as foreign merchants involved in overseas dealing, and as wholesale and sometimes retail merchants'. Jews often had more success than Gentiles because of their international links as a result of the global diasporic nature of their settlement patterns, although the Christian elites would certainly have outnumbered their Jewish counterparts.[51] The economic and financial success of both Jews and Gentiles in the eighteenth century clearly came about as a result of the growth of British economic and geopolitical power, based, in financial terms, in the City of London.[52] The story of the Jewish elite in this period, as reflected in the family history of the Gideons, consists of one of increasing integration which involved social mobility and the adoption of mainstream cultural norms, whether attending the theatre and opera, shedding traditional Jewish attire, marrying a Gentile or no longer keeping kosher.[53] As the eighteenth century progressed, Jewish settlement increasingly became Ashkenazi with newcomers originating in Germany and, to a lesser extent, Poland and Holland.[54]

Together with Jews, other foreigners, especially Germans, but also Dutch and Huguenots, played a role in the economic success of Britain during the seventeenth and eighteenth centuries, partly because of the relatively open attitude towards immigration compared with continental European states, reflected in a liberal naturalization regime and, once again, because of the burgeoning of international trade emanating from London. The Germans initially played a role in commerce with their home country but increasingly moved into trade with Russia and the Levant, as well as becoming involved in insurance and banking.[55] As in the case of Jews, the existence and further development of international networks played a role in German success in London in this period.[56] By the end of the eighteenth century several hundred merchants in London had non-British origins. The Germans included Andreas Grote from Bremen, who originally moved there as an agent and established a bank in 1776. The Baring banking house also originated in the port of Bremen as Johann Baring, the son of a cloth merchant, moved to Larkbear in Devon in 1717 and established a business as a wool merchant, accumulating significant wealth by the time of his death in 1748. His three sons, Francis, Charles and John, would establish the Barings banking house.[57]

THE NINETEENTH-CENTURY COSMOPOLITAN CITY OF ELITES

By the beginning of the nineteenth century, the city of London, at the centre of global trade and banking, had already become highly cosmopolitan, a process which would continue in the decades that followed, as the power of both the City and the Empire reached its zenith. While the City may have acted as the centre of the global financial and trading system which had emerged by the Victorian period, it interacted with smaller hubs, both within Britain and beyond. In the age of the Industrial Revolution, while Liverpool continued the international significance it had established during the slave trade, Manchester also became a global city.[58] Britain may have become the leading economic power during the course of the nineteenth century but, by the First World War, this dominance came under threat, especially from Germany and the United States which overtook it.[59] One way of understanding London's global position during the nineteenth century may consist of initial dominance followed by the beginnings of decline, but it might prove more useful to speak of interconnectedness or even entanglement. This entanglement brought economic elites from all over the world to London. In 1890 two native African merchants, Joseph Edward Biney and Joseph Etrrusion Ells, had purchased land laced with gold in the Ashanti nation. Biney actually served as the West African agent of the London merchants Smith and Cade.[60] This both illustrates the centrality of the City in Britain's global economic and political dominance and the fact that British decline remained relative,[61] taken over by the growing American and German industrial economies, but not in all sectors.

Understanding the international nature of trade, banking and industry during the nineteenth century requires a breakdown into its component parts. The banking system grew significantly during this period, due to the boom in industry and consequent international trade, leading to the development of a variety of types of banks, with a significant increase both in the number overall, especially in London, revolving around Lombard Street, and also in the numbers of people who worked in them.[62] The Victorian period saw the rise of the merchant bank, an 'amorphous' organization, which evolved gradually during this period, often from commercial ventures as the example of Nathan Mayer Rothschild in London will demonstrate.[63] The Victorian era also meant a growth of direct investment overseas and the consequent spread of British business all over the world,[64] once again a two-way process, which also brought business and banking from overseas to London, not simply in the case of individuals with foreign origins who had grown their banks organically such as the Rothschilds and the Barings, but also what would, by 1914, constitute multinationals. For example, Deutsche Bank, established in 1870, opened a branch in Old Street in 1873, followed by City branches of the Dresdner (1895) and the Diconto-Gesellschaft, although all of these would face liquidation during the First World War.[65] The growth of the industrializing German economy during the late nineteenth and early twentieth centuries also meant an increase in German direct investment in firms in Britain, especially in those sectors in which Germany had overtaken Britain such as chemicals and electrical engineering, although, once again, the government sequestered them all during the First World War. The other main rival to Britain's global economic power, the United States, opened up the most foreign-owned factories in Britain as a whole before 1945, part of a process of the growth of multinational companies, which often involved the marriage of businesses from more than one country. While this type of foreign involvement may have had a relatively limited impact before 1945,[66] it formed part of the process of globalization and entanglement. The role of London as the centre of imperial trade meant that it attracted merchants from all over the world.

Nineteenth-century industrial, banking and commercial globalization therefore gave rise to a cosmopolitan bourgeoisie. Because of its role as a centre of commerce, industry and finance, London acted as the focal point for this development, with banking constituting the driving force by the end of the nineteenth century in view of the vast range of financial enterprises which had emerged from the efforts of entrepreneurs but also through the establishment of joint-stock banks, which often came into existence as a result of mergers.[67] The international nature of the City of London meant that it attracted foreigners during the nineteenth century, continuing the process which took off with the arrival of Jews after readmission. It seems tempting to view the success of some nineteenth-century bankers in the same way as the post-1945 entrepreneurs who succeeded in London because they possessed unique skills and attributes which could include expertise in a particular field of trade or industry, superior education, family networks and a desire for success partly driven by religious motivation. Like some of the post-1945 newcomers, the success of the nineteenth-century merchants and bankers evolved over several generations.[68]

We can focus on two groups in particular in the form of Germans, both Jews and Gentiles, and Greeks, although we can briefly mention merchants and bankers from other countries including the United States, especially as Anglo-American trade developed in the early nineteenth century.[69] Perhaps the most visible example of American business success in Britain consisted of the Selfridges Department store, established by the Chicago businessman Harry Gordon Selfridge in 1909 and perhaps a symbol of the development of US economic power in Britain which would grow during the course of the twentieth century.[70] As an indication of the global migrant ownership of concerns in London by the early twentieth century, as well as the size of the London market, the small Armenian community owned thirteen carpet dealerships, while fourteen other members of this community established themselves as fur and skin merchants, mostly in the City of London.[71] An account of this community from 1901 claimed that 'during the last ten years Armenians have been quietly coming over to England establishing branch houses in connection with their home enterprises, and now the Englishman looks around him and finds in his midst a host of representatives of Armenian trade'. The sectors mentioned included 'electrical engineering, locomotives, steel rails, agricultural machinery, and many other things'.[72]

A Greek trading diaspora had emerged under the Ottoman Empire with a presence in the Russian, Habsburg and British empires, based upon family networks, but the open attitude towards migration of elites to Britain, and the consolidation of British power, helped the growth of Greek mercantile families in London, as well as Manchester, in the nineteenth century.[73] An important turning point in the development of the Greek mercantile community in London occurred in the 1820s as a result of the persecution of the population of Chios by the Ottomans, which led many of the most prominent and wealthiest Greeks to leave the island.[74] By 1839 twenty-one Greek merchants and bankers had established themselves in London, a figure which had grown to over seventy by the early 1860s.[75] They usually constituted members of larger Greek trading families, using their own ships and trading in specific locations.[76]

The Ralli brothers became the most successful Greek mercantile family with their first London branch opening in 1817 followed by a second in 1820.[77] In fact, the Londoners constituted part of a much wider network which also incorporated branches in Odessa, Constantinople, Marseilles and Liverpool.[78] The firm continued to grow both in London and on the continent and, as an indication of its truly international and networked nature, Stephen Ralli, the son of Augustus Ralli of Marseilles where he grew up, moved to work in the London office in 1851 with his uncle Pandias, taking over the running of the London branch when his uncle died in 1865. Pandias, the son of Stefanos, who had established a branch of the firm in Livorno, was born in Chios and had moved to London in the early 1820s. Pandias had overseen an expansion of the London branch and the opening of offices in the Middle East and India.[79] As early as 1837 an outlet in Taurid in Persia traded in silk. Developments in India began to occur from 1851 when John Ralli moved to Calcutta. Here the firm traded in all manner of Indian products from cotton to rice to indigo.[80] Ralli Brothers had interests stretching from New York to Russia by the middle of the nineteenth century, operating even further east than India in Japan. By 1860 it had become one of the largest and most global companies trading from the City of London with an estimated wealth of £1 million. As many as sixty-six members of the Ralli family may have worked in the global network.[81] By the 1930s it had become focused upon British India with branches in Bombay, Calcutta, Karachi and Madras. The head office remained in London and employed a predominantly Greek staff.[82]

The Ralli dynasty simply became the largest Greek commercial family operating globally from London,[83] as a series of others followed a similar path. They included the Rodocanachi[84] and the Ionidis, who established one of the first Greek London firms as early as 1815,[85] the Zarifi House and the Vagliano brothers.[86] London also became an important centre for Greek global shipping operations originating, once again, especially in Chios, although others came from Andros and Cephalonia during the course of the nineteenth and twentieth centuries. In London they worked with London firms who provided them with finance. As late as the 1980s 150 Greek shipping companies still existed in London, with 45 owned by Chiots. This elite group, like their early nineteenth-century predecessors, resided in exclusive parts of London, in this case Marble Arch and St John's Wood, and distinguished themselves, in the post-war period, from the poorer Greek Cypriots, with whom they nominally shared the same language and religion.[87] For the Greek merchants and shipping agents London provided global opportunities as the centre of international and imperial trade which survived into the second half of the twentieth century beyond the collapse of Empire.

German Gentiles and Jews also seized the opportunities available in London from the early nineteenth century, partly through the type of family networks which the Greeks utilized. By the middle of the century about 5 per cent of London Jewry, around 1,000 individuals or 200 families, belonged to the upper or upper middle class, some of whom had origins dating back to readmission.[88] Nathan Mayer Rothschild became one of the most famous, successful and wealthy of the German Jews to move to London from the end of the eighteenth century. Born in the Jewish quarter of Frankfurt in 1777 to a coin dealer, Mayer Amshel Rothschild, Nathan went to London in 1798 as the agent of his father's firm, which by that time traded in textiles, having already worked as a traveller and agent in Brussels, Paris and Basel. When he moved to London, where he remained for a year, Nathan did so with £20,000 from his father and worked for the branch of his father's firm which already existed in London, moving to Manchester in 1799 where he set up on his own as a textile trader. By 1810, having married Hannah Cohen, the daughter of Levi Barent Cohen, a wealthy Jewish Dutch merchant working in the City, which helped both his social standing and business opportunities, Nathan returned to London to act as a major financier for the government's Napoleonic war campaigns, working together with the continental branch of the firm, obtaining help from his brothers, which seems to have involved gold smuggling. The financing of this campaign proved the making of the English branch of the Rothschilds, bringing Nathan close to the centre of the British government, which he continued to help to bankroll beyond the Napoleonic Wars, contributing to the further growth of this firm.[89]

The success of Nathan Mayer Rothschild involved seizing the moment, clearly aided by a European-wide family financial network. Other highly successful German traders and financiers, building on the success of their eighteenth-century predecessors, also rose to prominence in London during the Napoleonic Wars, partly because of the occupation of Frankfurt and Hamburg by the French Emperor's armies between 1806 and 1812, as well as the blockade of the continent, which meant increasing numbers of agents from these and other German cities migrated to London.[90] In 1791 fourteen-year-old Frederick Huth, born in Harsefeld in 1777, moved to Hamburg to work as an apprentice in a Spanish firm, then progressed to Coruna as an agent for the company in 1797, but subsequently opened his own business in Spain. He moved to London in 1809 with 4,000 thalers as a commission agent, dealing primarily in tea and silk. The firm expanded to establish branches in other parts of England, as well as Hamburg and Bremen and, subsequently, America and 'East Asia', but continued with its headquarters in London into the late nineteenth century.[91] Meanwhile, Heinrich Goschen and Heinrich Fruhling from Bremen, involved in the Baltic trade, also established themselves in London.[92]

The most famous firm to emerge in London with origins in Hamburg at the time of the Napoleonic Wars, working on a scale comparable with the Rothschilds, consisted of the Schröders when the merchant Christian Mathias sent his sons Johann Frederick and Johann Heinrich to the British imperial capital. The family originated in Quackenbrück and had moved into trade during the eighteenth century, which meant relocation to Hamburg. By the end of the eighteenth century, Christian Mathias had established a leading international merchant family in the city. Hamburg is significant not simply because of the fact that expertise migrated from the city towards London during the Napoleonic Wars, but also because it acted as a global port on a similar standing to London, meaning that those merchants who migrated did so from one great early nineteenth-century trading city to another. The migration of Johann Frederick and Johann Heinrich became the first building block in an Anglo-German bank which also witnessed the movement of subsequent generations of the German banking family from Hamburg to London. J. Henry Schröder had established the original branch in London in 1818, after dissolving his partnership with his brother and would subsequently create a network of firms in London, Hamburg and Liverpool. From the 1840s the company diversified into merchant banking. J. Henry Schröder's son John Henry William Schröder became a partner in 1849 and moved to London in the following year.[93] By 1870 J. Henry Schröder & Co. had become the fourth largest bank in terms of capital.[94] In 1888, Bruno Schröder transferred to London from Hamburg as part of his commercial training and would return in 1892 to become a partner, essentially becoming head of the London firm from this time. By the 1890s he and his family lived in Kensington and would move to Mayfair in the following decade.[95]

The Rothschilds and the Schröders re-emphasize the global importance of London as a trading and financial centre which acted as the focal point to a series of international houses with branches in other global cities. In terms of ethnic and geographical origins by the 1870s these could fall into three categories: Jewish houses, which include not just Rothschilds, but also the Speyer brothers; Anglo-American, which include Baring and J. S. Morgan; and Anglo-German, which, in addition to Huth and Schröder, would further include Alexander Kleinwort and C. J. Hambro.[96]

We might view the Rothschilds and the Schröders as trailblazers for subsequent German and German Jewish international bankers with a key base in London, as others followed during the course of the nineteenth century. The Kleinwort Benson Bank came into existence in 1961 through the merger of two institutions with origins in Hamburg and the Lake District. The founder of the former, Alexander Friedrich Kleinwort, was born in Gerdeshagen to a merchant family in 1815 and moved with them to Altona in his childhood, following a downturn in his father's business. Alexander Friedrich initially worked in a series of firms in Hamburg but moved to Cuba in 1838 to take up a position as a clerk for a German firm, subsequently working for Drake Brothers, one of the most significant merchant houses in the country, and again indicating the global reach of British business, from 1840 in charge of European correspondence. He rapidly rose through this company and helped to establish a merchant banking house in London from the 1850s, which his son, Alexander Drake Kleinwort, born in Camberwell in 1858, would develop further. Alexander Friedrich Kleinwort differs from the Rothschilds and Schröders because family networks did not play a key role in his success, although he started a family banking dynasty himself. He essentially offers an example of a self-motivated and ambitious individual who took the right decisions enabling him to succeed in merchant banking, at a time when this sector continued to develop.[97] The Speyer banking house, like the Rothschilds, originated from the Jewish community of Frankfurt. By the second half of the nineteenth century it had three main branches in New York, Frankfurt and London. Edgar Speyer became chairman of the last of these in 1886 at the age of twenty-four and would play a major role in financing the expansion of the London Underground system, as well as moving to the centre of London society, becoming a British citizen at the age of twenty-nine, a process which came to halt when he fell victim to First World War Germanophobia.[98]

Saemy Japhet followed a similar path as revealed in his autobiography. The background to his migration lay in the fact that problems evolved for some older banks in Frankfurt during the 1880s and 1890s when Berlin became the banking capital of Germany, which meant that some Frankfurt businesses went into liquidation while others transferred to other European cities.[99] Born in Frankfurt in 1858 to a Hebrew teacher,[100] Japhet started work as 'a shy junior' in the banking firm of Emile Schwarzschild,[101] 'promoted a clerk with a yearly salary of M.1000 and I began to show some initiative'.[102] After an 'interruption in my work caused through my entry into the army' he started working in the Frankfurt Stock Exchange,[103] subsequently secured a post as the Frankfurt agent of the Hamburg firm Rennes, and on 28 November 1880 'I started business on my own account' in the form of a 'small brokerage business'.[104] This meant that he 'travelled a lot',[105] visiting London for the first time in 1886, acting also as an agent to another Frankfurt firm, Ransford and Schiff, which 'made an enormous impression upon me'.[106] He spent the next few years working in Amsterdam, Paris, Berlin and London, developing clients and connections and opening his office in 31 Throgmorton Street on 25 May 1896. By 1900 London became his head office with branches in Berlin, Frankfurt and Hamburg.[107] His firm survived both world wars, although it suffered as a result of the 1931 economic collapse in Germany, never returning to its previous strength.[108] Another self-made man' in 'the fullest sense of the term', who worked with Japhet, Sir Ernest Cassel reached the top of both the banking establishment and London's social elite, developing a close friendship with Edward VII.[109] Born to a Jewish banking family in Cologne in 1852, and therefore originating in solid upper middle-class stock, he migrated to Liverpool in 1869 to take up a position as a clerk with a firm of German grain merchants, Blessing, Braun and Co. The following year he moved to Paris to work for the Anglo-Egyptian bank, but he settled in London at the outbreak of the Franco-Prussian War in 1870 where he began working for another German Jewish firm, Bischoffsheim & Goldschmidt.[110] His father left Cassell a significant amount of money when he died in 1875 which allowed him, along with his ambition, risk taking and financial acumen, to become 'one of the richest lone wolves in European banking'. From the 1870s he had become involved in a wide variety of projects encompassing Britain, Europe, North and South America and Africa. He became both a financier and also got involved in industrial concerns, many of which he helped to purchase.[111]

Cassel symbolizes the openness and globality of the Victorian and Edwardian London economy and society. While he might, to some extent, have driven his own success through networking and hard work, a statement which would apply to all of the figures outlined above, virtually all of the Germans and Greeks previously discussed came from wealthy family mercantile backgrounds which gave them advantages over their competitors both in terms of the global networks that they provided but also in the sense that they had financial backing behind them. None of the figures discussed above went from rags to riches, in the way that a few twentieth-century migrants may have done. Instead, they generally went from rich to super-rich. The additional factors which helped this process included their entry into and, essentially, driving the rise of merchant baking, a system in which the boundaries between commerce and finance remained blurred, at least in the earlier decades of the nineteenth century.[112] Moving to London provided both social and economic opportunities as the migrants entered the centre of both British trade and commerce as well as high society.

MIGRANT ELITES SINCE 1914

The international bankers who moved to London during the course of the nineteenth century entered a city and country undergoing a phenomenal growth spurt. Those settling in London and other British cities seized their opportunities in a largely unregulated economy. As the twentieth century progressed the type of openings available to Nathan Mayer Rothschild or Saemy Japhet to develop major fortunes over a short period of time lessened, at least in the sense of establishing their own banking houses, even if, in virtually all of the cases described above, they formed a branch of a continental firm. The greater number of migrants who have moved to the capital since 1945 have opened more businesses but on a smaller scale. They share with their nineteenth-century predecessors drive and family support.

We can look at twentieth- and twenty-first-century migrant elites under a number of headings. The most prominent group falling into this category consists of Jews. The banking firms established during the nineteenth century would, in many cases, continue to thrive under the direction of the descendants of the original founders. At the same time, East European arrivals of the late nineteenth century and their descendants have moved to the top of the London social scale. Migration of Jews also occurred from other parts of Europe, especially Nazi Germany. The British state has always looked favourably upon foreigners who could invest in the country, despite the continual tightening of immigration controls since the beginning of the twentieth century, which literally meant that London had become the playground of the rich and famous by the beginning of the twenty-first century helped also by global economic liberalization, moving away from the more controlled economies of much of the twentieth century. Some of those who fall into the category of the super-rich parachuted in from outside while others have experienced social mobility, often through generations.

The consolidation of the Jewish elites in the twentieth century did not simply occur as a result of the continuing success of those families which emerged during the nineteenth century or even the social mobility of Russian Jews, but also the arrival of members of Jewish communities from other parts of the world. For example, the parents of Ralph Stern, Alfred and Lisa Stern, originated 'from a small village near Frankfurt' and from Essen respectively. Alfred migrated to London in 1906 to work as a button merchant with his brother Julius. He faced First World War internment followed by deportation to Germany but managed to return to the city after the Nazi takeover with the help of his brother who had remained. Alfred started a button factory in Long Lane in the City, destroyed by German bombs in 1940. The family subsequently moved to Tottenham to run another button factory, which survived until the end of the twentieth century.[113] Meanwhile Leon Aelion, born in Salonika in 1907, settled to London in 1927 via Turkey and France where he worked in the carpet trade.[114] David Elias moved to London from India (where his father ran a factory) with the help of various Jewish contacts who helped him purchase a house. He originally worked for David Ben-Gurion, the first prime minister of Israel from 1948 to 1953, which meant spending time in Israel, but Elias returned to London to establish his own business.[115]

The most significant Jewish elites who migrated to London and the rest of Britain during the twentieth century arrived from Nazi Germany, initially as long as Jewish charitable organizations agreed to financially guarantee them, a policy which lasted until 1938 when the British government introduced a more liberal policy in the light of increasing Nazi brutality exemplified by the *Kristallnacht* pogrom.[116] By the 1930s German Jewry constituted an overwhelmingly (generally upper) middle-class group and would, in the longer term in most cases, return to the employment which they had practised before emigrating, despite hostility in some professions in Britain. Those who moved as children without their parents, usually to live in middle-class homes, also generally had successful careers. However, as refugees, many of these German elites experienced difficulties readjusting to their foreign environment as well as coming to terms with the loss of home and family they had experienced.[117]

By the 1960s surveys revealed that the Anglo-Jewish community had a higher standard of living than any other ethnic group in the country as revealed by a series of indicators including the ownership of cars and domestic electrical appliances which far exceeded similar statistics for the population as a whole. By 1978 83.5 per cent of Jews in Redbridge owned their own homes compared with just 55 per cent for the population of the UK as a whole. Jews also revealed a much higher rate of university education.[118] Such trends have continued into the twenty-first century. Jews held higher educational qualifications than the population as a whole,[119] were more likely to work in 'real estate, renting and business activities', education and 'financial intermediation', and were also more likely to hold positions as 'managers and senior officials' as well as 'corporate managers', and 'managers and proprietors in services'.[120] The wealthiest Jews in Britain have included the descendants of both the nineteenth-century elites and the Russian refugees. We can reel out numerous names such as the Rothschilds, the Samuels, descended from Marcus Samuel who founded Shell, the Goldsmids and the Waley-Cohens amongst the former category, for example.[121] These had originated as international families and continued to remain so, despite their assimilation and Anglicization. These wealthy Jews became involved in all areas of the British economy. In the period between 1945 and 1965, of 108 people who made a personal fortune from property exceeding £1 million, focused especially upon London, 70 per cent had Jewish origins, the best known of whom included Charles Clore, Harry Hyams, Max Rayne and Harold Samuel.[122] We might see property speculation as offering the type of opportunities to entrepreneurs which merchant banking did during the eighteenth century, attracting both Jews and other ethnic minorities. The most economically successful descendants of East European refugees included Jack Cohen whose market stall established immediately after the First World War had become Tesco stores in 1932. By the 1950s it counted 150 shops and, by the end of the twentieth century, when Cohen had relinquished control, it had become the largest grocer in Britain.[123] Two other major high street retailing chains, Marks and Spencer and the clothing firm Montague Burton, also had East European Jewish origins, although their founders grew up in Chesterfield and Leeds respectively.[124] Marks and Spencer came into existence through the association of Michael Marks, a Polish immigrant, and Thomas Spence, 'a Yorkshireman and Gentile'. One of their earliest stores opened in Regent Street.[125] Similarly, the Glasgow-born Isaac Wolfson established the mail order company Great Universal Stores during the 1920s.[126] Such individual businesses represent the flagships of both London and Jewish entrepreneurial success. Others who operated on a smaller but national or international scale include, for example, Emmanuel Kaye, educated at Twickenham Technical College, who would, with J. R. Sharp, establish Lansing Bagnall, which became the largest European producer of electric lift trucks.[127] Meanwhile, Jack Dickmann established Fidelity Radio after initially opening his enterprise using his demobilization pay and a loan of £100 from his mother-in-law.[128]

Over the last two centuries it seems clear that the Jewish community of London has experienced a period of sustained business success from the Rothschilds to the descendants of the East Europeans who usually arrived penniless to settle in the East End. While German Jews in particular arrived as members of the European elite, the Russian refugees did not. Members of both groups, however, used their connections to maximize the success of their enterprises. They have had a profound influence on the London, British and global economy. We should, however, beware of generalization as the descendants of poorer Jews often took several generations to achieve a middle-class status while the vast majority would never have achieved the elite lifestyles and standards of wealth achieved by the leading figures in Anglo-Jewry.

The longevity of Jewish settlement in Britain, continuous since the readmission of the seventeenth century, helps further to explain their prominence as elite businessmen. Post-war arrivals to London have had less time to establish the types of global enterprises set up by Jewish migrants and their descendants, but some have done so, as we saw with the example of Asil Nadir, who worked from London to utilize his international networks in Cyprus and Turkey to establish a European-wide business empire.[129] While he does not quite represent a rags to riches story, he provides an example of an immigrant from a lower middle-class background who became a member of the international bourgeoisie. Other examples include Vijay and Bikhu Patel, who moved from Kenya to London in the 1960s and would establish the multimillion pharmaceutical wholesale business Waymade,[130] and Sir Gulam Noon, who developed a food empire after migration from India to London.[131]

On the one hand, some of the most successful of twentieth- and twenty-first-century migrants in Britain resemble the East European Jewish refugees to Britain in the sense that they emerge from relatively humble backgrounds, but with an international mindset because of their personal histories. On the other hand, some of the elite businessmen resemble the Rothschilds and the Speyers because they came from international business backgrounds, as a few examples illustrate. Stelios Hadjioannou, the founder of Easyjet and the various other Easy brands, achieved the status of 'the richest Cypriot in Britain' and the 48th richest person overall in Britain in 2018,[132] and has written a biographical sketch about himself in which his business advantages come through. He was actually born in Athens, the second son of Loucas Hadjioannou described as a 'self-made shipping magnate born in Cyprus'.[133] Lakshmi Mittal came from an even more privileged background and, while he has topped the list of Britain's richest Asians and Britain's richest person, he epitomizes the international bourgeoisie of the early twenty-first century, the scion of one of the richest and most established business families in India and also a symbol of business globalization, with London as one of the key centres of his empire.[134] Roman Abramowich, meanwhile, highly unusually, essentially constitutes a self-made man, almost moving from rags to riches, in the sense that he was not born into the type of privilege characterizing some of the other very wealthy individuals who settled in London in the early twenty-first century, although, like them, he managed to network with the correct people and seize his opportunities. Orphaned at the age of two, but adopted by his uncle, he moved rapidly to purchase Russian state oil shares when they became available for sale in the middle of the 1990s. By the following decade he had settled in London to become one of the richest men in Britain, while never cutting his ties to Russia,[135] although in 2018 he took out Israeli citizenship following a crackdown on Russian oligarchs in London, which meant he had difficulties renewing his visa.[136]

The British government pursued various policies to ensure that London and the country as a whole remained at the centre of globalization, including the use of special visas which allowed people who invest £1 million, £2 million or £10 million a fast track to permanent residence in the United Kingdom, overwhelmingly in London, dating back to the government of John Major in 1996. The countries who sent the most migrants to Britain under this scheme between 2008 and 2014 consisted of Russia (433) and China (419), with India (44) fifth in this list. At the same time, those who decided to settle in the UK only paid tax on their income earned within the country rather than that gained abroad, which in some ways made the country a tax haven, with the London super-rich making up 0.01 per cent of the British population, a few thousand people. By the beginning of the twenty-first century London had become a magnet for the world's billionaires. In some cases, the super-rich did not even settle in the metropolis, simply purchasing properties from abroad as investment, which added to the skyrocketing prices of London property and homes.[137] An analysis of the *Sunday Times Rich List* in 2018 comparing the people who managed to secure an entry in this year with those when this publication first emerged in 1989 points to the fact that in 1989 'only five Rich Listers (2.5%) were from ethnic minorities. By 2018 that number had risen to 86 (8.6%), 83 of them from the Asian community. Several of them arrived here as refugees.' At the same time the *Sunday Times Rich List* had become 'unquestionably more international. In 1989, Sweden, Germany, Canada and America were represented in our top 20.' In 2018 'India, Ukraine, Holland, Sweden, Russia, Canada, Italy, Saudi Arabia and Norway account for 13 of the 20 richest'. At the same time, indicating the increasing importance of globalization and entrepreneurship, the percentage of landowners had decreased significantly from 28.5 per cent to 2.9 per cent.[138]

We should not become fixated upon the super-rich in twenty-first-century London because, like their predecessors a hundred years earlier, they constitute a fraction of the overall population of the capital, concentrated in the wealthiest areas such as the City and Kensington. As we have seen from the naturalization certificates sampled at the start of this chapter, the international bourgeoisie in London in the late nineteenth and early twentieth centuries constituted a diverse group, which would continue into the second half of the twentieth century and accelerated in terms of numbers as a result of the banking and stock market liberalization from the 1980s. This brought growing numbers of foreign banks into the City, as well as increasing the staff they employed, both British and foreign,[139] facilitated further by free movement within the European Union, which meant that the educated middle class have migrated freely from one country and city to another.[140] These developments have not just brought bankers and stockbrokers to London, but also a variety of other employees dependent on these sectors. Donatella, a data analyst from Puglia, who studied economics at university in Italy, moved to London at the age of thirty-three to work in the International Finance Centre near the Stock Exchange. She described her friends as 'about 20 per cent English, 20 per cent Italian and 60 per cent international'.[141] One account of the overwhelmingly middle-class French population in London at the start of the twenty-first century divided it into two groups: the 'highly skilled, highly educated and highly sought after (euro)City (euro)stars'; and those 'seeking language skills, a new lifestyle, perhaps a new self and, above all, employment'.[142] London has proved attractive to young graduates from all over Europe, who recognized its importance as one of the economic hubs of Europe with truly global significance and greater job opportunities than some of the poorer European Union states.[143] London has also continued to attract large numbers of foreign students, whose numbers increased from the 1980s, despite the fact that the Thatcher government started charging them. While this took place throughout the country, the concentration of so many higher and further education institutes in the capital has made London especially attractive.[144]

LONDON AS THE CENTRE OF THE GLOBAL ELITE

As with the other social and economic groups we have examined, it becomes clear that London has always attracted the rich, entrepreneurial and highly educated throughout its history, in this particular case dating back to the Middle Ages. These elites have shaped this global city, especially those involved in finance, from the medieval Jews to the nineteenth-century Jewish immigrants from Germany in particular to those who arrived as a result of the liberalization of banking and the stock market from the 1980s. Clearly, the global importance of the City of London over the last two centuries has meant that it has proved a magnet to bankers. However, its global economic significance has also attracted merchants from all over the world. More recently, increasing numbers of professionals have made their way to London, although, as the analysis of the naturalization certificates indicated, the international bourgeoisie have always constituted a diverse group. As with the other two social groups we have tackled, an increase has taken place in the numbers of elites in the post-war period.

Those involved in trade, banking, large-scale retailing and industry lend themselves to division into two categories. First, those who moved to the country as wealthy men who used the opportunities provided by the global marketplace of London to become members of the super-rich, whether Sir Ernest Cassel or Sir Stelios Hadjioannou. These individuals came from already wealthy families, although they clearly had to undertake risk in order to succeed to a level that earned them knighthoods. The rags to riches stories seem more difficult to find. Roman Abramovich had made his way to the top of Russian society by the time he moved to London and essentially transplanted himself having already achieved billionaire status. Jack Cohen and Vijay and Bikhu Patel came from humble but not poor backgrounds. The importance of family comes through in virtually all of the economic elites, as indicated by the success of many Germans and Greeks who moved to London in the nineteenth century. Their financial and commercial networks meant they had relatives in cities throughout Europe and beyond which they used to their advantage. London stood at the centre of these networks which operated on a global scale.

6

RACISTS, FRIENDS AND LOVERS

There was very little work done in the East-end throughout the day. Shopkeepers of unequivocal British birth in the areas where rioting was most violent thought it wise to close their doors for the day, and in some of the streets which run off Commercial Road there was scarcely a shop which was not shuttered.

The damage done by the rioters was very great. Not content with smashing doors and looting the whole of the furniture and the contents of the shops, the interiors of the houses were in numerous instances greatly damaged. Staircases were hacked to pieces and ceilings were knocked down. Shops were completely wrecked before the police had time to arrive on the scene. At Poplar, for instance, in an area of a quarter of a mile half a dozen houses were attacked simultaneously by different crowds in the early afternoon. Before the constables were able to attempt to disperse the mob, horse-drawn carts, handcarts, and perambulators – besides the unaided arms of men, women, and children – had taken everything away from the wrecked houses. One saw pianos, chests of drawers, dressers, and the heaviest type of household furniture being carted triumphantly through the streets. 'Here is wealth for the taking,' said one man who had possession of several spring mattresses, and was calmly driving his over-loaded donkey-cart down C[h]risp Street.[1]

I am a wine waiter. I was born in Cyprus and came to this country in 1937. In 1948, I married Hella Drothea Bleicher. I have three children, two boys and a girl. They range between twelve and nine years. The accused is my mother. She came to this country . . . to live with me, my wife and my children . . .

My mother and my wife did not get along very much. My wife has been a little tired. She was going on holiday to her parents in Germany . . .

On Wednesday, 28th July, 1954, I last saw my wife about half-past eight in the morning . . . I was carrying out my duties at the Café until approximately 3 o'clock in the morning on the 29th July. I got home about half-past three that morning, to find that my wife was dead.[2]

First- and second-generation migrants in London have had a vast range of experiences in their relationships with white Britons. On the one hand racism always remains in the background, impacting on virtually every foreigner who has lived in the capital at some stage of their lives, no matter how mild or subtle such an experience may prove. At the other extreme comes the normality of interethnic relationships and marriages, not simply between white Britons and migrants and their descendants but also involving members of different migrant groups. In between come a variety of forms of interaction involving friendships, whether at school, in the workplace or in the social sphere.

As this book has argued throughout, migrants and their descendants form a key part of London society across the social scale, meaning that their experiences simply mirror those of the white majority. Interethnic interaction involves both the majority and the minority. In the case of hostility, the two actors have a different role to play, as either perpetrator or victim, whether the act of hostility remains mild or involves a physical attack, the latter of which impacted upon all ethnic groups in London for most of its history from medieval Jewry to post-war arrivals from the Empire and Commonwealth, although the final decades of the twentieth century witnessed the disappearance of the anti-immigrant riot in London. This would appear to suggest the emergence of a more inclusive and tolerant or cosmopolitan society. While we cannot dismiss this argument, cosmopolitanism and interethnic friendship and interaction have formed a key feature of London life for centuries, involving the whole social spectrum.

This chapter outlines the reality of interaction between different ethnic groups and individuals, from sex and love to violence. A simplistic analysis might argue that the last two hundred years have witnessed a decline in racism, as evidenced by the disappearance of the anti-immigrant riot, and the rise of tolerance, indicated by the acceptance of concepts of multiculturalism following the arrival, impact and political campaigning of black and Asian migrants after 1945.[3] But as indicated, for example, by the collection put together by George R. Sims, cosmopolitanism has always characterized London life.[4] Significantly, however, his collection appeared at the same time as the campaign for the Aliens Act of 1905, which set the template for all subsequent immigration controls in Britain, in which the arrival of visible numbers of newcomers from one particular area of the world, in this case East European Jews, led to a rise of xenophobia on the ground which interacted with receptive political elites to lead to the passage of new legislation. The crucible which fused together hostility on the ground with highbrow racism usually lay in London, whether in the antisemitic East End around 1900 or racist Notting Hill in the late 1950s. Yet to describe the East End or Notting Hill simply as racist and antisemitic during these years simplifies reality. While they may have become cauldrons of anti-immigrant hostility, they also represent symbols of multicultural London at those particular periods. Perhaps the racism, especially when manifested in violence, simply represents a type of thunderstorm, the final act of resistance before a new diverse reality.

While xenophobia may have become less violent and visible in recent decades, multicultural racism has characterized interethnic relations in London, reflecting the picture in the country as a whole.[5] Positive and negative reactions always run parallel and, in some cases, as with the Notting Hill riots, mixed-race relationships contributed to a rise of ethnic tensions.[6] While the anti-immigrant riot may have disappeared as a characteristic of London life by the 1960s, other forms of hostility towards newcomers certainly did not disappear as attacks upon individuals continued, brought to international attention by the murder of Stephen Lawrence in Eltham in 1993. Even in superdiverse London ethnic minorities and migrants would continue to face prejudice.

In twenty-first-century London the level of hostility experienced by migrants and their offspring varies from one ethnic group to another, determined by three factors in particular. First, the position on the social and economic ladder, so that those at the lower end of the scale already experience discrimination simply by virtue of the task which the labour market assigns them. Second, the level of integration, so that those born and educated in

London usually experience less hostility than their parents. Third, the level of difference from the white British, in which land of origin and colour play a key role. Combining these factors together, the experiences of a second-generation Irish person employed in an office environment would differ significantly from those of a black African immigrant cleaning the same office.

Nevertheless, this equation, while it may indicate reality in most cases, remains theoretical, as the example of the Germans during the First World War indicates. This largely integrated and invisible group, which had intermarried with Britons (especially German men with British women), experienced a tidal wave of state-supported xenophobia, most visible in rioting across London in May 1915, which essentially wiped out the German community of the capital. As in the case of the campaign to pass the Aliens Act of 1905 or the Commonwealth Immigrants Act of 1962, migrants become fair game during times of heightened ethnic tension.

RACISTS

Hostility from already established populations towards new foreign arrivals has formed part of the everyday experience of migrants and their offspring throughout the history of London and the country as a whole. The uniqueness of the British capital lies, once again, in its continuity as a city and, more especially, as a city of migrant settlement, which has meant that it has a history of racial and ethnic hostility covering almost a millennium if not more.

In the Middle Ages, when Jews focused on distinct parts of London, 'the vast majority of Gentiles . . . never knew a Jew at all intimately. Their first introduction was often a riot or some equally dramatic event', driven to violence by the stereotypes of Jews as Christ killers and moneylenders, which characterized medieval Christianity.[7] The major outbreaks of violence against London Jewry in this period occurred in September 1189 during the Coronation of Richard I against the background of the heightened religious tension of the First Crusade[8] and between 1262 and 1267, when Jews came under attack on several occasions, together with Italians, against the background of political and economic instability.[9]

In many ways the hostility towards medieval Jewry sets the pattern of events which would follow against subsequent minority groups in London's history at times of heightened political and economic tension. Together with violence a milder general xenophobia exists that usually focuses upon one particular group at a time. In the Middle Ages, until the expulsion of 1290, Jews unquestionably played this role. The 'London mob', which appears to have reached its apotheosis in the eighteenth century, meted out justice to those regarded as having broken real or imagined moral rules, including migrants, and, if we accept the existence of this random arbiter of right and wrong,[10] it would continue to function until the second half of the twentieth century.

One of the best recorded incidents of the xenophobic London mob in action in early modern London occurred on Evil May Day in 1517, when rioters attacked European merchants and financiers.[11] The violence was sparked off by 'an unfortunate coincidence of anti-alien tension on several levels at once' from English merchants who resented the competition they faced to the wider population, which became caught up in this proto-nationalist discourse leading to outbreaks of violence that lasted from 28 April to 1 May, which also resulted in the execution of rioters.[12] In the following century Huguenots would face hostility which would include violence in Spitalfields, where they worked as silk weavers, and in the City. In both cases natives viewed them as an economic threat undercutting local workers.[13]

A variety of migrants became victims of the London mob in the eighteenth century, especially Germans, Jews and above all Irish and other foreign Catholics, against the background of the ideological anti-Catholicism which complemented the development of Britishness during this period.[14] Antisemitism and attacks upon Jews also became a characteristic of London life at this time, complementing the integration which took place amongst the socially mobile Jews following readmission.

Although no specific strand of ideological Germanophobia existed in the eighteenth century, as would happen in the early twentieth, migrants from various parts of Germany who moved to London for a variety of reasons experienced attacks during this period. In the expanding city with dire social conditions in which burials exceeded baptisms, violence and xenophobia became a characteristic of everyday life, so that all 'foreigners . . . were liable to be roughly treated, or at least abused, by the mob'.[15] In 1709 the main victims consisted of the 13,000 to 15,000 refugees from the Palatinate who had to live in makeshift accommodation throughout London, including barns and warehouses, especially in Blackheath and Whitechapel Fields. Although, on the one hand, public and private charity raised £20,000 to support them, much public opinion united to oppose the refugees in a variety of ways, as British national consciousness began to develop following the Act of Union with Scotland in 1707, including the publication of leaflets leading to violent attacks, some of which involved axes.[16] The Brethren, a religious minority which moved to East London from Upper Silesia in the late 1730s, also experienced hostility including physical violence.[17]

Antisemitism in eighteenth-century London may have become so wide-spread that 'Jew-baiting became a sport, like cock-throwing, or bull-baiting or pelting some poor wretch in the pillory'.[18] Jewish itinerant traders suffered in particular, although attacks occasionally took place on the homes of wealthier London Jews, as happened in Duke's Place in 1763.[19] Such incidents occurred against the background of an underlying pre-modern type of anti-Jewish ideology which still viewed Jews as the killers of Christ and the enemies of Christian civilization. Much of this type of language came to the fore during the opposition to the campaign for the Jewish Naturalization Bill of 1753.[20] Antisemitism would evolve during the course of the eighteenth century to more modern manifestations which focused upon both the financial and consequently potential political power of the Jews, their apparent unchangeability and consequent inability to assimilate, but which also contained an anti-poverty aspect to it with a focus on second-hand clothes peddlers.[21]

The bullying and violence which impacted upon London Jewry focused to an even greater extent upon the Irish, perhaps because they counted significantly larger numbers and because anti-Catholicism acted as a more potent ideology. The Britishness which developed during the eighteenth century did so against the Catholic enemies of France and Spain. Catholic Ireland also fell into this orbit, which meant that the Irish in London, as well as other European Catholics who lived within the city, formed something of an enemy within.[22] Although anti-Catholicism remained a nationwide ideology, its main victims during the course of the eighteenth century lived in London, especially during the Gordon Riots of 1780, which represented the culmination of this type of prejudice in the history of London, as well as the worst example of civil disorder of any type, whether or not aimed against foreigners.

But other types of violence also took place against and involving the eighteenth-century Irish. This large community did not simply play the role of victims but could also fight back and even perpetrate violence, a situation which continued into the nineteenth century both in London and in other

British cities. In 1740, 'there was a general onslaught by a body of Irish upon the butchers of Claire Market' after 'some rash butchers' boys had ventured to burn a "Paddy" on St Patrick's day'. In 1763, meanwhile, 'a pitched battle' took place 'between a party of sailors and a number of Irish Chairmen in Convent Garden'.[23]

The culmination of the anti-Irish anti-Catholic feeling in London, the peak of the power of the London mob, came with the Gordon Riots of 1780. The name of these disturbances comes from Lord George Gordon, the leader of the Protestant Association of Great Britain that came into existence in order to oppose the Catholic Relief Act of 1778, which was primarily aimed at boosting recruitment into the British army by removing the requirement to condemn the Catholic Church when swearing allegiance to the British Crown, while also lifting restrictions on land ownership, preaching and publishing. The culmination of the Protestant Association's campaign came with the gathering of 44,000 signatures for a petition calling for the repeal of the 1778 Act. On Friday 2 June 1780 about 60,000 people gathered in St George's Field in Southwark to present the petition to Parliament. However, the protest quickly turned violent, leading to almost a week of rioting. On 2 June the crowd attacked the Chapels of the Bavarian and Sardinian ambassadors. On 3 June the rioters targeted a silk merchant from Cambray called Mr Malo and also attempted to attack Irish residents in Moorfield, but troops prevented them from doing so. By Monday 5 June rioting had gripped much of London. On 6 June fires illuminated the London skyline when the properties which came under attack included two Catholic schools. The culmination of the disturbances came on Black Wednesday (7 June). Houses, shops and offices occupied by Catholic merchants, businessmen, shopkeepers and justices faced attack, as did public houses in Golden Lane and Whitechapel and a Catholic distiller in Holborn. Rioting also broke out in Bermondsey and continued into the following day when the victims included the public houses and homes of Roman Catholics. By this time the disturbances had come to an end. They had resulted in 450 arrests and twenty-five hangings. The military, although initially remaining fairly passive, which facilitated the spread of the rioting, had killed 210 people on the streets, while seventy-five more died in hospital.

These events have given rise to a variety of interpretations. In the first place it seems obvious that the driving force consisted of anti-Catholicism and xenophobia because the victims were predominantly Irish and Europeans. They differ from any of the other riots against foreigners in the history of modern London because of the scale of the destruction involved, even though the attacks on Germans in May 1915 lasted for a similar length of time and also spread to the whole of London. But the Gordon rioters attacked churches, schools, rich and poor. Social protest also motivated the rioters as many of the victims consisted of large and small businessmen, as well as members of the Roman Catholic elite. However, at heart and at origin, they constituted the worst xenophobic riots in London's history. While they may not indicate the normal everyday experience of Irish and other Roman Catholics in eighteenth-century London, their scale and destructiveness, like the anti-German riots of May 1915, point to an intense hatred which had other numerous and milder manifestations.[24]

While nineteenth-century London may not have witnessed anti-immigrant disturbances on the scale of the Gordon Riots, anti-Catholic and anti-Irish prejudice remained strong despite, or perhaps because of, the fact that this religious group was increasingly moving towards equality with the Protestant majority population. By the end of the Victorian period, as anti-Catholicism had declined,[25] racism replaced it as the main driving force of anti-Irish prejudice at an ideological level,[26] although it proves difficult to identify a direct link between the racial ideology and the relationships between the Irish and the English on the ground. London does not seem to have experienced the type of sectarian violence between Catholics and Protestants which characterized other British cities during the Victorian period, especially Liverpool and Glasgow. Neither does it appear to have experienced any anti-Irish riots which occurred sporadically throughout the country,[27] but which declined as the century progressed, partly because the majority of the Irish in Britain and, more especially, London, either kept a low profile, especially during Fenian attacks, or even publicly pledged allegiance to the Queen.[28] But the Irish certainly experienced prejudice, which kept them at the bottom of the labour scale, partly driven by the emergence of 'No Irish Need Apply' notices, which began to appear in significant numbers in late Georgian and early Victorian London[29] and during the nineteenth century had become 'customary' in the capital, as well as Liverpool and Manchester, the three cities with the largest Irish populations.[30] The worst example of intercommunal violence involving the Irish in Victorian London occurred in Hyde Park in September and October 1862. It was sparked by English supporters of the Italian nationalist leader Giuseppe Garibaldi, who made anti-Papal speeches, leading Irishmen who had gathered in the park to react violently both here, in the immediate vicinity and in pubs in West London.[31]

Hostility towards the Irish subsided during the course of the nineteenth century, especially in London, due to a variety of factors, perhaps most importantly the declining numbers of migrants, who had peaked from the second half of the 1840s as a result of the Irish Famine, but also because of the integration that had taken place. This meant that the Irish became increasingly invisible, despite the growth of Roman Catholic churches and other bodies connected with them. By the end of the nineteenth century a new more visible minority caught the attention of newspapers, parliamentary opinion and the ethnic majority in London in the form of East European Jews, which also coincided with a decline of anti-Catholicism and a rise or, more accurately, the birth of, antisemitism not just in the imperial capital but across the whole of Europe.[32]

Public opinion in London, and in the country as a whole, usually focuses upon one group at one particular time, from the Georgian and Victorian Irish, through the Jews for much of the early twentieth century, Germans during the First World War, to people of colour after 1945. Migrants from western Europe also experienced hostility in Victorian and Edwardian London, especially Italians and Germans. Italians became victims of social hostility, revolving particularly around issues of noise, child exploitation and hygiene during the Victorian period. Italian street musicians became the objects of hostility because of the noise they made and the fact that they utilized children.[33] Since that time Italians have remained a fairly invisible and integrated group in London society except during the Second World War. Mussolini's declaration of war upon Britain on 10 June 1940 led to the outbreak of anti-Italian riots, especially in Soho, where the perpetrators included Greeks (probably Cypriots), while other attacks took place in Glasgow, Liverpool and South Wales. These disturbances took place against the background of a rise of wartime Italophobia, which also resulted in the internment and deportation of members of this minority.[34]

For most of the Victorian and Edwardian period Germans in London remained largely invisible in public consciousness. Explanations for this situation include a racialized discourse that developed during the late nineteenth century which viewed Germans as part of an Anglo-Saxon race,[35] although this may have had limited impact on relations on the ground. At the same time, Germans also became a generally integrated group, as indicated by their activities as small shopkeepers.[36] However, they got caught up in a series of wider xenophobic campaigns including those led by the crusading London City Mission,[37] the movement against street music, because of the presence of German brass bands in London, and the wider hostility towards aliens (primarily Jews), which led to the passage of the Aliens Act of 1905. Hostility also arose against Germans in particular trades,[38] especially waiting.[39] Occasional attacks also took place against this group, especially in connection with the rise of German imperial, military and naval power,[40] which during the First World War turned this minority from an integrated to an enemy group both within London and in the country as a whole, to an even greater extent than the Irish during the Gordon Riots. The most serious manifestation of London Germanophobia consisted of large-scale violence, which broke out on five main occasions: August 1914, October 1914, May 1915, June 1916 and July 1917. Apart from May 1915, the others remained focused in specific locations. Following the sinking of the Liverpool-based passenger liner *Lusitania* by a German submarine on 7 May resulting in the death of over 1,000 civilians, virtually every German-owned shop in London faced destruction as the capital became 'one vast riot area' between 11 and 15 May, mirroring the situation in the country as a whole, and resembling the situation during the Gordon Riots. While fewer fires may have broken out in May 1915 and the violence may not have appeared to threaten the British state, 866 people faced arrest while 1,950 persons claimed compensation under the Riot (Damages) Act.[41] The May 1915 disorder resembles the Gordon Riots because of the virulence of xenophobia with official backing as German males experienced internment and subsequent deportation while their wives and children also faced expulsion. The government confiscated any German property which had not faced destruction, whether it belonged to the local baker and butcher or the Deutsche or Dresdner Bank. London and British society's saturation with Germanophobia meant Germans had nowhere to hide, irrespective of their social status. Merchant bankers with German origins faced particular hostility in the press, leading most of them to offer public pledges of allegiance,[42] but the animosity proved too much for Edgar Speyer who sailed to New York, leaving behind his London and Norfolk residences.[43]

The intensity of the hatred experienced by Germans during the Great War has not impacted upon other minorities in quite the same way. Germanophobia returned during the Second World War when refugees from Nazism would experience internment and deportation in 1940 and 1941, although this episode remained short-lived, largely because of the realization that most of the victims consisted of Jews fleeing the Nazis.[44] Nevertheless, antisemitism remained a feature of London and British life from the middle of the nineteenth until the middle of the twentieth century, manifesting itself against the Jewish population on all sections of the social scale in a variety of ways. While the gaining of legal equality by Jews, driven by the London-based elites, during the course of the Victorian period may indicate both integration and a lessening of the religious-based Judeophobia which characterized the early modern period,[45] the end of the nineteenth century saw the birth of the modern concept of antisemitism throughout Europe fuelled by the rise of nationalism which turned Jewish minorities into internal enemies.[46] While elite integrated London Jewry may not have experienced any direct consequences of this new ideology, in the sense that it closed no doors to them, wealthy Jews became more visible. Antisemitic ideologues blamed the Jewish elite for aspects of Britain's foreign policy (especially Prime Minister Benjamin Disraeli, despite the fact that he had undergone baptism), including intervention in the Boer War.[47] Apart from the fact that their Jewish origins determined their actions, for antisemites, 'Good or bad, rich Jew or poor, tyrant or slave, money was almost bound to be at the root of his problem.'[48] With regard to the Jewish elite, financially driven hostility focused upon corrupt practices, especially during the so-called Marconi Crisis when radical right-wing journalists examined the actions of Sir Rufus Isaacs, the attorney general, and his brother Godfrey, essentially accusing them of insider trading of shares which potentially impacted upon Britain's security.[49] The hostility to the London Jewish elite reached a peak during the First World War when ideas of an enemy within focused attention upon Jews of German origin, claiming that they prevented a British victory because of their primary allegiances to Germany and to the 'Cult of the Coin'.[50] The end of the First World War did not mean an end to conspiratorial antisemitism as the type of ideas which circulated in interwar Germany also surfaced in interwar Britain, becoming linked to Bolshevism, while the *Protocols of the Elders of Zion*, an antisemitic forgery about clandestine Jewish power which had circulated since the end of the nineteenth century, gained traction in the immediate post-war years.[51]

Because British democracy remained ultimately stable in the interwar years, unlike in Germany, elite London Jewry experienced few consequences of the rise of conspiratorial antisemitism. Those at the sharp end of the rise of Judeophobia from the late nineteenth until the middle of the twentieth century were the refugees from Eastern Europe and their descendants, who became the central focus of the campaign that led to the passage of the Aliens Act of 1905, which frightened established Anglo-Jewry who distanced themselves from the East End immigrants in case the growing hostility against the newcomers impacted upon them.[52] The ideology against poor Jews focused upon their threat to sanitation, the fact that they might work for lower wages than native Londoners and therefore undercut them, and the idea that they had a negative impact upon housing by paying more for their rent and, contradictorily, living in overcrowded conditions. While much of this ideological hostility came from those on the extreme anti-immigrant right of British politics, trade unions also weighed in because of the issue of cheap labour.[53]

Those Jews concentrated in the East End of London experienced relatively little everyday hostility before the First World War, essentially because the concept of safety in numbers protected them. While some isolated attacks may have taken place in the East End,[54] the only place in Britain which witnessed an anti-Jewish riot before 1914 was South Wales in August 1911, an area that counted tiny numbers of Jews who became scapegoats during a coal-mining strike.[55] Against the background of the nationalism and xenophobia of the First World War, antisemitic riots broke out in the ghettoes of Leylands in Leeds and the East End in June and September 1917 respectively because of the unfounded perception that Jews avoided military service.[56]

Everyday antisemitism as experienced by London Jews continued during the interwar years. On the one hand this resulted from the fact that the second generation started breaking out of the constraints and safety of the East End, especially when they tried to move into the professions, when the idea that they faced a glass ceiling circulated amongst them, meaning that many opted for an easier path such as small-scale self-employment. These developments took place against the background of the fact that the majority of Londoners held antisemitic views, even during the Second World War,[57] when some members of the white majority expressed the type of virulent ideas circulating in Nazi Germany.[58] The 1930s also witnessed a growth in violent attacks on East End Jews as a result of the activism of the British Union of Fascists, although the local community fought back, especially during the Battle of Cable Street.[59]

Antisemitism remained strong in the early post-war decades. London Jews became victims of the nationwide attacks which took place in August 1947 following the murder of two kidnapped British sergeants by Irgun, a Zionist paramilitary organization in Palestine. The violence in London remained small in scale, largely because the Jewish community had already developed self-defence strategies against the British Union of Fascists during the 1930s.[60] However, the antisemitic mentality remained strong in the Bethnal Green of the 1950s, even though some of the Gentile population had developed a tolerant attitude.[61]

The decline in hostility towards Jews in Britain and London after 1945 can be explained by their increasing integration and social mobility as well as the fact that they became increasingly invisible because of the arrival of people of colour. While the Irish may also have become less obvious, hostility towards this group surfaced especially during the influx of the 1950s and 1960s, particularly once racists heard Irish accents, resulting in a confinement at the lower ends of the employment ladder and exclusion from much housing.[62] Stereotypes of the Irish, with deep historical roots,[63] survived into the 1980s revolving around the idea of this group as 'a stupid drunken, fractious and violent race' as 'Irish' jokes circulated both on the television and in everyday discourse.[64] Heightened IRA activity made the Irish in London and the country as a whole more visible and more likely to face discrimination. A Commission for Racial Equality report suggested that 25 per cent of those questioned had faced negative police reactions to their ethnicity.[65] One woman 'working in a civilian job for the Metropolitan Police' with an Irish boyfriend 'was told that unless she gave him up she would be moved from her job in a top security building. She gave up her job.'[66] Three Irish priests in London 'remembered receiving hate mail, abusive phone calls or being personally or verbally attacked after bombings in Britain'.[67] After the 1974 Birmingham and Guildford pub bombs, 'there was a small physical backlash in London in the form of two petrol bombs being thrown into an Irish-owned pub in Ealing and tobacconist's in Streatham, and a window at the Irish Embassy being smashed.'[68]

Although the Irish (as well as other white minorities)[69] faced hostility in post-war London, racists directed most of their fire at the more visible black and Asian people. Such hostility, as in the case of the Irish, came from both the organs of the state and the population as a whole. Focusing specifically upon the London black (more specifically African-Caribbean) community, some of the main hostility they have faced has come from the Metropolitan Police, which has had an 'unhappy dialogue' with black Londoners for decades.[70] Negative stereotyping of the black population by the force became clear by the early 1950s. A confidential report from 1952 accused black people of accentuating several problems including housing, resulting in overcrowding, public health, immorality (because of the 'absence of coloured women'), anti-social behaviour and unemployment. One solution put forward for these 'problems' was to control black immigration,[71] a widely shared view which led to the campaign resulting in the Commonwealth Immigrants Act of 1962. The move towards this legislation gained momentum as a result of the Notting Hill and Nottingham race riots between 23 August and 2 September 1958, leading the government to come to the conclusion that only limiting immigration could stop further incidents of this nature. In Notting Hill, which, like the East End at the beginning of the twentieth century, lay close to the corridors of power in Westminster, attacks upon people and property involving hundreds of people occurred between 30 August and 2 September.[72]

The Notting Hill riot remains the last large-scale attack upon immigrants in London, as well as a culmination of negative attitudes towards black people which had characterized their twentieth-century lives. They faced rioters in the East End in the post-war crisis of 1919,[73] while those who lived in the capital during the interwar years experienced the 'colour bar',[74] which lasted into the 1950s and beyond. The Test cricketer and black civil rights campaigner Learie Constantine had 'been refused rooms in hotels, asked to leave restaurants and so on'.[75] In fact, such experiences remain mild compared to those of many black people in post-war Britain. The Jamaican Wallace Collins recalled his 'first Saturday night in North London' in 1954 when, while crossing Hornsey Road, 'a big fellow with side-burns and blood oozing from his forehead' shouted 'You blacks, you niggers, why don't you go back to the jungle?'[76] More significant violence broke out against black people in Camden Town in August 1954, resulting in 'racial warfare' as the newcomers defended themselves.[77] Earlier, in July 1949, 'a crowd of 1,000 whites besieged a number of blacks who were staying in a local hostel, Carrington House'.[78] Murders also took place in the 1950s, most seriously that of Kelso Cochrane, an Antiguan carpenter attacked by a white gang and stabbed to death in Notting Hill on 17 May 1959.[79]

While rioting against black people may have disappeared during the course of the 1960s, violence did not. Over 100,000 racial attacks may have taken place on a nationwide basis during 1993,[80] the year of the murder of Stephen Lawrence, while sixty-three racist killings may have occurred in Britain between 1970 and 1985.[81] In 1986 one in four black residents living in the London Borough of Newham 'had been victims of some form of racial harassment in the previous twelve months'.[82] Such violence took place against the background of both official and unofficial prejudice with a race-obsessed media constantly campaigning for a reduction in black and Asian immigration.[83] The deprivation and police indifference and victimization, especially the use of stop-and-search tactics, which had characterized relations between the police and the black population, played a major role in the outbreak of the Brixton riots in April 1981[84] and the Broadwater Farm disturbances in Tottenham in October 1985 following the death of Cynthia Jarrett during a search of her home in 1985.[85] Essays written by students at the Metropolitan Police Training School in Hendon in 1982 revealed statements such as: 'quite frankly I don't have any liking whatsoever for wogs, nig nogs and Pakis'; and 'I think all blacks are pains and should be expelled from our country'.[86] The issue of police racism came to the forefront again following the murder of Stephen Lawrence by a gang of white youths in Eltham in April 1993, in a case resembling the killing of Kelso Cochrane. On this occasion media attention focused on the fact that the police had not done enough to bring the perpetrators to justice.[87] The spark for the Tottenham riots of August 2011, which became nationwide disturbances, consisted of the killing of another black man, Mark Duggan, by the Metropolitan Police.[88]

People of South Asian origin also faced both everyday prejudice and racial violence in the earlier post-war decades. While most Indians, Pakistanis and Bangladeshis arrived in Britain after the Notting Hill riots and did not become subjects of large-scale attacks, they became victims of a type of low level guerrilla warfare whereby small groups of white youths, usually skinheads, harassed individuals going about their daily business, although on some occasions these incidents became quite significant. While it developed into a nationwide phenomenon,[89] 'Paki-bashing' became particularly prevalent in London and, more especially, in the East End,[90] pointing to a continuity which links the racism of the 1970s and 1980s against South Asians with that which impacted upon Jews earlier in the twentieth century, especially in the 1930s.[91] As early as 1965 there was 'a growing mass hysteria against the Pakistanis' in the East End and the 'skinhead era' had arrived by 1970.[92] One sixteen-year-old son of a docker explained: 'They got a choice . . . We go up to them and say, "Hand over your wallet." If they don't, we give them a kicking. If they do, we probably give them a right old kicking anyway. They smell, don't they? It's all that garlic. I mean, they've no right to be ere.'[93] The victims in 1970 included two Asian employees of the London Chest Hospital in Bethnal Green, who attracted nationwide attention,[94] although the attacks would continue into the 1970s and beyond.[95] One woman born in Bangladesh who lived in Aldgate recalled: 'They call us "Pakis" and many other things. Some of them daub slogans on our door and one night some of them even pushed some dog's mess through our letter box'.[96] The activities of the National Front in the East End, following the example of the British Union of Fascists in the 1930s, aggravated the situation. Asians faced particular victimization when given homes in housing estates dominated by whites. This reflected a situation in which the Bangladeshi community faced more widespread local and metropolitan racism, which impacted upon their access to social services, education and housing, while the police failed to devote sufficient attention to the perpetrators of racial violence.[97]

A turning point in the history of racial violence in the East End occurred following the murder of Altab Ali, who worked in the clothing industry, in Adler Street on 4 May 1978. Both the local and metropolitan-wide reactions to this event, resulting in a series of protests and rallies, meant that racists moved out of the East End, or at least kept a low profile, as a series of emerging Bangladeshi community organizations, supported by the anti-racist movement developing elsewhere in London and beyond, began to transform the East End into a safe space for Asian migrants and their children in the form of Banglatown,[98] although attacks did not disappear completely, most notoriously in the case of seventeen-year-old student Quddus Ali, beaten by a group of eight racists in Whitechapel Road on 8 September 1993 and left in a coma for four months followed by permanent brain damage.[99] Despite this murder, the generally improving situation in the East End found reflection in Southall, which had also become a safe space for Asians by the end of the twentieth century, following earlier attacks upon the Sikh community, most notoriously the murder of Gurdip Singh Chaggar outside the Victory Pub in June 1976. The last stand of the racists in Southall occurred on 23 April 1979 when local Sikh activists together with anti-racists from other parts of London confronted a planned National Front march, although this event became notorious because of the murder of the New Zealand teacher Blair Peach by the Metropolitan Police Special Patrol Group.[100]

FRIENDS AND LOVERS

The above summary of racism and racial violence in the history of London provides the impression of a city in which migrants and their offspring have encountered hostility, including physical attack, as part of their everyday lives and, even worse, have become subject to large-scale rioting which has endangered their lives and property. Hundreds of people have perished as a result of the actions of thugs over the centuries. This violence represents the most potent manifestation of racism in London which, as we have seen, has impacted upon the working and living conditions of ethnic minorities in the capital. As in the case of these two aspects of their lives, attacks upon migrants and their offspring appear to decline over time as part of a process of integration, which, however, has often meant that racists have turned their attention to the next newly arrived group, who have not yet developed strategies of resistance. The above description also suggests that violent racism has declined with the passage of time. Certainly, the scale of destruction of the Gordon Riots did not resurface again, although the *Lusitania* riots became equally widespread over a century later when the capital had witnessed a significant geographical expansion. The events in Notting Hill in August and September 1958 represent the last large-scale attacks on immigrants. While we might argue, because of the dying out of the anti-immigrant riot, that London has become more tolerant, the capital has not moved from a situation of racist hell to multicultural paradise. Racists murdered scores of people from ethnic minority backgrounds in the capital in the final decades of the twentieth century.

However, interethnic friendships and relationships have characterized London throughout its history. While the latter prove relatively straightforward to measure both because statistics exist on them (at least in recent decades) and the fact that racists focus upon them because of their belief that they lead to 'miscegenation' and consequent racial decay, friendships do not attract the same amount of attention, perhaps because of their ubiquity or because they do not offer the same threat. A nationwide survey from 2004 claimed that '94 per cent of white people say most or all of their friends are of the same race, while 47 per cent of the ethnic minorities say white people form most or all of their friends'.[101] In fact, a closer analysis of the survey does not appear so stark when it comes to the white population[102] and it also points to the fact that a significant percentage of ethnic minorities mix with whites. At the same time, the concept of race proves highly problematic because it would not take into account friendships between different groups of whites (say the white British and people of Italian origin), Asians (for example Sikhs and Pakistanis) or blacks (i.e. Africans and African-Caribbeans). Most importantly for us, it takes no account of regional variation. While people from Cornwall or some large northern cities such as Newcastle and Sunderland may not have friends from a different 'race' because they do not come into contact with them, it seems inconceivable that this would happen in London by the end of the twentieth century at the latest because of the sheer diversity of the population. Clearly, much social activity takes place on religious and national grounds, resulting in the development of organizations operating along these lines, which means that members of minority groups often form friendships within their own family and community networks, although individuals make up their own minds about the extent to which they participate in such ethnic bodies and they do not represent all members of a particular ethnic group.[103] However, even New Zealanders in twenty-first-century London operate predominantly in friendship groups amongst their nationality built from the networks which helped them migrate,[104] a factor that applies to all ethnic groups in which networks play a central role in movement.

A historical survey of interethnic friendships and marriages in London's history over the last two centuries reveals their normality. As previously mentioned, relationships prove much easier to measure than friendships because of the attention which they attract. One of the key reasons for the development of mixed marriages and relationships is that males outnumber females amongst most migrant communities, often on a significant scale.

For two European groups in Victorian London, marriage outside their own national group became normal. Women never made up more than 30 per cent of the Italian community in England and Wales between 1861 and 1911, meaning that families with an English, rather than Italian, wife predominated, as demonstrated in the key settlement of Holborn. In 1871 out of 172 couples with an Italian husband, 119 (69 per cent) had an English wife, 45 an Italian, 7 an Irish wife, and one from another nationality, although by 1881 the majority of wives consisted of Italians.[105] Children with mixed national identities therefore became the norm in the Italian community in Victorian London. The same applies to the Germans. In the 1851 census German males outnumbered females by nine to one, but by 1891 the figure had changed to

60 per cent males and 40 per cent females. Consequently, in 1851 about two-thirds of all marriages in Whitechapel and St George's involved an English and a German partner, but by 1891, 60 per cent of marriages involved two Germans.[106] The normality of interethnic marriages points to the fact that friendships must have become equally widespread, despite the existence of a plethora of ethnic German organizations in London.[107]

The preponderance of exogamy amongst Germans and Italians attracted relatively little attention, presumably because this practice offered no threat to the survival of the 'white race'. This did not apply to the Chinese, another London group which had a significant over-representation of males. The numbers stood at ninety-seven males and twenty-three females in 1901 and 729 males and 465 females in 1931. In the former year an extraordinarily high 82 per cent of London Chinese males were single,[108] which meant that the number of 'London Chinese men married to white women is extremely small', at least at the start of the twentieth century,[109] although by the 1930s hundreds of Anglo-Chinese children may have lived in Limehouse.[110] Those couples who lived here before the First World War included 'Tsang Wah with a young wife, comely of face and sweet of voice'. Meanwhile, 'Ng Yong, the enterprising Chairman of the Chung Yee Tong, a prosperous benevolent society . . . was likewise married to an Englishwoman, now dead, whose portrait, with her infant, occupies a prominent place in his office'.[111] A racist account of the 'Cockney John Chinaman' from 1900, which described the Chinese as 'Celestials' because they came from the 'Celestial Empire', gave an example of one 'Chinaman' who married an Irish widow in a local church during an unostentatious ceremony and celebration. George Wade also claimed that the 'Celestials' interacted well with the local white population: 'There is seldom, or never, any quarrelling between them and their neighbours',[112] although the Chinese did face attack during the 1919 race riots in the docklands area.[113] After the Second World War, when the centre of the Chinese London community moved from Limehouse to Soho, unions involving two Chinese partners became the norm as 'more and more women are coming over here to work or to study' and 'to marry or to rejoin their husbands'.[114]

Although the family may represent the centre of Jewish life, interethnic friendships, relationships and marriages have characterized the Jewish experience to the same extent as antisemitic hostility. The focused Jewish settlement on the East End of London in the nineteenth and early twentieth centuries helped the perpetuation of endogamy but its breakdown meant an increase in exogamy and interethnic friendship, even though those who moved away from the East End tended to settle in new Jewish concentrations in north-east and north-west London.

Taking a long-term perspective, exogamy, conversion to Christianity and moving towards the centre of London and British society went hand in hand for the different waves of Jewish elites who made their way to Britain from the readmission to the nineteenth century.[115] In Georgian London where the 'Jewish poor and the Jewish petite bourgeoisie lived on very close physical terms to their non-Jewish peers . . . intimate and sustained socializing' became inevitable. The mixed marriages which took place amongst these social groups often involved a Gentile woman converting to Judaism.[116]

Immigration statistics suggest that more Jewish males than females arrived in London from Eastern Europe in the late Victorian and Edwardian years, which meant that in 1911 about 22 per cent of Russian-born men in Britain under forty-five had non-Russian wives. When the Jewish population reached its peak in the middle of the twentieth century, and developed a more even gender ratio, endogamy became the norm.[117] 'Most of the marriages that were solemnized in the local synagogues were invariably the end product of a dozen family meetings conducted on a business basis.'[118] However, some unions involving two Jews took place as a result of the fact that the partners met each other at a social event,[119] emphasizing that Anglicization had taken place, which was inevitable in view of the fact that the second generation attended English-speaking schools and increasingly worked with Gentiles. Nevertheless, while many London-born East End Jews in the interwar years may have used English as their everyday medium of communication and increasingly eaten foods influenced by growing up in London, they often worked and socialized in a predominantly Jewish milieu amongst Jewish friends, co-workers and rela-tives.[120] This meant that relationships and marriages outside their ethnic group did not become as necessary as they did for migrant groups such as the Victorian Chinese, Germans and Italians. Crucially, while Jewish men may have outnumbered women before the First World War, the gender ratio became increasingly even. Whereas in 1881 men made up just under 60 per cent of the Russian, Russian Polish and Romanian-born population of Britain, in 1921 women accounted for half of the Jewish population in Britain born outside the country.[121] Those born in Britain would also have had an equal gender ratio.

While some young Jewish men and women may have had sex before marriage, many did not in a situation in which family remained central to their lives.[122] Despite Anglicization at school, many would have socialized in an entirely Jewish environment even during their education, in overwhelmingly Jewish schools, which meant that most of their friends were also Jews.[123]

The post-war period witnessed the decline of the Jewish population of the East End and its traditions as the ghetto broke down and third-generation Jews and beyond increasingly moved into the professions, became more at ease in the company of Gentiles and consequently intermarried, especially as secularity became the norm for much of the population of London. Consequently, the number of Jews in Britain had declined to 259,927 by the 2001 census, having reached a peak of about half a million in the 1950s. The number of synagogue marriages fell from 1,830 in 1965 to 1,031 by 1992.[124] Those middle-class German Jews who escaped from the Nazis had already become integrated into German society, although they faced problems of ethnic identification when settling in London, but as many worked in the professions, they would encounter mainstream Londoners in their daily lives.[125] Some of those children who arrived with the Kindertransport, usually from integrated German backgrounds, would live with adopted Gentile parents and become assimilated into wider society, especially as they would never see their natural parents again.[126]

Interethnic relationships have formed a key aspect of the history of black settlement in London since the eighteenth century. The thousands of black people who lived in London after the abolition of slavery in 1807, overwhelmingly males, disappeared during the course of the nineteenth century as a result of intermarriage, as the small numbers of black people who settled in London during the nineteenth century could not replenish their numbers because no significant immigration of this group took place.[127]

In the middle of the twentieth century, when West Indian and African males outnumbered their female counterparts, mixed-race relationships became normal amongst these two groups, especially in the 'coloured quarter' in Stepney. Importantly, a reflection of the history of sex and marriage in the recent history of London, many of the relationships which took place here did not simply involve women born in London or other parts of Britain but also other ethnic groups. For example, one Swedish woman originally married to a drunken Englishman moved to Stepney where an African 'invited her to live with him . . . but she took to living as a prostitute with seamen and coloured men'. A woman from Ireland who had initially lived in 'a Midlands town with a fellow lodger' moved with her baby to Stepney but eventually developed a stable relationship with an African here so that 'after two and half years she bore a child and after three they got married'.[128] Most of the Stepney white women in mixed-race relationships originated in Britain, especially the north-east, Liverpool, Coventry and Hull, varying in age from sixteen to forty. While some were 'of the nicer type who have been genuinely attracted to the man and have married him for affection . . . the vast majority have come into the district with the deliberate intention of trading on the coloured man'. Even those who married often showed 'signs of being ashamed of their husbands because they are coloured, and have a distinct feeling that they have lowered themselves by the union' due to 'the general attitude of white people towards mixed marriages'. These unions resulted in the birth of 'half-caste children',[129] including Keith and Abby born to Kathleen and Sulaiman, who 'was bought up in Aden and went to sea at the age of 14' but worked as 'a stoker at Claridge's Hotel'. The family lived at 5 North East Passage, off Cable Street, which Kathleen kept 'scrupulously clean, without help'.[130] Higher up the social scale 'colonial students' had difficulty in developing relationships with white women of the same status during the 1950s, which meant that they gravitated towards either European or 'low-class women'.[131]

The racist attitudes towards relationships between black men and white women remained well into the second half of the twentieth century, but these unions became increasingly normal as the West Indian and African population increased. They involved both English and European women. For example, the Swedish 'street girl' Majbritt Morrison married the West Indian Raymond Morrison, whose relationship acted as a spark for the Noting Hill riots.[132] As well as condemning these mixed-race encounters, some contemporary commentators also pointed to the fact that according to 'English standards West Indian family life leaves a lot to be desired. Migrants come here accustomed to illegitimacy, domestic instability, paternal irresponsibility and inconsistent but repressive child-rearing practices', although some men adapted to English norms by helping with cooking, cleaning and child-rearing.[133] The relationships which developed clearly varied from the casual to the serious, often resulting in marriage despite the disapproval of such unions. Wallace Collins met Sylvia, 'a sexy type who swung her hips Monroe style' and 'worked as a typist in Shepherds Bush' in his 'stamping ground' of the Lyceum Ballroom. She suggested that they should get married after a few dates.[134] Collins also had a 'love affair' with 'Sybil, a sweet person, intelligent, easy to get along with and who oozed sincerity', and for whom marriage 'seemed an inevitable outcome'. Despite the fact that Sybil became pregnant and lost her job at the hospital where 'she was training to be a nurse', Collins decided to break off the relationship largely because of the hostility of her parents,[135] and married another West Indian woman with whom he emigrated to Canada.[136]

Despite the callousness of Collins, interracial mixing and relationships became increasingly normal from the 1960s and beyond into the twenty-first century. Apart from the workplace and the neighbourhood, black and white people encountered each other on a daily basis in everyday life including, for instance, on London Transport, which employed large numbers of West Indians. In Brixton newly arrived immigrants initially purchased groceries from predominantly white shopkeepers, until black people moved into this field of employment.[137] As we have seen from the experience of Wallace Collins, West Indian arrivals attended dance halls and other places of recreation frequented by the white majority, despite the fact that they might face hostility. Any unspoken or unofficial colour bars[138] in such places would have disappeared with the passage of the Race Relations Acts from 1965 to 1976.[139]

By the 1970s the 'interracial family' had become a feature of London life. The most common form of interethnic relationships continued to consist of black men marrying white women, often following the paradigm of the coloured quarter in the 1940s and 1950s with the males marrying below their social status, although other types of union also took place involving two people of higher status and often consisting of a white man and a black woman. In many cases, especially in the earlier post-war decades, relationships involving black and white people faced hostility from families, which sometimes meant that they failed.[140] Nevertheless by the beginning of the twenty-first century 40 per cent of 'native born Black Caribbean' males in Britain (of varying generations) had a native white partner, with the figure for foreign-born males standing at nearly 18 per cent. By this time a more tolerant attitude amongst both black and white people towards such relationships had developed.[141] At the time of the 2001 census 1.27 per cent of the British population described themselves as having a mixed-race identity, over half of whom involved a black and white partner.[142] By 2011, 5 per cent of the population of London described themselves as mixed race, more than double the next region, West Midlands, at 2.4 per cent.[143]

People of West Indian origin entered into mixed-race relationships to a greater extent than those from South Asia, partly because they felt closer to mainstream white society than did those from former British India who had their own distinct form of identity which revolved around the long-established religions in the subcontinent. Migration from South Asia initially displayed a significant over-representation of men who often wanted to return home after saving money, but this did not usually happen, which meant that pre-existing wives and families migrated to Britain instead. In the short term all-male households developed amongst the South Asian community in Britain. The 2001 census suggested that only 6 per cent of Indians, 4 per cent of Pakistanis and 3 per cent of Bangladeshis had married people outside their own ethnic group.[144]

Religion plays a key role in this situation and has meant the survival of the family as a strong unit into the twenty-first century amongst Sikhs, Hindus and Muslims. The early post-war migrants viewed relationships with white women 'in terms of values acquired in India and therefore reject them as being sexual'.[145] Such attitudes, however, did not prevent some Asian women from having children outside the traditional family unit by the end of the twentieth century[146] or mixed-race relationships. Pakistanis in the East End immediately after the war lived 'in bachelor establishments with a large number of men sharing a room. They obviously cannot have a normal sex life and this must no doubt impose a considerable psychological strain on them'.[147] Although marriage or 'temporary liaison' with a white woman is 'generally looked down on', those involved in such relationships included Ali, who lived with Molly, 'from a good home in Newcastle'. She had previously had a child with an Indian, married a second Indian with whom she had a second child, but left him because he 'beat her, starved her, and expected her to earn money for him on the streets', but then met Ali, with whom she had a further six children. However, she did not marry this 'man in a million' because she could not trace her previous husband to get divorced. Unfortunately, Molly died a few months after the birth of her eighth child.[148] As with West Indians, we should not become fixated with the inner-city immigrant entering into relationships with working-class women. Those higher on the social scale also did the same, as indicated by the story of one thirty-year-old graduate from Bombay who, while 'waiting in the rain' in the West End 'struck up a conversation' with 'a girl in a similar position' and after meeting her several times, proposed to her. The wife, a primary school teacher, 'is only part English and claims French, Spanish and even Indian descent', which would almost certainly have made her more willing to enter into such a marriage.[149] Couples negotiated religious difference in a variety of ways, sometimes involving conversion, especially in the case of Muslim wives.[150] Linda from Ballybrack, in Dublin, married her husband from Lebanon after meeting him in central London in 1991. She claimed that they had agreed that 'the child will be christened' and 'will be Catholic' and they had a Catholic wedding but that when their child Mara was born in 1993 'he turned round and said real bluntly "she's a Moslem and that's that" '. The husband became violent, Linda felt betrayed and moved into a refuge for battered Irish women.[151] This offers an example of two strong religions coming into conflict as such problems tend not to arise when one partner does not have such a strong belief, which also makes life easier after children arrive, as they can follow one religion.[152]

Irish women in London have differed from virtually all the other communities which have settled in the metropolis because they have outnumbered men in each census since 1861, peaking at 1,630 women for every 1,000 men in 1921, although the proportion has become more even since that time.[153] But this situation meant Irish women became more likely to marry somebody of another ethnicity than men, as we saw with the case of unions involving Italian men during the Victorian period. In 1971 only 46 per cent of women born in the Republic of Ireland had a husband born in the same country.[154] The most common form of interethnic marriage has probably involved an Irish woman and an Englishman,[155] although in some cases an Irish Catholic married an Irish Protestant.[156] Although Irish cultural expressions, revolving especially around the Roman Catholic Church, became a feature of London life from the Victorian period,[157] the consequences of intermarriage both for Irish 'mixed-race' children and for those of other ethnic groups consists of the development of an identity which fuses both.[158]

As in the case of the South Asian communities, family played a central role for both Greek and Turkish Cypriots, meaning that endogamy became the norm when the number of migrants from these communities peaked during the 1960s, in which unions involved family members and matchmakers bringing people together, often from the same villages, helped by the existence of a fairly even gender ratio that allowed the development of strong family units which, in the case of the Greeks, revolved around the Orthodox Church. However, by the end of the twentieth century, mirroring the rest of London society, the nuclear monocultural family had begun to break down, especially as the second generation began to develop relationships with a range of ethnic groups.[159] Chrisostomos Sosti provides an example of the early Cypriot family unit in London during the 1950s and 1960s. He moved to the heart of empire in 1955 with his five children. By 1966 his first three children, aged between twenty-one and twenty-five, had all married other Cypriots while his nineteen-year-old student son had a fiancée from his own ethnic group. The youngest daughter, Irene, could only go out with a chaperone.[160]

Before the growth of the post-war Cypriot community in London, an earlier, much smaller wave (of less than 1,000 people) had arrived during the 1930s, consisting overwhelmingly of males concentrated on Soho where they worked predominantly in the catering trade.[161] They included Stavros Christofis, who had migrated to London from Nicosia in 1937, where he had worked as a waiter, and secured a position as a sommelier in the Café de Paris. Stavros met the German Hella Bleicher, born in Wuppertal in 1917, who found herself in London when the Second World War broke out, bound for America, but could not complete her journey. They met in 1941 and married shortly afterwards, settling in Hampstead where Hella gave birth to three children with cross-cultural names, Nicholas, Peter and Stella. Hella subsequently worked as a ladies' belt-maker in a factory in the West End. Unfortunately, the story of this family has survived because of the actions of the mother of Stavros, Styllou, who had moved to London in July 1953 to live with her son. A clash of cultures and personality appears to have ensued between mother-in-law and daughter-in-law involving the Westernized Londoner and the newly arrived greener, who disapproved of the lifestyle and dress of the younger woman, which meant that they could not tolerate each other and both had to seek medical help for the stress which their relationship caused. Stavros developed a solution to this problem which involved sending his wife and three children back to Germany for a short break, during which time his mother would return to Cyprus. This did not happen, however, because, on the night of 28 July 1954, while Stavros was working at the Café de Paris, Styllou murdered Hella by hitting her over the head with a metal ash plate, then strangling her and finally setting her alight in the yard of their house after dousing her in petrol. Styllou denied carrying out the murder but became the penultimate woman to be hanged in Britain on 15 December 1954. The case made national headlines and appeared the story of London multi-ethnic glamour versus Cypriot tradition, in which the latter triumphed in a brutal fashion. Similarly, Ioannos Sotirious from Kentish Town faced conviction in August 1954 for kicking his wife, Anna, another Cypriot, in the stomach when she attended a party in Goodge Street without him, although it appears that this represented the final act in a doomed and abusive marriage. We need some perspective on these events, however, especially the case of the Christofis. Numerous violent marriages existed in 1950s London but few ended with the murder of a daughter by a mother-in-law. Styllou had actually previously faced trial for killing her own mother-in-law in Cyprus in 1925 by forcing a burning torch down the older woman's throat but appears to have escaped punishment because of the cruelty which she herself had faced. She may represent an extreme anti-multiculturalist, reminiscent of Asian women who carried out so-called 'honour killings' later in the twentieth century, desperate to maintain the ethnic identity of her grandchildren.[162]

FROM RACISTS TO FRIENDS AND LOVERS?

It may seem tempting to summarize the history of interethnic dialogue in London as moving from a situation in which hostility tends to greet the first generation but in which the offspring of the newcomers subsequently become assimilated into wider London society. The history of racism as indicated by the decline of the race riot and even the racial attack would appear to support this perspective. At the same time the experiences of various generations of Jews who have settled in the metropolis point to initial hostility followed by long-term integration and assimilation in which mixed marriages play a key role.

Yet the story told above points to the simplicity of this perspective. The proportion of men to women has proved especially important in the development of relationships in London's history, so that where one significantly outnumbers the other, mixed marriages become more likely, although the case of the male-only Asian household in the earlier post-war decades would suggest that we guard against this generalization. It seems clear that the move towards friendship between different ethnic groups becomes inevitable over time as they develop in the workplace, in social situations and, above all, in school, which really offers the key place where the melting pot evolves and from which friendships may last for decades, as well as laying the basis for interethnic friendship and acceptance of other ethnic groups, simply because it seems normal. This certainly represented my experience in Hornsey during the late 1960s and 1970s, meaning that I developed a fear of monoculture. In fact, this type of interethnic friendship from a young age, in which school plays a key role, has given rise to the idea of a new type of language variously described as creolization or multicultural London English.[163]

Ethnic settlement patterns may militate against the development of the melting pot, but the normality of positive interethnic interaction throughout London's history and the increasing numbers of mixed-race relationships supports this perspective, especially when we take into account the fact that official statistics work on the basis of crude ethnic groups along the line of races, which have become discredited, rather than also adding those which involve people with origins in different European states or different regions of Asia, for example. Millions of people born in London have had parents with different ethnicities and nationalities, meaning that the appearance of the average Londoner over the centuries has changed not simply due to migration but also due to interethnic relationships.

Racists, friends and lovers have lived side by side in the history of London. In fact, as we have seen, the fact that white women have entered into relationships with black men in particular contributed to rioting in 1919 and 1958, as well as condescending and racist comments from middle-class commentators. To return to our clichés, the melting pot survives in tandem with the kaleidoscope of ethnic neighbourhoods as well as alongside racist violence. The decline of the race riot suggests that friends and lovers have increasingly outnumbered the racists who characterized earlier centuries and decades. However, it seems that the only way to understand the history of interethnic interaction in London implies accepting the fact that racists, friends and lovers have always lived side by side.

7

RACISTS, REVOLUTIONARIES AND REPRESENTATIVES

I got up and expressed my opposition to the fascist . . . immediately a group of uniformed fascists pounced on me and forced me to leave the gallery. And I came down a number of steps from the gallery right the way down to the ground floor, and on either side of the staircase there were fascists every yard or so and on the way down they beat me and . . . split my head open. And when I got downstairs and I had blood pouring out of my head, and I was pushed into a waiting taxi and taken to a nearby doctor's surgery where I was stitched up.[1]

On Sunday last, a very numerous assembly of British and Foreign Socialists took place at the Institution, John Street, for the purpose of welcoming Wilhelm Weitling, the leader of the German Communists, who has recently arrived in this country after enduring imprisonment and persecution in Switzerland and Prussia, in consequence of his labours in the Communist cause. The meeting was also intended to introduce the members of the Rational Society to the Foreign Communists resident in London. There are two societies which hold regular meetings, the one composed of natives of France, the other of Germany and many of their numbers were present, with numerous continental friends besides.[2]

It may be considered rather rash and unwise on my part to stand before this House so immediately after my admission here: and my only excuse is that I am under a certain necessity to do so. My election for an English constituency is a unique event. For the first time during more than a century of

settled British rule, an Indian is admitted into the House as a member for
an English constituency.[3]

Along with its role as the centre of international finance, perhaps no other
aspect of the history of modern London indicates its unique global importance
as does its significance as a crucible for the development of international revolutionary ideas. London has played a role in the evolution of virtually every
radical political ideology over the last two centuries, whether communism,
pan-Africanism or a host of nationalist ideologies which led to the overthrow
of both the continental nineteenth-century empires and to British imperialism. It appears that every revolutionary leader of the period from the end of
the eighteenth to the middle of twentieth century spent time in London, from
Karl Marx, Lajos Kossuth and Giuseppe Garibaldi through to Vladimir Ilyich
Lenin, Jomo Kenyatta, Mahatma Gandhi – and beyond that, a series of governments in exile which based themselves in London waiting for the defeat of the
Nazis in Europe, perhaps most famously the Free French led by Charles de
Gaulle. The presence of the conservative but nationalist French leader points
to the fact that London has acted as home to political exiles from all parts of
the political spectrum, beginning with those fleeing the French Revolution in
the 1790s, although, while fascism may have had adherents in London, this
city played little role in the evolution of this ideology. For some political
thinkers spending time in the home of the mother of parliaments, their sojourn
proved fundamental in the evolution of their ideas including, for example,
Karl Marx and Mahatma Gandhi. While Gandhi may have moved to the
imperial capital voluntarily for the purpose of his legal education, Marx resembles countless other refugees who essentially spent time in London because it
proved the closest place to revolutionary activity taking place on the European
continent. London was almost a last resort but one which housed numerous
other exiles who may have shared similar ideas, facilitating the evolution of
communism and pan-Africanism, for example. However, revolutionaries did
not all share the same views, leading Marx to write about 'a great war between
frogs and mice'[4] when describing the mid-nineteenth-century German exiles
in London. These great men therefore simply serve as figureheads for much
larger movements which have existed in London's modern history. Some of
these well-known and lesser-known people may have spent the bulk of their
existence in London whereas others simply passed through, with London

acting as one outpost in a life of exile, as the example of Lenin would indicate, the capital playing a limited role in the development of their political thought. While many Europeans may have moved to London as a last resort, others subject to imperial rule deliberately moved to the heart of empire because of the presence of other nationalist intellectuals, in order to learn the workings of the British political system, to escape repression inflicted by the British Empire in their own homelands, or for employment and educational purposes. Although some of the revolutionaries, epitomized by Marx, may have spent some or most of their lives in London peacefully planning the overthrow of the British state, others took more direct violent action, from Irish nationalists beginning in the Victorian period to Islamists at the start of the twenty-first century.

The position of London as the home of the mother of parliaments has meant that a seat in the House of Commons has also acted as the ultimate goal for non-revolutionary migrants and their offspring. In fact, becoming an MP provides an indication not simply of the integration of those aspiring migrants but also of the integration of the community from which they have emerged, because representatives with ethnic minority backgrounds have often held seats in constituencies which count a large number of people with the same ethnicity, whether Irish, Jewish, African-Caribbean or South Asian. While a small number of Irish nationalists before the First World War may have held seats in constituencies outside London, because of the concentration of such a large percentage of migrants in the capital over the last two centuries, London has served as home not simply to the British Parliament but also to the most significant number of ethnic minority MPs during this time period. While migrants from post-1945 black and Asian backgrounds took decades to make a breakthrough into the House of Commons, the example of the late nineteenth- and early twentieth-century Indian MPs, as well as the numbers of people with Jewish backgrounds, from the Victorian elites to the representatives of East European Jews and their offspring, points to diversity in the British Parliament emerging primarily from London constituencies.

RACISTS

Although Britain and London may not have played a central role in the evolution of racist, fascist and xenophobic political parties in modern European history, a third aspect of the relationship between migration and the political evolution of London lies in the reaction of natives to the presence of migrants in their midst. While the most noticeable negative reaction on the ground has consisted of violence, the capital has proved fertile for the emergence of racist fringe groups focusing upon the immigrants who have settled in London. Although such groups have had virtually no political impact in terms of securing representatives even at a local council level, they have targeted specific areas, especially the East End, where their activities have led to the development of a hostile and violent environment, impacting upon the migrants who live in these locations. More importantly, although migrants who have made specific parts of London their home may have fallen victim to the racists, they have fought back either through violence or by joining anti-racist groups or both. The racist political activity may have grown organically, in the sense that it has emerged in areas of migrant concentration, but it has received outside interference from agitators.

This partly occurred during the Gordon Riots, for example, which broke out following an anti-Catholic meeting involving as many as 50,000 people led by Lord George Gordon and his Protestant Association opposing the Catholic Relief Act passed in 1778. The main centre of support for the Protestant Association was in London, indicated by the scale and widespread nature of the rioting which took place here.[5] While anti-Catholicism may have remained a feature of nineteenth-century Britain and while Irish immigrants may have faced prejudice as part of their everyday lives, the main anti-Catholic body that surfaced in the country during this period, in the form of the Orange Order, failed to gain a foothold in the capital. This meant that London did not experience the type of regular fighting between Roman Catholics and Protestants which characterized cities further north, especially Liverpool and Glasgow,[6] perhaps because a wider range of working-class identities offered themselves to Londoners, or perhaps because of the trauma of the memory of the Gordon Riots.

The xenophobia which characterized everyday life in Victorian London did not sustain any significant anti-Irish immigrant organizations here. The situation began to change at the end of the nineteenth century, especially in the East End as a reaction against the arrival of Jewish immigrants from Tsarist Russia, fuelled by the growing antisemitism throughout Europe at this time. The first group of any significance was the Society for the Suppression of

Destitute Aliens, founded in 1886 and partly financed by the antisemitic ideologue Arnold White, but it had little impact. There then followed the Association for Preventing the Immigration of Destitute Aliens, which actually counted members of both Houses of Parliament in its ranks but did not attract ordinary East Enders and also folded. Another group called the Immigration Reform Association came into existence in 1903 but had limited success. The most significant anti-Jewish immigrant grouping before the First World War was the British Brothers' League, established in 1901 under the leadership of Major William Evans-Gordon, Conservative MP for Stepney and a dominant political voice in the campaign which led to the Aliens Act of 1905. The League also received some support from most of the other East End MPs. The British Brothers' League claimed to count 45,000 members and also organized meetings in Leicester, Kettering and Bedford, but remained a primarily East End group, with activity and branches through much of this area. Some of the gatherings it held in the East End may have attracted as many as 4,000 people. The organization had died away after the passage of the Aliens Act of 1905, as its members and those who controlled it had achieved their aim.[7] A proposal to revive it in September 1918 fell on deaf ears,[8] but it had laid down something of a marker for interwar fascist activity in East London.

The state-led Germanophobia of the First World War, supported by an even more virulent public opinion, gave rise to a series of organizations which focused upon those German migrants who had settled in Britain, especially London. The capital became the centre of all manner of Germanophobic activity even after the widespread destruction of German property following the sinking of the *Lusitania* in 1915 and the wholesale internment after this violence.[9] A series of organizations played a role in leading anti-German demonstrations. In July 1917 the League of Londoners came into existence after a meeting at the Canon Street Hotel with a key aim of interning more alien enemies, and it organized a series of meetings in the capital during the summer of 1918.[10] The most significant Germanophobic body consisted of the British Empire Union, which may have counted 10,000 members by 1918 and aimed at 'the Extirpation – Root and Branch and Seed – of German Control and Influence from the British Empire'. It came into existence in April 1915 as the Anti-German Union and received a boost from the Germanophobic peak following the sinking of the *Lusitania*. Its first large meeting occurred in the Aeolian Hall in London in June 1915 and by the end of 1916 it had published the monthly *British Empire Union Monthly Record*, having changed its name in the spring of 1916. Ostensibly an Empire-wide organization with as many as 10,000 members, its base consisted of London, although branches existed throughout Britain and even in parts of the British Empire such as Canada, Hong Kong and the Bahamas. Active London branches included Croydon, Hampstead, Islington, Kingston, Walthamstow and Wandsworth. Unlike the British Brothers League and many of the twentieth-century organizations which would follow, its followers did not consist primarily of the lumpenproletariat, as the branches listed above lie in primarily middle-class areas. Although it opposed any group which appeared to threaten British victory, including pacifists, it focused primarily upon Germans. On 5 September 1915 the Anti-German Union held a meeting outside a German church in Forest Hill, repeating this process against a service in Walthamstow High Street on 27 May 1917. Its activities in the summer of 1916 included securing the closure of two London German restaurants which had managed to survive the *Lusitania* riots and protest meetings in Hyde Park following the death of Lord Kitchener after the boat he sailed in hit a German mine near Scapa Flow. In the summer of 1918 the organization held regular meetings in central London demanding the intensification of internment policy. Throughout the war it gained support from radical right-wing MPs. After the conflict it turned its attention to fighting communism and supporting the Empire, although it faded from the limelight.[11] Other racist groups which Emerged during the First World War included the Vigilantes and the National Party which counted MPs. These groups thrived in the xenophobic atmosphere of the First World War and its immediate aftermath in which the mistreatment of ethnic minorities became government policy.[12]

The shadow of the success of continental fascism hangs over radical right-wing politics in London and Britain as a whole because of the ultimate political failure of this ideology, returning no Members of Parliament and without success even at a local council level largely because of the long-term democratic traditions of Britain and the opposition which fascists faced from state forces.[13] Pressure groups or minor political parties, with little impact beyond the racist ideological level, included the early post-war Britons under the leadership of Henry Hamilton Beamish, who called for the extermination or expulsion of British Jews, as did the Imperial Fascist League under the leadership of Arnold Leese.[14]

The British Union of Fascists (BUF), founded by the former Conservative, Labour and New Party MP Sir Oswald Mosley in 1932, differed from the plethora of fringe organizations because it became a full-blown political party modelled on its continental counterparts with a paramilitary grouping in the form of the Blackshirts, a corporatist ideology and a strong strand of antisemitism by the middle of the 1930s evident in its newspaper, the *Blackshirt*. It remained a predominantly London-based group in terms of political activity and support.

The antisemitism of the BUF mirrored that of the Nazis as well as building upon British traditions. Standard ideas included Jews forming a state within a state, controlling the press, international finance and the established parties, and using their power for the benefit of their own race rather than the whole of the British population.[15] However, unlike the Nazis, the BUF did not develop a wide-ranging racialized biological concept of Jewish difference,[16] although it operated on 'an ethnocentric and conspiratorial framework',[17] with a racial basis.[18]

Antisemitism had become a core activity amongst BUF supporters by the middle of the 1930s, even though its membership and support remained limited in comparison with the mainstream political parties. It may have reached a peak of 50,000 during 1934 although the figure for most of the 1930s appears to have fluctuated between 15,000 and 20,000 with a focus on London and the south-east, especially the East End.[19] The organization received support from conservative newspapers, especially the *Daily Mail* during 1934,[20] as well as from some establishment figures.[21]

Some BUF activity took place outside the capital, including in Bristol, Worthing, Leicester and Bootle, although most of the provincial incidents involved anti-fascists standing up to their opponents.[22] This fringe group has attracted a mass of attention because it became the main British manifestation of the fascism that seized Europe, because its activities centred on London, and because of the violence which it carried out and which it caused amongst those who opposed it, especially Jews. Its actions in London included marches, beginning, on a significant scale, in June 1933 when 1,000 blackshirts made their way through the capital.[23] The organization really became front-page news during a meeting held at Olympia in the following June attended by 12,000 people, including 2,000 blackshirts but also about 500 left-wing opponents who entered the hall, resulting in violence, which led mainstream opinion to turn against the BUF.[24] On 28 October 1934 Mosley made a speech in the Royal Albert Hall which 'signalled the real beginning of the BUF's campaign against the Jews'.[25]

This also meant the move of the organization towards a focus upon the East End Jewish community which, in the early days of the BUF, had remained largely ignored as the first London branches surfaced in areas that included Fulham, Hampstead and Lewisham. Between 1934 and 1936 groupings emerged in Bow, Bethnal Green, Shoreditch, Limehouse and Hackney.[26] Between 1935 and 1939 the organization may have had a London-wide membership reaching a peak of 11,250 (but probably less) which, if we accept this total, included as many as 7,200 in the East End.[27] The members and supporters here came from a variety of working-class occupations, but especially the unskilled, as the semi-skilled and skilled would more likely have gravitated towards the Labour Party through union membership, but they also included some people from other social groups as well as Roman Catholics.[28] Whatever the nature and level of support in the area, and despite attempting to secure local power, the BUF did not even gain one local council seat in the East End.[29]

Its major impact in this area, however, came from the antisemitic campaign it launched, which had a variety of manifestations including the spreading of propaganda about the consequences of Jewish immigration for living standards, as well as suggesting a racial unity with Jews higher up on the social scale.[30] Reflecting the antisemitic discourse which had characterized London life since readmission, Jews 'were accused of clannishness and filthy habits; of swindling the innocent gentiles and depriving them of their jobs; of being, simultaneously, capitalist plutocrats and communist agitators'. Full-time troublemakers lived throughout the East End.[31] This spread of propaganda partly occurred through street meetings which could exceed 200 in a single month. More seriously, 'Jew-baiting' became a part of everyday life in the East End, including attacks upon individuals and their shops, as well as defacing Jewish property with fascist slogans. On more than one occasion hundreds of youths rampaged through the area and attacked a whole street, as in Mile End Road in October 1936. Between January and June of 1936, the Metropolitan Police received over fifty complaints about Jew-baiting, a figure that still stood at thirty-eight in the six months before the outbreak of the Second World War.[32]

The story of the East End in the interwar years does not, however, tell of the victory of the BUF, despite the terror which it may have inflicted upon local residents, but the fightback by the local Jewish community, especially the second generation which had developed its own sense of belonging and became attracted to radical ideologies including communism.[33] The symbolic clash between the local Jewish community, helped by anti-fascists who streamed into the area, and the British Union of Fascists occurred during the Battle of Cable Street on 4 October 1936. Following an intensification of activity in the East End throughout that year, the BUF had attempted to stage their largest march here on that day, involving 3,000 people. They were escorted by the police who, however, could not pass because of the barricades erected by anti-fascists in Cable Street, who significantly outnumbered their opponents (totalling hundreds of thousands according to some estimates), which led to the abandonment of the march.[34] Despite the fact that the BUF and other post-war racist activity in the East End did not cease with this event, the Battle of Cable Street has become a symbolic moment in the history of London from the point of view of East European Jews, anti-fascists, fascism,[35] and the policing of demonstrations in the capital, which helped to prevent a recurrence of the violence of this day.[36]

In fact, the activity of the BUF, as well as other antisemitic organizations, continued in the East End into the early days of the anti-fascist Second World War. In February 1940 the BUF contested a by-election in Silvertown, where it performed very badly. In May of that year 4,000 people attended a speech given by Oswald Mosley in Victoria Park. Most of this activity came to an end when the leading fascists faced internment from May 1940, although it did not cease completely.[37]

Liberation from internment at the end of the Second World War brought a resurrection of fascist activity. Mosley underwent something of a reincarnation with the formation of the Union Movement in 1948, which, although initially antisemitic and East End-based, became anti-black and campaigned in areas with West Indian settlers during the 1950s, including Brixton and Notting Hill, where its activities played a role in whipping up the local white population to participate in rioting in 1958.[38] Mosley made one of his first major post-war speeches in Kensington Town Hall in 1956 and from January 1958 his organization, replicating the pre-war East End activity, held regular well-attended meetings on Notting Hill street corners attended especially by white men.[39] Mosley's actions in West London intensified even further after the Notting Hill riots with an increase in meetings and the opening of an office and a bookshop in North Kensington. He stood as the Union Movement's candidate for North Kensington in the general election of October 1959, using overtly racist anti-immigrant and anti-black language. Despite the poisonous atmosphere which had developed here, Mosley only secured 7.5 per cent of the vote. Meanwhile, the more extreme White Defence League, which verged on neo-Nazism, fielded William Webster in St Pancras North on an anti-colour platform with the slogan 'Keep Britain White'. Webster worked together with John Bean, the director of policy at the National Labour Party, swallowed up by the White Defence League in 1960, to prevent the election of David Pitt, the black West Indian-born Labour candidate, in Hampstead, including instigating violence at election meetings in both Hampstead and St Pancras, as well as terrorizing Pitt by making abusive phone calls. Webster only obtained 4 per cent of the vote.[40] In the 1960s the West Midlands became a centre of racist politics, indicated by the Birmingham Immigration Control Association in the first half of the decade[41] and, in the second half, by the anti-immigration speeches of Enoch Powell, as an MP for Wolverhampton.[42]

The history of racist politics in Britain since the 1960s, initially primarily based in London but also impacting on the country as a whole, has a series of characteristics. In the first place, a small number of individuals have played a role in the various groups which have come and gone, essentially reconstructing themselves with new names. Mosley and his Union Movement remained active until the early 1970s, fighting a small number of elections in East End constituencies but securing a small slice of the vote.[43] Those who replaced Mosley included John Bean, Colin Jordan, Martin Webster, Nick Griffin and John Tyndall, with the most important parties being the British National Party and the National Front.[44] The latter came into existence in February 1966 as a result of the merger of a series of other fringe groups. Its white supremacist and corporatist fascist aims were to 'preserve our British native stock in the United Kingdom, to prevent interracial strife such as is seen in the United States of America, and to eradicate race-hatred, by terminating non-white immigration, with humane and orderly repatriation of non-white immigrants (and their dependants)'.[45] The National Front therefore primarily focused upon black and Asian immigrants, although it opposed what it saw as Jewish control and power. It claimed to have 13,000 members nationally by the end of the 1970s, although the true figure probably lay closer to around 5,000. Its highest levels of electoral support occurred in wards with high immigration or areas which neighboured such locations in places such as Leicester, Hackney and Walthamstow. Nevertheless, like all of its predecessors after 1919, it had no concrete electoral success, even at a local council level.[46]

In 1993 something of a shockwave went through British politics when the British National Party, emerging from the National Front, won a council seat on the Isle of Dogs in East London. This proved a false dawn, at least in the short run, but during the early twenty-first century the BNP won council seats in a variety of locations including Dagenham and Barking,[47] as well as a London Assembly seat in 2008.[48] The success at the 2009 European elections may have represented a more significant breakthrough when the BNP took two northern seats,[49] but this was not reflected in London, where it gained just 4.9 per cent of the vote.[50] This represented the high point of BNP activity, whose voters moved to supporting UKIP, pointing the way to the EU referendum when the anti-EU immigration north voted much more heavily in favour of leave than London, with the exception of white areas which had developed in the post-war period as a result of white flight such as Barking and Dagenham, and Havering.[51]

During the 1970s the East End as a centre of far right politics in Britain had come back to life, replicating the activities of the British Union of Fascists, with the victims now consisting of the Bangladeshi community rather than Jews and the National Front as the racist agitators. It had actually polled 7.6 per cent in Bethnal Green and Bow and 9.4 per cent in Hackney South and Shoreditch at the October 1979 general election.[52] Although this remained the peak of electoral support the organization arranged menacing meetings in Brick Lane on Sunday mornings around an NF banner which attracted skinheads. In September 1978 the National Front moved its headquarters from Teddington to Great Eastern Street in the heart of the East End. The Union Movement also operated in the area at this time, as evidenced by the ubiquity of its slogans and posters.[53] Osmar Gani remembered that between 1978 and 1979, in a carbon copy of events in the 1930s, 'you name it, you know BNP, National Front, they started to run, run amok. They would suddenly appear and you know smash people's windows etc, chase, attack.'[54] Furthermore, just as a combination of anti-racists (in the form of left-wing political groupings) and Jews fought off the BUF in the 1930s, new anti-racists joined together with the increasingly politicized Bangladeshi community. The latter flirted and worked with a series of groupings including Black Power, far left ideologies, with roots in Britain, Pakistan and Bangladesh, and trade unionism, before finally entering the local council chamber as Labour Party representatives from the 1980s.[55] In addition, a series of semi-political organizations such as women's groups and youth organizations surfaced, turning the East End from a hostile environment into Banglatown,[56] although, as we have seen, violence against this ethnic group continued into the 1990s.

The final elimination of fascism from East London, mirroring the death of racial violence, which it provoked, took a century from its first nascent appearance in the late Victorian period. Its demise appears to symbolize the move from racist to multicultural London, as white flight took away any potential support for such groups. However, we need to accept the fact that racist groupings have profoundly transformed the nature of political discourse in Britain so that multicultural London has developed at the same time as anti-immigrant discourse has entered the mainstream. The lessening in importance of the extreme right in inner London has taken place at a time when a significant percentage of the British population voted to leave the European Union due to free movement of people into the country. Significantly, the most diverse inner London boroughs, including Tower Hamlets, had counts against leaving of 2 to 1 while 60 per cent of Londoners voted to stay in the EU, a marked contrast to the 48.1 per cent in the country as a whole.[57] While the racists may not have disappeared from London, their support has gradually declined since the end of the nineteenth century.

REVOLUTIONARIES

Although fascism became rooted in some parts of the heart of Empire, London has also acted as home to some of the most important political revolutionary activists, from Karl Marx through to leading nationalists who would lead the movements which caused the collapse of the British Empire. While racists, who would include the aristocratic Oswald Mosley, fought for the streets of East London, intellectuals from Marx and Lenin through to Asian and African nationalists thought and networked in the heart of Empire. The imperial capital served both as a place of refuge for those fleeing from the political upheaval which characterized the development of Europe as it moved from autocracy to democracy from the French Revolution to the Second World War, and as a place where imperial subjects could spend time studying the workings of British democracy to realize that, as people of colour, they remained second-class citizens. At the same time, those born to working-class migrants have become attracted to a wide range of radical ideologies from communism to Islamism.

London played the role of safe haven to tens of thousands of European refugees who fled continental oppression from the French Revolution to the end of the Second World War, originating from all parts of the continent and with political ideas encompassing the entire political spectrum. In many cases London proved the last place of sanctuary, but its advantages consisted of its proximity to the continent and its role as the centre of British political, economic and intellectual life.

While this process pre-dates the French Revolution because of the stream of refugees entering the capital as a result of the Reformation,[58] this upheaval offers an important starting point for an analysis of refuge in the capital. Those who moved specifically from France during the nineteenth century illustrate the range of exiles who have lived in the British capital from monarchs to anarchists, mirroring the development of French history through the series of revolutions which took place from 1789 to 1870. While for some exiles London proved a final place of settlement because the regime which they supported had died forever in the transition from autocracy to democracy, others simply used it as a sojourn awaiting their chance to return back to their homeland once regime change occurred.[59] The Second World War may have become the period when London reached the height of its importance as the centre for French refugees, as governments in exile waited here for the tide to turn against Hitler, with De Gaulle's variation eventually proving victorious.[60] In fact, London during the Second World War acted as home to a variety of governments in exile, some of which would return as the successor regimes once the Nazis faced defeat.[61]

Others, as in the case of the Poles, would never achieve this aim and therefore spent the rest of their lives in London and other parts of the United Kingdom.[62] These Polish exiles followed in the footsteps of their countrymen who had previously lived in London fighting for the rebirth of the Polish state following the partitions of their country in the late eighteenth century and establishing the futile Polish Revolutionary Commune in the British capital, which only lasted for a few years in the late 1850s and early 1860s.[63] This group operated against the tide of history in contrast with those Polish exiles in London during the First World War who, however, played a relatively small role in the foundation of the Polish Republic in 1918.[64]

In the early nineteenth century, as nationalism transformed Italy from a geographical expression to a unified state, many of those caught up in the repression which accompanied this process spent time in London. Some, such as Giuseppe Mazzini, would return to the continent. Others would remain in the capital, including Gabriele Rossetti who reached London in 1824 after initially spending time in exile in Malta, following his role in Italian nationalist politics in Naples, which faced suppression in 1821, and who secured a chair in Italian at King's College London in 1831. One of the first Italian refugees was Ugo Foscolo, who arrived in London in September 1816, having first escaped to Switzerland.[65] In 1864 Garibaldi would spend a short time in London, feted as a hero, the symbol of freedom against continental oppression in a period when Britain stressed its position as a democracy in contrast to the regimes which existed in continental Europe.[66] The Hungarian revolutionary Lajos Kossuth had fulfilled a similar role when he visited Britain in 1851, the highlights of which included London public meetings which may have attracted between 50,000 and 200,000 people, partly because of the ground-work laid by Ferenc Pulszky, who constructed a Kossuth hero myth, similar to that of Garibaldi, which stressed the commonalities between Englishmen and Hungarians.[67]

Kossuth and the Italian aristocratic exiles who glided through the salons of London became some of the most respectable and celebrated of the thousands of Europeans who lived in Victorian London. Their peak numbers in the country as a whole may have reached 7,000 refugees by the early 1850s.[68] They were heavily concentrated in London, following the suppression of the 1848 revolutions,[69] and were allowed to enter the country because of a liberal and virtually non-existent immigration regime,[70] which came under threat because they did not all play the role of opponents of continental tyranny, an issue that came to a head with the attempted assassination of Napoleon III by the Italian nationalist Felice Orsini in Paris, with bombs actually made in Birmingham.[71]

The most numerous and diverse nineteenth-century European exiles were the Germans, whose numbers had started expanding from the 1830s. In 1834 a branch of the nationalist Young Germany came into existence in London and expanded further in 1836 following the expulsion of this organization from Switzerland. In 1840 Karl Schapper and a group of six other Germans established the German Workers Educational Association with a working-class base. This morphed into the Communist Correspondence Committee in 1847 and then the Communist League.[72] Following the failure of the 1848 revolutions numerous Germans entered London, including liberal nationalist celebrities such as Arnold Ruge, Gottfried Kinkel, Karl Heinrich Schaible and Carl Blind, who spent varying periods of time in the British capital.[73] More significantly in terms of global history, Karl Marx arrived in London in 1849, having paid two previous visits in the 1840s. He would spend the rest of his life in several homes in the world's capital, working in the British Museum to produce *Das Kapital*, as well as collaborating and falling out with both German and other revolutionaries who had made their home in London, playing a role in the International Association, which existed from 1855 to 1859 and the establishment of the First International in 1864. Clearly, London became pivotal in the development of communist ideology.[74] The more humble German refugees included Johann Georg Eccarius, initially a friend of Marx, but gradually rejected by him. Eccarius moved to London in 1846 to work as a tailor, joined the German Workers Educational Association and the League of the Just, played a role in the development of the latter into the Communist League and spoke as the representative of German workers at the 1864 foundation meeting of the First International. He served on the general council from 1864 to 1872 and held the position of general secretary from 1867 to 1871, as well as writing many tracts and articles. Eccarius married an Englishwoman, Isabella Sedgley, and became naturalized in 1872.[75]

London would continue as a centre of left-wing activity after Marx's death in 1883 as further repression on the continent created more refugees. A new wave of Germans arrived following the passage of Anti-Socialist Laws in 1878. They established a wide range of organizations covering the whole spectrum of left-wing politics, as well as joining the established groupings such as the German Workers Educational Association, which by this time had several branches in the East End and West End.[76] The most prominent of these late nineteenth-century exiles included Eduard Bernstein who did not move to the British capital until 1888, again following the pattern of choosing it as a refuge of last resort after banishment from Switzerland where he had run his *Sozialdemokrat* newspaper, which he brought with him. Once in London he interacted with a variety of German exiles and studied English politics, returning to Germany in 1901, where he would play a leading role in the Social Democratic Movement.[77]

Anarchism had also taken root in London by the late Victorian period, especially under the influence of German and Russian exiles. It became a public issue as a result of several small-scale attempted bombings, as well as the siege of Sidney Street, a battle between police and Latvian anarchists in 1911 which also implicated the Italian anarchist Enrico Malatesta, also living in London.[78] The leading German adherent of this ideology was Rudolf Rocker, born in Mainz in 1873, who had travelled through Europe as a bookbinding apprentice, during which time he moved from Marxism to libertarianism. He settled in Paris in 1893 and, two years later, moved to London, to produce anarchist propaganda for the purpose of smuggling it into Germany. He also became the leader of the Jewish anarchist movement in the East End, faced internment in Alexandra Palace during the First World War and returned to Germany in 1918, where he continued to play a role in extremist politics, fleeing to the United States when the Nazis seized power.[79]

Some of those escaping Hitler's seizure of power fled to London, including Social Democrats[80] who, nevertheless, would find that Nazi activity[81] also took place here, at the same time as attempted fascistization of the Italian community.[82] German intolerance in the process of moving from autocracy to democracy via fascism therefore sent thousands of refugees to London from the 1830s. Most of these exiles simply passed through and left little trace and had limited influence upon London politics, despite mixing with English radicals, as the Labour Party emerged as a moderate democratic trade union party in which the imperial capital did not play the decisive role.

The other major exporter of refugees to London from the early nineteenth to the early twentieth century was Russia and included the type of elite revolutionary figures which characterized the German émigrés, for example the anarchist Prince Kropotkin.[83] Like their German counterparts, these exiles interacted with English radicals, although, once again, they had a limited impact on the emerging labour movement, which focused on winning parliamentary seats.[84] The most famous of the Russian exiles who spent several spells in London before the First World War was Lenin. He first arrived with his wife from Munich in April 1902 as Dr and Mrs Richter using false passports, and were greeted by another Russian, who had fled Siberia, Nikolay Alekseev. They lived in a two-bedroom flat in Holford Square near King's Cross. Like his revolutionary predecessor, Karl Marx, Lenin spent much of his reading time in the British Museum, which he visited daily, partly as an escape from his Russian comrades who tried to visit him every day. However, he also attended London political meetings involving both the local population and his political colleagues from Russia. They included Trotsky, who lived in a Russian revolutionary commune in Sidmouth Street which acted as the base for the editing of the journal *Iskra*. Although Lenin would leave London for Geneva in May 1903, he actually returned to the heart of Empire in 1905, 1907, 1908 and 1911 to attend congresses of the Russian Social Democratic and Labour Party as well as to use the British Museum. London exile played an important role in the evolution of the movement which would overthrow Tsarism, although we need to see living in London as part of a process that had sent revolutionaries here during a prolonged period of absence from their homeland, waiting for their chance to pounce when it arrived, in this case in 1917.[85] In contrast to the early Victorian Germans, few of the Russians appear to have settled permanently in Britain, largely because the final German revolution in their lifetime occurred in 1848. Some of the German exiles, however, especially the liberals, accepted the new political reality and returned home.[86]

One group of refugees from Tsarist Russia did actually make their permanent homes in London, namely those who were fleeing antisemitism. While, as we have seen, some of the second generation drifted towards communism in the interwar years partly in opposition to the rise of fascism, others took a different revolutionary path by turning to Zionism, which had first emerged in London and Britain as a whole, reflecting its birth as a movement in the late nineteenth century. Despite the activity of several organizations, the East End of London did not become a strong base for Zionism, with the ideology proving more attractive to those Jews moving to the suburbs.[87]

The appearance of Zionism in London reflects the spread of nationalism from Europe to the rest of the world, which, in the case of the imperial capital, would manifest itself in the development of African and Indian movements to overthrow the British Empire. From 'the 1850s, in ever increasing numbers, African traders, chiefs, lawyers and doctors sent children to Britain from Sierra Leone and the Gold Coast for higher education, a few also coming from Lagos and the Oil Rivers'. This led to the formation of the Gold Coast Aborigines Protection Society, which sent deputations to London in order to attempt to improve the position of its people in Britain.[88] The later nineteenth century also saw the beginnings of formalized pan-Africanism, especially with the establishment of the African Association in London in 1897. The leading figure in this group was the Trinidad-born Henry Sylvester Williams.[89] It aimed at encouraging 'a feeling of unity' and facilitating 'friendly intercourse among Africans in general', as well as protecting 'the interests of all subjects claiming African descent' throughout the British Empire.[90] In 1900 there followed the Pan-African Conference, which also met in London, attended by both Africans and African Americans, to discuss the position of black people globally. It resulted in the transformation of the African Association into the Pan-African Association, which aimed at improving the position of Africans throughout the world. However, the organization remained short-lived because the black population of London consisted especially of transient students, while the group received limited support from white political parties.[91] In 1911 the Universal Race Congress met in London. As its name suggests, it brought together black and white people, including political activists, artists and academics, although much of its discussion focused upon the plight of Africa and Africans.[92]

New pan-African groupings came into existence in interwar Britain, including the African Progress Union, established in 1918, while, two years later, the second Pan-African Congress opened in Central Hall, Westminster, leading, after sessions in Brussels and Paris, to the formation of the Second Pan-African Association.[93] The West African Students Union, which emerged specifically in interwar London, developed into an instrument of African nationalism.[94] The League of Coloured Peoples became perhaps the most significant black political grouping in London during the 1920s and 1930s, led by a Jamaican doctor, Harold Moody, with its own journal the *Keys*. Established in 1931, it aimed at improving the position of its members and of black people throughout the world, including London, but fizzled out following the death of Moody in 1947.[95]

The development of black political consciousness in early twentieth-century London resembles the activities of refugees who made their way to Britain in the Victorian period, because in both cases such consciousness brought together educated individuals with a common cause. The Pan-African Association mirrors the International,[96] with black people taking the place of workers. In the case of black identity, this consciousness did not simply encompass politics, with an opposition to the global oppression of black people, but also black cultural life, especially music.[97] In one sense we can see London as central in the three points of what would become known as the Black Atlantic[98] by the end of the twentieth century, a link between the emergence of Garveyism and its desire to celebrate black identity based on African origins in New York and the emergence of black nationalism in Africa. A type of radical black internationalism developed in interwar London, which included the organizations listed above.[99] In addition to those individuals outlined above, key figures in the development of this consciousness included the Trinidad-born and US-educated communist George Padmore, whose geographical range also involved trips to Moscow and Germany in the early 1930s and whose London acquaintances included another Trinidadian, C. L. R. James. Like his white communist nineteenth-century predecessors, Padmore had a complex relationship with the Labour Party. He would play a key role in the campaign opposing the Italian invasion of Abyssinia.[100] Another key black nationalist figure, Jomo Kenyatta, also spent time in interwar London, in order to escape the totalitarian system of government established by the British in Kenya, interacting with Padmore and other figures in the Black Atlantic and illustrating the way in which the Empire decayed from its core.[101]

Radical black politics did not disappear in the post-war period, even though most black political activity revolved around the parliamentary system which allowed imperial and Commonwealth immigrants to vote because of their nationality status as Britons. Claudia Jones held more left-wing views. Born in Trinidad in 1915 she had grown up in Harlem, joined the Communist Party of the USA and fled to London at the height of McCarthyism after years of persecution. Here she worked with other black activists including the singer Paul Robeson, interacted with the Communist Party of Great Britain opposing colonialism and racial discrimination in Britain but, perhaps most famously, played a leading role in the establishment of the short-lived *West Indian Gazette* and, more significantly, the Notting Hill Carnival.[102] In the late 1960s, after the death of Claudia Jones in 1964, London also became a centre of Black Power with the emergence of a Black Panther Movement, following a visit by the American leader of the group, Stokely Carmichael, to attend the Congress on the Dialectics of Liberation in London in July 1967. The British group remained small compared with the US organization and fizzled out, like its American counterpart by the early 1970s, but Black Power attracted much public attention in Britain.[103] Its leading figures included, once again, Trinidadians in the form of the contrasting Michael De Freitas, a drifter and hustler who gradually moved towards this ideology after settling in London in the late 1950s,[104] and the more educated and purely political Darcus Howe, who faced trial (and acquittal) as one of the Mangrove Nine for allegedly inciting a riot, after taking part in a protest following the targeting by the police of the Mangrove restaurant in Notting Hill in which he worked,[105] as well as the Nigerian playwright Obi Egbuna, who spent time in prison for making a speech in Hyde Park threatening to kill police officers.[106] Perhaps the last revolutionary activity by the black community of London consisted of the Brixton and Broadwater Farm uprisings of the 1980s, again, like the protest which led to the Mangrove Nine Trial, caused by police repression.

Indian revolutionary activity in London began before the First World War. The short-lived London Indian Society established in 1865 campaigned for the interests of India, but perhaps the most radical act by Indians in London occurred in 1909 when Madan Lal Dhingra assassinated William Curzon Wyllie, who had served in India as a civil servant and soldier and was known to take a hardline position on Indian nationalism. By this time, India House, which aimed at Indian Independence, had opened in Highgate, attracting prominent nationalist thinkers and activists, including Dhingra. Indian women, notably Sophia Duleep Singh, also became active in the Women's Social and Political Union.[107] The India League, which became the main organization campaigning for independence within Britain during the interwar years, came into existence in 1916 and brought together a wide range of Indians including seamen, students and professionals led by Vengalil Krishnan Krishna Menon, although it only had a membership of 180.[108] The most famous Indian nationalist to visit London, Mahatma Gandhi, initially travelled to the imperial capital in order to study for the bar between 1888 and 1891 and interacted with the radical vegetarian movement and the theosophists, influenced by Indian religion. He returned in 1906 to lead a deputation to Parliament campaigning for the rights of Indians in South Africa and therefore established his reputation as a political campaigner in the heart of Empire. By the time of his next visit in 1909 he had turned against the imperial capital. He returned again in 1931 as a celebrity, the leader of the movement irreversibly leading India towards independence, having moved back to his homeland to take up the cause of liberation since his last visit.[109]

A Pan-Islamic Society came into existence as early as 1903, renamed the Central Islamic Society in 1910, with the aim of removing 'misconceptions prevailing among non-Muslims regarding Islam and Muslims'.[110] The more politically oriented Muslim League, a branch of the All-India Muslim League, founded in 1907, which acted as the basis for the development of the concept of Pakistan, emerged in London to campaign for Muslim rights and nationality at the seat of imperial power.[111]

The concept of a global Islamic political identity took off in Britain, as it did in the rest of the globe, at the end of the twentieth century. London has had two main roles in the history of this ideology. In the first place the concept of Londonistan emerged, which argued that the British capital 'had become the hub of the European terror networks' because of its 'large and fluid Muslim and Arab population' that 'fostered the growth of myriad radical Islamist publications spitting hatred of the West', while 'its banks were used for fundraising accounts funnelling money into extremist and terrorist organizations'. It served as home to radical preachers such as Abu Qatada, Omar Bakri Mohammed, Abu Hamza and Mohammed al-Massari,[112] with the Finsbury Park Mosque becoming a major focus for the spread of hatred.[113] At the same time, some of the long-term Islamic residents of London, including those who had experienced East End racism, became attracted to Islamism. For example, Ed Husain remembered: ' "Pakis! Pakis! F--- off back home!" the hoodlums would shout . . . I can still see a gang of shaven-headed tattooed thugs standing tall above, hurling abuse as we walked to the local library to return our books.'[114] Although Husain would adopt radical Muslim ideology, he would subsequently abandon this before the events of 7 July 2005, when three British-born individuals, of Pakistani origin, travelled to London from West Yorkshire together with a fourth from Aylesbury, born in Jamaica. They met in Luton and went on to detonate bombs on the London transport system which killed fifty-two people from the range of ethnic groups who lived in the capital, including Muslims.[115] In fact, the events of that particular day point to another interpretation for the bombing of London in the sense that it represented the centre of British power, anathema to British Muslims who blamed Tony Blair for the invasion of Iraq, as well as the headquarters of secularism and multiculturalism, which Islamists equally loathe.[116] Islamist attacks since July 2005 have focused upon London and have involved people from a variety of ethnic groups as well as from various parts of the country. Most symbolically, the

Houses of Parliament became the scene of clumsy but deadly attacks which involved driving cars into pedestrians from 2017.[117] At the same time some of the most famous Britons who made their way to Syria in the second decade of the twenty-first century became radicalized in their London homes, including Mohammed Emwazi (Jihadi John)[118] and Shamima Begum.[119]

REPRESENTATIVES

Like their Victorian and Edwardian Marxist predecessors, the Islamists bombing London had global ties, which, in many cases, involved travelling to Pakistan and Afghanistan for training.[120] Whereas communists aimed at world-wide proletarian revolution, Islamists bombed symbolic targets such as London. In some ways the Islamists have more in common with the Irish community in Britain because it also helped to give rise to 'home-grown terrorists', although the overwhelming majority of the Irish, like Muslims, had nothing to do with lethal violence. This statement applies to migrants in London and Britain generally, whose main engagement with politics has consisted of the parliamentary system, helped by the fact that those who migrated from different parts of the Empire had the same voting rights as Britons, as well as the fact that Britain has maintained a citizenship system based on *jus solis*, meaning that those born in Britain automatically gain the right to vote.

The Irish prove one of the best case studies for examining engagement with the democratic process in Britain, although we first need to recognize that Irish nationalists have carried out more attacks on London than any other political grouping from the Victorian period to the later twentieth century. Victorian violence sprang from the Fenian Irish Republican Brotherhood, a transnational organization with a headquarters in New York carrying out activities in both Ireland and on the British mainland. The IRB aimed at overthrowing British rule by violence and may have counted as many as 80,000 members in the United Kingdom in 1865, despite strong opposition towards it from the Roman Catholic Church. Its main attack on London occurred in 1868 on Clerkenwell jail, which, instead of freeing Fenian inmates, killed twenty residents who lived nearby. Such activity led 22,000 Irish people in London to present a petition declaring their loyalty to Queen Victoria.[121] During the 1930s an Irish Republican Army bombing campaign included fifty-four attacks in London during the first half of 1939.[122] The IRA campaign of the late twentieth century, which lasted from the 1970s until the 1990s, proved more destructive and resulted in more casualties, with London acting as the scene of some of the most high-profile incidents,[123] including the Balcombe Street siege in 1975,[124] during which time anyone living in London simply accepted IRA bombing as part of everyday life.

The majority of the London Irish during the nineteenth and twentieth centuries had a limited association with political violence, which tended to involve professionals from Ireland rather than the working-class settlers in the British capital or other parts of the country. Nevertheless, some people displayed sympathy with the objectives of Sinn Fein, helped by the fact that they became targets of heavy-handed metropolitan policing.[125] Since the Victorian period the Irish have found themselves caught between nationalists (whether violent or not) and working-class representatives. During the 1840s the Irish participated both in activities connected with the Repeal Association, aimed at the 1801 Act of Union between Britain and Ireland, and Chartism, whose leaders included Feargus O'Connor and James Bronterre O'Brien.[126] Later in the nineteenth century the Home Rule Confederation and the Irish National League campaigned on the mainland, with London acting as their administrative centre.[127] By 1900 the London Irish had become incorporated into London political structures, which meant both the emerging Labour Party and the liberals, although support for nationalism continued.[128] Despite Irish independence the immigrants retained the right to vote in British elections and gravitated overwhelmingly towards the working-class and trade union-based Labour Party, with as much as 80 per cent of this group voting for Labour nationally in the 1970 general election, although the level of voting participation may have remained low. Relatively few Irish people became local councillors, at least in the early post-war decades. However, Paddy O'Connor became Camden's first Irish-born mayor in 1966 and Michael O'Halloran became Labour MP for Islington North in 1969.[129]

Jews became involved in local London as well as parliamentary politics in a more direct way, explained at least partly by the social mobility of this group as well as the fact that some of its members arrived as elites. On the other hand, the working-class refugees of the late nineteenth century and their descendants remained loyal to the Labour Party deep into the following century. While MPs of Jewish origin came to represent constituencies throughout the country by the 1990s,[130] London proves especially important in the history of Jewish politics in Britain.

The early stages of this process ties in with the emancipation of Anglo-Jewry in the earlier nineteenth century, in other words the granting of full civil rights to this community, in which the ability to take seats in local and central government bodies proved a key development. Jews initially became representatives at the local level from the 1840s, while Lionel de Rothschild, the son of Nathan Meyer, became MP for the City of London in 1847. However, he could not take up his seat until 1858, having won on four different occasions, when the Jewish Relief Act of that year, which amended the oath taken by MPs, finally allowed him to enter the House of Commons.[131] This proved a turning point in Jewish political history in London and in the country as a whole. The number of Jewish MPs increased from three in 1859 to sixteen in December 1910, by which time they made up 2.4 per cent of the House of Commons, much higher than their percentage in the British population.[132] In view of the concentration of the Jewish community in London, its members played a particularly important role in local politics here. In 1910, while Jews formed a fraction of 1 per cent of the London County Council area, they provided over 10 per cent of councillors.[133] Whitechapel became a Jewish stronghold from 1885 until the First World War with a Jewish MP, initially Samuel Montagu and then his nephew Stuart (both Liberals), who by 1913 partly relied on a 40 per cent Jewish electorate.[134] After the First World War the East End became a Jewish Labour heartland, returning local councillors increasingly from the second-generation Russian immigrants.[135] While Jewish support for the Labour Party survived into the late twentieth century, a symbolic turning point was the election in 1959 of Margaret Thatcher as MP for Finchley, which had a large Jewish constituency.[136] The community turned increasingly towards the Conservatives as social mobility took place, further reflected in the presence of cabinet ministers with Jewish origins, a process that dates back to Disraeli's premiership in the 1870s.[137] We should not exaggerate the turn to the Tories because as late as 1981 those Jews elected to the Greater London Council consisted of one Conservative and six Labour representatives.[138]

By the end of the twentieth century people of colour had embraced democratic politics in the way in which Jews had done for over a hundred years, becoming representatives at both the national and the local level, in London and beyond. This process, however, began from the late Victorian period and the election of three Asian MPs for parliamentary seats in London before the Second World War, at a time when the South Asian community of the capital remained tiny and could not have influenced the election of these candidates. Dadabhai Naoroji became the first of these MPs. Born in Bombay in 1826, he supported home rule for India and sat as a Liberal on this platform for the seat of Finsbury Central between 1892 and 1895, having previously failed in his attempts to secure election in Holborn. He subsequently became the President of the Indian National Congress in 1906, after losing his seat in the 1895 election as a result of a national swing to the Tories.[139] Reflecting this trend, Mancherjee Bhownaggree became Conservative MP for the north-east division of Bethnal Green in that year. Born in Bombay in 1851, he initially worked as a journalist, moving into state service for various Indian officials before migrating to Britain in 1882 for the purpose of studying law and receiving a call to the bar at Lincoln's Inn in 1885. Despite standing as a Conservative he had previously supported Naoroji's election. Bhownaggree secured the candidacy of North East Bethnal Green as a third choice because the first two believed it an unwinnable seat. Unlike Naoroji he opposed home rule. Despite this, his interventions in Parliament tended to focus upon India, especially its economy and the drain of its resources. His defeat in 1906 reflected the landslide victory of the Liberal Party.[140] The third Indian MP in Britain came from the opposite end of the political spectrum in the form of Shapurji Saklatvala, who had familial links to the Tata business clan. The son of a merchant, he had initially worked in the family business and moved to Britain as a Tata representative in 1905 at the age of twenty-four, by which time he had become interested in Indian nationalism. Although initially gravitating towards the Liberals, he moved towards the Independent Labour Party and married an Englishwoman, Sarah Marsh. Saklatvala remained true to the Labour Party into the 1920s although by this time he had moved to Battersea, which had a tradition of radicalism and racial tolerance indicated by the fact that John Archer, the son of a ship's steward from Barbados and an Irish Catholic woman, had secured a seat on Battersea Council in 1906 for the Progressive Alliance of socialists, labourites, radicals and Liberals on a programme of the sensible self-government for the colonies, eventually becoming mayor of Battersea from 1913 to 1914 and remaining a leading local Labour Party activist into the 1920s. Saklatvala stood as the Labour Party candidate in the 1922 general election and won his seat, although he lost it in the following year. He won it back again in 1924, this time as a communist, and would remain MP here until 1929, taking up the cause of Indian independence.[141]

The election of Naoroji, Bhownaggree and Saklatvala, as well as John Archer on the local level, together with the importance of Jews in London politics, suggests a significant degree of tolerance in the British and imperial capital. This appeared to have lessened after the defeat of Saklatvala in the 1929 general election as the next black and Asian MPs did not enter the House of Commons until 1987, with three out of four, Diane Abbott in Hackney, Paul Boateng in Brent and Bernie Grant in Tottenham, representing London constituencies.[142] A simplistic explanation for this interregnum might suggest an intensification of racism in London and beyond, but we need to remember that those who moved to Britain from Empire and Commonwealth, especially West Indians and South Asians, together with smaller groupings such as Cypriots, had the right to vote. Yet they did not always exercise that right, especially those of African-Caribbean origin who tended to participate in the electoral process to a lesser extent than other sections of the population.[143] Once again, as in the case of Jews and Irish migrants, the majority of votes went towards the Labour Party, especially in the case of West Indians, although some movement has taken place towards the Conservatives amongst Asians in particular. Clearly, the concept of Asians proves too general here and it seems more likely that wealthier Gujaratis living in Wembley and Harrow would turn to the Conservatives than poorer Bangladeshis in the East End, although early twenty-first-century elections meant Labour tightened its grip on most of the capital, irrespective of ethnic group.[144] Of the 52 MPs classed as ethnic minorities elected in the 2017 general election, 14 stood for London seats, or about 27 per cent, a significant over-representation, although the remainder point to an increasing ethnic diversification of the United Kingdom as a whole.[145]

Moving away from parliamentary voting, post-war ethnic minorities have also done well in local elections in areas with concentrations of their own group, although they sat for constituencies throughout the capital. During the 1980s black and Asian people became mayors including, most famously, representing the Labour Party, Bernie Grant in Haringey before becoming an MP, Merle Amory in Brent and Linda Bellos in Lambeth. Two Greek Cypriots, Andreas Mikkides and Demetris Demetriou, held the same position in Haringey by the early 1990s.[146] In the East End Bangladeshis, like their Jewish predecessors earlier in the twentieth century, moved into the council chamber by the 1980s, in a process that emerged from the political activism in which they had participated during the course of the 1970s. This meant participation in mainstream Labour politics in Tower Hamlets, with Rushanara Ali becoming MP for Bethnal Green and Bow from 2010, following on from Oona King and, from 2005 to 2010, George Galloway, standing for Respect, with an opposition to Tony Blair's foreign policy, especially the invasion of Iraq.[147]

This type of Bengali political activism, which focused upon the East End and which involved both parliamentary and extra-parliamentary activity, also characterized not simply Jewish politics in London but also that of the emerging black community. We might see a progress from pan-Africanism in the earlier part of the century, through to campaigning against racial discrimination during the course of the 1950s and 1960s which helped the birth of Black Power, to a move into the Labour Party mainstream by the 1970s and 1980s through the aborted attempt to form black sections, by which time, although black London led the way on black political representation in Britain, it had become a national issue.[148] Bernie Grant indicates this process in action. Born to a middle-class family in Guyana in 1944, he moved to London in 1963 to join his mother who had migrated to the capital to undergo an ear operation. He initially lived in Hornsey and obtained a job as a clerk for British Rail. After studying for A levels at Tottenham Technical College, he undertook a degree in engineering at Herriot-Watt University in Edinburgh but left because he viewed the institution as racist. Although Grant flirted with the Black Panthers and revolutionary groupings his entry into the Labour Party came through a trade union route, while he worked for the Post Office, eventually becoming MP for Tottenham in 1987, via leadership of Haringey Council, a seat he held until his death in 2000. Standing firmly on the left of the Labour Party and therefore facing regular hostility,[149] Grant played a pioneering role, along with Diane Abbott, who consecutively represented the same constituency (allowing for boundary changes) for over thirty years, in the multiculturalization of London and British politics. They differed from Naoroji, Bhownaggree and Saklatvala because these three essentially represent a manifestation of imperial politics in the heart of Empire. In contrast, we might see Grant and Abbott as Empire coming home, the first two of four representatives in a process which would bring the descendants of the subjects of British imperialism into the heart of power. They led the way for the eventual election of Sadiq Khan, the son of an immigrant Pakistani bus driver, born in Tooting, as London mayor in 2016.[150] Ethnic minorities also play a significant role in the London Assembly, although they remain under-represented in relation to the make-up of the capital's population.[151]

RACISTS, REVOLUTIONARIES AND VOTERS

As the centre of political life in Britain and its Empire and the largest city in modern Europe, London has played a key role in the political development of all of these entities. It has attracted all manner of activists from nationalists and communists during the nineteenth century, often as the last place of refuge for Europeans expelled from every other capital on the continent, to those ultimately aiming to overthrow the British Empire by placing themselves at its heart in the early twentieth century. Because of the presence of so many political ideologues in London over the past two centuries, the city has played a key role in the development of global internationalist ideologies such as Marxism and anti-imperialism, although we should see it, especially in the case of the former, as one of many centres where such views emerged. We might also view London as a place where refugees remained in cold storage, waiting for their moment to return to the continent to seize the day whether in the middle of the nineteenth century, the aftermath of the First World War, or following the collapse of Nazi Europe.

While some of the revolutionaries who lived in London simply utilized it as a stepping stone, useful for maintaining their contacts and developing their ideas, others took more direct action by planting bombs, whether anarchist, Irish or Islamist. Killing people at the heart of power draws attention to the cause. While anarchists and Islamists may have ultimately achieved little, Irish Republican bombing played a role in the move towards Home Rule in the early twentieth century and the Good Friday Agreement in 1998. Bomb attacks have almost become a fact of everyday life in London since the middle of the nineteenth century.

Those with the right to vote in London have tended to use it, moving away from extra-parliamentary action and politics beyond the mainstream, whether communism or Black Power. There seems something of an inevitability in the victory of parliamentary politics illustrated by the examples of all of the major migrant groups who have settled in the capital, whether Jews, Irish, African-Caribbean or South Asian, usually involving a vote for the Labour Party. Once again, London has acted as the fulcrum for these processes although, by the twenty-first century, the ethnicization of politics had become a nationwide phenomenon.

This victory of democratic politics and the increasing move into the mainstream by ethnic minorities suggests the defeat of the racists. In reality, despite the heat which they may have generated from their opponents, racists have had little direct impact upon the politics of London. Those campaigning on an overtly racist platform have not secured a parliamentary seat for a London constituency and hardly any have held council seats. The fight over the East End, whether in the 1930s or the 1970s, represented a symbol for control of the capital, which, viewed retrospectively, could only result in the defeat of the racists who have taken the path of white flight. In political terms London would certainly appear more liberal than the rest of the country. Yet part of the reason for the failure of overtly racist parties, whether in London or in the rest of Britain, lies in the ability of the mainstream parties to adopt and adapt the policies of the racists. At the same time as ethnic minority voters became central in London politics, immigration controls became increasingly racist. This was evidenced by the passage of numerous controls aimed at specific groups since the Aliens Acts of 1905, in order to exclude Jews and emerging from the opposition to East End immigration from the 1880s.[152] It was replicated again in the 1950s when the Notting Hill riots helped to lead to the 1962 Commonwealth Immigrants Act, which stopped free movement from the Empire and Commonwealth to Britain.[153]

Ultimately, as this chapter has argued, London has acted as home to racists, revolutionaries and representatives, confirming its national and global importance. The capital has attracted people of all political persuasions, seeking either exile or a political education. It has become the focus of a variety of bombers, and it has acted, in the case of the East End in particular, as a symbolic battleground between racists and their opponents. While it may seem as though the latter proved victorious, their resistance actually ended in a score draw because of the evolution of immigration legislation. London also paved the way for the entry of ethnic minorities into the British parliamentary system because so many ethnic minority MPs, from Jews through to Asians, have represented London seats.

CHRISTIANS, HINDUS, JEWS, MUSLIMS AND SIKHS

At length, at a monthly conference held by the secretaries of the various Missionary Societies in London, it was a matter of discussion whether, while we are sending missionaries at a great cost into foreign lands, something ought not to be done by Christians for the inhabitants of those lands when they occasionally visit this country ... The sight of Hindoos, Chinamen, Negroes and other heathens in the streets of London, suggested this question to the consciences of more than one member of the conference, and it was determined to ascertain, by inquiry, what the effect of a visit to this Christian country had upon these heathen visitors. With this end in view, a few were spoken to in the streets, and the answers were most appalling – for the treatment they had received had evidently produced upon their minds the very reverse of a favourable impression of the Christian religion.[1]

... the East End Jews of the working class rarely attend the larger synagogues (except on the day of Atonement), and most assuredly they are not seat-holders. For the most part the religious-minded form themselves into associations (Chevras), which combine the functions of a benefit club for death, sickness, and the solemn rites of mourning with that of public worship and of the study of the Talmud. Thirty or forty of these Chevras are scattered throughout the Jewish quarters; they are of varying size as congregations, of different degrees of solvency as friendly societies, and of doubtful comfort and sanitation as places of public worship. Usually each Chevra is named after the town or district in Russia or Poland from which the majority of its members have emigrated; it is, in fact, from old associations – from ties of relationship and or friendship, or, at least, from the memory of a common home – that the new association springs.[2]

. . . you had the Regents Park Mosque but that came later so in Newham there wasn't a place where Muslims could congregate on a Friday. There wasn't a place where Muslims could send their children to read the Koran, there was no place where you could basically sit down and discuss Islam so my father was the first Muslim in Newham to set up a Madrisse – that is a school for teaching children and that was above his butcher shop.[3]

The period after the Second World War appears to have resulted in a funda-mental transformation in the belief system of the population of London, reflecting national, European and broader Western developments. Whereas the vast majority of Londoners before 1945 consisted of white Christians, the decades which followed witnessed the burgeoning of religions that did not have Jesus Christ at their centre. While Islam became increasingly visible by the beginning of the twenty-first century, the diversity of London's population by this period meant that this religion, and its politicization, simply became the most prominent manifestation of the globalization of belief in the British capital as, to take the example of those religions with origins in South Asia, Hinduism, Sikhism and Buddhism[4] also developed.

However, religious diversity in London has deep roots stretching back to the Middle Ages, as witnessed by the presence of a Jewish community, at least until 1290. The Reformation destroyed Catholic London, but in the move towards a Protestant majority, several significant developments took place. First, Protestantism split off into a variety of sects with London at their centre. At the same time, the challenge to Catholicism in the European continent, resulting in war and persecution, sent the first genuine (Protestant) refugees to Britain, centred on the Austin Friars Church in London. The seventeenth and eighteenth centuries witnessed further growth in religious diversity as a result of the arrival of French Huguenot refugees but also German Lutherans and Jews. At the same time, Roman Catholicism never disappeared from London and received a shot in the arm with the mass influx of Irish migrants in the nineteenth century, not simply to the imperial capital but also to the growing industrial centres in the north. By 1945, although a majority Anglican popula-tion lived in London, the capital also counted numerous nonconformists,

Roman Catholics, Jews and Orthodox Christians, each of whom had developed their own churches and related welfare organizations, which determined the nature of diversity in the British capital.

These religious structures present one way of understanding the impact of immigration on the religious life of London. The building of churches, synagogues, mosques, mandirs and gurdwaras signals the arrival of particular groups in significant numbers and also the claiming of space in the capital for a particular religion. The opening of a place of worship offers the clearest signal that a religious minority has established itself. Nevertheless, while the religious architectural history of London attests to the diversity of the capital, numerous individuals, especially those from beyond Europe, have either become missionary prey or have faced racism from the established churches.

Viewing religious diversity simply through the prism of churches and related welfare activity proves unsatisfactory because it does not account for individual choice or the change in practice over generations. The emergence and survival of London synagogues since readmission offers an important way of understanding the development of the Jewish community of London but it does not reveal the complex relationship which individuals have with their religion ranging from the devout to the lax. By the end of the twentieth century Jewishness emerged into a type of secular identity for some individuals who rarely attended religious services but maintained other traces of Jewish identity.

THE ORIGINS OF RELIGIOUS DIVERSITY IN LONDON

Because of the variety of ethnic groups living in London by the beginning of the twenty-first century it would seem undeniable that religious diversity increased in London after 1945. But it proves inaccurate to suggest that the British capital has moved from a situation of religious monopoly[5] to one in which parallel religions thrive, as this situation has always existed since the Reformation. The difference between the twenty-first century and the years before 1945 lies in the fact that the nature of diversity has changed. While Anglicanism coexisted with nonconformity, Roman Catholicism and Judaism, it has survived, albeit with low levels of practice, alongside what seem more dynamic non-Christian religions, especially Islam. However, the postwar period has also witnessed an increase in Roman Catholicism and

Orthodoxism because of the arrival of millions of people from Ireland and the European continent and beyond, meaning that the traditionally international religions such as Roman Catholicism attract worshippers with a variety of national origins, as it had done in Victorian London.[6]

In the medieval city the most significant religious minority consisted of the marginalized and persecuted Jews who, nevertheless, could practise their religion within the constraints that existed. This led to the evolution of rabbinic learning as well as the development of community organizations including synagogues and a burial place, although the former could fall victim to anti-Jewish rioters.[7]

A key turning point in the religious history of London, as in the rest of Western Europe, occurred as a result of the Reformation and, in the British case, the break with Rome. Apart from the religious chaos caused by this event, which resulted in persecution and the temporary coexistence of old and new religions,[8] the events in western Europe opened the door to the first genuine refugees to London, escaping from a well-founded fear of persecution as a result of the wars of religion taking place on the continent, where Roman Catholics and Protestants fought for supremacy throughout.[9] Although settlement took place in various parts of England, the largest and most important congregations centred on the Austin Friars church in London where Germans, French, Walloons and Flemings worshipped separately, arriving initially during the reign of Edward VI (1547–53), with the church receiving its Charter in 1550 under Johannes A. Lasco, a Polish nobleman, as superintendent and spiritual leader. The accession of the Catholic Queen Mary to the throne in 1553 forced the refugees to leave the country but they would return in larger numbers following Elizabeth's accession in 1558. By this time the church fell under the supervision of the Bishop of London as Lasco died in 1560. Other congregations, using new locations, also emerged in the capital during the course of the sixteenth century, with a significant early French religious gathering using a church in Threadneedle Street. These churches acted as the official face of the refugees. By the end of the sixteenth century Austin Friars had become the Dutch Church and would retain this name in the centuries which followed. By 1583, 1,850 people attended the Dutch Church and 1,650 the French Church, although some foreigners also participated in services in English places of worship.[10]

The seventeenth century increased the religious diversity of London even further because of the influx of further refugees and migrants. The most significant in terms of numbers consisted of French Huguenots fleeing the persecution of Protestantism in their homeland following the revocation of the Edict of Nantes, which had granted religious toleration in France, by Louis XIV in 1685. They focused especially upon London, further developing the French Church in Threadneedle Street, although twenty-three French congregations had emerged in the City and Westminster by 1700, together with others in Chelsea, Greenwich, Wandsworth and Wapping, and may have made up to 5 per cent of the population of the entire area in which they settled. Spitalfields became especially important with two places of worship opening by the end of the seventeenth century, increasing to nine by the end of the 1730s.[11]

Huguenots formed one element of the European influx which normalized religious diversity in the capital by the end of the seventeenth century. Distinctly German places of worship also appeared, as people from central Europe settled in the British capital for a variety of reasons, with concentrations emerging in various locations, especially the East End. The first of these churches, the Hamburg Lutheran, opened in the City in 1673, followed by three more by the close of the seventeenth century, aided by the passage of the Toleration Act of 1689 which allowed foreign congregations to practise in Britain without obtaining a Royal Charter. An increase in the German population of London during the eighteenth century resulted in the emergence of further places of worship, most significantly St George's Lutheran Church in Little Alie Street in Whitechapel, aimed especially at the sugar-baking community which had emerged here, and St John's Evangelical Church in Ludgate Hill. By the beginning of the nineteenth century, a German Roman Catholic church had also emerged in the City.[12] These institutions would act as the focal points for the development of German ethnicity during the Victorian period.

German religious life remained overwhelmingly concentrated on London during the seventeenth and eighteenth centuries and, while the same applies to Jews to a large extent, the period after 1700 also resulted in the rise of provincial Jewry.[13] Clearly, as in the case of the Germans, the place of worship became the centre of Jewish life. Those who settled following readmission did not face the level of violence experienced by their medieval predecessors, which consequently resulted in the evolution of long-standing synagogues throughout the capital, together with a range of charitable organizations associated with them and the birth of a Jewish bureaucracy aimed at protecting the interests of the Jewish community.

The main division of the early settlers consisted of that between the Sephardim community of predominantly Spanish and Portuguese origin, who tended to dominate the early Jewish history of London following readmission, and the central and northern European Ashkenazim, with different religious practices, who would soon become the predominant group because most migrants from the eighteenth century had this religious identity. The first place of worship for the Sephardim was the upper floor of a house in Creechurch Lane, establishing a temporary pattern imitated by subsequent Jewish and other settlers. The community quickly outgrew this short-term solution and constructed a purpose-built synagogue, Bevis Marks, in nearby Heneage Lane, opened in 1701.[14] The first Ashkenazi place of worship opened in Duke's Place in 1690 and would become a key centre for this form of Jewish ritual and identity during the course of the eighteenth century and beyond. Because of increasing numbers of worshippers, it would experience expansion during the middle of the eighteenth century and become known as the Great Synagogue.[15] Some members of the synagogue in Duke's Place from Hamburg quickly broke away and opened a new place of worship, the Hambro, completed in Fenchurch Street in 1726. In 1761 there followed a third Ashkenazi establishment, the New Synagogue.[16] These Jewish places of worship acted as the centre of a whole network of charitable and religious activity which determined the survival of this group and ensured the religious diversity of London, a pattern followed by all subsequent religious communities. By the middle of the eighteenth century there existed a Sephardic School of Girls, a Sephardic Orphanage and the Beth Holim, a hospital for the sick and aged. Similar activity developed for the Ashkenazi community, including a fund for the relief of poor orphans by Duke's Place in 1748 which subsequently expanded to include widows, poor brides and the sick.[17] The key bureaucratic structures of Anglo-Jewry also emerged during the course of the eighteenth century, including the establishment of the office of the Chief Rabbi in 1764, an indication of the spread of the Jewish community beyond London with authority emanating from the capital.[18] The Board of Deputies of British Jews, essentially the body which represents Jews in the political sphere, also surfaced in 1760, bringing together both Ashkenazi and Sephardic representatives.[19]

Unlike the Jewish community, the 'Roman Catholic Church in London was small and haphazardly organized as late as 1800', partly because of the draconian legislation that emerged during the Reformation, which would only disappear gradually during the course of the seventeenth, eighteenth and nineteenth centuries. Catholic worship remained illegal until 1791. One way around this problem for the London Irish consisted of worship in the chapels of European ambassadors, but this did not prove straightforward and three of these faced destruction during the Gordon Riots.[20] Secret places of worship known as mass-houses therefore emerged, which catered both for Irish migrants and for other Europeans living in London, although these also faced destruction during the Gordon Riots.[21]

OUTSIDERS

The development of organized Roman Catholicism in London, part of a national process, took place during the course of the nineteenth century, partly as a result of the actions of Roman Catholic missionaries who worked together with the re-established Church in Britain to gather converts and construct parishes. While many Irish Catholics may have welcomed this attention, meaning that they participated in the type of religion which they had practised in their homeland, other newcomers to London have either attracted the unwanted attention of Christian missionaries or have, at least in the short run, faced difficulty in establishing their own places of worship. This was especially the case of West Indians and Africans, some of whom theoretically came from a branch of a Church with a British basis which, however, did not always accept them as equals because of racial prejudice.

The Victorian capital teemed with missionaries who went after lost souls, whether foreign or poor, as darkest London became a mirror for the dark continent which European Christians viewed as a golden opportunity for expanding the faith. The London City Mission devoted particular attention to a wide variety of migrants. Those employed in 1851 for the purpose of 'visiting special classes of the population are to the police, 2; to omnibus stations, 1; to the Welsh, 2; to the Italians, 2; and to the Irish, 4'. Those concerned with Italians 'had distributed 147 copies of Italian scriptures'.[22] Despite the opening of St Peter's Roman Catholic Church in Clerkenwell in 1864, Italians continued to attract the attention of the London City Mission for decades after its establishment. An account from 1877 described them as 'a peculiar people in their present religious state of apathy and uncertainty, being in general disgusted with Romanism and suspicious of Protestantism'. The missionary concerned

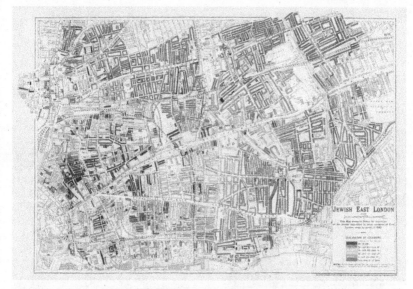

1. In the years leading up to the First World War the East End became the heartland of East European Jewish settlement in London and Britain as a whole, as shown in this contemporary map which accompanied the research of Charles Booth's *Survey of London*.

2. For much of the nineteenth century the most visible group in London consisted of the Irish, whose ethnicity revolved around their Roman Catholic religion, as illustrated in this photograph taken in the East End just before the First World War.

3. The Greek community which emerged in central London during the course of the nineteenth century offers an example of an elite diasporic group that made the global capital its home and used it to develop a vast commercial empire. At the centre of Greek Orthodox identity lay the Cathedral of St Sophia, opened in Bayswater in 1879.

4. The Irish navvy became a central feature of London life from the eighteenth century, playing a key role in numerous construction projects, as this early post-war image illustrates.

5. South Asian women became a central feature of the London economy from the 1970s. The first generation worked in a wide variety of jobs including at the Grunwick film processing laboratories in Dollis Hill, where they became involved in a bitter dispute.

6. From the end of the nineteenth century a series of migrant groups sustained the rag trade in London, including East European Jews, Cypriots (as in this 1980s photograph) and Bangladeshis.

7. After 1945 London Transport became one of many firms that directly imported people from the West Indies to work for them.

8. The size of the London market has offered enterprising migrants the opportunity to open up businesses of all sizes and in all fields, as demonstrated in this image from Haringey during the 1980s.

9. Italian migrants proved especially entrepreneurial and played a key role in the popularization of ice cream during the Victorian period.

10. From the re-admission of Jews to Britain in the middle of the seventeenth century, one of the key occupations – which would survive into Victorian Britain – was the recycling of clothes.

11. The Irish street seller became a feature of mid-Victorian Britain.

12. German and Jewish elites played an important role in the development of London banking from the end of the eighteenth century but would face intense hostility in the Germanophobic atmósphere of the Great War. This led some, such as Edgar and Leonora Speyer, to flee.

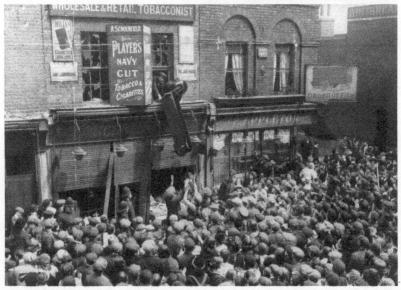

13. Violence has greeted most migrant groups that have settled in London but, during the nineteenth and twentieth centuries, none faced the scale of violence experienced by the Germans during the Great War. The attack on this property on Chrisp Street in the East End in May 1915 followed the sinking of the passenger liner *Lusitania* by a German submarine.

14. The Brixton riots of 1981 broke out as a reaction against inner-city deprivation and persecution which involved the Metropolitan Police.

15. During the 1970s, the East End became the site of violent activity involving the racist National Front which targeted the area's Bangladeshi community.

16. Despite the small numbers of people of colour living in London during the Victorian period, they attracted attention, especially from missionaries such as Joseph Salter who helped establish the Strangers Home for Asiatics, Africans and South Sea Islanders.

17. The Asians who appeared on the streets of London included this Hindu tract seller, identified by the social investigator Henry Mayhew in the 1850s.

18. Germans became a feature of London life from the end of the seventeenth century with the basis of their ethnic identity being the churches they established. This included St George's German Church on Little Alie Street which operated a whole social network including a school.

19. The history of Jewish London involves a succession of migrants. At the end of the nineteenth century the refugees from Eastern Europe had different religious practices from established and elite London Jews and therefore opened their own synagogues or *chevroth*, which survived into the post-Second World War period.

20. Religion operates as one of the key markers of ethnic diversity in London and the leaders of different communities have constructed grand religious spaces to signify their presence in the capital, as in the case of the London Central Mosque.

21. Victorian London acted as the site for the development of the symbol of British food, as the wider population developed a fondness for the consumption of Jewish fried fish.

22. Cosmopolitan food emerged in Soho from the end of the nineteenth century, a trend that would continue into the post-war period when the area became important for the Chinese restaurant trade.

23. Daniel Mendoza (pictured right in 1789) was the first London sporting celebrity of migrant origins.

24. Bill Richmond became the first black boxing celebrity in London at the start of the nineteenth century.

25. Walter Tull, who became famous both as a black British officer during the Great War and as a footballer, spent some of his career with Tottenham Hotspur.

26. The Bermuda-born Clyde Best became the first black footballer to appear weekly on London television screens for West Ham United during the 1960s and 1970s, and must have inspired countless Londoners to follow in his footsteps.

27. Germans became a central feature of the London concert scene, from Handel onwards, including Wilhelm Ganz who conducted the Philharmonic Society from 1879.

28. Despite the overwhelming whiteness of classical music before the First World War, the London-born Samuel Coleridge-Taylor became a prominent orchestral figure and composer.

29. The most famous classical music couple in Victorian London, the German-born conductor Otto Goldschmidt and the Swedish-born soprano Jenny Lind, lived in South Kensington.

30. As well as the European performers who dominated the classical music scene, the streets of Victorian London teemed with street players, including Italians.

31. In the post-war period London became central in the evolution of black music on a global scale. One of the earliest arrivals was the calypso artist Aldwyn Roberts, aka Lord Kitchener, who arrived on the *Empire Windrush* in 1948 singing 'London is the Place for Me'.

divided this community into the 'better class' which lived in Soho, who welcomed him into their homes and spoke with him, although he did 'not see much result'. The 'poorer classes' in Leather Lane in Clerkenwell proved difficult 'on account of their great ignorance, superstition, and slowness of understanding, truly requiring the simple milk of the Word', which meant that 'it is necessary to speak to them of subjects of which they have some slight knowledge', although the missionary concerned does not seem to have achieved many conversions as the Italians simply interpreted the information through their Roman Catholic upbringing.[23] By this time the London City Mission also devoted attention to French migrants in London,[24] as well as Scandinavians, especially sailors.[25] In view of their numbers, Irish migrants also received attention from this body.[26]

We can interpret the interest of the London missionaries in two different ways. On the one hand, we might view their activities as a type of internal imperialism, searching out souls for conversion in exactly the same way as their brethren in the British Empire. On the other hand, these individuals also had the ability to act as something of a safety net for those facing difficult circumstances, even though the ultimate aim may have consisted of conversion. In 1857 a series of London Protestant bodies, led by the Church of England's Church Missionary Society and receiving financial help from the recently converted Duleep Singh, the last Maharajah of the Punjab living in exile in Britain, established the Strangers Home for Asiatics, Africans and South Sea Islanders facing difficult conditions in West India Dock Road. The residents, especially sailors, paid £2 per month and, together with food and shelter, also received religious instruction from Protestant missionaries with some knowledge of India. Other institutes, aimed especially at sailors, emerged in late Victorian London, including the Asiatic Rest in East India Dock Road and St Luke's Lascar Mission in Victoria Dock Road.[27]

Joseph Salter became the most active missionary, and certainly the one who left the most detailed record of his activities amongst 'Asiatics', publishing two books on the subject.[28] Between 1853 and 1893 he took charge of Asians and Africans for the London City Mission and served as the religious instructor in the Strangers Home.[29] In typical missionary fashion, his two volumes consist of a combination of sympathy for those at the mercy of London life, a desire to assist them, and orientalist and racist language driven particularly by his strong Christian faith. In one sense Salter and his colleagues succeeded in their objectives because of the thousands of people they assisted,[30] although it seems less clear how many conversions actually took place. Salter provided examples of 'heathen strangers, reaching London in their blindness; who after a short residence in our shores . . . have obtained the bread of life, the glad tidings of salvation, and have taken it to the land of their nativity',[31] partly because of the fact that the Strangers Home acted as a repatriation agency for destitute people from the colonies.[32] On the other hand, some of Salter's colleagues and contemporaries consisted of converted Indians who settled in London.[33] In the 1850s Henry Mayhew had asserted that more than half of the fifty 'sellers of religious tracts' he identified 'are foreigners such as Malays, Hindoos, and Negroes. Of them, some cannot speak English, and . . . are Mahometans, or worshippers of Bramah'.[34] These had the advantage of command of Indian languages, although Salter and other white people had learnt them as part of their training, but this did not improve the conversion rates.[35]

The Strangers Home continued to exist into the twentieth century. An account from 1932 pointed to the fact that it provided 'lodgings, recreations, and three meals a day for men from India, Arabia, Africa, China, Straits of Malacca, New Zealand, Polynesia, the islands of the China Sea and the Indian Ocean'. In this environment 'the Asiatic stranger can find somebody who speaks his own tongue, and here he can rest secure from imposition'. This account focused upon the material benefits of the Home.[36] Other accounts of black and Asian people in the East End from the interwar years devoted more attention to their spiritual needs. For example, the Reverend George Mitchell hoped that 'the Chinese gospels and portions of the Bible are . . . as readily perused as they are cheerfully received', although his narrative, as we would expect, contained racist statements. 'The Chinaman still uses his chop-sticks and has not yet absorbed Western culinary civilization.'[37] Mitchell took pride in people he had converted (without providing figures) but mentioned Abdul 'who was a Brahmin . . . I baptised Abdul and gave him another name in place of his Indian one. Wherever he goes, his Bible goes with him and in Urdu he speaks to his countrymen about the Christian God.'[38]

In the post-war period, while the type of missionary conversion and overt racism which characterized earlier attitudes towards people from beyond Europe may have lessened, especially because of the role that the Churches have increasingly played in helping asylum seekers who have fallen through the state safety net in the early twenty-first century,[39] the arrival of a significant number of West Indian and African Christians reveals that the racial attitudes remained. In the early 1960s, 69 per cent of the former group settled in London had attended church services and 'have been welcomed by Christians and representatives from the London churches and have been given help in many ways'. Nevertheless, most West Indians only 'make contact with the Church when they wish to be married and when they have a baby to be baptised'. This lack of engagement partly evolved from the 'patronising attitude of so many English Churches towards West Indians'.[40] The newcomers felt alienated from the 'emptiness of the church, the drab and dark surroundings' which 'do not give West Indians the "uplift" which they expect'. This sense of alienation became accentuated if 'their presence causes comment', which meant 'they tend to go away with the impression that they are unwanted'. While they may appreciate the fact that the 'Vicar tries his best to provide a welcome . . . if the attitude of the congregation affects their sensitivity they tend to keep away in spite of these efforts'.[41] The British Council of Churches, responsible for all Protestant sects, took an official stance against racial discrimination and also encouraged ministers to reach out to people of colour.[42]

But negative experiences led to the development of Pentecostal sects with some basis in the homeland but essentially directed from the United States, including Seventh Day Adventists, the New Testament Church of God, the Church of God in Christ and the Church of God of Prophecy.[43] By the early 1990s two-thirds of black Christians in Britain belonged to black-led Churches, by which time more black people attended church than whites in some parts of London.[44] The Nigerian Yorùbá community in London developed their religion in a similar way to West Indians as they experienced 'a wall of separation in churches where white Christians would not sit next to a black fellow Christian on the pews'.[45] This community established a series of Pentecostal churches throughout the capital involving a variety of sects, most significantly the Cherubim and Seraphim Church which had already developed in Nigeria.[46] These places of worship have facilitated the emergence of black gospel music in London and in the United Kingdom as a whole, epitomized by Bazil Meade who founded the London Community Gospel Choir in 1983.[47] Another type of faith which emerged in London was Rastafarianism.[48] It counted believers in the capital by the end of the 1950s,[49] including in Portobello Road where 'they had a meeting hall'.[50]

RELIGIOUS STRUCTURES

The black Churches which emerged after 1945 followed, to some extent, the pattern of the European migrants who had settled in London in earlier centuries, although significant differences exist, including the fact that they did not emerge as a reaction to racism in the white Church. They resemble, as we shall see, the synagogues which emerged organically as a reaction against the practices of established Anglo-Jewry in the late nineteenth century. Jews, European Christians and, subsequently, Muslims, Sikhs and Hindus, have established places of worship as the centre of their communal life and as a demonstration of their presence in the world capital. The places of worship usually formed the focal point of a network of other activity, as the synagogues and German Churches established from the seventeenth century have demonstrated. The places of worship and the other bodies which have revolved around them partly represent an attempt by communal leaders to emphasize their ethnic and religious difference from the mainstream Anglican and other Protestant sects. However, individuals who theoretically have an allegiance to particular religious groups do not necessarily follow their lead.

The evolution of German Church activity during the nineteenth century demonstrates the centrality of religion for migrants in London in this period, even though, as we have seen by examining German political London, this did not constitute the only form of ethnic identity for this community. However, we might see it as a type of official German ethnicity. By 1905 over fifteen German places of worship existed in London concentrated in the areas in which this group had developed during the course of the nineteenth century, especially the East End but also, by this time, the West End, Islington and further south in Forest Hill and Camberwell where wealthier Germans had settled. Services also took place in the German Seaman's Church and the German Sailor's Home, both located in Stepney. St George's in the East remained in Little Alie Street, where it still stands today, and demonstrates how such churches formed the centre of ethnic life for Germans in Victorian London as the bodies connected to it included: a Ladies Clothing Society, providing clothes to children of poor German families; a fund for poor elderly Germans; a free library for members of the congregation; and, above all, St George's School, which may have provided free education to over 12,000 German children during the course of the nineteenth century. Similarly, St Bonifatius, the

German Catholic church which also catered for other nationalities and which occupied four different buildings during the course of the nineteenth century, ran its own classes and established societies aimed at a range of groups including female servants and families. These bodies received funding from wealthier members of the German community.[51] Despite the Germanophobia and upheavals of the First World War the German churches did not come under direct attack although they lost their congregations, which faced deportation and therefore needed rebuilding.[52] The German Evangelical Church in Sydenham and St Bonifatius fell victim to German bombs during the Second World War but then underwent reconstruction, although secularization has meant that the German churches have declined in importance despite the continuing large size of the German community in London.[53]

The development of the Italian community in Clerkenwell in the nineteenth century led to the establishment of St Peter's Church, consecrated in April 1863. Previous to this 'Rome sent a young Italian priest', Don Angelo Maria Baldacconi, from Siena in 1824 to look after the Italians here and also to direct them to the Sardinian Chapel in Lincoln's Inn Fields.[54] In 1905 George Sims described the 'ten o'clock mass' as well as the activities of the Sisters of Charity and the schools connected with St Peter.[55] Into the twentieth century the church remained a centre of Italian Catholicism, distinguishing itself from the mainstream Irish-centred strand of this religion with the school continuing to function, while the annual procession which took place here allowed a manifestation of Italian identity in the capital even as late as the 1990s, by which time an Italian church in Southwark had also opened.[56]

The Roman Catholics of London constituted a diverse group from a variety of locations in Europe in addition to Italy and Germany, including France, but, above all, from Ireland.[57] The number of Roman Catholics in London may have stood at around 15,000 at the start of the nineteenth century,[58] increasing to over 200,000 by the 1850s,[59] a figure maintained until the end of the Victorian period and consisting predominantly of Irish migrants,[60] although a small percentage of those moving from the Emerald Isle to the British capital consisted of Protestants.[61]

The influx of hundreds of thousands of Catholics to London, reflecting the picture in the rest of the country, transformed the Roman Catholic Church from 'a small, proud, rich, and unpopular body', consisting of the descendants of those individuals who had not converted to Protestantism during the

Reformation, but also the small numbers of early Victorian Irish migrants as well as some Europeans, into 'a large, prudent, poorer and popular body, with a vast majority of Irish adherents'.[62] Missionaries played a large role in this process, supported by some of the wealthier English Catholics who 'lavished funds on the mission to the Irish poor, upon charitable relief for their worst distresses, on self-help societies and soup kitchens, orphanages and almshouses, reformatories, convents, chapels and schools', driven by a Catholic revival of the 1840s. The missions partly evolved from the chapels of the Spanish, Sardinian and Bavarian ambassadors, but then became independent organizations, often with a base in Rome, including Jesuits.[63] The hard work and devotion of missionaries proved fundamental in the development of the Catholic faith in Britain,[64] as did the re-establishment of the Roman Catholic hierarchy following the passage of the Catholic Relief Act of 1829, which meant the development of a parish and diocese system based upon the established Church and the installation of archbishops.[65] By the 1805s a vibrant Roman Catholic life had developed in London counting as many as 150 'Romish priests', while the number of churches and chapels had also increased, focusing not simply on Westminster and Southwark but throughout the expanding metropolis where Irish Catholics had settled. Convent and monastic life had also come to London by the 1850s.[66] The Roman Catholic social system which emerged in London and other British cities also had schooling at its heart.[67] By the second half of the nineteenth century a 'Roman Catholic culture' had developed, which both encouraged the retention of Irish Catholic identities but also 'helped migrants to adapt to urban society and to develop wider loyalties', inculcating a 'heavy dose of social discipline'.[68] In the East End several churches emerged during the Victorian era[69] and the Catholic Church here, as elsewhere, 'provided one of the main centres for community expression' with the priests 'moulding the community, restraining its excesses and relieving its suffering'.[70]

By the time of the arrival of the post-war Irish migrants, Roman Catholicism had become firmly established and the number of people practising this religion had increased through the generations. However, the increase in the numbers of Irish from the 1940s resulted in the type of missionary activity which had taken place in the previous century if not quite on the same scale, again partly as an attempt to keep the newcomers within the Irish Catholic fold but also in order to keep them away from the temptations of sex and drink.[71] 'After mass on Sunday was the best time to meet Irish people.' The Victorian churches 'were full every Sunday' and in some cases 'there was an overspill with the women going in and the men remaining outside kneeling on the pavement'. The church did not simply provide spiritual nourishment, it also 'served as a point of continuity for life in the homeland'.[72] Apart from the church, the other important Irish Catholic spaces were the schools so that attendance at them 'was very much the norm for the Irish in London'. As well as providing a Catholic education, these institutions also 'put on Irish dancing and music concerts'.[73]

Orthodox Christianity in London has a similar trajectory to Roman Catholicism (although the chronology differs) in the sense that it began as an elite religion but turned into a mass belief, if not on the same scale. The Greek and Russian varieties remain interlinked although, by the end of the nineteenth century, the former had more securely established itself and also became more prominent. The first Greek Orthodox church appears to have come into existence at the end of the seventeenth century, driven forward by the Archbishop of Samos, in Greek Street, but it only appears to have lasted for one year after its opening due to the lack of a congregation, and it was taken over by French Huguenots in 1682. The Greek population of London then worshipped at the Russian Orthodox Church, which used homes in various West End locations and whose establishment partly came through the efforts of Greek and Greek Cypriot clergymen.[74] The development of the wealthy Greek merchant community in nineteenth-century London meant the establishment of an independent Greek Orthodox religious community. The group initially worshipped in the Russian Orthodox church, by this time located in the Russian Embassy in Welbeck Street. However, in 1837 a chapel opened in one of the houses in Finsbury Square where the wealthy Greek community became concentrated, but this only served as a temporary solution and in 1850 a purpose-built church opened at Great Winchester Street, London Wall. However, the increasing numbers, wealth and integration, but not assimilation, of the Greek community in the second half of the Victorian period indicated a desire to make a grand statement, leading to the establishment of a committee to build a permanent establishment in the form of St Sophia, which opened in Moscow Road in Bayswater in 1879, and which became a cathedral in 1922.

By the time the Greek Cypriot community began to arrive from the 1930s onwards, Greek Orthodox churches had also opened in Liverpool and

Manchester, but St Sophia tended not to attract the newcomers from Cyprus, originally catering for about sixty or seventy wealthy Greek families.[75] The newcomers from predominantly rural backgrounds had worshipped in the autonomous Cypriot Orthodox Church in their homeland and established their own places of worship, usually utilizing establishments which belonged to other Christian denominations. Orthodoxism has had almost the same role in modern Greek identity as the practice of Judaism for Jews, a statement which applies to both Greeks and Cypriots. The latter consider 'the Church as the guardian of their Hellenic culture, against the menacing forces of various nations that occupied Cyprus over the centuries'. On national holidays Cypriot priests in London delivered 'from their pulpits the most fiery praise of Cypriot and Greek cultures'. The first Cypriot church opened in Camden Town in 1948, followed by a second in Kentish Town in 1959, a third in Camberwell in 1963 and a fourth in Hammersmith in 1965.[76] By the 1990s the number of Greek Orthodox churches in London and its suburbs had increased to thirty-two, while others emerged to serve the small communities of Greek Cypriots outside the capital.[77] The Greek Orthodox churches have formed the centre of Cypriot Christian ethnicity in London, acting as the base for many of the Greek (evening) schools which emerged in the British capital, although some of these subsequently moved to council buildings often with help from the Cyprus government and parents in London. These establishments had the aim of preserving knowledge of the mother tongue for the second generation and preventing rapid assimilation. The calendar of the devout Greek Cypriot revolves around the major Christian ceremonies, especially Christmas, New Year and Easter, which, in Cyprus, determined the diet of the community. London life, education in English, secularization and exogamy have seriously eroded the power of the Church, which, in the early post-war decades, was responsible for virtually all marriages involving Greek Cypriots.[78]

Similar to both Roman Catholicism and Greek Orthodoxism, Judaism underwent a transformation as a result of the arrival of a new poor community, this time from the last quarter of the nineteenth century. This means that in all three of these religions we need to fully accept that distinct variations exist in those who practise them from a national, social and denominational perspective.

The overarching structures which emerged during the eighteenth century, including the Board of Deputies, became formalized during the course of the nineteenth, and would increasingly become the official political voice of

Anglo-Jewry into the twentieth century and beyond,[79] while the Chief Rabbi and his office also developed further.[80] The first half of the nineteenth century also witnessed a proliferation of Jewish charities totalling around fifty by 1844.[81] Many of them came together through the establishment of the Board of Guardians in 1859 by seventeen men who met in the Great Synagogue for the purpose of assisting their poorer co-religionists through the opening of schools, the encouragement of Jews into apprenticeships, especially by opposing practices which discriminated against them, and the provision of poor relief when necessary. The Board of Guardians became especially active in helping the large number of East European Jews who arrived from the 1880s, although, by this time, it also encouraged repatriation and further travel to America as a solution to the problem of poverty.[82] By the beginning of the twentieth century Anglo-Jewry, with the majority of its adherents based upon London, but with communities throughout the country, had developed an extraordinary range of local and national organizations both religious and secular.[83] In 1870 the United Synagogue came into existence, which aimed at keeping the London congregations together as Jews moved into the suburbs.[84] A Jewish court or Beth Din, which aimed at interpreting Jewish law and ritual, had also come into existence by the nineteenth century. Around 1900 the court sat twice a week and consisted of the Chief Rabbi and his two assessors, regulating the details of religious observance and also acting as a court of arbitration on issues which included matrimonial disputes, family quarrels and industrial matters.[85] The Schechita had emerged in London in 1804, with responsibility for 'organising and supervising the supply of kosher meat to the Jewish public', and by the 1920s it acted as the supervising agency for matters of food for all of the different Jewish communities which had emerged by this time.[86]

The East European Jewish refugees who settled in London at the end of the nineteenth century felt alienated from the social background, imposing grandeur and ritual of the established Ashkenazi Jews and their services,[87] who also displayed hostility towards them. This meant that the newcomers organically established their own places of worship, independent *hebroth* or *chevroth*, 'in any back- or upstairs-room, attic, or hut that could be found fit for the purpose', as they could not afford the luxurious surroundings of their established co-religionists,[88] which they also viewed as lacking piety. However, these early solutions remained temporary as some of the congregations took over disused churches in the East End with decreasing numbers of Christian worshippers, some previously used by the disappearing Huguenots.[89] The religious practices of the established Jewish community in London had experienced change in the early nineteenth century, which brought the services and the function of the rabbi closer to that of Protestant Christian norms.[90] The nineteenth century also witnessed the beginnings of Reform Judaism, consisting of Ashkenazi and Sephardic believers and emerging from the West London Synagogue in 1840 to grow into one of the key structures in Jewish belief in London and Britain in the years that followed.[91] The newcomers established the Federation of Synagogues in 1887 to hold together the new *chevroth* and *hebroth*.[92] The mutual distrust between native and foreign Jews revolved around religious practice and class, area of origin, outward appearance and numbers, so that the established community feared that the influx of so many newcomers who settled in 'ghettos' would lead to an upsurge of antisemitism which would undermine the gains they had made during the nineteenth century. Established Jewry made efforts to speed up the integration process by setting up a series of organizations such as the East End Scheme, aimed at holding separate services in the major Ashkenazi synagogues, as well as opening youth and sporting groups in the East End. Meanwhile, the immigrants also established their own religious schools, continuing the practices of Eastern Europe.[93]

As the twentieth century progressed, however, and the migrants and their descendants experienced upward social mobility, the Federation of Jewish Synagogues also became part of established Anglo-Jewry. During the interwar years the migration out of the East End ghetto meant the establishment of new synagogues in the suburbs, building upon a construction phase which involved both the United Synagogue and the Federation of Synagogues in the late nineteenth century.[94] This process continued into the 1920s and 1930s, especially in Golders Green and Hendon.[95] The first religious service in Hendon took place in the house of H. Berman in Alderton Crescent in 1925, but the movement from the East End and the arrival of Jewish refugees from the Nazis meant that by 1940 the Hendon synagogue, consecrated in 1929, had become the sixth largest of the United Synagogue congregations and the second largest by 1950.[96] Nevertheless, during the early 1930s the Jewish East End remained very much alive. A total of fifty-six out of 139 synagogues in Greater London lay in the City and Stepney, meaning that 'their membership constitutes over 40 per cent of the total synagogue membership of the metropolitan and extra-metropolitan districts'. The *chevroth* also continued to exist, although the 'small inconvenient buildings of a generation ago have been enlarged or remodelled in many instances, or have expanded into a few large synagogues as in Spitalfields, Whitechapel and Bethnal Green', accommodating hundreds of worshippers.[97] Further out the West Ham Synagogue, consecrated in 1911, had established itself with its network of educational and charitable activities,[98] a pattern repeated in the West End of London[99] and, in fact, across the whole of the capital as Jewish structures firmly established this community as a core part of London life,[100] building from the foundations of the seventeenth and eighteenth centuries and the expansion of the Victorian and Edwardian years.[101] The communal structures of Anglo-Jewry survived into the post-war period, by which time the four main congregations consisted of Sephardic, Reform, Orthodox and the expanding Ultra-Orthodox, around the Union of Orthodox Hebrew congregations.[102] While the first three have witnessed increasing assimilation, which has meant a decline in communal activity, and while Golders Green has maintained a Jewish character,[103] the most dynamic, Ultra-Orthodox group has emerged in Stamford Hill, even establishing its own synagogues reminiscent of its late nineteenth-century predecessors.[104]

In post-war London the most dynamic religions have essentially originated in the Middle East and South Asia, especially Islam, but also Hinduism and Sikhism, with the first two counting more adherents than Judaism could attract even at its high point. Islam in particular has a complexity even more marked than Judaism, in view of the diverse origins and religious practices of its adherents. All of these major world religions have profoundly changed post-war London as a result of the evolution of places of worship, which has also meant a development of the type of communal organization that characterized the Jewish community.

Islam differs from Judaism in the sense that its history in Britain does not remain tied to London in quite the same way, a process which has continued subsequently because of the settlement of so many Indians and Pakistanis, although not people with Middle Eastern origins, in towns in the Midlands and north of England. While Joseph Salter and other London missionaries worked with 'Asiatics' in London, Islam emerged in a formalized way in the north-east, Cardiff and Liverpool because of the presence of Muslim sailors, with the first mosques founded in Liverpool and Woking largely as a result of the efforts of British converts.[105]

The East London Mosque became the first to emerge in the world capital. Its origins lay in a public meeting held at the Ritz Hotel in 1910 for the purpose of raising the funding necessary for constructing it, attended by various Muslim and non-Muslim dignitaries, who realized the necessity of building a mosque in East London because of the presence of many people of Islamic faith in the area, including from the part of British India which would subsequently become Bangladesh. However, the establishment of this place of worship took decades, during which time the Muslim population of the area increased further, especially as a result of further immigration from the Bangladesh region. It practised in three converted houses in Commercial Road in 1941 and then moved to a prefabricated structure in Fieldgate Street in 1975 and then into the large purpose-built mosque in Whitechapel in 1975,[106] which became the most significant Muslim place of worship in this part of London. Before the completion of this building early post-war workers utilized the less glamorous place of worship which preceded it, whereas 'richer people' tended to attend the Islamic Cultural Centre[107] that would become the London Central Mosque. This was the other imposing Islamic space in London with origins as far back as the 1920s, which did not finally open until 1977, following the raising of enough funds to build the impressive structure in the grounds of Regent's Park.[108] These two institutions symbolize the acceptance of religious diversity as a fact of life in the evolution of post-war London and, along with the Ismaili Cultural Centre in South Kensington, constitute the most ostentatious Islamic structures in the capital. In fact, the first London mosque in a purpose-built Islamic building opened in Southfields in 1926.[109] The arrival of hundreds of thousands of Muslims in London, reflecting the millions who have settled in Britain and the rest of Western Europe, has transformed the religious architecture of the capital. By 2000 over 150 mosques existed in London,[110] a figure which would increase significantly in the first two decades of the twenty-first century, reflecting Muslim concentrations in East London in particular, although Muslim sites of worship have emerged throughout the capital, wherever people of Islamic faith have settled.[111] While the larger mosques may have emerged with international Islamic funding, the proliferation of places of worship has evolved as a result of limited community resources. This has meant that, in the short term, some prayers took place in house mosques, reflecting the *chevroth* of the late nineteenth-century Jewish community, which would emerge into purpose-built structures with imams and classes as communities became established and raised funding. As these buildings have proliferated they have become increasingly sensitive to the objections of already existing communities. Even more than Judaism, it seems difficult to speak of a British or London Islam because of the diversity of the believers of this faith, either because of the wide range of origins of the newcomers or the different religious practices and rituals. They incorporate not simply people from South Asia and the Middle East but also, for instance, Turkish Cypriots and Somalis. Nevertheless, the type of bureaucratic struc- tures which characterize Judaism have also emerged, although the headquar- ters does not always lie in London, as indicated by the Bradford Council of Mosques. Since the rise of Islamism, central government has tasked Muslim bodies and individual mosques with reporting and eradicating any preachers with suspect political beliefs.[112]

The more purely South Asian religions in the form of Hinduism and Sikhism have also made their presence felt in post-war London, although not on the same scale as Islam because they count fewer believers. The earlier Hindu settlers, like their Muslim counterparts, tended to make do with the spaces available for worship, often their own homes, with the first Hindu temple in the United Kingdom emerging in a house in Leicester in 1969. Early mandirs in London opened in Wandsworth in 1975 (Gujaratis), Southall (Punjabis) and Brixton (Indians migrating from the Caribbean, to which the British Empire had transported them from the nineteenth century).[113] By the end of the twentieth century the centre of Hindu life in London had moved to Wembley, symbolized by the spectacular Shri Swaminarayan Mandir in Neasden opened in August 1995, the largest Hindu temple outside India. The funding came from the efforts of British Hindus and utilized a workforce of about 2,000 people, some of them volunteers. The driving body behind its construction was the Swaminarayan Hindu Mission and had the aim of making the mandir a type of headquarters for British Hindus, as well as serving as a statement about the presence of this religion in London and in the United Kingdom, resembling some of the largest cathedrals in London and in Britain in view of its scale. The mandir came with a community centre,[114] reflecting the role of this temple, as in the case of the other major London religions, as the centre of religious life and community activity for this reli- gious group. Like Judaism and Islam, Hinduism, reflecting the situation in India, has a complex of subdivisions in which caste has played a central role in the evolution of places of worship driven by caste associations and temple groupings.[115]

Sikh religion developed at the beginning of the twentieth century and the first significant gurdwara emerged in a house in Shepherd's Bush, becoming the focal point for the entire Sikh community in Britain in the earlier twentieth century. The arrival of new settlers in the post-war years led to the emergence of further places of worship, with Southall becoming a major centre because of the concentration of Sikhs here. By 1997 London counted thirty-one gurdwaras while in March 2003 the largest Sikh place of worship outside India opened, the Singh Sabha Gurdwara in Southall. The proliferation of temples can be explained not only by the growth of the Sikh population but also by the structures which have emerged to develop them in the form of organizations operating at both a local and a national level, and by the fact that, as in the Hindu case, the temples have emerged on a caste basis, despite the scriptural opposition of this religion to this way of dividing people.[116]

INDIVIDUAL BELIEF AND IDENTITY

The ways in which migrant beliefs have emerged in modern London have close similarities, indicating the centrality of religion in the capital's recent history, despite the rise of secularism. The pattern generally involves the arrival of a new community who gradually develop the confidence and wealth to open up their own places of worship, initially humble and basic but increasingly grandiloquent and a closer reflection of the buildings in their homeland. As we have seen, all of the major world religions which have emerged in London in recent centuries have divisions, according to area of origin, class or caste and religious ritual. Hinduism, Sikhism and Judaism, for example, have developed parallel bureaucratic organizations to run the places of worship which they have established. The emergence of these structures clearly has the function of community building while the construction of the large places of worship announces to the wider London public as well as to the British population and even the world, in view of London's global significance, that a particular community has arrived.

However, we need to ask what significance churches, synagogues, mosques, gurdwaras and mandirs have beyond statements about the presence of a particular group in the world capital. Do they simply constitute symbolic spaces, or do they actually attract believers? In the case of those places of worship which emerge organically, the answer remains yes. But we need to examine the extent to which devotion actually occurs.

At the beginning of the twentieth century Richard Mudie-Smith's survey of religious life in London both outlined the diverse places of worship in the capital, incorporating all denominations, and tackled the issue of attendance at services. While one in three of the population of Ealing participated in morning prayers, the figure for Willesden dipped to one in fifteen.[117] Although Mudie-Smith claimed that 'the outstanding lesson' of his survey 'is that the power of preaching is undiminished' he also asserted that his census 'emphatically enforced' the fact that 'the majority of the inhabitants remain, owing to either indifference or hostility, uninfluenced and untouched'.[118] The same would apply to some of the migrant-based religions if we use Mudie-Smith's statistics. The census claimed that 26,612 people attended services at the 66 synagogues listed, less than 20 per cent of the Jewish population of the time.[119] Meanwhile, 1,522 people attended services at the 15 German places of worship in London on the Sunday of the census, at a time when the German population of the capital stood at 27,427 or just 5.5 per cent.[120]

We can look at the larger migrant religious groups in the capital in the form of Roman Catholics, Jews and Muslims in more detail, examining both service attendance and individual identity. Post-Famine Ireland experienced a 'devotional revolution' helped by the spread of modern communications, the penetration of the English language and the destruction of traditional peasant society, which 'paved the way for an assertion of liturgical practice and richer visual symbolism'.[121] In London the new zeal manifested itself in Roman Catholic missionary work carried out by both the Irish and other Europeans.[122] However, while all Irish Catholics in London may have had their children baptized in the 1830s, only about 10 per cent of parishioners 'fulfilled their Easter duties in 1837',[123] although between 25 and 30 per cent of the 'baptised population' may have attended services later in the century.[124] Most migrants and their English-born children may have taken part 'in the major Catholic rituals marking birth and probably death' but far fewer attended regular services. Mixed marriages, irreligious parents, Protestant schools and anti-Catholicism impacted upon the extent of devotion.[125] Henry Mayhew found that 'some of the Irish Roman Catholics', especially the poorest and those who had resided in England for 'many years', had 'become indifferent to their creed'. But others displayed a high level of devotion, including one man who claimed to attend mass every Sunday and to pray 'mysilf ivery night for a blissin'. One house Mayhew entered contained 'a sanctuary to pray before every night and morning, and even in the day'.[126] At the beginning of the twentieth century accounts of Irish devotional practice came to similar contradictory conclusions as Mayhew. 'Catholicism in London may be regarded as a single force, and as such stands out as one of the greatest of the religious influences', yet it seemed in the process of losing more believers than gaining converts.[127] An article on the London Irish claimed that the Catholic Church had a greater 'hold' on women than men while one priest claimed that he and his colleagues 'retain little real hold upon London Irishmen of the third generation, though they feel sure of the first and second'.[128] This same complex dichotomy also applies to the post-war era.[129]

An examination of Anglo-Jewry demonstrates a constant process of assimilation of the differing flows that have entered London over the centuries, followed by a devotional reinvigoration when a new stream arrives while, by the end of the twentieth century, Jewishness had moved from a religious into an increasingly secular identity as much as a religious practice for many people. Some assimilation into majority society either through marriage or conversion or both took place rapidly and had involved the different groups of Jews which migrated to London from the eighteenth century.[130] Religious attendance rates in the middle of the nineteenth century, something of an interregnum in terms of a reinvigoration of the Jewish community, may have stood at about 10 per cent nationally and perhaps slightly higher in London.[131] Mayhew claimed that the eight synagogues he identified 'are not well attended, the congregations being smaller than those in the Church of England'. For the 'street-Jews, religion is little known among them, or little cared for'.[132] The number of seat holders in synagogues increased during the late nineteenth century throughout the capital, both in the established places of worship and as a result of the construction of new ones, the former partly because of the social mobility of already resident Jews.[133] When Beatrice Potter examined the religious activity of the East European newcomers she identified the 'religious-minded' and the 'devout', confirming Mudie-Smith's statistics. Such individuals 'early in the morning, or late at night . . . meet to recite the morning and evening prayers, or to decipher the sacred book of the Talmud'. However, she also described 'some 20,000 to 30,000 Jews – men, women, and children – too poor or too indifferent to attend regularly a place of worship'.[134] Perhaps as many as half of immigrant Jews belonged to some sort of *hebroth*, although this does not mean that they attended regular services as many Jews even worked on the Sabbath.[135]

The offspring of the East European immigrants had an even more ambivalent attitude towards their religion, even though many of them benefited from Jewish institutions, especially schools. The future Leeds University maths professor Selig Brodetsky attended the Jews Free School before the First World War. 'This was a very important institution' maintained by Jewish philanthropy and situated in the East End at this time:

> One of the attractions of the school was that every pupil was given a suit of clothes and a pair of boots each year. It was important help for families like ours, struggling with poverty. The school gave a reasonable amount of Jewish education, far more than most children get today. But orthodox Jews found it inadequate and supplemented it.
>
> We were sent to the Brick Lane Talmud Torah, the most important orthodox Cheder in London, run by the orthodox Machsike Synagogue next door.[136]

Both the Jews Free School and religious education continued into the interwar years and beyond with the former moving its location as a result of suburbanization. Although synagogue attendance and marriage increased, the explanation for this lies in the natural growth of the Jewish population which had arrived before the First World War, rather than because of increased devotion of the second generation, whose observance declined, despite the continued celebration of key days and rituals, such as bar mitzvah.[137] One account of the East End from 1931 claimed that 'the younger generation appears to gently but decidedly be breaking away. They marry outside their faith, they eat what they will, they observe Shabos or not, as they fancy; and if they attend the synagogue at all they attend it perfunctorily, once a year, at Yom Kippur.'[138]

Although London Jews reached their numerical peak in the early post-war years, by the early 1960s the 'basic fact of religious life in Anglo-Jewry is that the great bulk of the community has only the slightest concern with Judaism' even though the 'casual observer might not think such is the case' because of the apparent strength of institutional religion as seen through buildings and fund raising.[139] Twenty years later the same still seemed to apply. While the vast majority of Jews in the London Borough of Redbridge claimed membership and affiliation of a synagogue, only about 10 per cent of the Jews here went to services regularly. This was close to the figure for church attendance for outer London although far more people attended on religious festivals, especially Yom Kippur, as well as during weddings and bar mitzvahs, while others claimed to follow some religious festivals at home. By this time, attendance of religious schools had also declined.[140] These trends continued into the twenty-first century by which time some of those who described themselves as Jewish never attended synagogue and essentially held on to this concept in a secular way of attending events such as Jewish book week.[141] Despite the apparent decline in observance, we should remember that regular synagogue attendance remained the preserve of a minority throughout the history of Jewish settlement in London and despite the increasing number of religious buildings. At the same time, we should not forget that the ultra-orthodox Hasidic Jews, based around Stamford Hill and Clapton, whose numbers have increased, lead devout lives in which religion remains central to their entire existence, whether through social activities, schooling or food.[142]

In fact, keeping kosher offers one way of measuring Jewish observance because in traditional Judaism food 'does not occupy a segment of the observant Jew's daily or weekly routine but provides the framework in which, in theory, he or she lives all of his or her life'.[143] However, the extent to which Jewish migrants and their descendants ate kosher rather than Jewish food, which they had picked up in their continental environment, remains open to question, despite the organizations that had emerged to police the implementation of kashrut.[144] A 1911 *Jewish Chronicle* article on East End Jewish restaurants claimed that 'ninety per cent of these establishments are unworthy of the name of restaurant or, indeed, of kosher'.[145] Keeping kosher may have reached its peak in the early post-Second World War years. While those attending Jewish schools could eat the correct meals, the Kosher School Meals Service came into existence in 1953 to provide food for those children attending state schools and by 1956 it provided 1,500 meals daily in Golders Green, Edgware, Finchley and Hendon. The service continued into the 1960s but appears to have ceased in 1972 due to a decline in kashrut observance and a shift in government policy requiring parents to pay for meals at school. Just as the Kosher School Meals Service declined, and probably reflecting the ageing of the Jewish community, the Hospital Kosher Meals Service came into existence in 1968. By 1988 this facility provided approximately 17,000 dishes per month in 250 different hospitals in greater London. But the post-war period witnessed a gradual decline in kosher retail outlets. On a national scale the number of kosher butchers declined from 198 in 1956 to 73 in 1979 and just 26 by 2005. In the 1980s just six kosher grocers and delicatessens existed in London.[146]

It proves difficult to generalize about the practice of Islam in London in view of the hundreds of thousands of adherents of this religion in the British capital, the different forms of beliefs, the geographic origins and the range of generations. Immigrants from Bangladesh and Pakistan certainly made much effort to adhere to their beliefs. During the 1960s about 80 per cent of Pakistanis in London fasted during the month of Ramadan, although attendance at mosques remained limited outside holy days.[147] Haji Shirajul Islam, born in 1912 in what would become Bangladesh and settling in the East End of London after which he opened restaurants in several parts of London, recalled that in 1971 he 'went back' to his 'religious practice. I never stopped being a Muslim, but my business used to distract me from practising. Then I started to pray five times again.' He also made a pilgrimage to Mecca and 'built an orphanage near Maulvi Bazar'. He 'never drank alcohol, and I wouldn't even have it in my restaurants'.[148] Most members of a group of twenty Bangladeshis between the ages of fifty-eight and seventy-two living in Camden in the middle of the 1990s prayed five times a day 'as prescribed by Islamic teaching' and the majority of the men attended the local mosque. Many went to daily prayers and nearly all participated in Friday service, while the women practised their religion at home. Islam played a central role for the entire group.[149] More broadly, many Muslim homes became Islamized, especially once women joined their husbands from South Asia during the 1960s and 1970s meaning, for example, the closing of curtains to protect women from the 'external gaze', a front door inscribed with Arabic calligraphy, the removal of shoes and the use of Islamic art to decorate walls. Muslim homes also act as the site of Muslim ritual, especially praying five times per day.[150] Perhaps the most significant indication of the presence of Islam consists of the celebration of religious festivals, especially the end of Ramadan, which has become a public spectacle.[151] One of the main ways of attempting to keep the second and subsequent generations in the Islamic fold has been through religious education and the opening up of a network of schools similar to that established by Jews, Roman Catholics and numerous other migrant religions in London.[152]

MIGRANT RELIGIOUS SPACE AND THE EVOLUTION OF LONDON

Religious diversity has characterized the evolution of London since the Reformation as Protestant refugees from the continent moved to the British capital to escape persecution and established their own churches, followed from the seventeenth century by the first of many streams of Jews who constructed their own sacred spaces. The Irish and other Europeans did the same from the nineteenth century while the period since the end of the Second World War has seen the emergence of numerous mosques, some of them with origins in the earlier twentieth century. The place of worship usually forms part of a wider welfare and educational network which attempts to reconnect with believers from the homeland.

Many of the places of worship evolve organically as the examples of the late nineteenth-century East End synagogues or the early post-war mosques and gurdwaras indicate. These emerged because groups of people wished to continue the religious practice of the place from which they had originated. Over time, as the communities grew and the migrants experienced social mobility and increasing wealth, more permanent places of worship in specially designated buildings have emerged to replace the makeshift places of devotion. However, some of the most spectacular buildings, including the London Central Mosque[153], have relied on outside help just as the Roman Catholic churches constructed in nineteenth-century London liaised with Rome. The development of purpose-built places of worship suggests the making of a statement by the world's great religions whose believers have settled in London. The British capital appears a place where different religions vie for believers and, while some missionary work has certainly occurred, religious tension has remained largely absent from London as the different religious buildings which have emerged have essentially existed side by side, as the example of the East End would indicate.[154]

In some cases, places of worship have moved from one community to another as believers have assimilated into wider society. A building on the corner of Brick Lane and Fournier Street in Spitalfields provides an excellent example of this process. It first functioned as the Huguenot La Neuve Église in

1743. By the end of the nineteenth century it became the Machzike Hadath, the Spitalfields Great Synagogue. Bangladeshi migrants purchased it in 1976 and transformed it into the Jamme Masjid, erecting a minaret in 2009.[155] The history of this building points to assimilation, suburbanization and the decline of devotion, as well as the migration history of the East End.

However, the statistics used in this chapter have suggested that only a minority of migrants have ever participated in religious services, a statement that applies to all faiths including Protestantism. While religious practice may appear to have declined, it started from a fairly low base as contemporary commentators always asserted. On the other hand, some people have chosen to practise their faith as individuals in their own home, as the example of Jews and Muslims indicates.

We need to return to the issue of the uniqueness of London. A diversification of worship characterizes cities throughout Britain and the whole of Western Europe after 1945 in particular. Groups such as the Federation of Synagogues or the United Synagogue operated as national bodies concerned with Jews throughout Britain, even though most of this community lived in London. These bodies had their headquarters in London. Some religions have counted more believers outside London than within it, including Catholicism and Islam, although Greek Orthodoxism remains firmly focused upon the metropolis. The uniqueness of London once again lies in the level of diversity, as the above survey has indicated, as well as longevity, dating back to the Reformation. Few if any other cities in either Britain or anywhere else in the world could match London from this point of view.

On the other hand it would prove difficult to describe London as a leading religious capital. It has not played the same global role as it has in the exportation of political power through the British Empire or as the global headquarters of capitalism and finance. These two facts ensure that London has never had any particular spirituality connected with it. In fact, this concept seems the very antithesis to life in the world's capital. No major world religion has ever emerged from London and the city does not act as the headquarters of any global belief, even Anglicanism (despite St Paul's Cathedral and Westminster Abbey), which is centred on Canterbury. In religious terms London has received and hosted beliefs that have originated from further east, including virtually all forms of Christianity. Migrants have created their own spaces either organically or with outside help. For many settlers, even into the nineteenth and twentieth centuries and beyond, religion has formed the key aspect of their identity, maintaining their connection with the homeland. This process has characterized modern migration throughout the world because in many, if not most, cases religious belief has more of a pull than national identity. There seems no reason to dispute the assertion that, as in the case of the United States during the nineteenth century, the 'first concern of the immigrants ... was with their churches',[156] a statement which would apply to London and which would extend to synagogues, mandirs, mosques and gurdwaras, whatever the level of attendance. As we have seen, whether or not migrants participate in services, their religions have formed the central marker of their identity, and the building and practice of new religions act as a key symbol of the role of London as a world city, the central indicator of the durability and breadth of its diversity.

9

THE RESTAURANT

But what is this? – this most delectable odour which assails us? – this bubbling, frizzling sound that meets our ears? That makes the nostrils of Judah distend, the eyes of Israel dilate with joy, while the lips water with expectation? – Fried fish. A fish-shop throws its cheerful glare into the chilly night. We will halt for a moment and inspect its interior – one of many of a similar character which abound in the neighbourhood.

The first thing which arrests our attention, after having feasted our eyes upon the rows of crisp brown fish that decorate the window, is the large fire within, which has a fiercely jolly look, like the face of a giant who has taken to drinking; but which comforts us nevertheless, till we forget this raw December, which encompasses us about. The shop is tenanted by a family of five – a mother, her three daughters and an only son, the heir to the house of Manasseh.[1]

Whether you choose fried sliced chicken with mushrooms, bamboo shoots and water chestnuts for 2s. and 2d., or fried cuttlefish with mixed vegetables for 3s. 6d. at the Shanghai in Greek Street, or boiled noodles with shredded chicken and vegetables for 4s. 0d. at Ley On's in Wardour Street (both in Soho) it is essential to order a portion of rice, plain boiled, or fried as well.[2]

Luigi Azario was born in 1855 at Pettinengo, near Biella – the Manchester of Italy – and started his catering career at the Grand Hotel Nice, under Mr César Ritz, afterwards taking service at the Grand Hotel Du Parc at

Vichy. He arrived in London in 1877, and was employed at the Café Monico when it was first opened. Afterwards he established a modest restaurant of his own in High Holborn, and in 1898 built the Florence, which has since become one of the best-known restaurants of the West End, specially noted, perhaps, for the excellence and moderate price of its *table d'hôte* dinners and suppers, served in the Victoria Saloon, a magnificent apartment which will comfortably fit 200 guests.[3]

While the evolution of modern London remains inconceivable without the role of migrants, they may have had a more profound impact upon eating out than any other aspect of the history of the city. In the first place they have opened and staffed some of the most famous restaurants in the world. But this only tells one side of the story because settlers from Europe and beyond have, at the other end of the scale, also opened up establishments which serve up the dishes that characterize mass consumption, from the first fish and chip shops in the East End to the Chinese and Indian restaurants of the post-war period and the vast range of foreign food establishments which exist in the global capital of the twenty-first century. While, on the one hand, these restaurants cater for the ethnic majority, which increasingly became a vanishing concept, many migrants have also opened up restaurants for their countrymen as such establishments form a key part of local ethnic economies. The constant supply of staff from the continent and the food they have brought with them have profoundly changed the eating patterns of Londoners over the last two hundred years. While, on the one hand, the West End may have acted as home to some of the world's leading restaurants since the Victorian period, fish and chips has a similar chronology, meaning that migrants have impacted the eating habits of all sections of the population in both social and geographical terms, even though Soho in particular may have acted as a funnel through which culinary cosmopolitanism initially arrived in London. On the other hand the Jewish East End gave birth to fish and chips.

By the beginning of the twentieth century there 'were about a dozen restaurants in London which could most appropriately be called Grand Restaurants' where 'the cream of London society settled down nightly to enjoy themselves'.[4] In fact, the concept of the restaurant lay in the origins of the word as a French 'restorative broth', which only became 'a space for urban sociability' at the end of the eighteenth century. By the 1820s Parisian restaurants had emerged into the familiar patterns of today, spreading gradually beyond Paris to other French regions and other countries and cities, including London, during the Victorian period, aided by both French and other continental immigrants.[5] Restaurants accompanied the 'rise of gastronomy' caused by the expansion of the middle classes in London during the nineteenth century, a development reflected elsewhere in Britain, Europe and the United States. This not only led to an increase in the number of restaurants during the late Victorian years, but also hotels, where dining became an important activity. This accompanied the 'diffusion of French cuisine', in which French chefs played a large role.[6] In fact, the global nature of this development, with London acting as a key centre, explains the fact that not only waiters but also other hotel and restaurant staff consisted of migrants.

These, however, formed the tip of the iceberg of eating out in London, which had a long history and which encompassed a whole variety of other establishments including the purveyors of street food and drink, including whelks, baked potatoes, ham sandwiches, slices of pineapple and ice cream identified by Henry Mayhew,[7] and other equally modest establishments. By 1910 the number of 'dining rooms, refreshment rooms and restaurants' in London stood at just under 2,000.[8] The range of places to eat out would have attracted the entire population of the world city.

London had already become something of a culinary cosmopolis during the seventeenth century, indicated most obviously by the opening of Europe's first coffee house during the 1650s through the efforts of Pasqua Rosee, an ethnic Armenian from Smyrna. By 1663 eighty-two such establishments existed in the City of London, increasing to 551 by 1739, outnumbered, however, by the 8,000 gin palaces. By 1815 the coffee bubble had burst as the figure declined to twelve coffee houses.[9] They came back to life in the post-war period, although Mayhew identified 'coffee stall keepers' during the 1850s.[10]

We can best understand the influence of migrants on London's eating establishments by focusing upon three themes. First, the foreigners who have played a central role in the evolution of the restaurant trade since the nineteenth century, because they have provided so much of the staffing from owners through to chefs, waiters and even cleaners. While these types of restaurants may have introduced French haute cuisine into London, migrants also brought with them a wide variety of other products, which often became assimilated into the British mainstream and attracted the label of British – most obviously

Jewish fried fish, which joined together with potatoes to become fish and chips, and, more recently, curry. Indian restaurants (usually run by Bangladeshis) which sold curry marketed themselves as exotic and foreign from the end of the nineteenth century, as did owners of a series of establishments that sold other cuisines, which became a feature of life in the West End, more especially Soho, by the early twentieth century. These restaurants differ from those establishments catering for members of migrant communities, opened up by people with the same origins, which have tended to serve food closer to products eaten in the homeland than those restaurants established for the wider London population, although some overlap exists.

EUROPEAN MIGRANTS AND THE EVOLUTION OF
EATING OUT IN LONDON

Migrants established two of the most famous dining houses in Britain before 1914. First, the Café Royal in Regent Street, originally opened by Daniel de Nicols, a French wine merchant, who moved to England in 1862.[11] Similarly, César Ritz founded the hotel which bears his name in 1906. Ritz offers an example of the international nature of caterers before 1914. Born in Niederwald in 1850, the thirteenth son of a Swiss shepherd, he began his career as a waiter in Brieg in the 1860s, after which he moved to Paris where he took management positions in a series of hotels. By the 1880s he owned his own hotel and restaurant. He moved to London in 1889 where he became manager of the recently opened Savoy and imported a predominantly continental staff, above all the chef Auguste Escoffier. He then brought together a Ritz Hotel syndicate in 1896 with international financial backing, which led to the opening of the Paris Ritz in 1898, followed by the London version in 1906.[12]

Quite a different type of establishment also came into existence as a result of immigration, this time as part of the Lyons group. This firm originated in the business dealings of Samuel and Henry Gluckstein, German Jews who moved to London in 1841 and established their name as a tobacco firm. Out of this emerged J. Lyons in 1894, with the name originating from another descendant of Jewish immigrants, Joseph Lyons, born in Southwark in 1847. Catering always played a large role in the activities of Lyons, although its business dealings encompassed a broad sweep of food provision by the middle of the twentieth century.[13] The catering outlets appealed to a wide range of classes.

At the top, the Trocadero restaurant opened in Piccadilly in 1896.[14] Simultaneously, the firm also established teashops appealing 'to ladies shopping, to clerks who would return home for a hot evening meal' having had a light lunch in a teashop, and 'above all, at the turn of the century and after the First World War, to the growing army of London typists. Respectability, quality, cheapness, speed and cleanliness became the Lyons watchwords.' The year 1909 saw the opening of the first corner house,[15] a development which would become a mass phenomenon during the interwar years.[16] Clearly, Lyons played an important role in the spread of eating out from the end of the nineteenth century for both the working and lower middle classes as dozens of teashops had opened in London by 1939.[17]

Lyons tended to rely on native-born female staff,[18] unlike the higher-class establishments which had evolved in London during the nineteenth century and acted as a magnet for an army of continental caterers, including cooks.[19] Those who gained celebrity status included Charles Elmé Francatelli, born in 1805 in London 'of Italian extraction', educated in France and serving as chef to Queen Victoria in 1841–2.[20] Alexis Soyer, born in France in 1810, was initially employed in his homeland, before moving to London in 1831. As well as working in several clubs, before modern hotels and restaurants had fully developed, he published a series of volumes, aimed at all classes of British society.[21] At the start of the twentieth century Auguste Escoffier became the most famous celebrity chef in London. Born in the Côte d'Azur in 1846, he moved to the metropolis in 1887 to work in the Savoy, by which time he had reached the height of his career. He followed César Ritz to the Carlton Hotel. While in London, he published his monumental *Guide Culinaire.*[22]

Francatelli, Soyer and Escoffier form the celebrity tip of an iceberg of foreign chefs before 1945, originating especially in France, Switzerland, Germany and Italy, whose total numbers on a national scale had reached 2,447 by 1901, making this one of the most important occupations for foreigners.[23] A few portraits help to bring these statistics to life. In 1911 Rudolph von Görög of the New Gallery Restaurant in Regent Street won the Grand Prix at the Culinary Exhibition in Paris. Born in Budapest in 1878, he initially worked in the Grand Hotel in his native city, before moving to Paris and then to the Carlton in London, where he worked under Escoffier.[24] Antoine Moisy, meanwhile, 'chef de cuisine at the Kensington Palace Mansions' in 1904, was born in Alsace-Lorraine and had worked in Paris, before serving as a cook to an officers' mess in the French army regiment he joined. Following a spell in Germany, he obtained a job in Birmingham, after which he took up appointments in Newcastle, Blackpool, Aldershot and Dover. He then returned to Germany before moving to his post in Kensington Palace Mansions.[25] Another Frenchman, Angel Cabrol, 'in charge of the high-class "confiserie" of Lyons Corner House in Coventry Street' in London, had made his way to this position via a series of appointments in France, Spain, Portugal and London.[26] While these three individuals did not obtain celebrity status, they provide examples of highly successful chefs, who migrated in search of the best possible position, which London establishments offered. A series of organizations emerged from the beginning of the twentieth century to represent the interests of the hidden army of continental cooks, including the Society of German Chefs,[27] the Italian Club of Culinary Art,[28] the Italian Culinary Society[29] and the Société Culinaire Française de Londres.[30]

Migrants also found employment as managers of hotels and restaurants. Many of these had made their way up from waiters, a profession in which continental Europeans have played a central role since the first London restaurants opened. Before 1945, German, Swiss, French and Italian nationals predominated. Waiting offered an occupational path, in which moving from one European location to another formed part of an apprenticeship system, with the hope of eventually securing a permanent position as a maître d'hôtel.

In 1911 about 10 per cent of waiters and waitresses in restaurant work in London were German.[31] By the early 1930s about 122,000 people found employment in the hotel and catering trade in the capital. Although they included Britons, 'foreign staff are still demanded by hotels and restaurants of the most expensive type, where, in consequence, they tend to congregate, accounting in these cases for perhaps 90 per cent of the kitchen staff and 70 per cent of the waiting staff'. This situation arose not 'due to race prejudice, but rather to the natural preference of a person in a position of responsibility to have around him assistants of the sort with whom he can most easily work, since it is on him that the blame for any contretemps will first fall'.[32]

Migrants also worked harder for longer hours. Before 1914 German waiters laboured up to fifteen hours per day. In contrast to Englishmen, who demanded a fixed wage, foreigners relied upon tips, from which they could make £2 per week. Germans had also had formal training, which accounted for their 'neatness and civility'. Those who intended to return home would accept lower wages to obtain experience, although others remained and rose to become hotel and restaurant managers and went on to employ other foreigners in turn,[33] a practice, which, as we have seen, continued into the 1930s. Waiters who lived in Soho displayed a preparedness to 'perform the lowest duties at the lowest wage', with a view to a 'rise in their profession'.[34]

Spending time abroad seems to have formed part of a type of apprenticeship system so that owners of hotels in Germany and Switzerland sent their sons 'to foreign countries to pick up as many languages as possible and to learn their profession from the very lowest rungs of the social ladder', with the aim of eventually becoming 'hotel proprietors and responsible persons'.[35] Charles Meschini, whose father owned the Hôtel du Lac in Switzerland, worked in London, Zurich, Lucerne and Genoa, but then took more long-term positions in London.[36]

Most foreign waiters in London did not, however, come from such privileged backgrounds. Obituaries and autobiographies of those who progressed to senior positions indicate this, although for each of these individuals we probably need to count dozens of others who remained junior waiters, or simply held positions at lesser-known establishments. Paolo Contarini, born to a shoemaker in Ravenna in 1894, became a waiter at a local hotel where he undertook a range of tasks and learnt French, English and German. At thirteen he moved to Genoa, after his father had a stroke, and then to Santa Margherita on the Italian Riviera, where his command of languages increased. He then worked in France and moved to employment in a small Soho restaurant, eventually establishing himself at the Savoy after 1945.[37] Meanwhile, Jules Ribstein actually seems to have made his way to London as a refugee following the Franco-Prussian War.[38]

The presence of large numbers of foreign waiters in London led to the establishment of societies which looked after their interests, often branches of bodies with headquarters on the continent. As early as 1869 a German Waiters Club existed in London.[39] Three decades later, the London and Provincial Hotel Employees Society, based in Tottenham Court Road, acted as an employment agency and provided shelter to its members.[40] One of the largest bodies was the Ganymede Friendly Society for Hotel and Restaurant Employees, a branch of an international association established in 1878, with headquarters in central London. It may have counted 10,000 members in 1907.[41] Other Edwardian bodies included the International Hotel Employees Society and the

London Hotel and Restaurant Employees Society.[42] These groups were aimed primarily at Germans. Similarly, the Caterers Employees Union had its headquarters in Hamburg.[43] This body devoted considerable attention to the working conditions of those involved in the catering trade.[44] At least two Swiss organizations existed in London before 1914. The Geneva Association, established in 1877, had 140 branches by 1911. One of the largest was in London, with a membership of 2,029. Other branches served Ramsgate and Margate, Manchester, Bradford, Bournemouth and Liverpool.[45] The Union Helvetica, an international body with over 2,000 members, opened in London in 1889 and by 1900 counted 400 Swiss members.[46]

This grouping appears to have survived the First World War, unlike the German organizations and the Geneva Association, which faced closure as a result of the Germanophobia that arose during the conflict.[47] But the Geneva Association opened again during the late 1920s.[48] Although the closure of German waiters' groupings happened as a direct result of the First World War, this development had roots in nationalistic and xenophobic resentment at the dominance of foreigners in the restaurant trade, which began to surface before 1914. This led to the formation of the Loyal British Waiters Society in 1910 whose aims included 'the displacement of the foreigner and re-instating the Britisher'.[49] The Germanophobia of the First World War meant that the wish of the Loyal British Waiters Society came true as German waiters became symbols of the paranoid xenophobia of the war, meaning that they nearly all lost their jobs and usually faced internment.[50] But the German waiter made a reappearance during the 1920s, joined by other Europeans, particularly Italians, concentrated especially upon Soho, where they, in turn, would face dismissal, internment and deportation following Mussolini's declaration of war on Britain in June 1940.[51]

The importance of European staff in London restaurants continued after 1945. The Ritz appointed its first chef from the British Isles, Michael Quinn, as late as the 1980s.[52] Despite Quinn, staff with origins on the continent continued to play an important role in many of the higher-class London hotels and restaurants. In 1946 the Association Culinaire Française had 400 members and its staff bureau aimed at 'hotels and restaurants who require a chef, cook or assistant'.[53] Many of those employed in senior positions had worked on the London scene for decades and retired in the first post-war decades. For instance, A. Avignon, who had served as chef de cuisine in the Ritz from 1928, ceased working in 1955, replaced by another Frenchman, Edouard Peray, who had previously worked in several British establishments including the Midland Hotel in Belfast and Brown's in London.[54] Similarly, in 1957 Jack Pedersen, a Dane who had moved to London in 1912 and had worked in several leading British hotels and restaurants, beginning in the kitchens of the Carlton Hotel under Escoffier, retired as general manager of Scott's Restaurant in Piccadilly.[55] As late as 1975 Eugène Kaufeler, who had moved from Switzerland to the Dorchester in 1936, held the position of head chef at the hotel, which he had acquired in 1950.[56]

A new group of Europeans, Greek Cypriots, also became significant in London catering from the interwar years. The majority of the 6,000 to 8,000 members of this community who lived in London in 1938 'work in hotels and restaurants', almost exclusively 'in the West End at such places as the Savoy, Berkeley, Grosvenor House, Piccadilly, Chez Quaglino, Park Lane, Monaco etc. Indeed, it is difficult to find a hotel or restaurant in the West End where no Cypriots are employed as waiters, commis-waiters, or kitchen hands.'[57] This situation continued into the post-war period. In 1952 catering accounted for 49 per cent of Cypriot male employment in London, although this figure had decreased to 30.5 per cent by 1958. With a high propensity for self-employment, Greek Cypriots opened their own catering establishments, especially in the fish and chip trade, as well as a range of other areas, without any indication of the ethnicity of the owner.[58] One Cypriot who moved to Kentish Town in 1948 at the age of sixteen worked in a restaurant as a waiter, married a Cypriot, opened up a café in North London, and subsequently owned three restaurants.[59] Cypriots, both Turkish and Greek, became involved in the running of Wimpy bars, part of a franchise system which allowed people to own such outlets.[60]

Like Cypriots, Italians continued to play a role in the post-war catering scene in London by opening establishments which did not overtly market their national origins, including coffee and sandwich bars, building upon businesses which this group had run during the interwar years serving food, milk and tea, imitating the Lyons outlets. By 1960 about 200 coffee bars existed in the West End. Their number would subsequently decline because they provided small profit margins which meant that some owners turned to cafés and trattorias. The invention of the espresso machine in 1946 had helped the initial emergence of the coffee bar.[61] Many Italians opened central London sandwich bars aimed at office workers. For instance, J. Cacchioli bought a shop in Hanover Square for £5,000, spent a further £7,000 converting it and opened it as the Queen's Soup and Sandwich Bar in July 1960. 'From seven in the morning until seven at night customers can choose from the six soups and 150 types of sandwiches served there.'[62] Higher up on the social scale, one of the most famous Italian restaurateurs in twentieth-century London, Mario Gallati, who worked in a variety of high-class West End establishments after he moved to the British capital in the Edwardian era, reopened the Caprice in Arlington Street in Green Park, a dining establishment for London's cosmopolitan high society.[63]

Unrestricted European Union migration and a further expansion of high-class and chain restaurants in London, as well as an increase in the number of meals eaten outside the home,[64] meant that the patterns established during the Victorian era involving the recruitment of continental employees to work in hotels and restaurants continued into the twenty-first century. This led one celebrity chef to complain that 'Lots of people from eastern Europe and elsewhere come here and work in restaurants without having the level of English or the skills they should have.'[65] By 2017 European Union nationals may have made up as much as 34 per cent of employees in hotels and 26 per cent in restaurants in London.[66] By this time about '10 per cent of all employed migrants are working in hotels and restaurants compared with only 3 per cent of UK-born Londoners; and an astonishing 60 per cent of all workers in London's hotels and restaurants are migrants',[67] making London an extreme case of catering dependence on migrants even though this forms part of a global pattern.[68]

One type of eating out in which migrants have made a deep impact has been fish and chips. Jewish fried fish eaten and sold by East End Jews during the early nineteenth century united with chips by the end of the Victorian era. The National Federation of Fish Fryers carried out a survey in the 1960s, which concluded that the first fish and chip shop was the Jewish Joseph Malins, which opened in Old Ford Road in 1860.[69] Jews continued to sell this food into the twentieth century. *Kelly's Post Office London Directory* from 1923 lists 776 individuals who owned fried fish shops. A total of 148 of these have either obviously Jewish names, or at least central European names. Those in the former category include eighteen Cohens, eleven Isaacs and eleven Levys. Although many of these remain concentrated in East London as a whole, rather than the inner East End (E1), some of them had premises in other parts of London. Eight of the eighteen Cohens lay in the core East End, together with others in Stratford, Great Western Road (W9) and Pentonville Road (N1). Those owned by individuals called Levy included properties in New Cross Road and Cartwright Gardens (WC1), while Isaac included only three properties in the East End heartland. Overall, the 148 Jewish-sounding fish-and-chip shops in London represented over 19 per cent of the total. The list in *Kelly's* also contains a small number of shops owned by people with Italian names.[70] The Jewish fish and chip shop owners included the father and uncles of Jessica Gould. Her grandparents, all from Russia, initially worked in the garment industry. While the shop of her father failed, those of her uncles succeeded, 'cause they were in the right spots' in the West End. The locations of shops owned by her family included Commercial Road, Hammersmith and Soho.[71]

Jews would continue in the London fish and chip trade into the post-war period, but by this time new ethnic groups also played a role. *Kelly's Directories* outline the importance of Greek Cypriots in particular. In 1954 we can identify 16 Greek names amongst the fried fish shops listed, together with 23 Italians out of a total of around 800. At this stage Jews remained important. Nevertheless, because not all owners name their shops after themselves and do not always give them a name suggesting their place of origin, these figures are only the lowest possible estimate of migrant influence.[72] By 1975, when the number of London fried fish shops remained similar, at least 150 recognizably Greek Cypriot-owned businesses existed in the capital, although this again does not reflect the true picture. If we add to this those names of Turkish Cypriot, Chinese, Italian and other foreign origins, then it seems clear that migrants had come to play a major role in the fried fish trade by this time,[73] a process which would continue as increasing diversification occurred in subsequent decades.[74]

FOREIGN FOOD FOR LONDONERS

Migrants have therefore played a central role in the evolution of eating out in establishments which seem to sell British food, even though, in the case of both French haute cuisine and fried fish, a process of assimilation into the mainstream took place during the course of the Victorian and Edwardian eras. Migrants have, however, also sold overtly foreign products to Londoners, a process that began in the late nineteenth century, especially, but not exclusively, in Soho, and which spread to the rest of London and the country as a whole, in the post-war years.

Continental restaurants which advertised themselves as such began to emerge during the late nineteenth century. The first 'Franco-Italian Restaurants' drew most of their clientele from French immigrants lodging around Soho, 'but their novel cuisines and modest charges soon appealed to "Bohemian" English artists, actors and authors, though not until somewhat later to the great and not so good of the *"fin de siècle"*'. They included Pinoli's, Monico's, Romano's, Oddedino's, Frascati's, Kettner's and the Criterion.[75] The earliest foreign restaurants which attracted an English clientele included Rouget's in Carlisle Street in Leicester Square, which 'gives English and French dishes capitally done'.[76] The Maison Dorée in Glasshouse Street, meanwhile, whose 'chef is an importation from the Parisian Maison Dorée', seemed to have served a mixture of dishes which would merit the description of French and English.[77]

By the beginning of the twentieth century, London food critics recognized the existence of restaurants according to nationality. One of the most famous eating out guides of this period, by Nathaniel Newnham Davis, categorized the 122 restaurants mentioned in his book. These included seven 'small French' restaurants, distinguished from eleven described as serving 'Haute Cuisine Française', and listed some of the most famous in the capital, such as the Cecil and the Savoy, which essentially served international French food aimed at the highest classes of society. Davis also listed thirteen Italian restaurants and four which served German food. The major concentration of small French and Italian London eateries before 1914 was in Soho.[78] One of these was Restaurant au Bienvenu, in Greek Street, described in the *Caterer* as 'A Soho Snail Restaurant', although snails simply represented 'the great speciality of the establishment'.[79] Davis offered a description of Pagani's, in Great Portland Street, slightly to the north of Soho, which he described as 'À la carte Italian', although what he actually ate there seems to have little connection with any concept of Italian food, including 'Bortsch soup . . . the customary Sunday soup at Pagani's'.[80]

Also in central London lay Appenrodt's, a patisserie which supplied both Germans and other Londoners.[81] A similar West End establishment to Appendrodt's was Rumpelmayer's, 'a byword for recherché pastry and chic confectionery', which opened a London branch to follow the 'half a dozen' which existed on the continent.[82] Meanwhile, an Austro-Hungarian restaurant opened in Regent Street in 1910 serving a range of recognizably central European dishes including goulash, 'soup with liver dumplings', 'carp with paprika' and 'Viennese veal scollops'. This establishment had the same ownership as the Vienna Café in Oxford Street, which offered coffee, confectionery, pastries and food.[83]

All of these Victorian and Edwardian continental eateries remained within central London, suggesting that the only people who would have used them were the international and, especially, 'artistic' bourgeoisie. The Viennese coffee shops, which may have attracted a slightly broader clientele than restaurants such as Pagani's, sold a distinctively central European product. But it proves difficult to identify a specifically Italian cuisine in the restaurants described by Davis, certainly not of the type which would emerge after 1945. The menu at Pagani's essentially consisted of continental haute cuisine, indicated, above all, by the fact that this restaurant, like other high-class establishments in central London, carried French menus. The Italian nature of these restaurants comes from ownership rather than food. The categorizations produced by Davis clearly used no scientific method. The dominance of French-inspired haute cuisine in central London and elsewhere before 1914[84] meant that all other methods of cooking had to assimilate into the descriptions it offered. At this stage in the history of Italian food in London, a significant space had not yet opened up for a distinct product appealing to a wide cross section of British society.

Some changes took place during the interwar years, although the above assertions still remain largely true. Italian caterers did not generally sell a distinct cuisine. New establishments included the Taverna Medicea, opened in Soho by B. Calderoni and Francesco Barbieri in 1928 with Italian décor.[85] Meanwhile, 'Mr L. Donzelli and Mr Maccagno' established Luigi's grill in Jermyn Street in 1936. 'Lunches and dinners will be featured, and all service will be à *la carte*.'[86] One of the most famous interwar Italian restaurants, Romano's, which opened before 1914, simply served haute cuisine.[87]

But establishments which sold distinct national cuisines did increase during the interwar years. The 'higher class' Tuscan Restaurant, which began in Shaftesbury Avenue in 1921, imported Florentine chefs and printed a menu partly in Italian and French, which included 'Antipasto', 'Ravioli al Brodo' and 'Mandorino al Fiorentina'. By 1925 this had become part of a chain owned by the Mecca Café Company featuring an English menu with no trace of Italian influence, other than, perhaps, macaroni cheese.[88] Another 'genuine Italian',

Gennaro, opened in New Compton Street serving dishes which would become part of the mainstream Italian menu after 1945, including macaroni, 'prosciutto Italiano', minestrone, ravioli, 'fritto misto' and various risottos.[89]

A variety of other international restaurants also emerged in interwar London. One guide to eating out from 1924 by Elizabeth Montizambert gave a list of nineteen such establishments, including five French, five Italian, two Spanish, one Greek, one Jewish, one Armenian, one Russian, one Chinese and two Indian.[90] Similarly, Thomas Burke claimed that 'the field of choice is bewildering' in central London. Interestingly, he puts this down to 'the coming of petrol transport', which meant that 'central London receives everyday not only its constant people, but a large section of the seven Home Counties'.[91] Writing thirteen years after Montizambert, he listed considerably more foreign restaurants than she did, including five Spanish, three German, one Japanese, six Indian, three Hungarian and one Swedish, together with Italian, 'French or mainly French', 'Old English' and Chinese.[92]

Many of the European restaurants which became established during the interwar years therefore served food that moved away from French haute cuisine. A handful of Spanish restaurants fit into this description. The Espagnol in Dean Street seems to have targeted primarily the small Spanish community in London, with a menu in Spanish, including Jerez kidneys, Cuban rice and omelette with capsicum.[93] The Spanish Restaurant in Swallow Street, near Piccadilly, became one of the most famous eating establishments in interwar London, receiving attention in many guides to eating out in the capital. Alfred Foster, for instance, wrote that, upon entering it, you 'are transported to Spain'.[94] 'As for the menu the dishes are Spanish if one chooses à la carte and the table d'hôte is composed of the usual French dishes.'[95] Foster 'insisted on purely native dishes' beginning with 'succulent juicy Spanish olives' with 'a glass of perfect sherry', followed by a Spanish omelette, 'Paella à la Valenciana' and a dessert, all washed down with Rioja.[96] This restaurant clearly did well, expanding its premises at the end of the 1930s.[97]

Greek restaurants serving a distinct cuisine had also appeared by the interwar years, including Demos in Shaftesbury Avenue, which featured 'pilaffs, ragouts, and various fish dishes'.[98] The White Tower in Percy Street, owned by Yianni Stasis, stood on the site of a former French restaurant, and in outward appearance at least did not flaunt its national identity.[99] The first Greek restaurant of all appears to have been the Salonika, in Beak Street in the West End, owned by a native of Athens, Christos Pandelis. The clientele included members of the London Greek community. The menu offers a fascinating insight into both the transformation of food in the migration process and its reporting by the London catering press. Although 'pickled young vine leaves are much used in cooking', the dolmades consisted of 'portions of forcemeat, which are wrapped in the leaves of a lettuce with melted butter poured over and broth added. After cooking, the dolmas, as they are termed, are carefully arranged on some rice which has been boiled in stock, and a lemon sauce is poured over all.'[100] The *Hotel Review* described 'sour cream', presumably plain yoghurt, as a 'national delicacy'.[101] Although such products, particularly the latter, would become familiar in Britain by the end of the twentieth century, at this stage they either attracted almost orientalist attention, because of their exoticism, or simply had a wrong description attached to them.

Some foreign restaurants had also reached the suburbs by the interwar years, although diners outside central London did not sample particularly exotic fare as the menus remained 'haute cuisine'. For instance, the Valchera Reataurant in Richmond, owned by the Jacomelli family, which hailed from Ticino in Switzerland, 'would probably be called a Swiss restaurant'. But 'you could tell immediately it was a classical French cuisine'. The menu included a wide range of dishes from risotto to Welsh rarebit.[102]

By 1939 some Londoners had also tasted food with origins beyond Europe, especially from China and India. Chinese cuisine reached national attention in 1884 during the Health Exhibition in London, which hosted an international range of exhibits, including a Chinese restaurant with a menu in French and a combination of dishes varying from bird's nest soup to 'Vermicelli Chinoise à la Milanaise'. The restaurant received a wide range of reactions, both positive and negative.[103]

But few Londoners would have sampled either the food on offer here or in the Chinese restaurants in the East End of London.[104] Instead, those adventurous and wealthy enough to try such exotic produce would probably have eaten in the establishments which started to appear in central London from the Edwardian period. Although these form the beginnings of the Westernized Chinese menu in Britain, part of their appeal lay in the unique meals they sold. The *Hotel Review* of April 1914 recommended 'bird's nests, shark's fin, bamboo shoots and noodles' served in the Cathay in Piccadilly, which stood on five floors by 1916. While it still served 'bird's nest or shark's fin', customers had to give half a day's notice for these. Westernized dishes included chop suey, chicken with pineapple and chicken with almonds and bamboo shoots.[105]

During the interwar years the Westernized menu increasingly came to dominate, as globalized Chinese food developed, even though some of the curiosities of dishes, such as bird's nest and shark's fin soup, still survived in some restaurants. But these essentially represented the exotic in an otherwise increasingly standardized menu aimed at Western tastes. The range of dishes, now numbered, began to become a feature of Chinese restaurants. Immediately after the First World War the management of the Cathay appears to have opened the Chinese Café in Oxford Street, which listed '271 items on the menu, all numbered'. While it served bird's nest and shark's fin soup at half a day's notice, most of the dishes on the menu, 'which is printed in English, are modified to suit western palates', which meant that about 90 per cent of the clientele consisted of Europeans. It could actually cater for 250 and employed 30 staff in 2 kitchens.[106] By the Second World War at least nine Chinese restaurants existed in London, the majority of them in Soho. Ley-On's in Wardour Street became the most popular with Westerners.[107]

This desire for the exotic (albeit modified for Western palates) represents one of the main reasons for the development of both Chinese and Indian food in Britain, as does cheapness in the case of the former.[108] The history of Indian food, or, more accurately, its Anglo-Indian manifestation, curry, has a tenuous connection with the small number of Indians who lived in London before 1945. This differs from the Chinese migrants who opened the initial restaurants in the East End of London. The first establishments of the nineteenth century usually targeted natives, especially people who had lived in the Raj who had a taste for the exotic.

The first Indian restaurant in London, the Hindoostane Coffee House, appears to have opened in 1809 in Portman Square and was primarily aimed at a higher class of clientele.[109] This institution did not last for long, a fate which befell several other curry houses during the late Victorian and Edwardian periods, including one in New Bond Street opened by 'Pheroze Langrane, an Indian Lady'.[110] In 1904 Mahomed Futymed, the 'late Indian chef of the Trocadero Restaurant' in Piccadilly, 'opened a restaurant on the first floor of the "Prince Rupert" ' nearby. Further fleeting Indian restaurants also opened in Holborn and Shepherd's Bush before 1914.[111]

In 1919 Indian Restaurants Ltd, a firm established by an Indian barrister and an Indian doctor, operated two establishments, including one in Rupert

Street, but the company had wound up by 1921.[112] The longest-lasting Indian restaurant in London, Veereswamy's in Swallow Street, came into existence in 1926, established by Edward Palmer, after he had served food at the Empire Exhibition in Wembley in 1924. It catered both for wealthy Londoners and for returned Anglo-Indians.[113] By this time a couple of restaurants in the capital also catered for Indian students. At the same time, other cafés which served Indian sailors also appeared in the East End, acting as 'the roots from which Indian restaurants in Britain were to grow'.[114]

The foreign restaurant would move out of the West End heartland to the whole of London and the country as a whole after the Second World War. This development has a variety of explanations. The business approach, which sees it as an opportunity for financial success and social mobility, offers a starting point.[115] A more market-based approach would point to the idea that the expanding restaurant sector led to increasing specialization, 'as businesses try to secure a share of the market'.[116] It proves difficult to view the provision of food offered by ethnic minorities in restaurants as anything other than a product, as a business transaction, which means that migrants construct meals that would appeal to the wider population, rather than serving the foods which they eat at home. Even before 1945 the few Chinese and Indian restaurants in London sold constructed meals, explained by the doyen of Chinese food writers, Kenneth Lo, in the former case, as the difference between Chinese food in the West and Chinese food in China.[117] Curry represents the ultimate constructed product as it 'bears very little resemblance to the food British Asians eat in their homes'.[118] The post-war years also witnessed an increasing diversification of national cuisines on offer in restaurants. *Harden's London Restaurants* from 1998 lists over forty different types of food according to ethnicity, region or nationality, including, apart from the obvious culprits such as Chinese, Greek, Indian and Italian, others as diverse as British, French, Burmese, Argentinian, Japanese, Afghan and Sudanese.[119] However, by 2018 *Harden's* had increased this range to almost sixty, some of which involved groupings such as West African, South American and central and Eastern European,[120] and it seems likely that the range of restaurants in London matches the range of ethnic groups.

While a post-war revolution may have occurred in the proliferation of restaurants serving foods with origins from all over the world, it built upon those establishments which already existed before 1945 and in the immediate post-war years. Central London, and Soho in particular, continued as the focus of many of these. By the second half of the 1940s the concept of eateries selling distinct ethnic, regional or national cuisines had established itself. They thrived despite the 'pinch of austerity' as rationing continued, which meant difficulties in obtaining products such as 'macaroni, olive oil, salamé, cheese, wines, cunning spices, caviare'.[121] A guide to Soho claimed that it was not 'easy to say that one restaurant is French, another Italian and a third exclusively Greek'.[122]

Despite this assertion, others marketed themselves along particular national lines. A guide to *Dining Round London* from 1947 divided restaurants in the capital, essentially in the centre, into various categories, including, along ethnic and national lines, 'Cuisine Française', Hungarian, Greek, 'Chop Suey', 'Slavonic', Spanish and 'Scandinavian'. The four Greek restaurants mentioned, the Crete, Elysée, White Tower and Akropolis, 'are owned and mainly run by Greek Cypriots'. Most of the Chinese restaurants lay in or around Soho. Slavonic included Polish.[123] The 'over 400 restaurants and cafés' in Soho included 'French, Italian, Greek, Cypriot, Jewish, Russian, Danish, Chinese' and Spanish.[124] Such places sold food that bore a resemblance to the products eaten in the places from which they claimed to originate. For example, Goya, owned 'by a sad-eyed little Cypriot with generations of catering experience behind him, takes great pains over native dishes like *moussaka* and *shish kebab*'.[125]

An expansion of restaurants marketing a distinct ethnic cuisine occurred outside central London, as well as within it, during the course of the 1950s, as indicated by editions of *The Good Food Guide*, originally published from 1951.[126] In 1954 we learn of the Parthenon restaurant in Golders Green, which offered a variety of dishes including kebabs, 'escalope of kidney Marsala', 'Ravioli Maison' and lamb cutlets.[127] While most of the restaurants listed in the 1961 Egon Ronay guide lay in central London, it also mentions the Andalucia and the Trattoria Romana in Hampstead, the Café Royal in Wimbledon, owned by the 'Anglo-Swiss-Italian', Maitre Rampoldi, and Casa Cominetti in Lewisham.[128]

Greek Cypriots and Italians operated many of the earliest overtly foreign restaurants of the immediate post-war years. Coffee bars offered 'simple Italian dishes which soon became very popular including spaghetti Bolognese, ravioli, pizza and minestrone'. These, however, differed from the trattoria, with Italian names, which 'became extremely popular with the newly affluent classes for whom a meal' at the established central London Italian eateries 'was financially out of the question'.[129] The Ristorante Ferrovia in Walham Green Arcade,

Fulham Broadway, offers an example of these new Italian restaurants, actually opened in 1962 by a firm called Dino's, which owned another five establishments. The 'Italian specialities' here included pizza napoletana, tagliatelle bolognese and lasagne verdi al forno.[130] Fulham counted other similar eateries including 'Il Porcellino of Florence . . . which is run by three gentlemen who immediately inspire confidence with names like Mario, Franco and Luciano'.[131]

Like their Italian counterparts, Greek Cypriots increasingly established restaurants which served an interpretation of Greek food, a generic concept covering dishes served in both Greece and Cyprus. It bore a limited resemblance to the predominantly vegetarian pulses, which many of the migrants would have eaten in their villages of origin.[132] The menu usually included various types of kebabs (the central feature), together with roast lamb (*kleftikon*) and chicken, fish, dolmades, mousaka, halloumi, Greek salad, dips and pitta bread. By the middle of the 1960s the *Good Food Guide* included ten Greek restaurants in London, many of them in the suburbs.[133] The same publication provided the names of seventeen such eateries in 1985.[134] The Cyprus government actually claimed that over 300 existed in London by 1968.[135] A product connected with Greek restaurants, but which developed a life of its own, sold by Greeks but, more especially, Turkish Cypriots and Turks, was the kebab, leading to the development of the kebab shop. These tend to sell a variety of products, especially burgers and often pizza or fish and chips, and may have totalled 125 by 1978.[136]

The migration of Chinese people to Britain from the 1950s had close connections with the evolution of restaurants. Most of the migrants originated in Hong Kong, which experienced a series of economic problems. An increase in movement occurred during the early 1960s due to the impending introduction of the Commonwealth Immigrants Act of 1962, which severely curtailed migration from the Empire and Commonwealth to Britain. The developing Chinese restaurant sector acted as an important pull factor in attracting the Chinese, so that a type of recruitment developed during the 1950s, formalized in the establishment of the Association of Chinese Restaurants in 1961. Even after 1962 movement for the purpose of staffing the restaurant trade continued, as owners could import people from Hong Kong if they could prove the need for them and an absence of native workers, who could do the same job.[137]

The development of the Chinese restaurant went through a series of phases. In the immediate post-war period establishments began to open up outside both Limehouse and Soho in Kensington, Chelsea, Croydon, Harrow, Ealing and Purley,[138] as well as the provinces. By the middle of the 1950s approximately 300 Chinese restaurants may have existed in Britain.[139] The real boom in the growth of the Chinese restaurants' trade (when they began to become part of the British way of eating out) occurred from the middle of the 1950s to the middle of the 1960s. This nationwide explosion meant that Britain counted as many as 2,500 Chinese restaurants by 1965. A survey carried out by Unilever into dining habits during that year indicated that 31 per cent of people who regularly dined out had eaten Chinese.[140] As we would expect, London became the city with the largest number of Chinese restaurants in Britain by the end of the 1960s, counting as many as 200.[141] Expansion would continue after this time with the development of the takeaway, which a Chinese family could open 'for a fraction of the price' of a restaurant, and by 1984 Britain counted as many as 7,000 Chinese restaurants and takeaways, a remarkable increase from the handful based in London of the late 1940s.[142] Despite the threat of McDonaldization,[143] expansion continued even further so that, by 1997, about 9,000 takeaways and 3,000 restaurants existed on a national scale, meaning that Chinese food had become part of British life, as the outlets which sold them had literally become ubiquitous.[144] Post-war growth in London, outside Soho, and Britain as a whole formed part of a global phenomenon, 'Chinese Food Abroad' in the words of Kenneth Lo, whereby a distinct product surfaced for Western tastes. Chinese restaurants in Soho, which numbered about 100 by the 1980s, served both this type of Chinese food as well as products more commonly eaten in the homeland.[145]

Indian food, in contrast, remains rooted in the culinary exchange which took place in the Raj and spread to Britain after the arrival of Indian, or, more accurately, Bangladeshi migrants. Most accounts of the growth of Indian restaurants in the post-war period point to the role of sailors from Sylhet, originally forming part of East Pakistan after partition, which became Bangladesh during the early 1970s. Many of these had served as cooks on British-owned ships and would often take over 'bombed out cafés in need of renovation' in the East End during the immediate post-war years, serving a combination of native foods and curry. The early clientele in these establishments included other South Asians[146] and 'ordinary Englishmen' who had 'spent a year or more in the Far East, in India, Burma, Malaya' during the war and had sampled curries or chappatis.[147] The dishes that would come to dominate, based upon the culinary constructions which had occurred in the Raj during the previous century, included vindaloo, korma and madras.[148]

The few hundred Indian restaurants, which existed on a national basis during the early 1960s, had increased to around 3,000 by the early 1980s and 7,516 by 1998, including 1,431 in London.[149] Most of the expansion therefore took place during the 1970s and 1980s. The explanation would largely lie in the fact that, while more than one group of South Asians have opened restaurants, Bangladeshis, who pioneered the post-war curry house, have seen the restaurant trade as a way of business success, despite the long hours involved, small profits and increasing numbers of restaurant failures. A shortage of staff from the middle of the 1970s meant an importation of people directly from Bangladesh using work permits, following the earlier Chinese pattern, because it 'was usually hopeless trying to teach British workers how to prepare and cook Asian food'.[150] In 1995 Bangladeshis owned 7,000 of the 8,000 Indian restaurants in the United Kingdom, while by the end of the 1990s there were 70,000 Bangladeshi waiters and cooks on a nationwide scale.[151]

Bangladeshis take the main responsibility for menu changes since the late 1960s, which has seen various fads. The first of these, the spread of tandoori, lasted from the end of the 1960s until the 1980s. By the 1980s the balti (meaning bucket in Hindi) had emerged. This dish originated in Pakistani-run restaurants in Birmingham. By the end of the twentieth century vegetarian restaurants run by Indians rather than Bangladeshis had also emerged, especially in London and the Belgrave area of Leicester, the heart of the Gujarati community in the city. Das Sreedharan, a trained accountant born in Kerala, presents an alternative story to the Bangladeshi paradigm. While he claimed that he had an interest in food from his childhood, catering offered a good business opportunity. At the end of 2006 he owned eight London outlets, although these seem to have declined to just two by 2018. They served South Indian food and the development of such higher-class establishments reflected patterns in Chinese food in the same period in the capital. The growth of the Indian restaurant trade has also meant the emergence of firms to supply them.[152]

It proves impossible to speak of the history of the foreign restaurant without referring to the spread of American fast food from the 1970s, linked with the growth of corporate America[153] and contrasting with the family businesses established by migrants. The first twelve Kentucky Fried Chicken outlets opened in London in 1970 when Ray Allen bought the rights to the US corporation.[154]

McDonald's arrived a few years later, opening its first UK restaurant in Woolwich in 1974,[155] with 'plans for further developments in Greater London already well advanced' (in Catford and Croydon) following the opening of the second branch in Seven Sisters Road in Holloway in the spring of 1975.[156] By 1997 the McDonald's outlets in Britain may have totalled 1,400,[157] although these remain significantly fewer than the number of Chinese and Indian restaurants. An estimate from 1993 pointed out that the 3,614 chain-owned outlets which existed in that year, while threatening independent takeaway owners, only represented 9.5 per cent of all takeaways, meaning that over 30,000 independent outlets existed throughout the country.[158] By 2000 Britain counted 1,000 McDonald's restaurants, 600 Kentucky Fried Chicken outlets, 400 Burger King and 286 Pizza Express.[159] Figures from 1997 which point to over £1 billion spent on burgers, £838 million on pizza and £515 million on fried chicken,[160] need to take into account the fact that chains only account for a fraction of the total. Migrants have also opened some chains, including Costa Coffee[161] and Pizza Express.[162]

RESTAURANTS FOR MIGRANTS

As well as establishing places to eat out for natives, settlers from Europe and beyond have also opened restaurants for members of their own community, as eating out plays a key role in socialization. While dining out had solidified on class lines by the end of the nineteenth century, from fish and chips to the Ritz, a clear ethnic element had also emerged. If eating out worked according to class and taste,[163] it also functioned along the lines of national origin and religion. Places where members of minorities have eaten out in London have played a role in bringing them together and perpetuating the existence of an ethnic community as such restaurants develop in immigrant quarters alongside shops selling foods from the homeland.

This becomes clear when examining the Jewish community, whose religion determines their food which, in theory, means the necessity for the establishment of kosher restaurants even though few Jewish restaurants actually sold kosher produce.[164] An early kosher establishment consisted of Goldstein's in Bloomfield Street, London Wall, '3 Minutes from the Bank', advertising in the *Jewish Chronicle* from the early 1880s.[165] It sold typically Ashkenazi products including 'fimsell', 'matsoklese', 'sauerkraut', 'kugel' and 'apple staffen', although some of the other dishes could have come from any middle-class restaurant in late nineteenth-century London, including smoked salmon, fried plaice, 'filleted steak' and roast chicken.[166] Cohn's in Houndsditch came 'under supervision of the Beth Din' and by the 1930s catered 'for weddings, bar-mitzvahs, etc.' It became one of the Jewish restaurants 'of the better class', which 'cater more particularly for the English Jew', in contrast to the numerous other establishments in the East End, 'some being mostly frequented by aliens from Eastern Europe'.[167] Many Jewish establishments had a relatively short lifespan. For instance, 'The Kosher Restaurant Company' survived, as a public limited company, from 1881 until 1905.[168] Similarly, Kosher Caterers, which appears to have been an attempt to open a chain as 'proprietors and/or managers of restaurants, cafes, hotels and dining-rooms either generally or on "Kosher Restaurant" lines', only lasted from 1926 to 1929.[169]

But some establishments survived from the Edwardian years into the interwar period and beyond including Bloom's, which, along with Rakusens, provided kosher food on a national scale.[170] Abrahamson's, meanwhile, lay in the West End, which by the interwar years, had a concentration of kosher restaurants to serve the Jewish community which had emerged in this part of London.[171] In 1908 Abrahamson's in Oxford Street described itself as 'The Only Kosher Restaurant in the West End'.[172] Another advertisement from the following year asserted that it served 'First Class Cuisine. Strictly Orthodox'. Its wares included 'Tongues, Worsht & Smoked Beef, Olives, Cucumbers, Biscuits, Pastries, Gateaux, Almond Puddings, Motzas, and Confectionery of every kind'.[173] By 1921 Abrahamson's could cater for 'Weddings or Receptions' of up to 100 persons.[174]

Sam Stern's, an East End establishment, became one of the most famous Kosher restaurants of the interwar years. This firm originally began as an outside caterer, based in Smith Street in Stepney. In 1927 Sam Stern bought a warehouse in Mansell Street, which, in the following year, he opened as 'Stern's Hotel and Restaurant', acting both as a venue for functions, especially weddings, and as a restaurant. Although it appears to have attracted a high-class clientele, a menu from the 1930s would suggest that it must have appealed to a wide range of social groups from a variety of Jewish backgrounds. It included a range of straightforward dishes available in any 1930s restaurant, such as egg mayonnaise, grapefruit and sardines as starters, while the main meals included fried fish, roast beef, roast lamb and mint sauce, together with strained prunes, apples or pears for dessert. These came with some recognizably Jewish dishes, including salt or pickled herring, lockshen, farfel and fried worsht and eggs. But the majority of the dishes would not look out of place on any British restaurant menu of the 1930s. Sam Stern died in 1951 and his restaurant closed in the following year. His premises had catered for over 6,000 Jewish weddings.[175]

Kosher restaurants and catering establishments had clearly become part of the life of the Jewish community in Britain before 1945. While kosher food remains part of the menu, Jewish dishes, reflecting the process of Jewish acculturation, increasingly incorporated dishes which the rest of the population consumed. Cohn's and Abrahamson's, which would seem to cater for a more middle-class clientele, contained more recognizably Jewish dishes on their menu before 1914 than Stern's. The latter appears to have had a more universal group of customers during the 1930s, suggesting, perhaps, a fairly rapid assimilation into the norms of British eating patterns, while still, once again, adhering to the basics of the kosher diet. Interestingly, reflecting the extent to which food has become multiculturalized for all sections of London society, the seventeen kosher restaurants authorized by the Kashrus Commission in 2005 included Isola Bella Café, La Fiesta, Tasti Pizza and Kaifeng.[176] In addition to these, Jewish-style restaurants have also emerged.[177] As in the pre-war period, these establishments appeal almost exclusively to a Jewish clientele.

Numerous German restaurants and drinking establishments emerged in London before the outbreak of the First World War, playing a central role in the life of this group in the imperial capital. Beer proved especially important, leading to the development of a series of breweries including the Austro-Bavarian Lager Beer Company, based in Tottenham during the 1880s, the Kaiser Lager Beer Company (1884–90) and the English Lager Beer Company.[178] German beer halls had also developed in London by the end of the nineteenth century. These included 'The Imperial' in Newgate Street, which claimed to sell 'exquisite German food' and 'German and English beers'.[179] By the beginning of the twentieth century the largest 'beer hall' appears to have been 'Ye Olde Gambrinus', with branches in both Regent Street and Glasshouse Street in Piccadilly. This firm gave itself various plaudits including 'The Home of Lager Beer in England' and 'the Largest Original Beer Hall in England'. Its drinks included genuine Munich Pschorrbräu and genuine Kulmbacher 'Mönchshof' on tap.[180]

Beer was not the only attraction for enticing German diners out of their homes, although it may have proved the most attractive, especially for males, who would have dominated the clientele of the beer halls. A few did not make this beverage the main feature of their advertising. These included Keller's restaurant of London Wall, a 'cheap and respectable house', which, in 1869, sold a 'selection of German, English and French dishes', including 'four types of soup', 'two types of fish', 'four types of joints', together with 'English and German style vegetables', and would probably have attracted a more even gender balance.[181]

After beer, but far less important, cakes featured as the most common bait for London's Germans eating away from home, perhaps attracting more women and children, although those who frequented the beer halls may have simply eaten their pastries earlier in the day. Thus Wolff's Conditorei in Broad Street advertised 'fine chocolate confectionery' and a 'list of unsurpassable cakes'.[182] The Wiener Café, also in the City, sold Viennese coffee, chocolate and tea, together with 'French and Viennese cakes'.[183] Appenrodt's advertised pastries amongst its many products.[184]

A variety of places therefore existed in Victorian and Edwardian London for the substantial German community, which would face destruction and elimination as a result of Germanophobia during the First World War.[185] Although the range of German eating establishments would never reach their pre-war peak after 1918, restaurants 'specialising in German, Austrian and Swiss cuisine abounded' in the London of the 1930s, including Schimdt's in Charlotte Street and Appenrodt's.[186]

The Chinese restaurants which emerged before 1945 primarily targeted the small communities which had evolved in London. In the years leading up to the First World War 'there were some 30 Chinese shops and restaurants along two streets' in the East End of London, Pennyfields and Limehouse Causeway, 'patronized exclusively, or almost exclusively, by Chinese'.[187] A 1908 article with the orientalist heading of 'London's Chinatown: Its Restaurants and Opium Dens' involved a food critic entering the East End of London, rather like a missionary discovering China, looking for a specific restaurant. 'Lacking some clue as to its whereabouts, the casual visitor might wander about for many hours without "striking" the precise locality. Local shopkeepers betray a sublime ignorance of any Chinatown in their midst.' When he eventually reaches Limehouse Causeway, 'the spot which a stranger in search of Chinatown should make for', he enters the sought-after location. Interestingly, the dishes on offer include chop suey, the ultimate example of Chinese food for Westerners, although the author claims that, at 6d. per bowl, it 'is the standing dish of the poorer orders'. He also points out that 'knives and forks are never seen' and proceeds to describe the use of chopsticks.[188] In 1916 another restaurant in Limehouse Causeway sold chop suey together with 'birds nests and water melon, whole chicken stuffed with birds' nests and soup, duck with orange peel and soup, and fried chicken with shark's belly'.[189]

The restaurants established by the Chinese community managed to attract some natives, even when situated in Limehouse. As they spread out towards the West End of London during the interwar years the clientele became increasingly mixed. These differ from the special case of kosher restaurants which peddled a cuisine with religious restrictions and did not attract Gentiles. While many of the German restaurants which advertised in the London German press, enticing customers primarily with beer, probably had a predominantly German customer base before 1914, others, most notably Appenrodt's, both a delicatessen and a café, certainly attracted a variety of Londoners. With the exception of kosher restaurants, it proves difficult to speak of purely ethnic minority restaurants simply frequented by members of specific communities.

Since 1945, as we have seen, the ethnic restaurant has become inextricably linked with the history of eating out in London, but some establishments in areas with concentrations of specific groups attract a clientele from that particular migrant community. By the twenty-first century it proves possible to find restaurants selling every type of cuisine in London, from Afghan to West Indian, in a situation of superdiversity, and it would certainly seem that some of these establishments would primarily serve their own people. They form part of a wider ethnic food economy with specialist shops and, in the case of larger communities, suppliers which sometimes operate on a nationwide basis.[190] In 1981, 67 per cent of customers of Asian-owned restaurants in Ealing, which included Southall, were Asians, concentrated around Southall Broadway. This situation continued after that time, as Southall proved the centre of Sikh life in the capital and also acted as home to shops selling a variety of South Asian products.[191] Smaller communities have also established restaurants appealing predominantly to their own people. For example, a Korean restaurant, Asadal, opened in New Malden in 1991 to cater for the Korean community which had emerged here from the 1960s and which may have totalled 12,000 people by 2017, from both North and South Korea. In fact, Asadal represents one of many Korean restaurants here as New Malden had developed into a key centre of Korean settlement in London.[192] We can also give the example of a Vietnamese restaurant in Deptford, run by a woman who left Vietnam in 2000 to join her family in London and who took over the site from a previous Vietnamese owner in 2004. She received initial financial support from family members. Her establishment employed four people, all Vietnamese, including her sister. None spoke good English, including the owner, and the clientele consisted primarily of Vietnamese locals. She faced competition from 700 other 'ethnic' restaurants in Deptford.[193] This situation replicates itself in other parts of London throughout the post-war period. While some establishments may attract a clientele from their own community, especially in areas in which a specific group concentrates, all businessmen would want as large a share of the market as possible.

MIGRANTS AND LONDON RESTAURANTS

What does this survey of eating out in London tell us about its relationship with migration? In the first place, it points to the fact that newcomers have driven the evolution of the restaurant. The history of high-end cuisine, or the restaurant, seems inconceivable without a constant stream of restaurateurs, chefs and waiters from its inception in the Victorian period. Europeans have arrived with more culinary knowledge and a willingness to work harder than natives. They have developed chains of migrants which have operated throughout this entire period, whether from France, Germany, Italy, Cyprus or Eastern Europe.

These Europeans, together with newcomers from the continent, introduced foreign foods to Londoners and marketed them as such. At the top level this process began in the West End and would spread to the rest of London society and to the rest of the country from the 1950s and, more especially, the 1960s. Eventually, the restaurants and takeaways which sold Italian, Chinese and Indian food moved into the mainstream, becoming part of London and national cuisine. The pioneer for this process consisted of fish and chips, with fried fish regarded as a Jewish food before the middle of the nineteenth century but, when combined with chips sometime in the late Victorian period, developed an association with the British working classes and, from the 1960s, with the British. Part of the reason for the British association was that foods had developed a national identity by this time and those who sold them marketed them along such lines, which meant that fish and chips became the food of the British.[194] Those who open new restaurants largely do so as business opportunities and offer an excellent example of migrant entrepreneurialism. In most cases, the clientele has consisted of Londoners as a whole, although, especially in the period before 1945 and in the case of establishments opened in areas with significant concentrations of one particular group, they tried to offer food reminiscent of the homeland in contrast with, for example, Chinese food in the West and the curry menu initially eaten by the British in India. While, in the early twentieth century, if we exclude the by then assimilated fish and chips, most Londoners would not have tasted 'foreign food', which remained confined to the West End, to the Limehouse Chinese, the East and West End Germans and to the East End Jews, one hundred years later superdiversity and marketing of food along ethnic lines have ensured that most of the ethnically diverse population of London ate at a range of restaurants divided along ethnic lines. Pizza, which became a mass product in Britain in the last few decades of the twentieth century, largely due to the efforts of national chains in the case of that eaten outside the home,[195] had ceased to have a nationality in the same way as fish and chips and in a similar way to Chinese and Indian food, even though the people who sold these latter two products tended to originate from Hong Kong and Bangladesh respectively.

It seems tempting to view the foreign restaurant as a symbol of multicultural and superdiverse London, a situation in which all ethnic groups can sample the food of their neighbours from a different ethnic group, especially if we take a long-term perspective and accept that foods sold by foreign restaurants eventually make it into the mainstream. Clearly this does not always happen because, while this statement might apply to fish and chips and curry, the situation for kosher remains quite different, while, for example, restaurants in Southall Broadway have an overwhelming majority of South Asian customers.

Does the alimentary history of London have any unique aspects or does it reflect developments occurring elsewhere? In terms of the history of the high-class restaurant, it seems clear that this concept emerged in early nineteenth-century Paris and that it would spread to the rest of Europe, including London, over the next century. Yet by the outbreak of the First World War the British capital, with its concentration of both native and migrant elites, acted as home to some of the world's great restaurants, a status it has retained. This caused the arrival of legions of foreign waiters who established branches of their continental trade unions in London, as the heart of Empire formed one of the most important stops in the training of such people, together with chefs. Some of those who had a stint of employment in London worked not simply in other European capitals but also in some provincial hotels and restaurants as some of the portraits above indicate.

The diversity of cuisine available by the beginning of the twenty-first century seems quite unique, reflecting the range of populations which had settled in the British capital by this time. Some of these may sell niche products confined to specific ethnic groups which the wider population may not sample and may remain unusual outside the land of origin. On the other hand the British capital also acts as home to numerous Chinese restaurants peddling a global standardized product. Fish and chips originated in London and the first curry houses appeared here and spread to the rest of the country.

London has unquestionably played the role of the food capital of Britain because of the number and range of places to eat out which it has housed. It has also become globally important for the same reason, although other major capitals might also claim the title of food capital of the world, especially Paris since the end of the eighteenth century. The uniqueness of the British capital would again have to revolve around the level of diversity, not simply in terms of the range of ethnic cuisines, catering for both specific ethnic groups and the population at large, but also because of the range of social groups which have sampled such products. These range from fish and chips sold in Malins to Peach Melba, which, while it may have become rather staid and hackneyed, came to life when Escoffier named the dish after the Australian coloratura soprano Dame Nellie Melba in the Carlton Hotel.[196]

10

FIGHTERS AND FOOTBALLERS

Shortly after my return to town, I was induced to engage in another pugilistic contest; for being present one day in company with a young man at a fight at Kentish Town, my friend happened to be grossly insulted by a man, whom I challenged in consequence, and we accordingly set to, when after a contest of about half an hour, he was forced to give in, being so severely beaten as to be scarcely able to stand, and, indeed, he was obliged to be carried off the field.[1]

Of all the conversations myself and Ossie engaged in during the long months preceding the World Cup, moving to England wasn't one of them. We just hadn't considered the prospect. But when Ossie contacted me with news of the proposed deal I was instantly interested. Before I knew it we were sat in a hotel in Buenos Aires alongside the manager of Tottenham Hotspur, Keith Burkinshaw, and an interpreter.[2]

It was supposed to be the fulfilment of my life's ambition. Since I could run all I ever wanted was to become a professional footballer. And there I was, only twenty years old, about to make my debut in the Second Division for one of the biggest clubs in London in a local derby against Crystal Palace.

It should have been one of the greatest days of my life, not a nightmare that came back again and again.

But this debut wasn't the Hollywood version. This was the snarling, nasty, eighties-Britain version. It was a miserable evening but we were winning 1-0 thanks to [a] goal from popular winger Clive Walker, and the last few minutes were ticking by.

The manager John Neal leant over and told me to warm up, I was coming on. I stood up and ran along the side of the Selhurst Park pitch.

Nothing could have prepared me for what happened next. As I'm stretching and running, I hear loud individual voices through the noise: 'Sit down you black cunt', 'You fucking wog – fuck off!' Over and over again. Lots of different people. I hardly dared look around. They were right behind me. I snatched a glimpse. They were all wearing blue shirts and scarves – Chelsea fans, my side's fans, faces screwed with pure hatred and anger all directed at me.[3]

The history of football in London and the participation of migrants and ethnic minorities within it acts as a key symbol of the relationship between migration and globalization, as well as illustrating the forces of multiculturalism and racism in action. It resembles other aspects of the migration history of the British capital in the sense that the period before the Second World War and even before the 1980s appears one dominated by the white British in terms of the professionals who played this sport. However, as in the case of much else in the migration history of London, scratch below the surface and there emerges a longer history of migrant participation involving the Irish in particular, as well as a few people of Jewish, African and Caribbean origin. While the global and multi-ethnic football team may have become the norm by the end of the twentieth century, symbolized especially by Arsenal and Chelsea fielding teams consisting almost entirely of foreigners by 1999,[4] a situation which became normal for these two clubs in the twenty-first century,[5] Arsenal had a tradition of importing Irish players,[6] reflecting the long history of the global migration of footballers.[7] On the one hand we can see the dominance of foreign players in London football as a key symbol of the extent and nature of globalization in the early twenty-first century, especially as London teams simply replicate the situation amongst football clubs not just in the rest of England but also in much of the rest of Europe, indicated not simply by the playing staff but also by managers and owners. Whereas Arsenal may have had the same French-born manager, Arsène Wenger, from 1996 to 2018, Chelsea changed managers regularly and did not appoint a single British manager in the same period. On the one hand the migration of foreign footballers to

London and elsewhere involves global superstars, perhaps similar to financial and commercial elites who have settled in the capital, especially with the absurd salaries which footballers earned by the beginning of the twenty-first century, symbolizing the inequality which accompanies globalization.[8] In reality, most of these footballers, unlike other elites in twenty-first-century London, did not find themselves born into a high social status, although exceptions exist including Gianluca Vialli, who came from a 'privileged' background,[9] and Eden Hazard, whose mother and father both played football, which provided the type of inside knowledge necessary to succeed in many professions. The fact that Hazard's educated parents then became teachers would have provided a further advantage,[10] although supportive and educated parents form an aspect of numerous sporting success stories, as the example of one of Hazard's Chelsea teammates, the Brazilian-born David Luiz, also the son of teachers, indicates.[11]

However, numerous footballers, especially according to their autobiographies, have had to overcome disadvantage, driven forward by their ability and determination, as well as their families. For the sons of West Indian and African immigrants who became professionals in the late twentieth century, these disadvantages included racism, epitomized by the story of Paul Canoville. On the one hand the multinational, multi-ethnic and multiracial London football teams offer the best indication of the nature of London at the beginning of the twentieth century, which includes social inequality. However, London football also demonstrates that racism has not disappeared. While Arsenal's supporters may reflect their players in terms of their ethnic backgrounds, the same does not apply to Chelsea, West Ham or Millwall, each of which had previous associations with racist political groups in London. At the same time, while the sons of African and West Indian immigrants have become the mainstay of London football teams since the 1980s, they have recruited virtually no children of those originating in South Asian communities.

FIGHTERS

The British, London and global history of football takes off in its current organized and regulated form from the end of the nineteenth century.[12] However, the issues which arise with regard to migrant and minority participation on the London scene emerged over a hundred years earlier in the sport of boxing during the 'English Golden Age',[13] initially in the form of bare-knuckle fighting.[14] In the late eighteenth and early nineteenth centuries both upwardly mobile second-generation sporting migrants and black foreigners played a role in London fighting, setting the pattern which would last into the twentieth century and beyond and replicated by football. 'The participation of minorities in boxing started almost with the inception of the sport in the eighteenth century and prevails (with various peaks and lows) until today',[15] but so does the presence of outsiders, especially black men, who arrived in Britain and London, sometimes already as stars, to take the boxing scene by storm.

A series of long and detailed histories of boxing written during the course of the nineteenth and into the twentieth centuries, often focusing upon the personalities of the ring, provide an indication of the importance of minorities and outsiders in the evolution of this sport. However, it is important to realize that, while Jews and black men became some of the major celebrities of the sport, they remained a minority, unlike the situation in the Premier League in the twenty-first century. At the same time, while London played a central role in the evolution of boxing, it developed into a national sport, with some of the great fights described in the early histories of this activity taking place outside London.

A focus upon Jews, however, reveals that London, from where all of the champions of this ethnicity evolved, from the end of the eighteenth century until the twentieth, remained their key playground. On the one hand, we might view Jewish participation as a symbol of 'the extent to which lower-class Jews adopted the habits and tastes of their peers . . . both as spectators and as participants',[16] a statement that applies both to the late eighteenth century and to the first half of the twentieth. Boxing provides a good indication of integration or even assimilation, a drifting away from the norms of Judaism, or even 'a parting of the ways'.[17] On the other hand, boxing, as well as other sporting activities involving Jews, illustrates 'emancipation through muscles'. They offer an alternative perspective to the position of Jews as part of the elites of London, British and European society,[18] and become especially relevant as a reaction against the slurs of antisemites about the lack of physical prowess of Jews, especially in the first half of the twentieth century.[19] Boxing became attractive to second-generation Jews whether in London, the United States or elsewhere, because 'entry into the sport was dependent on ability alone and . . . anti-Semitism played no role in the progress of the Jewish prize fighter'.[20]

The early London Jewish boxers included Dutch Sam, his son Young Dutch Sam, Aby Belasco, Isaac Bittoon, Izzy Lazarus and, above all, Daniel Mendoza,[21] although between 1760 and 1820 'there were at least thirty Jewish prize-fighters'.[22] In April 1824 we learn of a boxing match between Barney Aaron, 'the light-weight champion of the twelve tribes', and Peter Warren in Colacbrook, 'eighteen miles from London'. In the evening before the contest the area around Petticoat Lane in East London 'was occupied in frying fish and cooking other victuals for refreshment on the road' for those Jews who would make the journey to watch Aaron box.[23] At the same time, Jewish women also became involved in pugilism.[24] One of the earliest histories of British boxing included a portrait of Dutch Sam (1775–1816), 'about five feet six inches and a half, weighing only nine stone four pounds, (never exceeding eight) and rather of a robust make; and who has, notwithstanding, vanquished some of the best ten and twelve *stone* bruisers in the country'. He possessed a 'sharp and penetrating eye' and 'his distances are excellently judged, rendering his blows, powerful and effective'. Among those of 'his own persuasion (the Jews) he is an object of great notoriety, and no money is ever wanting to back him upon any pugilistic occasion'.[25] Young Dutch Sam (1808–43) 'was also a heralded fighter, feared and famed for his graceful, accurate, and powerful blows'.[26] Aby Belasco (1817–24) 'was in his day a boxer of superior talent, a master of the science, not wanting for game, not deficient in strength, of an athletic make, a pene-trating eye, and in the ring full of life and activity'.[27] Meanwhile, the same history of boxing from which this portrait emerges, published in the early twentieth century, described Isaac Bittoon, 'a Jew of great strength, coolness, some skill in singlestick, fencing, and with the gloves, and well-known for more than thirty years to the ring-going world'.[28]

Daniel Mendoza (1765–1836) became the most famous of the early Jewish boxers, partly because of his status as 'British Champion' from 1792 to 1795, partly because he moved from fighting to training, but what 'really set Mendoza apart was the fact that he was the only eighteenth century boxer to write an autobiography',[29] part of a wider process of self-publicity which made him the leading boxing celebrity of his time.[30] The early nineteenth-century history of boxing described him as 'one of the most elegant and scientific Pugilists in the whole race of Boxers and might be termed a complete artist. His theoretic acquirements were great, and his practice truly extensive. He rose up like a phenomenon in the pugilistic hemisphere, and was a star of the first brilliancy for a considerable period.'[31] His autobiography claimed that he 'was born on the fifth day of July, 1764, in the parish of Aldgate, London. My parents, who were of the Jewish persuasion, were by no means in affluent circumstances; they might however be considered as in the middling class of society.'[32] He attended a Jewish School which he left at thirteen and acquired a series of jobs before demonstrating fighting ability, partly through self-defence, sometimes as a result of antisemitic slurs. 'Faced with the prejudice of his non-Jewish neighbours, he responded to anti-Semitic taunts with his fists.'[33] On one occasion, in Northampton, he came across 'a young man who was considered as the bully of the place', who declared that 'it was a pity we were not sent to Jerusalem'.[34] He had become fully engaged in the ring by 1783 and shortly afterwards opened a school of boxing in Capel Court, behind the Royal Exchange, marrying a Jewish woman, Esther, in May 1787.[35] Mendoza fought as a Jew largely because of the endemic antisemitism that existed in Georgian England, which ascribed this assignation to him as well as to other boxers of his faith, but partly as a way of increasing the tribalism associated with this sport.[36] Mendoza participated in his last fight in 1820 against Tom Owen, a Hampshire innkeeper in Banstead Downs, who, although just six years his junior, beat him so badly that he never came out of retirement again.[37] As well as his autobiography Mendoza also published a volume on *The Art of Boxing*, which further helped to cement his celebrity status.[38] Despite this fact, he actually died a pauper in 1836.[39] This narrative should not obscure the brutality of the sport in which Mendoza became involved and in which extreme violence, involving both the sporting stars and the spectators, became part of the entire spectacle.[40]

Black boxers also became a feature of the Georgian prize-fighting scene, most famously Bill Richmond and Tom Molineux, whose colour became central to their identity.[41] Richmond, born a slave in Cuckold's Town (now Port Richmond) in New York City in 1763, liberated himself by the end of the following decade and joined the British army during the American War of Independence, moving to England as the valet of General Hugh Percy who had seen him box against two Hessian soldiers. Percy took Richmond to England, where he became apprenticed to a knife grinder but also became involved in various fights in a similar way to Mendoza because of the prejudice he faced, on one occasion after having the racial slur 'black devil' directed against him. He moved to London in 1804 where he would become a professional boxer, with his first fight taking place in Wimbledon Common on 23 January. He became a leading figure in the boxing fraternity for the following decade, retiring in 1815 and running a pub in St Martin's Street in Westminster. He died in 1829. He became a celebrity in a similar way to Mendoza and also attracted the racial description of the 'Black Terror'. But he had become integrated into and part of London society,[42] a path which black footballers would follow at the end of the twentieth century, again having to face and overcome prejudice. Following in the footsteps of Richmond, Tom Molineux, born in Richmond, Virginia, on 23 March 1784, gained his freedom after beating another slave in a fight and by 1804 made his living as a boxer in New York. He sailed across the Atlantic in 1809 and claimed to hold the title of champion of America. Richmond coached him in London even though he had doubts about his technique and ability. Molineux's first fight took place in Tothill Fields in Westminster on 24 July 1810 and he continued to box throughout the country until 1815, after which he tried coaching but died penniless in 1818, having fallen victim to alcohol abuse and suffering from the injuries he had sustained.[43] The other black boxers in early nineteenth-century England included: Massa Kendrick from St Kitts, who fought between 1819 and 1826; Sambo Sutton, an American whose first London fight took place in Seven Dials and who would continue boxing until 1848; Young Richmond, the son of Bill, who however, only remained active from 1821 to 1822; Bob Travers, born in Richmond, Virginia, in 1836, who fought throughout Britain between 1854 and 1864; Bob Smith, another American who fought from 1863 to 1866; and John Perry, from Nova Scotia, active from 1846 to 1850.[44]

Irish fighters also became a feature of the London boxing scene, the most famous of whom included Andrew Gamble, who had made his name in Dublin and moved to London at the beginning of the nineteenth century. His defining victory took place on Wimbledon Common in December 1800 against the English champion Jim Belcher, in front of an enormous crowd which included the London Irish and even people who had travelled from Ireland to watch, with the ethnicity of the two fighters becoming a key issue. Meanwhile, Dan Dogherty's first fight in London took place against 'a Jew' on Willesden Green in June 1806 and he then became involved in contests throughout the capital over the next few years, as well as fighting further afield, especially after 1810. Dogherty subsequently trained the Irish fighter Dan Donnelly.[45]

Black, Jewish and Irish boxers, marketed through ethnic identity, had a violent space available to them on the London boxing scene from the eighteenth into the nineteenth century. The headquarters of boxing had moved to the United States by the 1880s,[46] by which time the settlement of East European Jews in the East End of London provided the basis for a new wave of second-generation migrant boxers at the start of the twentieth century. While, from the point of view of community elders, this sport served as an evil which took young Jews away from their religion, it also played a role in 'ironing out the ghetto bend', together with other sporting activities run by a series of organizations from the late Victorian and Edwardian years, which, mimicking the mainstream emerging boy scouts and girl guides, aimed at turning Jewish youth into good British citizens. The most famous groups were the Jewish Lads and Girls Brigade, founded in 1895 and operating on a national level, supported by the established Anglo-Jewish Goldsmid family, who, like other members of their social and ethnic milieu, feared that the influx of the new Jewish migrants could undermine their own position. Such organizations aimed at social and ethnic engineering, maintaining the Jewishness of the migrant children, increasingly born in London, as well as turning them into good Englishmen and women.[47] In 1903 the *Jewish Year Book* listed eighteen 'Clubs and Athletic Societies' based in London both in the East End and beyond.[48]

London Jewry became involved in all manner of competitive sports by the early twentieth century: ping pong, football, athletics, wrestling and boxing.[49] Within the youth organizations boxing had the particular role of training young men, who had a tendency to indiscriminate fighting, to control their aggression as well as strengthening them, serving as a protection in case of attack by non-Jews, which proved successful in a competitive sense as the London Jewish Lads Brigade won the Prince of Wales Boxing Shield, aimed at all youths, regularly during the interwar years. Out of the ghetto, helped by the Jewish sporting organizations which had developed, there emerged significant numbers of Jewish professional boxers, as well as promoters. Jews also played a role in the development of the boxing venues which emerged in the East End, including Harry Jacobs, Victor Berliner and Jack Solomons. While the youth clubs may have played some role in the training of the professional fighters, some had also honed their skills on the streets, like their contemporary Gentile counterparts[50] and resembling some of their predecessors of previous centuries.

261

The most famous names before the First World War included Abe Attell, Leach Cross, Battling Levinsky, Harry Lewis, Charlie Goodman, Matt Wells, Cockney Cohen and Young Joseph.[51]

Ted Kid Lewis and Jack Kid Berg became the most famous London Jewish boxers of the interwar years. Both had parents employed in classic Jewish trades in the East End. Lewis 'was born Gershon Mendeloff, son of Solomon Mendeloff, cabinet-maker, on 28 October 1893. Place of birth, 56 Umberston Street, St-George's in the East, in the heart of what was then, in fact if not in name, the Jewish East End'.[52] The biography of Lewis written by his son stresses the poverty which the Mendeloffs endured, although entry into the Jews Free School for him, as with other successful contemporaries, acted as a spur for his development. Like Mendoza, Gershon recalled having to defend himself against antisemitic slurs, in his case on his way to school. He initially worked for his father, but he appears to have decided to become a professional fighter by the age of ten. He developed his skills in the Judean Club in Princes Square, where he also chose the name Kid Lewis, to which he later added 'Ted' in the United States. He became a professional in his early teens and would start fighting in Premierland in the East End, which would become a major Jewish boxing venue. Lewis went on to hold a variety of boxing titles, including a world championship, and moved to the USA, becoming a global boxing celebrity.[53] Jack Kid Berg, the Whitechapel Windmill, fourteen years younger than Lewis, followed a similar path. He was born Judah Bergman above a fish and chip shop in Cable Street where his father, a tailor, rented a two-bedroom apartment, although the family of seven children would subsequently move to larger premises. Judah joined the Victoria Club and played a variety of sports. He made his Premierland debut in 1923, the first time he wore boxing gloves. Although he tried to become an apprentice to a cabinet-maker and to a barber, he soon became a professional boxer at fourteen and his career path would follow that of Lewis, which involved holding a variety of titles and spending time in the USA.[54]

Jewish boxers would disappear in the post-war period as a result of the social mobility of the group from which they emerged. Lewis, Berg and others moved upward as a result of their success in the ring. Berg would subsequently become a film stuntman, while his daughter became an artist and he managed to buy property for his parents and sisters.[55] In the place of Jews, following the patterns of other aspects of the history of London migration, came new groups to take their place in boxing, especially those of West Indian origin including Maurice Hope, Lloyd Honeghan, Nigel Benn, Michael Watson, Lennox Lewis and Chris Eubank. They held a variety of titles between them, although few obtained the celebrity status of Berg and Lewis, with the exception of Eubank. In contrast to their Jewish predecessors, they did not emerge from an East End production line. They originated in a variety of West Indian islands and grew up or lived in a variety of London locations.[56]

Frank Bruno became perhaps the most famous post-war black British boxer, establishing the type of celebrity second only to fellow white South Londoner, Henry Cooper, even though the main claim to sporting glory in both cases consisted of nearly beating world champions Cassius Clay and Mike Tyson respectively. Bruno grew up in South London, the son of a Jamaican nurse and a Dominican bakery worker, who died when Bruno was fourteen. Although he came from the type of secure family unit characteristic of the East End Jewish boxers, he was sent to Oak Hall School in Sussex at the age of ten in 1971 for disruptive behaviour, which proved important in his development as a boxer. He carried out factory and construction work, but became a professional in 1982 and fought until 1996. He subsequently moved into television and acting work and also became known because of his bipolar disorder, which led him to campaign for awareness of mental health.[57]

The participation of London boxers from ethnic minority backgrounds has a long history. On the one hand we might see fighting as an opportunity available to those from working-class or lower middle-class backgrounds who often have secure family backgrounds. Most of the life stories point to an engagement with boxing at the street level from an early age, often, in the case of Jews, as a protection against antisemitism, although racism does not appear to have played a major role in Frank Bruno's move into boxing. In the case of the East End Jews in the early twentieth century a type of production line appears to have developed in which boys learnt their trade in the youth clubs and then moved into a professional career. Perhaps boxing, and sport more generally, 'profits from failure: the failure of black kids to integrate more satisfactorily, gain qualifications more readily, find careers more easily'.[58] Teachers and the education system as a whole increasingly directed black pupils towards sport from the 1970s.[59] However, this seems an unfair assessment for those who succeed.

FOOTBALLERS

The trajectory of football differs from boxing because it developed as a sport in the late nineteenth century and because of the fact that, while elite migrants and the offspring of working-class settlers dominated the professional game by the twenty-first century, they remained largely absent in the early days of the sport with the exception of a handful of Jewish and black players. The Irish really formed the first significant ethnic group to ply their trade as professionals in the football league. The increase in numbers of black players took off during the course of the 1980s, while foreign elites became prominent during the 1990s. London proves especially important in the story of the multiculturalization and globalization of football because of the number of professional football teams in the capital, the fact that it counted some of the least English teams by the twenty-first century (especially Arsenal and Chelsea), and because London teams (again especially Arsenal and Chelsea) have attracted some of the most prominent stars in world football.

Before the Second World War, London and English clubs essentially remained a preserve of the English, with some exceptions originating especially in other parts of the United Kingdom, as well as Ireland, both north and south. In addition, a small number of Jews also made it as professional footballers, including Louis Bookman, an Irish Jew of East European origin who played for a variety of English clubs, including Bradford, West Bromwich Albion and Luton, and the Leeds-born Leslie Goldberg, who represented his home town team as well as Reading, and who changed his name to Gaunt.[60] The most famous London Jewish footballer of the earlier twentieth century was David Hyman 'Harry' Morris (1897–1985), who had taken a similar path to contemporaneous East End boxers. Born in Brick Lane in 1897 he attended the Jews' Free School as well as the Brady Street Boys Club. He played for Fulham, Brentford and Millwall but then moved to Swansea and made his name at Swindon.[61] But no conveyor belt existed, as in the case of boxing, which turned the East End Jews into footballers, as few if any others became professional in this sport.

A similarly small number of black people played professional football in the early days of the sport. A handful of pioneers appeared before the Second World War with limited connections to London. Arthur Wharton, a Ghanaian with Caribbean and Scottish ancestry, played for Rotherham, Sheffield United,

Stockport County and, especially, Preston North End during a career that lasted from 1886 until 1902.[62] Walter Tull, the most famous of the earliest black footballers, had a different trajectory and family history, beginning his short career with Tottenham Hotspur. Born in 1888 in Folkestone to a Barbadian father and a Kentish white woman, his mother died of cancer in 1895. His father died two years later and, despite the fact that he had married another woman, Walter ended up in an orphanage in Bethnal Green in 1898, where he played as a left back for the institution's football team. In 1908 he joined a local amateur club, Clapton FC. In the following year he moved to Tottenham Hotspur, but he would only play for them until 1911, after which he joined Northampton Town. He has become famous partly because of his status as a pioneer footballer but more especially because he became the first and only black British officer commanding white troops in the First World War; he was killed in action in France in March 1918 and was awarded the British War and Victory Medal as well as a recommendation for a Military Cross.[63]

A handful of other black and Asian footballers had careers with clubs outside London during the interwar years, including Alfred Charles, Salim Bachi Khan, Hong Y. Soo, Gil Heron and Roy Brown.[64] In the earlier post-war decades the most famous players included Albert Johanneson, who played for Leeds United and became the first black player to appear in an FA Cup Final in 1965, and Steve Mokone of Coventry City and Cardiff City.[65] From a purely economic perspective, the fact that more black players did not break through during the 1960s and 1970s, at a time when the Commonwealth population of London and Britain as a whole increased, was probably because the need for their labours had not yet arisen. At the same time, football had not become globalized on the scale which would happen at the end of the twentieth century, while the second generation had also not yet evolved.[66]

An important breakthrough for black footballers in the 1980s, especially if we focus on the London clubs, came in the form of the West Ham winger Clyde Best, because he appeared on television screens on almost a weekly basis, certainly in the London area, in the football highlights shows of the BBC and ITV, *Match of the Day* and *The Big Match* respectively. He therefore acted as the pioneering role model to the children of West Indian immigrants reaching their teens, who realized that a career in football, which they played on a daily basis in the playground and at youth clubs, was now possible. In fact, shortly before the arrival of Clyde Best, the mixed-race John Charles, born in Canning

Town, East London, in 1944 to a Grenadian seaman and a local woman, played for West Ham between 1963 and 1969, making 117 appearances.[67] Clyde Best took a different path. Born in Bermuda in 1951 to a respectable lower middle-class family, he played international football for his island of birth from the age of fifteen and moved to London to play for West Ham in 1968, spending his first few days with the mother of John Charles and then settling in Plaistow. He signed a professional contract the following spring and made his debut in the 1969–70 season against Arsenal, alongside World Cup winners Bobby Moore, Geoff Hurst and Martin Peters as well Frank Lampard and Billy Bonds. Best would become a fixture in the West Ham team of the first half of the 1970s and, on one occasion, against Tottenham in April 1972, he turned out in a team with two other black players, the first time three black footballers had played for the same team in England. The other two were Clive Charles, the brother of John, who made just twelve appearances for West Ham, and Ade Coker, born in Lagos in 1954, who had moved to London to join his family in 1965 and who played just nine times for West Ham. Best made 221 appearances between 1969 and 1975 and then moved on to play for Tampa Bay Rowdies.[68]

Black players would become a permanent feature of the London, English and global football scene by the early 1980s, but before examining them, we need to focus on a group which had provided numerous footballers for London and English teams from the early days of the professional game at the end of the nineteenth century. In terms of statistics, between 1888 and 1939 a total of 167 professional footballers migrated from Northern Ireland to play in England, while a further 95 came over from Ireland, together with 24 others who simply gave Ireland as their place of birth, making a grand total of 286. In the post-war period the figure increased significantly: 500 moved from the Republic of Ireland in the years 1945–2010, either as a result of a transfer, as trainees or as juniors, and 417 from Northern Ireland.[69] In the years 1888 to 2010 as many as 1,203 footballers in England therefore had birthplaces in Ireland.

Numerous explanations have emerged for this development. On the one hand we can see this as part of the overall process which has sent the Irish to Britain in terms of Ireland acting as a ready and close (geographical) supplier of cheap labour in football, as in other sectors of the British economy. In such a hypothesis, the Irish labour market remains subservient to the British, which means that the latter can pull in employees in all sectors from Ireland. More generally those who have made their living from football have had a higher degree of mobility than most of the rest of the population in all parts of the British Isles since the inception of the professional game. Pay provides a key indication of the economic subservience of Irish to English football. Those who plied their trade in Ireland could earn considerably more in Great Britain than they could in their homeland while, for those at the top of football in particular, the prestige of playing in one of the greatest leagues in the world, with potential glory in the form of English and European trophies, also proved a great pull. Networks also developed, both in terms of the regional and school origins of the players, aided by scouting involving the teams for which the migrants played.[70]

The English teams which attracted the largest numbers of Irish players included Manchester United, Liverpool, Everton and, in the case of London, Millwall and, above all, Arsenal.[71] The last of these has a tradition of recruiting Irish footballers dating back to the nineteenth century; one example is Patrick Farrell, born in Belfast in 1872, who joined Woolwich Arsenal, based in Plumstead at that time, in 1897. In the same season David Hannah arrived in London. Early twentieth-century players included Maurice Connor, born in Dundee in 1877 of Irish parents, who arrived in 1902, although he made only a handful of appearances and then moved to Brentford in exchange for Wexford-born Tommy Shanks. The height of Irish influence at Arsenal lasted from the 1970s until the 1990s when the star players included Liam Brady, Pat Jennings, Sammy Nelson, David O'Leary, Niall Quinn, Pat Rice and Frank Stapleton, together with, in the years 1976–83, an Irish manager in the form of Terry Neil. Liam Brady acted as the key midfield creator in his spell which lasted from 1973 to 1980.[72] Born in Dublin in 1956 as the seventh child of a docker, he initially went for a trial at Arsenal at the age of fifteen. Although he did not want to go back to the British capital when he returned home to Dublin because of homesickness, caused by leaving Ireland at such a young age, he became an apprentice in 1971 and lived with a Mr and Mrs Rowland who helped him settle in London. Much of his early period consisted of becoming fit and integrated into the professional ethos of the club.[73]

The number of Irish-born footballers playing in the Premier League after its formation in 1992 declined in comparison with those in the First Division,[74] even though, in 2012, 241 professional footballers (including forty-eight in the Premier League) in the entire English game hailed from Ireland.[75] The key reason for this relative decline lies in the globalization of football that took place from the last decade of the twentieth century, which meant that Ireland became just one potential source of talent for English and London clubs, aided by the Bosman ruling by the European Court of Justice in 1995, allowing footballers to move at the end of their contract without a fee, and the ability of sportsmen to migrate freely within the European Union. While the mass migration of footballers did not begin in the 1990s, the increasing globalization of the sport meant that the traditional paths of migration which, for example, took the Irish to Britain, no longer acted as the only options for these players, who increasingly moved as elites, headhunted by clubs not just in London and England but across Europe, where the largest and most successful clubs lay. The large clubs in Spain, Italy, Germany, France and England that regularly play in the Champions League and therefore pay the highest salaries essentially act as globalized companies that can pick and choose whichever players they want. They receive the highest revenues as a result of the development of pay TV and the fact that other globalized companies utilize the success of these clubs as brands to sell their own products by pouring in billions of pounds worth of sponsorship. A pattern of elite migration established by Spanish and Italian clubs from the 1950s had therefore become the norm across the continent by the beginning of the twenty-first century although, while smaller London clubs such as Millwall and Brentford could not attract the most talented and expensive players in the same way as Arsenal or Chelsea, they also experienced some globalization. Because of the international reach and level of funding available in the English game, smaller Premier League teams such as Watford or West Ham have attracted players from some former European elite clubs in, for example, the Netherlands or Portugal.[76]

Table 4 provides an indication of the globalization of the professional game in London, focusing upon the twelve professional teams in the English capital between 1970 and 2010.[77] The Britishness of London football teams proves remarkable, with just thirteen sportsmen originating from outside the United Kingdom and Ireland as late as 1990, double the number of 1970. After 1990 these figures changed drastically, reaching 120 foreign-born footballers or 22.2 per cent in the UK by 2000 and 147 or 38.5 per cent by 2010. The two teams which lead the way in this sense are Arsenal and Chelsea,

Table 4: Footballers Playing for London Teams and Born Outside the UK and Ireland, 1970–2010

Team	1970 Total (and per cent)	1980 Total (and per cent)	1990 Total (and per cent)	2000 Total (and per cent)	2010 Total (and per cent)
Arsenal	0	0	1 (3.4)	21 (43.8)	24 (77.4)
Brentford	1 (5.5)	0	1 (4.0)	3 (7.9)	0
Charlton	1 (4.1)	2 (8.7)	0	9 (19.6)	5 (18.5)
Chelsea	0	1 (3.5)	3 (12.5)	22 (42.3)	51 (64.7)
Crystal Palace	1 (3.7)	0	0	7 (19.5)	7 (26.9)
Fulham	0	0	1 (5.0)	9 (23.7)	22 (64.7)
Millwall	0	0	0	1 (2.2)	2 (7.7)
Orient	0	1 (2.8)	1 (4.5)	3 (7.9)	5 (23.8)
QPR	0	1 (3.7)	1 (3.8)	5 (8.9)	11 (36.6)
Tottenham	1	3 (9.0)	2 (8.0)	12 (26.0)	16 (34.7)
Watford	1 (3.0)	1 (5.5)	0	10 (22.2)	2 (7.1)
West Ham	1 (3.4)	0	3 (11.1)	18 (35.3)	42 (47.6)
Total	6 (2.0)	9 (2.8)	13 (4.5)	120 (22.2)	147 (38.5)

Source: Rothmans Football Yearbook 1970–71 (London, 1970); *Rothmans Football Yearbook 1980–81* (London, 1980); *Rothmans Football Yearbook, 1990–91* (London, 1990); *Rothmans Football Yearbook, 2000–2001* (London, 2000); Glenda and Jack Rollin, *Sky Sports Football Yearbook, 2010–11* (London, 2010).

the most prominent London clubs in terms of ground capacity and trophy success during this period. In fact, the figures of 77.4 per cent of foreign-born footballers playing for Arsenal and 64.7 per cent for Chelsea respectively in 2010 underestimate the true situation in the early twenty-first century because they include all squad members. In reality, both of these teams have rarely played with more than three British players during this period and have often fielded none. Clear variations exist between the Premier League clubs and those which did not make it into this division in the form of Brentford, Millwall and Leyton Orient. Millwall stands out in particular, perhaps attracting so few foreign players because of the racist reputation of its fans, which has also meant that relatively few black players have ever worn the club's shirt.[78]

The 1990s onwards also witnessed an increase in the number of black footballers in both London and English teams as a whole. A combination of migrants and second-generation players with origins from other parts of the world would leave the white British and, even more so, the white English, in a minority. For example, just eleven from fifty-one players in the Chelsea squad of 2010–11 came from white English backgrounds (none originated from other parts of the British Isles).[79] Many of those playing for Chelsea by this time consisted of black players born abroad, including José Bosingwa, Didier Drogba, Michael Essien, Salomon Kalou and Florent Malouda, originating from a variety of African states in this case, although often coming through other European Union countries.

An examination of a series of football biographies and autobiographies, often written with the aid of 'ghostwriters', gives a personal insight into the increasing numbers of foreign and black players who started populating the London game in the late twentieth and early twenty-first centuries. These narratives build upon a genre which had emerged after the Second World War and which had initially told the story of white footballers, with celebrity at its centre. Although many of these accounts may have limited literary value, the passage to Britain proves especially interesting for London footballers with foreign origins, after which these type of stories often then fade into details of matches and success or, sometimes, failure through personal frailty.[80]

Although, as a black player with foreign origins, Clyde Best proved a pioneer, he impacted more upon those born in Britain with West Indian and African parents than upon those born abroad who played for London clubs. As Table 4 demonstrates, his arrival proved something of a false dawn from the point of view of significant football immigration. The same applies to the movement of the two Argentinians who arrived to play for Tottenham Hotspur, Osvaldo Ardiles and Ricky Villa, immediately after Argentina won the World Cup in their home country in 1978. This represented something of a unique coup, which involved Keith Burkinshaw, the English manager of a newly promoted team travelling to Argentina to persuade the two players to move, which he did, offering more money than they could earn in their home country with a limited involvement of the type of football agents who subsequently took control of the lives of many sports stars, and also breaking the patterns of top-class South Americans moving to the elite continental European clubs. Both Villa and Ardiles came from strong family units, the latter from a solid middle-class background, as he actually studied for a law degree. Ardiles in particular became a permanent fixture in the London football scene, eventually becoming manager of Tottenham, if only for a brief and unsuccessful spell. At the height of terrace victimization of black players these Argentinians played for Spurs during the Falklands War of 1982 and faced vilification in the press, especially as traitors, which effectively ended Villa's career in England, and led Ardiles to spend a season on loan at Paris St Germain.[81]

While John Barnes became one of the first black players to play for England,[82] his birthplace was in Kingston, Jamaica, the son of a colonel who moved to London in 1976 to take up a position as Jamaican military attaché. The family settled in affluent Hampstead and John attended Marylebone Grammar School, although he quickly turned his attention to football. His talent emerged at Stow Boys' Club and he signed for Watford in 1981, where he would remain until 1987, during which time he established himself as an England international. He then joined Liverpool where the level of racial abuse shocked him,[83] even though he had experienced it at Watford, especially when playing against Millwall, West Ham and Chelsea, whose fans 'showered me with spit and abuse. Banana after banana came flying from the terrace throngs towards me; hundreds of them.'[84]

Barnes fitted in somewhere between the foreign-born Clyde Best and the scores of British-born black footballers who came to prominence during the course of 1980s, with whom he had more in common than, for example, subsequent black immigrants such as Thierry Henry and Didier Drogba. Their life stories do not feature significant experiences of racism because by the time they arrived to play for the most diverse clubs in London, in the form of Arsenal and Chelsea respectively, John Barnes and his British-born black contemporaries had essentially defeated the terrace racism which had characterized the 1980s. Although born to working-class immigrant parents from the West Indies in Paris in 1977, Henry, guided by his father, became an elite sportsman from the age of thirteen when he joined L'Institut National de Football in Clairefontaine, established to school the best French footballers. Before arriving at Arsenal in 1999 he had already played for Monaco and Juventus and won the World Cup with France in 1998, and would subsequently move to Barcelona. He made his name at Arsenal, an elite club for an elite sportsman whose life after he escaped from his humble background in Paris[85] resembles that of elites in other professions who have made careers in London, the privileged schooling he received paving the way for his career success. Didier Drogba also became a member of the London elite, once he arrived at Chelsea in 2004, having spent a season with Marseilles from 2003 to 2004, although the trajectory of his life differs from Henry. Born in Abidjan in the Ivory Coast in 1978 to a bank employee, he had a good start in life and his move into a football career was because his uncle Michel already played professional football in France. Didier migrated to live with his uncle in a traumatic episode for a five-year-old and he played for a series of smaller clubs before eventually signing for Marseilles.[86] As well as black players who entered the English game via France, essentially constituting a group which could invite the description 'twice migrants',[87] other groups moved directly from Africa to London and other English clubs including South Africans, both black and white, a process with a long history, which intensified from the 1990s.[88]

Henry and Drogba arrived in London at a time when race was subsiding as an issue in English football, for they became heroes to their supporters in the same way as their white British and European counterparts, especially Henry at Arsenal. Football has become one of the most diverse aspects of London and British life in which ability determines success. This has meant that some of the British-born black stars by the early twenty-first century had the same sort of protection as Henry and Drogba. Ian Wright represents something of a transitional figure in that he bridges the gap between the earlier pioneers who bore the brunt of the racial abuse, such as Paul Canoville and John Barnes, and those who would not experience it, like Drogba and Henry, together with British-born players such as Sol Campbell and Rio Ferdinand. Wright has published two autobiographies. The first, from 1996, at the height of his Arsenal-playing career, focused on his progression from a South London childhood, where he came from a solid family background, but where he proved disruptive in school and even spent five nights in Chelmsford Prison for motoring offences. However, he had turned to football with the encouragement of secondary-school teachers and took a circuitous route to the path of becoming a professional as he spent his late teens working mostly in labouring jobs, eventually joining Crystal Palace in 1985 at the age of twenty-one.[89] Although Wright's first book tackled the issue of race and racism,[90] he dealt with it in a more circumspect way in his 2016 autobiography, fifteen years after retiring, stating that he had mixed feelings about this issue, believing that during his 'time as a footballer people in general – especially in London – have become less bigoted', which he attributed to 'the crackdown on racially offensive behaviour' and the fact that racial mixing between children helped to eliminate the prejudice. He also pointed to the increase in the numbers of black players and remembered that while at Crystal Palace, where he played until 1991, his team included Mark Bright, John Salako, Andy Gray and Tony Finnigan.[91] By the time Wright arrived at Arsenal the club already counted a series of black players, including Paul Davies, Michael Thomas and David Rocastle, again illustrating the way in which football teams had become multi-racial by the beginning of the 1990s, although these players had experienced some of the worst examples of racism. On one occasion, playing at Millwall on the right wing, Rocastle experienced chants of 'You Black Bastard', while children 'were encouraged to throw bananas on the pitch' as Rocastle's boots and jersey became 'peppered with phlegm, as large sections of the crowd tried to make the case that the majestic winger was the uncivilised one'.[92] Rocastle came from a similar South London Caribbean background to Wright and spent most of his career playing for London clubs, particularly Arsenal during his prime but also Chelsea as his talents waned.[93]

It is important to stress the centrality of London in the multiculturalization of English football. The capital has proved key to all aspects of the history of black Britain,[94] including football. This becomes clear not only from considering the playing personnel of London clubs, whether the elite Premier League clubs of Arsenal and Chelsea, or the established top-flight club of West Ham United which, by 2006, could count sixty players from black African, Caribbean and Latin American backgrounds since the pioneering John Charles, Clyde Best and Ade Coker.[95] Of the 259 black professional footballers in the English League in 1999, 69, or 26.6 per cent, played for London clubs, while 97, or 37.4 per cent, were born in the capital.[96] These statistics reflect the demographic reality of the concentration of Britain's black population in London, as well as the capital as a centre of black life in Britain. While the story of the so-called 'three degrees', Brendon Batson, Laurie Cunningham and Cyrille Regis, who played for West Bromwich Albion at the same time during 1978–9, remains a West Midlands one, all three grew up in London.[97]

We can conclude this survey of London and its black footballers by briefly examining two twenty-first-century stories. Sol Campbell, who played most of his career for Tottenham and Arsenal, came from a background similar to that of David Rocastle and Ian Wright. He was born in Newham in 1974, the son of Jamaican immigrants. His father Sewell had worked for London Transport and his mother Wilhelmina in a series of factories.[98] Although he made his name with Manchester United, during which time he also captained England, the mixed-race Rio Ferdinand was born in King's College Hospital in London in 1978 to a St Lucian-born father, Julian, and a half-Irish mother Angelina. He grew up on the Friary Estate, Peckham, pointing to the support of his parents and his schoolteachers in his success. He began and ended his career with West Ham and Queens Park Rangers respectively.[99]

Campbell and Ferdinand entered football in the golden age of financial wealth and prove the possibility of this sport acting as a vehicle for social mobility with the right familial and educational support. However, it seems likely that numerous boys from all ethnic backgrounds have had their dreams crushed either because they have not had the mental strength or ability to succeed or because injury has not allowed them to progress in the professional game.[100] In between the superstars, who produce the autobiographies or have biographies written about them, come numerous other professional footballers who spend their lives in football without either failing or reaching the heights of Premier League and international glory. Leroy Rosenior offers a good example of a black Londoner who fits this description. Born in 1964, his parents actually came from Sierra Leone, although, like many of his more successful contemporaries and successors, he grew up in South London, studying for A levels and beginning his career with Fulham.[101] He described its home ground, Craven Cottage, as 'an oasis from the vicious chants' which characterized other grounds such as Stamford Bridge.[102] Rosenior also played for Queens Park Rangers, West Ham and Charlton, and viewed racism as an additional problem facing black players.[103]

RACISM

The world of the London football team appears to have defeated racism in the second decade of the twenty-first century in view of the global origins of the players, either in the first or second generation. However, discrimination would appear to have survived in a number of other ways. First, because of the almost total absence of players from South Asian backgrounds, the most numerous ethnic group in London society. At the same time, while the colour of the players may have changed, few black people have made it into either management or coaching. Finally, the fans of some of the London clubs have tended to remain white and they drove the terrace racism which reached its height in the last three decades of the twentieth century, especially in the case of Chelsea, Millwall and West Ham, although, in other instances – especially Arsenal and, to a lesser extent, Tottenham – the makeup of the fans reflects the ethnicity of the players, especially since the 1990s.

In the 2003–4 season the first-team squads of the entire English Football League and Premier League counted just five players of Asian origin (including two of mixed Asian and white parentage), which seems remarkable in view of the hundreds, if not thousands, of people of African heritage who have played the game from the 1980s.[104] Zeshan Rehman became the first player of South Asian origin to play in the Premiership for Queens Park Rangers in 2008, although he did not progress to a stellar career.[105] In view of the percentage of people of Asian origin in London and in the country as a whole,[106] these statistics seem shocking.

A variety of explanations have emerged to account for this state of affairs, including those revolving around racial prejudice. Extending the definition of Asian more widely, footballers from South Korea, Japan and China have played for both London and other English clubs, usually because of a global scouting system but also due to the impact of these countries and their players at the World Cup. India, Pakistan, Bangladesh and Sri Lanka, however, where the South Asian community of London and the country as a whole originate, have never qualified for the World Cup Finals and neither do they have powerful professional football leagues, as football comes behind cricket as a national pastime. This has meant that English and London clubs do not recruit football players directly from these countries, unlike those from Africa such as the Ivory Coast or Cameroon – often via France as in the case of Didier Drogba – who have made an impact on the global stage. Exceptions to this rule include Chelsea, who have sought an 'Asian Star', in a scheme which 'offers children of Asian heritage between the ages of eight and twelve the opportunity to win a 12-month placement within the Chelsea FC Foundation Elite Training Centre'. But, by 2016, 'despite being in its ninth year, no winner has been signed to Chelsea's academy permanently'.[107]

Some explanations for the absence of Asian footballers, especially when they involve scouts, point to the international nature of the playing staff and essentially maintain that British Asians do not have the skill or physical strength to compete in the professional game – theories that partly emerge from stereotypes which developed during British imperial control of India.[108]

This might seem especially surprising in view of the emergence of the Asian football leagues both in London and in other parts of the country, therefore helping to break down the idea that Asians simply participate in sports more popular in their countries of origin such as cricket and hockey.[109] In London, for example, there has emerged an Asian Premier League, founded in 1993, which includes mostly Asian players but also accepts those from other ethnic groups, reflecting multicultural London. At the same time a Bangladesh Football Association also exists.[110] This mirrors the activities of other migrant groups including a Cypriot Football League of England (essentially London), and, historically, Wingate FC which developed as an amateur Jewish club playing in the Middlesex League and the London League from the 1940s. Although Wingate players Ivor Harrison and Bernard Black signed for Queens Park Rangers and Millwall respectively, Cypriots, Jews and Asians have provided few players to London football teams,[111] meaning that the explanations for the lack of Asian players may also apply to these two groups, even though they form smaller communities. Other theories for the absence of Asian professional footballers point to the fact that scouting networks do not even bother with this group because of the belief that they could not make it as professionals.[112]

Despite the thousands of black footballers who have plied their trade in London, few have become managers, a situation which applies not just to the global capital but to the whole of English and European football. Exceptions with a London connection include Ruud Gullit, the first black coach in the Premier League era, who managed Chelsea from 1997 to 1998, and Chris Hughton the former Tottenham full back born in Forest Gate to a Ghanaian postman and an Irish mother, who has coached several Premier League clubs. However, in 2014 just 19 out of 552 (3.3 per cent) people in coaching roles in professional football in England came from black and ethnic minority backgrounds, while first-team managers in the English professional game counted just 2 from 92 (2.2 per cent) in the form of Londoner Chris Powell, who then took charge of Huddersfield Town, and the mixed-race Keith Curle. The reasons for the absence of black managers and coaches resemble those which hinder Asian footballers in the form of stereotypes about administrative ability as well as the difficulty of breaking into coaching networks.[113]

Despite changes which have taken place in the ethnic makeup of London football fans in recent decades, they do not, as a collective, reflect the diversity of the players they watch. An analysis of the history of the fan base would point to the fact that the inner-city London clubs which emerged in the late nineteenth century tended to draw support from the white working-class communities that surrounded them. These groups included Jews, who began to follow London teams, especially, but not exclusively, Tottenham Hotspur in the years before the First World War. This link developed further in the interwar years when as many as a third, or 11,000, of the regular spectators at White Hart Lane may have consisted of Jews. One of the main reasons for this connection is the geographical proximity of Jewish settlement to White Hart Lane. Glory hunting may also have played a role in this development, as the closest clubs to the East End were Leyton Orient and West Ham, although the movement out of the East End brought some second-generation Jews closer to White Hart Lane in areas such as Tottenham, Hackney, Golders Green and Finchley. Other Jews who migrated to North London supported Arsenal with encouragement from the club itself, including its highly successful manager of the 1930s, Herbert Chapman. The link between Tottenham and its Jewish fans would survive into the twenty-first century, further helped by the fact that the club had Jewish ownership but also because of the rise of racism amongst supporters of other London teams. They started to use the words 'Yid' and 'Yiddo' to describe Tottenham fans who, however, reclaimed the phrase to describe themselves, along with Star of David flags. While overt racism existed amongst Tottenham fans directed against black players and post-war migrants when this became fashionable during the 1970s, a movement developed amongst supporters called 'Spurs Against the Nazis', which helped to stamp it out. In the early twenty-first century Tottenham Hotspur has an ethnically diverse fan base beyond the descendants of late nineteenth-century Jewish immigrants, reflecting the range of groups which live in its catchment area.[114]

By this time Arsenal had become the true symbol of London football multi-culturalism. As we have seen, this manifested itself in management in the form of the long reign of Arsène Wenger from 1996 to 2018, who simply recruited according to talent without any consideration of ethnicity and nationality. Although this may have caused some hostility from other football managers and the British press,[115] Arsenal had developed an extraordinarily diverse range of fans evident to anyone attending a match involving the club but also by the emergence of Arsenal Fan TV, which was forced by the club to rebrand itself as AFTV in August 2018.[116] Although this group of supporters proved instrumental in the dismissal of Wenger in 2018, its broadcasts demonstrate the range of ethnic groups which support this club, especially those of African, African-Caribbean and mixed-race heritage.[117]

While Arsenal may have moved towards a situation of multi-ethnic support, they counted racist supporters in the same way as other clubs during the 1970s and 1980s, linked not simply with the abuse of black players but also with the rise of football hooliganism, as well as recruitment by far-right political groups. In the case of London, the three clubs which became especially associated with these phenomena were Chelsea, West Ham and Millwall. Chelsea and West Ham became linked with hooligan gangs in the form of the Chelsea Head Hunters and the Intercity Firm respectively, even though one of the leading figures in the latter was Cass Pennant, born to a Jamaican mother but adopted by a white family in Kent. Partly as a result of the efforts of bodies such as Kick It Out and the government to eliminate violence from football grounds, but also because of the demographic change in London society, the association between violence, football and racism had declined by the end of the twentieth century, especially in London, despite occasional flare-ups. However, Arsenal and Tottenham offer examples of the changing fan base of London clubs. In the case of West Ham, despite the decline of the Intercity Firm, the numerous black players who have worn the team's colours and the fact that the area in which the Boleyn Ground and the London Stadium lies has become increasingly Asian, its fan base has remained overwhelmingly white, despite the white flight which has taken place from the area. The support of the team amongst those who left the area represents a symbolic link to their London birthplaces, an assertion which would also apply, for instance, to middle-aged Chelsea supporters.[118]

THE BEAUTIFUL GAME IN THE GLOBAL CAPITAL

Football encapsulates the significance of migration in the evolution of London in a way which few other aspects of its recent history can replicate. In the first place, an examination of the playing staff of London teams illustrates both the way in which free movement of labour has increasingly characterized the demographics of the global capital from the 1990s but also the opportunities available to the second generation, at least in the case of those with African and West Indian origins. While the Irish provided labour for many clubs in London and beyond during their early history, they became less important, as did their counterparts in the wider economy, as migration became increasingly globalized and Europeanized by the end of the twentieth century. The fan base reflects these changes especially in the case of Arsenal and Tottenham, if not quite to the same degree amongst other London clubs. London football reflects the situation amongst other English clubs although, once again, Arsenal and, in this case, Chelsea, have a level of uniqueness because of the extent of dominance of foreign and black players, which contrasts, especially in the London case, with smaller clubs such as Brentford, Millwall and Orient. The diversity of the playing staff finds reflection in the rest of Europe as football acts as a key symbol of late twentieth-century globalization. While Spanish clubs may have similar recruitment practices to those in London and the English League as a whole, a significant difference lies in the fact that few second-generation migrants have come through in the same way as they have in England, France, the Netherlands and, more recently, Germany.

Despite the fact that elements of racism may exist in London and English football, it has largely disappeared. Perhaps the fact that so many black boys born in (especially South) London have become footballers may reflect the failure of the education system which has marginalized them and stereotyped them as athletic, but the biographies of those who have become professional footballers, dedicating their lives to the sport, becoming both rich and famous, motivated in their childhoods by teachers and parents, gives the lie to this suggestion. Asians who have not had the same level of success may point to the survival of racism, as does the absence of the black coach and manager which seems especially surprising in view of the vast numbers of black players. We cannot ignore the role of networks and career paths which appear to last for decades or even centuries. While only a handful of London Jews may have become professional footballers, they have been significantly over-represented as boxers, from Daniel Mendoza to Ted Kid Lewis and Jack Kid Berg. These types of networks, as well as the role models which develop, help to explain the attraction of football to black boys. In this sense we have to stress Clyde Best, who must have influenced people born in the early and mid-1960s such as David Rocastle, Ian Wright and Leroy Rosenior, as they watched him on their television screens playing for West Ham alongside the core of the 1966 England World Cup winning team.

While, on the one hand, football offers an opportunity for extreme social mobility to a small minority of the population, both black and white, ultimately based on ability, with intervening factors such as scouts and networks, it also demonstrates the inequality that characterizes the capital and its migrant populations. This is because of the way in which the professional game has imported elite foreign players on astronomical salaries, again especially in the case of Arsenal and Chelsea, although even those playing outside the Premier League may earn salaries far in excess of even high-earning Londoners.

The number of professional clubs based in London makes it unique on a global scale, as no other city could come close to boasting twelve professional teams. While all of these have developed multi-ethnic, multiracial and international teams, the Premier League teams, especially Arsenal and Chelsea, lead the way in this sense, again by any global international comparisons. The number of black footballers emerging from (especially South) London also make this city distinct.

11

HANDEL TO TEMPAH

When I first saw Sir August Manns (then Mr A. Manns) he was a member of the Crystal Palace Orchestra, conducted by Herr Schallehn, wearing a uniform, and the band played under a stand in the open air. Manns helped the conductor by arranging his compositions for the orchestra which Herr Schallehn put on the programmes as his own. Later on Manns became the conductor himself, and after a little while he and the members of his orchestra were allowed by the directors to discard the uniforms for ordinary civilian dress. It was then that Manns instituted and celebrated Saturday afternoon concerts, which he conducted with so much ability for so many years.[1]

The Italian tribe of street musicians may be dealt with as a group. There are the bag-pipers, the children with the accordion and the triangle, the organ-man and the monkey, and the hurdy-gurdy grinder, all of whom hail from the neighbourhood of Clerkenwell.[2]

London is the place for me
London this lovely city
You can go to France or America,
India, Asia or Australia
But you must come back to London city.[3]

Music, the restaurant and football have all relied heavily on migrants for their evolution in London. Those involved in these three activities stand out partly because moving from one place to another, whether within or across national borders, forms an accepted part of their search for work, promotion and, in the case of footballers and musicians, glory.[4] While this becomes clear from the 1990s in the case of football, migrant musicians, like restaurant staff, became involved in the development of the capital's entertainment from top to bottom. They did so as performers, managers or composers and writers in all genres from the dissemination of the classical tradition – aided especially by Italians, Germans and other continental Europeans from the early eighteenth century onwards, epitomized by Handel – through to the impact of migrants with African heritage in the twentieth century, who have influenced the development of jazz, calypso, reggae and grime, making London a key focal point in the evolution of the musical Black Atlantic.[5]

While, from the point of view of classical players, managers and composers, at least since Handel, musicians have essentially spread the continental classical tradition, in the case of those of African heritage a type of cultural transfer[6] has taken place, meaning that rhythms and lyrics brought from the United States, the West Indies and Africa further developed in London to evolve into a new form of cultural production such as grime. People with origins in Africa have also played the central role in the performance of these genres.

On a visit to London in 1855 Richard Wagner took an extreme position in his condemnation of the classical tradition in the city, feeling as though 'eternal night were closing around me' and comparing London with Dante's *Inferno* because of what he viewed as the lack of imagination in programming, including 'the ridiculous Mendelssohn worship',[7] the original victim of his antisemitism.[8] Although Wagner claimed during his visit that the orchestra he conducted consisted 'almost exclusively of Englishmen, that is clever machines which cannot be got into the right swing',[9] foreign players in London became so widespread that their presence led to bouts of xenophobia. As early as 1728 Daniel Defoe complained about 'heaps of foreign musicians', especially those from Italy, supported by the nobility and gentry ahead of 'anything English'. Defoe suggested the development of a system of advanced musical education to produce native-born performers.[10] During the Victorian period the presence of foreign street musicians in London led to a parliamentary and press campaign, combining issues of poverty and xenophobia, to control their numbers.[11] During the 1920s and 1930s the newly formed Musicians Union made an attempt to prevent the entry of foreign performers so that British ensembles could find employment instead. The object of their ire included jazz bands, classical orchestras and groups which performed in restaurants. In fact, the Union persuaded the Ministry of Labour to introduce a work permit system which gave preference to musicians born in Britain, but this led to complaints from promoters and other employers.[12] The *Musicians Journal* published an article written by W. Batten, the joint secretary of the London branch of the Musicians Union, entitled 'The Invasion of Alien Musicians', claiming that when 'individual alien musicians' are allowed in as 'star artists ... when they once settle in this country they never return, especially Americans'.[13] Meanwhile, Captain Humphries, the entertainment manager of the Café de Paris in London, claimed that, despite the expense of hiring 'alien bands', it felt under an obligation to do so because neighbouring establishments did the same and therefore might attract 'custom from his own restaurant'.[14] Although the hostility towards foreign musicians would continue into the post-war period, transnational employee organizations also emerged to represent the interests of performers across national borders.[15]

Despite episodes of xenophobia in the London musical scene, xenophilia became stronger, partly driven by the fact that both music and musicians inevitably migrate so that, while national traditions of music may emerge, the process of cultural transfer involving both sound and people mean that such traditions cannot remain sealed off from external influences, even if they may develop national-level identities, at least in the short run. As examples we could cite the music of Elgar in the late nineteenth century, the English Folk Revival of the interwar years, both of which, however, had little connection with London, or the British popular music which developed in the 1950s. While from Handel to Elgar music and musicians crossed European boundaries, during the twentieth century both performers and their tunes have increasingly spanned global and consequently racial divides. The German assertion that nineteenth-century Britain constituted a 'Land ohne Musik' (land without music), while an exaggeration, partly explains the arrival of foreign musicians to Victorian London and the eras before and since. The constant settlement and visits by musicians to the British capital since the early eighteenth century meant that London did not become a city without music, even if the tunes and those who played them often originated from abroad.[16]

Some music makers, such as Haydn, Mozart and Wagner, simply passed through London and had a relatively fleeting, but sometimes rich, encounter with the imperial capital. Despite the hostility which they faced, especially from middle-class opinion, itinerant street musicians in Victorian London brought the capital to life.[17] Others, perhaps most importantly of all Handel, who settled in London in 1712, spent a large portion of their lives in the metropolis, having a profound influence on music-making. However, as well as music crossing borders with the arrival of performers, it has also evolved within the metropolitan environment from the second generation, who create their own genres and traditions, again by drawing on outside influences. The development of bhangra, in which London has played a role together with other British cities with Punjabi populations, offers a good example of this process, as does the rise of gospel performance. Music has played a role in the construction of migrant identities within London as musical genres which evolved after 1945 illustrate.

As in the case of the rise of the restaurant, the London 'market', as a result of the population size, has meant that the metropolis has housed a vast range of musical venues, proving again that the city does not play the role of the heart of the land without music. This market did not simply support grand music-making, it also allowed continental musicians to pick up pennies from the Victorian poor and working classes. Londoner Thomas Burke provided an indication of the range of musical activity available to the city's residents in an account he published in 1915 about the imperial capital's nightlife. His descriptions include those of music halls, partly a vehicle for working- and lower middle-class jingoism, yet Burke mentions 'Mr Francioli' as his favourite conductor in this environment.[18] Burke's survey also included a tour of much of the capital, including Jewish Whitechapel, Chinese Limehouse, Italian Clerkenwell, Scandinavian Shadwell, Russian Stepney, as well as a 'French Night' in Old Compton Street. These 'nights out' all involved an element of music, although Burke's descriptions included dining and other entertainments. He also described 'The Opera and the Promenades', which included numerous performers from all over the world. During the interwar years, which resulted in significant developments in popular music and dance connected especially with the arrival and dissemination of jazz from America,[19] Soho, which featured in Burke's narrative, had become a centre of music and entertainment in which international performers played a key role.[20]

MIGRANTS AND THE EVOLUTION OF THE EUROPEAN
CLASSICAL TRADITION

Migration played a central role in the evolution of the classical tradition in London and Britain as a whole, involving both celebrity composers and an army of orchestral musicians, who hailed especially from Italy and Germany.[21] While serious music-making may have developed from the end of the seventeenth century, it really began to take off during the course of the eighteenth, especially from the 1780s onwards, although before this time a steady development occurred caused by increasing commercialization and the early development of public concerts. Some aristocrats employed their own musicians while, from the 1730s, an amateur Philharmonic Society met in the Crown and Anchor in Arundel Street. By 1740 this counted twenty-two members. The founding of the Italian Opera in London in 1728 played a central role in the development of classical music, especially with the influence of Handel, and meant the importation of numerous Italian players, as Defoe made clear. London dominated the British music scene in the eighteenth century, indicated by the Italian Opera, the development of orchestral music and the performances in Vauxhall Gardens, which included not just Handel's music but also pieces by other composers. As many as 1,500 musicians had their base here in the middle of the eighteenth century. Performances also took place in theatres, while subscription concerts had also evolved. The Academy of Ancient Music also came into existence in the Anchor Tavern in 1726, while performances took place in other public houses and gentlemen's clubs, together with a variety of other locations in the City and Westminster.

By the time of Haydn's arrival in 1791 considerable professionalization had developed as the London music scene offered a whole range of events from oratorios at Covent Garden and nightly concerts in Vauxhall to organ recitals in Tottenham Court Road, often performed by professional orchestras. Such developments occurred against the background of the evolution of subscription concerts, fuelled by the arrival of Haydn's music in the 1780s, even before the man himself set foot in the capital. They further helped the growth of the London music scene, assisted by the efforts of the German-born violinist and impresario Johann Peter Salomon, who then brought Haydn to London and helped to popularize his music through such subscription concerts. At the same time Franz Cramer, another German, organized similar performances, in which the music of Mozart, along with Haydn, played a prominent role.[22]

The foundation of the Philharmonic Society in London in 1813 signalled an important turning point in the professionalization and stabilization of orchestral music in the imperial capital. On 24 January a group of friends met in the house of Henry Dance, brother of an experienced London musician, William. They signed a document declaring that the object of the new organization lay in promoting 'the performance, in the most perfect manner possible, of the best and most approved instrumental music'. The group would comprise thirty members and they devised a complicated administrative structure. The first concerts took place at the Argyll Rooms and were attended by over 600 people although they subsequently changed their venues. The Society gave birth to the Philharmonic Orchestra, which would subsequently evolve into the Royal Philharmonic, a mainstay in the history of London concert life since that time and the second oldest orchestra in the world. It would introduce the work of numerous continental composers to London and British audiences.[23]

Musical entertainment continued to develop during the course of the nineteenth century and a significant expansion occurred in the 1870s and 1880s. It was assisted by the growth of free trade leading to the importation of cheap instruments, the development of conservatoires, the growth of musical education, and an increase in the number of professional musicians, especially in London. These processes continued into the twentieth century when London would remain home to world-class orchestras that, in addition to the Philharmonic, included the London Symphony Orchestra and the London Philharmonic, which made use of the South Bank Centre opened in 1951, while the Henry Wood Promenade Concerts came into existence in 1895.[24] In the late Victorian period opera, featuring both Italian and German composers, remained a key element in London's musical life.[25] 'The Opera' and 'The Promenades' feature in Thomas Burke's 1915 account. He listed the leading continental and American celebrity performers and composers of the day and asserted that: 'No artist of any kind in music – singer, pianist, violinist, conductor – considers himself as established until he has appeared in London and received its award of merit; and whatever good things may be going in other continental cities we know that, with the least possible waste of time, those good things will be submitted to us for our sealing judgment.'[26]

Foreigners played a central role in the evolution of classical music in Britain, clearly centred on London, from top to bottom, as in the restaurant trade, as players and administrators, while European celebrities regularly visited the city, in some cases – above all Handel – spending a great part of their life in the global capital. As Burke indicates, London formed a key stop in the European music scene, largely because of the size of the audiences in a city with a large middle class. Statistics, profiles of lesser-known musicians and accounts of celebrities help to illustrate the importance of foreigners in London's musical history.

Between 1750 and 1850 people born in Britain made up 75 per cent of British musicians, while 4 per cent came from Ireland, 8.6 per cent from Italy, 7.3 per cent from Germany, 2.5 per cent from France, together with another 2.5 per cent from other locations. Of these musicians, 56.1 per cent spent the bulk of their careers in London.[27] Of the thirty original members of the Philharmonic Society, about a third were continental Europeans.[28] The performers at the fourth concert included 'a negro violinist, George Augusts Polgreen Bridgetown', while the other violinists were P. Spagnoletti, Johann Salomon, Franz Cramer and Jospeh Moralt.[29] Foreigners who conducted the Philharmonic Society included the Prague-born Ignaz Moscheles from 1832 to 1841 and the German Wilhelm Ganz from 1874.[30]

During the eighteenth century Italian string players became especially important, following in the footsteps of Nicola Matteis who performed in London during the 1670s. After 1700 the expansion of the city and the increasing leisure time of its growing middle classes, which led to the growth in public performances, created the opportunities for further migration of both Italian and other string players. They brought the music of their home-land with them, including that of Corelli and Vivaldi, while Italians and others also became administrators, as with the foundation of the Philharmonic Society.[31] Felice Giardini, born in Turin in 1716 of French parentage, initially travelled to Berlin and subsequently to Paris, arriving in London during the 1750s, by which time he had established a significant reputation. His life in the capital involved performing, organizing concerts and teaching, so that he became a leading musical figure there during the second half of the eighteenth century whether in the Italian Opera or in the Bach-Abel concerts.[32] Another violinist, Giovanni Battista Viotti, born in Piedmont in 1755, had travelled throughout Europe, especially Paris, before eventually moving to London in

1792. He spent much of the remainder of his life there until his death in 1824. Viotti had moved to the city initially as an exile from the French Revolution, taking up the opportunities available in London at the time, playing in Salomon's concerts, and managing at the King's Theatre during his initial spell there.[33] Muzio Clementi, a contemporary of Viotti and, like him, a founder member of the Philharmonic Society, was born in Rome in 1752, the eldest son of a silversmith, and moved to England in 1766, initially to Dorset, to provide music for the home of the novelist Peter Beckford. Clementi appears to have settled in London in 1773 and would spend much of the rest of his life here as composer and virtuoso, although like his Italian contemporaries he also travelled to other parts of Europe until his death in 1832.[34] Finally, the double bass virtuoso, Domenico Dragonetti (1763–1846), who had spent his formative years in Venice, moved to London in 1794 where he would remain for the rest of his life, again playing a role in the key musical activities and events of the time, including at the King's Theatre, the Ancient Concerts and the Philharmonic Society.[35] Giacomo Rossini also made a visit to London during the 1820s, conducting his own and other musical works as a celebrity.[36]

German and other continental musicians had also settled in London and contributed to the city's music scene at around the same time as the Italian string players, attracted to the British capital by the greater opportunities and advanced in their virtuosity by better musical education in their homeland as well as pushed away by political instability on the continent. The newcomers found employment as composers, soloists and leaders as well as instrumental performers, while English regiments also employed German military bandsmen. Other Germans became established as music publishers and instrument manufacturers. They played a role in many of the leading metropolitan musical ventures of the time. Hundreds of Germans worked in London between 1750 and 1850. Handel, who first arrived in 1710, clearly stands out but other notable names include Johann Christopher Pepuch, who migrated to London in 1700 and composed, conducted and administrated there. John Frederick Lampe moved to England in 1725 and played the bassoon at the opera. Carl Friedrich Baumgarten arrived from Lübeck in 1757 and quickly obtained a post as an organist, becoming leader of the Haymarket Theatre in 1763 and also working as a composer.[37]

Born in 1685 in Halle, Georg Friedrich Handel had already made his name as a performer and composer in Germany and Italy before he visited London for the first time, therefore mirroring the lives of numerous other itinerant musicians, albeit moving in a different orbit, by taking a circuitous route to the metropolis. A turning point occurred in 1710, when he became kapellmeister of the court of Hanover, arriving in London in the autumn of that year, four years before the succession of the Hanoverian elector to the English throne as George I, and although he would lose this position before the accession took place, Handel subsequently received further support from the monarchy. He remained in London until his death in 1759 concentrating on composition, especially of operas, but also orchestral pieces, including the *Water Music* and *Music for the Royal Fireworks*, church music, oratorios and keyboard pieces. He worked for the Royal Academy of Music, composing operas in Italian, and his presence in London clearly helped to attract the Italian musicians who migrated to the British capital to perform the Italian operas which he produced. Handel seems like a Titan in the London, British and German musical scene, in the case of the last of these representing the first step, along with his contemporaries Bach and Telemann, in the development of the Western canon. He played a role in bringing music to the centre of London's cultural life, and his death appears to have left a vacuum never to be filled again.[38]

Two other central European Titans spent time in eighteenth-century London, although the shorter length of their stays meant that they did not have the influence of Handel and neither did they leave a vacuum in the same way as he did. Mozart visited as a child prodigy with his father Leopold and his sister Nannerl from 1764 to 1765, during which time they initially lived in St Martin's Lane but subsequently moved to Chelsea. The spell in the British capital involved playing before the Royal Family, through the intervention of the London resident Johann Christian Bach, as well as performing in public, while Mozart wrote his first three symphonies here. The impact of London on the Mozarts and the Mozarts on London appears limited. Many of Wolfgang's major works did not receive their first performances here until the 1790s and beyond.[39] In contrast, Haydn had already achieved celebrity status before his visits to London in 1791 and 1794, as ensembles and orchestras performed his works, while his scores circulated in the capital. His visits inspired him to write his London symphonies. Haydn had a significant influence on performance, as his works became a key part of the repertoire in the late eighteenth and early nineteenth centuries.[40]

Perhaps the most well-received celebrity composer who visited London during the course of the nineteenth century was Felix Mendelssohn who, along with Haydn, had a profound influence on the popularity of the oratorio in Victorian England.[41] Despite the misery of Wagner's first visit in 1855, he returned in a triumphant fashion in 1877 'in the zenith of his fame', helped by the efforts of the Wagner Society of Great Britain, founded in 1873,[42] during which time a Wagner Festival took place at the Royal Albert Hall.[43] Numerous other celebrity composers also spent time in nineteenth-century London, especially working with the Philharmonic Society.[44]

These celebrities constituted just one element of the continued impact of continental, especially German, musicians in London. Many more took up longer-term or more permanent residence. The most famous included Sir Charles Hallé, who founded the Manchester orchestra which bears his name. He moved to Britain after the failure of the French Revolution in Paris of 1848, although his reasons for fleeing involved the possibility of securing a position in England, as London in particular retained the significance it had developed during the eighteenth century.[45] The Hungarian Hans Richter became conductor of the Hallé in 1899 and would hold the post until 1911, having previously performed in St James's Hall in London.[46]

The capital remained the centre of musical life in the Victorian period and Germans in particular, but also others, played a leading role in its development. The Neapolitan Michael Costa (1808–84) and the German August Manns (1825–1907) led the evolution of musical life at Crystal Palace, which acted as a magnet for international players whether settled in London or simply visiting the capital for performing purposes, as well as becoming central in the development of music performance more generally.[47] Costa had initially arrived in 1829 with the intention of conducting at the Birmingham Festival but quickly moved to London, after the committee rejected him because of his youth. He established himself as perhaps the leading musical figure in the capital during the nineteenth century, initially working for the Italian Opera, establishing the Royal Italian Opera and becoming conductor of the Philharmonic, as well as a leading light in the development of music at Crystal Palace. He helped to professionalize conducting and orchestral playing and also wrote his own operas. Manns was born in Pomerania and had a musical education in Germany, moving to London in 1854 to take up the position of sub-conductor and clarinettist in the Crystal Palace Orchestra. At the time it was conducted by another German, Henry Schallehn, who Manns succeeded in 1855.[48]

As the brief profile of Costa indicates, elite musical migrants from countries outside German-speaking Europe also made their way to London during the nineteenth century, although he essentially followed in the footsteps of previous Italians who migrated for employment purposes. François Hippolyte Bartholemon became one of the most famous Frenchmen to move to London in the eighteenth century. Born in Bordeaux to a French father and Irish mother, he had made it to Britain via an Irish regiment and started performing in public as a violinist in London from 1764. He subsequently composed and played a leading role at the Italian Opera and became a key figure in London musical life in the second half of the eighteenth century, also working as a concert promoter.[49] Wilhelm Kuhe, meanwhile, born to a musical family in Prague in 1823, moved to London in 1845 and would become a leading impresario and performer.[50]

One of the most distinctive performers and composers of the nineteenth-century London music scene was Samuel Coleridge-Taylor. Although born in Holborn in 1875 to a local woman, Alice Hare Martin, his father, Daniel Hughes Taylor, had moved to the heart of Empire from Sierra Leone in order to study medicine. Samuel's father, however, returned home, leaving his mother to bring him up with the help of her parents, although Alice subsequently remarried. Samuel played music at home and at school and entered the Royal College of Music in 1890 on the basis of his ability as a violinist. After his study Coleridge-Taylor would become one of the most prominent British composers of his generation and was supported by Elgar. He produced several key works including *Hiawatha's Wedding Feast* and taught at the Trinity College of Music and the Guildhall School of Music, but he died in 1912 at the age of thirty-seven. He seems almost a unique figure in the musical history of London as a man of colour who succeeded in the classical world, despite some racism which he faced, which his talent nevertheless overcame. Clearly, he differs from the continental migrants and also from the post-war black second generation.[51]

Coleridge-Taylor essentially formed part of the native-born London musical scene of the late Victorian and Edwardian periods. As we have seen, migrants played a central role in the development of this London scene from the early eighteenth century as performers, writers, conductors and impresarios, and it seems that the impact of continental Europeans arose from a type of vacuum in English musical life which did not produce great musicians for most of these two centuries. Instead, they would emerge from the continent, especially Germany. The elite players described above resemble the other highly skilled migrants who have moved to London, in the sense that they formed part of an itinerant profession who progressed to the imperial capital because of the opportunities which it offered. Although, in many cases, it simply formed one stop in their careers, others would spend the bulk of their lives here.

Musical migration continued into the twentieth century and beyond as London remained a key location on the global classical music scene while musicians have continued to wander. The rise of the Nazis forced some German Jewish musical refugees to London. In fact, German Jews had already made their way to the imperial capital during the course of the nineteenth century as part of the wider migration of their countrymen in this profession rather than as a result of antisemitism. They included Otto Goldschmidt (1829–1907), who arrived in London in 1858, took up the position of Vice-Principal of the Royal Academy of Music and formed the London Bach Choir in 1875. He married the more famous Swedish soprano Jenny Lind, one of the most celebrated voices of the nineteenth century, and they shared a home in South Kensington. Other German Jewish musical figures in Britain before the Nazi period included Georg Henschel (1850–1934) and Carl Rosa (1842–89), together with the Prague-born Ignaz Moscheles (1794–1870). Nazi persecution would send composers, musicologists and performers to London and the rest of Britain.[52]

VICTORIAN STREET PERFORMERS

At the same time as the Victorian middle and upper classes listened to the music of Wagner conducted by Michael Costa and August Manns, the urban poor and proletariat heard street performers who moved to London for the same reasons as their more illustrious counterparts. They were attracted by the economic opportunities available in such a large city but also, again like the concert-hall performer, they constituted part of networks which brought them to the heart of Empire, as their connections with people already present in London acted as a key reason for their migration.

Once again, as with much else in Victorian London, Henry Mayhew acts as an essential and empathetic guide to identifying street musicians with origins in a variety of international locations, although other contemporary publications operated on racial stereotypes partly because of a middle-class campaign to eliminate street music from the metropolis, a campaign in which the mathematician Charles Babbage and the MP Michael T. Bass played a leading role, with support from Charles Dickens and Thomas Carlyle. This led to the passage of several pieces of legislation, above all the Street Music (Metropolis) Act of 1864. The opponents focused not simply on the fact that uncontrolled music playing outside the sealed environment of the concert hall disturbed middle-class peace but also on the fact that Italian musicians exploited children by bringing them to London, while others caused street accidents.[53]

Racial and class stereotypes surfaced in numerous publications which tried to classify the musicians performing on the streets of Victorian London. An 1852 article on 'The Music Grinders of the Metropolis' divides them into nine categories as follows: the 'hand-organist is most frequently a Frenchman of the departments, nearly always a foreigner'; the 'monkey-organist is generally a native of Switzerland or the Tyrol' and 'carries a doctored, and flannel-swathed instrument'; the 'handbarrow-organist is not uncommonly some lazy Irishman'; the 'handcart-organists'; the 'horse-and-cart-organists'; the 'blind bird-organist' made up of Englishmen, Irishmen, Frenchmen, Italians and Savoyards; 'piano-grinders' who came from Italy and 'are never in tune, and therefore never worth hearing'; 'flageolet-organists and pianists', actually viewed positively; and the 'hurdy-gurdy player' described as 'a most horrid grinder'.[54] Babbage devised a table in which he matched nationalities to instruments as follows: Italians and organs; Germans and brass bands; Indians and tom-toms; the English and 'brass bands, fiddles, &c.'[55] Another campaign to suppress street music, with less support and hostility than that of the 1850s and 1860s, developed in the 1890s. One article from 1892 divided performers into 'the tolerable and the intolerable' and identified a range of nationalities including: Scottish bagpipe players; the 'Italian tribe', who included bagpipers, children with an accordion and a triangle, organ grinders with monkeys and hurdy-gurdy players; Indian tom-tom players; and German brass bands.[56] An article from 1896 claimed 'foreigners, of course, predominate, and for a very good reason: they earn far more here than they could earn at home.' One Italian organ grinder with a monkey claimed: 'I can get nothing in my own country but macaroni . . . Here I can get both macaroni and roast beef.'[57]

Mayhew took an empathetic view of street musicians, partly because he spoke directly to them, identifying a series of groups. While they formed a key element of the musical life of Victorian London, they also constituted part of the wider community of people identified by Mayhew who made their lives by selling products on the street, in this case music, and therefore had as much in common with the city's hawkers or destitute as they did with their illustrious counterparts playing in the Crystal Palace and other London concert venues. Those interviewed by Mayhew included a twenty-five-year-old French hurdy-gurdy player from Dijon, who 'voyaged for seventeen years' and performed with his dancing children and his violin-playing wife.[58] Mayhew also spoke to 'Arab' and 'East Indian' tom-tom players, who 'within the last few years . . . have occasionally made their appearance on London's streets'. While Mayhew described them in orientalist language, focusing on their appearance and skin colour, he allowed them to speak at length.[59] In contrast, an article from 1892 described one Indian tom-tom player as 'intolerable' as he used an instrument 'of a very primitive kind', producing a noise described as 'mournful monotony'.[60]

The geographic origin of the largest number of London's foreign street musicians throughout the Victorian period, as Mayhew and numerous other commentators recognized,[61] was Italy, although such street musicians also performed in other European cities, including Paris and Berlin, as well as New York. Italian street performers were already living in London before the nineteenth century, but the increasing emigration from Italy and the economic opportunities offered by the growth of the imperial capital increased their numbers during the Victorian period. However, despite the objections which performances by both Italians and other groups caused amongst middle-class opinion, it seems unlikely that their numbers ever totalled more than a thousand. The peak national figure of 2,237 was achieved in 1901 while 412 resided in Holborn in 1881, although others lived in Hammersmith at this time. The Italians made their way to London through networks which, on the one hand, brought them to the capital, especially from the Como, Parma, Lucca and Liri valleys in central and northern Italy. These networks also sent children to London, with the knowledge of their parents, to work for padrones – a type of evil stepfather, as portrayed in London public opinion – who exploited and mistreated them, sending them out onto the streets to perform. Although both British and Italian authorities made efforts to reduce the exploitation of children, they performed on the streets until the late Victorian period, by which time they also originated from Naples.[62] Some of the performing children worked with their families, as in the case of the Italian harper whose 'parents have long been established in England and have a regular home in Deptford'. One of his sisters 'plays the fiddle admirably' and they also performed in other large towns during the winter and at the seaside in the summer.[63] Some of those who lived in Holborn also worked as family units.[64]

After Italians, the most prominent nationality in the London street musical scene consisted of Germans, essentially brass bands, in an age when this type of ensemble also developed on a significant scale amongst Englishmen.[65] The German musicians also seem to have employed children, in this case boys with 'very poor parents' of between twelve and fourteen years of age, who were 'imported' into Britain 'by a speculating master, who very scantily provides for their necessaries of life, and who sends them out in small companies of 4 or 6, and by their earnings, reaps a bountiful harvest', while keeping them in petty slavery.[66] This 'importation' continued into the 1890s, although perhaps no longer involving children, when one bandmaster brought over people 'from the agricultural parts of Germany' and paid for their fares, uniforms, and board and lodging. 'Fulham is their headquarters and Sunday their practice day'.[67] Mayhew interviewed a bandsman from Oberfeld near Hanover, who played in a group of seven who could each earn between six and eight shillings per day. He stated that he wanted to save enough money to return to Hanover. 'We all live together ze seven of us. We have three rooms to sleep in and one to eat in. We are all single men but one; and his wife, a German woman, lives wis us, and cooks for us. She and her husband have a bedroom to zemselves.' The interviewee claimed that they played in London for half of the year and then performed elsewhere in the country for the rest of the time.[68] The German brass bands sometimes included string players and others dressed in military uniforms.[69]

BLACK MUSIC IN LONDON

Henry Mayhew, along with other Victorian commentators, also identified black (faced) performers in the metropolis. While they may have had limited impact on the musical scene in Victorian London in the way that Germans did, during the course of the twentieth century black people would become the most important musical migrants in the global capital, originating from

America, Africa and the West Indies and therefore placing London at the heart of the Black Atlantic. Like the Germans, some black performers simply spent short sojourns in the metropolis, playing to an admiring audience. Others would spend most of their lives here and would have a profound impact on the evolution of specific genres, as would their offspring, in this sense distinguishing them from the Germans. These genres have included jazz, ska, reggae and rap (grime).[70]

A music and dance tradition had developed amongst the London black community, which had survived the departure from Africa during the course of the eighteenth century, holding this grouping together, but it also transferred to Europeans in the capital who participated in dancing. This African dance also seems to have led to the development of the quadrille. Black people also became employed in military bands, and were often recruited outside Britain.[71]

Black (and black-faced) musicians became a feature of Victorian London's streets almost as common as Germans and Italians. In 1839 an individual called Peter 'held a dialogue between himself and his master . . . accompanied with a guitar'.[72] Mayhew identified 'Street Negro Serenaders', described as Ethiopian. One interviewee claimed that 'Nigger bands vary from four to seven, and have numbered as many as nine; our band is now six.' He continued: 'Regent-street, and Oxford-street and the greater part of St James's, are our best places. The gentry are our best customers.' London acted as home to '50 Ethiopian serenaders', although only 'one of the street nigger-singers is a real black – an African'. These 'Ethiopians' consisted of black-faced minstrels, a genre imported from the United States in the early nineteenth century. They became a feature of the London music hall into the late Victorian period and survived into the television age until 1978, despite the racist overtones. Those interviewed by Mayhew included Irish and 'Scotch niggers'.[73]

However, in addition to these mock black people performing in Victorian London, individuals of genuine African descent also made an appearance, most famously the Fisk Jubilee Singers, formed in 1867 at Fisk University in Tennessee, in the aftermath of the American Civil War and the abolition of slavery in the United States. They had already toured America from 1871, essentially singing black spiritual music, during which time they received critical acclaim but also experienced everyday racism and abuse, including exclusion from hotels.[74]

The fame of the Fisk Jubilee Singers overcame this hatred and they became global stars, receiving invitations to perform in Britain and Europe, beginning and emanating from London. However, even the experience of sailing across the Atlantic proved racially problematic, because 'the managers discovered that no American steamship would take African Americans as passengers', which meant that they sailed on the British ship *Batavia*.[75] Despite the endemic racism which existed in the heart of Empire, their celebrity status meant they had a different experience from that of their homeland, helped by the fact that aristocracy and royalty feted them. The philanthropic Lord Shaftesbury sponsored the visit. Arriving in Liverpool, the Fisk Jubilee Singers took up residence in a house in Upper Norwood in south-east London. The first performance of the eleven singers took place in Wills's Rooms on 6 May 1873 in front of 600 members of the aristocracy.[76] They also performed for Queen Victoria, at the home of the Duke and Duchess of Argyle in Kensington shortly afterwards. She enjoyed their singing and recorded in her journal on the same night that: 'They are real Negroes come from America & have been slaves. They sing extremely well together.'[77] The fact that the Queen received them so favourably meant that doors opened to them throughout her realm and those they met included Gladstone, Disraeli, the Archbishop of Canterbury and Jenny Lind.[78] The Fisk Jubilee Singers also sang in public, especially in churches and chapels, most notably in the Metropolitan Tabernacle, founded by the Victorian Baptist preacher Charles Haddon Surgeon and the largest church in London. Their well-attended concert resulted in a collection of £220. The troupe spent a total of three months in London, after which they embarked upon a tour of much of Great Britain including Scotland and Ireland, returning for a final concert in London in Exeter Hall on 31 March 1874.[79]

The Fisk Jubilee Singers would return to London in the following year, having cemented their celebrity status during their original visit to the heart of Empire and Great Britain as a whole, to the extent that people followed them around in 1875, as well as overcoming some barriers in the United States, sailing back on an American ship. Once again, they both sang in public and met members of the British establishment. Their fame also reached continental Europe which they toured in 1875 and 1877.[80]

As 'real Negroes' the Fisk Jubilee Singers offered an alternative to minstrelsy and paved the way for other black performers both in London and elsewhere. By the Edwardian period hundreds worked in the entertainment industry in

Britain, often as curiosities because of their colour playing stereotypical roles, sometimes almost as equals to their white counterparts. Belle Davis, a mixed-race woman born in New Orleans in about 1874, became a popular star of the London music hall in the first two decades of the twentieth century, making appearances in the rest of the country and then moving to France in the 1920s. Meanwhile, the first all-black musical, *In Dahomey*, with a storyline involving a return to Africa, moved from New York to the Shaftesbury Theatre in 1903, and would then tour other parts of Britain. Although still operating on racial lines, *In Dahomey* signified a breakthrough both in the United States and in Britain.[81]

The interwar years witnessed the beginning of a significant cultural transfer involving black musicians, most significantly jazz artists. 'Music was an ever-present part of black sociability and anticolonial activity in early to mid-twentieth century London', and it also appealed to a broad section of the London population during these years. This meant that by the 1930s the heart of Empire 'was "swinging" to the sounds emanating from black America', often involving black American performers, despite the objections of the Musicians Union.[82] Not all of the black stars of the London jazz scene originated in the United States, as others came from the West Indies, perhaps most famously Leslie Hutchinson. He was born in Grenada in 1900 and moved to Harlem in 1916, then on to Paris where he met F. Scott Fitzgerald and Cole Porter. Hutchinson travelled to London in 1927 which, like many of his early post-war West Indian migrant successors, he came to view as his home because of his belief in the strength of the imperial connection. Despite the inevitable racism which he faced, Hutch, as he became known, turned into one of the most famous performers in London during the course of the 1930s with his own band, which, for instance, appeared at the London Palladium in November 1931. Although he went out of fashion in the early post-war decades, he made something of a comeback, without quite re-establishing his pre-war status.[83] Interwar London also welcomed American performers, perhaps most famously the actor, singer and political activist Paul Robeson, who starred in concerts, plays and films while in the capital from the 1920s to the 1950s. Although, like the first Fisk Jubilee Singers, Robeson and his wife, Essie, experienced less overt prejudice in the imperial capital than they did in their homeland, the Savoy Grill refused him admission to a party given in his honour because of his colour.[84]

Interwar London became the scene for the development of a variety of music involving black performers. Some sung in the classical tradition including, for instance, the South Carolina-born Edmund Jenkins, who studied and then taught clarinet at the Royal College of Music. Some of these sojourners included traces of their ethnicity in their writing and performance, whether from the West Indies or the United States.[85] Black people from all over the world recorded songs in the heart of Empire, which had become a major centre for the production of music.[86]

The main contribution of black and white Americans to the development of music in London and the rest of Britain during the first half of the twentieth century consisted, as indicated above, of the transfer of the mediums of blues, swing and jazz. Some of the first jazz performers arrived during the course of the First World War, including Dan Kildare's Clef Club Orchestra, a black group formed in New York in 1910, which played in the Ciro Club behind the National Gallery. The leader of the band, the pianist Dan Kildare, was from Kingston, Jamaica.[87] The year 1919 has become accepted as the beginning of jazz in Britain because of the arrival in London of the all-white Original Dixieland Jazz Band and the all-black Southern Syncopated Orchestra.[88] The 1920s would witness further black and white American bands in London, a process which would continue for the rest of the twentieth century as jazz went through a whole series of transformations.[89]

Black jazz musicians moved to and performed in London throughout the course of the twentieth century and beyond, originating not simply from the United States but also from the West Indies and Africa, stressing the importance of London both to the dissemination of jazz in Britain but also as a capital of the black diaspora. In view of the racism which continued to exist in the capital and in the country as a whole, the reception of early jazz combined both fear and fascination, reflecting the musical history of the imperial capital since the dominance of the London music scene by Italians and Germans during the eighteenth and nineteenth centuries. Black American musicians became increasingly ubiquitous during the course of the 1920s and 1930s, including Duke Ellington and Louis Armstrong who performed during the latter decade. By the 1930s West Indians became especially visible in the capital, including the trumpeter Leslie Thompson, born in Kingston, Jamaica, in 1901 and originally moving to Britain in 1919 to study at the military musical training centre at Kneller Hall in Twickenham. He went back to

Jamaica but returned in 1929 to become a key figure on the London musical scene. Although, like his fellow West Indian Leslie Hutchinson, his fame would decline, the educated Thompson retrained to become a probation officer in 1963. By this time a new wave of West Indians, part of the Windrush generation, were performing in London jazz clubs. The 1960s also resulted in the arrival of black musicians fleeing the apartheid regime in South Africa while, by the 1980s, descendants of West Indian migrants had also entered the London jazz scene.[90] One of the most famous post-war London jazz clubs, which would host the leading musicians of this genre, came into existence in 1961 as a result of the efforts of an East Ender descended from Jewish immigrants: Ronnie Scott's, located in the key entertainment heartland of Soho.[91]

Black and white musical migrants acted as one key ingredient in the evolution of jazz in Britain, helped by the commercialization of this genre from the 1920s involving record companies, music criticism and writing, especially in the form of *Melody Maker*, and making jazz, in its various forms, one of the most popular and enduring styles of popular music during the twentieth century. As we have seen from Ronnie Scott himself, a tenor saxophonist, this popularization involved the adoption of jazz by the majority population both in London and in Britain as a whole, reflecting the transatlantic transmission of this form which impacted on the whole of Europe, meaning that mainstream society both listened to and played jazz. London played a key role in its diffusion because of its role as a centre of entertainment, re-emphasizing the city's global status.[92]

After 1945 London acted as the centre of a whole series of developments in the history of pop music, involving both migrants and their offspring, as well as the native-born white population, especially from the Beatles onwards, despite the origins of this and other subsequent pop groups from other parts of Britain. Popular music, whether or not it came through London, acted as a key symbol of the globalization of Britain.[93]

London has proved especially important in the evolution of music genres produced by individuals with origins in the West Indies and Africa. One of these was calypso, a form which has its origins in Trinidad connected with carnival and originally sung in French creole. Lord Kitchener (Aldwyn Roberts), one of three entertainers who arrived on the *Empire Windrush*, became the most significant figure involved in the transmission of calypso to London, although his positive portrayal of his life in the metropolis, especially in 'London is the Place for Me', did not reflect the racial realities faced by other West Indians. The metropolis acted as a base for the export of calypso to other parts of the world including Nigeria and Ghana, meaning that this genre, with origins in the Caribbean diaspora from Africa, experienced a kind of return home via the London recording business.[94] Within Britain the influence of Trinidad made itself felt in the development of the steel-pan movement, in which London played a key role.[95]

A similar process of globalization due to forced and voluntary migration resulted in the development of ska and subsequently reggae. Ska had its genesis in the West Indies, with its roots similar to those of calypso, and both were influenced by American jazz during the 1940s and 1950s. Ska then migrated to London, to a greater extent even than calypso, because some of the first ska records released in the early 1960s, perhaps most famously 'My Boy Lollipop' in 1964 sung by Millie Small, which demonstrates a combination of heavy beat, jazz and emerging pop rhythms, followed shortly after by the Migil 5's 'Mockin' Bird Hill' and Georgie Fame's 'Yeh Yeh' (both white), demonstrates yet another element in the complex process of cultural transfer characterizing the evolution of popular music. This might also be described as the cultural appropriation of black music by wider white society, a process which characterized jazz and continued in the case of ska into the 1960s as it further evolved. On the other hand some of the ska groups which would evolve during the course of the 1960s counted both black and white members.[96]

Ska helped to prepare the way for another related form of music with origins in Jamaica – reggae. A significant factor in the transformation of ska to reggae lay in the increasing importance of the bass, helped by the evolution of sound systems, while the reggae lyricist dealt with themes such as captivity and inequality, as well as using biblical references, assisted by the conversion of many reggae musicians to Rastafarianism during the 1960s and 1970s. Many black musicians migrated to London during this period, although, as we have seen, black music had already evolved in the capital, including, at a grassroots level, in Notting Hill from the 1950s. The establishment of Island Records by the white Jamaican Chris Blackwell facilitated this process, helping both the importation of Jamaican music and the development of London reggae involving either Jamaican immigrants such as Desmond Dekker and Jimmy Cliff or native-born Londoners including Janet Kay and the band Musical Youth. While, in one sense, reggae may have evolved from Jamaica and developed into a symbol of Rastafarian identity, on the other hand it quickly became commercialized, if not quite mainstream, which meant it also attracted white audiences. Reggae and ska, which have evolved in a variety of ways in terms of the music and performers they have produced over the years, demonstrate how black musicians and music have penetrated London, British and global consciousness.[97]

At the beginning of the twenty-first century London-born musicians of African origin began to emerge, for example Tinie Tempah and Dizzee Rascal. They have become two of the leading performers of the London music style named grime, which was clearly influenced by rhythms derived from the globalization of rap and largely evolved from the inner city in terms of both its performers and the themes it tackles.[98] The son of Nigerian parents, Rosemary and Patrick Okogwu, the young Patrick (Tinie Tempah) was born in 1988 and grew up in the Aylesbury Council Estate in Walworth with two younger brothers and a sister. His father became a social worker while his mother worked for the NHS. Tinie secured three A levels when he left school.[99] He came after Dizzee Rascal, one of his influences born in Bow in 1984 as Dylan Kwabena Mills to a Nigerian father and a Ghanaian mother. Dylan's father died in 1987 when he was just three, which meant he had quite a different childhood from Tempah, often involving violence, but he would emerge as a grime artist by his late teens.[100]

A final type of black music which emerged in London in the second half of the twentieth century, again a manifestation of the Black Atlantic, with origins in Africa and the black population of the United States, was gospel music, sung in the capital and elsewhere in both West Indian and then African churches. This form in London has its origins in the Fisk Jubilee Singers. In fact, one of its members, Thomas Rutling, moved to the imperial capital in 1905 and tried to give recitals in nonconformist churches, but a lack of interest forced him to settle in Harrogate, where he remained until his death in 1915. In the meantime, the singing of gospel music had taken off in the United States where it had become big business. In London, both in churches and beyond, it developed as a result of West Indian and, especially, Jamaican migration and settlement after the Second World War. The Harmoniser Gospel Group performed in London black churches of a variety of denominations and then also sang in the provinces, changing its name to eventually become the Harmonisers and acquiring national fame. This group prepared the way for an even more famous ensemble in the form of the London Community Gospel Choir, led by Bazil Meade, a native of Montserrat, who settled in Clapton with his parents in 1960. He had initially performed with other gospel choirs, including the Overcomers and the Persuaders, and helped to form the London Community Gospel Choir partly as a reaction against the negative images of black youth following the Brixton riots of 1981 and evolving from the Latter Rain Outpuring Revival Choir, in which Meade played a key role. The London Community Gospel Choir would establish both a national and international reputation and provide inspiration for the development of further London black choirs,[101] offering an alternative London black music story to ska, reggae and grime, even though it has similar origins in the United States, Africa and the West Indies.

OTHER ETHNICITIES AND IDENTITIES

People from the Caribbean and Africa therefore played a central role in the evolution of the London music scene from the 1960s, building upon the pioneering jazz performers of the early twentieth century and also confirming the metropolis as a focal point in the Black Atlantic. The numerous other migrant groups which have made their home in London have also developed their own types of music usually involving an interaction with their place of origin. However, they have not become as globalized as the genres which have emerged in the Black Atlantic, as record labels have not picked them up in the same way as those of African heritage who, since the jazz age, have remained central to the development of popular music and its marketing.

We should also bear in mind that some migrants and migrant groups produce music which demonstrates little resemblance to the areas from which they emerge. Cat Stevens (aka Yusuf Islam), for example, symbolizes the complexity of London identities through his musical phases. Born to a Greek Cypriot father, Stavros Georgiou, and a Swedish mother, Ingrid Wickam, in 1948, Steven Demetre Georgiou grew up in Soho and worked in the family restaurant. His music, whether pop, protest, spiritual or Islamic, reveals little trace of his ethnic origins. His transformations and lack of an obvious ethnic identity symbolize the fluid identities of some Londoners who become fully assimilated, although one could argue that the conversion to Islam filled some sort of spiritual gap which Greek Orthodoxy would have provided for his ancestors.[102] Another

London Greek Cypriot who became even more globally famous than Cat Stevens, namely George Michael – again the result of the marriage of an immigrant from Cyprus to a Londoner from another ethnic group (Kyriacos Panayiotou, anglicized to Jack Panos, and Lesley Harrison, who had a Jewish mother) – reveals even less of his ethnicity in his music, although he symbolizes the normality of ethnic mixing and cultural production in post-war London.[103]

An examination of Jewish involvement in music reveals that this group has participated more deeply in this area of London life as a result of the longer history and larger numbers which this group has counted in the capital's modern history. Jews played a role as music hall entertainers, bandleaders, agents and entrepreneurs during the course of the nineteenth and twentieth centuries. Prominent post-war pop stars with Jewish origins include Helen Shapiro and Marc Bolan. Alma Cogan, born in the Jewish East End, had a Russian-born father and a mother born in the East End to Russian parents.[104]

Bolan and Shapiro, like Cat Stevens, are examples of fully assimilated Londoners who moved into the pop mainstream. The first generation, on the other hand, tends to demonstrate a desire to directly reproduce the music of the homeland. In later nineteenth-century London, while August Manns conducted at Crystal Palace and German brass bands marched through the streets of London, other Germans had established a whole series of singing clubs to perform songs from their homeland, although these tended to attract the German elites, as honorary members of the Liederkranz, including Max Bruch and Richard Wagner.[105] Fifty years later, visitors to Soho could eat in Italian restaurants which played Italian music and where dancing from the homeland also took place, performed in one case by 'a jazz band on the ground floor, another on the second floor, and two accordionists at the top'.[106] For Latin American migrants to post-war London, salsa music and dancing became a key component of identity.[107]

Irish music in London also played a key role in the maintenance of identity, involving the transplantation of melodies and dance forms and the evolution of new types of performance. At the same time Irish musicians have always formed part of the mainstream London, national and international scene. While some transplantation of traditional Irish dance forms may have occurred from the nineteenth century, the Gaelic revival, the cultural aspect of the growth of Irish nationalism during this period, helped to invigorate and reinvent this tradition. It manifested itself musically in the emergence of the Irish Folk Song Society of London, as well as the development of pipe bands, although the latter also had connections with the Roman Catholic Church and the London Irish connection to the military. The decades after 1945 also witnessed a flowering of Irish music in London, especially of a form that remained unorganized in pubs located in areas of Irish settlement. Irish dance halls also developed which included performances from Irish showbands, consisting of electric guitar and bass, drums, piano and a lead singer who played cover versions of contemporary pop songs, an importation from Ireland demonstrating another combining and crossing of cultures. At the same time Irish folk song also developed in the capital.[108] Ireland also provided more mainstream musicians on the London scene whose ethnicity remained in the background. The most prominent composer of the Elizabethan Age, John Dowland, may have hailed from Dublin.[109] Some of the most famous British performers in the post-war period had Irish ancestry, including Elvis Costello and Dusty Springfield in the case of those born in London, and perhaps most importantly the Pogues, who had close connections to Ireland because of their birth or parents, and also because of their musical punk style.[110]

Asian music and musicians in London and in Britain more broadly resemble the story of the Irish. Neither community has played the same role as Italians, Germans and black people. In the case of Asian music, London forms one urban location in a wider national picture. In the first place, as in the case of the Irish, some direct transplantation took place from the homeland so that, for example, Bengali settlers in the East End of London probably brought their own music and songs with them from the end of the nineteenth century. Bhangra music emerged from Punjabi settlers and their music in Sikh and Hindu temples, weddings and festivals. Bhangra came to fruition in the early 1980s through a combination of the songs and music of the settlers directly from India combined with the business acumen and technical skills of the Punjabis who had moved to Britain via East Africa, giving rise to groups which performed and signed recording contracts while the same music was performed at weddings and festivals. By the 1990s Asian bands had also emerged.[111]

LONDON AS THE GLOBAL MUSIC CAPITAL

The centrality of London in the development of a wide variety of musical genres from classical to grime makes it unique simply because of its longevity. As in the case of food one of the key reasons for its importance lies in the concentration of its population, creating a demand for restaurants and for entertainment, with music at its heart. In both cases, without denying the existence and evolution of indigenous influences, migrants have played a central role in the development of the London scene.

Cultural transfer has clearly taken place often involving several stages. Gospel music, for example, has its origins in Africa and was further developed in the Caribbean, helped by American influences. It then migrated to London with West Indians and, in a type of returning to Africa in reverse, received a new lease of life following the arrival of fresh streams of African immigrants in the late twentieth century. A similar process led to the development of grime. Perhaps London acts as a type of entrepôt, through which musical forms pass, sometimes remaining and at other times experiencing re-export, in the case of grime back to the United States as well as globally. While, on the one hand, London serves as a key focus in the Black Atlantic, it also plays the same role in the global music scene per se, indicated by its importance as a recording capital from the early twentieth century.

In terms of many of the stories told above, musicians have simply used London as a residence because of the demand for entertainment. This clearly applies to some of the German composers and performers from Handel and Haydn through to August Manns, as well as to the Italian-born Costa and the numerous Italian-born string players of the eighteenth and early nineteenth centuries. For classical music London has therefore not acted as a key point in the development of particular genres in the way it has done for those emerging in the Black Atlantic. While Handel and Haydn composed some of their key works in the British capital, in the case of classical music London has played less of a role as an entrepôt but more that of a place for consumption of the imported music, rather like the numerous other products which enter the city.

As in the case of the history of the restaurant, London has not simply acted as the playground of the rich and famous but also as a site for the development of popular music, best illustrated in the case of forms originating in Africa. While jazz, reggae and grime may have become global international products, the same does not apply to the music of other less visible migrant groups such as the Irish and South Asians, although all migrant communities have their own distinct music which uses elements from both the homeland and London and therefore remains internationalized if not commercialized on a global scale.

12

MIGRANTS AND THE GLOBAL CITY

From the Romans until the twenty-first century migrants and settlers have played a central role in the development of the city which would, by the nineteenth century, become the capital of the world because of the size of its population and its economic and political power. Although London may have experienced relative decline from the zenith of its influence and status in the late Victorian era, it has remained the most important metropolis in Europe and also one of the leading cities in the world, whatever time period we may examine. Even after the final collapse of Empire during the 1960s, while it may have remained in a kind of limbo for several decades, seeking a post-imperial role together with the country of which it formed the capital, London rose to prominence again at the end of the twentieth century to become the leading financial capital in Europe, due to the easing of financial trading rules worldwide, a position it had originally established from the eighteenth century because of the role of the City in financing the expansion of the British Empire. The London metropolis needs understanding initially because of its importance as the centre of the global financial and imperial system from the middle of the eighteenth century, but from this arose its importance in the other spheres considered by this volume.

The book has demonstrated the uniqueness of London in terms of its long history of immigration, the fact that at least half of most migrant populations in Britain have concentrated here, but also in its level of diversity, which becomes apparent from the end of the Second World War and established by the beginning of the twenty-first century. By that time not only did every nation state in the world count people in London but every London borough housed significant numbers of migrants – even if a difference in this sense exists between, for example, the inner London Haringey and the outer London Brentwood.[1]

These three unique aspects in London's migratory history can be better appreciated if we consider a series of other interlinked features: demography; globality; employability; social mobility; and a revisiting of diversity. These five headings help us to achieve a deeper understanding of the relationship between migration, globality and diversity, especially through the prism of employment because the discussions have demonstrated that, while London has for most of the last three centuries constituted the political and financial capital of the world, this has fed into its importance as a global work centre. It has attracted people from Britain, Europe and the rest of the world seeking employment in all sectors of the economy, from cleaners – even though those working in this area may endeavour to secure better-paid employment – to hawkers, to musicians, footballers and political and financial elites.

DEMOGRAPHY

London's role as a magnet attracting Britons, Europeans and people from all over the world has meant that, for much of the last three centuries, it remained, in terms of population, either the largest city in the world or one of the largest. No other British settlement could compete with it for almost its entire history, while it became the largest European city by the early nineteenth century. These numbers and statistics have a significant impact on its history of migration and diversity.

It seems most useful to tackle the issue of the relationship between demography, migration and diversity through the concept of success breeds success. While London may have become a domestic population magnet for much of the early modern period, its population did not expand significantly until the early nineteenth century because high mortality rates had wiped out any increases in the numbers of births and immigration from other parts of the country which fed its growing commercial and industrial activity. Medical and sanitary advances in the nineteenth century, in particular, helped the steady growth in the population of London, assisted further by increases in internal and international migration.

During the early modern period and even until the first half of the twentieth century, London therefore essentially acted as a magnet for internal migrants although, after the Act of Union between Great Britain and Ireland in 1800, this would include Ireland and the Irish, a group which has had a profound influence upon London's demographic and broader history for hundreds of years. While the Irish remained visible and foreign because of their Roman Catholicism from the Reformation onwards, London's population continued to increase primarily as a result of internal migration until well into the twentieth century, although, by 1945, the Jewish community, which like the Irish, had always had a presence in London (except during the period of expulsion, 1290–1656), became visible and centrally important in the development of numerous aspects of London life. The emigration of white British Londoners who had helped build the metropolis from the Victorian period created a vacuum filled by migrants from the Empire and Commonwealth. They proceeded to transform, literally, the face of the capital, whose peak population size of 1939 did not return until the second decade of the twenty-first century, by which time more white flight had taken place while the areas of origin of international settlers had diversified even further. Gentrification of the inner city has not significantly changed the ethnic make-up of the capital since the end of the twentieth century, because no clear evidence has emerged to demonstrate the ethnicity and nationality of those moving into areas originally inhabited by the white working classes and then reconfigured by the post-war settlers.[2]

To return to the concept of success brings success, this manifests itself in two ways in terms of the demographic history of London. First, the ever increasing size of the metropolis has meant that it has provided work opportunities to millions of people in all sectors of the economy and, as the city grew, these opportunities increased even further. The size of the London economy has allowed people involved in all types of economic activity to live in the city to find employment in service sectors in order to support the elites, whether governmental, financial, industrial or cultural. As London children (like me) learn from their childhood, London plays the role of capital in all sectors whether demographic, political, administrative or cultural, for example. It is, quite simply, the capital of everything, certainly in a British context, and has been even globally in many senses for much of the last two centuries. This included the centre of industry, often ignored in the telling of the Industrial Revolution which tends to focus on the English Midlands and north as well as on Wales and Scotland. From the Victorian period onwards London's factories produced all manner of goods while the physical growth of the capital attracted millions of people to construct and maintain the millions of buildings, especially homes, which have emerged, a role in which migrants, from the Victorian Irish onwards, have played a key role.

The idea of success breeding success also operates when considering the streams of migrants who have moved to the world's capital over the last two hundred years, because population movement across international borders usually works through networks. This means that initial small numbers of settlers act as the basis for the development of communities, despite the attempts of the British state, backed by a hostile media, to reduce the stream of migration into the global capital since the passage of the Aliens Act of 1905. Thus, the initial Bangladeshi sailors who settled in the East End of London in the early post-war period, with possible connections to the late nineteenth-century lascars, acted as the basis for the development of Banglatown by the end of the twentieth century. Similarly, the Greek Cypriot community which evolved in 1930s Soho would act as the foundation for relatives who followed after 1945 although, in this case, the focus shifted away from the West End towards North London. For the different streams of Jews who moved to the metropolis from the middle of the seventeenth century, whose areas of origins changed, the attraction of the capital lay in the fact that, while antisemitism remained part of everyday life in London, the city acted as a beacon of hope against the violent state-supported prejudice which Jews experienced on the continent, whether in the Iberian Peninsula, Russia or Germany.

EMPLOYABILITY

The freedoms of London, especially in contrast to European cities, acted as a key factor in attracting all manner of refugees to the metropolis: the exiles escaping the French Revolution in the 1790s,[3] German revolutionaries in the Victorian period, governments in exile during the Second World War, those fleeing persecution in the Cold War, and the global crisis which followed the end of this conflict from the end of the 1990s – even though, by this time, British refugee policy limited and controlled those who could enter and settle in London.[4]

However, this book has revealed London as the work capital of Britain and Europe and, for much of the past two hundred years, the world. The numerous personal accounts quoted essentially tell the story of foreigners moving to London in search of employment, as that remains the main motivation for migration for the vast majority of those who have settled in the metropolis. Once again, the economic significance of London, its size and the scale of the economy have all combined together to bring in people from all over the world working in all manner of occupations throughout the social scale and, increasingly, throughout the entire geographical area covered by the metropolis.

As the book has argued, one of the unique factors about this city lies in its ability to attract people throughout the economic and social scale. The idea of London acting as a magnet for cheap labour offers just one explanation as to why this metropolis has proved such an important global magnet. Clearly, most of those who have entered the city seeking employment have worked in low-end manual and service-sector jobs since the eighteenth century, as the example of the long history of the Irish in the London building trade demonstrates. However, numerous other social groups have settled in the city. Few other international urban centres could claim the range and scale of global elites. The importance of London as an international financial centre from the eighteenth century has proved fundamental, a status which European Jews helped to cement from the Napoleonic period onwards and which attracted bankers from other parts of Europe over the following century. The proportion of foreign bankers may have remained stable or declined during the course of the twentieth century but the 'Big Bang' in financial services at the end of that century gave the City of London a new lease of life and power comparable with its Victorian and Edwardian status. This in turn helped to create a new service sector to provide for the needs of the growing international bourgeoisie with a key centre in the City, whether, for example, as cleaners or restaurant staff. But these elites have also included individuals who moved to London directly as a consequence of the opportunities which the presence of British and international bankers provided. The arrival of classical musicians from the early eighteenth century occurred because of the employment opportunities which no other city could offer, because none had such a developed middle and upper middle class, both foreign and domestic born. The presence of a large bourgeoisie offered all types of job openings from those working in classical music to those who founded the restaurant trade as waiters, cooks and owners. Musicians and waiters filled a skills gap. Trained in occupations which had emerged on the European continent, they transferred their abilities to the

European city where the greatest economic opportunities existed. As we have seen, during the course of the twentieth century London also attracted a new group of musicians from Black America and the West Indies in particular, who imported jazz but also helped to develop musical forms such as ska and reggae. Similarly, the presence of a dozen football teams in London meant that it had become well positioned to develop some of the most globalized football teams in the world whether in terms of ownership or from the point of view of the playing staff. Arsenal and Chelsea in particular illustrate this process.

But between Nathan Mayer Rothschild, as a banking elite, and Didier Drogba, as a sporting superstar, the Irish builders from the eighteenth century onwards and the South Asian women preparing aeroplane food in West London in the second half of the twentieth century, come numerous others. They have settled in London and established all types of small businesses, from the Jewish and Irish street-peddlers interviewed by Henry Mayhew, many of whom existed on tiny profit margins (if any), to the plethora of migrant shop-keepers and restaurant owners residing in the capital in the second half of the twentieth century.

The size of the London economy therefore offers the key explanation as to why people from all over the globe have settled to work in such a wide range of occupations throughout the social scale. While the international impor-tance of the London economy determines its size, this globality is also reflected in the range of occupations which foreigners undertake within the city. But the central point to re-emphasize here is the position of London as work capital. Those who have settled in the metropolis have usually devoted their lives to work, the reason they moved. The Irish navvies who have settled in the capital since the eighteenth century did so for the purpose of labouring in London's streets, a pattern which continued into the second half of the twentieth century. The life of Donall MacAmlaigh,[5] one of hundreds of thousands of Irishmen working in the London building trade over centuries, offers just one example of the centrality of employment for manual workers who surrendered their rural existence for a supposedly better life, even though the reality of employment proved different. Many of MacAmlaigh's post-war single male contemporaries worked long hours and spent much of their leisure time simply drinking, although other Irishmen and women established a better equilibrium in their lives.[6] Meanwhile, higher up the social scale, the life of the Turkish Cypriot immigrant Asil Nadir offers an example of another individual whose London life essentially revolved around work, on this occa-sion through the establishment of an international business empire, which, however, crashed in the 1990s. Clyde Best's life revolved around football, an artist much like the classical music performers who migrated to London in pursuit of their artistic goals. Idolized by West Ham fans in the early 1970s, his career would fizzle out in the second half of that decade when he moved to the United States.

These examples demonstrate that the London economy has, for centuries, had an insatiable appetite for labour. Until the twentieth century those who settled in the capital were primarily English people who would often pay with their lives in their search for employment because of the insanitary conditions existing there. The examples of the Irish drinkers and the failed businessmen such as Asil Nadir demonstrate that the London economy eats up and spits out people on all parts of the social scale. Working hard, the purpose of moving to the capital, does not guarantee success or social mobility. African cleaners who take on several jobs at once to make ends meet seem to have little prospect of achieving social mobility because of both racism and the fact that they cannot earn and save enough money to purchase a house.

SOCIAL MOBILITY

While the London economy may have essentially enslaved numerous migrants and also ruined the lives of countless others, experiences of work remained mixed. Social mobility has also characterized the lives of migrant settlers in London, although it appears to have become increasingly difficult in recent decades because of the rise in house prices at a much faster rate than wages, placing this key determinant of upward progress out of the reach of most migrants. In contrast, my father, Nestoras Panayi, a pastry cook, who spent his early London days in a bedsit in Leman Street in the heart of the East End in 1958 had, by the middle of the 1960s, purchased a four-bedroom three-storey house in Crouch End, after going through other forms of accommodation, including living with relatives in various parts of North London and the ownership of a smaller house in Essex Road. A mortgage from the local council, no longer an option, helped him to buy his house at 61 Uplands Road. My father settled in London at a time of population decline, which made housing affordable to newly arrived immigrants. This was in contrast to the situation by the beginning of the twenty-first century when significant population growth, largely the result of European Union migration, meant that property purchases remained out of reach for much of the population of London, whether immigrant or not, other than for those who already owned a flat or a house.

Buying a house offers a key indicator of social mobility (even though some Europeans may not have this ambition because it is customary to rent in their own countries), but others also exist. Migrants from all areas of the world played a leading role in the development of the London economy by establishing businesses of all sizes. While nineteenth-century German migrants (both Jewish and Gentile) such as Nathan Mayer Rothschild or Saemy Japhet may have started from a high base because they already had expertise and training in the business world, their entry into London finance turned them into some of the richest individuals in Britain and therefore the world. Asil Nadir may provide a twentieth-century parallel, again because he had some business experience but utilized the opportunities available in London to establish a nationwide and global business empire, albeit one that failed. Lower down the social scale come the army of immigrant small businessmen who have opened tens (perhaps hundreds) of thousands of shops and eating establishments since the Victorian period. Some groups such as the Greek Cypriots and East African Asians already arrived with either a sense of financial and economic independence because of the normality of property ownership (in the case of the former) or because they had previous experience of running a business (for those arriving from East Africa).

However, social mobility really needs understanding through generations and the best example consists of the East European Jews who moved into the East End in the Victorian and Edwardian periods. The most typical pattern here was of a Jewish settler living in crowded accommodation in a large family unit somewhere in Stepney in which either the father or the father and mother both worked in sweated industries, especially the boot, shoe and tailoring trades. When we move forward to the interwar years, the children tend to have moved into new types of occupations including hairdressing and taxi driving, occupations suggesting the early stages of upward mobility. Just as significantly, while many of the immigrant parents did not speak English, their children became fully fluent, often from attending educational establishments, especially the Jews Free School, opened by previous waves of Jewish settlers. A further key element in the process of interwar social mobility was the move out of the East End, usually collectively, to emerging suburbs in areas such as Golders Green and Finchley. By the 1960s the East European Jewish community, which by this time had entered a third generation, had become focused in outer North London boroughs, especially Barnet and Redbridge, while social surveys demonstrated that the London Jews had become the most prosperous community in the capital and in the country as a whole, by which time the religious devotion of the descendants of the immigrants had often declined into a type of secular Jewishness.[7] The East European Jews built upon the pattern which had characterized their predecessors who had moved into London from a variety of European states during the seventeenth and eighteenth centuries.

This gradual intergenerational process offers one way of understanding London social mobility. As we have seen, this sometimes occurs more rapidly, especially in the age of celebrity and pay inequality from the late twentieth century. Footballers with African and African-Caribbean heritage have moved from inner-city working-class backgrounds, often in South London, to global superstar status, playing for one of the big London clubs or, in the case of Rio Ferdinand, Manchester United. This pattern is replicated in the careers of rap musicians such as Dizzee Rascal.

Social mobility does not inevitably happen, however. Many of Henry Mayhew's Jewish and Irish street-sellers would have died in poverty. It seems difficult to imagine how the African and South American labourers living in contemporary London could experience the type of upward social mobility characterizing Jewish settlement. Except if we remember the fact that a Jewish male with several children living in a street off Whitechapel working long hours in 1900 could not have imagined that his grandchildren would achieve some of the highest standards of living in London by the 1960s. This would appear something of a fantasy for the army of builders, office cleaners and security guards who lubricate London and who send their children to inner-city schools. While education may provide a way forward for their offspring it seems inconceivable that the London property market could open up for them in the way that it did for the numerous communities which settled in the metropolis from the 1880s until the 1980s. Perhaps the offspring of Latin Americans and Africans will enjoy social mobility without property ownership, as renting may become increasingly the norm.

DIVERSITY

Clearly, one of the truly unique aspects of the migration history of London is the level of diversity which exists, to the extent that the concept of superdiversity has emerged in order to explain the variety of ethnic groups now living in the metropolis. Every nation state in the world can count members in London today.[8] While the numbers of migrants and their offspring living in London by the end of the twentieth century may constitute a new development, the presence of people from all over the world does not because the global economic, political and cultural significance of the former heart of Empire always attracted a diverse range of people. As the chapters above have clearly demonstrated, the difference lies in the variety and size of communities. Before 1945 Irish and Jewish settlers became highly visible, especially when they arrived in large numbers in the early and late Victorian periods respectively. However, by the second half of the nineteenth century public attention also focused upon the Chinese, South Asians and black population of London, concentrated especially upon the East End, closer to the river than the Jewish settlers, despite small numbers. By this time European groups had also become a feature of London, especially Germans and Italians, although they, along with the French and Africans, had lived in London for centuries.

The increasing diversity of London from the second half of the twentieth century has meant that migrants live all over the city, even though boroughs closer to the centre tend to count the highest numbers of foreigners and the widest range of groups. This represents a change from the Victorian era, partly as a result of the expansion and growth of the city. The East End has experienced centuries of migrant settlement from the Huguenots onwards because it has existed as a built-up area for a longer period than other parts of the capital, especially the suburbs stretching in all directions, which emerged from the mid-Victorian period and which experienced white flight after the Second World War, creating space for the newly arrived migrants from all over the Empire and Commonwealth. In addition to the East End, the other area which has a long tradition of settlement is Soho. Whereas the East End has become associated with poor migrant settlement, both because of economic realities but also the way in which London and wider opinion has constructed it, Soho by contrast has been associated with cosmopolitanism. It almost seems as if these two areas in core London symbolize the positive and negative aspects of migration.

The type of ghettoization associated with the East End appears to have spread out to the rest of London in the post-war period, in the sense that specific groups have settled in specific locations, perhaps creating the type of ghettoes which emerged in Spitalfields with the Huguenots. Except for the fact that such settlements do not remain sealed and always comprise other populations. Although we might argue that West Indian settlement spread out from the core of Brixton, Greek Cypriots moved northwards from Camden Town, while Bangladeshis have concentrated in East London, for example, in reality these groups have not monopolized these areas and, over time, have broken down. Cosmopolitanism seems more appropriate when describing London by the early twenty-first century, because ghettoes no longer exist as people of different ethnic groups live next to each other. Diversity in many parts of London has become so ingrained that the type of violent racism which characterized the East End in the 1930s and 1970s appears consigned to the past.

Cosmopolitanism has also developed because of the reality of interethnic marriage and relationships, which has meant that the face of Londoners literally looks different in 2019 from 1819 or 1919. Mixed-race children and those born to parents from two completely different ethnic groups have become normal, a development which has roots dating back to the nineteenth century as we saw with regard to, for example, Italians, Irish, Germans and Chinese, and even earlier in the case of the London black population which emerged from slavery. Groups who have no easy supply of migrants to replenish them, such as Greek Cypriots, will die out in the same way that the Huguenots and eighteenth-century black people did.

This image of a cosmopolitan fairyland needs some qualification. White British and white Europeans tend to secure jobs higher up on the social scale than, especially, Latin Americans and black Africans in the early twenty-first century, replicating patterns which existed, for example, during the nineteenth century when the Germans and the Irish lay at the bottom of the employment ladder. On the other hand, London has provided opportunities for business success for members of all ethnic groups partly because of the presence of ethnic economies but also because many migrants have simply moved into the manufacture and selling of mainstream products.

The lives of migrant Londoners simply mirror people either born in the city or who have moved to it from other parts of Great Britain. Immigration took off after 1945 when the supply of Britons dried up. While immigrants may practise different religions, at least temporarily, and eat different foods, their foods and their religion become part of the London kaleidoscope. Just as importantly, they lead lives which parallel those of white Britons. The stories of the Irish navvy would equally apply to English or Scottish labourers in the early post-war period, as well as Sikhs and West Indians. Multi-ethnic work-forces characterized the building trade and factories after 1945, and even though ethnic concentration in the rag trade may have continued, Jewish and Cypriot factory owners employed a variety of ethnic groups. To give another example, the stories of Irish and black footballers would also apply to those born of white British parentage who come from similar social stock and who have viewed a football career with the same excitement as those with migrant backgrounds, many of whom, both black and white, ultimately pursue fairly mundane careers.[9]

Diversity has simply become a fact of life in London, evolving over hundreds of years but intensifying after 1945. Migrants constitute real Londoners because they live next to their white British counterparts and to people of various different ethnic groups. Their lives therefore run parallel to their neigh-bours, with whom they intermarry to produce children different from those of the Victorian period, although even then children of mixed ethnicity, but mostly white, had become a feature of the metropolis.

GLOBALITY

The diversity of London may characterize other cities both within Great Britain and other parts of the world, although not to such an extent, but few other cities can match its superdiversity or cosmopolitanism because few can count such a large population or such a wide range of groups within them. This range and the ability to absorb have shaped London for centuries, simply intensifying after 1945.

The level of diversity links to the globality of London, which has character-ized its evolution since the early modern period. Its origins lie as an outpost of the first great European Empire established by the Romans, although London would remain fairly peripheral within this entity during and after its existence. London ultimately becomes global because of its role as the heart of Empire backed up by the fact that it served as the commercial and banking capital of the world by the eighteenth century. If globalization reached a new peak during the course of the nineteenth century, the city which lay at the very heart of this globalization or, to put it another way, the heart of this globalization, was London. Not only did it serve as the centre of global political power, it also became the greatest financial, commercial and industrial city in existence for most of the nineteenth and early twentieth centuries. This was the reason that London could attract so many people, which also made it, for much of the nineteenth century, the largest city in the world. While its importance may have declined during the course of the twentieth century, it has remained at the centre of globalization, especially as a result of the renaissance of the 1990s, although decline had only remained relative following imperial collapse by the 1960s.

Goods, services and ideas have passed through London throughout its history of globalization and to these we need to add people. While, on the one hand, we can think globally, in terms of the origins of goods, on the other hand we also need to focus upon the European relationship of London because, despite Empire, London has, since the eighteenth century, remained the most important European city precisely because it could multitask in terms of commerce, political power, high culture, food and industry, to give just a few examples. Its magnetic pull therefore lay in its position both as a global centre and as the major European city. It has had the ability to attract individuals involved in all walks of life, from those who spent time in the heart of Empire to perfect their political ideas, whether Marx or Lenin, or even to plan the overthrow of a regime in the case of individuals such as Gandhi or Jomo Kenyatta whose anti-imperial ideas partly crystallized as a result of spending time in London, to the German musicians and conductors who settled here because of the economic opportunities which existed. The globality attracted numerous European bankers from the Napoleonic period. London's role as the centre of the slave trade in the early modern period meant that it became the centre of black settlement in Europe, albeit forced, during the seventeenth and eighteenth centuries. The Empire came home after the Second World War, as hundreds of thousands of predominantly rural and working-class migrants moved to the dying heart of Empire and to other parts of Britain as a result of the British Nationality Act of 1948, which theoretically allowed the entire population of the Empire to settle in the capital, although this door quickly closed.[10]

Migration to the British and former imperial capital constitutes a key part of the globality of London and has done for hundreds of years, indicated from the early modern period by the presence of the human commodity of slaves, who would gradually become emancipated. Peoples from the Empire continued to move to its heart during the course of the nineteenth century, although this involved small numbers as the most important migrants originated in Ireland and continental Europe. The post-war years saw the true globalization of immigration into London and elsewhere in Britain, precisely at the time when the Empire collapsed from the 1940s to the 1960s. Yet, because of the pulling power of London, at the same time as these movements occurred from the Empire and Commonwealth, older streams of migrants from Europe and Ireland also proceeded to the British capital. Despite increasingly controlled migration regimes which have characterized Britain and the rest of the world since the Second World War, migration has continued on a significant scale because London has retained the same characteristics as a centre of global finance, trade, culture and politics that it possessed when it reached its Victorian zenith. Immigration remains intertwined with London's global history.

NOTES

CHAPTER 1

1. Paul Cohen-Portheim, *The Spirit of London* (London, 1935), p. 1.
2. 'Our City of Nations', *Chambers's Journal* (1891), pp. 453–5.
3. This phrase has become popular in academic circles through the now classic work produced by Stephen Castles, Hein de Haas and Mark J. Miller, *The Age of Migration: International Population Movements in the Modern World*, 5th edn (Palgrave, 2013), which focuses upon the period since the end of the Second World War.
4. For broader definitions of multiculturalism see, for example: Peter Kivisto, *Multiculturalism in a Global Society* (Oxford, 2002); and Tariq Modood, *Multiculturalism: A Civic Idea*, 2nd edn (Cambridge, 2013).
5. Saskia Sassen, *The Global City: New York, London, Tokyo*, 2nd edn (Princeton, NJ, 2001); Greg Clark, *The Making of a World City: London 1991 to 2021* (Chichester, 2015); Ernst Karpf, *Eine Stadt und ihre Einwanderer: 700 Jahre Migrationsgeschichte in Frankfurt am Main* (Frankfurt, 2013); Doreen Massey, *World City* (Cambridge, 2007).
6. Sassen, *The Global City*; Massey, *World City*. For the post-war British consensus see, for example, Kevin Hickson, 'The Postwar Consensus Revisited', *Political Quarterly*, vol. 75 (2004), pp. 142–53.
7. Despite the expulsion of 1290, Jews continued to live in London until their readmission into England in 1656, although they could not replenish themselves on the same scale as they did before 1290 or after 1656. See David S. Katz, *The Jews in the History of England, 1485–1850* (Oxford, 1994).
8. Steven Vertovec, 'Super-Diversity and its Implications', *Ethnic and Racial Studies*, vol. 30 (2007), pp. 1024–54, has pioneered this concept.
9. See, especially, Colin Holmes, 'Cosmopolitan London', in Anne J. Kershen, ed., *London the Promised Land? The Migrant Experience in a Capital City* (Aldershot, 1997), pp. 10–37, who concentrates on the period from the late nineteenth to the late twentieth century. Judith R. Walkowitz, *Nights Out: Life in Cosmopolitan London* (London, 2012), focuses upon Soho in the interwar years, as did Count E. Armfelt, 'Cosmopolitan London', in George R. Sims, ed., *Living London: Its Work and Its Play, Its Humour and Its Pathos, Its Sights and Its Scenes*, vol. 1 (London, 1902), pp. 241–7. See also Mica Nava, *Visceral Cosmopolitanism: Gender, Culture and the Normalisation of Difference* (Oxford, 2007), which focuses upon London.
10. An excellent work on this continuity is Anne J. Kershen, *Strangers, Aliens and Asians: Huguenots, Jews and Bangladeshis in Spitalfields, 1660–2000* (London, 2005).
11. This theme receives detailed attention in Chapter 2 below.
12. See the classic Marxist-inspired account in the form of Stephen Castles and Godula Kosack, *Immigrant Workers and Class Structure into Western Europe* (London, 1973).

13. See Jon May, Jane Wills, Kavita Datta, Yara Evans, Joanna Herbert and Cathy McIlwaine, 'Global Cities at Work: Migrant Labour in Low-Paid Employment in London', *London Journal*, vol. 35 (2010), pp. 85–99.
14. See Chapter 5.
15. See Chapter 4.
16. Ralph Merrifield, *Roman London* (London, 1969), p. 13.
17. Roy Porter, *London: A Social History* (London, 1994), p. 21.
18. Grace Derwent, *Roman London* (London, 1968), p. 85.
19. Merrifield, *Roman London*, p. 30.
20. See Chapter 5 for more information on European merchants.
21. Christopher Hibbert, *London: The Biography of a City* (Harmondsworth, 1977), p. 7; Nick Merriman, 'The Invisible Settlers: From Prehistoric Times to Huguenots', in Nick Merriman, ed., *The Peopling of London: Fifteen Thousand Years of Settlement from Overseas* (London, 1993), p. 32.
22. As argued by Patrice L. R. Higonnet, *Paris: Capital of the World* (London, 2002), although he accepts that Paris did not have the political or economic power of London, focusing, instead, upon the cultural importance of the French capital.
23. Porter, *London*, p. 1.
24. Stephen Alford, *London's Triumph: Merchant Adventurers and the Tudor City* (Kindle, 2017), p. ix.
25. Ibid.
26. Robert O. Bucholz and Joseph P. Ward, *London: A Social and Cultural History, 1550–1750* (Cambridge, 2012), p. 2.
27. Roger Finlay, *Population and Metropolis: The Demography of London, 1580–1650* (Cambridge, 1981), pp. 51, 59–69; Stena Nenadic, ed., *Scots in London in the Eighteenth Century* (Lewisburg, PA, 2010); Emrys Jones, ed., *The Welsh in London, 1500–1800* (Cardiff, 2001).
28. George Rudé, *Hanoverian London* (London, 1971), p. ix.
29. Ibid., p. x.
30. Jerry White, *London in the Eighteenth Century: A Great and Monstrous Thing* (London, 2013), pp. 167–9.
31. Ibid., pp. 85–162; Rudé, *Hanoverian London*, pp. 5–8; M. Dorothy George, *London Life in the Eighteenth Century* (Harmondsworth, 1966), pp. 116–57.
32. John Garwood, *The Million-Peopled City: Or, One Half of the People of London Made Known to the Other Half* (London, 1853).
33. Ibid.
34. J. Thompson and Adolphe Smith, *Street Life in London* (London, 1877).
35. Henry Mayhew, *London Labour and the London Poor*, 4 vols (originally 1861, London, 1968).
36. Charles Booth, ed., *Life and Labour of the People in London*, 9 vols (London, 1892).
37. Sims, ed., *Living London*.
38. Lynda Nead, *Victorian Babylon: People, Streets and Images in Nineteenth-Century London* (London, 2000), deals with the issues outlined in the subtitle to her book.
39. Martin Daunton, 'London and the World', in Celina Fox, ed., *London: World City, 1800–1840* (London, 1992), p. 35.
40. Leonard Schwarz, *London in the Age of Industrialisation* (Cambridge, 2004), p. 12.
41. Daunton, 'London and the World'.
42. Stephen Inwood, *A History of London* (London, 1998), pp. 411–12; K. Schürer and Joe Day, 'Migration to London and the Development of the North-South Divide, 1851–1951', *Social History*, vol. 44 (2019), pp. 26–56.
43. Schwarz, *London in the Age of Industrialisation*, pp. 149–55.
44. Nead, *Victorian Babylon*.
45. David R. Green, *From Artisans to Paupers: Economic Change and Poverty in London, 1790–1870* (Aldershot, 1995), p. 3.

46. Jerry White, *London in the Nineteenth Century: 'A Human Awful Wonder of God'* (London, 2007), p. 68.
47. Gareth Stedman Jones, *Outcast London: A Study in the Relationship between Classes in Victorian Society* (Harmondsworth, 1984).
48. Sims, *Living London*.
49. Ford Madox Ford, *The Soul of London: A Survey of a Modern City* (London, 1905).
50. Jonathan Schneer, *London 1900: The Imperial Metropolis* (London, 1999); Felix Driver and David Gilbert, 'Heart of Empire? Landscape, Space and Performance in Imperial London', *Environment and Planning D*, vol. 16 (1998), pp. 11–28.
51. Jerry White, *London in the Twentieth Century: A City and Its People* (London, 2008), p. 27.
52. Ibid., p. 26.
53. Inwood, *A History of London*, pp. 707–73.
54. Green, *From Artisans to Paupers*, p. 154.
55. Cohen-Portheim, *Spirit of London*, p. 103.
56. See Jerry White, *Campbell Bunk: The Worst Street in North London Between the Wars* (London, 1986).
57. Walkowitz, *Nights Out*; Stephen Graham, *Twice Round the London Clock and More London Nights* (London, 1933).
58. Porter, *London*, pp. 406–12.
59. White, *London in the Twentieth Century*. Steen Eiler Rasmussen, *London: The Unique City* (London, 1937), takes a longer-term perspective to planning.
60. Inwood, *A History of London*, p. 894.
61. White, *London in the Twentieth Century*, p. 60.
62. Inwood, *A History of London*, pp. 895–902.
63. Clark, *The Making of a World City*, p. 35.
64. Ibid.
65. Ibid., pp. 37–45.
66. https://www.london.gov.uk/press-releases/mayoral/london-population-confirmed-at-record-high, Mayor of London, London Assembly Press Release, 'London Population Confirmed at Record High', 2 February 2015, accessed 17 November 2017; *Evening Standard*, 22 June 2017.
67. Chris Hamnett, *Unequal City: London in the Global Arena* (Abingdon, 2003), pp. 103–27. Jane Wills, Kavita Datta, Yara Evans, Joanna Herbert, Jon May and Cathy McIlwaine, *Global Cities at Work: New Migrant Divisions of Labour* (London, 2010), p. 1, accept that 'migrants have long populated the lower echelons of the London labour market' but assert that 'London has become almost wholly reliant on foreign-born workers to do the city's "bottom-end" jobs'.
68. Merriman, 'Invisible Settlers', pp. 28–9.
69. Simon Webb, *Life in Roman London* (Stroud, 2011), p. 11.
70. Peter Ackroyd, *London: The Biography* (London, 2001), pp. 10–17; Merrifield, *Roman London*, pp. 11–15.
71. John Morris, *Londinium: London in the Roman Empire* (London, 1982), p. 6.
72. Ibid.
73. Derwent, *Roman London*, p. 12.
74. Merrifield, *Roman London*, p. 147.
75. Ibid., pp. 147–9; Merriman, 'Invisible Settlers', pp. 29–31.
76. Webb, *Life in Roman London*, pp. 42–54; Derwent, *Roman London*, pp. 23–30.
77. Merriman, 'Invisible Settlers', p. 32.
78. Inwood, *A History of London*, pp. 34–41.
79. Ibid., pp. 42–50; Merriman, 'Invisible Settlers', pp. 32–4.
80. Paul Hyams, 'The Jewish Minority in Medieval England, 1066–1290', *Journal of Jewish Studies*, vol. 25 (1974), p. 271; A. M. Hyamson, *The History of the Jews in England* (London, 1908), p. 107.
81. Joe Hillaby, 'The London Jewry: William I to John', *Transactions of the Jewish Historical Society of England*, vol. 33 (1992–4), pp. 8–12.

82. H. G. Richardson, *The English Jewry under Angevin Kings* (London, 1960), p. 277.

83. Hyamson, *History of the Jews*, p. 108.

84. Ibid., p. 18.

85. Hyams, 'Jewish Minority', p. 277.

86. Joe Hillaby, 'London: The Thirteenth-Century Jewry', *Transactions of the Jewish Historical Society of England*, vol. 33 (1990–2), pp. 100–2.

87. Ibid., pp. 286–7.

88. Hillaby, 'The London Jewry', pp. 26–30.

89. Ibid., pp. 30–40.

90. Hillaby, 'London', pp. 134–7.

91. Robin R. Mundill, *England's Jewish Solution: Experiment and Expulsion* (Cambridge, 1998).

92. T. H. Lloyd, *England and the German Hanse, 1157–1611: A Study in their Trade and Commercial Diplomacy* (Cambridge, 1991); Panikos Panayi, *German Immigrants in Britain during the Nineteenth Century, 1815–1914* (Oxford, 1995), pp. 3–6; Joseph P. Huffman, *Family, Commerce and Religion in Cologne: Anglo-German Emigrants, c.1000–c.1300* (Cambridge, 1998), pp. 175–96.

93. T. H. Lloyd, *Alien Merchants in England in the High Middle Ages* (Brighton, 1982); Sylvia L. Thrupp, 'Aliens in and Around London in the Fifteenth Century', in A. E. J. Hollaender and William Kelloway, eds, *Studies in London History: Presented to Philip Edmund Jones* (London, 1969), pp. 251–72.

94. Beverly A. Dougherty, 'German and Italian Merchant Colonies in Early Modern England', in Victor N. Zakharov, Gelina Harlaftis and Olga Katsiardi-Hering, eds, *Merchant Colonies in the Early Modern Period* (London, 2012), pp. 35–9; Suzanne Dempsey, 'The Italian Community in London during the Reign of Edward II', *London Journal*, vol. 18 (1993), pp. 14–22; Terri Colpi, *The Italian Factor: The Italian Community in Great Britain* (Edinburgh, 1991), pp. 25–6.

95. Jacob Selwood, *Diversity and Difference in Early Modern London* (Farnham, 2010); Alford, *London's Triumph*, p. 16.

96. Lien Bich Luu, *Immigrants and the Industries of London* (Aldershot, 2005).

97. Martin Holmes, 'Evil May-Day 1517: The Story of a Riot', *History Today*, vol. 15 (September 1965), pp. 642–50; Irene Scouloudi, 'Alien Immigration in London, 1558–1640', *Proceedings of the Huguenot Society of London*, vol. 16 (1938), pp. 27–49; Michael Wyatt, *The Italian Encounter with Tudor England: A Cultural Politics of Translation* (Cambridge, 2005).

98. C. W. Chitty, 'Aliens in England in the Sixteenth Century', *Race*, vol. 8 (1966), pp. 129–45; David Ormond, *The Dutch in London: The Influence of an Immigrant Community* (London, 1973); Panayi, *German Immigrants*, pp. 7–8; Andrew Pettegree, *Foreign Protestant Communities in Sixteenth-Century London* (Oxford, 1986); Randolph Vigne and Charles Littleton, eds, *From Strangers to Citizens: The Integration of Immigrant Communities in Britain, Ireland and Colonial America, 1550–1750* (Brighton, 2001), pp. 7–105.

99. Mark Greengrass, 'Protestant Exiles and their Assimilation in Early Modern England', *Immigrants and Minorities*, vol. 4 (1985), pp. 67, 71; Greg Parker, *Probate Inventories of French Immigrants in Early Modern London* (London, 2016).

100. Kershen, *Strangers, Aliens and Asians*, pp. 76–83, 109–14, 168–72; Robin D. Gwynn, *Huguenot Heritage: The History and Contribution of the Huguenots in Britain* (London, 1988), pp. 32–7, 67–9, 110–28.

101. Peter Fryer, *Staying Power: The History of Black People in Britain* (London, 1984), pp. 67–236; Kenneth Little, *Negroes in Britain* (London, 1972), pp. 187–229; James Walvin, *Black and White: The Negro and English Society, 1555–1945* (London, 1973); Edward Scobie, *Black Britannia: A History of Blacks in Britain* (Chicago, IL, 1972); Norma Myers, *Reconstructing the Black Past: Blacks in Britain, 1780–1830* (London, 1996).

102. Kevin O'Connor, *The Irish in Britain* (Dublin, 1974).

103. See the classic pioneering account by M. Dorothy George, *London Life in the Eighteenth Century* (Harmondsworth, 1966), pp. 116–31.

104. See Chapter 6 below.
105. Craig Bailey, *Irish London: Middle-Class Migration in the Global Eighteenth Century* (Liverpool, 2013).
106. See, especially, Todd Endelman, *The Jews of Georgian England: Tradition and Change in a Liberal Society* (Philadelphia, PA, 1979).
107. Panikos Panayi, 'Germans in Eighteenth-Century Britain', in Panikos Panayi, ed., *Germans in Britain since 1500* (London, 1996), pp. 29–48.
108. Key works on nineteenth-century globalization include: Gary B. Magee and Andrew S. Thompson, *Empire and Globalisation: Networks of People, Goods and Capital, c.1850–1914* (Cambridge, 2010); Eric Hobsbawm, *The Age of Empire, 1875–1914* (Harmondsworth, 1987), especially pp. 56–83; C. A. Bayly, *The Birth of the Modern World, 1780–1914* (Oxford, 2004); and Jürgen Osterhammel, *The Transformation of the World: A Global History of the Nineteenth Century* (Oxford, 2014).
109. For New York see Nancy Foner, *From Ellis Island to JFK: New York's Two Great Waves of Immigration* (London, 2000). Higonnet, *Paris*, p. 242, claims that the French capital cannot compare itself to New York during the nineteenth century in terms of the number of migrants who passed through.
110. Klaus J. Bade, *Migration in European History* (Oxford, 2003), pp. 53–164.
111. Marjory Harper and Stephen Constantine, *Migration and Empire* (Oxford, 2014).
112. M. A. Jones, 'The Role of the United Kingdom in the Transatlantic Emigrant Trade, 1815–1875' (University of Oxford D.Phil thesis, 1955); Harold Pollins, *Hopeful Travellers: Jewish Migrants and Settlers in Nineteenth-Century Britain* (London, 1991), p. 25; Ulrike Kirchberger, *Aspekte deutsch-britischer Expansion: Die Überseeinteressen der deutschen Migranten in Großbritannien in der Mitte des 19. Jahrhunderts* (Stuttgart, 1999), pp. 29–55.
113. See the classic orientalist, evangelizing yet still useful Joseph Salter, *The Asiatic in England* (London, 1873).
114. See Rosina Visram, *Asians in Britain: 400 Years of History* (London, 2002), originally published as *Ayahs, Lascars and Princes: Indians in Britain 1700–1947* (London, 1986).
115. Panayi, *German Immigrants in Britain during the Nineteenth Century*, pp. 178–9.
116. See below, pp. 22–3.
117. Mayhew, *London Labour and the London Poor*, vol. 1, p. 104.
118. Garwood, *Million-Peopled City*, pp. 244–313.
119. Ibid., p. 314.
120. F. A. Fahy and D. J. O'Donoghue, *Ireland in London* (Dublin, 1889).
121. Ibid., p. 8.
122. Lynn Hollen Lees, *Exiles of Erin: Irish Immigrants in Victorian London* (Manchester, 1979).
123. See, for example: William Evans-Gordon, *The Alien Immigrant* (London, 1903); C. Russell and H. D. Lewis, *The Jew in London: A Study of Racial Character and Present-day Characteristics* (London and New York, 1901).
124. Aubrey Newman, ed., *The Jewish East End* (London, 1981).
125. Mordechai Rozin, *The Rich and the Poor: Jewish Philanthropy and Social Control in Nineteenth-Century London* (London, 1999).
126. Panikos Panayi, 'Germans in London', in Merriman, *The Peopling of London*, pp. 112–14.
127. Olive Besagni, *A Better Life: A History of London's Italian Immigrant Families in Clerkenwell's Little Italy in the 19th and 20th Centuries* (London, 2011), pp. 9–16; Lucio Sponza, 'Italians in London', in Merriman, *The Peopling of London*, pp. 130–4; David R. Green, 'Little Italy in Victorian London: Holborn's Italian Community', *Camden History Review*, vol. 15 (1988), pp. 2–6.
128. See the relevant contributions to Debra Kelly and Martyn Cornick, eds, *A History of the French in London: Liberty, Equality, Opportunity* (London, 2013).
129. Thimotheous Catsiyannis, *The Greek Community of London* (London, 1993), pp. 28–605.
130. Keith Sword, 'The Poles in London', in Merriman, *The Peopling of London*, p. 156.
131. See, for example, Marika Sherwood, *Origins of Pan-Africanism: Henry Sylvester Williams, Africa, and the African Diaspora* (London, 2011).

132. Elleke Boehmer, *Indian Arrivals, 1870–1915: Networks of British Empire*, by (Oxford, 2015).

133. As originally investigated by Visram, *Ayahs, Lascars and Princes*.

134. John Seed, 'Limehouse Blues: Looking for Chinatown in the London Docks, 1900–40', *History Workshop Journal*, Issue 62 (2006).

135. David Dee, *The 'Estranged' Generation? Social and Generational Change in Interwar British Jewry* (Basingstoke, 2017).

136. See, for example, Marion Berghahn, *Continental Britons: German-Jewish Refugees from Nazi Germany* (Oxford, 1988).

137. Seán Hutton, 'The Irish in London', in Merriman, *The Peopling of London*, pp. 123–4.

138. James J. Barnes and Patience P. Barnes, 'London's German Community in the Early 1930s', in Panayi, *Germans in Britain since 1500*, pp. 131–46.

139. Michel Rapoport, 'The London French from the Belle Epoque to the End of the Inter-War Period', in Kelly and Cornick, *A History of the French in London*; Besagni, *A Better Life*, pp. 18–26.

140. Claudia Baldoli, 'The Remaking of the Italian Community in London: L'Italia Nostra and the Creation of a Little Fascist Italy during the 1930s', *London Journal*, vol. 26 (2001), pp. 23–34; James J. and Patience P. Barnes, *Nazis in Pre-war London, 1930–1939: The Fate and Role of German Party Members and British Sympathizers* (Brighton, 2005).

141. As an introduction to South Asian settlement see, for example, the relevant contributions to Rehana Ahmed and Sumita Mukherjee, eds, *South Asian Resistances in Britain 1858–1947: Interactions and Models of Resistance* (London, 2011). A good introduction to black settlement is Marc Matera, *Black London: The Imperial Metropolis and Decolonization in the Twentieth Century* (Berkeley, CA, 2015).

142. Seed, 'Limehouse Blues'; George H. Mitchell, *Down in Limehouse* (London, 1925), pp. 20–2; H. V. Morton, *H. V. Morton's London* (London, 1944), pp. 9–12, 335–7, 354–6, 389–91.

143. J. A. G. Roberts, *From China to Chinatown: Chinese Food in the West* (London, 2002), pp. 155–9.

144. Walkowitz, *Nights Out*; Panikos Panayi, *Spicing Up Britain: The Multicultural History of British Food* (London, 2008), pp. 84–93.

145. See, for example: Anthony Glees, *Exile Politics during the Second World War: The German Social Democrats in Britain* (Oxford, 1982); Martin Conway and José Gotovich, eds, *Europe in Exile: European Exile Communities in Britain, 1940–45* (Oxford, 2001); Nicolas Atkin, *The Forgotten French: Exiles in the British Isles, 1940–44* (Manchester, 2003).

146. See two volumes by Stephen Bourne: *Mother Country: Britain's Black Community on the Home Front, 1939–45* (Stroud, 2010); and *The Motherland Calls: Britain's Black Servicemen and Women* (Stroud, 2012).

147. According especially to Fryer, *Staying Power*. More recently see Miranda Kaufmann, *Black Tudors: The Untold Story* (London, 2017), for a series of biographies of free blacks, with a focus on London.

148. Greater London Authority, *The World in a City: An Analysis of the 2001 Census Results* (London, 2005), pp. 15–17, 70–2.

149. Philip E. Ogden, 'Foreword', in Anne J. Kershen, ed., *London the Promised Land Revisited: The Changing Face of the London Migrant Landscape in the Early 21st Century* (London, 2015), p. xvii.

150. Anne O'Grady, *Irish Migration to London in the 1940s and 1950s* (London, 1988).

151. V. D. Lipman, *A History of the Jews in Britain Since 1858* (Leicester, 1990), p. 233, speaks of 300,000 Jews in London at the end of the Second World War.

152. Michael Banton, *The Coloured Quarter: Negro Immigrants in an English City* (London, 1955); Ruth Glass, *Newcomers: The West Indians in London* (London, 1960); Sheila Patterson, *Dark Strangers: A Study of West Indians in London* (Harmondsworth, 1965). See also Clair Wills, *Lovers and Strangers: An Immigrant History of Post-War Britain* (London, 2017).

153. See, for example, 'The Cypriots in London', *Manchester Guardian*, 14 August 1954; Martin Kettle, 'Famagusta, N16', *New Society*, 26 March 1981; Vic George and Geoffrey Millerson, 'The Cypriot Community in London', *Race*, vol. 8 (1967), pp. 277–92; Robin Oakley, *Changing Patterns of Distribution of Cypriot Settlement* (Coventry, 1987).

154. Sheila Patterson, 'The Poles: An Exile Community in Britain', in James L. Watson, ed., *Between Two Cultures: Migrants and Minorities in Britain* (Oxford, 1977), p. 223, describes London as 'by far the largest Polish settlement' in the United Kingdom.

155. Vered Amit Talai, *Armenians in London: The Management of Social Boundaries* (Manchester, 1989).

156. Geoff Dench, *The Maltese in London: A Case Study in the Erosion of Ethnic Consciousness* (London, 1975).

157. Sponza, 'Italians in London', pp. 135–6.

158. See especially Vaughan Robinson, *Transients, Settlers and Refugees: Asians in Britain* (Oxford, 1986).

159. Ceri Peach, 'South Asian Migration and Settlement in Great Britain, 1951–2001', *Contemporary South Asia*, vol. 15 (2006), pp. 134–6; Greater London Authority, *The World in a City*, p. 18.

160. As an introduction see Panikos Panayi, 'Cosmopolis: London's Ethnic Minorities', in Andrew Gibson and Joe Kerr, eds, *London from Punk to Blair* (London, 2003), pp. 67–71. This theme receives more attention in Chapter 2 below.

161. *Guardian*, 14 February 2003.

162. Ogden, 'Foreword', p. xvii.

163. Greater London Authority, *Londoners Born Overseas, Their Age and Year of Arrival* (London, 2013), pp. 7, 9, 10.

164. Naomi Pollard, Maria Latorre and Dhananjayan Sriskandarajah, *Floodgates or Turnstiles? Post-EU Enlargement Migration Flows to (and from) the UK* (London, 2008).

165. For Australasians see: Dylan Nichols, *What Are You Doing Here? The Question of Australians in London* (Brighton, 2007); and David Conradson and Alan Latham, 'Friendship, Networks and Transnationality in a World City: Antipodean Transmigrants in London', *Journal of Ethnic and Migration Studies*, vol. 31 (2005), pp. 287–305. For the French see Kelly and Cornick, *A History of the French in London*. For Americans see Allison Lockwood, *Passionate Pilgrims: The American Traveller in Great Britain, 1800–1914* (London, 1981).

166. C. McIlwaine, J. C. Cock and B. Linneker, *No Longer Invisible: The Latin American Community in London* (London, 2011); Patria Roman-Velazquez, *The Making of Latin London: Salsa Music, Place, and Identity* (Aldershot, 1999).

167. Anne J. Kershen, 'London's Migrant Landscape in the 21st Century', in Kershen, *London the Promised Land Revisited*, p. 19.

168. This phrase was used by Heinrich Dorgeel, *Die Deutsche Colonie in London* (London, 1881), p. 17.

169. See Chapter 7.

170. As an introduction to the national picture see Tony Kushner and Katherine Knox, *Refugees in an Age of Genocide: Global, National and Local Perspectives During the Twentieth Century* (London, 1999), pp. 217–395.

171. See Chapter 11 below.

172. Castles, de Haas and Miller, *Age of Migration*, p. 40.

173. Ibid.

174. Patrick Manning, *Migration in World History*, 2nd edn (London, 2013), pp. 9–10.

175. Panayi, *German Immigrants*; Kirchberger, *Aspekte deutsch-britischer Expansion*.

176. Lucio Sponza, *Italian Immigrants in Nineteenth-Century Britain* (Leicester, 1988), p. 36.

177. Kershen, *Strangers, Aliens and Asians*, pp. 43–8; Katy Gardner, *Age, Narrative and Migration: The Life Course of Bengali Elders in London* (Oxford, 2002); Caroline Adams, *Across Seven Seas and Thirteen Rivers: Life Stories of Pioneer Sylhetti Settlers in Britain* (London, 1987).

178. Maritsa V. Poros, *Modern Migrations: Gujarati Indian Networks in New York and London* (Stanford, CA, 2011).

179. Kathy Burrell, 'Introduction: Migration to the UK from Poland: Continuity and Change in East-West European Mobility', in Kathy Burrell, ed., *Polish Migration to the UK in the 'New' European Union: After 2004* (Farnham, 2009), pp. 1–19.

180. Richardson, *English Jewry*, pp. 6–14.

181. Cecil Roth, *The Rise of Provincial Jewry: The Early History of the Jewish Communities in the English Countryside* (London, 1950).

182. Bill Williams, *The Making of Manchester Jewry, 1740–1875* (Manchester, 1976).

183. Joseph Buckman, *Immigrants and the Class Struggle: The Jewish Immigrant in Leeds, 1880–1914* (Manchester, 1983).

184. Ben Braber, *Jews in Glasgow 1879–1939: Immigration and Integration* (London, 2007).

185. Frank Neal, *Sectarian Violence: The Liverpool Experience, 1819–1914* (Manchester, 1988).

186. T. P. MacDermott, 'Irish Workers in Tyneside in the Nineteenth Century', in Norman McCord, ed., *Essays in Tyneside Labour History* (Newcastle-upon-Tyne, 1977), pp. 59–85.

187. Ray Costello, *Black Liverpool: The Early History of Britain's Oldest Black Community 1730–1918* (Liverpool, 2001), pp. 8–10; Kathy Burrell, ' "The World in One City": Migrant Lives in Liverpool', *North West Geography*, vol. 17 (2017), pp. 11–18. For post-war migration to Newcastle see Sarah Hackett, *Foreigners, Minorities and Integration: The Muslim Immigrant Experience in Britain and Germany* (Manchester, 2013).

188. White, *London in the Nineteenth Century*.

189. Foner, *From Ellis Island to JFK*.

190. See, for example: Hartmut Keil and John B. Jentz, eds, *German Workers in Industrial Chicago, 1850–1910: A Comparative Perspective* (DeKalb, IL, 1983); Michael Innis-Jiménez, *Steel Barrio: The Great Mexican Migration to South Chicago, 1915–1940* (New York, 2013); and Roland L. Guyotte and Barbara M. Posadas, 'Interracial Marriages and Transnational Families: Chicago's Filipinos in the Aftermath of World War II', *Journal of American Ethnic History*, vol. 9 (1990), pp. 26–48.

191. But see Karpf, *Eine Stadt und ihre Einwanderer*.

192. An excellent account of migration to ancient Rome is Laurens E. Tacoma, *Moving Romans: Migration to Rome in the Principate* (Oxford, 2016). For more recent movement see Jacqueline Andall, *Gender, Migration and Domestic Service: The Politics of Black Women in Italy* (Aldershot, 2000).

193. While there are many studies of a variety of migrant groups in Paris, there exists no volume which has taken a long-term perspective tackling the history of foreign settlers in the city.

194. See two publications by Jacob Selwood: *Diversity and Difference in Early Modern London*, pp. 24–43; and 'Jewish Immigration, Anti-Semitism and the Diversity of Early Modern London', *Jewish Culture and History*, vol. 10 (2008), pp. 1–22.

195. James Ewing Ritchie, *The Religious Life of London* (London, 1870), p. 14.

196. Ibid., pp. 16–75.

197. C. Maurice Davies, *Unorthodox London: Or Phases of Religious Life in the Metropolis* (London, 1873).

198. Richard Mudie-Smith, ed., *Religious Life in London* (London, 1904).

199. Sims, *Living London*.

200. See above, p. 6.

201. W. W. Simpson, 'The Council of Citizens of East London: A Postscript', in Newman, *Jewish East End*, pp. 315–21.

202. JML/1988.525.2, 'Our East London: The Growth of Its Religions', Second Bulletin issued by the School's Committee of the Council of Citizens of E. London, Spring 1950.

203. JML/1988.525.1, 'Our East London: How We Came Here', First Bulletin issued by the School's Committee of the Council of Citizens of E. London, Winter 1949.

204. These articles appeared in 2005 for which see https://www.theguardian.com/uk-news/series/london, accessed 15 December 2017.

205. Philip Baker and Jeehoon Kim, *Global London: Where to Find almost Everything Ethnic and Cultural in the Multilingual Capital* (London, 2003).

206. For critiques of diversity and superdiversity, as well as investigations of cosmopolitanism see, for example: Vertovec, 'Super-Diversity'; Ranji Devadason, 'Cosmopolitanism, Geographical Imaginaries and Belonging in North London', *Urban Studies*, vol. 47 (2010), pp. 2945–63; Susanne Wesendorf, 'Commonplace Diversity and the "Ethos of Mixing": Perceptions of Difference in a London Neighbourhood', *Identities*, vol. 20 (2013), pp. 407–22; Gerd Baumann, *Contesting Culture: Discourses of Identity in Multi-Ethnic London* (Cambridge, 1996); John Nagle, *Multiculturalism's Double Bind: Creating Inclusivity, Cosmopolitanism and Difference* (Farnham, 2009). These themes receive more attention below, especially in Chapters 2 and 7.

207. For a discussion of cultural transfer and migration see Stefan Manz and Panikos Panayi, 'Refugees and Cultural Transfer to Britain: An Introduction', in Stefan Manz and Panikos Panayi, eds, *Refugees and Cultural Transfers to Britain* (Abingdon, 2013), pp. 11–19.

208. See Chapter 11 below.

209. Panikos Panayi, *Fish and Chips* (London, 2014).

CHAPTER 2

1. William Evans-Gordon, *The Alien Immigrant* (London, 1903), pp. 6–7.

2. A. N. Wilson, *London: A Short History* (London, 2004), p. 128.

3. Kellow Chesney, *The Victorian Underworld* (Harmondsworth, 1972).

4. Henry Mayhew, *London Labour and the London Poor*, vol. IV (originally 1861; London, 1968), p. 419.

5. Ibid., p. 421.

6. Ibid., p. 425.

7. Henry Mayhew, *London Labour and the London Poor*, vol. I (originally 1861, London, 1968), pp. 109–13; Jacqueline Turton, 'Mayhew's Irish: The Irish Poor in Mid Nineteenth-Century London', in Roger Swift and Sheridan Gilley, eds, *The Irish in Victorian Britain: The Local Dimension* (Dublin, 1999), pp. 122–55.

8. M. Dorothy George, *London Life in the Eighteenth Century* (Harmondsworth, 1966), pp. 122–3.

9. Joseph Salter, *The East in the West or Work Among the Asiatics and Africans in London* (London, 1896), p. 37.

10. Joseph Salter, *The Asiatic in England* (London, 1873), p. 182.

11. THLHA/P/RAM/3/2/3, 'The Coloured Population in Stepney', February 1950.

12. THLHA/P/RAM/3/2/7, '[Confidential] Report on Investigation into Conditions of the Coloured Population in a Stepney Area', n.d.

13. See A. E. Musson, 'The Great Depression in Britain, 1873–1896: A Reappraisal', *Journal of Economic History*, vol. 19 (1959), pp. 199–228.

14. Rosemary Ashton, *Little Germany: Exile and Asylum in Victorian Britain* (Oxford, 1986), pp. 225–8; Francesca M. Wilson, *They Came as Strangers: The Story of Refugees to Great Britain* (London, 1959), p. 129.

15. Leopold Katscher, 'German Life in London', *Nineteenth Century*, vol. 21 (1887), p. 732.

16. Panikos Panayi, *German Immigrants in Britain during the Nineteenth Century, 1815–1914* (Oxford, 1995), pp. 112–15.

17. Lucio Sponza, *Italian Immigrants in Nineteenth-Century Britain* (Leicester, 1988), pp. 163–81; John E. Zucchi, *The Little Slaves of the Harp: Italian Child Street Musicians in Nineteenth-Century Paris, London and New York* (London, 1992), pp. 76–110; J. Thompson and Adolphe Smith, *Street Life in London* (London, 1877), pp. 86–8.

18. Mordechai Rozin, *The Rich and the Poor: Jewish Philanthropy and Social Control in Nineteenth-Century London* (Brighton, 1999); Anne Kershen, *Strangers, Aliens and Asians: Huguenots, Jews and Bangladeshis in Spitalfields, 1660–2000* (London, 2005), pp. 114–22;

Susan L. Tananbaum, *Jewish Immigrants in London, 1880–1939* (London, 2014), pp. 55–69.

19. J. H. Stallard, *London Pauperism amongst Jews and Christians* (London, 1867), pp. 5–6.
20. Geoffrey Alderman, *Modern British Jewry* (Oxford, 1992), pp. 110–15.
21. Tananbaum, *Jewish Immigrants in London*, p. 57; Aubrey Newman, 'The Poor Jews' Temporary Shelter: An Episode in Migration Studies', *Transactions of the Jewish Historical Society of England*, vol. 40 (2005), pp. 14–56.
22. See Alderman, *Modern British Jewry*, p. 104.
23. Max Cohen, *I Was One of the Unemployed* (London, 1945), which does not provide specific dates of his experiences.
24. NA/CO/876/88, *SS Empire Windrush* – Jamaican Unemployed: Memorandum by the Secretary of State for the Colonies, Arthur Creech Jones, 15 June 1948'; Edward Pilkington, *Beyond the Mother Country: West Indians and the Notting Hill White Riots* (London, 1988), p. 20.
25. Wilmoth George Brown, *Windrush to Lewisham: Memoirs of 'Uncle George'* (London, 1999), pp. 13–16.
26. See, especially, Tony Kushner, *Remembering Refugees: Then and Now* (Manchester, 2006).
27. Tony Kushner and Katherine Knox, *Refugees in an Age of Genocide: Global, National and Local Perspectives During the Twentieth Century* (London, 1999), pp. 64–100.
28. See, for example, the relevant contributions to W. E. Mosse, et al., eds, *Second Chance: Two Centuries of German-Speaking Jews in the United Kingdom* (Tübingen, 1991); and the essays by Marian Malet and Stefan Howald in Marian Malet and Anthony Grenville, eds, *Changing Countries: The Experience and Achievement of German-Speaking Exiles from Hitler in Britain, 1933 to Today* (London, 2002).
29. See, for example, Diana Kay and Robert Miles, *Refugees or Migrant Workers? European Volunteer Workers in Britain* (London, 1992); and Keith Sword, 'The Poles in London', in Nick Merriman, ed., *The Peopling of London: Fifteen Thousand Years of Settlement from Overseas* (London, 1993), p. 157.
30. In 1956 as many as 22,000 Hungarians fled to Britain following the crushing of the revolution by the Soviet Union. While they faced initial housing problems, their status as victims of communism at the height of the Cold War meant that they received a favourable reception. See Kushner and Knox, *Refugees in an Age of Genocide*, pp. 241–61.
31. William G. Kuepper, G. Lynne Lackey and E. Nelson Swinerton, *Ugandan Asians in Great Britain: Forced Migration and Social Absorption* (London, 1975).
32. ECHP/2013_esch_UgAs_16, Interview with Keshavji Mandali, 12 March 2013.
33. NA/HO376/193, Cypriot Refugees in Haringey.
34. Alice Bloch, *The Migration and Settlement of Refugees in Britain* (Basingstoke, 2002), pp. 147–53.
35. Tendayi Bloom, 'London's "Ghosts": The Capital and the UK Policy of Destitution of Refused Asylum-Seekers', in Anne J. Kershen, ed., *London the Promised Land Revisited: The Changing Face of the London Migrant Landscape in the Early 21st Century* (London, 2015), pp. 77–96.
36. Parvati Nair, 'Undocumented and Unseen: The Making of the Everyday in the Global Metropolis of London 2015', in Kershen, *London the Promised Land Revisited*, pp. 100–1.
37. Refugee Action London Migrant Homelessness Conference, *Report* (London, 2013).
38. Amnesty International, *Down and Out in London: The Road to Destitution for Rejected Asylum Seekers* (London, 2006), p. 26.
39. Ben Judah, *This is London* (London, 2016).
40. Although the word 'antisemitism' may have emerged in late nineteenth-century Germany with the development of ideas of racial superiority, hatred of Jews based on their religion and their moneylending had a long history. As an introduction see Robert Wistrich, *Antisemitism: The Longest Hatred* (New York, 1991). The current book follows Anthony Julius, *Trials of the Diaspora: A History of Anti-Semitism in England* (Oxford, 2010), which uses the phrase for the persecution of Jews since the Middle Ages.

41. Joe Hillaby, 'London: The Thirteenth-Century Jewry', *Transactions of the Jewish Historical Society of England*, vol. 33 (1990–2), pp. 90–1.

42. Aubrey Newman, ed., *The Jewish East End, 1840–1939* (London, 1981).

43. Lloyd P. Gartner, *The Jewish Immigrant in England, 1870–1914*, 3rd edn (London, 2010), pp. 143–5.

44. Kershen, *Strangers, Aliens and Asians*.

45. *Report of the Royal Commission on Alien Immigration*, vol. 3 (London, 1903), pp. 70–1; Chaim Bermant, *Point of Arrival: A Study of London's East End* (London, 1975); Lynn Hollen Lees, *Exiles of Erin: Irish Immigrants in Victorian London* (Manchester, 1979), pp. 57, 67–8; Douglas Jones, 'The Chinese in Britain: The Origins and Development of a Community', *New Community*, vol. 14 (1987), p. 399.

46. Henrietta Adler, 'Jewish Life and Labour in East London', in Sir Hubert Llewellyn Smith, ed., *New Survey of London Life and Labour*, vol. 6 (London, 1934), pp. 268–97.

47. Michael Banton, *The Coloured Quarter: Negro Immigrants in an English City* (London, 1955).

48. Katy Gardner, *Age, Narrative and Migration: The Life Course of Bengali Elders in London* (Oxford, 2002).

49. Geoff Dench, *The Maltese in London: A Case Study in the Erosion of Ethnic Consciousness* (London, 1975).

50. John Marriot, *Beyond the Tower: A History of East London* (London, 2011).

51. Panikos Panayi, 'Germans in Eighteenth-Century Britain', in Panikos Panayi, ed., *Germans in Britain since 1500* (London, 1996), pp. 29–48.

52. John Seed, 'Limehouse Blues: Looking for Chinatown in the London Docks, 1900–40', *History Workshop Journal*, Issue 62 (2006), pp. 58–85; Salter, *The East in the West*.

53. Marriot, *Beyond the Tower*, pp. 169–91.

54. V. D. Lipman, 'Jewish Settlement in the East End – 1840–1940', in Newman, *Jewish East End*, pp. 17–40.

55. Caroline Adams, *Across Seven Seas and Thirteen Rivers: Life Stories of Pioneer Sylhetti Settlers in Britain* (London, 1987).

56. See two of the classic studies of the history of migrant settlement in the USA, which take these two contrasting perspectives: Oscar Handlin, *The Uprooted: The Epic Story of the Great Migration that Made the American Peoples*, 2nd edn (Boston, MA, 1973); and John Bodnar, *The Transplanted: A History of Immigrants in Urban America* (Bloomington, IN, 1985).

57. R. Kalman, 'The Jewish East End: Where Was It?', in Newman, *Jewish East End*, pp. 3–15.

58. Bernard Gainer, *The Alien Invasion: The Origins of the Aliens Act of 1905* (London, 1972).

59. C. Russell and H. S. Lewis, *The Jew in London: A Study of Racial Character and Present-day Conditions* (London and New York, 1901), p. 2.

60. Ibid., p. 10.

61. See the classic Léon Poliakov, *The History of Anti-Semitism*, vol. 4, *Suicidal Europe, 1870–1933* (Oxford, 1985). For the British context see the equally classic Colin Holmes, *Anti-Semitism in British Society, 1876–1939* (London, 1979), pp. 36–120.

62. George A. Wade, 'Israel in London: How the Hebrew Lives in Whitechapel', *English Illustrated Magazine*, vol. 23 (1900), pp. 401–10.

63. James Strang, 'The Jewish Colony in London', *Good Words*, vol. 40 (1899), pp. 815–19.

64. See David Englander, 'Booth's Jews: The Presentation of Jews and Judaism in "Life and Labour of the People of London" ', *Victorian Studies*, vol. 32 (1989), pp. 551–71.

65. Walter Besant, *East London* (London, 1903), pp. 193–203.

66. Adler, 'Jewish Life and Labour in East London', pp. 268–98. See the contemporaneous H. L. Trachtenberg, 'Estimate of the Jewish Population of London', *Journal of the Royal Statistical Society*, vol. 46 (1933), pp. 87–99, which uses a statistical methodology to study its subject.

67. Thomas Burke, *The Real East End* (London, 1932), pp. 46–7.

68. William Baker, 'Zangwill, Israel', *Oxford Dictionary of National Biography*, https://doi.org/10.1093/ref:odnb/37087, accessed 25 January 2017.

69. Israel Zangwill, *Children of the Ghetto* (London, 1902).

70. Ibid., pp. 48–9.
71. See also the account in William J. Fishman, *East End 1888* (London, 1988), pp. 131–76.
72. Selig Brodetsky, *Memoirs: From Ghetto to Israel* (London, 1960), p. 17.
73. Ibid., pp. 23–6.
74. Ralph L. Finn, *No Tears in Aldgate* (Bath, 1963), p. 12.
75. Ralph L. Finn, *Grief Forgotten: The Tale of an East End Jewish Boyhood* (London, 1985), p. 56.
76. Willy Goldman, *East End: My Cradle* (London, 1988), pp. 84–8, 95–103.
77. Ibid., pp. 17–22; Finn, *No Tears in Aldgate*, pp. 62–7.
78. Brodetsky, *Memoirs*, pp. 27–51, had an education which allowed him to study at Cambridge.
79. Harry Blacker, *Just Like It Was: Memoirs of the Mittel East* (London, 1974), p. 15.
80. For an introduction to these themes see, for instance: Gartner, *Jewish Immigrant*, pp. 187–291; and Newman, 'Synagogues of the East End', in Newman, *Jewish East End*, pp. 217–21.
81. David Dee, *The 'Estranged' Generation? Social and Generational Change in Interwar British Jewry* (Basingstoke, 2017), pp. 149–204. Religion receives more attention in Chapter 8 below.
82. Lynn H. Lees, 'Patterns of Lower-Class Life: Irish Slum Communities in Nineteenth-Century London', in Stephan Thernstrom and Richard Sennett, eds, *Nineteenth-Century Cities: Essays in the New Urban History* (London, 1969), pp. 359–85; 'The London Irish', *Blackwood's Edinburgh Magazine*, vol. 170 (1901), pp. 124–34; John A. Jackson, 'The Irish in East London', *East London Papers*, vol. 6 (1963), pp. 105–19.
83. Panayi, *German Immigrants*, pp. 94–8.
84. Count E. Armfelt, 'German London', in George R. Sims, ed., *Living London: Its Work and Its Play, Its Humour and Its Pathos, Its Sights and Its Scenes*, vol. 3 (London, 1902), p. 104.
85. Panayi, *German Immigrants*, p. 99.
86. Seed, 'Limehouse Blues'; Sascha Auerbach, *Race, Law and 'The Chinese Puzzle' in Imperial Britain* (Basingstoke, 2012), pp. 15–88; Gregor Benton and Terence Gomez, *The Chinese in Britain, 1800–Present: Economy, Transnationalism and Identity* (Basingstoke, 2008), pp. 25–7; Ng Kwee Choo, *The Chinese in London* (London, 1968), pp. 16–20; George Wade, 'The Cockney John Chinaman', *English Illustrated Magazine*, vol. 23 (1900), pp. 301–7; Hermann Scheffauer, 'The Chinese in England: A Growing National Problem', *London Magazine*, vol. 26 (June and July 1911), pp. 465–80, 645–57; Min-Chien T. Z. Tyau, *London Through Chinese Eyes, or, My Seven and a Half Years in London* (London, 1920), pp. 302–17; Panikos Panayi, *Spicing Up Britain: The Multicultural History of British Food* (London, 2008), p. 74; Virginia Berridge, 'East End Opium Dens and Narcotic Use in Britain', *London Journal*, vol. 4 (1978), pp. 3–28; Marek Kohn, *Dope Girls: The Birth of the British Drug Underground* (London, 1992).
87. Banton, *Coloured Quarter*, pp. 13, 92, 94, 96.
88. Ibid., pp. 126–49.
89. See the variety of documents in NA/MEPO2/9047.
90. Bangladeshis would have seen themselves as such from 1972 when Bangladesh came into existence, previously existing as East Pakistan after the partition of India in 1947 and securing independence from the rest of Pakistan in 1972 after a bitter war.
91. Banton, *Coloured Quarter*, p. 96.
92. Hamza Alavi, *The Pakistanis in London* (London, 1963), p. 2.
93. Kershen, *Strangers, Aliens and Asians*, p. 183; Tower Hamlets Research Briefing, *Ethnicity in Tower Hamlets: Analysis of 2011 Census Data*, https://www.towerhamlets.gov.uk/Documents/Borough_statistics/Ward_profiles/Census-2011/RB-Census2011-Ethnicity-2013-01.pdf, accessed 26 January 2018; Gardner, *Age, Narrative and Migration*, pp. 85–144.
94. THLHA/LC502, Danielle Lamarche, 'Housing Needs of Bangladeshis in Tower Hamlets', 1986.
95. John Eade, *The Politics of Community: The Bangladeshi Community in East London* (Aldershot, 1989), pp. 20–7.
96. Nazneen Ahmed, Jane Garnett, Ben Gidley, Alana Harris and Michael Keith, 'Shifting Markers of Identity in East London's Diasporic Religious Spaces', *Ethnic and Racial Studies*, vol. 39 (2016), pp. 223–42.

97. Kershen, *Strangers, Aliens and Asians*, p. 181.

98. As an introduction see Graham Davis, 'Little Irelands', in Roger Swift and Sheridan Gilley, eds, *The Irish in Britain, 1815–1939* (London, 1989), pp. 104–33.

99. George, *London Life*, p. 121.

100. Ibid., p. 122.

101. According to ibid., p. 125, using similar stereotypes to eighteenth- and nineteenth-century commentators.

102. Lees, *Exiles of Erin*, p. 63.

103. Ibid., p. 88.

104. Samuel Garratt, *The Irish in London* (London, 1852), p. 188.

105. John Denvir, *The Irish in Britain* (London, 1892), p. 393.

106. Ibid., p. 392.

107. Ibid., pp. 393–4.

108. Bernard Canon Bogan, 'History of Irish Immigration to England: The Irish in Southwark', *Christus Rex*, vol. 12 (1958), pp. 38–50.

109. Sponza, *Italian Immigrants*, p. 19.

110. David R. Green, 'Little Italy in Victorian London: Holborn's Italian Community', *Camden History Review*, vol. 15 (1988), pp. 2–6.

111. Olive Besagni, *A Better Life: A History of London's Italian Immigrant Families in Clerkenwell's Little Italy in the 19th and 20th Centuries* (London, 2011), pp. 9–27.

112. Count E. Armfelt, 'Italy in London', in Sims, *Living London*, vol. 1, pp. 183–9.

113. James Strang, 'The Italian Colony in London', *Good Words*, vol. 40 (1899), p. 121.

114. Ibid., p. 123.

115. Ibid., p. 125.

116. Roy F. Haddon, 'A Minority in a Welfare State Society: The Location of West Indians in the London Housing Market', *New Atlantis*, vol. 1 (1970), p. 85.

117. NA/MEPO2/9047, J. Waring Sainsbury, 'The Coloured Population of London', 21 January 1952.

118. NA/MEPO2/9047, R. Garvey, 'The Coloured Population of London', 1 April 1952.

119. Ruth Glass, *Newcomers: The West Indians in London* (London, 1960), pp. 5–20; John Western, *Passage to England: Barbadian Londoners Speak of Home* (Minneapolis, MI, 1992), pp. 67–86.

120. Haddon, 'Minority', pp. 95–109.

121. Sheila Patterson, *Dark Strangers: A Sociological Study of the Absorption of a Recent West Indian Migrant Group in Brixton, South London* (London, 1963).

122. John Davis, 'Rents and Race in 1960s London: New Light on Rachmanism', *Twentieth Century British History*, vol. 12 (2001), pp. 69–92; Shirley Green, *Rachman: The Slum Landlord Whose Name Became a Byword for Evil* (London, 1979); Pilkington, *Beyond the Mother Country*.

123. Elizabeth Burney, *Housing on Trial: A Study of Immigrants and Local Government* (London, 1967), pp. 110–46; Lord Scarman, *The Scarman Report: The Brixton Disorders, 10–12 April 1981* (Harmondsworth, 1982).

124. Patterson, *Dark Strangers*, pp. 251–77.

125. Ferdinand Dennis, *Behind the Front Lines: Journey into Afro-Britain* (London, 1988), pp. 187–216.

126. Gurharpal Singh and Darshan Singh Tatla, *Sikhs in Britain: The Making of a Community* (London, 2006), pp. 63–4; Neil Chippendale, *Reminiscences from the Asian Community in Hounslow* (London, 1993).

127. Brett Bebber, ' "We Were Just Unwanted": Bussing, Migrant Dispersal and South Asians in London', *Journal of Social History*, vol. 48 (2015), pp. 635–61.

128. Ceri Peach, 'Does Britain Have Ghettos?', *Transactions of the Institute of British Geographers*, New Series, vol. 21 (1996), pp. 232–4; Nissa Finney and Ludi Simpson, *'Sleepwalking to Segregation?' Challenging Myths About Race and Immigration* (Bristol, 2009).

129. See, for example, Ted Cantle, *Community Cohesion: A New Framework for Race and Diversity* (Basingstoke, 2005).

130. David Cesarani, 'A Funny Thing Happened on the Way to the Suburbs: Social Change in Anglo-Jewry Between the Wars, 1914–1945', *Jewish History and Culture*, vol. 1 (1998), pp. 5–26; Dee, *'Estranged' Generation?*.

131. Panikos Panayi, *Immigration, Ethnicity and Racism in Britain, 1815–1945* (Manchester, 1994), p. 55.

132. Adler, 'Jewish Life', pp. 271–2, 296; V. D. Lipman, *History of the Jews in Britain since 1858* (Leicester, 1990), pp. 207–8.

133. Todd M. Endelman, *The Jews of Britain 1656–2000* (London, 2002), pp. 230–1; Stanley Waterman and Barry A. Kosmin, 'Ethnic Identity, Residential Concentration and Social Welfare: The Jews in London', in Peter Jackson, ed., *Race and Racism: Essays in Social Geography* (London, 1987), pp. 263–4; Barry A. Kosmin and Nigel Gizzard, *Jews in an Inner London Borough: A Study of the Jewish Population of the London Borough of Hackney based on the 1971 Census* (London, 1971); David Graham, Marlena Schmool and Stanley Waterman, *Jews in Britain: A Snapshot from the 2001 Census* (London, 2007), pp. 23–37.

134. Stanley Waterman and Barry A. Kosmin, 'Residential Patterns and Processes: A Study of Jews in Three London Boroughs', *Transactions of the Institute of British Geographers*, vol. 13 (1988), p. 93.

135. Geoffrey Alderman, *The History of the Hendon Synagogue* (London, 1978); Pam Fox, *The Jewish Community of Golders Green: A Social History* (Stroud, 2016), pp. 22–3.

136. Fox, *The Jewish Community of Golders Green*, p. 25.

137. Ibid., pp. 31, 35, 50, 52; Alderman, *History of the Hendon Synagogue*.

138. Fox, *The Jewish Community of Golders Green*, p. 69.

139. Panikos Panayi, *An Immigration History of Britain: Multicultural Racism Since 1800* (London, 2010), p. 102; Bernard Wasserstein, *Vanishing Diaspora: The Jews of Europe Since 1945* (London, 1996).

140. Enda Delaney, *The Irish in Post-War Britain* (Oxford, 2007), p. 88.

141. Lees, 'Patterns of Lower-Class Life', p. 365.

142. Delaney, *Irish in Post-War Britain*, pp. 88–95; Bronwen Walter, 'Contemporary Irish Settlement in London: Women's Worlds, Men's Worlds', in Jim MacLaughlin, ed., *Location and Dislocation in Contemporary Irish Society: Emigration and Identities* (Cork, 1997), pp. 61–93; Tom Connor, *The London Irish* (London, 1987), pp. 25–32; Catherine Dunne, *An Unconsidered People: The Irish in London* (Dublin, 2003), pp. 11–14; Maria Maguire, *The Irish in Ealing: An Invisible Community* (London, 1989); Judy Chance, 'The Irish in London: An Exploration of Ethnic Boundary Maintenance', in Jackson, *Race and Racism*, pp. 142–60; Martin Mac an Ghaill, 'The Irish in Britain: The Invisibility of Ethnicity and Anti-Irish Racism', *Journal of Ethnic and Migration Studies*, vol. 26 (2000), pp. 137–47.

143. See below, p. 50.

144. Anna Hassiotis, *The Greek Cypriot Community in Camden* (London, 1989); Evan Smith and Andrekos Varnava, 'Creating a "Suspect Community": Monitoring and Controlling the Cypriot Community in Inter-War London', *English Historical Review*, vol. 132 (2017), pp. 1149–81; Vic George and Geoffrey Millerson, 'The Cypriot Community in London', *Race*, vol. 8 (1967), pp. 277–92.

145. Robin Oakley, *Changing Patterns of Distribution of Cypriot Settlement* (Coventry, 1987).

146. Jeffrey Leeuwenberg, *The Cypriots in Haringey* (London, 1979); Fuat Alkan, *Cypriots in Haringey* (London, 1979).

147. Martin Kettle, 'Famagusta, N16', *New Society*, 26 March 1981.

148. 'Turks in Green Lane', *Guardian*, 21 January 2005; 'Little Istanbul', *Evening Standard*, 3 January 2013.

149. Trevor R. Lee, *Race and Residence: The Concentration and Dispersal of Immigrants in London* (Oxford, 1977).

150. Brown, *Windrush to Lewisham*, pp. 28–36.

151. Bishop Theoditus of Nazianzos, 'History of the Greek Cathedral of Saint Sophia in London', in George Kakavas, ed., *Treasured Offerings: The Legacy of the Greek Orthodox*

Cathedral of St. Sophia London (London, 2002), pp. 21–6; Jonathan Harris, 'London's Greek Community', in idem, pp. 3–8; Timotheous Catsiyannis, *The Greek Community of London* (London, 1993), pp. 44–53, 355–7, 405–12.

152. John Sweeney, 'Among the Russians', *Time Out*, 9–15 April 1986, pp. 18–21.
153. Mark Hollingsworth and Stewart Lansley, *Londongrad: From Russia with Cash: The Inside Story of the Oligarchs* (London, 2009), pp. 24, 117–29.
154. Ramy M. K. Aly, *Becoming Arab in London: Performativity and the Undoing of Identity* (London, 2015), pp. 50–1.
155. Ibid., pp. 52–69.
156. Laura Hunt Yungblut, *Strangers Settled Here Amongst Us: Policies, Perceptions and the Presence of Aliens in Elizabethan England* (London, 1996), pp. 19–22.
157. Craig Bailey, *Irish London: Middle-Class Migration in the Global Eighteenth Century* (Liverpool, 2013).
158. Armfelt, 'German London', pp. 59–62.
159. Panayi, *Germans Immigrants*, pp. 100–1.
160. William F. Brand, *London Life Seen with German Eyes* (London, 1902), p. 117.
161. V. D. Lipman, 'The Rise of Jewish Suburbia', *Transactions of the Jewish Historical Society of England*, vol. 21 (1968), pp. 78–103.
162. Gerry Black, *Living Up West: Jewish Life in London's West End* (London, 1994); V. D. Lipman, 'The Structure of London Jewry in the Mid-Nineteenth Century', in H. J. Zimmels, J. Rabinowitz and Israel Feinstein, eds, *Essays in Honor of Chief Rabbi Israel Brodie* (London, 1967), pp. 258–72.
163. JML/Oral History Collection Transcript 370, Interview with Sid Spellman, n.d.
164. Black, *Living Up West*, pp. 55–69.
165. Armfelt, 'Cosmopolitan London', in Sims, *Living London*, vol. 1, p. 241.
166. Black, *Living Up West*, pp. 55–69.
167. Armfelt, 'Cosmopolitan London', p. 242; Panayi, *Spicing Up Britain*, pp. 79–93, 164–6; Lucio Sponza, 'The Anti-Italian Riots, June 1940', in Panikos Panayi, ed., *Racial Violence in Britain in the Nineteenth and Twentieth Centuries* (London, 1996), p. 131; Judith R. Walkowitz, *Nights Out: Life in Cosmopolitan London* (London, 2012), pp. 1–15, 92–246; Arthur Sherwell, *Life in West London: A Study and a Contrast* (London, 1901), p. 59.
168. Helen Evangelou, *Tales from Riding House Street: A Faded London House and the Cypriots Who Lived in It* (London, 2018), pp. 4, 47.
169. Banton, *Coloured Quarter*; A. R. Mannick, *Mauritians in London* (Mayfield, 1987), pp. 15–16.
170. Tower Hamlets Research Briefing, *Ethnicity in Tower Hamlets: Analysis of 2011 Census Data*, https://www.towerhamlets.gov.uk/Documents/Borough_statistics/Ward_profiles/Census-2011/RB-Census2011-Ethnicity-2013-01.pdf, accessed 5 February 2018.
171. Tim Butler and Chris Hamnett, *Ethnicity, Class and Aspiration: Understanding London's New East End* (Bristol, 2011).
172. Greater London Authority, *The World in a City: An Analysis of the 2001 Census Results* (London, 2005), p. 19.
173. GLA Intelligence, *Census Information Scheme, Local Areas of Ethnic Group Concentration* (London, 2014).
174. See the list and map in 'London: A World in One City', *Guardian*, 21 January 2005.
175. Cathy McIlwaine, Juan Camilo Cock and Brian Linneker, *No Longer Invisible: The Latin American Community in London* (London, 2011), pp. 33, 137; Patria Román-Velázquez, *The Making of Latin London: Salsa Music, Place, and Identity* (Aldershot, 1999), pp. 51–4.
176. Gardner, *Age, Narrative and Migration*; Tarek Qureshi, *Living in Britain, Growing Old in Britain: A Study of Bangladeshi Elders in London* (London, 1998).
177. As claimed by Ranji Devadason, 'Cosmopolitanism, Geographical Imaginaries and Belonging in North London', *Urban Studies*, vol. 47 (2010), pp. 2945, 2948.
178. Susanne Wessendorf, 'Commonplace Diversity and the "Ethos of Mixing": Perceptions of Difference in a London Neighbourhood', *Identities*, vol. 20 (2013), pp. 407–22.

179. Francis Dodsworth, Elena Vaccelli and Sophie Watson, 'Shifting Religions and Culture's in London's East End', *Material Religion*, vol. 9 (2013), pp. 86–112. Religion receives detailed attention in Chapter 8.

180. See the argument put forward by Gerd Baumann, *Contesting Culture: Discourses of Identity in Multi-Ethnic London* (Cambridge, 1996).

181. See Finney and Simpson, '*Sleepwalking to Segregation?*'.

CHAPTER 3

1. James Greenwood, *The Wilds of London* (London, 1874), p. 265, describing working conditions for German employees in a sugar bakery owned by one of their countrymen in Back Church Lane, Whitechapel.

2. Donall MacAmlaigh, *An Irish Navvy: The Diary of an Exile* (originally London, 1964; Cork, 2018, reprint), describing a job in 1957.

3. Museum of London, Oral History Archive, 93/131, Interview with Handley Best.

4. Greenwood, *Wilds of London*, p. 264.

5. Stephen Castles, et al., *Here for Good: Western Europe's New Ethnic Minorities* (London, 1984); Dudley Baines, 'European Labour Markets, Emigration and Internal Migration', in Timothy J. Hatton and Jeffrey G. Williamson, eds, *Migration and the International Labour Market* (London, 1994), pp. 35–54.

6. See, for instance: Ian R. G. Spencer, *British Immigration Policy: The Making of Multi-Racial Britain* (London, 1997); Kathleen Paul, *Whitewashing Britain: Race and Citizenship in the Post-war Era* (Ithaca, NY, 1997).

7. Greater London Authority, *London Divided: Income, Inequality and Poverty in the Capital* (London, 2002), p. xii. See Chapter 6 for more on racism.

8. Jon May, Jane Wills, Kavita Datta, Yara Evans, Joanna Herbert and Cathy McIlwaine, 'Global Cities at Work: Migrant Labour in Low-Paid Employment in London', *London Journal*, vol. 35 (2010), pp. 85–99.

9. Kavita Datta, Cathy McIlwaine, Yara Evans, Joanna Herbert, Jon May and Jane Wills, 'From Coping Strategies to Tactics: London's Low-Pay Economy and Migrant Labour', *British Journal of Industrial Relations*, vol. 45 (2007), p. 410.

10. Ian Gordon, Tony Travers and Christine Whitehead, *The Impact of Recent Immigration on the London Economy* (London, 2007), p. 48.

11. See Nick Buck, et al., *Life and Labour in Contemporary London* (London, 2002).

12. Panikos Panayi, *An Immigration History of Britain: Multicultural Racism Since c.1800* (London, 2010), p. 20.

13. Florian Shyllon, *Black People in Britain, 1555–1833* (London, 1977), pp. 20–1, 179–86; Gretchen Gerzina, *Black London: Life Before Emancipation* (New Brunswick, NJ, 1995), pp. 43–52.

14. Shyllon, *Black People in Britain*, p. 160.

15. Ibid., pp. 162–5.

16. Leopold Katscher, 'German Life in London', *Nineteenth Century*, vol. 21 (1887), p. 733.

17. Lucio Sponza, *Italian Immigrants in Nineteenth-Century Britain* (Leicester, 1988), p. 330.

18. Ibid.

19. Lara Marks, 'Race, Class and Gender: The Experience of Jewish Prostitutes and Other Jewish Women in the East End of London at the Turn of the Century', in Joan Grant, ed., *Women, Migration and Empire* (Stoke-on-Trent, 1996), p. 32; Panikos Panayi, 'The German Poor and Working Classes in Victorian and Edwardian London', in Geoffrey Alderman and Colin Holmes, eds, *Outsiders and Outcasts* (London, 1993), p. 61.

20. NA/MEPO2/558/6.

21. Marks, 'Race, Class and Gender', pp. 44–5.

22. Kellow Chesney, *The Victorian Underworld* (Harmondsworth, 1972), p. 367.

23. NA/MEPO2/558.

24. Rosina Visram, *Asians in Britain: 400 Years of History* (London, 2002), pp. 14–20, 54.
25. Joseph Salter: *The Asiatic in England: Sketches of Sixteen Years Work Among Orientals* (London, 1873); *The East in the West or Work Among the Asiatics and Africans in Britain* (London, 1896).
26. See Jacqueline Jenkinson, *Black 1919: Racism, Riots and Resistance in Imperial Britain* (Liverpool, 2009). See also Chapter 6 below which tackles racial violence.
27. Laura Tabili, 'The Construction of Racial Difference in Twentieth-Century Britain: The Special Restriction (Coloured Alien Seamen) Order, 1925', *Journal of British Studies*, vol. 33 (1994), pp. 54–98.
28. THLHA/P/RAM/3/2/7, '[Confidential] Report on Investigation into Conditions of the Coloured Population in a Stepney Area' (nd), pp. 11–12.
29. Michael Banton, *The Coloured Quarter: Negro Immigrants in an English City* (London, 1955), pp. 127–9.
30. As an introduction see: Frank V. Dawes, *Not in Front of the Servants: Domestic Service in England, 1850–1939* (London, 1973); and Frank Edward Huggett, *Life Below Stairs: Domestic Servants in England from Victorian Times* (London, 1977).
31. Panikos Panayi, *German Immigrants in Britain during the Nineteenth Century, 1815–1914* (Oxford, 1995), pp. 136–7.
32. Tony Kushner, 'An Alien Occupation: Jewish Refugees and Domestic Service in Britain, 1933–1948', in Werner E. Mosse, et al., eds, *Second Chance: Two Centuries of German-Speaking Jews in the United Kingdom* (Tübingen, 1991), pp. 553–78.
33. Linda McDowell, *Migrant Women's Voices: Talking About Life and Work in the UK Since 1945* (London, 2016), pp. 93–8; Diana Kay and Robert Miles, *Refugees or Migrant Workers? European Volunteer Workers in Britain* (London, 1992).
34. McDowell, *Migrant Women's Voices*, pp. 99–100.
35. Gordon, Travers and Whitehead, *Impact of Recent Immigration*, pp. 46–57.
36. See Peter Hall, *London Voices, London Lives: Tales from a Working Capital* (Bristol, 2007), especially Chapter 9.
37. Buck, et al., *Life and Labour in Contemporary London*.
38. Gordon, Travers and Whitehead, *Impact of Recent Immigration*, pp. 47–52.
39. Jane Wills, Kavita Datta, Yara Evans, Joanna Herbert, Jon May and Cathy McIlwaine, *Global Cities at Work: New Migrant Divisions of Labour* (London, 2010), pp. 59–93.
40. B. Akíntúndé Oyètádé, 'The Yorùbá Community in London', *African Languages and Cultures*, vol. 6 (1993), p. 75.
41. Andrew Gimson, 'Backbone of England', *Spectator*, 1 June 2002.
42. Pam Decho and Claire Diamond, *Latin Americans in London: A Select List of Prominent Americans in London, c. 1880–1996* (London, 1998), pp. 1, 14–16.
43. Cathy McIlwaine, Juan Camilo Cock and Brian Linneker, *No Longer Invisible: The Latin American Community in London* (London, 2011), pp. 10–12.
44. Ibid., pp. 41, 43, 48–9.
45. Kjartan Páll Sveinsson, *Bolivians in London: Challenges and Achievements of a London Community* (London, 2007), p. 4.
46. McIlwaine, Cock and Linneker, *No Longer Invisible*, p. 56.
47. Yara Evans, Jane Wills, Kavita Datta, Joanna Herbert, Cathy McIlwaine, Jon May, Father José Osvaldo de Araújo, Ana Carla França and Ana Paula França, *Brazilians in London: A Report for the Strangers into Citizens Campaign* (London, 2007), p. 12.
48. McIlwaine, Cock and Linneker, *No Longer Invisible*, pp. 62–9.
49. Katie Wright, ' "It's a Limited Kind of Happiness": Barriers to Achieving Human Well-being among Peruvian Migrants in London and Madrid', *Bulletin of Latin American Research*, vol. 29 (2010), pp. 367–83.
50. Ben Judah, *This is London* (London, 2016).
51. Hsiao-Hung Pai, *Chinese Whispers: The True Story behind Britain's Hidden Army of Labour* (London, 2008).
52. Parvati Nair, 'Undocumented and Unseen: The Making of the Everyday in the Global Metropolis of London 2015', in Anne J. Kershen, ed., *London the Promised Land Revisited:*

The Changing Face of the London Migrant Landscape in the Early 21st Century (London, 2015), pp. 103–4.

53. Graham Davis, *The Irish in Britain* (Dublin, 1991), pp. 83–123.
54. Jeffrey Williamson, 'The Impact of the Irish on British Labour Markets during the Industrial Revolution', in Roger Swift and Sheridan Gilley, eds, *The Irish in Britain, 1815–1939* (London, 1989), pp. 134–62.
55. M. Dorothy George, *London Life in the Eighteenth Century* (Harmondsworth, 1966), p. 120.
56. Lynn Hollen Lees, *Exiles of Erin: Irish Immigrants in Victorian London* (Manchester, 1979), pp. 94–5.
57. John A. Jackson, 'The Irish in East London', *East London Papers*, vol. 6 (1963), pp. 108–9.
58. Lynn Hollen Lees, 'Patterns of Lower-Class Life: Irish Slum Communities in Nineteenth-Century London', in Stephan Thernstrom and Richard Sennett, eds, *Nineteenth-Century Cities: Essays in the New Urban History* (London, 1969), pp. 368–9.
59. Charles Manby Smith, *Curiosities of London Life, or, Phases, Physiological and Social, of the Great Metropolis* (London, 1853), pp. 135–8.
60. Gerard Leavey, Sati Sembhi and Gill Livingston, 'Older Irish Migrants Living in London: Identity, Loss and Return', *Journal of Ethnic and Migration Studies*, vol. 30 (2004), pp. 767–9.
61. Clair Wills, *An Immigrant History of Post-War Britain* (London, 2017), pp. 46–50.
62. Miki Garcia, *Rebuilding London: Irish Migrants in Post-War Britain* (Dublin, 2015), p. 62.
63. Tom O'Connor, *The London Irish* (London, 1987), p. 35.
64. Maria Maguire, *The Irish in Ealing: An Invisible Community* (London, 1989), p. 22.
65. Ibid.; Enda Delaney, *The Irish in Post-War Britain* (Oxford, 2007), pp. 116–26.
66. Christine Wall, Linda Clarke, Charles McGuire and Olivia Muñoz-Rojas, *Building the South Bank Arts Centre: The Art of Concrete* (London, 2014).
67. Christine Wall, Linda Clarke, Charles McGuire and Olivia Muñoz-Rojas, *Building the Barbican, 1962–1982: Taking the Industry out of the Dark Ages* (London, 2014).
68. BI/CPWB/1/5, Interview with Noel Clarke, 2011.
69. BI/CPWB/1/4, Interview with Michael Houlihan, 2011.
70. BI/CPWB/1/8, Interview with Tony McGing, 2011.
71. BI/CPWB/4/1, Interview with Jim McDonald, 2012.
72. BI/CPWB/1/5, Interview with Noel Clarke, 2011.
73. BI/CPWB/1/4, Interview with Michael Houlihan, 2011.
74. Geoffrey Randall, *Over Here: Young Irish Migrants in London: Education, Training, Employment, Housing, Health, Anti-Irish Racism* (London, 1990), pp. 14, 24–8, 33.
75. O'Connor, *London Irish*, p. 39.
76. Panayi, *German Immigrants*, pp. 121–3; Hans Rössler, ' "Die Zuckerbäcker waren vornehmlich Hannoveraner": Zur Geschichte der Wanderung aus dem Elbe-Weser-Dreieck in die Britische Zuckerindustrie', *Jahrbuch der Männer vom Morgenstern*, vol. 81 (2003).
77. Panayi, *German Immigrants*, pp. 123–4.
78. Quoted in ibid., p. 124.
79. Geoffrey Alderman, *Modern British Jewry* (Oxford, 1992), p. 121.
80. John Marriot, *Beyond the Tower: A History of East London* (London, 2011), Chapter 8.
81. Alderman, *Modern British Jewry*, pp. 121–2.
82. J. A. Dyche, 'The Jewish Workman', *Contemporary Review*, vol. 73 (1898), p. 46.
83. Lloyd P. Gartner, *The Jewish Immigrant in England, 1870–1914*, 3rd edn (London, 2010), pp. 57–8.
84. Alderman, *Modern British Jewry*, p. 121.
85. William J. Fishman, *East End 1888* (London, 1988), p. 61; David Feldman, *Englishmen and Jews: Social Relations and Political Culture, 1840–1914* (London, 1994), pp. 186–8.
86. Willy Goldman, *East End: My Cradle* (London, 1988), p. 85.
87. William Evans-Gordon, *The Alien Immigrant* (London, 1903), pp. 10–11.
88. London Correspondent of the Board of Trade, *Report of the Board of Trade on the Sweating System at the East End of London* (London, 1887), p. 7.

89. *First Report of the Select Committee of the House of Lords on the Sweating System* (London, 1888), p. 525.

90. Beatrice Potter, 'The Tailoring Trade', in Charles Booth, *Life and Labour of the People in London*, 1st Series, vol. 4 (1970 reprint), p. 66.

91. Fishman, *East End 1888*, pp. 60–81.

92. Peter Elman, 'The Beginnings of the Jewish Trade Union Movement in England', *Transactions of the Jewish Historical Society of England*, vol. 17 (1952), pp. 53–62; James A. Schmiechen, *Sweated Industries and Sweated Labour: The London Clothing Trades, 1860–1914* (London, 1984), pp. 104–14; Anne J. Kershen, *Uniting the Tailors: Trade Unionism among the Tailoring Workers of London and Leeds, 1870–1939* (Ilford, 1995); Feldman, *Englishmen and Jews*, pp. 215–30.

93. Gerry Black, *Living Up West: Jewish Life in London's West End* (London, 1994), p. 55.

94. William I. Massil, *Immigrant Furniture Workers in London, 1881–1939 and the Jewish Contribution to the Furniture Trade* (London, 1997).

95. Sam Clarke, *Sam: An East End Cabinetmaker* (London, 1930).

96. Henrietta Adler, 'Jewish Life and Labour in East London', in Sir Hubert Llewellyn Smith, ed., *New Survey of London Life and Labour*, vol. 6 (London, 1934), pp. 285–6.

97. David Dee, *The 'Estranged' Generation? Social and Generational Change in Interwar British Jewry* (Basingstoke, 2017), pp. 93–111.

98. See especially W. D. Rubinstein, *A History of the Jews in the English-Speaking World: Great Britain* (Basingstoke, 1996), pp. 400–7.

99. Selig Brodetsky, *Memoirs: From Ghetto to Israel* (London, 1960).

100. Sheila Patterson, *Immigrants in Industry* (London, 1968), pp. 173–204.

101. See the analysis of Telelux, Chocolac and Polplastics in ibid., pp. 293–390.

102. Kim McPherson and Julia Gaitskell, *Immigrants and Employment: Two Case Studies in East London and in Croydon* (London, 1969).

103. Hastings Donnan, 'Inter-ethnic Friendship, Joking and Rules of Interaction in a London Factory', in Ladislav Holy, ed., *Knowledge and Behaviour* (Belfast, 1976), pp. 81–99.

104. Banton, *Coloured Quarter*, pp. 132, 139–41.

105. James Wickenden, *Colour in Britain* (London, 1958), p. 37.

106. Albert Hyndman, 'The West Indian in London', in S. K. Ruck, ed., *The West Indian Comes to England: A Report Prepared for the Trustees of the London Parochial Charities by the Family Welfare Association* (London, 1960), p. 105.

107. Simon Taylor, *A Land of Dreams: A Study of Jewish and Caribbean Migrant Communities in England* (London, 1993), pp. 87–90.

108. Marcus Collins, 'Pride and Prejudice: West Indian Men in Mid-Twentieth Century Britain', *Journal of British Studies*, vol. 40 (2001), p. 401.

109. Hyndman, 'West Indian in London', p. 105.

110. See, for example, Ruth Glass, *Newcomers: The West Indians in London* (London, 1960), pp. 69–70.

111. Collins, 'Pride and Prejudice', pp. 399–402; Hyndman, 'West Indian in London', pp. 106–7.

112. See below, pp. 82–3.

113. Sheila Patterson, *Dark Strangers: A Sociological Study of the Absorption of a Recent West Indian Migrant Group in Brixton, South London* (London, 1963), pp. 101–25.

114. Nancy Foner, *Jamaica Farewell: Jamaican Migrants in London* (London, 1979), pp. 86–123.

115. David F. Kohler, *The Employment of Black People in a London Borough* (London, 1974).

116. Jerry White, *London in the Twentieth Century: A City and Its People* (London, 2008), pp. 75–87.

117. Panayi, *Immigration History*, pp. 117–18.

118. See Chapter 4.

119. R. B. Davison, *Black British Immigrants to England* (London, 1966), p. 89.

120. NA/DO35/9501, 'Employment of Pakistanis in the United Kingdom, 16 May 1958'.
121. Rachel Leeser, Marian Storkey, Eileen Howes and Doreen Kenny, *Without Prejudice? Exploring Ethnic Differences in London* (London, 2000), pp. 111–15.
122. See Chapter 4.
123. Stella Mascarenhas-Keyes, *Goans in London: Portrait of a Catholic Asian Community* (London, 1979), pp. 28–9, 45–6.
124. Tarek Qureshi, *Living in Britain, Growing Old in Britain: A Study of Bangladeshi Elders in London* (London, 1998), p. 15.
125. Hamza Alavi, *The Pakistanis in London* (London, 1963), pp. 3–4; LMA/Acc/1888/398, London Council of Social Services, 'East Pakistanis in London', 1967.
126. He recounts his story to Katy Gardner, *Age, Narrative and Migration: The life Course and Life Histories of Bengali Elders in London* (Oxford, 2002), p. 96.
127. Samir Shah, *Immigrants and Employment in the Clothing Industry: The Rag Trade in London's East End* (London, 1975); Naila Kabeer, *The Power to Choose: Bangladeshi Women and Labour Market Decisions in London and Dhaka* (London, 2000), pp. 193–212; Anne Kershen, *Strangers, Aliens and Asians: Huguenots, Jews and Bangladeshis in Spitalfields, 1660–2000* (London, 2005), p. 179.
128. Kabeer, *The Power to Choose*, p. 212.
129. Ibid., pp. 232–5.
130. Gurharpal Singh and Darshan Singh Tatla, *Sikhs in Britain: The Making of a Community* (London, 2006), p. 147.
131. McDowell, *Migrant Women's Voices*, pp. 69–70.
132. Ibid., pp. 72–3.
133. Joe Rogaly, *Grunwick* (Harmondsworth, 1977), pp. 22–8; Jack McGowan, ' "Dispute", "Battle", "Siege", "Farce"? Grunwick 30 Years On', *Contemporary British History*, vol. 22 (2008), pp. 383–406; Striking Women, The Grunwick Dispute, http://www.striking-women.org/module/striking-out/grunwick-dispute, accessed 5 March 2018.
134. Kay and Miles, *Refugees or Migrant Workers?*, pp. 101–4.
135. Terri Colpi, *The Italian Factor: The Italian Community in Great Britain* (Edinburgh, 1991), pp. 144–7.
136. See Patterson, *Immigrants in Industry*.
137. John Stuart McDonald and Leatrice D. McDonald, *The Invisible Immigrants* (London, 1972), p. 22.
138. Ibid., pp. 32–7, provides an analysis of the national picture.
139. Sarah Ladbury, *A Report on the Social and Working Lives of the Greek and Turkish Cypriot Communities in London* (Southall, 1979), p. 19.
140. Floya Anthias, *Ethnicity, Class, Gender and Migration: Greek Cypriots in Britain* (Aldershot, 1992), p. 53.
141. Vic George and Geoffrey Millerson, 'The Cypriot Community in London', *Race*, vol. 8 (1967), pp. 282–3. See Ladbury, *Report*, p. 20, for figures from the 1970s.
142. Vic George, 'The Assimilation of Cypriot Immigrants in London', *Eugenic Review*, vol. 58 (1966), p. 189.
143. See Chapter 4.
144. George, 'Assimilation', p. 189.
145. Ladbury, *Report*, pp. 19–34; F. M. Bhatti, *Turkish Cypriots in London* (Birmingham, 1981), pp. 6–8, 10–14.
146. Alkan Fuat, *Cypriots in Haringey* (London, 1980), p. 12.
147. See Chapter 9.
148. See Chapter 4.
149. Panayi, *German Immigrants*, pp. 70, 133–4; Gregory Anderson, 'German Clerks in England, 1870–1914: Another Aspect of the Great Depression Debate', in Kenneth Lunn, ed., *Hosts, Immigrants and Minorities: Historical Responses to Newcomers in British Society* (Folkestone, 1980), pp. 201–21.
150. See Chapters 9 and 11.

151. Sponza, *Italian Immigrants*, pp. 75–93; Colpi, *The Italian Factor*, pp. 38–41; David R. Green, 'Little Italy in Victorian London: Holborn's Italian Community', *Camden History Review*, vol. 15 (1988), pp. 2, 4–5; George R. Sims, 'Trips Around Town, III: Round Little Italy', *Strand Magazine*, vol. 29 (1905), p. 515.

152. See above, p. 64.

153. Enda Delaney, *Demography, State and Society: Irish Migration to Britain, 1921–1971* (Liverpool, 2000), pp. 112–59.

154. Kay and Miles, *Refugees or Migrant Workers?*; J. A. Tannahill, *European Volunteer Workers in Britain* (Manchester, 1958); Elizabeth Stadulis, 'The Resettlement of Displaced Persons in the United Kingdom', *Population Studies*, vol. 5 (1952), pp. 207–37.

155. See, for example, Louise Ryan, 'Passing Time: Irish Women Remembering and Re-telling Stories of Migration to Britain', in Panikos Panayi and Kathy Burrell, eds, *Histories and Memories: Migrants and their History in Britain* (London, 2006), pp. 191–209.

156. Anne Lynch, *The Irish in Exile* (London, 1988), pp. 11–14.

157. Garcia, *Rebuilding London*, pp. 92–7; Delaney, *Irish in Post-War Britain*, pp. 91–2.

158. MLOHC, 93.132, Rory O'Connell interview of Elma Sampson, 30 April 1993.

159. ECHP, Redbridge Nurses Project, 2000_esch_nurs_01, Judith Garfield interview of Ruth Barnett, 6 September 2000.

160. Julian Simpson, *Migrant Architects of the NHS: South Asian Doctors and the Reinvention of British General Practice (1940s–1980s)* (Manchester, 2018).

161. Garcia, *Rebuilding London*, pp. 87–90; Dennis Brooks, *Race and Labour in London Transport* (London, 1975), pp. 26–8.

162. Brooks, *Race and Labour in London Transport*; Patterson, *Dark Strangers*, pp. 95–8; John Western, *A Passage to England: Barbadian Londoners Speak of Home* (Minneapolis, MI, 1992), pp. 87–109; London Transport Museum, *Sun a-shine, Rain a-fall: London Transport's West Indian Workforce* (London, 1994).

163. Gareth Stedman Jones, *Outcast London: A Study in the Relationship between Classes in Victorian Society* (Harmondsworth, 1984), pp. 19–155.

164. See the classic T. Coleman, *The Railway Navvies: A History of the Men Who Made the Railways* (London, 1965), and the account of MacAmlaigh, *An Irish Navvy*, who worked in several parts of the country.

165. Panayi, *Immigration History*.

CHAPTER 4

1. Henry Mayhew, *London Labour and the London Poor*, vol. 1 (originally 1861; London, 1968), p. 104.

2. JML, Oral History Collection Transcript No. 17, Interview with Henry Goldring, 21 May 1985.

3. GLA Economics, *The Contribution of Asian-Owned Businesses to London's Economy* (London, 2005), p. vii.

4. Ibid., p. 4.

5. Panikos Panayi, *An Immigration History of Britain: Multicultural Racism Since 1800* (London, 2010), p. 116.

6. Panikos Panayi, 'Anti-German Riots in London During the First World War', *German History*, vol. 7 (1989), p. 193. See below for more details of these businesses.

7. Andrew Godley, *Jewish Immigrant Entrepreneurship in New York and London, 1880–1914: Enterprise and Culture* (Basingstoke, 2001), p. 54.

8. Noi Isaakovich Barou, *Jews in Work and Trade* (London, 1946), pp. 5–6.

9. Gregor Benton and Terence Gomez, *The Chinese in Britain, 1800–Present: Economy, Transnationalism, Identity* (Basingstoke, 2011), p. 134.

10. London Development Agency, *Redefining London's BME-Owned Businesses* (London, 2005), pp. 23–5; John Kitching, David Smallbone and Rosemary Athayde, 'Ethnic

Diasporas and Business Competitiveness: Minority-Owned Enterprises in London', *Journal of Ethnic and Migration Studies*, vol. 35 (2009), pp. 689–705.

11. Sheila Patterson, 'The Poles: An Exile Community in Britain', in James L. Watson, ed., *Between Two Cultures: Migrants and Minorities in Britain* (Oxford, 1977), p. 221. Marta Rabikowska and Kathy Burrell, 'The Material Worlds of Recent Polish Migrants: Transnationalism, Food, Shops and Home', in Kathy Burrell, ed., *Polish Migration in the UK in the 'New' European Union After 2004* (Farnham, 2009), pp. 211–32.

12. Cathy McIlwaine, Juan Camilo Cock and Brian Linneker, *No Longer Invisible: The Latin American Community in London* (London, 2011); Kjartan Páll Sveinsson, *Bolivians in London: Challenges and Achievements of a London Community* (London, 2007); Yara Evans, Jane Wills, Kavita Datta, Joanna Herbert, Cathy McIlwaine, Jon May, Father José Osvaldo de Araújo, Ana Carla França and Ana Paula França, *Brazilians in London: A Report for the Strangers into Citizens Campaign* (London, 2007)

13. These receive fuller attention in Chapter 5.

14. See Chapter 9.

15. James B. Jefferys, *Retail Trading in Britain, 1830–1950* (Cambridge, 1954), pp. 1–39; Molly Harrison, *People and Shopping* (London, 1975), pp. 91–116.

16. London Development Agency, *Redefining London's BME-Owned Businesses*, p. 22.

17. As an indication see Philip Baker and Jeehoon Kim, *Global London: Where to Find almost Everything Ethnic and Cultural in the Multilingual Capital* (London, 2003).

18. The pioneering works on migrant foodways, focusing upon the USA, are: Linda Keller Brown and Kay Mussell, eds, *Ethnic and Regional Foodways in the United States: The Performance of Group Identity* (Knoxville, TN, 1985); and Hasia R. Diner, *Hungering for America: Italian, Irish and Jewish Foodways in the Age of Migration* (London, 2001).

19. See below, pp. 93–4.

20. See below, pp. 101–3.

21. Godley, *Jewish Immigrant Entrepreneurship*, p. 96.

22. GLA Economics, *Contribution of Asian-owned Businesses*, p. 11.

23. See Chapter 5.

24. See below, p. 97.

25. Hilary Metcalf, Tariq Modood and Satnam Virdee, *Asian Self-Employment: The Interaction of Culture and Economics in England* (London, 1996), pp. 3–6; Howard E. Aldrich, John C. Cater, Trevor P. Jones and David McEvoy, 'Business Development and Self-Segregation: Asian Enterprise in Three British Cities', in Ceri Peach, Vaughan Robinson and Susan Smith, eds, *Ethnic Segregation in Cities* (London, 1981), pp. 170–88; Mark S. Brown, 'Religion and Economic Activity in the South Asian Population', *Ethnic and Racial Studies*, vol. 23 (2000), pp. 1,035–61; Trevor Jones, 'Small Asian Businesses in Retreat? The Case of the UK', *Journal of Ethnic and Migration Studies*, vol. 29 (2003), pp. 485–500.

26. Max Weber, *The Protestant Ethic and the Spirit of Capitalism* (originally 1904, London, 1976 edn).

27. Despite its title the article by Brown, 'Religion and Economic Activity in the South Asian Population', pp. 1035–61, deals with a whole variety of factors in trying to explain the entrepreneurial activities of this diverse group.

28. Anuradha Basu and Esser Altinay, 'The Interaction between Culture and Entrepreneurship in London's Immigrant Businesses', *International Small Business Journal*, vol. 20 (2002), pp. 371–93.

29. Michael H. Lyon and Bernice J. M. West, 'London Patels: Caste and Commerce', *Journal of Ethnic and Migration Studies*, vol. 21 (1995), pp. 399–419; Parvin Patel and Mario Rutten, 'Patels of Central Gujarat in Greater London', *Economic and Political Weekly*, vol. 334 (1999), pp. 952–4.

30. See Chapter 3.

31. Floya Anthias, *Ethnicity, Class, Gender and Migration: Greek Cypriots in Britain* (Aldershot, 1992), p. 58.

32. Pnina Werbner, *The Migration Process: Capital, Gifts and Offerings among British Pakistanis* (Oxford, 1990), pp. 50–78.

33. Basu and Altinay, 'The Interaction between Culture and Entrepreneurship', p. 374.

34. Benton and Gomez, *The Chinese in Britain*, pp. 135–6.

35. Metcalf, Modood and Virdee, *Asian Self-Employment*, p. 24.

36. See the discussion on Jewish exploitation in Chapter 4. For Germans see below, pp. 101–3. For early twenty-first-century London see: Basu and Altinay, 'Interaction between Culture and Entrepreneurship', pp. 385–6; and Akin Fadahunsi, David Smallbone and Salinder Supri, 'Networking and Ethnic Minority Enterprise Development: Insights from a North London Study', *Journal of Small Business and Enterprise Development*, vol. 7 (2000), pp. 233–4.

37. Godley, *Jewish Immigrant Entrepreneurship*, p. 93.

38. Fadahunsi, Smallbone and Supri, 'Networking and Ethnic Minority Enterprise Development', pp. 232–3.

39. See, for example, Lien Bich Luu, *Immigrants and the Industries of London* (Aldershot, 2005).

40. Anne J. Kershen, *Strangers, Aliens and Asians: Huguenots, Jews and Bangladeshis in Spitalfields, 1660–2000* (London, 2005), pp. 166–72.

41. Godley, *Jewish Immigrant Entrepreneurship*, pp. 129–30.

42. M. Dorothy George, *London Life in the Eighteenth Century* (Harmondsworth, 1966), p. 120.

43. Mayhew, *London Labour and the London Poor*, vol. 1, p. 104.

44. Panayi, *Immigration History*, pp. 222–4.

45. Mayhew, *London Labour and the London Poor*, vol. 1, p. 104.

46. Lynn Hollen Lees, *Exiles of Erin: Irish Immigrants in Victorian London* (Manchester, 1979), pp. 39–44.

47. Mayhew, *London Labour and the London Poor*, vol. 1, p. 104.

48. Ibid., p. 104.

49. Ibid., p. 105.

50. Ibid., pp. 106–7.

51. Ibid., pp. 117–18.

52. Lynn H. Lees, 'Patterns of Lower-Class Life: Irish Slum Communities in Nineteenth-Century London', in Stephan Thernstrom and Richard Sennett, eds, *Nineteenth-Century Cities: Essays in the New Urban History* (London, 1969), pp. 368–74.

53. 'The London Irish', *Blackwood's Edinburgh Magazine*, vol. 170 (1901), p. 127.

54. Seán Sorohan, *Irish London during the Troubles* (Dublin, 2012), p. 8.

55. Anne Pimlott Baker, 'Murphy, James [John] (1913–2009)', *Oxford Dictionary of National Biography*, https://doi.org/10.1093/ref:odnb/102053, accessed 4 January 2019.

56. See the discussion in Judy Chance, 'The Irish in London: An Exploration of Ethnic Boundary Maintenance', in Peter Jackson, ed., *Race and Racism: Essays in Social Geography* (London, 1987), pp. 142–60.

57. Dorothy Davis, *A History of Shopping* (London, 1966), pp. 251–75.

58. See below, pp. 101–3.

59. Panikos Panayi, *Spicing Up Britain: The Multicultural History of British Food* (London, 2008), pp. 44–6, 128.

60. Mayhew, *London Labour and the London Poor*, vol. 1, p. 114, suggests that Irish street-sellers drank less than their English counterparts and points to the preference for whisky. 'The London Irish', p. 127, claimed that: 'A prosperous week means, too often, a Saturday spent in "booze" – the very day on which they should be making most money.' For early post-war Irish migrant drinking and its causes see Clair Wills, *Lovers and Strangers: An Immigrant History of Post-War Britain* (London, 2017), pp. 123–40.

61. These elites receive consideration in Chapter 5.

62. Todd M. Endelman, *The Jews of Britain, 1656–2000* (London, 2002), pp. 42–3.

63. Todd M. Endelman, *The Jews of Georgian England: Tradition and Change in a Liberal Society* (Ann Arbor, MI, 1999), p. 119.

64. Ibid., p. 120.
65. Ibid., p. 122, also points out that some Jews became assimilated into the London poor through conversion and intermarriage.
66. Henry Mayhew, *London Labour and the London Poor*, vol. 2 (originally 1861; London, 1968), p. 118.
67. Ibid., p. 119.
68. Ibid., p. 121.
69. Ibid., p. 122.
70. Ibid., pp. 124–5.
71. Harold Pollins, *Economic History of the Jews in England* (London, 1982), pp. 126–7.
72. George A. Wade, 'Israel in London: How the Hebrew Lives in Whitechapel', *English Illustrated Magazine*, vol. 23 (1900), p. 404.
73. David Powell, *Counter Revolution: The Tesco Story* (London, 1991), pp. 1–24.
74. See Chapter 3.
75. Panayi, *Spicing Up Britain*, pp. 46–9.
76. Mayhew, *London Labour and the London Poor*, vol. 2, p. 121.
77. *Jewish Chronicle*, 7 January 1921. The schechita board regulated Jewish butchers and slaughtering.
78. *Jewish Chronicle*, 2 April 1897.
79. *Jewish Chronicle*, 2 November 1888.
80. *Jewish Chronicle*, 2 April 1909.
81. Chaim Lewis, *A Soho Address* (London, 1965), p. 20.
82. Ibid., p. 23.
83. Sir Hubert Llewellyn Smith, *The New Survey of London Life and Labour*, vol. 3, *London Industries*, II (London, 1933), pp. 47–8.
84. William D. Rubinstein, *A History of the Jews in the English-Speaking World: Great Britain* (Basingstoke, 1996), pp. 418–19.
85. See, for example, *Jewish Chronicle*, 2 November 1980, 8 October 1982, 8 March 1985.
86. LMA Acc/2805/7/9/8, 'Draft of Kosher Meat Trade in the UK', 31 May 1979; United Synagogue Kashrut Board, *The Really Jewish Food Guide, 2005/5765* (London, 2005), pp. 137–9, 142–4.
87. JML/1990.10, '100 Years in the Baking: Leaflet Produced in the Centenary Year of the Grodzinksi Bakery, Telling their Story', 1988.
88. Henrietta Adler, 'Jewish Life and Labour in East London', in Llewellyn Smith, ed., *New Survey of London Life and Labour*, vol. 6 (London, 1934), p. 287.
89. Barou, *Jews in Work and Trade*, p. 6.
90. David Dee, *The 'Estranged' Generation? Social and Generational Change in Interwar British Jewry* (Basingstoke, 2017), pp. 113–16.
91. Geoffrey Alderman, *Modern British Jewry* (Oxford, 1992), p. 335.
92. See, for example, Stephen Aris, *The Jews in Business* (London, 1970), esp. pp. 86–111.
93. Rachel Lichtenstein, 'Cecil Gee', in Elizabeth Selby, ed., *Moses and Mr Fish* (London, 2016), pp. 39–49.
94. Panayi, *Spicing Up Britain*, p. 80.
95. Harold Pollins, 'German Jews in British Industry', in Werner E. Mosse, et al., eds, *Second Chance: Two Centuries of German-Speaking Jews in the United Kingdom* (Tübingen, 1991), pp. 373–7.
96. Pam Fox, *The Jewish Community of Golders Green: A Social History* (Stroud, 2016), pp. 118–40.
97. David Graham, Marlena Schmool and Stanley Waterman, *Jews in Britain: A Snapshot from the 2001 Census* (London, 2007), p. 88.
98. Panikos Panayi, *The Enemy in Our Midst: Germans in Britain During the First World War* (Oxford, 1991). See also Chapter 6 for the anti-German rioting.
99. Graham Jeffcoate, *Deutsche Drucker und Buchhändler in London, 1680–1811: Strukturen und Bedeutung des Deutschen Anteils am englischen Buchhandel* (Berlin, 2015).

100. Panikos Panayi, *German Immigrants in Britain during the Nineteenth Century, 1815–1914* (Oxford, 1995), pp. 120–1.
101. Arthur Shadwell, 'The German Colony in London', *National Review*, vol. 26 (1896), p. 808.
102. Panayi, *German Immigrants*, p. 131.
103. *Caterer*, 15 November 1912.
104. Panayi, *German Immigrants,* p. 120.
105. Ibid., pp. 131–2.
106. *Post Office London Directory, 1913* (London, 1913), p. 258.
107. *Hermann*, 4 August 1866.
108. *Hermann*, 2 January 1869.
109. *Londoner General Anzeiger*, 1 May 1904.
110. *Londoner General Anzeiger*, 3 March 1909.
111. *Londoner General Anzeiger*, 25 December 1909, 6 January 1912.
112. *Londoner General Anzeiger*, 6 January 1900, 3 January 1914.
113. Panayi, *The Enemy in Our Midst*.
114. *Hotel Review*, June 1940.
115. *Caterer*, 11 September 1936.
116. See the work of Lucio Sponza especially: *Divided Loyalties: Italians in Britain during the Second World War* (Frankfurt, 2000); 'The Anti-Italian Riots, June 1940', in Panikos Panayi, ed., *Racial Violence in Britain in the Nineteenth and Twentieth Centuries* (London, 1996), pp. 131–49; and 'The British Government and the Internment of Italians', in David Cesarani and Tony Kushner, eds, *The Internment of Aliens in Twentieth-Century Britain* (London, 1993), pp. 125–46.
117. Giorgio Riello, 'The Taste of Italy: Italian Businesses and the Culinary Delicacies of Georgian London', *London Journal*, vol. 31 (2006), pp. 201–22.
118. See Chapter 3.
119. C. Carter Blake, 'Italian Produce', *Food Journal*, 1 January 1874, pp. 447–9. See also Lucio Sponza, *Italian Immigrants in Nineteenth-Century Britain* (Leicester, 1988), pp. 101–3.
120. Lucio Sponza, 'Italian "Penny Ice-Men" in Victorian London', in Anne J. Kershen, ed., *Food in the Migrant Experience* (Aldershot, 2002), pp. 17–41. See also the description in J. Thomson and Adolphe Smith, *Street Life in London* (London, 1877), pp. 53–8.
121. Felicity Kinross, *Coffee and Ices: The Story of Carlo Gatti in London* (Sudbury, 1991).
122. Basil Crowhurst, *A History of the British Ice Cream Industry* (Westerham, 2000), pp. 11–17; Terri Colpi, *The Italian Factor: The Italian Community in Great Britain* (Edinburgh, 1991), pp. 58–60, 81–2.
123. Alkan Fuat, *Cypriots in Haringey* (London, 1980), p. 11.
124. Martin Kettle, 'Famagusta, N16', *New Society*, 26 March 1981.
125. Fuat, *Cypriots in Haringey*, p. 11.
126. Hatice Abdullah and Mark Sinker, *Departures and Arrivals: Turkish Cypriots who Came to England between 1934 and 1963* (London, 2006), pp. 84–7.
127. The above account is constructed from the following: Bilge Nevzat, *The Turquoise Conspiracy: Asil Nadir, the Collapse of Polly Peck and the Persecution of a Family* (London, 1999); David Barchard, *Asil Nadir and the Rise and Fall of Polly Peck* (London, 1992); Tim Hindle, *Asil Nadir: Fugitive from Injustice* (London, 1993); and Raymond Zelker, *The Polly Peck Story: A Memoir* (London, 2001).
128. *Financial Times*, 23 August 2012.
129. Chinese catering is discussed in Chapter 9.
130. Herman Scheffauer, 'The Chinese in England: A Growing National Problem', *London Magazine*, vol. 26 (1911), p. 646.
131. Benton and Gomez, *The Chinese in Britain*, pp. 89–90, 99–102.
132. Ibid., pp. 102–6; George Wade, 'The Cockney John Chinaman', *English Illustrated Magazine*, vol. 23 (1900), p. 304; Virginia Berridge, 'East End Opium Dens and Narcotic Use in Britain', *London Journal*, vol. 4 (1978), pp. 3–28.

133. Anthony Shang, *The Chinese in Britain* (London, 1984), pp. 9–10.

134. *Caterer*, 15 July 1916.

135. *Caterer*, 15 July 1908.

136. Townley Searle, *Strange News from China: A First Chinese Cookbook* (London, 1932), pp. 32–3.

137. James L. Watson, *Emigration and the Chinese Lineage: The* Mans *in Hong Kong and London* (London, 1975), pp. 116–19; Anthony Shang, 'The Chinese in London', in Nick Merriman, ed., *The Peopling of London: Fifteen Thousand Years of Settlement from Overseas* (London, 1993), p. 93; Ng Kwee Choo, *The Chinese in London* (London, 1968), pp. 31–2, 47–78.

138. See Chapters 3 and 9.

139. Rashmi Desai, *Indian Immigrants in Britain* (London, 1963), p. 57.

140. Rozina Visram, *Asians in Britain: 400 Years of History* (London, 2002), p. 279.

141. Desai, *Indian Immigrants*, pp. 56–67.

142. Aldrich, Cater, Jones and McEvoy, 'Business Development and Self-Segregation', pp. 172, 178, 188.

143. Harald Tambs-Lyche, *London Patidars: A Case Study in Urban Ethnicity* (London, 1980), pp. 32, 38.

144. Ibid., pp. 54–78.

145. Ibid., p. 86.

146. Patel and Rutten, 'Patels of Central Gujarat in Greater London', pp. 952–4.

147. Metcalf, Modood and Virdee, *Asian Self-Employment*, pp. 22–3.

148. Maritsa V. Poros, *Modern Migrations: Gujarati Indian Networks in New York and London* (Stanford, CA, 2011), p. 84.

149. MLOHC/93/120, Interview by Rory O'Connell of Ajit Rai, 23 March 1993.

150. Panikos Panayi, 'The Spicing Up of English Provincial Life: The History of Curry in Leicester', in Kershen, *Food in the Migrant Experience*, pp. 54–5; Sharbani Basu, *Curry: The Story of the Nation's Favourite Dish* (Stroud, 2003), pp. 52–103; Richard Tames, *Feeding London: A Taste of History* (London, 2003), p. 120.

151. George Kay, *Food Supply and Ethnic Minorities: Its Availability and Quality* (London, 1986), p. 22.

152. GLA Economics, *Contribution of Asian-Owned Businesses*, pp. 13–14.

153. See Virinder S. Kalra, *From Textile Mills to Taxi Ranks: Experiences of Migration, Labour and Social Change* (Farnham, 2000), which focuses upon Lancashire and, in particular, Oldham.

154. David Smallbone, Marcello Bertotti and Ignatius Ekanem, 'Diversification in Ethnic Minority Business: The Case of Asians in London's Creative Industries', *Journal of Small Business and Enterprise Development*, vol. 12 (2005), pp. 41–56.

155. Parminder Bhachu, *Dangerous Designs: Asian Women Fashion the Diaspora Economies* (London, 2004).

156. Susan Okokon, *Black Londoners: A History* (Stroud, 2009), pp. 83–4

157. Tony Wade, *How they Made a Million: The Dyke and Dryden Story* (London, 2001), p. 27.

158. Ibid., pp. 27–83.

159. Okokon, *Black Londoners*, p. 83.

160. For an indication of this range see: ibid., pp. 83–105; and Emete Wanohogo, *Black Women Taking Charge: Profiles of Black Women Entrepreneurs* (London, 1997).

161. But see Chapter 6.

162. See Chapter 9.

CHAPTER 5

1. Saemy Japhet, *Recollections of My Business Life* (London, 1931), p. 62.

2. 'Africans in London', *Economist*, 11 March 1950.

3. See, for example, the discussion in Eric Hobsbawm, 'The Example of the English Middle Classes', in Jürgen Kocka and Allen Mitchell, eds, *Bourgeois Society in Nineteenth-Century Europe* (Oxford, 1993), pp. 127–50.

4. Ulrike Kirchberger, *Aspekte deutsch-britischer Expansion: Die Überseeinteressen der deutschen Migranten in Großbritannien in der Mitte des 19. Jahrhunderts* (Stuttgart, 1999), pp. 202–347.

5. Panikos Panayi, *The Germans in India: Elite European Migrants in the British Empire* (Manchester, 2017), pp. 40–72. Before 1833, German missionary organizations could not operate in India.

6. See Chapter 7.

7. Colin Holmes, *John Bull's Island: Immigration and British Society, 1871–1971* (Basingstoke, 1988), pp. 34–5.

8. Min-Chien T. Z. Tyau, *London through Chinese Eyes, or, My Seven and a Half Years in London* (London, 1920), pp. 303–8.

9. Szeming Sze, 'Chinese Students in Great Britain', *Asiatic Review*, vol. 27 (1931), p. 311.

10. Ibid., p. 312.

11. Ng Kwee Choo, *The Chinese in London* (London, 1968), p. 14.

12. For the total number of Chinese students in the UK in 2016 see UK Council for International Student Affairs, 'International (non-UK) students in UK HE in 2016–17', https://ukcisa. org.uk/Research--Policy/Statistics/International-student-statistics-UK-higher-education, accessed 9 July 2018.

13. As an introduction see Hans Werner Debrunner, *Presence and Prestige: Africans in Europe: A History of Africans in Europe Before 1918* (Basel, 1979), pp. 368, 384, 389.

14. 'Africans in London', p. 519. Hakim Adi, 'West African Students in Britain, 1900–60: The Politics of Exile', in David Killingray, ed., *Africans in Britain* (Ilford, 1994), pp. 107–28, provides an outline history of students from one particular part of Africa.

15. Christopher Roy Zembe, *Zimbabwean Communities in Britain: Imperial and Post-Colonial Identities and Legacies* (Basingstoke, 2018), pp. 218–23.

16. Shompa Lahiri, *Indians in Britain: Anglo-Indian Encounters, Race and Identity, 1880–1930* (London, 2000); A. Martin Wainwright, *'The Better Class' of Indians: Social Rank, Imperial Identity and South Asians in Britain, 1858–1914* (Manchester, 2008); Antoinette M. Burton, *At the Heart of the Empire: Indians and the Colonial Encounter in Late-Victorian Britain* (London, 1998).

17. *Naturalization Act of 1870*.

18. The naturalization certificates of those described in this paragraph can be found in NA/ HO334/1.

19. NA/HO334/1/119; NA/HO1/165/A119.

20. NA/HO1/165/A124.

21. NA/HO1/165/A153.

22. NA/HO1/165/A137.

23. NA/HO1/165/A97; NA/HO1/165/A98.

24. These naturalization certificates are in NA/HO334/1.

25. NA/HO334/5.

26. NA/HO334/40.

27. NA/HO334/137.

28. Daniel Gorman, *Imperial Citizenship: Empire and the Question of Belonging* (Manchester, 2007), pp. 19–28.

29. According to the 1911 census, London served as home to 5,352 Americans, for which see 'A Vision of Britain Through Time', *1911 Census General Report with Appendices*, Table 109, http://www.visionofbritain.org.uk/census/table/EW1911GEN_M109, accessed 9 July 2018. See also: Alison Lockwood, *Passionate Pilgrims: The American Traveller in Great Britain, 1800–1914* (London, 1981); and Brian M. Norton, *Americans in London: An Anecdotal Street Guide to the Homes and Haunts of Americans from John Adams to Fred Astaire* (London, 1988).

30. NA/HO334/137/5529.
31. Panikos Panayi, *The Enemy in Our Midst: Germans in Britain During the First World War* (Oxford, 1991), pp. 188–91.
32. Timotheous Catsiyannis, *The Greek Community of London* (London, 1993), pp. 45–6, 405–12.
33. See Chapter 2.
34. See, for example, Ulrike Kirchberger, 'Deutsche Naturwissenschaftler im britischen Empire: Die Erforschung der au Bereuropäischen Welt im Spannungsfeld zwischen deutschem und britischen Imperialismus', *Historische Zeitschrift*, vol. 271 (2000), pp. 621–60.
35. Panikos Panayi, *German Immigrants in Britain during the Nineteenth Century* (Oxford, 1995), p. 138.
36. See John R. Davis, 'Friedrich Max Müller and the Migration of German Academics to Britain in the Nineteenth Century', in Stefan Manz, Margrit Schulte Beerbühl and John R. Davis, eds, *Migration and Transfer from Germany to Britain, 1660–1914* (Munich, 2007), pp. 93–106. More generally, Tamson Pietsch, *Empire of Scholars: Universities, Networks and the British Academic World, 1850–1939* (Manchester, 2013).
37. Marion Berghahn, *Continental Britons: German-Jewish Refugees from Nazi Germany* (Oxford, 1988), pp. 77–106. See also the relevant contributions to Werner E. Mosse, et al., eds, *Second Chance: Two Centuries of German-Speaking Jews in the United Kingdom* (Tübingen, 1991).
38. Craig Bailey, *Irish London: Middle-Class Migration in the Global Eighteenth Century* (Liverpool, 2013), pp. 19–156.
39. F. A. Fahy and D. J. O'Donoghue, *Ireland in London* (Dublin, 1889). See also Tony Murray, *London Irish Fictions: Narrative, Diaspora and Identity* (Liverpool, 2012), pp. 21, 34.
40. Jeffrey P. Green, *Black Edwardians: Black People in Britain, 1901–1914* (London, 1998).
41. Susan Okokon, *Black Londoners: A History* (Stroud, 2009), p. 30; Verna Wilkins, *Rudolph Walker OBE* (London, 2008).
42. Okokon, *Black Londoners*, p. 170.
43. Sukhdev Sandhu, *London Calling: How Black and Asian Writers Imagined a City* (London, 2004).
44. Okokon, *Black Londoners*, p. 167.
45. Cecil Roth, *A History of the Jews in England* (Oxford, 1964), pp. 1–90; P. Hyams, 'The Jewish Minority of Medieval England', *Journal of Jewish Studies*, vol. 25 (1974), pp. 270–93.
46. Roth, *A History of the Jews in England*, pp. 105–13; Joe Hillaby, 'London: The Thirteenth-Century Jewry', *Transactions of the Jewish Historical Society of England*, vol. 33 (1990–2), pp. 102–5.
47. Hillaby, 'London', pp. 107–53, outlines the major Jewish lending families in thirteenth-century London.
48. David S. Katz, *The Jews in the History of England, 1485–1850* (Oxford, 1994), pp. 110–34; Todd M. Endelman, *The Jews of Britain, 1656–2000* (London, 2002), pp. 20–5.
49. Endelman, *Jews of Britain*, pp. 27–30; David Cesarani, 'The Forgotten Port Jews of London: Court Jews who were also Port Jews', in David Cesarani, ed., *Port Jews: Jewish Communities in Cosmopolitan Trading Centres, 1550–1950* (London, 2002), pp. 116–21.
50. Paul H. Emden, *Jews of Britain: A Series of Biographies* (London, 1943), pp. 15, 27–31.
51. William D. Rubinstein, *A History of the Jews in the English-Speaking World: Great Britain* (Basingstoke, 1996), pp. 64, 66, 67.
52. Endelman, *Jews of Britain*, p. 48.
53. Todd M. Endelman, *The Jews of Georgian England: Tradition and Change in a Liberal Society* (Ann Arbor, MI, 1999), pp. 121–8.
54. Endelman, *Jews of Britain*, p. 42.
55. Margrit Schulte Beerbühl, *The Forgotten Majority: German Merchants in London, Naturalization and Global Trade 1660–1815* (Oxford, 2014).
56. Margrit Schulte Beerbühl, 'Commercial Networks, Transfer and Innovation: The Migration of German Merchants to England', in Manz, Beerbühl and Davis, *Migration and Transfer from Germany to Britain*, pp. 25–7.

57. John Orbell, 'Baring, Sir Francis, First Baronet', *Oxford Dictionary of National Biography*, https://doi-org.proxy.library.dmu.ac.uk/10.1093/ref:odnb/1382, accessed 17 May 2018; Panikos Panayi, 'Germans in Eighteenth-Century Britain', in Panikos Panayi, ed., *Germans in Britain since 1500* (London, 1996), pp. 34–5; Philip Ziegler, *The Sixth Great Power: The History of One of the Greatest of All Banking Families, the House of Barings, 1762–1929* (New York, 1988).

58. Stanley Chapman, *Merchant Enterprise in Britain: From the Industrial Revolution to World War I* (Cambridge, 1992), pp. 129–66.

59. Eric Hobsbawm, *Industry and Empire* (London, 1969), pp. 172–94.

60. Jonathan Schneer, *London 1900: The Imperial Metropolis* (London, 1999), p. 72.

61. Ibid., pp. 64–92, analyses the power of the City in 1900.

62. Karl Erich Born, *International Banking in the 19th and 20th Centuries* (Leamington Spa, 1983), pp. 1–184; David Kynaston, *City of London* (London, 2012); Jerry White, *London in the Nineteenth Century: 'A Human Awful Wonder of God'* (London, 2007), pp. 163–72.

63. Stanley Chapman, *The Rise of Merchant Banking* (London, 1984), p. 57.

64. Gary B. Magee and Andrew S. Thompson, *Empire and Globalisation: Networks of People, Goods and Capital in the British World, c.1850–1914* (Cambridge, 2010), pp. 117–23.

65. Manfred Pohl, 'Deutsche Bank London Agency Founded 100 Years Ago', in Deutsche Bank, ed., *Studies on Economic and Monetary Problems and on Banking History* (Frankfurt, 1988), pp. 233–45; Panayi, *Enemy*, pp. 132–49.

66. Antje Hagen, *Deutsche Direktinvestitionen in Grossbritannien, 1871–1918* (Stuttgart, 1997); Geoffrey Jones, 'Foreign Multinationals and British Industry before 1945', *Economic History Review*, 2nd series, vol. 61 (1988), pp. 429–53.

67. Charles A. Jones, *International Business in the Nineteenth Century: The Rise and Fall of a Cosmopolitan Bourgeoisie* (Brighton, 1987), pp. 153–65; Youssef Cassis, *City Bankers, 1890–1914* (Cambridge, 1994).

68. Stanley Chapman, 'Ethnicity and Money Making in Nineteenth-Century Britain', *Renaissance and Modern Studies*, vol. 38 (1995), p. 21.

69. Chapman, *Merchant Enterprise*, pp. 149–53.

70. Lindy Woodhead, *Shopping, Seduction and Mr Selfridge* (London, 2007).

71. Joan George, *Merchants to Magnates, Intrigue and Survival: Armenians in London, 1900–2000* (London, 2009), pp. 234–5.

72. *Directory of Armenians in London* (London, 1901), pp. 253–4.

73. Maria Christina Chatziioannou, 'Greek Merchants in Victorian England', in Dimitris Tziovas, ed., *Greek Diaspora and Migration since 1700: Society, Politics and Culture* (Farnham, 2009), pp. 45–60.

74. Catsiyannis, *Greek Community of London*, pp. 39–40.

75. Ibid., pp. 45–6; Maria Christina Chatziioannou and Gelina Harlaftis, 'From the Levant to the City of London: Mercantile Credit in the Greek International Commercial Networks of the Eighteenth and Nineteenth Centuries', in Philip L. Cottrell, Evan Lange and Ulf Olsson, eds, *Centres and Peripheries in Banking: The Historical Development of Financial Markets* (Aldershot, 2007), pp. 29–30.

76. Chatziioannou and Harlaftis, 'From the Levant to the City of London', p. 27.

77. Catsiyannis, *Greek Community of London*, p. 44.

78. John Gennadius, *Stephen A. Ralli: A Biographical Memoir* (London, 1902), pp. 21–2.

79. Timotheous Catsiyannis, *Pandias Stephen Rallis, 1793–1865: The Founder of the Greek Community in London* (London, 1986), pp. 29, 47–8.

80. Vikram Doctor, 'Ralli Brothers', *Economic Times*, 2 August 2015; LMA/CLC/B/186/MS23836, ms history, 'The House of Ralli Brothers', by Leoni M. Calvocoressi, 1952.

81. Chatziioannou and Harlaftis, 'From the Levant to the City of London', p. 31; 'The Late Mr. Stephen A. Ralli', *The Times*, 30 April, 1902.

82. LMA/CLC/B/186/MS23834, Ralli Brothers Limited Collection, 'Report to the Chairman on Organisation and Activities, with Suggestions for Improvements, Including Statistical and Financial Data about the Period 1931–8'.

83. LMA/CLC/B/186/MS23836, 'Chronological Account of the Firm, 1818–1936, Compiled 1906 (printed)'.

84. Timotheous Catsiyannis, *The Rodocanachi of London: A Pictorial History* (London, 1987); Chatziioannou and Harlaftis, 'From the Levant to the City of London', p. 32.

85. Alexander C. Ionides Junior, *Ion: A Grandfather's Tale* (Dublin, 1927); Timotheous Catsiyannis, *Constantine Ionidis-Ipliktsis 1775–1852 and the Ionidi Family* (London, 1988).

86. Chatziioannou and Harlaftis, 'From the Levant to the City of London', pp. 33–4.

87. Gelina Harlaftis, *A History of Greek-Owned Shipping: The Making of an International Tramp Fleet, 1830 to the Present Day* (London, 1996), pp. 194–203; Mai Wann, *Chiot Shipowners in London: An Immigrant Elite* (Coventry, 1987).

88. V. D. Lipman, 'The Structure of London Jewry in the Mid-Nineteenth Century', in H. J. Zimmels, J. Rabinowitz and Israel Feinstein, eds, *Essays in Honour of Chief Rabbi Israel Brodie* (London, 1967), pp. 257–8.

89. Victor Gray and Melanie Aspey, 'Nathan Mayer Rothschild', *Oxford Dictionary of National Biography*, https://doi.org/10.1093/ref:odnb/24162, accessed 4 January 2019; Herbert H. Kaplan, *Nathan Mayer Rothschild and the Creation of a Dynasty* (Stanford, CA, 2006); Niall Ferguson, *The World's Banker: The History of the House of Rothschild* (London, 1998), pp. 91–118; Charles Buxton, ed., *Memoirs of Sir Thomas Fowell Buxton* (London, 1852), pp. 288–90; Richard Davis, *The English Rothschilds* (London, 1983); Stanley Chapman, *N. M. Rothschild, 1777–1836* (London, 1977); Stanley Chapman, 'The Establishment of the Rothschilds as Bankers', *Jewish Historical Studies*, vol. 29 (1982–6), pp. 177–93; Victor Gray, 'An Off-Hand Man: The Character of Nathan Rothschild', in Victor Gray and Melanie Aspecy, eds, *The Life and Times of N. M. Rothschild* (London, 1998), pp. 14–24; Jules Ayer, *A Century of Finance, 1804–1904: The London House of Rothschild* (London, 1905).

90. Panayi, *German Immigrants in Britain*, pp. 18–19.

91. Heinrich Gerdes, 'Ein Sohn Gerdes als Grosskaufmann in London', *Stader Archiv*, vol. 14 (1924), pp. 409.

92. Panayi, *German Immigrants in Britain*, p. 19; Stanley Chapman, 'The International Houses: The Continental contribution to British Commerce', *Journal of European Economic History*, vol. 6 (1977), p. 12.

93. Richard Roberts, *Schroders: Merchants & Bankers* (Basingstoke, 1992), pp. 3–42.

94. Ibid., p. 44; Chapman, *Rise of Merchant Banking*, p. 44.

95. Roberts, *Schroders*, pp. 117–20.

96. This is the categorization put forward by Chapman, *Rise of Merchant Banking*, p. 44. See also: Cassis, *City Bankers*, pp. 214–20; and Perch Arnold, *The Bankers of London* (London, 1938), p. 55. Carl Joachim Hambro actually came from a Jewish family in Copenhagen. For an introduction to his life and career see Andrew St George, 'Hambro, Baron Carl Joachim', *Oxford Dictionary of National Biography*, https://doi.org/10.1093/ref:odnb/48884, accessed 23 May 2018.

97. Jehanne Wake, *Kleinwort, Benson: A History of Two Families in Banking* (Oxford, 1987).

98. Antony Lentin, *Banker, Traitor, Scapegoat, Spy? The Troublesome Case of Sir Edgar Speyer* (London, 2013).

99. Panayi, *German Immigrants*, pp. 71–2.

100. John Orbell, 'Japhet, Saemy', *Oxford Dictionary of National Biography*, https://doi.org/10.1093/ref:odnb/48906, accessed 4 January 2019.

101. Japhet, *Recollections*, p. 7.

102. Ibid., p. 22.

103. Ibid., p. 23.

104. Ibid., pp. 24, 25.

105. Ibid., p. 35.

106. Ibid., p. 40.

107. Ibid., pp. 51, 62, 76.

108. Orbell, 'Japhet, Saemy'.
109. Cecil Roth, 'The Court Jews of Edwardian England', *Jewish Social Studies*, vol. 5 (1943), p. 362.
110. Chapman, *Rise of Merchant Banking*, pp. 45–6; Kurt Grunwald, ' "Windsor-Cassel" – The Last Court Jew: Prolegomena to a Biography of Sir Ernest Cassel', *Leo Baeck Yearbook*, vol. 14 (1969), p. 123; Pat Thane, 'Sir Ernest Joseph Cassel', *Dictionary of Business Biography* (London, 1984), p. 604.
111. Grunwald, ' "Windsor-Cassel" ', pp. 119–61; Pat Thane, 'Financiers and the British State: The Case of Sir Ernest Cassel', *Business History*, vol. 17 (1986), pp. 80–9.
112. See Chapman, *Rise of Merchant Banking*.
113. 'Ralph Stern', in David Stebbing, ed., *Jewish Memories of the Twentieth Century* (Stanmore, 2003), pp. 297–8.
114. JML, Oral History Collection Transcript 231, Interview of Leon Aelion by Judith Evans, 4 March 1992.
115. JML, Oral History Collection Transcript 233, Interview of Sophie and David Elias by Judith Devons, 10 March 1992. He moved to London during the 1940s or 1950s but the interview does not make clear the exact date.
116. Geoffrey Alderman, *Modern British Jewry* (Oxford, 1992), pp. 274–80; Louise London, 'British Immigration Policy Control Procedures and Jewish Refugees, 1933–1939', in Mosse, et al., *Second Chance*, pp. 485–517.
117. The story of German Jewish refugees from the Nazis can be traced in the following: Mosse, *Second Chance*; Berghahn, *Continental Britons*; Gerhard Hirschfeld, ed., *Exile in Great Britain: Refugees from Hitler's Germany* (Leamington Spa, 1984); Daniel Snowman, *The Hitler Emigrés: The Cultural Impact on Britain of Refugees from Nazism* (London, 2003); Marian Malet and Anthony Grenville, eds, *Changing Countries: The Experience and Achievement of German-Speaking Exiles from Hitler in Britain, 1933 to Today* (London, 2002); Peter Alter, ed., *Out of the Third Reich: Refugee Historians in Post-War Britain* (London, 1998); and J. M. Ritchie, *German Exiles: British Perspectives* (New York, 1997).
118. Rubinstein, *A History of the Jews in the English-Speaking World*, pp. 400–1.
119. David Graham, Marlena Schmool and Stanley Waterman, *Jews in Britain: A Snapshot from the 2001 Census* (London, 2007), pp. 79–87.
120. Ibid., p. 91.
121. These are some of the names covered by Chaim Bermant, *The Cousinhood: The Anglo-Jewish Gentry* (London, 1971).
122. Stephen Aris, *The Jews in Business* (London, 1970), esp. pp. 186–206.
123. Ibid., pp. 144–58; David Powell, *Counter Revolution: The Tesco Story* (London, 1991); Andrew Seth and Geoffrey Randall, *The Grocers: The Rise of the Supermarket Chains* (London, 2001), pp. 23–51.
124. For Montague Burton see the relevant contributions to Elizabeth Selby, ed., *Moses and Mr Fish* (London, 2016). Aris, *The Jews in Business*, pp. 159–76, deals with the history of Marks and Spencer.
125. Emden, *Jews of Britain*, p. 478.
126. Geoffrey Alderman, 'Wolfson, Sir Isaac, First Baronet', *Oxford Dictionary of National Biography*, https://doi.org/10.1093/ref:odnb/50705, accessed 24 May 2018.
127. Harold Pollins, *Economic History of the Jews in England* (London, 1982), p. 223.
128. 'Mister Fidelity', *JC Audio-Visual Supplement*, 20 July 1973, p. vi.
129. See Chapter 4.
130. *Daily Telegraph*, 13 April 2014.
131. Sir Gulam Noon, *Noon with a View: Courage and Integrity* (Dunbeath, 2008).
132. *Parikiaki*, 17 May 2018, using the *Sunday Times Rich List*.
133. Sir Stelios Haji-Ioannou: Official Biography, http://stelios.org/about-me/biography.html, accessed 24 May 2018.
134. 'Lakshmi Mittal Talks to the FT', *FT*, 22 December 2006. *Sunday Times Rich List*, 3 April 2005.

135. Dominic Midgley and Chris Hutchins, *Abramovich: The Billionaire from Nowhere* (London, 2006).

136. *Guardian*, 28 May 2018.

137. Vidya Ram, 'Britain Proposes Controversial Changes to Investor Visas', *Businessline*, 26 February 2014; Mark Hollingsworth and Stewart Lansley, *Londongrad: From Russia with Cash: The Inside Story of the Oligarchs* (London, 2009), p. 24; John Lanchester, 'Why the Super-Rich Love the UK', *Guardian*, 24 February 2012; Geoffrey DeVerteuil and David Manley, 'Overseas Investment into London: Imprint, Impact and Pied-à-terre Urbanism', *Environment and Planning A*, vol. 49 (2017), pp. 1308–23.

138. *Sunday Times*, 13 May 2018.

139. Anthony D. King, *Global Cities: Post-Imperialism and the Internationalization of London* (Abingdon, 2015), pp. 89–93.

140. Adrian Favell, *Eurostars and Eurocities: Free Movement and Mobility in an Integrating Europe* (Oxford, 2008).

141. Ibid., pp. 42–5.

142. Saskia Huc-Hepher and Helen Drake, 'From the 16ème to South Ken? A Study of the Contemporary French Population in London', in Debra Kelly and Martyn Cornick, *A History of the French in London: Liberty, Equality, Opportunity* (London, 2013), p. 399.

143. Russell King, Aija Lulle, Francesca Conti and Dorothea Mueller, 'Eurocity London: A Qualitative Comparison of Graduate Migration from Germany, Italy and Latvia', *Comparative Migration Studies*, vol. 4 (2016), pp. 1–22.

144. King, *Global Cities*, pp. 128–311.

CHAPTER 6

1. *The Times*, 13 May 1915.

2. NA/PCOM91721, CHRISTOFI, Styllou Pantopiou: convicted at Central Criminal Court (CCC) on 28 October 1954 of murder; sentenced to death, executed 15 December 1954.

3. For an outline of post-war developments see, for example, Harry Goulbourne, *Race Relations in Britain Since 1945* (Basingstoke, 1998).

4. See the relevant chapters on migrant groups in George R. Sims, ed., *Living London*, 3 vols (London, 1902–3).

5. Panikos Panayi, *An Immigration History of Britain: Multicultural Racism Since c.1800* (London, 2010).

6. See below, p. 160.

7. Paul Hyams, 'The Jewish Minority in Medieval England, 1066–1290', *Journal of Jewish Studies*, vol. 25 (1974), pp. 277, 278.

8. Joe Hillaby, 'The London Jewry: William I to John', *Transactions of the Jewish Historical Society of England*, vol. 33 (1992–4), pp. 26–30.

9. Joe Hillaby, 'London: The Thirteenth-Century Jewry', *Transactions of the Jewish Historical Society of England*, vol. 33 (1990–2), pp. 134–7.

10. See, for example: George Rudé, 'The London Mob of the Eighteenth Century', *Historical Journal*, vol. 2 (1959), pp. 1–18; Robert B. Shoemaker, *The London Mob: Violence and Disorder in Eighteenth-Century England* (London, 2004).

11. C. W. Chitty, 'Aliens in England in the Sixteenth Century', *Race*, vol. 8 (1966), p. 131.

12. Martin Holmes, 'Evil May-Day 1517: The Story of a Riot', *History Today*, vol. 15 (September 1965), pp. 642–9.

13. Anne J. Kershen, *Strangers, Aliens and Asians: Huguenots, Jews and Bangladeshis in Spitalfields, 1660–2000* (London, 2005), pp. 194–6.

14. Considered by Linda Colley, *Britons: Forging the Nation, 1707–1837* (London, 1994).

15. M. Dorothy George, *London Life in the Eighteenth Century* (Harmondsworth, 1966), p. 137.

16. Panikos Panayi, *German Immigrants in Britain during the Nineteenth Century, 1815–1914* (Oxford, 1995), p. 13; Philip Otterness, *Becoming German: The 1709 Palatine Migration to New York* (Ithaca, NY, 2004), pp. 57–77.

17. Panayi, *German Immigrants in Britain during the Nineteenth Century*, p. 14.

18. George, *London Life*, p. 137.

19. Todd M. Endelman, *The Jews of Georgian England: Tradition and Change in a Liberal Society* (Ann Arbor, MI, 1999), pp. 114–15.

20. Ibid., pp. 86–93; Anthony Julius, *Trials of the Diaspora: A History of Anti-Semitism in England* (Oxford, 2010), pp. 251–5; Thomas W. Perry, *Public Opinion, Propaganda and Politics in Eighteenth-Century England: A Study of the Jew Bill of 1753* (Cambridge, MA, 1962).

21. Endelman, *Jews of Georgian England*, pp. 95–110.

22. Colley, *Britons*.

23. George, *London Life*, pp. 124–5.

24. The best accounts and interpretations of the Gordon riots include: Ian Haywood and John Seed, eds, *The Gordon Riots: Politics, Culture and Insurrection in Late Eighteenth-Century Britain* (Cambridge, 2012); George Rudé, 'The Gordon Riots: A Study of the Rioters and their Victims', *Transactions of the Royal Historical Society*, vol. 6 (1956), pp. 93–114; Clive Bloom, *Violent London: 2000 Years of Riots, Rebels and Revolts* (Basingstoke, 2010), pp. 119–32; John Paul De Castro, *The Gordon Riots* (London, 1926); John Stevenson, *Popular Disturbances in England, 1700–1870* (London, 1979), pp. 78–83; Shoemaker, *London Mob*, pp. 140–2; Christopher Hibbert, *King Mob: The Story of Lord George Gordon and the London Riots of 1780* (London, 1958).

25. E. R. Norman, *Anti-Catholicism in Victorian England* (London, 1968).

26. L. P. Curtis, *Anglo-Saxons and Celts* (New York, 1968).

27. Frank Neal, *Sectarian Violence: The Liverpool Experience, 1819–1914* (Manchester, 1988); Tom Gallagher, *The Uneasy Peace: Religious Tension in Modern Glasgow, 1819–1940* (Manchester, 1987); Walter L. Arnstein, *Protestant Versus Catholic in Mid-Victorian Britain* (London, 1982).

28. Alan O'Day, 'Varieties of Anti-Irish Behaviour in Britain, 1846–1922', in Panikos Panayi, ed., *Racial Violence in Britain in the Nineteenth and Twentieth Centuries* (London, 1996), pp. 36, 28–9.

29. Donald M. MacRaild, ' "No Irish Need Apply": The Origins and Persistence of a Prejudice', *Labour History Review*, vol. 78 (2013), p. 275.

30. Ibid., p. 277.

31. Sheridan Gilley, 'The Garibaldi Riots of 1862', *Historical Journal*, vol. 16 (1973), pp. 697–732.

32. O'Day, 'Varieties of Anti-Irish Behaviour', discusses the rise and fall of anti-Irish prejudice. Roman Catholic bodies in London are discussed in Chapter 8. For the growth of antisemitism see below, pp. 144–51.

33. Lucio Sponza, *Italian Immigrants in Nineteenth-Century Britain* (Leicester, 1988), pp. 119–265; John E. Zucchi, *The Little Slaves of the Harp: Italian Child Street Musicians in Nineteenth-Century Paris, London and New York* (London, 1992), pp. 76–110.

34. Lucio Sponza, *Divided Loyalties: Italians in Britain during the Second World War* (Frankfurt, 2000). For the situation in Scotland see Wendy Ugolini, *Experiencing the War as the 'Enemy Other': Italian Scottish Experience in World War II* (Manchester, 2011). For Cypriots in Soho see Evan Smith and Andrekos Varnava, 'Creating a "Suspect Community": Monitoring and Controlling the Cypriot Community in Inter-War London', *English Historical Review*, vol. 132 (2017), pp. 1149–81.

35. Panayi, *German Immigrants*, pp. 209–14.

36. See Chapter 4.

37. This published the *London City Mission Magazine*, which essentially attacked any activity in London, whether religious or not, which did not follow Protestant norms, as a justification for missionary work.

38. Panayi, *German Immigrants*, pp. 224–8.

39. Panikos Panayi and Stefan Manz, 'The Rise and Fall of Germans in the British Hospitality Industry, c1880–1920', *Food and History*, vol. 11 (2013), pp. 258–9.

40. Panayi, *German Immigrants*, pp. 232–51.

41. Panikos Panayi, 'Anti-German Riots in London During the First World War', *German History*, vol. 7 (1989), pp. 184–203.

42. Panikos Panayi, *The Enemy in Our Midst: Germans in Britain During the First World War* (Oxford, 1991).

43. Antony Lentin, *Banker, Traitor, Scapegoat, Spy? The Troublesome Case of Sir Edgar Speyer* (London, 2013).

44. Good introductions to this episode include: François Lafitte, *The Internment of Aliens* (originally 1940; London, 1988); Ronald A. Stent, *A Bespattered Page? The Internment of His Majesty's 'Most Loyal Enemy Aliens'* (London, 1980); and Peter and Leni Gillman, *'Collar the Lot': How Britain Interned and Expelled Its Wartime Refugees* (London, 1980).

45. See specially M. C. N. Salbstein, *The Emancipation of the Jews in Britain: The Question of the Admission of the Jews to Parliament* (London, 1982).

46. As an introduction see Léon Poliakov, *The History of Anti-Semitism*, vol. 4, *Suicidal Europe, 1870–1933* (Oxford, 1985).

47. Colin Holmes, *Anti-Semitism in British Society, 1876–1939* (London, 1979), pp. 49–88; David Feldman, *Englishmen and Jews: Social Relations and Political Culture, 1840–1914* (London, 1994), pp. 94–120; Julius, *Trials of the Diaspora*, pp. 268–76.

48. Edgar Rosenberg, *From Shylock to Svengali: Jewish Stereotypes in English Fiction* (Stanford, CA, 1960), p. 262.

49. Holmes, *Anti-Semitism*, pp. 70–7.

50. Ibid., pp. 121–40; Panayi, *Enemy*, pp. 163–4, 175. The concept of the 'Cult of the Coin' came from J. H. Clarke, *England under the Heel of the Jew* (London, 1918).

51. Holmes, *Anti-Semitism*, pp. 141–74.

52. For this distancing, see, for example, Feldman, *Englishmen and Jews*, pp. 291–352.

53. The best introductions to the anti-alien mentality include: Bernard Gainer, *The Alien Invasion: The Origins of the Aliens Act of 1905* (London, 1972); John A. Garrard, *The English and Immigration, 1880–1910* (London, 1971); and Kershen, *Strangers, Aliens and Asians*, pp. 198–209.

54. Gainer, *The Alien Invasion*, pp. 56–9.

55. Geoffrey Alderman, 'The Anti-Jewish Riots of August 1911 in South Wales', *Welsh History Review*, vol. 6 (1972), pp. 190–200; Colin Holmes, 'The Tredegar Riots of 1911: Anti-Jewish Disturbances in South Wales', *Welsh History Review*, vol. 11 (1982), pp. 214–25.

56. Holmes, *Anti-Semitism*, pp. 128–37; Julia Bush, *Behind the Lines: East London Labour 1914–1919* (London, 1984), pp. 165–92.

57. Tony Kushner, 'The Impact of British Anti-semitism, 1918–1945', in David Cesarani, ed., *The Making of Modern Anglo Jewry* (Oxford, 1990), pp. 191–208; David Dee, *The 'Estranged' Generation? Social and Generational Change in Interwar British Jewry* (London, 2017), pp. 104–22.

58. Tony Kushner, *The Persistence of Prejudice: Anti Semitism in British Society during the Second World War* (Manchester, 1989).

59. This incident receives more attention in Chapter 7.

60. Tony Kushner, 'Antisemitism and Austerity: The August 1947 Riots in Britain', in Panayi, *Racial Violence*, pp. 150–70.

61. James H. Robb, *Working-Class Anti-Semite: A Psychological Study in a London Borough* (London, 1954).

62. Tom O'Connor, *The London Irish* (London, 1987), pp. 21–4; John Corbally, 'The Jarring Irish: Postwar Immigration to the Heart of Empire', *Radical History Review*, no. 104 (2009), pp. 103–25; Mairtin Mac an Ghaill, 'The Irish in Britain: The Invisibility of Ethnicity and Anti-Irish Racism', *Journal of Ethnic and Migration Studies*, vol. 26 (2000), pp. 137–47.

63. See, for example, Sheridan Gilley, 'English Attitudes towards the Irish, 1789–1900', in Colin Holmes, ed., *Immigrants and Minorities in British Society* (London, 1978), pp. 81–110.

64. LMA/GLC/DG/PUB/01/159/1464, 'Policy Report on the Irish Community', 1984. See also: Christie Davis, 'The Irish Joke as a Social Phenomenon', in John Durant and Jonathan Miller, eds, *Laughing Matters: A Serious Look at Humour* (London, 1988), pp. 44–65; and Liz Curtis, Jack O'Keefe and Claire Keatinge, *Hearts and Minds: Anam Agus Intinn: The Cultural Life of London's Irish Community* (London, 1987), pp. 3–7.

65. Mary Hickman and Bronwen Walter, *Discrimination and the Irish Community in Britain* (London, 1997).

66. Ibid., p. 182.

67. Seán Sorohan, *Irish London during the Troubles* (Newbridge, 2012), p. 89.

68. Ibid., p. 90.

69. T. R. Fyvel, *The Insecure Offenders: Rebellious Youth in the Welfare State* (Harmondsworth, 1963), pp. 13, 34, 100–2, discusses attacks by 'Teddy Boys' on Cypriots during the 1950s.

70. James Whitfield, *Unhappy Dialogue: The Metropolitan Police and Black Londoners in Post-War Britain* (Cullompton, 2004).

71. NA/MEPO2/9047, J. Waring, 'The Coloured Population of London', 21 January 1952.

72. Edward Pilkington, *Beyond the Mother Country: West Indians and the Notting Hill White Riots* (London, 1988), pp. 53–124; Robert Miles, 'The Riots of 1958: The Ideological Construction of Race Relations as a Political Force in Britain', *Immigrants and Minorities*, vol. 3 (1984), pp. 352–75; Michael Rowe, *The Racialization of Disorder in Twentieth-Century Britain* (Aldershot, 1998), pp. 105–34.

73. Jacqueline Jenkinson, *Black 1919: Riots, Racism and Resistance in Imperial Britain*, (Liverpool, 2009), pp. 77–8.

74. Harold A. Moody, *The Colour Bar* (London, 1945), tackles this issue in London, Britain and globally.

75. Learie Constantine, *Colour Bar* (London, 1954), p. 67.

76. Wallace Collins, *Jamaican Migrant* (London, 1965), p. 57.

77. Ruth Glass, *Newcomers: The West Indians in London* (London, 1960), p. 129.

78. Colin Holmes, *John Bull's Island: Immigration and British Society, 1871–1971* (Basingstoke, 1988), p. 256.

79. Mark Holden, *Murder in Notting Hill* (Winchester, 2011).

80. Tony Kushner, 'The Fascist as "Other"? Racism and Neo-Nazism in Contemporary Britain', *Patterns of Prejudice*, vol. 28 (1994), p. 37.

81. Keith Tompson, *Under Siege: Racial Violence in Britain Today* (London, 1988), p. 171.

82. Commission for Racial Equality, *Living in Terror: A Report on Racial Harassment in Housing* (London, 1987), p. 9.

83. Two excellent contemporary accounts of race relations in the 1960s are: Dilip Hiro, *Black British, White British* (London, 1971); and Sheila Patterson, *Immigration and Race Relations in Britain, 1960–1967* (London, 1969).

84. Lord Scarman, *The Scarman Report: The Brixton Disorders, 10–12 April 1981* (Harmondsworth, 1982).

85. Rowe, *Racialization of Disorder*, pp. 135–61.

86. Quoted in Paul Gordon, *White Law: Racism in the Police, Courts and Prisons* (London, 1983), pp. 71–2.

87. Brian Cathcart, *The Case of Stephen Lawrence* (London, 1999); Sir William MacPherson, *The Stephen Lawrence Inquiry* (London, 1999).

88. Daniel Briggs, *The English Riots of 2011: A Summer of Discontent* (Hook, 2012).

89. Geoffrey Pearson, ' "Paki-Bashing" in a North East Lancashire Cotton Town: A Case Study and its History', in Geoff Mungham and Geoffrey Pearson, eds, *Working-Class Youth Culture* (London, 1976), pp. 48–81.

90. See especially Bethnal Green and Stepney Trades Council, *Blood on the Streets* (London, 1978).

91. Christopher T. Husbands, 'East End Racism, 1900–1980: Geographical Continuities in Vigilantist and Extreme Right-wing Political Behaviour', *London Journal*, vol. 8 (1982), pp. 3–26.

92. Kenneth Leech, *Brick Lane 1978: The Events and their Significance* (London, 1994), p. 7.

93. Colin Smith, 'Skinhead Terror in Bethnal Green', *Observer*, 5 April 1970.
94. Louise London, 'The East End of London: Paki-Bashing in 1970', *Race Today*, vol. 5 (1973), p. 337.
95. NA/FCO37/1878, Attacks on Bangladeshis in East London, 1976–7.
96. Ethnic Communities Oral History Project, *Asian Voices: Life Stories from the Indian Sub-Continent* (London, 1993), p. 12.
97. Bethnal Green and Stepney Trades Council, *Blood on the Streets*.
98. See especially: Leech, *Brick Lane 1978*; Mohamad Ali Ashgar, 'Bangladeshi Community Organisations in East London: A Case Study Analysis' (unpublished University of Birmingham PhD thesis, 1994); Kershen, *Strangers, Aliens and Asians*, pp. 209–17.
99. Georgie Wemyss, *The Invisible Empire: White Discourse, Tolerance and Belonging* (Abingdon, 2016), p. 72.
100. Michael A. E. Dummett, *Southall, 23 April 1979: The Report of the Unofficial Committee of Enquiry* (London, 1980); David Ransom, *The Blair Peach Case: Licence to Kill* (London, 1980).
101. As reported by Vikram Dodd, '90% of Whites Have Few or No Black Friends', *Guardian*, 19 July 2004.
102. Ibid. added together the 54 per cent who stated: 'All my close friends are white' with the 23 per cent, 'Almost all my close friends are white', and 17 per cent, 'Most of my close friends are white.' For the original survey see: YOUGOV, 'Survey for Commission for Racial Equality', https://d25d2506sfb94s.cloudfront.net/today_uk_import/YG-Archives-lif-commracial-RacialEquality-040728.pdf, accessed 11 July 2018.
103. Panayi, *An Immigration History*, pp. 136–99.
104. David Conradson and Alan Latham, 'Friendship, Networks and Transnationality in a World City: Antipodean Transmigrants in London', *Journal of Ethnic and Migration Studies*, vol. 31 (2005), pp. 287–305.
105. Sponza, *Italian Immigrants*, p. 59.
106. Panayi, *German Immigrants*, pp. 109–10.
107. Ibid., pp. 145–99.
108. Ng Kwee Choo, *The Chinese in London* (London, 1968), pp. 11–12.
109. Hermann Scheffauer, 'The Chinese in England: A Growing National Problem', *London Magazine*, vol. 26 (June and July 1911), p. 646.
110. John Seed, 'Limehouse Blues: Looking for Chinatown in the London Docks, 1900–40', *History Workshop Journal*, Issue 62 (2006), p. 67.
111. Scheffauer, 'Chinese in England', p. 646.
112. George Wade, 'The Cockney John Chinaman', *English Illustrated Magazine*, vol. 23 (1900), pp. 302–4.
113. Jenkinson, *Black 1919*, p. 90; Sascha Auerbach, *Race, Law and 'The Chinese Puzzle' in Imperial Britain* (Basingstoke, 2012), pp. 152–68.
114. Choo, *Chinese in London*, p. 12.
115. Todd M. Endelman, *Radical Assimilation in English Jewish History, 1656–1945* (Bloomington and Indianapolis, IN, 1990).
116. Endelman, *Jews of Georgian England*, pp. 267–9.
117. Panayi, *Immigration History*, p. 102.
118. Harry Blacker, *Just Like It Was: Memoirs of the Mittel East* (London, 1974), p. 53.
119. Dee, *'Estranged' Generation?*, pp. 46–7.
120. Ibid., passim; Susan L. Tananbaum, *Jewish Immigrants in London, 1880–1939* (London, 2014).
121. Tananbaum, *Jewish Immigrants in London*, p. 27.
122. Dee, *'Estranged' Generation?*, p. 49.
123. Autobiographies which confirm this situation include: Blacker, *Just Like it Was*; Harold Rosen, *Are You Still Circumcised? East End Memories* (Nottingham, 1999); and Ralph L. Finn, *No Tears in Aldgate* (Bath, 1963).
124. Panayi, *Immigration History*, p. 102.

125. Marion Berghahn, *Continental Britons: German-Jewish Refugees from Nazi Germany* (Oxford, 1988).

126. Vera K. Fast, *Children's Exodus: A History of the Kindertransport* (London, 2011).

127. Peter Fryer, *Staying Power: The History of Black People in Britain* (London, 1984), pp. 235–6; James Walvin, *Black and White: The Negro and English Society, 1555–1945* (London, 1973), pp. 189–201. Norma Myers, *Reconstructing the Black Past: Blacks in Britain, 1780–1830* (London, 1996), suggests that, rather than disappearing, this community may simply have slipped out of the public gaze following the abolition of slavery.

128. Michael Banton, *The Coloured Quarter: Negro Immigrants in an English City* (London, 1955), pp. 155–6.

129. THLHA/P/RAM/3/2/7, '[Confidential] Report on Investigation into Conditions of the Coloured Population in a Stepney Area', c.1944.

130. THLHA/P/RAM/3/1/15, 'Papers re Kathleen and Sulaiman Wrsma who ran a lodging house at 5 North East Passage, mainly for Somalis 1944–1951'.

131. A. T. Carey, *Colonial Students: A Study of the Social Adaptation of Colonial Students in London* (London, 1956), pp. 121–5.

132. Majbritt Morrison, *Jungle West 11* (London, 1964); Pilkington, *Beyond the Mother Country*, pp. 5–6.

133. Katrin Fitzherbert, *West Indian Children in London* (London, 1967), pp. 33, 38. See also: Albert Hyndman, 'The West Indian in London', in S. K. Ruck, ed., *The West Indian Comes to England: A Report Prepared for the Trustees of the London Parochial Charities by the Family Welfare Association* (London, 1960), pp. 119–51; Marcus Collins, 'Pride and Prejudice: West Indian Men in Mid-Twentieth Century Britain', *Journal of British Studies*, vol. 40 (2001), pp. 402–10; and Clive Webb, 'Special Relationships: Mixed Race Couples in Post-War Britain and the United States', *Women's History Review*, vol. 26 (2017), pp. 110-29.

134. Collins, *Jamaican Migrant*, p. 64.

135. Ibid., pp. 85–91.

136. Ibid., pp. 99–102, 122.

137. Sheila Patterson, *Dark Strangers: A Study of the Absorption of a Recent West Indian Migrant Group in Brixton, South London* (London, 1963), pp. 239–44.

138. Ibid., pp. 244–50; Pilkington, *Beyond the Mother Country*, pp. 41–52; Clair Wills, *Lovers and Strangers: An Immigrant History of Post-War Britain* (London, 2017), pp. 211–19.

139. Panayi, *Immigration History*, pp. 269–70.

140. C. T. Kannan, *Inter-Racial Marriages in London: A Comparative Study* (London, 1972); Susan Benson, *Ambiguous Ethnicity: Interracial Families in London* (Cambridge, 1981); Yasmin Alibhai-Brown, *The Colour of Love: Mixed Race Relationships* (London, 1992).

141. Suzanne Model and Gene Fisher, 'Unions Between Blacks and Whites: England Compared with the USA', *Ethnic and Racial Studies*, vol. 25 (2002), pp. 728–54.

142. France Winddance Twine, *A White Side of Black Britain: Interracial Intimacy and Racial Literacy* (London, 2010), p. 14.

143. Office for National Statistics, 'Ethnicity and National Identity in England and Wales: 2011', https://www.ons.gov.uk/peoplepopulationandcommunity/culturalidentity/ethnicity/articles/ethnicityandnationalidentityinenglandandwales/2012-12-11, accessed 16 July 2018.

144. Panayi, *Immigration History*, pp. 104–5.

145. Rashmi Desai, *Indian Immigrants in Britain* (London, 1963), p. 122.

146. Rachana Sinha, *The Cultural Adjustment of Asian Lone Mothers Living in London* (Aldershot, 1998).

147. Hamza Alavi, *The Pakistanis in London* (London, 1963), p. 5.

148. THLHA/P/RAM/3/1/2, Papers re Molly Ullah (d 1946) and Mahomar Ali and their family of 24 Fenton Street, 1946–1947.

149. Desai, *Indian Immigrants in Britain*, p. 129.

150. See the example of Nicola and Mabroor Bhatty, in Alibhai-Brown, *Colour of Love*, pp. 191–8.

151. Anne Holohan, *Working Lives: The Irish in Britain* (Hayes, 1995), pp. 93–8.

152. Kannan, *Inter-racial Marriages in London*, pp. 79–105.

153. Bronwen Walter, 'Contemporary Irish Settlement in London: Women's Worlds, Men's Worlds', in Jim MacLaughlin, ed., *Location and Dislocation in Contemporary Irish Society: Emigration and Identities* (Cork, 1997), pp. 63–6.

154. Sorohan, *Irish London*, p. 102.

155. Breda Gray, 'From "Ethnicity" to "Diaspora": 1980s Emigration and "Multicultural" London', in Andy Bielenberg, ed., *The Irish Diaspora* (Harlow, 2000), pp. 78–9.

156. Sorohan, *Irish London*, p. 102.

157. For the importance of Roman Catholicism see Chapter 8. For more recent increasingly secular expressions of Irishness in London see, for example: Gerard Leavey, Sati Sembhi and Gill Livingston, 'Older Irish Migrants Living in London: Identity, Loss and Return', *Journal of Ethnic and Migration Studies*, vol. 30 (2004), pp. 763–79; and Mary Kells, *Ethnic Identity Amongst Young Irish Middle-Class Migrants in London* (London, 1995).

158. See Kannan, *Inter-Racial Marriages in London*.

159. F. M. Bhatti, *Turkish Cypriots in London* (Birmingham, 1981), pp. 6–8; Floya Anthias, *Ethnicity, Class, Gender and Migration: Greek Cypriots in Britain* (Aldershot, 1992), pp. 118–27; Vic George, 'The Assimilation of Cypriot Immigrants in London', *Eugenics Review*, vol. 58 (1966), pp. 191–2; Alkan Fuat, *Cypriots in Haringey* (London, 1980), p. 13.

160. KCL/GDA/7/AV1, BBC TV Documentary film entitled *Minorities in Britain: The Cypriot Community*, 1966.

161. Smith and Varnava, 'Creating a "Suspect Community" ', pp. 1151–2.

162. The most important source for the case of the Christofis is NA/PCOM91721, CHRISTOFI, Styllou Pantopiou: convicted at Central Criminal Court (CCC) on 28 October 1954 of murder; sentenced to death, executed 15 December 1954. But see also, for example: LMA/CLA/003/PR/04/003, Correspondence and Papers Relating to Styllou Christofi; Jean Christou, ' "Middle Aged, Unattractive and Foreign": The Cypriot Murderess', *Cyprus Mail*, 31 January 2016; Phillip Jones, *Quickly to Her Fate* (Barton-on-Sea, 2010); Patrick Wilson, *Murderess: A Study of the Women Executed in Britain since 1843* (London, 1971), pp. 303–7; Annette Ballinger, *Dead Women Walking: Executed Women in England and Wales, 1900–1955* (Aldershot, 2000), pp. 158–65; Mark Aston, *Foul Deeds and Suspicious Deaths in Hampstead, Holborn and St Pancras* (London, 2005), pp. 160–4. For the case of Ioannos and Ann Sotirious see *Hampstead and Highgate Express*, 24 August 1954. For honour killings in early twenty-first-century London see Veena Meetoo and Heidi Safia Mirza, ' "There is Nothing 'Honourable' about Honour Killings": Gender, Violence and the Limits of Multiculturalism', *Women's Studies International Forum*, vol. 30 (2007), pp. 187–200.

163. See, for example: Roger Hewitt, *White Talk Black Talk: Inter-Racial Friendship and Communication amongst Adolescents* (Cambridge, 1986); Jenny Cheshire, Paul Kerswill, Sue Fox and Eivind Torgersen, 'Contact, the Feature Pool and the Speech Community: The Emergence of Multicultural London English', *Journal of Sociolinguistics*, vol. 15 (2011), pp. 151–96.

CHAPTER 7

1. JML, Oral History Collection Transcript 99, Interview of Albert Booth by Mark Burman, 5 October 1987, describing his experiences of attending the British Union of Fascist Meeting at Olympia on 7 June 1934.

2. J. Watson, *Young Germany* (London, 1844), p. 9.

3. Opening statement from Dadabhai Naoroji's maiden speech in the House of Commons on 9 August 1892, after his election as MP for Finsbury Central, quoted in Dadabhai Naoroji, *Speeches and Writings of Dadabhai Naoroji* (Madras, 1918), p. 121.

4. *Marx and Engels Collected Works*, vol. 12 (London, 2010), p. 488. For more information on the range of German socialist beliefs in Victorian London see Christine Lattek, *Revolutionary Refugees: German Socialism in Britain, 1840–1860* (London, 2006).

5. See Chapter 6.

6. Donald M. MacRaild, *Faith, Fraternity and Fighting: The Orange Order and Irish Migrants in Northern England, c. 1850–1920* (Liverpool, 2005); Frank Neal, *Sectarian Violence: The Liverpool Experience, 1819–1914* (Manchester, 1988); Tom Gallagher, *The Uneasy Peace: Religious Tension in Modern Glasgow, 1819–1940* (Manchester, 1987).

7. Christopher T. Husbands, 'East End Racism, 1900–1980: Geographical Continuities in Vigilantist and Extreme Right-wing Political Behaviour', *London Journal*, vol. 8 (1982), pp. 7–12; Bernard Gainer, *The Alien Invasion: The Origins of the Aliens Act of 1905* (London, 1972), pp. 60–4, 67–73; Colin Holmes, *Anti-Semitism in British Society, 1876–1939* (London, 1979), pp. 89–97; Nick Toczek, *Haters, Baiters and Would-Be Dictators: Anti-Semitism and the UK Far-Right* (Abingdon, 2016), pp. 74–82.

8. Julia Bush, *Behind the Lines: East London 1914–1919* (London, 1984), p. 184.

9. Panikos Panayi, *The Enemy in Our Midst: Germans in Britain during the First World War* (Oxford, 1991), pp. 217–20.

10. Ibid., p. 209.

11. Panikos Panayi, 'The British Empire Union in World War I', in Tony Kushner and Kenneth Lunn, eds, *The Politics of Marginality: Race, the Radical Right and Minorities in Twentieth-Century Britain* (London, 1990), pp. 113–28.

12. Panayi, *Enemy*, pp. 209–15; W. D. Rubinstein, 'Henry Page Croft and the National Party, 1917–22', *Journal of Contemporary History*, vol. 9 (1974), pp. 129–48; G. R. Searle, *Corruption in British Politics, 1895–1930* (Oxford, 1987), pp. 255–68.

13. Mike Cronin, ed., *The Failure of British Fascism: The Far Right and the Fight for Political Recognition* (Basingstoke, 1996); Richard Thurlow, 'The Failure of British Fascism', in Andrew Thorpe, ed., *The Failure of Political Extremism in Inter-War Britain* (Exeter, 1989), pp. 67–84.

14. Holmes, *Antisemitism*, pp. 141–74; Gisela C. Lebzelter, *Political Antisemitism in England, 1918–1939* (New York, 1978), pp. 49–85; Richard Thurlow, *Fascism in Britain* (Oxford, 1987), pp. 62–91.

15. Lebzelter, *Political Antisemitism in England*, pp. 91–2.

16. Daniel Tilles, *British Fascist Antisemitism and Jewish Responses, 1932–40* (London, 2015), p. 57–74.

17. Holmes, *Antisemitism*, p. 180.

18. Lebzelter, *Political Antisemitism in England*, p. 92.

19. Thurlow, *Fascism in Britain*, pp. 122–5.

20. Martin Pugh, *Hurrah for the Blackshirts! Fascists and Fascism in Britain Between the Wars* (London, 2006), pp. 149–50.

21. Thurlow, *Fascism in Britain*, pp. 135–40.

22. See the table constructed by Michael Rowe, *The Racialisation of Disorder in Twentieth-Century Britain* (Aldershot, 1998), pp. 78–9.

23. Thurlow, *Fascism in Britain*, p. 99.

24. Ibid., pp. 101–3; Lebzelter, *Political Antisemitism in England*, pp. 105–6.

25. W. F. Mandle, *Anti-Semitism and the British Union of Fascists* (London, 1968), p. 13.

26. D. S. Lewis, *Illusions of Grandeur: Mosley, Fascism and British Society, 1931–81* (Manchester, 1987), p. 105.

27. Thomas P. Linehan, *East London for Mosley: The British Union of Fascists in East London and South-West Essex, 1933–40* (London, 1996), p. 198.

28. Ibid., pp. 89–94, 208–21.

29. Husbands, 'East End Racism', p. 13.

30. Lewis, *Illusions of Grandeur*, p. 106.

31. William J. Fishman, 'A People's Journée: The Battle of Cable Street (October 4th 1936)', in Frederick Krantz, ed., *History from Below: Studies in Popular Protest and Popular Ideology in Honour of George Rudé* (Montreal, 1985), p. 383.

32. Lewis, *Illusions of Grandeur*, pp. 106–7.
33. David Dee, *The 'Estranged' Generation? Social and Generational Change in Interwar British Jewry* (London, 2017), pp. 205–72; Henry Felix Srebrnik, *London Jews and British Communism, 1935–1945* (Ilford, 1995); Elaine Smith, 'Jews and Politics in the East End of London, 1918–1939', in David Cesarani, ed., *The Making of Modern Anglo-Jewry* (Oxford, 1990), pp. 141–62.
34. Lewis, *Illusions of Grandeur*, pp. 114–43; Fishman, 'A People's Journée'; Rowe, *Racialisation of Disorder*, pp. 84–9.
35. Tony Kushner and Nadia Valman, eds, *Remembering Cable Street: Fascism and Anti-Fascism in British Society* (London, 2000).
36. Robert Benewick, *Political Violence and Public Order* (London, 1969); Richard Thurlow, 'The Authorities and the Anti-Jewish Disturbances in the 1930s', in Panikos Panayi, ed., *Racial Violence in Britain in the Nineteenth and Twentieth Centuries* (London, 1996), pp. 112–30.
37. Tony Kushner, *The Persistence of Prejudice: Antisemitism in Britain during the Second World War* (Manchester, 1989), pp. 14–47; Thurlow, *Fascism in Britain*, pp. 188–232.
38. Husbands, 'East End Racism', pp. 14–15; Thurlow, *Fascism in Britain*, pp. 243–6.
39. Edward Pilkington, *Beyond the Mother Country: West Indians and the Notting Hill White Riots* (London, 1988), p. 100.
40. Ruth Glass, *Newcomers: The West Indians in London* (London, 1960), pp. 179–90; Nigel Copsey, *Contemporary British Fascism: The British National Party and the Quest for Legitimacy* (Basingstoke, 2004), pp. 2–8.
41. Paul Foot, *Immigration and Race in British Politics* (Harmondsworth, 1965), pp. 195–215.
42. See, for example, Nicholas Hillman, 'A Chorus of "Execration"? Enoch Powell's "Rivers of Blood" Forty Years On', *Patterns of Prejudice*, vol. 42 (2008), pp. 83–104.
43. Husbands, 'East End Racism', pp. 14–15.
44. Copsey, *Contemporary British Fascism*.
45. Sheila Patterson, *Immigration and Race Relations in Britain, 1960–1967* (London, 1969), pp. 382–5.
46. Stan Taylor, *The National Front in English Politics* (London, 1982); Christopher T. Husbands, *Racial Exclusionism and the City: The Urban Support of the National Front* (London, 1983); Michael Billig, *Fascists: A Social Psychological Profile of the National Front* (London, 1978).
47. Copsey, *Contemporary British Fascism*; Matthew J. Goodwin, 'The Extreme Right in Britain: Still an "Ugly Duckling" but for How Long?', *Political Quarterly*, vol. 78 (2007), pp. 241–50.
48. *Guardian*, 3 May 2008.
49. BBC News, 'BNP Secures Two European Seats', http://news.bbc.co.uk/1/hi/uk_politics/8088381.stm, accessed 20 August 2018.
50. BBC News, 'European Election 2009: London', http://news.bbc.co.uk/1/shared/bsp/hi/elections/euro/09/html/ukregion_39.stm, accessed 20 August 2018.
51. The Electoral Commission, 'EU Referendum Results', https://www.electoralcommission.org.uk/find-information-by-subject/elections-and-referendums/past-elections-and-referendums/eu-referendum/electorate-and-count-information, accessed 20 August 2018.
52. Husbands, 'East End Racism', p. 15.
53. Kenneth Leech, *Brick Lane 1978: The Events and their Significance* (London, 1994), pp. 11–12.
54. THLHA/O/BEE/7, The Bengali East End, Interview with Osmar Gani, October 2011.
55. Leech, *Brick Lane 1978*; Sarah Glynn, *Class, Ethnicity and Religion in the Bengali East End: A Political History* (Manchester, 2015), pp. 32–174; Stephen Ashe, Satnam Virdee and Laurence Brown, 'Striking Back against Racist Violence in the East End of London, 1968–1970', *Race and Class*, vol. 58 (2016), pp. 34–54.
56. Mohamad Ali Ashgar, 'Bangladeshi Community Organisations in East London: A Case Study Analysis' (unpublished University of Birmingham PhD thesis, 1994); THLHA/I/AVU/A/11/4, Publications of the Bangladeshi Youth Front.

57. The Electoral Commission, 'EU Referendum Results', https://www.electoralcommission.org. uk/find-information-by-subject/elections-and-referendums/past-elections-and-referendums/ eu-referendum/electorate-and-count-information, accessed 21 August 2018.

58. See Chapter 8.

59. See the relevant contributions to Debra Kelly and Martyn Cormack, eds, *A History of the French in London: Liberty, Equality, Opportunity* (London, 2013).

60. Nicholas Atkin, *The Forgotten French: Exiles in the British Isles* (Manchester, 2003).

61. See contributions to Martin Conway and José Gotovich, eds, *Europe in Exile: European Exile Communities in Britain, 1940–45* (Oxford, 2001).

62. See Wojciech Rojek, 'The Government of the Republic of Poland in Exile, 1945–92', in Peter D. Stachura, ed., *The Poles in Britain, 1940–2000: From Betrayal to Assimilation* (London, 2004), pp. 33–47.

63. Peter Brock, 'The Polish Revolutionary Commune in London', *Slavonic and East European Review*, vol. 35 (1956), pp. 116–28.

64. Norman Davies, 'The Poles in Great Britain, 1914–1919', *Slavonic and East European Review*, vol. 50 (1972), pp. 63–89.

65. Margaret C. W. Wicks, *The Italian Exiles in London, 1816–48* (New York, 1968 reprint); Carlo Maria Franzero, *A Life in Exile: Ugo Foscolo in London* (London, 1977).

66. Marcella Pellegrino Sutcliffe, 'Garibaldi in London', *History Today*, vol. 64 (April 2014), pp. 42–9.

67. Dénes A Jánosy, *Great Britain and Kossuth* (Budapest, 1937); Zsuzsanna Lada, 'The Invention of a Hero: Lajos Kossuth in England (1851)', *European History Quarterly*, vol. 43 (2013), pp. 5–26.

68. Bernard Porter, *The Refugee Question in Mid-Victorian Politics* (Cambridge, 1979), p. 16.

69. Sabine Freitag, ed., *Exiles from European Revolutions: Refugees in Mid-Victorian England* (Oxford, 2003).

70. Porter, *Refugee Question*, p. 3.

71. Ibid., pp. 126–99.

72. Panikos Panayi, *German Immigrants in Britain during the Nineteenth Century, 1815–1914* (Oxford, 1995), pp. 193–4.

73. Rosemary Ashton, *Little Germany: Exile and Asylum in Victorian England* (Oxford, 1986), pp. 139–87.

74. Asa Briggs and John Callow, *Marx in London* (London, 2007); Gareth Stedman Jones, *Karl Marx: Greatness and Illusion* (London, 2016), pp. 314–588; Communist Party of Great Britain, *London Landmarks: A Guide with Maps to Places where Marx, Engels and Lenin Lived and Worked* (London, 1963), pp. 2–4.

75. Panikos Panayi, 'Eccarius, John George', *Oxford Dictionary of National Biography*, https:// doi.org/10.1093/odnb/9780198614128.013.101085, accessed 12 October 2018.

76. Panayi, *German Immigrants*, pp. 196–7.

77. Eduard Bernstein, *My Years in Exile: Reminiscences of a Socialist* (London, 1921); James W. Hulse, *Revolutionists in London: A Study of Five Unorthodox Socialists* (Oxford, 1970), pp. 138–65.

78. Rudolf Emil Martin, *Anarchismus und seine Träger* (Berlin, 1887); John Quail, *The Slow Burning Fuse: The Lost History of British Anarchists* (London, 1978); Colin Rogers, *The Battle of Stepney: The Sidney Street Siege* (London, 1981).

79. William J. Fishman, *East End Jewish Radicals, 1875–1914* (London, 1975); Rudolf Rocker, *The London Years* (originally 1956; Nottingham, 2005); Margaret Vallance, 'Rudolf Rocker: A Biographical Sketch', *Journal of Contemporary History*, vol. 8 (1973), pp. 75–96.

80. Anthony Glees, *Exile Politics during the Second World War: The German Social Democrats in Britain* (Oxford, 1982).

81. James J. and Patience P. Barnes, *Nazis in Pre-War London, 1930–1939: The Fate and Role of German Party Members and British Sympathisers* (Brighton, 2005).

82. Claudia Baldoli, 'The Remaking of the Italian Community in London: L'Italia Nostra and the Creation of a Little Fascist Italy during the 1930s', *London Journal*, vol. 26 (2001), pp. 23–34.

83. John Slatter, ed., *From the Other Shore: Russian Political Emigrants in Britain, 1880–1917* (London, 1984); Hulse, *Revolutionists*, pp. 54–73, 166–91.

84. Barry Hollingsworth, 'The Society of Friends of Russian Freedom: English Liberals and Russian Socialists', *Oxford Slavonic Papers*, vol. 3 (1970); Anat Vernitski, 'Russian Revolutionaries and English Sympathizers in 1890s London: The Case of Olive Garnett and Sergei Stepniak', *Journal of European Studies*, vol. 35 (2005), pp. 299–314.

85. L. Muravyova, and I. Sivolap-Kaftanova, *Lenin in London: Memorial Places* (Moscow, 1983); Helen Rappaport, *Conspirator: Lenin in Exile* (London, 2009).

86. Ashton, *Little Germany*.

87. Geoffrey Alderman, 'The Political Impact of Zionism in the East End of London Before 1940', *London Journal*, vol. 9 (1983), pp. 35–8; Elaine Smith, 'East End Jews in Politics, 1918–1939: A Study in Class and Ethnicity' (unpublished Leicester University PhD thesis, 1990), pp. 165–9; Dee, *'Estranged' Generation?*, pp. 244–51.

88. Hans Werner Debrunner, *Presence and Prestige: Africans in Europe: A History of Africans in Europe Before 1918* (Basel, 1979), pp. 369–72.

89. Owen Charles Mathurin, *Henry Sylvester Williams and the Origins of the Pan-African Movement, 1869–1911* (London, 1976); Marika Sherwood, *Origins of Pan-Africanism: Henry Sylvester Williams, Africa, and the African Diaspora* (London, 2012); Hakim Adi, *Pan-Africanism: A History* (London, 2018).

90. Ron Ramdin, *The Making of the Black Working Class in Britain* (Aldershot, 1987), pp. 49–50.

91. Ibid., pp. 52–5; Immanuel Geiss, *The Pan-African Movement* (London, 1974), pp. 177–92; Peter Fryer, *Staying Power: The History of Black People in Britain* (London, 1984), pp. 281–7.

92. Susan D. Pennybacker, 'The Universal Races Congress, London Political Culture, and Imperial Dissent, 1900–1939', *Radical History Review*, Issue 92 (2005), pp. 103–17.

93. Geiss, *Pan-African Movement*, pp. 240–9.

94. Ibid., pp. 297–303; Hakim Adi, *West Africans in Britain, 1900–1960: Nationalism, Pan-Africanism and Communism* (London, 1998).

95. Ibid., pp. 100–29; Roderick J. MacDonald, 'Dr Harold Arundel Moody and the League of Coloured Peoples, 1931–1947: A Retrospective View', *Race*, vol. 14 (1973), pp. 291–310; Daniel Whittall, 'Creating Black Places in Imperial London: The League of Coloured Peoples and Aggrey House, 1931–1943', *London Journal*, vol. 36 (2011), pp. 225–46; Edward Scobie, *Black Britannia: A History of Blacks in Britain* (Chicago, IL, 1972), pp. 141–52.

96. Julius Braunthal, *History of the International, 1864–1914* (London, 1966).

97. See especially Marc Matera, *Black London: The Imperial Metropolis and Decolonization in the Twentieth Century* (Oakland, CA, 2015), pp. 145–99. Black music in interwar London receives more attention in Chapter 11.

98. Paul Gilroy, *The Black Atlantic: Modernity and Double Consciousness* (London, 1993).

99. Minkah Makalani, *In the Cause of Freedom: Radical Black Internationalism from Harlem to London, 1917–1939* (Chapel Hill, NC, 2011).

100. Susan D. Pennybacker, *From Scottsboro to Munich: Race and Political Culture in 1930s Britain* (Princeton, NJ, 2009), pp. 66–101.

101. Hakim Adi, 'African Political Thinkers, Pan-Africanism and the Politics of Exile c.1850–1970', in Stefan Manz and Panikos Panayi, eds, *Refugees and Cultural Transfers to Britain* (Abingdon, 2013), pp. 149–50.

102. Marika Sherwood, et al., *Claudia Jones: A Life in Exile* (London, 1999); Buzz Johnson, *'I Think of My Mother': Notes on the Life and Times of Claudia Jones* (London, 1985); Carole Boyce Davies, *Left of Karl Marx: The Political Life of Black Communist Claudia Jones* (London, 2007); Jan Carew, 'Paul Robeson and W. E. Dubois in London', *Race and Class*, vol. 46 (2004), pp. 39–48; Ishmahil Blagrove, *Carnival: A Photographic and Testimonial History of the Notting Hill Carnival* (London, 2014).

103. Anne-Marie Angelo, 'The Black Panthers in London, 1967–1972: The Diasporic Struggle Navigates the Black Atlantic', *Radical History Review*, vol. 103 (2009), pp. 17–35; R. E. R. Bunce and Paul Field, 'Obi B. Egbuna, C. L. R. James and the Birth of Black Power in

Britain: Black Radicalism in Britain', *Twentieth Century British History*, vol. 22 (2011), pp. 391–414.

104. John L. Williams, *Michael X: A Life in Black and White* (London, 2008); Michael Abdul Malik, *Michael de Freitas to Michael X* (London, 1968).

105. Robin Bunce and Paul Field, *Darcus Howe: A Political Biography* (London, 2014).

106. Obi Egbuna, *Destroy this Temple* (London, 1971).

107. Rosina Visram, *Asians in Britain: 400 Years of History* (London, 2002), pp. 124, 149–68.

108. Ibid., pp. 321–40; Michael H. Fisher, Shompa Lahiri and Shinder Thandi, *A South Asian History of Britain* (Oxford, 2007), pp. 136–42.

109. James D. Hunt, *Gandhi in London* (New Delhi, 1993).

110. Humayun Ansari, *'The Infidel Within': Muslims in Britain Since 1800* (London, 2004), pp. 84–92.

111. Muhammad Yusuf Abbasi, *London Muslim League (1908–1928): An Historical Study* (Islamabad, 1988).

112. Melanie Philips, *Londonistan* (New York, 2006), p. xi.

113. Sean O'Neill and Daniel McGrory, *The Suicide Factory: Abu Hamza and the Finsbury Park Mosque* (London, 2006).

114. Ed Husain, *The Islamist* (London, 2007), p. 2.

115. Milan Rai, *7/7: The London Bombings, Islam and the Iraq War* (London, 2006); *Report of the Official Account of the Bombings in London on 7th July 2005* (London, 2006).

116. For interpretations of the causes of the 7 July attacks, and the growth of Islamic fundamentalism in Britain and beyond, see: Rai, *7/7*; and Robert S. Leiken, *Europe's Angry Muslims: The Revolt of the Second Generation* (Oxford, 2015), pp. 117–216.

117. *Guardian*, 22 March 2017, 3 June 2017, 15 August 2018.

118. Robert Verkaik, *Jihadi John: The Making of a Terrorist* (London, 2016).

119. Shamima Begum's story receives detailed coverage in *The Times* during February and March 2019.

120. Rai, *7/7*; Leiken, *Europe's Angry Muslims*; *Report of the Official Account of the Bombings in London*.

121. Donald MacRaild, *Irish Migrants in Modern Britain, 1750–1922* (Basingstoke, 1999), pp. 138–42; John Newsinger, *Fenians in Mid-Victorian Britain* (London, 1994); Patrick Quinlivan and Paul Rose, *The Fenians in England, 1865–1872* (London, 1982).

122. Enda Delaney, *The Irish in Post-War Britain* (Oxford, 2007), pp. 118–19.

123. Tim Pat Coogan, *The IRA* (New York, 2002), pp. 385–91, 513–21, 585–8; Gary McGladdery, *The Provisional IRA in England: The Bombing Campaign, 1973–1997* (Dublin, 2006).

124. Steven P. Moysey, *The Road to Balcombe Street: The IRA Reign of Terror in London* (Binghamton, NY, 2008).

125. Mo Moulton, *Ireland and the Irish in Interwar England* (Cambridge, 2014), pp. 102–34; Seán Sorohan, *Irish London during the Troubles* (Dublin, 2012), pp. 60–100.

126. Graham Davis, *The Irish in Britain* (Dublin, 1991), pp. 159–90; Lynn Hollen Lees, *Exiles of Erin: Irish Immigrants in Victorian London* (Manchester, 1979), pp. 210–31.

127. Alan O'Day, 'The Political Organization of the Irish in Britain, 1867–90', in Roger Swift and Sheridan Gilley, eds, *The Irish in Britain, 1815–1939* (London, 1989), pp. 183–211.

128. Lees, *Exiles of Erin*, p. 242; Steven Fielding, *Class and Ethnicity: Irish Catholics in England, 1880–1939* (Buckingham, 1993), pp. 88–92, 118–26; John Hutchison, 'Diaspora Dilemmas and Shifting Allegiances: The Irish in London between Nationalism, Catholicism and Labourism (1900–22)', *Studies in Ethnicity and Nationalism*, vol. 10 (2010), pp. 107–25.

129. Sorohan, *Irish London*, pp. 56–7.

130. See the list in BI/ROTH/5/4, List of Jews in the 1987–1992 Parliament.

131. Rudolf Muhs, 'Jews of German Background in British Politics', in Werner E. Mosse, et al., eds, *Second Chance: Two Centuries of German-Speaking Jews in the United Kingdom* (Tübingen, 1991), p. 177; Panikos Panayi, *An Immigration History of Britain: Multicultural Racism Since 1800* (London, 2010), pp. 266–7.

132. Geoffrey Alderman, *The Jewish Community in British Politics* (Oxford, 1983), p. 174.

133. Geoffrey Alderman, *London Jewry and London Politics, 1889–1986* (London, 1989), p. 30.

134. Kenneth Lunn, 'Parliamentary Politics and the "Jewish Vote" in Whitechapel, 1906–1914', in Aubrey Newman, ed., *The Jewish East End, 1840–1939* (London, 1981), pp. 255–66.

135. Smith, 'East End Jews in Politics', pp. 48–101.

136. Alderman, *London Jewry*, p. 109.

137. Panayi, *Immigration History*, pp. 267–8.

138. Alderman, *London Jewry*, p. 181.

139. Omar Ralph, *Naoroji: The First Asian MP* (St John's, Antigua, 1997); R. P. Masani, *Dadabhai Naoroji: The Grand Old Man of India* (London, 1939).

140. John R. Hinnels and Omar Ralph, *Sir Mancherjee Merwanjee Bhownaggree K.C.I.E., Order of the Lion and the Sun of Persia: 1851–1933* (London, 1995).

141. Marc Wadsworth, *Comrade Sak: Shapurji Saklatvala MP* (Leeds, 1998); Mike Squires, *Saklatvala: A Political Biography* (London, 1990); Panchanan Saha, *Shapurji Saklatvala: A Short Biography* (Delhi, 1970); Barry Kosmin, 'Political Identity in Battersea', in Sandra Williamson, et al., *Living in South London: Perspectives on Battersea, 1871–1971* (Aldershot, 1982), pp. 17–50; Barry Kosmin, 'J. R. Archer (1863–1932): A Pan-Africanist in the Battersea Labour Movement', *New Community*, vol. 7 (1978–9), pp. 430–6; Sean Creighton, 'John Archer and the Politics of Labour in Battersea (1906–32)', *Immigrants and Minorities*, vol. 28 (2010), pp. 183–202.

142. The fourth, Keith Vaz, stood for Leicester East.

143. Zig Layton-Henry, 'The Electoral Participation of Black and Asian Britons: Integration or Alienation', *Parliamentary Affairs*, vol. 38 (1985), pp. 307–18; Martin Fitzgerald, *Political Parties and Black People: Participation, Representation and Exploitation* (London, 1984), pp. 70–86.

144. 'London Election Results Map', *Evening Standard*, 9 June 2017.

145. 'List of ethnic minority politicians in the United Kingdom', https://en.wikipedia.org/wiki/List_of_ethnic_minority_politicians_in_the_United_Kingdom, accessed 11 September 2018.

146. Panayi, *Immigration History*, p. 273. London Strategic Policy Unit, *Black Councillors in Britain* (London, 1987), provides a full list of the hundreds of black and Asian councillors in London during the 1980s.

147. Glynn, *Class, Ethnicity and Religion*, pp. 147–74, 215–39.

148. Trevor Carter, *Shattering Illusions: West Indians in British Politics* (London, 1986); Kalbir Shukra, *The Changing Face of Black Politics in Britain* (London, 1998); Kennetta Hammond Perry, *London is the Place for Me: Black Britons, Citizenship, and the Politics of Race* (Oxford, 2015).

149. Eric A. Grant, *Dawn to Dusk: A Biography of Bernie Grant MP* (London, 2006).

150. *Guardian*, 7 December 2017.

151. London Assembly Members, https://www.london.gov.uk/people/assembly, accessed 17 June 2019.

152. Gainer, *Alien Invasion*.

153. Robert Miles, 'The Riots of 1958: The Ideological Construction of Race Relations as a Political Force in Britain', *Immigrants and Minorities*, vol. 3 (1984), pp. 252–75; Perry, *London is the Place for Me*, pp. 153–86.

CHAPTER 8

1. Joseph Salter, *The Asiatic in England: Sketches of Sixteen Years Work Among Orientals* (London, 1873), pp. i–ii.

2. Beatrice Potter, 'The Jewish Community', in Charles Booth, ed., *Life and Labour of the People in London*, First Series, vol. 3, *Poverty* (London, 1904), p. 169.

3. MLOHC/99.87, Interview by Irna Imran of Iftikhar Din, 30 March 1998.

4. While Chinese people constituted 24 per cent of the 152,000 Buddhists in the 2001 UK census, the largest ethnic group practising this religion consisted of 'white' converts at 38.79 per cent, for which see Robert Black, 'Buddhism', in Linda Woodhead and Rebecca Catto, eds, *Religion and Change in Modern Britain* (Abingdon, 2012), pp. 131–43.

5. Matthew Guest, Elizabeth Olson and John Wolfe, 'Christianity: Loss of Monopoly', in Woodhead and Catto, *Religion and Change in Modern Britain*, pp. 57–79.

6. Francis Dodsworth, Elena Vacchelli and Sophie Watson, 'Shifting Religions and Cultures in London's East End', *Material Religion*, vol. 9 (2013), pp. 86–113.

7. Paul Hyams, 'The Jewish Minority in Medieval England, 1066–1290', *Journal of Jewish Studies*, vol. 25 (1974), pp. 284–6; Joe Hillaby, 'London: The Thirteenth-Century Jewry', *Transactions of the Jewish Historical Society of England*, vol. 33 (1990–2), pp. 100–2.

8. Susan Brigden, *London and the Reformation* (London, 2014).

9. Wolfgang Palaver, Harriet Rudolph and Dietmar Regensburger, *The European Wars of Religion: An Interdisciplinary Reassessment of Sources, Interpretations, and Myths* (Abingdon, 2015).

10. Andrew Pettegree, *Foreign Protestant Communities in Sixteenth-Century London* (Oxford, 1986); Panikos Panayi, *German Immigrants in Britain during the Nineteenth Century* (Oxford, 1995), pp. 7–8; David Ormond, *The Dutch in London: The Influence of an Immigrant Community* (London, 1973), p. 7; Jacob Selwood, *Diversity and Difference in Early Modern London* (Farnham, 2010), pp. 30–2.

11. Robin D. Gwynn, *Huguenot Heritage: The History and Contribution of the Huguenots in Britain* (London, 1988), pp. 36–7; Anne J. Kershen, *Strangers, Aliens and Asians: Huguenots, Jews and Bangladeshis in Spitalfields, 1660–2000* (London, 2005), pp. 76–83; Elizabeth Randall, 'A Special Case? London's French Protestants', in Debra Kelly and Martyn Cornick, eds, *A History of the French in London: Liberty, Equality, Opportunity* (London, 2013), pp. 13–42.

12. Panikos Panayi, 'Germans in Eighteenth-Century Britain', in Panikos Panayi, ed., *Germans in Britain since 1500* (London, 1996), pp. 41–2; Heinrich Dorgeel, *Die Deutsche Colonie in London* (London, 1881), pp. 42–5.

13. Cecil Roth, *The Rise of Provincial Jewry: The Early History of the Jewish Communities in the English Countryside* (London, 1950).

14. Paul Lindsay, *The Synagogues of London* (London, 1993), pp. 38–41; Anne Kershen, 'The Jewish Community in London', in Nick Merriman, ed., *The Peopling of London: 15,000 Years of Settlement from Overseas* (London, 1993), p. 139.

15. Cecil Roth, *The Great Synagogue London, 1690–1940* (London, 1950).

16. W. D. Rubinstein, *A History of the Jews in the English-Speaking World: Great Britain* (Basingstoke, 1996), p. 62; Lindsay, *The Synagogues of London*, pp. 45–7.

17. Israel Finestein, *A Short History of Anglo-Jewry* (London, 1957), pp. 59, 73.

18. Rubinstein, *History of the Jews*, p. 62.

19. Aubrey Newman, *The Board of Deputies of British Jews* (London, 1982), pp. 2–5.

20. Lynn Hollen Lees, *Exiles of Erin: Irish Immigrants in Victorian London* (Manchester, 1979), pp. 172, 174.

21. JML/1988.525.2, 'Our East London: The Growth of Its Religions', Second Bulletin issued by the School's Committee of the Council of Citizens of E. London', Spring 1950.

22. *London City Mission Magazine*, June 1851, pp. 124–5.

23. *London City Mission Magazine*, 1 September 1877, pp. 189–90.

24. Ibid., pp. 216–22.

25. *London City Mission Magazine*, 1 November 1892, pp. 258–9.

26. John Garwood, *The Million-Peopled City: Or, One Half of the People of London Made Known to the Other Half* (London, 1853), pp. 286–98.

27. A. Martin Wainwright, *The 'Better Class' of Indians: Social Work, Imperial Identity, and South Asians in Britain 1858–1914* (Manchester, 2008), pp. 71–4; Rozina Visram, *Asians in Britain: 400 Years of History* (London, 2002), pp. 59–61.

28. Joseph Salter, *The Asiatic in England; The East in the West or Work Among the Asiatics and Africans in London* (London, 1896).

29. Wainwright, *'Better Class'*, pp. 74–5.

30. Visram, *Asians in Britain*, p. 61.

31. Salter, *The Asiatic in England*, p. 170.

32. Visram, *Asians in Britain*, p. 60.

33. Ibid., pp. 61–2; Wainwright, *'Better Class'*, pp. 83–92; Salter, *The Asiatic in England*, pp. 165–81.

34. Henry Mayhew, *London Labour and the London Poor*, vol. I (originally 1861; London, 1968), p. 242.

35. Michael H. Fisher, Shompa Lahiri and Shinder Thandi, *A South Asian History of Britain: Four Centuries of People from the Indian Sub-Continent* (Oxford, 2007), pp. 97–8.

36. Thomas Burke, *The Real East End* (London, 1932), p. 64.

37. George H. Mitchell, *Down in Limehouse* (London, 1925), p. 21.

38. Ibid., p. 37.

39. See, for example, Church Response for Refugees, https://www.forrefugees.uk, accessed 9 October 2018.

40. Clifford D. Hill, *West Indians and the London Churches* (Oxford, 1963), pp. 5, 7, 29, 50.

41. Albert Hyndman, 'The West Indian in London', in S. K. Ruck, ed., *The West Indian Comes to England: A Report Prepared for the Trustees of the London Parochial Charities by the Family Welfare Association* (London, 1960), p. 79.

42. Sheila Patterson, *Immigration and Race Relations in Britain, 1960–1967* (London, 1969), pp. 325–9.

43. Malcolm J. C. Calley, 'Pentecostal Sects among West Indian Migrants', *Race*, vol. 3 (1962), pp. 55–64.

44. Hermione Harris, *Yoruba in Diaspora: An African Church in London* (Basingstoke, 2008), p. 4; B. Akíntúndé Oyètádé, 'The Yorùbá Community in London', *African Languages and Cultures*, vol. 6 (1993), p. 74.

45. Oyètádé, 'The Yorùbá Community in London', p. 70.

46. Ibid., pp. 78, 90; Harris, *Yoruba in Diaspora*.

47. Bazil Meade, *A Boy, A Journey, a Dream: The Story of Bazil Meade and the London Community Gospel Choir* (Oxford, 2011).

48. Ernest Cashmore, *Rastaman: The Rastafarian Movement in England* (London, 1979).

49. Sheila Patterson, *Dark Strangers: A Sociological Study of the Absorption of a Recent West Indian Migrant Group in Brixton, South London* (London, 1963), pp. 352–5.

50. ML/99.35, Interview by Alan Dein of Vincent Reid, April 1998.

51. Panayi, *German Immigrants*, pp. 150–9, 166–7; Susanne Steinmetz, 'The German Churches of London', in Panayi, *Germans in Britain Since 1500*, pp. 49–71.

52. Friedeborg L. Müller, *History of German Lutheran Congregations in England, 1900–1950* (Frankfurt, 1987).

53. Lothar Kettenacker, 'The Germans after 1945', in Panayi, *Germans in Britain Since 1500*, pp. 195–6.

54. Olive Besagni, *A Better Life: A History of London's Italian Immigrant Families in Clerkenwell's Little Italy in the 19th and 20th Centuries* (London, 2011), pp. 10–12.

55. George R. Sims, 'Trips around Town: III: Round Little Italy', *Strand Magazine*, vol. 29 (1905), pp. 511–12.

56. Terri Colpi, *The Italian Factor: The Italian Community in Great Britain* (London, 1991), pp. 236–7; Besagni, *A Better Life*, pp. 18–19, 23–4.

57. 'The Roman Catholic Church', in Charles Booth, ed., *Life and Labour of the People in London*, Third Series, vol. 7, *Religious Influences* (London, 1902), pp. 241–58.

58. John Denvir, *The Irish in Britain* (London, 1892), p. 101.

59. Lees, *Exiles*, p. 180.

60. Donald M. MacRaild, *Irish Migrants in Modern Britain* (Basingstoke, 1999), p. 83.

61. Ibid., pp. 100–22. Other parts of England counted a higher percentage of Protestants.

62. David Fitzpatrick, ' "A Particular Tramping People": The Irish in Britain, 1801–70', in W. E. Vaughan, ed., *A New History of Ireland*, vol. 5 (Oxford, 1989), p. 651.

63. Sheridan Gilley, 'The Roman Catholic Mission to the Irish in London, 1840–1860', *Recusant History*, vol. 10 (1969–70), pp. 123–45.

64. Graham Davis, *The Irish in Britain* (Dublin, 1991), pp. 142–3.

65. MacRaild, *Irish Migrants*, pp. 81–2.

66. Garwood, *The Million-Peopled City*, pp. 308–12; James Ewing Ritchie, The *Religious Life of London* (London, 1870), pp. 60–5.

67. Mary Hickman, *Religion, Class and Identity* (Aldershot, 1995), pp. 121–202; Lees, *Exiles*, pp. 197–203.

68. Lees, *Exiles*, p. 193.

69. JML/1988.525.2, 'Our East London: The Growth of Its Religions', Second Bulletin issued by the School's Committee of the Council of Citizens of E. London', Spring 1950; John A. Jackson, 'The Irish in East London', *East London Papers*, vol. 6 (1963), p. 115.

70. Jackson, 'The Irish in East London'.

71. Enda Delaney, *The Irish in Post-War Britain* (Oxford, 2007), pp. 129–49; Clair Wills, *Lovers and Strangers: An Immigrant History of Post-War Britain* (London, 2017), pp. 123–40.

72. Anne O'Grady, *Irish Migration to London in the 1940s and 1950s* (London, 1988), p. 13.

73. Seán Sorohan, *Irish London during the Troubles* (Dublin, 2012), p. 26.

74. M.-N. B., *History of the Russian Orthodox Church in London, 1707–1977* (London, 1978), p. 6; Christopher Birchall, *Embassy, Emigrants and Englishmen: The Three Hundred Year History of a Russian Orthodox Church in London* (New York, 2014), pp. 1–10, 13–15, 48–9; Jonathan Harris, 'London's Greek Community', in George Kakavas, ed., *Treasured Offerings: The Legacy of the Greek Orthodox Cathedral of St. Sophia, London* (London, 2002), pp. 4–5.

75. Theodore Dowling and E. W. Fletcher, *Hellenism in England* (London, 1915), pp. 86–7, 114–15; Bishop Theodoritos of Nazianos, 'History of the Greek Cathedral of Saint Sophia in London', in Kakavas, *Treasured Offerings*, pp. 23–6; Michael Constantinides, *The Greek Orthodox Church in London* (Oxford, 1933), pp. 50–1.

76. Vic George and Geoffrey Millerson, 'The Cypriot Community in London', *Race*, vol. 8 (1967), p. 290.

77. Panikos Panayi, *An Immigration History of Britain: Multicultural Racism Since c.1800* (London, 2010), p. 156.

78. George and Millerson, 'Cypriot Community in London', p. 291; Floya Anthias, *Ethnicity, Class, Gender and Migration: Greek Cypriots in Britain* (Aldershot, 1992), pp. 124–7; Zena Theodorou and Sav Kyriacou, 'Cypriots in London', in Merriman, *Peopling of London*, pp. 102–4; Anna Hassiotis, *The Greek Cypriot Community in Camden* (London, 1989); Pamela Constantinides, 'The Greek Cypriots: Factors in the Maintenance of Ethnic Identity', in James L. Watson, ed., *Between Two Cultures: Migrants and Minorities in Britain* (Oxford, 1977), pp. 286–7.

79. Newman, *Board of Deputies*.

80. Michaal Goulston, 'The Status of the Anglo-Jewish Rabbinate, 1840–1914', *Jewish Journal of Sociology*, vol. 10 (1968), pp. 55–82.

81. Finestein, *Short History of Anglo-Jewry*, p. 118.

82. V. D. Lipman, *A Century of Social Service* (London, 1959), pp. 1, 8, 76–137.

83. These are listed in *Jewish Year Book, 1903–4* (London, 1903).

84. Aubrey Newman, *The United Synagogue, 1880–1970* (London, 1977).

85. Potter, 'Jewish Community', pp. 176–8.

86. LMA/Acc/2805/4/1/91, Letter from the Chief Rabbi of 22 April 1927.

87. Stephen Sharot, 'Religious Change in Native Orthodoxy in London, 1870–1914: Rabbinate and Clergy', *Jewish Journal of Sociology*, vol. 15 (1973), pp. 167–87.

88. Geoffrey Alderman, *Modern British Jewry* (Oxford, 1992), pp. 142–5.

89. JML/1988.525.2, 'Our East London: The Growth of Its Religions', Second Bulletin issued by the School's Committee of the Council of Citizens of E. London', Spring 1950.

90. Steven Singer, 'The Anglo-Jewish Ministry in Early Victorian London', *Modern Judaism*, vol. 5 (1985), pp. 279–99.

91. Anne J. Kershen and Jonathan A. Romain, *Tradition and Change: A History of Reform Judaism in Britain, 1840–1895* (London, 1995).

92. Alderman, *Modern British Jewry*, pp. 142–5, 154.

93. Todd M. Endelman, 'Native Jews and Foreign Jews in London', 1870–1914', in D. Berger, ed., *The Legacy of Jewish Emigration and its Impact* (New York, 1983), pp. 109–29.

94. Judy Glasman, 'London Synagogues in the Late Nineteenth Century: Design in Context', *London Journal*, vol. 13 (1988), pp. 143–54.

95. Pam Fox, *The Jewish Community of Golders Green: A Social History* (Stroud, 2016), pp. 79–117.

96. Geoffrey Alderman, *The History of the Hendon Synagogue* (London, 1978), p. 1.

97. Henrietta Adler, 'Jewish Life and Labour in East London', in Sir Hubert Llewellyn Smith, ed., *New Survey of London Life and Labour*, vol. 6 (London, 1934), pp. 277–8.

98. Howard Bloch, *Earlham Grove Shul* (London, 1997).

99. Gerry Black, *Living Up West: Jewish Life in London's West End* (London, 1994), pp. 112–232.

100. Susan L. Tananbaum, *Jewish Immigrants in London, 1880–1939* (London, 2014).

101. Elkan Nathan Adler, *A History of the Jews in London* (Philadelphia, PA, 1930).

102. Todd M. Endelman, *The Jews of Britain, 1656–2000* (London, 2002), pp. 239–40; James Parkes, 'The History of the Anglo-Jewish Community', in Maurice Freedman, ed., *A Minority in Britain: Social Studies of the Anglo-Jewish Community* (London, 1955), pp. 16–36; Adolph G. Brotman, 'Jewish Communal Organization', in Julius Gould and Shaul Esh, eds, *Jewish Life in Modern Britain* (London, 1964), pp. 1–26; David Englander, 'Integrated but Insecure: a Portrait of Anglo-Jewry at the Close of the Twentieth Century', in Gerald Parsons, ed., *The Growth of Religious Diversity in Britain* (Abingdon, 1993), pp. 95–131.

103. Fox, *Jewish Community of Golders Green*.

104. Englander, 'Integrated but Insecure', pp. 114–19.

105. Humayun Ansari, *'The Infidel Within': Muslims in Britain Since 1800* (London, 2004), pp. 121–44; Sophie Gilliat-Ray, *Muslims in Britain: An Introduction* (Cambridge, 2010), pp. 32–41.

106. Humayun Ansari, 'Introduction', in Humayun Ansari, ed., *The Making of the East London Mosque* (Cambridge 2011), p. 1.

107. Hamza Alavi, *The Pakistanis in London* (London, 1963).

108. Shahed Saleem, *The British Mosque: An Architectural and Social History* (Swindon, 2018), pp. 133–47.

109. Ibid., pp. 35–43.

110. Fatima Gailani, *The Mosques of London* (Henstridge, 2000), p. 15.

111. See the maps in Saleem, *British Mosque*, pp. 272–3.

112. Gilliat-Ray, *Muslims in Britain*; John Wolffe, 'Fragmented Universality', in Parsons, *Growth of Religious Diversity*, pp. 133–72; Alkan Fuat, *Cypriots in Haringey* (London, 1980), p. 33.

113. Steven Vertovec, 'Community and Congregation in London Hindu Temples: Divergent Trends', *New Community*, vol. 18 (1992), pp. 251–64.

114. *Daily Telegraph*, 19 August 1995; Deborah Singmaster, 'Hindu Architecture Transcends its Suburban Context: The Shri Swaminarayan Mandir in Neasden is the First Traditional Hindu Complex to be Built Outside the Indian Subcontinent', *Architects Journal*, 21 December 1995, pp. 20–1.

115. Terence Thomas, 'Hindu Dharma in Dispersion', in Parsons, *Growth of Religious Diversity*, pp. 173–204.

116. Gurharpal Singh and Darshan Singh Tatla, *Sikhs in Britain: The Making of a Community* (London, 2006), pp. 60–93; Gerd Bauman, *Contesting Culture: Discourses of Identity in Multi-Ethnic London* (Cambridge, 1996), pp. 109–16.

117. Richard Mudie-Smith, ed., *Religious Life in London* (London, 1904), p. 441.

118. Richard Mudie-Smith, 'Methods and Lessons of the Church', in ibid., pp. 7, 10.

119. 'Table Showing Attendance at Synagogues in London', in ibid., p. 265. The total number of Jews in Britain at this time stood at between 150,000 and 250,000, the majority of whom would have resided in London, for which see Panikos Panayi, *Immigration, Ethnicity and Racism in Britain, 1815–1945* (Manchester, 1994), p. 51.

120. Panayi, *German Immigrants*, pp. 97, 151.
121. MacRaild, *Irish Migrants*, p. 80.
122. Sheridan Gilley,'Catholic Faith of the Irish Slums: London, 1840–70', in H. J. Dyos and M. Wolff, eds, *The Victorian City: Images and Realities* (London, 1973), pp. 837–53.
123. Lees, *Exiles of Erin*, p. 180.
124. Davis, *The Irish in Britain*, p. 140.
125. Lees, *Exiles of Erin*, pp. 182–3.
126. Mayhew, *London Labour*, vol. I, pp. 107–8.
127. 'The Roman Catholic Church', p. 251.
128. 'The London Irish', *Blackwood's Edinburgh Magazine*, vol. 170 (1901), pp. 132–3.
129. Delaney, *Irish in Post-War Britain*, pp. 129–75.
130. Todd M. Endelman, *Radical Assimilation in English Jewish History, 1656–1945* (Bloomington, IN, 1990).
131. V. D. Lipman, 'A Survey of Anglo-Jewry in 1851', *Transactions of the Jewish Historical Society of England*, vol. 17 (1951–2), p. 186.
132. Henry Mayhew, *London Labour and the London Poor*, vol. II (originally 1861; London, 1968), p. 126.
133. Stephen Sharot, 'Religious Change in Native Orthodoxy in London, 1870–1914: The Synagogue Service', *Jewish Journal of Sociology*, vol. 15 (1973), pp. 58–61.
134. Potter, 'Jewish Community', pp. 169, 172.
135. Lloyd P. Gartner, *The Jewish Immigrant in England, 1870–1914*, 2nd edn (London 1973), pp. 192–7.
136. Selig Brodetsky, *Memoirs: From Ghetto to Israel* (London, 1960), pp. 27–8.
137. David Dee, *The 'Estranged' Generation? Social and Generational Change in Interwar British Jewry* (London, 2017), pp. 155–91.
138. Thomas Burke, *The Real East End* (London, 1932), pp. 45–6.
139. Norman Cohen, 'Trends in Anglo-Jewish Religious Life', in Gould and Esh, *Jewish Life in Modern Britain*, p. 42.
140. Barry A. Kosmin and Caren Levy, *Jewish Identity in an Anglo-Jewish Community* (London, 1983).
141. Hariet Becher, Stanley Waterman, Barry Kosmin and Katarina Thomson, *A Portrait of Jews in London and the South-East: A Community Study* (London, 2002); David Graham, *Secular or Religious: The Outlook for London's Jews* (London, 2003).
142. Englander, 'Integrated but Insecure', pp. 114–19.
143. Todd M. Endelman, ' "Practices of a Low Anthropological Level": A Schechita Controversy of the 1950s', in Anne J. Kershen, *Food in the Migrant Experience* (Aldershot, 2002), p. 81.
144. Panikos Panayi, 'The Anglicisation of East European Jewish Food in Britain', in Stefan Manz and Panikos Panayi, eds, *Refugees and Cultural Transfers to Britain* (Abingdon, 2013), pp. 177–80.
145. *Jewish Chronicle*, 9 March 1911.
146. Panayi, 'Anglicisation', pp. 180–5.
147. Alavi, *Pakistanis in London*, p. 6.
148. Caroline Adams, *Across Seven Seas and Thirteen Rivers: Life Stories of Pioneer Sylhetti Settlers in Britain* (London, 1987), pp. 107–8.
149. Tarek Qureshi, *Living in Britain, Growing Old in Britain: A Study of Bangladeshi Elders in London* (London, 1998), pp. 30–1.
150. Gilliat-Ray, *Muslims in Britain*, pp. 137–8.
151. Wolffe, 'Fragmented Universality', p. 154.
152. Gilliat-Ray, *Muslims in Britain*, pp. 146–56; Ansari, *'The Infidel Within'*, pp. 317–40.
153. Wolffe, 'Fragmented Universality', p. 147.
154. Dodsworth, Vacchelli and Watson, 'Shifting Religions'; Nazneen Ahmed, Jane Garnett, Ben Gidley, Alana Harris and Michael Keith, 'Shifting Markers of Identity in East London's Religious Spaces', *Ethnic and Racial Studies*, vol. 39 (2016), pp. 223–42.

155. Anne J. Kershen, 'Time when England said "Welcome" ', *Church Times*, 12 June 2015.
156. Will Herberg, *Protestant-Catholic-Jew: An Essay in American Religious Sociology* (Chicago, IL, 1983), p. 14.

CHAPTER 9

1. Watts Phillips, *The Wild Tribes of London* (London, 1855), pp. 66–7.
2. T. A. Layton, *Dining Round London* (London, 1947), p. 47.
3. *Caterer*, 15 January 1908.
4. Gregory Houston Bowden, *British Gastronomy: The Rise of the Great Restaurants* (London, 1975), pp. 15, 17.
5. Rebecca L. Sprang, *The Invention of the Restaurant: Paris and Modern Gastronomic Culture* (London, 2000), pp. 1–2.
6. John Burnett, *England Eats Out: A Social History of Eating Out in England from 1830 to the Present* (London, 2004), pp. 66–98, 137–64.
7. Henry Mayhew, *London Labour and the London Poor*, vol. I (originally 1861; London, 1968), pp. 158–212; Edwina Ehrman, Hazel Forsyth, Lucy Peltz and Cathy Ross, *London Eats Out: 500 Years of Capital Dining* (London, 1999), pp. 84–5.
8. Brenda Assael, *The London Restaurant, 1840–1914* (Oxford, 2018), p. 17.
9. Jonathan Morris, *Coffee: A Global History* (London, 2018), pp. 44, 48–9.
10. Mayhew, *London Labour*, pp. 183–6.
11. Guy Deghy and Keith Waterhouse, *Café Royal: Ninety Years of Bohemia* (London, 1955); *Caterer*, 15 June, 15 February 1898.
12. Hugh Montgomery-Massingberd and David Watkin, *The London Ritz: A Social and Architectural History* (London, 1989), pp. 9–13, 16–18, 22, 64; Compton Mackenzie, *The Savoy of London* (London, 1953), pp. 40, 55–8; Marie Louise Ritz, *César Ritz: Host to the World* (Toronto, 1938); Stanley Jackson, *The Savoy: A Century of Taste* (London, 1989), pp. 24–31.
13. Peter Bird, *The First Food Empire: A History of J. Lyons & Co.* (Chichester, 2000), pp. 2–24.
14. *Caterer*, 15 October 1896.
15. D. J. Richardson, 'J. Lyons & Co. Ltd.: Caterers & Food Manufacturers, 1894 to 1939', in D. J. Oddy and Derek S. Miller, eds, *The Making of the Modern British Diet* (London, 1976), pp. 164–9.
16. *Caterer*, 15 June 1923.
17. Bird, *First Food Empire*, pp. 41–2.
18. Ibid., pp. 43–6.
19. Debra Kelly, 'A Migrant Culture on Display: The French Migrant and French Gastronomy in London (Nineteenth to Twenty-First Centuries)', *Modern Languages Open* (2016), pp. 1–31; Valerie Mars, 'Experiencing French Cookery in Nineteenth-Century London', in Debra Kelly and Martyn Cornick, eds, *A History of the French in London: Liberty, Equality, Opportunity* (London, 2013), pp. 217–40.
20. Anne Currah, *Chef to Queen Victoria: The Recipes of Charles Elmé Francatelli* (London, 1973), pp. 19–20.
21. Ruth Brandon, *The People's Chef: Alexis Soyer, a Life in Seven Courses* (Chichester, 2005); Helen Morris, *Portrait of a Chef: The Life of Alexis Soyer, Sometime Chef to the Reform Club* (Cambridge, 1938); Elizabeth Ray, *Alexis Soyer: Cook Extraordinary* (Lewes, 1991); Ruth Cowen, *Relish: The Extraordinary Life of Alexis Soyer, Victorian Celebrity Chef* (London, 2006).
22. Kenneth James, *Escoffier: King of Chefs* (London, 2002); Timothy Shaw, *The World of Escoffier* (London, 1994); Auguste Escoffier, *A Guide to Modern Cookery* (London, 1909); F. Ashburner, 'Escoffier, Georges Auguste (1846–1935)', *Oxford Dictionary of National Biography*, http://www.oxforddnb.com/view/article/50441, accessed 11 October 2018.
23. *Census of England and Wales, 1901, Summary Tables, Area, Housing and Population* (London, 1903), p. 270.

24. *Restaurant*, April 1911.
25. *Caterer*, 15 April 1904.
26. *Restaurant*, May 1912.
27. *Fach-Zeitung des Bundes Deutscher Köche*, 1 September 1902, 15 December 1902.
28. *Caterer*, 15 May 1901.
29. *Caterer*, 20 March 1931, 19 February 1937; *Hotel Review*, November 1927, December 1927.
30. *Caterer*, 15 December 1892; *Hotel Review*, December 1928.
31. *Census of England and Wales, 1911: Birthplaces* (London, 1915), pp. 220–8, 230–4.
32. Sir Hubert Llewellyn Smith, *The New Survey of London Life and Labour*, vol. 8, *London Industries*, III (London, 1934), pp. 203, 220.
33. Panikos Panayi, *German Immigrants in Britain during the Nineteenth Century, 1815–1914* (Oxford, 1995), p. 125.
34. Smith, *New Survey of London*, p. 220.
35. *London Hotel and Restaurant Employees Gazette*, 6 September 1890.
36. *London Hotel and Restaurant Employees Gazette*, 15 January 1908.
37. Paolo Contarini, *The Savoy Was My Oyster* (London, 1976).
38. *Caterer*, 16 April 1923.
39. *Hermann*, 2 January 1869.
40. *Londoner General Anzeiger*, 10 July 1901.
41. Panayi, *German Immigrants*, pp. 192–3; *Caterer*, 15 April 1907.
42. Panayi, *German Immigrants*, p. 193.
43. *Revue*, 1 July 1907.
44. *Revue*, 16 February 1907, 15 March 1909.
45. *Restaurant*, November 1911; *Hotel Review*, February 1914.
46. *Rütli*, 6 October 1900.
47. Panikos Panayi, *The Enemy in Our Midst: Germans in Britain during the First World War* (Oxford, 1991), pp. 157, 198; *Caterer*, 15 October 1918.
48. *Hotel Review*, July 1928, June 1929.
49. Panayi, *German Immigrants*, p. 227; *Restaurateur*, January 1914.
50. Panikos Panayi and Stefan Manz, 'The Rise and Fall of Germans in the British Hospitality Industry, c.1880–1920', *Food and History*, vol. 11 (2013), pp. 259–64.
51. Judith R. Walkowitz, *Nights Out: Life in Cosmopolitan London* (London, 2012), pp. 92–143.
52. Montgomery-Massingberd and Watkin, *London Ritz*, p. 164.
53. *Caterer*, 29 November 1946.
54. *Caterer*, 23 April 1955.
55. *Caterer*, 14 December 1957.
56. *Caterer*, 17 April 1975.
57. NA/CO67/303/6, Employment of Cypriots in London as Waiters, 1939.
58. 'The Cypriots in London', *Manchester Guardian*, 14 August 1954; Vic George and Geoffrey Millerson, 'The Cypriot Community in London', *Race*, vol. 8 (1967), pp. 283–4. Fish and chips receive attention below.
59. Floya Anthias, *Ethnicity, Class, Gender and Migration: Greek Cypriots in Britain* (Aldershot, 1992), pp. 55–6.
60. LMA/Acc/3527/384, *Wimpy Times*, Spring 1971.
61. Ehrman, Forsyth, Peltz and Ross, *London Eats Out*, pp. 93–5; Burnett, *England Eats Out*, p. 268.
62. *Caterer*, 30 July 1960.
63. Mario Gallati, *Mario of the Caprice: The Autobiography of a Restaurateur* (London, 1960). This restaurant has continued to thrive, for which see https://www.le-caprice.co.uk, accessed 18 October 2018.
64. Burnett, *England Eats Out*, pp. 290–2.
65. Antony Worrall Thompson in the *Independent*, 11 May 2006.
66. KPMG, *Labour Migration in the Hospitality Sector: A KPMG Report for the British Hospitality Association* (2017), p. 4.

67. Tom Baum, *Migrant Workers in the International Hotel Industry* (Geneva, 2012), p. 35.
68. Ibid.
69. Panikos Panayi, *Fish and Chips: A History* (London, 2014), pp. 14–15, 114–22; John K. Walton, *Fish and Chips and the British Working Class* (Manchester, 1992), pp. 23–6.
70. *The Post Office London Directory with County Suburbs for 1923* (London, 1923), pp. 2410–11.
71. Interview with Jessica Gould, 13 April 2004.
72. *Post Office London Directory for 1954* (London, 1954), pp. 2252–3.
73. *Kelly's Post Office London Directory* (London, 1975), pp. 1837–9.
74. See, for instance, *Kelly's Post Office Directory for London 1984* (London, 1984), pp. 1889–92.
75. Burnett, *England Eats Out*, pp. 95–6.
76. Anonymous, *London at Dinner: Or Where to Dine* (London, 1858), p. 12.
77. *Food Journal*, 1 June 1870.
78. Nathaniel Newnham Davis, *Dinners and Diners: Where and How to Dine in London*, 2nd edn (London, 1901), pp. xxi–xxiv.
79. *Caterer*, 15 January 1910.
80. Davis, *Dinners and Diners*, pp. 221–7.
81. See below, p. 250.
82. *Caterer*, 15 July 1907.
83. *Caterer*, 15 December 1908, 15 June 1910.
84. Priscilla Parkhurst Ferguson, *Accounting for Taste: The Triumph of French Cuisine* (London, 2004).
85. *Caterer*, 20 February 1928.
86. *Caterer*, 25 September 1936.
87. *Hotel Review*, June 1921; Guy Deghy, *Paradise in the Strand: The Story of Romano's* (London, 1958).
88. *Caterer*, 15 April 1921, 16 March 1925.
89. *Caterer*, 15 November 1921. Walkowitz, *Nights Out*, pp. 92–144, considers other Italian restaurants.
90. Elizabeth Montizambert, *London Discoveries in Shops and Restaurants* (London, 1924), p. 117.
91. Thomas Burke, *Dinner is Served! Or Eating Round the World in London* (London, 1937), p. 12.
92. Ibid., pp. 72–5.
93. *Caterer*, 15 March 1922.
94. Alfred Edye Manning Foster, *London Restaurants* (London, 1924), p. 84.
95. Eileen Hooton-Smith, *The Restaurants of London* (London, 1928), pp. 102–3.
96. Foster, *London Restaurants*, p. 84.
97. *Caterer*, 13 May 1938, 21 July 1939.
98. Burke, *Dinner is Served!*, p. 48.
99. Richard Tames, *Feeding London: A Taste of History* (London, 2003), pp. 116, 117.
100. *Caterer*, 15 July 1920.
101. *Hotel Review*, June 1922.
102. British Library, National Sound Archive, National Life Story Collection, 'From Source to Salespoint', Interview with Peter Jacomelli, 2000.
103. J. A. G. Roberts, *China to Chinatown: Chinese Food in the West* (London, 2002), pp. 140–4.
104. See below, p. 240.
105. *Caterer*, 15 June 1916.
106. *Caterer*, 15 October 1919; Foster, *London Restaurants*, pp. 87–90.
107. M. P. Lee, *Chinese Cookery* (London, 1943), p. 72; Roberts, *China to Chinatown*, p. 157.
108. Jack Goody, *Food and Love: A Cultural History of East and West* (London, 1998), p. 161.
109. *Daily Telegraph*, 30 September 2005; *Independent*, 30 September 2005; Peter and Colleen Grove, *Curry Culture: A Very British Love Affair* (Surbiton, 2005), pp. 29–31.

110. *Food and Cookery*, May and June 1898.
111. *Caterer*, August 1912, May 1915; Pat Chapman, *Curry Club Bangladeshi Restaurant Curries* (London, 1996), p. 9.
112. *Caterer*, 15 September 1919; NA/BT31/24215/151722, Indian Restaurants Ltd, 1919.
113. Lizzie Collingham, *Curry: A Biography* (London, 2005), p. 219; Hooton-Smith, *Restaurants of London*, pp. 87–9.
114. Collingham, *Curry*, pp. 218, 219.
115. This perspective is discussed in Chapter 4.
116. Alan Warde and Lydia Martens, *Eating Out: Social Differentiation, Consumption and Pleasure* (Cambridge, 2000), p. 26.
117. Kenneth Lo, *Chinese Food* (Newton Abbot, 1972).
118. Vicky Bhogal, *A Year of Cooking Like Mummyji* (London, 2005), p. 10.
119. *Harden's London Restaurants* (London, 1997), pp. 188–201.
120. https://www.hardens.com, accessed 12 October 2018.
121. Stanley Jackson, *An Indiscreet Guide to Soho* (London, 1946), p. 68.
122. Ibid., p. 70.
123. Layton, *Dining Round London*, pp. 42–53.
124. Jackson, *Indiscreet Guide to Soho*, pp. 68–90.
125. Ibid., p. 74.
126. Alan Warde, 'Continuity and Change in British Restaurants, 1951–2001: Evidence from the *Good Food Guide*', in Marc Jacobs and Peter Scholliers, eds, *Eating Out in Europe: Picnics, Gourmet Dining and Snacks Since the Late Eighteenth Century* (Oxford, 2003), pp. 229–43.
127. *Good Food Guide* (London, 1954), p. 369.
128. *Egon Ronay Recommends Eating Places in London and Round Britain* (London, 1961), pp. 17, 27, 29, 78.
129. Terri Colpi, *The Italian Factor: The Italian Community in Great Britain* (Edinburgh, 1991), pp. 140–1.
130. *Caterer's Journal*, September 1961, May 1962.
131. *Caterer*, 18 August 1962.
132. Sandra Lysandrou, *Cyprus Cooking for Friends: Traditional and Modern Recipes from Cyprus Including Taverna Meze and Sweets* (Nicosia, 1994); Nearchos Nicolaou, *Cooking from Cyprus: Including Selected Recipes of Taverna Meze*, 10th edn (Nicosia, 1990); *The Times*, 19 June 1968.
133. *Good Food Guide 1965–6* (London, 1966), p. 639.
134. *Good Food Guide 1985*, p. 450.
135. *The Times*, 19 June 1968.
136. *Fast Food*, November 1978.
137. Roberts, *China to Chinatown*, pp. 172–6; James L. Watson, *Emigration and the Chinese Lineage: The* Mans *in London and Hong Kong* (London, 1975); Susan Chui Chie Baxter, 'A Political Economy of the Ethnic Chinese Catering Industry' (unpublished University Aston PhD thesis, 1988), pp. 107–12; House of Commons, Second Report from the Home Affairs Committee, Session 1984–5, *Chinese Community in Britain*, vol. 1, *Report together with Proceedings of the Committee* (London, 1985), p. ix; *The Times*, 2 October 1961; Ng Kwee Choo, *The Chinese in London* (London, 1968), pp. 36–8.
138. Bowden, *British Gastronomy*, p. 150.
139. Watson, *Emigration*, p. 73.
140. *Daily Mail*, 15 October 1965.
141. Choo, *Chinese in London*, p. 29.
142. Anthony Shang, *The Chinese in Britain* (London, 1984), pp. 25–6.
143. See below, p. 246.
144. Mintel, Leisure Intelligence, *Ethnic Restaurants*, January 1998, p. 14.
145. Shang, *Chinese in Britain*, p. 28.
146. Collingham, *Curry*, pp. 215–22.

147. *Restaurant Trade Journal*, July 1946.
148. Collingham, *Curry*, pp. 54, 115.
149. Pat Chapman, *The Good Curry Guide to Indian Restaurants* (Haslemere, 1983), p. 5; *Guardian*, 9 December 1992; Pat Chapman, *The 1999 Good Curry Guide* (London, 1998), p. 19.
150. *Caterer*, 13 March 1975.
151. Chapman, *Curry Club Bangladeshi Restaurant Curries*, p. 14; Chapman, 1999 *Good Curry Guide*, p. 15.
152. http://rasarestaurants.com, accessed 16 October 2018; Shrabani Basu, *Curry: The Story of the Nation's Favourite Dish* (Stroud, 2003), pp. 134–202; Collingham, *Curry*, pp. 231–8; Monder Ram, Tahir Abbas, Blihar Sanghera and Guy Hillin, ' "Currying Favour with the Locals": Balti Owners and Business Enclaves', *International Journal of Entrepreneurial Behaviour and Research*, 6 (2000); interview with Das Sreedharan, 9 June 2004; Panikos Panayi, 'The Spicing up of English Provincial Life: The History of Curry in Leicester', in Anne J. Kershen, ed., *Food in the Migrant Experience* (Aldershot, 2002), pp. 60–2.
153. Tom Royle, *Working for McDonald's in Europe: The Unequal Struggle* (London, 2000); Eric Schlosser, *Fast Food Nation* (London, 2002).
154. *Caterer*, 1 January 1970.
155. *Daily Telegraph*, 12 November 2014.
156. *Caterer*, 27 March 1975.
157. George Ritzer, *The McDonaldization of Society*, New Century Edition (London, 2000), p. 220.
158. Stephen Ball, 'Whither the Small Independent Takeaway?', *International Journal of Contemporary Hospitality Management*, 8 (1996), p. 27.
159. Burnett, *England Eats Out*, p. 313.
160. Mintel, Leisure Intelligence, *Ethnic Restaurants*, p. 10.
161. Colpi, *Italian Factor*, p. 143; Morris, *Coffee*, pp. 108–9.
162. 'A Slice of the Action', *Observer Food Monthly*, 9 February 2003.
163. See Stephen Mennell, *All Manners of Food: Eating and Taste in England and France from the Middle Ages to the Present* (Oxford, 1985).
164. See Chapter 8 above.
165. *Jewish Chronicle*, 2 November 1883.
166. *Caterer*, 15 January 1898.
167. *Jewish Review and Advertiser*, 1931.
168. NA/BT31/2762/15403, Kosher Restaurant Company Ltd, 1881–1905.
169. NA/BT31/29446/212572, Kosher Caterers Ltd, 1926.
170. JML/1983/370, 'Bloom with Good Food'.
171. Gerry Black, *Living Up West: Jewish Life in London's West End* (London, 1994), pp. 70–4; Ehrman, Forsyth, Peltz and Ross, *London Eats Out*, p. 99.
172. *Jewish Chronicle*, 6 November 1908.
173. *Jewish Chronicle*, 2 April 1909.
174. *Jewish Chronicle*, 14 January 1921.
175. JML/1986.136.11.1, 'Sam Stern, Kosher Caterer'; JML/1986.136.4, 'Menu from Sam Stern's Hotel and Kosher Restaurant, 1930–9'.
176. United Synagogue Kashrut Board, *The Really Jewish Food Guide, 2005/5765* (London, 2005), p. 145.
177. Linda Zeff, *Jewish London* (London, 1986), pp. 23, 50–1.
178. Stefan Manz, *Migranten und Internierte: Deutsche in Glasgow, 1864–1918* (Stuttgart, 2003), pp. 135–6; *Caterer*, 15 January 1883.
179. *Londoner Courier*, 18 June 1884.
180. *Londoner General Anzeiger*, 6 January 1904, 4 May 1904, 3 March 1909.
181. *Hermann*, 2 January 1869.
182. Ibid.

183. *Londoner General Anzeiger*, 3 January 1900.
184. *Londoner General Anzeiger*, 6 January 1900.
185. Panayi, *Enemy*.
186. James J. and Patience P. Barnes, 'London's German Community in the Early 1930s', in Panikos Panayi, ed., *Germans in Britain since 1500* (London, 1996), p. 132.
187. Roberts, *China to Chinatown*, pp. 155–6.
188. *Caterer*, 15 July 1908.
189. *Caterer*, 15 July 1916.
190. Philip Baker and Jeehoon Kim, *Global London: Where to Find almost Everything Ethnic and Cultural in the Multilingual Capital* (London, 2003).
191. Howard E. Aldrich, John C. Cater, Trevor P. Jones and David McEvoy, 'Business Development and Self-Segregation: Asian Enterprise in Three British Cities', in Ceri Peach, Vaughan Robinson and Susan Smith, eds, *Ethnic Segregation in Cities* (London, 1981), p. 179.
192. Leo Benedictus, 'Koreans in New Malden', *Guardian*, 21 January 2005; Orla Ryan, 'Meet the North Korean Exiles of New Malden', *Financial Times*, 24 August 2017.
193. John Kitching, David Smallbone and Rosemary Athayde, 'Ethnic Diasporas and Business Competitiveness: Minority-Owned Enterprises in London', *Journal of Ethnic and Migration Studies*, vol. 35 (2009), p. 697.
194. Panayi, *Fish and Chips*, pp. 78–122.
195. Colpi, *Italian Factor*, p. 143; 'A Slice of the Action'.
196. James, *Escoffier*, pp. 173–4.

CHAPTER 10

1. Daniel Mendoza, *Memoirs of the Life of Daniel Mendoza* (London, 1816), pp. 23–4.
2. Ricky Villa, Joel Miller and Frederico Ardiles, *And Still Ricky Villa: My Autobiography* (Kingston upon Thames, 2010), pp. 92–3.
3. Paul Canoville, *Black and Blue: How Racism, Drugs and Cancer Almost Destroyed Me* (London, 2008), p. 4.
4. Jonathan Magee and John Sugden, ' "The World at their Feet": Professional Football and International Labour Migration', *Journal of Sport and Social Issues*, vol. 26 (2002), p. 421.
5. See the first team squads of these two clubs at the beginning of the 2018–19 season, which indicate that in the case of Chelsea they include just five English players along with Welsh Ethan Ampandu of the total first team squad, for which see chelseafc.com, https://www.chelseafc.com/en/teams/first-team?pageTab=players, accessed 26 October 2018 and, in the case of Arsenal, the same number of Englishmen, for which see arsenal.com, https://www.arsenal.com/first-team/players, accessed 26 October 2018.
6. See below, pp. 266–8.
7. Matthew Taylor, 'Global Players? Football Migration and Globalization, c. 1930–2000', *Historical Social Research*, vol. 31 (2006), pp. 7–30; Patrick McGovern, 'Globalization or Internationalization? Foreign Footballers in the English League, 1946–95', *Sociology*, vol. 36 (2002), pp. 23–42.
8. These issues receive attention from Richard Giulianotti and Roland Robertson, 'The Globalization of Football: A Study in the Globalization of the "Serious Life" ', *British Journal of Sociology*, vol. 55 (2004), pp. 545–68. For an intellectualization of Arsène Wenger's reign at Arsenal see David Horspool, 'Farewell Shrug', *TLS*, 16 May 2018. For the thirteen foreign Chelsea managers during this period see https://www.chelseafc.com/en/about-chelsea/history/former-managers, accessed 26 October 2018.
9. Gianluca Vialli and Gabriele Marcotti, *The Italian Job: A Journey to the Heart of Two Great Footballing Cultures* (London, 2006), p. 21.
10. 'Les Hazard, une famille de foot', *Le Parisien*, 13 May 2011.
11. *Chelsea FC Official Matchday Programme versus Watford*, 21 October 2017, pp. 38–9.

12. See, for example: Jim Walvin, *The People's Game: The Social History of British Football* (London, 1975); Matthew Taylor, *The Association Game: A History of British Football* (Harlow, 2008); David Goldblatt, *The Ball is Round: A Global History of Football* (London, 2007).

13. Kasia Boddy, *Boxing: A Cultural History* (London, 2008), pp. 26–109.

14. Dennis Brailsford, *Bareknuckles: A Social History of Prize Fighting* (Cambridge, 1988).

15. Ruti Ungar and Michael Berkowitz, 'From Daniel Mendoza to Amir Khan: Minority Boxers in Britain', in Michael Berkowitz and Ruti Ungar, eds, *Fighting Back? Jewish and Black Boxers in Britain* (London, 2007), p. 5.

16. Todd M. Endelman, *The Jews of Georgian England: Tradition and Change in a Liberal Society* (Ann Arbor, MI, 1999), p. 219.

17. David Dee, *Sport and British Jewry: Integration, Ethnicity and Anti-Semitism, 1890–1970* (Manchester, 2013), pp. 111–16.

18. See the range of contributions to Michael Brenner and Gideon Reuveni, eds, *Emancipation through Muscles: Jews and Sports in Europe* (Lincoln, NE, 2006).

19. For the case of London see Dee, *Sport and British Jewry*, pp. 196–202.

20. Alan Bodner, *When Boxing was a Jewish Sport* (London, 1997), p. 7.

21. Endelman, *Jews of Georgian England*, p. 219; Fred Henning, *Fights for the Championship: The Men and their Times*, vol. 1 (London, 1902), p. 106.

22. Bodner, *When Boxing was a Jewish Sport*, p. 7.

23. *Morning Chronicle*, 7 April 1824.

24. Endelman, *Jews of Georgian England*, p. 220.

25. Pierce Egan, *Boxiana or Sketches of Ancient and Modern Pugilism*, vol. 1 (London, 1830), pp. 322, 323.

26. Ungar and Berkowitz, 'From Daniel Mendoza to Amir Khan', p. 5.

27. Henry Downes Miles, *Pugilistica: The History of English Boxing* (Edinburgh, 1906), vol. 1, p. 482.

28. Ibid., p. 230.

29. Peter M. Briggs, 'Daniel Mendoza and Sporting Celebrity: A Case Study', in Tom Mole, ed., *Romanticism and Celebrity Culture, 1750–1850* (Cambridge, 2009), p. 103.

30. John Whale, 'Daniel Mendoza's Contests of Identity: Masculinity, Ethnicity and Nation in Georgian Prize-Fighting', *Romanticism*, vol. 14 (2008), p. 264.

31. Egan, *Boxiana*, pp. 254–5.

32. Mendoza, *Memoirs*, p. 2. Tony Gee, 'Mendoza, Daniel', *Oxford Dictionary of National Biography*, https://doi.org/10.1093/ref:odnb/18556, accessed 29 October 2018, and Lewis Edwards, 'Daniel Mendoza', *Transactions of the Jewish Historical Society of England*, vol. 15 (1946), p. 75, suggest a birthdate of 1765.

33. Ronald Schechter and Liz Clarke, *Mendoza the Jew: Boxing, Manliness and Nationalism, a Graphic History* (New York, 2014), p. xv.

34. Mendoza, *Memoirs*, pp. 33–4.

35. Edwards, 'Daniel Mendoza', pp. 76–7.

36. Whale, 'Daniel Mendoza's Contests of Identity', pp. 266–9; Endelman, *Jews of Georgian England*, pp. 220–3.

37. Simon Schama, 'The King's Pugilist: Daniel Mendoza (1764–1836)', in Franklin Foer and Marc Tracey, eds, *Jewish Jocks: An Unorthodox Hall of Fame* (New York, 2012), p. 11; Gee, 'Mendoza'.

38. Daniel Mendoza, *The Art of Boxing* (London, 1789).

39. Gee, 'Mendoza'.

40. Brailsford, *Bareknuckles*.

41. Adam Chill, 'The Performance and Marketing of Minority Identity in Late Georgian Boxing', in Berkowitz and Ungar, *Fighting Back?*, pp. 44–6.

42. Luke G. Williams, *Richmond Unchained: The Biography of the World's First Black Sporting Superstar* (Stroud, 2015); T. J. Desch Obi, 'Black Terror: Bill Richmond's Revolutionary Boxing', *Journal of Sport History*, vol. 36 (2009), pp. 99–114; Vincent Carretta, 'Richmond,

Bill', *Oxford Dictionary of National Biograpahy*, https://doi.org/10.1093/ref:odnb/71635, accessed 30 October 2018.

43. Bill Calogero, 'Tom Molineaux: From Slave to American Heavyweight Champion', in Colleen Aycock and Mark Scott, eds, *The First Black Boxing Champions: Essays on Fighters of the 1800s to the 1920s* (Jefferson, NC, 2011), pp. 9–21; Nat Fleischer, *Black Dynamite: The Story of the Negro in the Ring from 1782 to 1938*, vol. 1 (New York, 1938), pp. 34–45.

44. Fleischer, *Black Dynamite*, pp. 64–92.

45. Egan, *Boxiana*, pp. 239–42, 478–80; Chill, 'Performance', pp. 41–3.

46. Boddy, *Boxing*, p. 110.

47. Sharman Kaddish, *A Good Jew or a Good Englishman? The Jewish Lads' and Girls' Brigade, 1895–1995* (London, 1995); Susan L. Tananbaum, 'Ironing out the Ghetto Bend: Sports, Character and Acculturation among Jewish Immigrants in Britain', *Journal of Sport History*, vol. 31 (2004), pp. 53–75.

48. *Jewish Year Book, 1903–4* (London, 1903), pp. 104–8.

49. J. Hollander, 'Sport in the East End', *World Jewry*, 14 November 1935.

50. Dee, *Sport and British Jewry*, pp. 44–7, 109–13; Jack Solomons, *Solomons Tells All* (London, 1951).

51. Jack Harding with Jack Berg, *Jack Kid Berg: The Whitechapel Windmill* (London, 1987), p. 24.

52. Morton Lewis, *Ted Kid Lewis: His Life and Times* (London, 1990), p. 3.

53. See ibid for the full life story.

54. Harding and Berg, *Jack Kid Berg*.

55. 'This is Your Life', Jack Kid Berg, originally broadcast in 1987, available at https://www.youtube.com/watch?v=Ae_yky14xtI

56. Ungar and Berkowitz, 'From Daniel Mendoza to Amir Khan', p. 8; Richard Holt and Tony Mason, *Sport in Britain 1945–2000* (Oxford, 2000), pp. 86, 144.

57. Various biographies and autobiographies of Frank Bruno have emerged including: Frank Bruno with Norman Giller, *Frank Bruno: From Zero to Hero* (London, 1996); and Frank Bruno with Kevin Mitchell, *Frank: Fighting Back* (London, 2005). See also: Jack Friedman and Laura Sanderson, 'British Champ Frank Bruno Steels Himself for Iron Mike', *People*, 20 February 1989; and Lucy Clarke-Billings, 'Boxing Legend Frank Bruno Admitted to Hospital after Bipolar Disorder Relapse', *Daily Telegraph*, 18 September 2015.

58. Ernest Cashmore, *Black Sportsmen* (London, 1982), p. 207.

59. Ibid., pp. 98–110.

60. Anthony Clavane, *Does Your Rabbi Know You're Here? The Story of English Football's Forgotten Tribe* (London, 2012), pp. 9–21, 27–48.

61. Ibid., pp. 21–6; Dee, *Sport and British Jewry*, pp. 94–5.

62. Phil Vasili, *Colouring Over the White Line: The History of Black Footballers in Britain* (London, 2000), pp. 17–27; Al Hamilton and Rodney Hinds, *Black Pearls of Soccer: The A–Z of Black Footballers in the English Game* (London, 1999), p. 8.

63. Hamilton and Hinds, *Black Pearls of Soccer*, pp. 8–9; Phil Vasili, 'Walter Daniel Tull, 1888–1918: Soldier, Footballer, Black', *Race and Class*, vol. 38 (1996), pp. 51–69.

64. Vasili, *Colouring Over the White Line*, pp. 61–7.

65. Ibid., pp. 126–54; Hamilton and Hinds, *Black Pearls of Soccer*, p. 9.

66. See the analysis in Vasili, *Colouring Over the White Line*, pp. 99–126.

67. Brian Belton, *The Black Hammers: The Voice of West Ham's Ebony Heroes* (Hove, 2006), pp. 1–13.

68. Ibid., pp. 23–41; Clyde Best with Andrew Warshaw, *The Acid Test: The Autobiography of Clyde Best* (Liverpool, 2016). The career statistics of Clive Charles and Ade Coker can be found on Barry Hugman's Footballers, http://hugmansfootballers.com

69. Conor Curran, *Irish Soccer Migrants: A Social and Cultural History* (Cork, 2017), pp. 105, 125, 127.

70. Connor Curran, 'Irish-born Players in England's Football Leagues, 1945–2010: An Historical and Geographical Assessment', *Sport in Society*, vol. 19 (2016), pp. 74–94; Richard Elliot, 'Football's Irish Exodus: Examining the Factors Influencing Irish Player

Migration to English Professional Leagues', *International Review for the Sociology of Sport*, vol. 51 (2016), pp. 147–61; Patrick McGovern, 'The Irish Brawn Drain: English League Clubs and Irish Footballers, 1946–1995', *British Journal of Sociology*, vol. 51 (2000), pp. 401–18; Ann Bourke, 'The Road to Fame and Fortune: Insights on the Career Paths of Young Irish Professional Footballers in England', *Journal of Youth Studies*, vol. 5 (2002), pp. 375–89.

71. Curran, *Irish Soccer Migrants*, pp. 128–35.

72. Stephen McGarrigle, *Green Gunners: Arsenal's Irish* (Edinburgh, 1991).

73. Liam Brady, *So Far so Good: A Decade in Football* (London, 1980), pp. 11–32.

74. Kevin O'Neill, *Where Have All the Irish Gone? The Sad Demise of Ireland's Once Relevant Footballers* (Worthing, 2017); Connor Curran, 'The Migration of Irish-Born Footballers to England, 1945–2010', *Soccer and Society*, vol. 16 (2015), pp. 367–9.

75. Seamus Kelly, 'The Migration of Irish Professional Footballers: The Good, the Bad and the Ugly', in Richard Elliott and John Harris, eds, *Football and Migration: Perspectives, Places, Players* (London, 2012), p. 77.

76. Pierre Lanfranchi and Matthew Taylor, *Moving with the Ball: The Migration of Professional Footballers* (Oxford, 2001); Magee and Sugden, ' "The World at their Feet" '; Giulianotti and Robertson, 'Globalization of Football'; McGovern, 'Globalization or Internationalization?'.

77. The table excludes Barnet and Wimbledon because they did not constitute part of the Football League and Premier League for the whole of the period under consideration.

78. Garry Robson, *'No One Likes Us, We Don't Care': The Myth and Reality of Millwall Fandom* (Oxford, 2000).

79. Glenda and Jack Rollin, *Sky Sports Football Yearbook, 2010–11* (London, 2010), pp. 449–51.

80. Joyce Woolridge, 'These Sporting Lives: Football Autobiographies 1945–1980', *Sport in History*, vol. 28 (2008), pp. 620–64; Matthew Taylor, 'From Source to Subject: Sport, History, and Autobiography', *Journal of Sport History*, vol. 35 (2008), pp. 469–91.

81. Villa, Miller and Ardiles, *And Still Ricky Villa*; Ossie Ardiles with Marcela Mora y Araujo, *Ossie's Dream: The Autobiography of a Football Legend* (London, 2009).

82. The first, Viv Anderson, came from Nottingham and made his name for Nottingham Forest, the club he played for during his England debut in 1978, although he starred for Arsenal from 1984 to 1987, for which see, for example, Emy Onuora, *Pitch Black: The Story of Black British Footballers* (London, 2015), pp. 29–36.

83. Dave Hill, *Out of His Skin: The John Barnes Phenomenon* (London, 1989), pp. 11–60; John Barnes, *The Autobiography* (London, 1999), pp. 7–108.

84. Barnes, *The Autobiography*, p. 93.

85. Oliver Derbyshire, *Thierry Henry: The Biography* (London, 2005); Philippe Auclair, *Thierry Henry: Lonely at the Top* (London, 2012).

86. Didier Drogba, *Commitment: My Autobiography* (London, 2015).

87. This phrase comes from Parminder Bhachu, *Twice Migrants: East African Sikh Settlers in Britain* (London, 1985), to describe those Sikhs who had moved from the Punjab to East Africa under the British Empire and then proceeded to Britain during the 1960s and 1970s.

88. Football Unites, Racism Divides, Ruth Johnson, Howard Holmes and Phil Vasili, 'South African Footballers in Britain', http://www.furd.org/default.asp?intPageID=22&intResourceID=90, accessed 7 November 2018.

89. Ian Wright, *Mr Wright: The Explosive Autobiography of Ian Wright* (London, 1996), pp. 33–67.

90. Ibid., pp. 101–8.

91. Ian Wright, *A Life in Football: My Autobiography* (London, 2016), Chapter 21.

92. James Leighton, *Rocky: The Tears and Triumphs of David Rocastle* (London, 2016), pp. 12–13.

93. Ibid., *passim*.

94. See especially: Marc Matera, *Black London: The Imperial Metropolis and Decolonization in the Twentieth Century* (Berkeley, CA, 2015); and Kennetta Hammond Perry, *London is the Place for Me: Black Britons, Citizenship and the Politics of Race* (Oxford, 2016).

95. Belton, *Black Hammers*.

96. I have developed these statistics by utilizing the player profiles provided by Hamilton and Hinds, *Black Pearls of Soccer*. In addition to the twelve teams listed in Table 4 these authors also count Barnet and Wimbledon.

97. The rather simplistic account in Onuora, *Pitch Black*, pp. 37–48, does not point this out.

98. Simon Astaire, *Sol Campbell: The Authorised Biography* (London, 2014).

99. Wesley Clarkson, *Rio Five Star: The Biography* (London, 2014); Stephen Bourne, *Speak of Me as I Am: The Black Presence in Southwark Since 1600* (London, 2005), pp. 84–5.

100. For black players see Cashmore, *Black Sportsmen*.

101. Leroy Rosenior, *'It's Only Banter': The Autobiography of Leroy Rosenior* (Worthing, 2017), pp. 21–57.

102. Ibid., p. 87.

103. Ibid., pp. 79–94.

104. Daniel Burdsey, 'Obstacle Race? "Race", Racism and the Recruitment of British Asian Professional Footballers', *Patterns of Prejudice*, vol. 38 (2004), pp. 279–80.

105. Daniel Kilvington, 'British Asians and Football: How the "Beautiful Game" Needs to Change', *The Conversation*, 29 November 2017.

106. See Chapter 1 above.

107. Daniel Kilvington, *British Asians, Exclusion and the Football Industry* (London, 2016), pp. 101–2.

108. See Daniel Burdsey, *British Asians and Football: Culture, Identity and Exclusion* (Abingdon, 2018), pp. 16–31.

109. Jas Bains and Sanjeev Johal, *Corner Flags and Corner Shops* (London, 1998), pp. 33–50.

110. Kilvington, *British Asians*, pp. 101–2.

111. Cypriot Football League of England, http://www.kopaleague.com/l/fg/1_481600611.html, accessed 8 November 2018; Clavane, *Does Your Rabbi Know You're Here?*, pp. 135–6.

112. Burdsey, *British Asians and Football*, pp. 46–53.

113. Sports People's Think Tank and Network Fare, 'Ethnic Minorities and Coaching in Elite Level Football in England: A Call to Action', 2014, http://thesptt.com/wp-content/uploads/2015/10/We-speak-with-one-voice-REPORT.pdf, accessed 8 November 2018; Steven Bradbury, 'Institutional Racism, Whiteness and the Under-Representation of Minorities in Leadership Positions in Football in Europe', *Soccer & Society*, vol. 14 (2013), pp. 296–314; Onuora, *Pitch Black*, pp. 241–64; Hamilton and Hinds, *Black Pearls of Soccer*, pp. 18–19.

114. Dee, *Sport and British Jewry*, pp. 13, note, 32, 96–9; Clavane, *Does Your Rabbi Know You're Here?*, pp. 90–7; John Efron, 'When is a Yid Not a Jew? The Strange Case of Supporter Identity at Tottenham Hotspur', in Brenner and Reuveni, *Emancipation through Muscles*, pp. 235–56; Emma Poulton, 'Towards Understanding: Antisemitism and the Contested Uses and Meanings of "Yid" in English Football', *Ethnic and Racial Studies*, vol. 39 (2016), pp. 1,981–2,001.

115. David Ranc, *Foreign Players and Football Supporters: The Old Firm, Arsenal, Paris Saint-German* (Manchester, 2012), pp. 129–62.

116. *Evening Standard*, 14 August 2018.

117. AFTV, https://www.youtube.com/channel/UCBTy8j2cPy6zw68godcE7MQ, accessed 9 November 2018.

118. Brett Bebber, *Violence and Racism in Football* (London, 2012); Les Back, Tim Crabbe and John Solomos, *The Changing Face of Football: Racism, Identity and Multiculture in the English Game* (Oxford, 2001); Cass Pennant, *Cass* (London, 2008); Ignacio Ramos Gay, ' "Black Blokes Who Spoke Like East-Enders": Nation, Race and Hooliganism in Cass Pennant's *Cass*', *Journal of Postcolonial Writing*, vol. 52 (2016), pp. 13–25; Jon Garland and Michael Rowe, *Racism and Anti-Racism in Football* (Basingstoke, 2001); Jack Fawbert, ' "Wot, No Asians?" West Ham United Fandom, the Cockney Diaspora and the "New" East Enders', in Daniel Burdsey, ed., *Race, Ethnicity and Football: Persisting Debates and Emergent Issues* (Abingdon, 2012), pp. 175–90.

CHAPTER 11

1. Wilhelm Ganz, *Memories of a Musician* (London, 1913), p. 119.
2. Gilbert Guerdon, 'Street Musicians', *Strand Magazine*, vol. 3 (1892), p. 65.
3. Lord Kitchener, 'London is the Place for Me', 1948, from Island Lyrics, http://www.island-lyrics.com/lyrics-lord_kitchener_lyrics-london_is_the_place_for_me_1960s.htm, accessed 28 November 2018.
4. For the mobility of musicians see Angèle David-Guillou, 'Early Musicians' Unions in Britain, France, and the United States: On the Possibilities and Impossibilities of Transnational Militant Transfers in an International Industry', *Labour History Review*, vol. 74 (2009), pp. 293–4.
5. Paul Gilroy, *The Black Atlantic: Modernity and Double Consciousness* (London, 1993).
6. For an introduction to the relationship between migration and cultural transfer in Britain see Stefan Manz and Panikos Panayi, 'Refugees and Cultural Transfer to Britain: An Introduction', in Stefan Manz and Panikos Panayi, eds, *Refugees and Cultural Transfers to Britain* (Abingdon, 2013), pp. 2–31.
7. Letter from Richard Wagner to Franz Liszt, 16 May 1855, in Frances Hueffer, ed., *Correspondence of Wagner and Liszt*, vol. 2 (London, 1881), pp. 84–7.
8. Richard Wagner, *Das Judenthum in der Musik* (Leipzig, 1869).
9. Wagner to Liszt, 16 May 1855, pp. 84–5.
10. Daniel Defoe, *Augusta Triumphans: Or, the Way to Make London the Most Flourishing City in the Universe* (London, 1728), pp. 16–23.
11. See below, pp. 292–5.
12. Martin Cloonan and Matt Brennan, 'Alien Invasions: The British Musicians' Union and Foreign Musicians', *Popular Music*, vol. 32 (2013), pp. 279–82.
13. See the relevant, undated, edition of the *Musicians Journal* in NA/LAB2/1188/EDAR528/1929.
14. NA/LAB2/1188/EDAR528/1929, Mr Reid, Admission of Alien Bands, 14 October 1930.
15. Cloonan and Brennan, 'Alien Invasions'; David-Guillou, 'Early Musicians' Unions'.
16. See, for example: Nicholas Temperley, 'Xenophilia in British Musical History', in Bennett Zon, ed., *Nineteenth-Century British Musical Studies*, vol. 1 (Aldershot, 1999), pp. 3–19; Andrew Blake, *The Land without Music* (Manchester, 1977); Jon Stratton, *When Music Migrates: Crossing British and European Racial Faultlines, 1945–2010* (London, 2016); Nabeel Zuberi, *Sounds English: Transnational Popular Music* (Chicago, IL, 2001).
17. Tabitha Bolam, 'Class and the Reception of European Street Musicians in Victorian London' (unpublished De Montfort University BA History dissertation, 2016).
18. Thomas Burke, *Nights in Town: A London Autobiography* (London, 1915), pp. 36–9. Dave Russell, *Popular Music in England, 1840–1914*, 2nd edn (Manchester, 1997), pp. 105–67, provides a good introduction to music hall performers, audiences, the importance of London in their evolution, as well as a nuanced analysis of the meaning of songs.
19. James J. Nott, *Music for the People: Popular Music and Dance in Interwar Britain* (Oxford, 2002). See also the description of the evolution of jazz below.
20. Judith R. Walkowitz, *Nights Out: Life in Cosmopolitan London* (London, 2012).
21. See the description of their role in Reginald Nettel, *The Orchestra in England: A Social History* (London, 1946), p. 17.
22. Cyril Ehrlich, *The Music Profession in Britain since the Eighteenth Century: A Social History* (Oxford, 1985), pp. 4–6; Betty Matthews, *The Royal Society of Musicians of Great Britain: A List of Members, 1738–1984* (London, 1985), pp. 1–3; Deborah Rohr, *The Careers of British Musicians 1750–1850: A Profession of Artisans* (Cambridge, 2001), pp. 9–19, 41–51; Simon McVeigh, *Concert Life in London from Mozart to Haydn* (Cambridge, 1993), pp. 3–7; C. F. Pohl, *Mozart und Haydn in London*, 2 vols, vol. 1 (Vienna, 1867), pp. 3–6.
23. Cyril Ehrlich, *First Philharmonic: A History of the Royal Philharmonic Society* (Oxford, 1995); Robert Elkin, *Royal Philharmonic: The Annals of the Royal Philharmonic Society*

(London, 1946); George Hogarth, *The Philharmonic Society of London* (London, 1862); Myles Birket Foster, *The History of the Philharmonic Society of London, 1813–1912* (London, 1912).

24. Ehrlich, *Music Profession*.

25. Paul Rodmell, *Opera in the British Isles, 1875–1918* (Farnham, 2013), Chapters 2–3.

26. Burke, *Nights in Town*, pp. 131–3.

27. Rohr, *Careers of British Musicians*, pp. 29–30.

28. See the list in Foster, *History of the Philharmonic Society*, pp. 5–6.

29. Ibid., pp. 5–7.

30. Panikos Panayi, *German Immigrants in Britain during the Nineteenth Century* (Oxford, 1995), p. 130.

31. Simon McVeigh, 'Italian Violinists in Eighteenth-Century London', in Reinhard Strohm, ed., *The Eighteenth-Century Diaspora of Italian Music and Musicians* (Turnhout, 2001), pp. 139–76.

32. Simon McVeigh, 'Felice Giardini: A Violinist in Late Eighteenth-Century London', *Music & Letters*, vol. 64 (1983), pp. 162–72.

33. Warwick Lister, *Amico: The Life of Giovanni Battista Viotti* (Oxford, 2009); Rohan H. Stewart-MacDonald, 'Viotti as Concert and Operatic Manager during his "First" London Period (1792–1798)', in Massimiliano Sala, ed., *Giovanni Battista Viotti: A Composer Between Two Revolutions* (Bologna, 2006), pp. 121–54.

34. Leon Plantinga, *Clementi: His Life and Music* (London, 1977).

35. Fiona M. Palmer, *Domenico Dragonetti in England (1794–1846): The Career of a Double Bass Virtuoso* (Oxford, 1997).

36. Benjamin Walton, 'Rara Avis or Fuzzy Turnip: Rossini as Celebrity in 1820s London', in Tom Mole, ed., *Romanticism and Celebrity Culture, 1750–1850* (Cambridge, 2009), pp. 81–101.

37. F. Anne M. R. Jarvis, 'German Musicians in London, c. 1750–1850', in Stefan Manz, Margrit Schulte Beerbühl and John R. Davis, eds, *Migration and Transfer from Germany to Britain, 1660–1914* (Munich, 2007), pp. 37–47; Herma Fiedler, 'German Musicians in England and their Influence to the End of the Eighteenth Century', *German Life and Letters*, vol. 4 (1939), pp. 7–11; Simon McVeigh, *The Violinist in London's Concert Life, 1750–1914: Felice Giardini and his Contemporaries* (London, 1989), pp. 89–90.

38. Fiedler, 'German Musicians in England', pp. 6–11; P. Robinson, *Handel and his Orbit* (London, 1908); John Mainwaring, *Memoirs of the Life of the Late George Friedrich Handel* (London, 1760); Donald Burrows, *Handel*, 2nd edn (Oxford, 2012); Jonathan Keates, *Handel: The Man & His Music* (London, 2008); Nicholas Temperley, 'Handel's Influence on English Music', *Monthly Musical Record*, vol. 100 (1960), pp. 163–74.

39. Leo Hughes, 'The Mozarts' London', in John Glowacki, ed., *Paul A. Pisk: Essays in His Honour* (Austin, TX, 1966), pp. 103–15; Pohl, *Mozart und Haydn in London*, pp. 93–149.

40. *English Musical Gazette and Monthly Intelligencer*, 1 March, 1 April, 1 May 1819; Christopher Roscoe, 'Haydn and London in the 1780s', *Music and Letters*, vol. 49 (1968), pp. 203–12; H. V. F. Somerset, 'Joseph Haydn in England', *Music and Letters*, vol. 13 (1932), pp. 272–85; Pohl, *Mozart und Haydn in London*, vol. 2.

41. See, for example, Frances Hueffer, *Half a Century of Music in London* (London, 1889), p. 29; Wilhelm Kuhe, *My Musical Recollections* (London, 1896).

42. Hueffer, *Half a Century of Music in London*, pp. 63–73.

43. Nettel, *Orchestra in England*, p. 220.

44. Ehrlich, *First Philharmonic*; Foster, *History of the Philharmonic Society*.

45. C. E. and Marie Halle, *Life and Letters of Sir Charles Halle: Being an Autobiography with Correspondence and Diaries* (London, 1896), pp. 92–7; Michael Kennedy, 'Hallé, Sir Charles', *Oxford Dictionary of National Biography*, https://doi.org/10.1093/ref:odnb/12006, accessed 20 November 2018.

46. Nettel, *Orchestra in England*, pp. 222–6.

47. Michael Musgrave, *The Musical Life of Crystal Palace* (Cambridge, 1995).

48. John Goulden, *Michael Costa: England's First Conductor: The Revolution in Musical Performance in England, 1830–1880* (London, 2016); Michael Musgrave, 'Changing Values in Nineteenth-Century Performance: The Work of Michael Costa and August Manns', in Christina Bashford and Leanne Langley, eds, *Music and British Culture, 1785–1914: Essays in Honour of Cyril Ehrlich* (Oxford, 2000), pp. 169–91; 'Mr August Manns', *Musical Times and Singing Class Circular*, vol. 39 (1898), pp. 153–9.

49. McVeigh, *The Violinist in London's Concert Life*, pp. 99–106.

50. Kuhe, *My Musical Recollections*.

51. W. C. Berwick Sayers, *Samuel Coleridge Taylor Musician: His Life and Letters* (London, 1915); Jeffrey Green, *Samuel Coleridge Taylor, a Musical Life* (London, 2011).

52. Erik Levi, 'The German-Jewish Contribution to Musical Life in Britain', in Werner E. Mosse, et al., eds, *Second Chance: Two Centuries of German-Speaking Jews in the United Kingdom* (Tübingen, 1991), pp. 275–95; Charmian Brinson and Richard Dove, *Politics by Other Means: The Free German League of Culture in London 1939–1946* (London, 2010), pp. 92–106; Carole Rosen, 'Lind [married name Lind-Goldschmidt], Jenny [Johanna Maria]', *Oxford Dictionary of National Biography*, https://doi.org/10.1093/ref:odnb/16671, accessed 21 November 2018.

53. Bolam, 'Class and the Reception of European Street Musicians', pp. 25–39; Panayi, *German Immigrants*, pp. 219–21; J. Cuthbert Halden, 'The Regulation of Street Music', *Nineteenth Century*, vol. 39 (1896), pp. 950–6; Michael T. Bass, *Street Music in the Metropolis: Correspondence and Observations on the Existing Law, and Proposed Amendments* (London, 1864); Lucio Sponza, *Italian Immigrants in Nineteenth-Century Britain* (Leicester, 1988), pp. 141–9; Charity Organization Society, *Report of the Committee of the Charity Organisation Society Appointed to Inquire into the Employment of Italian Children for Mendicant and Immoral Purposes* (London, 1877); Charles Babbage, *Passages from the Life of a Philosopher* (London, 1864), pp. 337–62.

54. Charles Manby Smith, 'Music Grinders of the Metropolis', *Chambers's Edinburgh Journal*, vol. 17 (1852), pp. 197–201.

55. Babbage, *Passages*, p. 339.

56. Gilbert Guerdon, 'Street Musicians', *Strand Magazine*, vol. 3 (1892), pp. 64–72.

57. Halden, 'Regulation of Street Music', p. 953.

58. Henry Mayhew, *London Labour and the London Poor*, vol. 3 (originally 1861; London, 1968), pp. 171–7.

59. Ibid., pp. 185–9.

60. Guerdon, 'Street Musicians', p. 67.

61. Mayhew, *London Labour*, pp. 177–81.

62. John Zucchi, *Little Slaves of the Harp: Italian Child Street Musicians in Nineteenth-Century Paris, London and New York* (London, 1992); 'The Italian Organ-Grinder', *Charity Organisation Review*, vol. 10 (1894), pp. 407–13; Sponza, *Italian Immigrants*, pp. 31–51, 54, 141–61.

63. J. Thompson and Adolphe Smith, *Street Life in London* (London, 1877), p. 87.

64. Guerdon, 'Street Musicians', pp. 66–7.

65. Russell, *Popular Music in England*, pp. 205–47.

66. *London City Mission Magazine*, 2 January 1865.

67. Guerdon, 'Street Musicians', p. 10.

68. Mayhew, *London Labour*, vol. 3, p. 164.

69. Panayi, *German Immigrants*, p. 128.

70. As a general introduction to black music in twentieth-century Britain, focused upon London, see: Paul Oliver, ed., *Black Music in Britain* (Milton Keynes, 1990); Jon Stratton and Nabeel Zuberi, eds, *Black Popular Music in Britain since 1945* (London, 2016); and Lloyd Bradley, *Sounds like London: 100 Years of Black Music in the Capital* (London, 2013).

71. Rodriguez King-Dorset, *Black Dance in London, 1730–1850: Innovation, Tradition and Resistance* (London, 2008); Peter Fryer, *Staying Power: The History of Black People in Britain* (London, 1984), pp. 79–88.

72. John Thomas Smith, *The Cries of London* (London, 1839), p. 51.

73. Mayhew, *London Labour*, pp. 190–4; George F. Rehin, 'Blackface Street Minstrels in Victorian London and its Resorts: Popular Culture and its Racial Connotations as Revealed in Polite Opinion', *Journal of Popular Culture*, vol. 15 (1981), pp. 19–38; Derek B. Scott, *Sounds of the Metropolis* (Oxford, 2011), pp. 144–70; Michael Pickering, *Blackface Minstrelsy in Britain* (Aldershot, 2008); *Independent*, 28 August 1992.

74. Toni P. Anderson, *'Tell Them We Are Singing for Jesus': The Original Fisk Jubilee Singers and Christian Reconstruction, 1871–1878* (Macon, GA, 2010), pp. 117–20; J. B. T. Marsh, *The Story of the Jubilee Singers with their Songs*, rev edn (Boston, MA, 1880), pp. 1–47.

75. Anderson, *Tell Them We Are Singing for Jesus'*, p. 122.

76. Andrew Ward, *Dark Midnight When I Rise: The Story of the Jubilee Singers, Who Introduced the World to the Music of Black America* (New York, 2001), pp. 201–9.

77. Stephen Bourne, *Speak of Me As I Am: The Black Presence in Southwark since 1600* (London, 2005), pp. 32–3.

78. Ward, *Dark Midnight When I Rise*, pp. 216–28.

79. Bourne, *Speak of Me as I Am*, p. 33; Marsh, *The Story of the Jubilee Singers*, pp. 58–74.

80. Marsh, *The Story of the Jubilee Singers*, pp. 75–100; Anderson, *'Tell Them We Are Singing for Jesus'*, pp. 130–1.

81. Bourne, *Speak of Me as I Am*, pp. 36–41; Jeffrey Green, *Black Edwardians: Black People in Britain,1901–1914* (London, 1988), pp. 80–114.

82. Marc Matera, *Black London: The Imperial Metropolis and Decolonization in the Twentieth Century* (Oakland, CA, 2015), pp. 145, 149–50.

83. Charlotte Breese, *Hutch* (London, 1999).

84. Martin Duberman, *Paul Robeson* (London, 1989), pp. 87–125; Matera, *Black London*, pp. 286–98; Sean Creighton, 'Paul Robeson's British Journey', in Neil A. Wynn, ed., *Cross the Water Blues: African American Music in Europe* (Jackson, MI, 2007), pp. 112–27; Jan Carew, 'Paul Robeson and W. E. B. Du Bois in London', *Race & Class*, vol. 46 (2004), pp. 39–48; Colin Holmes, *John Bull's Island: Immigration and British Society, 1871–1971* (Basingstoke, 1988), p. 153.

85. Jeffrey Green, 'Afro-American Symphony: Popular Black Concert Hall Peformers', in Oliver, *Black Music in Britain*, pp. 36–43.

86. John Cowley, 'uBungca (Oxford Bags): Recordings in London of African and West Indian Music in the 1920s and 1930s', *Musical Traditions*, no. 12 (Summer 1994), pp. 13–26.

87. Howard Rye, 'Fearsome Means of Discord: Early Encounters with Black Jazz', in Oliver, *Black Music in Britain*, pp. 46–8.

88. Catherine Parsonage, *The Evolution of Jazz in Britain, 1880–1935* (Aldershot, 2005), pp. 122–62.

89. See, for example: Hilary Moore, *Inside British Jazz: Crossing Borders of Race and Class* (Abingdon, 2016); and Roberta Freund Schwartz, *How Britain Got the Blues: The Transmission and Reception of American Blues Style in the United Kingdom* (Aldershot, 2007).

90. Matera, *Black London*, pp. 145–99; Andrew Simons, 'Black British Swing: The African Diaspora's Contribution to England's Own Jazz of the 1930s and 1940s', in Andy Linehan, ed., *Aural History: Essays on Recorded Sound* (London, 2001), pp. 117–38; Leslie Thompson with Jeffrey Green, *Swing from a Small Island: The Story of Leslie Thompson* (London, 2009); Catherine Parsonage, 'Fascination and Fear: Responses to Early Jazz in Britain', in Wynn, *Cross the Water Blues*, pp. 84–96; Jason Toynbee, Catherine Tackley and Mark Doffman, 'Another Place, Another Race? Thinking Through Jazz, Ethnicity and Diaspora in Britain', in Jason Toynbee, Catherine Tackley and Mark Doffman, eds, *Black British Jazz: Rules, Ownership and Performance* (Aldershot, 2014), pp. 2–6; Bradley, *Sounds like London*, pp. 91–129.

91. John Fordham, *Ronnie Scott's at Fifty* (Loughton, 2009).

92. In addition to Parsonage, *The Evolution of Jazz in Britain*, and Schwarz, *How Britain Got the Blues*, the key works on the history of jazz in Britain are David Boulton, *Jazz in Britain* (London, 1958), and two volumes by Jim Goldbolt, *A History of Jazz in Britain, 1919–50* (London, 1984) and *A History of Jazz in Britain 1950–1970* (London, 1989). The transatlantic transmission of jazz receives attention in contributions to Wynn, *Cross the Water Blues*.

93. Zuberi, *Sounds English*, pp. 1–130; Paul du Noyer, *In the City: A Celebration of London Music* (London, 2009).

94. John Cowley, 'London is the Place: Caribbean Music in the Context of Empire, 1900–60', in Oliver, *Black Music in Britain*, pp. 58–76; Hugh Hodges, 'Kitchener Invades England: The London Calypsos of Aldwyn Roberts', *Wasafiri*, vol. 20 (June 2005), pp. 24–30.

95. Tom Chatburn, 'Trinidad All Stars: The Steel Pan Movement in Britain', in Oliver, *Black Music in Britain*, pp. 118–36.

96. Heather Augustyn, *Ska: The Rhythm of Liberation* (Plymouth, 2013); Stratton, *When Music Migrates*, pp. 37–58.

97. Bradley, *Sounds like London*, pp. 209–54; Simon Jones, *Black Culture, White Youth: The Reggae Tradition from JA to UK* (Basingstoke, 1988); 'Reggae: The Rhythm of Roots', *Sunday Times Magazine*, 28 August 1989.

98. Hattie Collins, *This is Grime* (London, 2016); Dan Hancox, *Inner City Pressure: The Story of Grime* (London, 2018).

99. *Guardian*, 23 May 2004, 2 August 2017.

100. Alex Kitts, *Dizzee Rascal: Tales from Da Corner* (London, 2001); Paul Lester, *Bonkers: The Story of Dizzee Rascal* (London, 2010).

101. Bazil Meade, *A Boy, a Journey, a Dream: The Story of Bazil Meade and the London Community Gospel Choir* (Oxford, 2011); Steve Alexander Smith, *British Black Gospel: The Foundations of this Vibrant UK Sound* (Oxford, 2009).

102. See Andrekos Varnava, 'Yusuf Islam (aka Cat Stevens) and his Anti-War and Pro-Peace Protest Songs: From Hippy Peace to Islamic Peace', *Contemporary British History* (published online 3 October 2018).

103. There are many biographies of George Michael including Emily Herbert, *George Michael: The Life 1963–2016* (New York, 2017).

104. Edward Nicholas Philip Marshall, 'Ambivalent Images: A Survey of Jewish Involvement and Representation in the British Entertainment Industry,1880–1980' (unpublished Royal Holloway, University of London PhD thesis, 2010); Sandra Caron, *Alma Cogan: A Memoir* (London, 1991).

105. Heinrich Dorgeel, *Die Deutsche Colonie in London* (London, 1881), pp. 70–3.

106. Stephen Graham, *Twice Round the London Clock, and, More London Nights* (London, 1933), pp. 98–104.

107. Patria Roman-Velazquez, *The Making of Latin London: Salsa Music, Place, and Identity* (Aldershot, 1999).

108. Reginald Richard Hall, 'Irish Music and Dance in London 1890–1970: A Sociocultural History' (unpublished University of Sussex PhD thesis, 1994); Rebecca S. Miller, 'Hucklebucking at the Tea Dances: Irish Showbands in Britain, 1959–1969', *Popular Music History*, vol. 9 (2014), pp. 225–47.

109. David Greer, 'Dowland, John (1563?–1626)', *Oxford Dictionary of National Biography*, https://doi-org.proxy.library.dmu.ac.uk/10.1093/ref:odnb/7962, accessed 28 November 2018; F. A. Fahy and D. J. O'Donoghue, *Ireland in London* (Dublin, 1889), pp. 16, 42, 43, 44, 47, 65, 73, 83, 87, 136, 139, 143.

110. Sean Campbell, *'Irish Blood, English Heart': Second-Generation Irish Musicians in England* (Cork, 2011).

111. Swadhinata Trust, 'A History of Bengali Music and Musicians in the UK', https://www.swadhinata.org.uk/a-history-of-bengali-music-and-musicians-in-the-uk, accessed 28 November 2018; Zuberi, *Sounds English*, pp. 181–236; Rehan Hyder, *Brimful of Asia: Negotiating Ethnicity on the UK Music Scene* (Aldershot, 2004); Gurharpal Singh and Darshan Singh Tatla, *Sikhs in Britain: The Making of a Community* (London, 2006), pp. 198–204; Sabita Banerji and Gerd Baumann, 'Bhangra 1984–8: Fusion and Professionalization in a Genre of South Asian Dance Music', in Oliver, *Black Music in Britain*, pp. 137–52; Gurdeep Khabra, 'Music in the Margins? Popular Music Heritage and British Bhangra Music', *International Journal of Heritage Studies*, vol. 20 (2014), pp. 343–55.

CHAPTER 12

1. Greater London Authority, *The World in a City: An Analysis of the 2001 Census Results* (London, 2005), pp. 19, 70–1.
2. Centre for Analysis of Social Exclusion, *Gentrification of London: A Progress Report, 2001–13* (London, 2016), makes no mention of race or ethnicity, a gap which exists in all literature on London gentrification.
3. Kirsty Carpenter, *Refugees of the French Revolution: Émigrés in London, 1789–1802* (Basingstoke, 1999).
4. Alice Bloch, *The Migration and Settlement of Refugees in Britain* (Basingstoke, 2002).
5. Donall MacAmlaigh, *An Irish Navvy: The Diary of an Exile* (originally London, 1964; Cork, 2018, reprint).
6. Clair Wills, *An Immigrant History of Post-War Britain* (London, 2017), pp. 123–40.
7. The best exponent of this basically positive narrative consists of W. D. Rubinstein, *A History of the Jews in the English-Speaking World: Great Britain* (Basingstoke, 1996), pp. 94–427.
8. Greater London Authority, *The World in a City*, pp. 70–1.
9. Martin Roderick, *The Work of Professional Football: A Labour of Love?* (Abingdon, 2006).
10. See Kathleen Paul, *Whitewashing Britain: Race and Citizenship in the Post-War Era* (Ithaca, NY, 1997).

BIBLIOGRAPHY

ARCHIVAL MATERIAL

BISHOPSGATE INSTITUTE

ROTH/5/4, List of Jews in the 1987–1992 Parliament.

JEWISH MUSEUM LONDON

1983/370, 'Bloom with Good Food'.
1986.136.4, 'Menu from Sam Stern's Hotel and Kosher Restaurant, 1930–9'.
1986.136.11.1, 'Sam Stern, Kosher Caterer'.
1988.525.1, 'Our East London: How We Came Here', First Bulletin issued by the School's Committee of the Council of Citizens of E. London', Winter 1949.
1988.525.2, 'Our East London: The Growth of Its Religions', Second Bulletin issued by the School's Committee of the Council of Citizens of E. London', Spring 1950.
1990.10, '100 Years in the Baking: Leaflet Produced in the Centenary Year of the Grodzinksi Bakery, Telling their Story', 1988.

KING'S COLLEGE LONDON, GREEK DIASPORA ARCHIVE

GDA/7/AV1, BBC TV Documentary film entitled *Minorities in Britain: The Cypriot Community*, 1966.

LONDON METROPOLITAN ARCHIVES

Acc/1888/398, London Council of Social Services, 'East Pakistanis in London', 1967.
Acc/2805, Office of the Chief Rabbi.
Acc/3527/384, *Wimpy Times*, Spring 1971.
CLA/003/PR/04/003, Correspondence and Papers Relating to Styllou Christofi.
CLC/B/186, Ralli Brothers Limited.
GLC/DG/PUB/01/159/1464, 'Policy Report on the Irish Community', 1984.

NATIONAL ARCHIVES, LONDON

Board of Trade, BT31.
Colonial Office, CO67, CO876.
Dominions Office and Commonwealth Relations Office, DO35.
Foreign and Commonwealth Office, FCO37.
Home Office, HO1, HO334, HO376.
Metropolitan Police, MEPO2.
Ministry of Labour, LAB2.
Prisoners and Prison Staff, PCOM.

TOWER HAMLETS LOCAL HISTORY ARCHIVE

I/AVU/A/11/4, Publications of the Bangladeshi Youth Front.
LC502, Danielle Lamarche, 'Housing Needs of Bangladeshis in Tower Hamlets', 1986.
P/RAM, Personal Papers of Edith Ramsey.

ORAL HISTORY SOURCES

BISHOPSGATE INSTITUTE

Constructing Post-War Britain
    CPWB/1/5, Interview with Noel Clarke, 2011.
    CPWB/1/4, Interview with Michael Houlihan, 2011.
    CPWB/1/8, Interview with Tony McGing, 2011.
    CPWB/4/1, Interview with Jim McDonald, 2012.

BRITISH LIBRARY, NATIONAL SOUND ARCHIVE

National Life Story Collection, 'From Source to Salespoint', Interview with Peter Jacomelli, 2000.

EASTSIDE COMMUNITY HERITAGE PROJECT

Redbridge Nurses Project, 2000_esch_nurs_01, Judith Garfield interview of Ruth Barnett, 6 September 2000.
Ugandan Asians Project, 2013_esch_UgAs_16, Interview with Keshavji Mandali, 12 March 2013.

INTERVIEWS CARRIED OUT BY PANIKOS PANAYI

Interview with Jessica Gould, 13 April 2004.
Interview with Das Sreedharan, 9 June 2004.

JEWISH MUSEUM LONDON

Oral History Collection Transcript 17, Interview with Henry Goldring, 21 May 1985.

BIBLIOGRAPHY

Oral History Collection Transcript 99, Interview of Albert Booth by Mark Burman, 5 October 1987.
Oral History Collection Transcript 231, Interview of Leon Aelion by Judith Evans, 4 March 1992.
Oral History Collection Transcript 233, Interview of Sophie and David Elias by Judith Devons, 10 March 1992.
Oral History Collection Transcript 370, Interview with Sid Spellman, n.d.

MUSEUM OF LONDON, ORAL HISTORY COLLECTION

93/120, Interview by Rory O'Connell of Ajit Rai, 23 March 1993.
93/131, Interview with Handley Best, n.d.
93.132, Interview by Rory O'Connell of Elma Sampson, 30 April 1993.
99.35, Interview by Alan Dein of Vincent Reid, April 1998.
99.87, Interview by Irna Imran of Iftikhar Din, 30 March 1998.

TOWER HAMLETS LOCAL HISTORY ARCHIVE

O/BEE/7, The Bengali East End, Interview with Osmar Gani, October 2011.

PRINTED WORKS

OFFICIAL PUBLICATIONS

1911 Census General Report with Appendices, Table 109, http://www.visionofbritain.org.uk/census/table/EW1911GEN_M109, accessed 9 July 2018.
Census of England and Wales, 1901, Summary Tables, Area, Housing and Population (London, 1903).
Census of England and Wales, 1911: Birthplaces (London, 1915).
Commission for Racial Equality, *Living in Terror: A Report on Racial Harassment in Housing* (London, 1987).
First Report of the Select Committee of the House of Lords on the Sweating System (London, 1888).
GLA Economics, *The Contribution of Asian-Owned Businesses to London's Economy* (London, 2005).
GLA Intelligence, *Census Information Scheme, Local Areas of Ethnic Group Concentration* (London, 2014).
Greater London Authority, *London Divided: Income, Inequality and Poverty in the Capital* (London, 2002).
Greater London Authority, *Londoners Born Overseas, Their Age and Year of Arrival* (London, 2013).
Greater London Authority, *The World in a City: An Analysis of the 2001 Census Results* (London, 2005).
House of Commons, Second Report from the Home Affairs Committee, Session 1984–5, *Chinese Community in Britain*, vol. 1, *Report together with Proceedings of the Committee* (London, 1985).
Kelly's Post Office Directory for London 1984 (London, 1984).
Kelly's Post Office London Directory (London, 1975).
London Correspondent of the Board of Trade, *Report of the Board of Trade on the Sweating System at the East End of London* (London, 1887).
London Development Agency, *Redefining London's BME-Owned Businesses* (London, 2005).

London Strategic Policy Unit, *Black Councillors in Britain* (London, 1987).

Lord Scarman, *The Scarman Report: The Brixton Disorders, 10–12 April 1981* (Harmondsworth, 1982).

MacPherson, Sir William, *The Stephen Lawrence Inquiry* (London, 1999).

Naturalization Act of 1870.

Office for National Statistics, 'Ethnicity and National Identity in England and Wales: 2011', https://www.ons.gov.uk/peoplepopulationandcommunity/culturalidentity/ethnicity/articles/ethnicityandnationalidentityinenglandandwales/2012-12-11, accessed 16 July 2018.

Post Office London Directory, 1913 (London, 1913).

Post Office London Directory with County Suburbs for 1923 (London, 1923).

Post Office London Directory for 1954 (London, 1954).

Report of the Official Account of the Bombings in London on 7th July 2005 (London, 2006).

Report of the Royal Commission on Alien Immigration (London, 1903).

Tower Hamlets Research Briefing, *Ethnicity in Tower Hamlets: Analysis of 2011 Census Data*, https://www.towerhamlets.gov.uk/Documents/Borough_statistics/Ward_profiles/Census-2011/RB-Census2011-Ethnicity-2013-01.pdf, accessed 26 January 2018.

NEWSPAPERS, PERIODICALS AND YEARBOOKS

Caterer
Caterer's Journal
Charity Organisation Review
Chelsea FC Official Matchday Programme
Cyprus Mail
Daily Mail
Daily Telegraph
English Musical Gazette and Monthly Intelligencer
Evening Standard
Fach-Zeitung des Bundes Deutscher Köche
Fast Food
Financial Times
Food and Cookery
Food Journal
Good Food Guide
Guardian
Hampstead and Highgate Express
Hermann
Hotel Review
Jewish Chronicle
Jewish Review and Advertiser
London City Mission Magazine
London Hotel and Restaurant Employees Gazette
Londoner Courier
Londoner General Anzeiger
Manchester Guardian
Morning Chronicle
Musical Times and Singing Class Circular
Observer
Observer Food Monthly
Parikiaki
Le Parisien
People
Restaurant

Restaurant Trade Journal
Revue
Rothmans Football Yearbook
Sunday Times
Sunday Times Rich List
Time Out
The Times
TLS
World Jewry

AUTOBIOGRAPHIES, BIOGRAPHIES, BIOGRAPHICAL SKETCHES AND MEMOIRS

Abdullah, Hatice and Sinker, Mark, *Departures and Arrivals: Turkish Cypriots who Came to England between 1934 and 1963* (London, 2006).

Adams, Caroline, *Across Seven Seas and Thirteen Rivers: Life Stories of Pioneer Sylheti Settlers in Britain* (London, 1987).

Alderman, Geoffrey, 'Wolfson, Sir Isaac, First Baronet', *Oxford Dictionary of National Biography*, https://doi.org/10.1093/ref:odnb/50705, accessed 24 May 2018.

Ardiles, Ossie with Araujo, Marcela Mora y, *Ossie's Dream: The Autobiography of a Football Legend* (London, 2009).

Ashburner, F., 'Escoffier, Georges Auguste (1846–1935)', *Oxford Dictionary of National Biography*, http://www.oxforddnb.com/view/article/50441, accessed 11 October 2018.

Astaire, Simon, *Sol Campbell: The Authorised Biography* (London, 2014).

Auclair, Philippe, *Thierry Henry: Lonely at the Top* (London, 2012).

Ayer, Jules, *A Century of Finance, 1804–1904: The London House of Rothschild* (London, 1905).

Babbage, Charles, *Passages from the Life of a Philosopher* (London, 1864).

Baker, Anne Pimlott, 'Murphy, James [John] (1913–2009)', *Oxford Dictionary of National Biography*, https://doi.org/10.1093/ref:odnb/102053, accessed 4 January 2019.

Baker, William, 'Zangwill, Israel', *Oxford Dictionary of National Biography*, https://doi.org/10.1093/ref:odnb/37087, accessed 25 January 2017.

Barchard, David, *Asil Nadir and the Rise and Fall of Polly Peck* (London, 1992).

Barnes, John, *The Autobiography* (London, 1999).

Belton, Brian, *The Black Hammers: The Voice of West Ham's Ebony Heroes* (Hove, 2006).

Berkowitz, Michael and Ungar, Ruti, eds, *Fighting Back? Jewish and Black Boxers in Britain* (London, 2007).

Bernstein, Eduard, *My Years in Exile: Reminiscences of a Socialist* (London, 1921).

Best, Clyde with Warshaw, Andrew, *The Acid Test: The Autobiography of Clyde Best* (Liverpool, 2016).

Blacker, Harry, *Just Like It Was: Memoirs of the Mittel East* (London, 1974).

Brady, Liam, *So Far so Good: A Decade in Football* (London, 1980).

Brand, William F., *London Life Seen with German Eyes* (London, 1902).

Brandon, Ruth, *The People's Chef: Alexis Soyer, A Life in Seven Courses* (Chichester, 2005).

Briggs, Asa and Callow, John, *Marx in London* (London, 2007).

Briggs, Peter M., 'Daniel Mendoza and Sporting Celebrity: A Case Study', in Tom Mole, ed., *Romanticism and Celebrity Culture, 1750–1850* (Cambridge, 2009).

Brodetsky, Selig, *Memoirs: From Ghetto to Israel* (London, 1960).

Brown, Wilmoth George, *Windrush to Lewisham: Memoirs of 'Uncle George'* (London, 1999).

Bruno, Frank with Giller, Norman, *Frank Bruno: From Zero to Hero* (London, 1996).

Bruno, Frank with Mitchell, Kevin, *Frank: Fighting Back* (London, 2005).

Bunce, Robin and Field, Paul, *Darcus Howe: A Political Biography* (London, 2014).

Bunce, R. E. R. and Field, Paul, 'Obi B. Egbuna, C. L. R. James and the Birth of Black Power in Britain: Black Radicalism in Britain', *Twentieth Century British History*, vol. 22 (2011).

Burrows, Donald, *Handel*, 2nd edn (Oxford, 2012).

Buxton, Charles, ed., *Memoirs of Sir Thomas Fowell Buxton* (London, 1852).

Calogero, Bill, 'Tom Molineaux: From Slave to American Heavyweight Champion', in Colleen Aycock and Mark Scott, eds, *The First Black Boxing Champions: Essays on Fighters of the 1800s to the 1920s* (Jefferson, NC, 2011).

Canoville, Paul, *Black and Blue: How Racism, Drugs and Cancer Almost Destroyed Me* (London, 2008).

Carew, Jan, 'Paul Robeson and W. E. Dubois in London', *Race and Class*, vol. 46 (2004).

Caron, Sandra, *Alma Cogan: A Memoir* (London, 1991).

Carretta, Vincent, 'Richmond, Bill', *Oxford Dictionary of National Biography*, https://doi.org/10.1093/ref:odnb/71635, accessed 30 October 2018.

Catsiyannis, Timotheous, *Constantine Ionidis-Ipliktsis 1775–1852 and the Ionidi Family* (London, 1988).

Catsiyannis, Timotheous, *Pandias Stephen Rallis, 1793–1865: The Founder of the Greek Community in London* (London, 1986).

Catsiyannis, Timotheous, *The Rodocanachi of London: A Pictorial History* (London, 1987).

Chapman, Stanley, 'The Establishment of the Rothschilds as Bankers', *Jewish Historical Studies*, vol. 29 (1982–6).

Chapman, Stanley, *N. M. Rothschild, 1777–1836* (London, 1977).

Chill, Adam, 'The Performance and Marketing of Minority Identity in Late Georgian Boxing', in Michael Berkowitz and Ruti Ungar, eds, *Fighting Back? Jewish and Black Boxers in Britain* (London, 2007).

Chippendale, Neil, *Reminiscences from the Asian Community in Hounslow* (London, 1993).

Clarke, Sam, *Sam: An East End Cabinetmaker* (London, 1930).

Clarkson, Wesley, *Rio Five Star: The Biography* (London, 2014).

Cohen, Max, *I Was One of the Unemployed* (London, 1945).

Collins, Wallace, *Jamaican Migrant* (London, 1965).

Contarini, Paolo, *The Savoy Was My Oyster* (London, 1976).

Cowen, Ruth, *Relish: The Extraordinary Life of Alexis Soyer, Victorian Celebrity Chef* (London, 2006).

Creighton, Sean, 'John Archer and the Politics of Labour in Battersea (1906–32)', *Immigrants and Minorities*, vol. 28 (2010).

Creighton, Sean, 'Paul Robeson's British Journey', in Neil A. Wynn, ed., *Cross the Water Blues: African American Music in Europe* (Jackson, MI, 2007).

Currah, Anne, *Chef to Queen Victoria: The Recipes of Charles Elmé Francatelli* (London, 1973).

Davies, Carole Boyce, *Left of Karl Marx: The Political Life of Black Communist Claudia Jones* (London, 2007).

Davis, Richard, *The English Rothschilds* (London, 1983).

Derbyshire, Oliver, *Thierry Henry: The Biography* (London, 2005).

Drogba, Didier, *Commitment: My Autobiography* (London, 2015).

Duberman, Martin, *Paul Robeson* (London, 1989).

Edwards, Lewis, 'Daniel Mendoza', *Transactions of the Jewish Historical Society of England*, vol. 15 (1946).

Egan, Pierce, *Boxiana or Sketches of Ancient and Modern Pugilism*, vol. 1 (London, 1830).

Egbuna, Obi, *Destroy this Temple* (London, 1971).

Emden, Paul H., *Jews of Britain: A Series of Biographies* (London, 1943).

Escoffier, Auguste, *A Guide to Modern Cookery* (London, 1909).

Ethnic Communities Oral History Project, *Asian Voices: Life Stories from the Indian Sub-Continent* (London, 1993).

Evangelou, Helen, *Tales from Riding House Street: A Faded London House and the Cypriots Who Lived in It* (London, 2018).

Ferguson, Niall, *The World's Banker: The History of the House of Rothschild* (London, 1998).

Finn, Ralph L., *Grief Forgotten: The Tale of an East End Jewish Boyhood* (London, 1985).

Finn, Ralph L., *No Tears in Aldgate* (Bath, 1963).

Fleischer, Nat, *Black Dynamite: The Story of the Negro in the Ring from 1782 to 1938*, vol. 1 (New York, 1938).

Franzero, Carlo Maria, *A Life in Exile: Ugo Foscolo in London* (London, 1977).

Gallati, Mario, *Mario of the Caprice: The Autobiography of a Restaurateur* (London, 1960).

Ganz, Wilhelm, *Memories of a Musician* (London, 1913).

Gee, Tony, 'Mendoza, Daniel', *Oxford Dictionary of National Biography*, https://doi.org/10.1093/ref:odnb/18556, accessed 29 October 2018.

Gennadius, John, *Stephen A. Ralli: A Biographical Memoir* (London, 1902).

Gerdes, Heinrich, 'Ein Sohn Gerdes als Grosskaufmann in London', *Stader Archiv*, vol. 14 (1924).

Goldman, Willy, *East End: My Cradle* (London, 1988).

Goulden, John, *Michael Costa: England's First Conductor: The Revolution in Musical Performance in England, 1830–1880* (London, 2016).

Grant, Eric A., *Dawn to Dusk: A Biography of Bernie Grant MP* (London, 2006).

Gray, Victor, 'An Off-Hand Man: The Character of Nathan Rothschild', in Victor Gray and Melanie Aspecy, eds, *The Life and Times of N. M. Rothschild* (London, 1998).

Gray, Victor and Aspey, Melanie, 'Nathan Mayer Rothschild', *Oxford Dictionary of National Biography*, https://doi.org/10.1093/ref:odnb/24162, accessed 4 January 2019.

Green, Jeffrey, *Samuel Coleridge Taylor, a Musical Life* (London, 2011).

Greer, David, 'Dowland, John (1563?–1626)', *Oxford Dictionary of National Biography*, https://doi-org.proxy.library.dmu.ac.uk/10.1093/ref:odnb/7962, accessed 28 November 2018.

Grunwald, Kurt, ' "Windsor-Cassel" – The Last Court Jew: Prolegomena to a Biography of Sir Ernest Cassel', *Leo Baeck Yearbook*, vol. 14 (1969).

Halle, C. E. and Marie, *Life and Letters of Sir Charles Halle: Being an Autobiography with Correspondence and Diaries* (London, 1896).

Hamilton, Al and Hinds, Rodney, *Black Pearls of Soccer: The A–Z of Black Footballers in the English Game* (London, 1999).

Harding, Jack with Berg, Jack, *Jack Kid Berg: The Whitechapel Windmill* (London, 1987).

Henning, Fred, *Fights for the Championship: The Men and their Times*, vol. 1 (London, 1902).

Herbert, Emily, *George Michael: The Life 1963–2016* (New York, 2017).

Hill, Dave, *Out of His Skin: The John Barnes Phenomenon* (London, 1989).

Hindle, Tim, *Asil Nadir: Fugitive from Injustice* (London, 1993).

Hinnells, John R. and Ralph, Omar, *Sir Mancherjee Merwanjee Bhownaggree K.C.I.E., Order of the Lion and the Sun of Persia: 1851–1933* (London, 1995).

Hodges, Hugh, 'Kitchener Invades England: The London Calypsos of Aldwyn Roberts', *Wasafiri*, vol. 20 (June 2005).

Hueffer, Frances, ed., *Correspondence of Wagner and Liszt*, vol. 2 (London, 1881).

Hughes, Leo, 'The Mozarts' London', in John Glowacki, ed., *Paul A. Pisk: Essays in His Honour* (Austin, TX, 1966).

Hulse, James W., *Revolutionists in London: A Study of Five Unorthodox Socialists* (Oxford, 1970).

Hunt, James D., *Gandhi in London* (New Delhi, 1993).

Husain, Ed, *The Islamist* (London, 2007).

Ionides Junior, Alexander C., *Ion: A Grandfather's Tale* (Dublin, 1927).

James, Kenneth, *Escoffier: King of Chefs* (London, 2002).

Jánosy, Dénes A., *Great Britain and Kossuth* (Budapest, 1937).

Japhet, Saemy, *Recollections of My Business Life* (London, 1931).

Johnson, Buzz, *'I Think of My Mother': Notes on the Life and Times of Claudia Jones* (London, 1985).

Jones, Gareth Stedman, *Karl Marx: Greatness and Illusion* (London, 2016).

Kaplan, Herbert H., *Nathan Mayer Rothschild and the Creation of a Dynasty* (Stanford, CA, 2006).

Keates, Jonathan, *Handel: The Man & His Music* (London, 2008).

Kennedy, Michael, 'Hallé, Sir Charles', *Oxford Dictionary of National Biography*, https://doi.org/10.1093/ref:odnb/12006, accessed 20 November 2018.

Kinross, Felicity, *Coffee and Ices: The Story of Carlo Gatti in London* (Sudbury, 1991).

Kitts, Alex, *Dizzee Rascal: Tales from Da Corner* (London, 2001).

Kosmin, Barry, 'J. R. Archer (1863–1932): A Pan-Africanist in the Battersea Labour Movement', *New Community*, vol. 7 (1978–9).

Kuhe, Wilhelm, *My Musical Recollections* (London, 1896).

Lada, Zsuzsanna, 'The Invention of a Hero: Lajos Kossuth in England (1851)', *European History Quarterly*, vol. 43 (2013).

Leighton, James, *Rocky: The Tears and Triumphs of David Rocastle* (London, 2016).

Lentin, Antony, *Banker, Traitor, Scapegoat, Spy? The Troublesome Case of Sir Edgar Speyer* (London, 2013).

Lester, Paul, *Bonkers: The Story of Dizzee Rascal* (London, 2010).

Lewis, Chaim, *A Soho Address* (London, 1965).

Lewis, Morton, *Ted Kid Lewis: His Life and Times* (London, 1990).

Lichtenstein, Rachel, 'Cecil Gee', in Elizabeth Selby, ed., *Moses and Mr Fish* (London, 2016).

Lister, Warwick, *Amico: The Life of Giovanni Battista Viotti* (Oxford, 2009).

MacAmlaigh, Donall, *An Irish Navvy: The Diary of an Exile* (originally London, 1964; Cork, 2018, reprint).

Mainwaring, John, *Memoirs of the Life of the Late George Friedrich Handel* (London, 1760).

Malik, Michael Abdul, *Michael de Freitas to Michael X* (London, 1968).

Marsh, J. B. T., *The Story of the Jubilee Singers with their Songs*, rev. edn (Boston, MA, 1880).

Marx and Engels Collected Works, vol. 12 (London, 2010).

Masani, R. P., *Dadabhai Naoroji: The Grand Old Man of India* (London, 1939).

Mathurin, Owen Charles, *Henry Sylvester Williams and the Origins of the Pan-African Movement, 1869–1911* (London, 1976).

Matthews, Betty, *The Royal Society of Musicians of Great Britain: A List of Members, 1738–1984* (London, 1985).

McDowell, Linda, *Migrant Women's Voices: Talking About Life and Work in the UK Since 1945* (London, 2016).

McGarrigle, Stephen, *Green Gunners: Arsenal's Irish* (Edinburgh, 1991).

McVeigh, Simon, 'Felice Giardini: A Violinist in Late Eighteenth-Century London', *Music & Letters*, vol. 64 (1983).

McVeigh, Simon, *The Violinist in London's Concert Life, 1750–1914: Felice Giardini and his Contemporaries* (London, 1989)

Meade, Bazil, *A Boy, a Journey, a Dream: The Story of Bazil Meade and the London Community Gospel Choir* (Oxford, 2011).

Mendoza, Daniel, *The Art of Boxing* (London, 1789).

Mendoza, Daniel, *Memoirs of the Life of Daniel Mendoza* (London, 1816).

Midgley, Dominic and Hutchings, Chris, *Abramovich: The Billionaire from Nowhere* (London, 2006).

Morris, Helen, *Portrait of a Chef: The Life of Alexis Soyer, Sometime Chef to the Reform Club* (Cambridge, 1938).

Morrison, Majbritt, *Jungle West 11* (London, 1964).

Muravyova, L. and Sivolap-Kaftanova, I., *Lenin in London: Memorial Places* (Moscow, 1983).

Musgrave, Michael, 'Changing Values in Nineteenth-Century Performance: The Work of Michael Costa and August Manns', in Christina Bashford and Leanne Langley, eds, *Music and British Culture, 1785–1914: Essays in Honour of Cyril Ehrlich* (Oxford, 2000).

Naoroji, Dadabhai, *Speeches and Writings of Dadabhai Naoroji* (Madras, 1918).

Nevzat, Bilge, *The Turquoise Conspiracy: Asil Nadir, the Collapse of Polly Peck and the Persecution of a Family* (London, 1999).

Noon, Sir Gulam, *Noon with a View: Courage and Integrity* (Dunbeath, 2008).

Obi, T. J. Desch, 'Black Terror: Bill Richmond's Revolutionary Boxing', *Journal of Sport History*, vol. 36 (2009).

Onuora, Emy, *Pitch Black: The Story of Black British Footballers* (London, 2015).

Orbell, John, 'Baring, Sir Francis, First Baronet', *Oxford Dictionary of National Biography*, https://doi.org/10.1093/ref:odnb/48906, accessed 4 January 2019.

Orbell, John, 'Japhet, Saemy', *Oxford Dictionary of National Biography*, https://doi.org/10.1093/ref:odnb/48906, accessed 22 May 2018.

Palmer, Fiona M., *Domenico Dragonetti in England (1794–1846): The Career of a Double Bass Virtuoso* (Oxford, 1997).

Panayi, Panikos, 'Eccarius, John George', *Oxford Dictionary of National Biography*, https://doi.org/10.1093/odnb/9780198614128.013.101085, accessed 12 October 2018.

Pennant, Cass, *Cass* (London, 2008).

Plantinga, Leon, *Clementi: His Life and Music* (London, 1977).

Pohl, C. F., *Mozart und Haydn in London*, 2 vols (Vienna, 1867).

Ralph, Omar, *Naoroji: The First Asian MP* (St John's, Antigua, 1997).

Rappaport, Helen, *Conspirator: Lenin in Exile* (London, 2009).

Ray, Elizabeth, *Alexis Soyer: Cook Extraordinary* (Lewes, 1991).

Ritz, Marie Louise, *César Ritz: Host to the World* (Toronto, 1938).

Roberts, Richard, *Schroders: Merchants & Bankers* (Basingstoke, 1992).

Robinson, P., *Handel and his Orbit* (London, 1908).

Rocker, Rudolf, *The London Years* (originally 1956; Nottingham, 2005).

Roscoe, Christopher, 'Haydn and London in the 1780s', *Music and Letters*, vol. 49 (1968).

Rosen, Carole, 'Lind [married name Lind-Goldschmidt], Jenny [Johanna Maria]', *Oxford Dictionary of National Biography*, https://doi.org/10.1093/ref:odnb/16671, accessed 21 November 2018.

Rosen, Harold, *Are You Still Circumcised? East End Memories* (Nottingham, 1999).

Rosenior, Leroy, *'It's Only Banter': The Autobiography of Leroy Rosenior* (Worthing, 2017).

Roth, Cecil, 'The Court Jews of Edwardian England', *Jewish Social Studies*, vol. 5 (1943).

Saha, Panchanan, *Shapurji Saklatvala: A Short Biography* (Delhi, 1970).

Sayers, W. C. Berwick, *Samuel Coleridge Taylor Musician: His Life and Letters* (London, 1915).

Schama, Simon, 'The King's Pugilist: Daniel Mendoza (1764–1836)', in Franklin Foer and Marc Tracey, eds, *Jewish Jocks: An Unorthodox Hall of Fame* (New York, 2012).

Schechter, Ronald and Clarke, Liz, *Mendoza the Jew: Boxing, Manliness and Nationalism, A Graphic History* (New York, 2014).

Selby, Elizabeth, ed., *Moses and Mr Fish* (London, 2016).

Shaw, Timothy, *The World of Escoffier* (London, 1994).

Sherwood, Marika, et al., *Claudia Jones: A Life in Exile* (London, 1999).

Solomons, Jack, *Solomons Tells All* (London, 1951).

Somerset, H. V. F., 'Joseph Haydn in England', *Music and Letters*, vol. 13 (1932).

Squires, Mike, *Saklatvala: A Political Biography* (London, 1990).

Stewart-MacDonald, Rohan H., 'Viotti as Concert and Operatic Manager during his "First" London Period (1792–1798)', in Massimiliano Sala, ed., *Giovanni Battista Viotti: A Composer Between Two Revolutions* (Bologna, 2006).

St George, Andrew, 'Hambro, Baron Carl Joachim', *Oxford Dictionary of National Biography*, https://doi.org/10.1093/ref:odnb/48884, accessed 23 May 2018.

Stebbing, David, ed., *Jewish Memories of the Twentieth Century* (Stanmore, 2003).

Sutcliffe, Marcella Pellegrino, 'Garibaldi in London', *History Today*, vol. 64 (April 2014).

Temperley, Nicholas, 'Handel's Influence on English Music', *Monthly Musical Record*, vol. 100 (1960).

Thane, Pat, 'Financiers and the British State: The Case of Sir Ernest Cassel', *Business History*, vol. 17 (1986).

Thane, Pat, 'Sir Ernest Joseph Cassel', *Dictionary of Business Biography* (London, 1984).

Thompson, Leslie with Green, Jeffrey, *Swing from a Small Island: The Story of Leslie Thompson* (London, 2009).

Ungar, Ruti and Berkowitz, Michael, 'From Daniel Mendoza to Amir Khan: Minority Boxers in Britain', in Michael Berkowitz and Ruti Ungar, eds, *Fighting Back? Jewish and Black Boxers in Britain* (London, 2007).

Vallance, Margaret, 'Rudolf Rocker: A Biographical Sketch', *Journal of Contemporary History*, vol. 8 (1973).

Varnava, Andrekos, 'Yusuf Islam (aka Cat Stevens) and his Anti-War and Pro-Peace Protest Songs: From Hippy Peace to Islamic Peace', *Contemporary British History* (published online, 3 October 2018).

Vasili, Phil, *Colouring Over the White Line: The History of Black Footballers in Britain* (London, 2000).

Vasili, Phil, 'Walter Daniel Tull, 1888–1918: Soldier, Footballer, Black', *Race and Class*, vol. 38 (1996).

Verkaik, Robert, *Jihadi John: The Making of a Terrorist* (London, 2016).

Vernitski, Anat, 'Russian Revolutionaries and English Sympathizers in 1890s London: The Case of Olive Garnett and Sergei Stepniak', *Journal of European Studies*, vol. 35 (2005).

Vialli, Gianluca and Marcotti, Gabriele, *The Italian Job: A Journey to the Heart of Two Great Footballing Cultures* (London, 2006).

Villa, Ricky, Ardiles, Federico and Miller, Joel, *And Still Ricky Villa: My Autobiography* (Kingston upon Thames, 2010).

Wade, Tony, *How They Made a Million: The Dyke and Dryden Story* (London, 2001).

Wadsworth, Marc, *Comrade Sak: Shapurji Saklatvala MP* (Leeds, 1998).

Wake, Jehanne, *Kleinwort, Benson: A History of Two Families in Banking* (Oxford, 1987).

Walton, Benjamin, 'Rara Avis or Fuzzy Turnip: Rossini as Celebrity in 1820s London', in Tom Mole, ed., *Romanticism and Celebrity Culture, 1750–1850* (Cambridge, 2009).

Wanohogo, Emete, *Black Women Taking Charge: Profiles of Black Women Entrepreneurs* (London, 1997).

Western, John, *Passage to England: Barbadian Londoners Speak of Home* (Minneapolis, MI, 1992).

Whale, John, 'Daniel Mendoza's Contests of Identity: Masculinity, Ethnicity and Nation in Georgian Prize-Fighting', *Romanticism*, vol. 14 (2008).

Wilkins, Verna, *Rudolph Walker OBE* (London, 2008).

Williams, John L., *Michael X: A Life in Black and White* (London, 2008).

Williams, Luke G., *Richmond Unchained: The Biography of the World's First Black Sporting Superstar* (Stroud, 2015).

Wright, Ian, *A Life in Football: My Autobiography* (London, 2016).

Wright, Ian, *Mr Wright: The Explosive Autobiography of Ian Wright* (London, 1996).

Zelker, Raymond, *The Polly Peck Story: A Memoir* (London, 2001).

Ziegler, Philip, *The Sixth Great Power: The History of One of the Greatest of All Banking Families, the House of Barings, 1762–1929* (New York, 1988).

CONTEMPORARY ACCOUNTS OF LONDON AND ITS MIGRANT GROUPS

Adler, Elkan Nathan, *A History of the Jews in London* (Philadelphia, PA, 1930).

Adler, Henrietta, 'Jewish Life and Labour in East London', in Sir Hubert Llewellyn Smith, ed., *New Survey of London Life and Labour*, vol. 6 (London, 1934).

'Africans in London', *Economist*, 11 March 1950.

Ahmed, Nazneen, Garnett, Jane, Gidley, Ben, Harris, Alana and Keith, Michael, 'Shifting Markers of Identity in East London's Diasporic Religious Spaces', *Ethnic and Racial Studies*, vol. 39 (2016).

Alavi, Hamza, *The Pakistanis in London* (London, 1963).

Aldrich, Howard, Carter, John C., Jones, Trevor P. and McEvoy, David, 'Business Development and Self-Segregation: Asian Enterprise in Three British Cities', in Ceri Peach, Vaughan Robinson and Susan Smith, eds, *Ethnic Segregation in Cities* (London, 1981).

Aly, Ramy M. K., *Becoming Arab in London: Performativity and the Undoing of Identity* (London, 2015).

Amnesty International, *Down and Out in London: The Road to Destitution for Rejected Asylum Seekers* (London, 2006).

Anonymous, *London at Dinner: Or Where to Dine* (London, 1858).

Ansari, Humayun, 'Introduction', in Humayun Ansari, ed., *The Making of the East London Mosque* (Cambridge 2011).

Anthias, Floya, *Ethnicity, Class, Gender and Migration: Greek Cypriots in Britain* (Aldershot, 1992).

Armfelt, Count E., 'Cosmopolitan London', in George R. Sims, ed., *Living London: Its Work and Its Play, Its Humour and Its Pathos, Its Sights and Its Scenes*, vol. 1 (London, 1902).

Armfelt, Count E., 'German London', in George R. Sims, ed., *Living London: Its Work and Its Play, Its Humour and Its Pathos, Its Sights and Its Scenes*, vol. 3 (London, 1902).

Armfelt, Count E., 'Italy in London', in George R. Sims, ed., *Living London: Its Work and Its Play, Its Humour and Its Pathos, Its Sights and Its Scenes*), vol. 1 (London, 1902).

Arnold, Percy, *The Bankers of London* (London, 1938).

Baker, Philip and Kim, Jeehoon, *Global London: Where to Find almost Everything Ethnic and Cultural in the Multilingual Capital* (London, 2003).

Banton, Michael, *The Coloured Quarter: Negro Immigrants in an English City* (London, 1955).

Barou, Noi Isaakovich, *Jews in Work and Trade* (London, 1946).

Bass, Michael T., *Street Music in the Metropolis: Correspondence and Observations on the Existing Law, and Proposed Amendments* (London, 1864).

Basu, Anuradha and Altinay, Esser, 'The Interaction between Culture and Entrepreneurship in London's Immigrant Businesses', *International Small Business Journal*, vol. 20 (2002).

Baumann, Gerd, *Contesting Culture: Discourses of Identity in Multi-Ethnic London* (Cambridge, 1996).

Becher, Hariet, Waterman, Stanley, Kosmin, Barry and Thomson, Katarina, *A Portrait of Jews in London and the South-east: A Community Study* (London, 2002).

Benson, Susan, *Ambiguous Ethnicity: Interracial Families in London* (Cambridge, 1981).

Besant, Walter, *East London* (London, 1903).

Bethnal Green and Stepney Trades Council, *Blood on the Streets* (London, 1978).

Bhatti, F. M., *Turkish Cypriots in London* (Birmingham, 1981).

Blagrove, Ishmahil, *Carnival: A Photographic and Testimonial History of the Notting Hill Carnival* (London, 2014).

Blake, C. Carter, 'Italian Produce', *Food Journal*, 1 January 1874.

Bloom, Tendayi, 'London's "Ghosts": The Capital and the UK Policy of Destitution of Refused Asylum-Seekers', in Anne J. Kershen, ed., *London the Promised Land Revisited: The Changing Face of the London Migrant Landscape in the Early 21st Century* (London, 2015).

Booth, Charles, ed., *Life and Labour of the People in London*, 9 vols (London, 1892).

Brooks, Dennis, *Race and Labour in London Transport* (London, 1975).

Buck, Nick, et al., *Life and Labour in Contemporary London* (London, 2002).

Burke, Thomas, *Dinner is Served! Or Eating Round the World in London* (London, 1937).

Burke, Thomas, *Nights in Town: A London Autobiography* (London, 1915).

Burke, Thomas, *The Real East End* (London, 1932).

Burney, Elizabeth, *Housing on Trial: A Study of Immigrants and Local Government* (London, 1967).

Butler, Tim and Hamnett, Chris, *Ethnicity, Class and Aspiration: Understanding London's New East End* (Bristol, 2011).

Calley, Malcolm J. C., 'Pentecostal Sects among West Indian Migrants', *Race*, vol. 3 (1962).

Carey, A. T., *Colonial Students: A Study of the Social Adaptation of Colonial Students in London* (London, 1956).

Cathcart, Brian, *The Case of Stephen Lawrence* (London, 1999).

Centre for Analysis of Social Exclusion, *Gentrification of London: A Progress Report, 2001–13* (London, 2016).

Chance, Judy, 'The Irish in London: An Exploration of Ethnic Boundary Maintenance', in Peter Jackson, ed., *Race and Racism: Essays in Social Geography* (London, 1987).

Charity Organization Society, *Report of the Committee of the Charity Organisation Society Appointed to Inquire into the Employment of Italian Children for Mendicant and Immoral Purposes* (London, 1877).

Cheshire, Jenny, Kerswill, Paul, Fox, Sue and Torgersen, Eivind, 'Contact, the Feature Pool and the Speech Community: The Emergence of Multicultural London English', *Journal of Sociolinguistics*, vol. 15 (2011).

Choo, Ng Kwee, *The Chinese in London* (London, 1968).

Cohen-Portheim, Paul, *The Spirit of London* (London, 1935).

Conradson, David and Latham, Alan, 'Friendship, Networks and Transnationality in a World City: Antipodean Transmigrants in London', *Journal of Ethnic and Migration Studies*, vol. 31 (2005).

Constantine, Learie, *Colour Bar* (London, 1954).

Constantinides, Michael, *The Greek Orthodox Church in London* (Oxford, 1933).

Constantinides, Pamela, 'The Greek Cypriots: Factors in the Maintenance of Ethnic Identity', in James L. Watson, ed., *Between Two Cultures: Migrants and Minorities in Britain* (Oxford, 1977).

Curtis, Liz, O'Keefe, Jack and Keatinge, Claire, *Hearts and Minds: Anam Agus Intinn: The Cultural Life of London's Irish Community* (London, 1987).

Datta, K., McIlwaine, C., Evans, Y., Herbert, J. and Wills, J., 'From Coping Strategies to Tactics: London's Low-Pay Economy and Migrant Labour', *British Journal of Industrial Relations*, vol. 45 (2007).

Davies, C. Maurice, *Unorthodox London: Or Phases of Religious Life in the Metropolis* (London, 1873).

Davis, Nathaniel Newnham, *Dinners and Diners: Where and How to Dine in London*, 2nd edn (London, 1901).

Defoe, Daniel, *Augusta Triumphans: Or, the Way to Make London the Most Flourishing City in the Universe* (London, 1728).

Deghy, Guy, *Paradise in the Strand: The Story of Romano's* (London, 1958).

Deghy, Guy and Waterhouse, Keith, *Café Royal: Ninety Years of Bohemia* (London, 1955).

Dench, Geoff, *The Maltese in London: A Case Study in the Erosion of Ethnic Consciousness* (London, 1975).

Dennis, Ferdinand, *Behind the Front Lines: Journey into Afro-Britain* (London, 1988).

Denvir, John, *The Irish in Britain* (London, 1892).

Devadason, Ranji, 'Cosmopolitanism, Geographical Imaginaries and Belonging in North London', *Urban Studies*, vol. 47 (2010).

DeVerteuil, Geoffrey and Manley, David, 'Overseas Investment into London: Imprint, Impact and Pied-à-terre Urbanism', *Environment and Planning A*, vol. 49 (2017).

Directory of Armenians in London (London, 1901).

Dodsworth, Francis, Vacchelli, Elena and Watson, Sophie, 'Shifting Religions and Cultures in London's East End', *Material Religion*, vol. 9 (2013).

Donnan, Hastings, 'Inter-Ethnic Friendship, Joking and Rules of Interaction in a London Factory', in Ladislav Holy, ed., *Knowledge and Behaviour* (Belfast, 1976).

Dorgeel, Heinrich, *Die Deutsche Colonie in London* (London, 1881).

Dummett, Michael A. E., *Southall, 23 April 1979: The Report of the Unofficial Committee of Enquiry* (London, 1980).

Dunne, Catherine, *An Unconsidered People: The Irish in London* (Dublin, 2003).

Dyche, J. A., 'The Jewish Workman', *Contemporary Review*, vol. 73 (1898).

Eade, John, *The Politics of Community: The Bangladeshi Community in East London* (Aldershot, 1989).

Egon Ronay Recommends Eating Places in London and Round Britain (London, 1961).

Evans, Yara, Wills, Jane, Datta, Kavita, Herbert, Joanna, McIlwaine, Cathy, May, Jon, Araújo, Father José Osvaldo de, França, Ana Carla and França, Ana Paula, *Brazilians in London: A Report for the Strangers into Citizens Campaign* (London, 2007).

Evans-Gordon, William, *The Alien Immigrant* (London, 1903).

Fadahunsi, A., Smallbone, D. and Supri, S., 'Networking and Ethnic Minority Enterprise Development: Insights from a North London Study', *Journal of Small Business and Enterprise Development*, vol. 7 (2000).

BIBLIOGRAPHY

Fahy, F. A. and O'Donoghue, D. J., *Ireland in London* (Dublin, 1889).

Fawbert, Jack, ' "Wot, No Asians?" West Ham United Fandom, the Cockney Diaspora and the "New" East Enders', in Daniel Burdsey, ed., *Race, Ethnicity and Football: Persisting Debates and Emergent Issues* (Abingdon, 2012).

Fitzherbert, Katrin, *West Indian Children in London* (London, 1967).

Foner, Nancy, *Jamaica Farewell: Jamaican Migrants in London* (London, 1979).

Ford, Ford Madox, *The Soul of London: A Survey of a Modern City* (London, 1905).

Fordham, John, *Ronnie Scott's at Fifty* (Loughton, 2009).

Foster, Alfred Edye Manning, *London Restaurants* (London, 1924).

Foster, Myles Birket, *The History of the Philharmonic Society of London, 1813–1912* (London, 1912).

Fuat, Alkan, *Cypriots in Haringey* (London, 1980).

Gailani, Fatima, *The Mosques of London* (Henstridge, 2000).

Garcia, Miki, *Rebuilding London: Irish Migrants in Post-War Britain* (Dublin, 2015).

Gardner, Katy, *Age, Narrative and Migration: The Life Course of Bengali Elders in London* (Oxford, 2002).

Garratt, Samuel, *The Irish in London* (London, 1852).

Garwood, John, *The Million-peopled City: Or, One Half of the People of London Made Known to the Other Half* (London, 1853).

George, Vic, 'The Assimilation of Cypriot Immigrants in London', *Eugenic Review*, vol. 58 (1966).

George, Vic and Millerson, Geoffrey, 'The Cypriot Community in London', *Race*, vol. 8 (1967).

Glass, Ruth, *Newcomers: The West Indians in London* (London, 1960).

Gordon, Ian, Travers, Tony and Whitehead, Christine, *The Impact of Recent Immigration on the London Economy* (London, 2007).

Graham, David, *Secular or Religious: The Outlook for London's Jews* (London, 2003).

Graham, Stephen, *Twice Round the London Clock and More London Nights* (London, 1933).

Greenwood, James, *The Wilds of London* (London, 1874).

Guerdon, Gilbert, 'Street Musicians', *Strand Magazine*, vol. 3 (1892).

Haddon, Roy F., 'A Minority in a Welfare State Society: The Location of West Indians in the London Housing Market', *New Atlantis*, vol. 1 (1970).

Halden, J. Cuthbert, 'The Regulation of Street Music', *Nineteenth Century*, vol. 39 (1896).

Hall, Peter, *London Voices, London Lives: Tales from a Working Capital* (Bristol, 2007).

Harden's London Restaurants (London, 1997).

Harris, Hermione, *Yoruba in Diaspora: An African Church in London* (Basingstoke, 2008).

Hassiotis, Anna, *The Greek Cypriot Community in Camden* (London, 1989).

Hill, Clifford D., *West Indians and the London Churches* (Oxford, 1963).

Hogarth, George, *The Philharmonic Society of London* (London, 1862).

Hollingsworth, Mark and Lansley, Stewart, *Londongrad: From Russia with Cash: The Inside Story of the Oligarchs* (London, 2009).

Hooton-Smith, Eileen, *The Restaurants of London* (London, 1928).

Hueffer, Frances, *Half a Century of Music in London* (London, 1889).

Hyndman, Albert, 'The West Indian in London', in S. K. Ruck, ed., *The West Indian Comes to England: A Report Prepared for the Trustees of the London Parochial Charities by the Family Welfare Association* (London, 1960).

Jackson, Stanley, *An Indiscreet Guide to Soho* (London, 1946).

Jackson, Stanley, *The Savoy: A Century of Taste* (London, 1989).

Jewish Year Book, 1903–4 (London, 1903).

Judah, Ben, *This is London* (London, 2016).

Kabeer, Naila, *The Power to Choose: Bangladeshi Women and Labour Market Decisions in London and Dhaka* (London, 2000).

Kannan, C. T., *Inter-Racial Marriages in London: A Comparative Study* (London, 1972).

Katscher, Leopold, 'German Life in London', *Nineteenth Century*, vol. 21 (1887).

Kells, Mary, *Ethnic Identity Amongst Young Irish Middle-Class Migrants in London* (London, 1995).

Kettle, Martin, 'Famagusta, N16', *New Society*, 26 March 1981.

King, Anthony D., *Global Cities: Post-Imperialism and the Internationalization of London* (Abingdon, 2015).

King, Russell, Lulle, Aija, Conti, Francesca and Mueller, Dorothea, 'Eurocity London: A Qualitative Comparison of Graduate Migration from Germany, Italy and Latvia', *Comparative Migration Studies*, vol. 4 (2016).

Kitching, John, Smallbone, David and Athayde, Rosemary, 'Ethnic Diasporas and Business Competitiveness: Minority-Owned Enterprises in London', *Journal of Ethnic and Migration Studies*, vol. 35 (2009).

Kohler, David F., *The Employment of Black People in a London Borough* (London, 1974).

Kosmin, Barry A. and Gizzard, Nigel, *Jews in an Inner London Borough: A Study of the Jewish Population of the London Borough of Hackney based on the 1971 Census* (London, 1971).

Ladbury, Sarah, *A Report on the Social and Working Lives of the Greek and Turkish Cypriot Communities in London* (Southall, 1979).

Layton, T. A., *Dining Round London* (London, 1947).

Leavey, Gerard, Sembhi, Sati and Livingston, G., 'Older Irish Migrants Living in London: Identity, Loss and Return', *Journal of Ethnic and Migration Studies*, vol. 30 (2004).

Lee, Trevor R., *Race and Residence: The Concentration and Dispersal of Immigrants in London* (Oxford, 1977).

Leech, Kenneth, *Brick Lane 1978: The Events and their Significance* (London, 1994).

Leeser, Richard, Storkey, Marian, Howes, Eileen and Kenny, Doreen, *Without Prejudice? Exploring Ethnic Differences in London* (London, 2000).

Leeuwenberg, Jeffrey, *The Cypriots in Haringey* (London, 1979).

Lindsay, Paul, *The Synagogues of London* (London, 1993).

London, Louise, 'The East End of London: Paki-Bashing in 1970', *Race Today*, vol. 5 (1973).

'The London Irish', *Blackwood's Edinburgh Magazine*, vol. 170 (1901).

London Transport Museum, *Sun a-shine, Rain a-fall: London Transport's West Indian Workforce* (London, 1994).

Lyon, M. H. and West, B. J. M., 'London Patels: Caste and Commerce', *Journal of Ethnic and Migration Studies*, vol. 21 (1995).

Mannick, A. R., *Mauritians in London* (Mayfield, 1987).

Maguire, Maria, *The Irish in Ealing: An Invisible Community* (London, 1989).

Mascarenhas-Keyes, Stella, *Goans in London: Portrait of a Catholic Asian Community* (London, 1979).

Massey, Doreen, *World City* (Cambridge, 2007).

May, Jon, Wills, Jane, Datta, Kavita, Evans, Yara, Herbert, Joanna and McIlwaine, Cathy, 'Global Cities at Work: Migrant Labour in Low-Paid Employment in London', *London Journal*, vol. 35 (2010).

Mayhew, Henry, *London Labour and the London Poor*, 4 vols (originally 1861; London, 1968).

McDonald, John Stuart and Leatrice, D., *The Invisible Immigrants* (London, 1972).

McIlwaine, Cathy, Cock, Juan Camilo and Linneker, Brian, *No Longer Invisible: The Latin American Community in London* (London, 2011).

McPherson, Kim and Gaitskell, Julia, *Immigrants and Employment: Two Case Studies in East London and in Croydon* (London, 1969).

Mitchell, George H., *Down in Limehouse* (London, 1925).

Montizambert, Elizabeth, *London Discoveries in Shops and Restaurants* (London, 1924).

Moody, Harold A., *The Colour Bar* (London, 1945).

Morton, H. V., *H. V. Morton's London* (London, 1944).

Moysey, Steven P., *The Road to Balcombe Street: The IRA Reign of Terror in London* (Binghamton, NY, 2008).

Mudie-Smith, Richard, ed., *Religious Life in London* (London, 1904).

Nair, Parvati, 'Undocumented and Unseen: The Making of the Everyday in the Global Metropolis of London 2015', in Anne J. Kershen, ed., *London the Promised Land Revisited: The Changing Face of the London Migrant Landscape in the Early 21st Century* (London, 2015).

BIBLIOGRAPHY

Nava, Mica, *Visceral Cosmopolitanism: Gender, Culture and the Normalisation of Difference* (Oxford, 2007).

Nichols, Dylan, *What Are You Doing Here? The Question of Australians in London* (Brighton, 2007).

O'Connor, Tom, *The London Irish* (London, 1987).

O'Neill, Sean and McGrory, Daniel, *The Suicide Factory: Abu Hamza and the Finsbury Park Mosque* (London, 2006).

'Our City of Nations', *Chambers's Journal* (1891).

Oyètádé, B. Akíntúndé, 'The Yorùbá Community in London', *African Languages and Cultures*, vol. 6 (1993).

Patel, Parvin and Rutten, Mario, 'Patels of Central Gujurat in Greater London', *Economic and Political Weekly*, vol. 334 (1999).

Patterson, Sheila, *Dark Strangers: A Sociological Study of the Absorption of a Recent West Indian Migrant Group in Brixton, South London* (London, 1963).

Patterson, Sheila, *Immigrants in Industry* (London, 1968).

Patterson, Sheila, *Immigration and Race Relations in Britain, 1960–1967* (London, 1969).

Patterson, Sheila, 'The Poles: An Exile Community in Britain', in James L. Watson, ed., *Between Two Cultures: Migrants and Minorities in Britain* (Oxford, 1977).

Philips, Melanie, *Londonistan* (New York, 2006).

Phillips, Watts, *The Wild Tribes of London* (London, 1855).

Qureshi, Tarek, *Living in Britain, Growing Old in Britain: A Study of Bangladeshi Elders in London* (London, 1998).

Rabikowska, Marta and Burrell, Kathy, 'The Material Worlds of Recent Polish Migrants: Transnationalism, Food, Shops and Home', in Kathy Burrell, ed., *Polish Migration in the UK in the 'New' European Union After 2004* (Farnham, 2009).

Rai, Milan, *7/7: The London Bombings, Islam and the Iraq War* (London, 2006).

Randall, Geoffrey, *Over Here: Young Irish Migrants in London: Education, Training, Employment, Housing, Health, Anti-Irish Racism* (London, 1990).

Ransom, David, *The Blair Peach Case: Licence to Kill* (London, 1980).

Ritchie, James Ewing, *The Religious Life of London* (London, 1870).

Robb, James H., *Working-Class Anti-Semite: A Psychological Study in a London Borough* (London, 1954).

Robson, Garry, *'No One Likes Us, We Don't Care': The Myth and Reality of Millwall Fandom* (Oxford, 2000).

Rogaly, Joe, *Grunwick* (Harmondsworth, 1977).

Roman-Velazquez, Patria, *The Making of Latin London: Salsa Music, Place, and Identity* (Aldershot, 1999).

Russell, C. and Lewis, H. D., *The Jew in London: A Study of Racial Character and Present-day Characteristics* (London and New York, 1901).

Ryan, Orla, 'Meet the North Korean Exiles of New Malden', *Financial Times*, 24 August 2017.

Salter, Joseph, *The Asiatic in England: Sketches of Sixteen Years Work Among Orientals* (London, 1873).

Salter, Joseph, *The East in the West or Work Among the Asiatics and Africans in London* (London, 1896).

Scheffauer, Hermann, 'The Chinese in England: A Growing National Problem', *London Magazine*, vol. 26 (June and July 1911).

Shadwell, Arthur, 'The German Colony in London', *National Review*, vol. 26 (1896).

Shah, Samir, *Immigrants and Employment in the Clothing Industry: The Rag Trade in London's East End* (London, 1975).

Sherwell, Arthur, *Life in West London: A Study and a Contrast* (London, 1901).

Sims, George R., ed., *Living London: Its Work and Its Play, Its Humour and Its Pathos, Its Sights and Its Scenes*, 3 vols (London, 1902–3).

Sims, George R., 'Trips Around Town, III: Round Little Italy', *Strand Magazine*, vol. 29 (1905).

Singmaster, Deborah, 'Hindu Architecture Transcends its Suburban Context: The Shri Swaminarayan Mandir in Neasden is the First Traditional Hindu Complex to be Built Outside the Indian Subcontinent', *Architects' Journal*, 21 December 1995.

Sinha, Rachana, *The Cultural Adjustment of Asian Lone Mothers Living in London* (Aldershot, 1998).

Smallbone, D., Bertotti, M. and Ekanem, I., 'Diversification in Ethnic Minority Business: The Case of Asians in London's Creative Industries', *Journal of Small Business and Enterprise Development*, vol. 12 (2005).

Smith, Charles Manby, *Curiosities of London Life, or, Phases, Physiological and Social, of the Great Metropolis* (London, 1853).

Smith, Charles Manby, 'Music Grinders of the Metropolis', *Chambers's Edinburgh Journal*, vol. 17 (1852).

Smith, Hubert Llewellyn, *The New Survey of London Life and Labour*, 9 vols (London, 1930–5).

Smith, John Thomas, *The Cries of London* (London, 1839).

Stallard, J. H., *London Pauperism amongst Jews and Christians* (London, 1867).

Strang, James, 'The Italian Colony in London', *Good Words*, vol. 40 (1899).

Strang, James, 'The Jewish Colony in London', *Good Words*, vol. 40 (1899).

Sveinsson, Kjartan Páll, *Bolivians in London: Challenges and Achievements of a London Community* (London, 2007).

Sweeney, John, 'Among the Russians', *Time Out*, 9–15 April 1986.

Sze, Szeming, 'Chinese Students in Great Britain', *Asiatic Review*, vol. 27 (1931).

Talai, Vered Amit, *Armenians in London: The Management of Social Boundaries* (Manchester, 1989).

Tambs-Lyche, Harald, *London Patidars: A Case Study in Urban Ethnicity* (London, 1980).

Thompson, J. and Smith, Adolphe, *Street Life in London* (London, 1877).

Trachtenberg, H. L., 'Estimate of the Jewish Population of London', *Journal of the Royal Statistical Society*, vol. 46 (1933).

Tyau, Min-Chien T. Z., *London Through Chinese Eyes, or, My Seven and a Half Years in London* (London, 1920).

Vertovec, Steven, 'Community and Congregation in London Hindu Temples: Divergent Trends', *New Community*, vol. 18 (1992).

Wade, George A., 'The Cockney John Chinaman', *English Illustrated Magazine*, vol. 23 (1900).

Wade, George A., 'Israel in London: How the Hebrew Lives in Whitechapel', *English Illustrated Magazine*, vol. 23 (1900).

Walter, Bronwen, 'Contemporary Irish Settlement in London: Women's Worlds, Men's Worlds', in Jim MacLaughlin, ed., *Location and Dislocation in Contemporary Irish Society: Emigration and Identities* (Cork, 1997).

Wann, Mai, *Chiot Shipowners in London: An Immigrant Elite* (Coventry, 1987).

Waterman, Stanley and Kosmin, Barry, 'Ethnic Identity, Residential Concentration and Social Welfare: The Jews in London', in Peter Jackson, ed., *Race and Racism: Essays in Social Geography* (London, 1987).

Waterman, Stanley and Kosmin, Barry, 'Residential Patterns and Processes: A Study of Jews in Three London Boroughs', *Transactions of the Institute of British Geographers*, vol. 13 (1988).

Watson, J., *Young Germany* (London, 1844).

Watson, James L., *Emigration and the Chinese Lineage: The Mans in Hong Kong and London* (London, 1975).

Wessendorf, Susanne, 'Commonplace Diversity and the "Ethos of Mixing": Perceptions of Difference in a London Neighbourhood', *Identities*, vol. 20 (2013).

Whitfield, James, *Unhappy Dialogue: The Metropolitan Police and Black Londoners in Post-War Britain* (Cullompton, 2004).

Wills, Jane, Datta, Kavita, Evans, Yara, Herbert, Joanna, May, Jon and McIlwaine, Cathy, *Global Cities at Work: New Migrant Divisions of Labour* (London, 2010).

Wright, Katie, ' "It's a Limited Kind of Happiness": Barriers to Achieving Human Well-being among Peruvian Migrants in London and Madrid', *Bulletin of Latin American Research*, vol. 29 (2010).

Zangwill, Israel, *Children of the Ghetto* (London, 1902).

Zeff, Linda, *Jewish London* (London, 1986).

HISTORICAL AND OTHER PUBLISHED WORKS

Abbasi, Muhammad Yusuf, *London Muslim League (1908–1928): An Historical Study* (Islamabad, 1988).

Ackroyd, Peter, *London: The Biography* (London, 2001).

Adi, Hakim, 'African Political Thinkers, Pan-Africanism and the Politics of Exile c.1850–1970', in Stefan Manz and Panikos Panayi, eds, *Refugees and Cultural Transfers to Britain* (Abingdon, 2013).

Adi, Hakim, *Pan-Africanism: A History* (London, 2018).

Adi, Hakim, *West Africans in Britain, 1900–1960: Nationalism, Pan-Africanism and Communism* (London, 1998).

Adi, Hakim, 'West African Students in Britain, 1900–60: The Politics of Exile', in David Killingray, ed., *Africans in Britain* (Ilford, 1994).

Ahmed, Rehana and Mukherjee, Sumita, eds, *South Asian Resistances in Britain 1858–1947: Interactions and Models of Resistance* (London, 2011).

Alderman, Geoffrey, 'The Anti-Jewish Riots of August 1911 in South Wales', *Welsh History Review*, vol. 6 (1972).

Alderman, Geoffrey, *The History of the Hendon Synagogue* (London, 1978).

Alderman, Geoffrey, *The Jewish Community in British Politics* (Oxford, 1983).

Alderman, Geoffrey, *London Jewry and London Politics, 1889–1986* (London, 1989).

Alderman, Geoffrey, *Modern British Jewry* (Oxford, 1992).

Alderman, Geoffrey, 'The Political Impact of Zionism in the East End of London Before 1940', *London Journal*, vol. 9 (1983).

Alford, Stephen, *London's Triumph: Merchant Adventurers and the Tudor City* (Kindle, 2017).

Alibhai-Brown, Yasmin, *The Colour of Love: Mixed Race Relationships* (London, 1992).

Alter, Peter, ed., *Out of the Third Reich: Refugee Historians in Post-War Britain* (London, 1998).

Andall, Jacqueline, *Gender, Migration and Domestic Service: The Politics of Black Women in Italy* (Aldershot, 2000).

Anderson, Gregory, 'German Clerks in England, 1870–1914: Another Aspect of the Great Depression Debate', in Kenneth Lunn, ed., *Hosts, Immigrants and Minorities: Historical Responses to Newcomers in British Society* (Folkestone, 1980).

Anderson, Toni P., *"Tell Them We Are Singing for Jesus": The Original Fisk Jubilee Singers and Christian Reconstruction, 1871–1878* (Macon, GA, 2010).

Angelo, Anne-Marie, 'The Black Panthers in London, 1967–1972: The Diasporic Struggle Navigates the Black Atlantic', *Radical History Review*, vol. 103 (2009).

Ansari, Humayun, *'The Infidel Within': Muslims in Britain Since 1800* (London, 2004).

Aris, Stephen, *The Jews in Business* (London, 1970).

Arnstein, Walter L., *Protestant Versus Catholic in Mid-Victorian Britain* (London, 1982).

Ashe, Stephen, Virdee, Satnam and Brown, Laurence, 'Striking Back against Racist Violence in the East End of London, 1968–1970', *Race and Class*, vol. 58 (2016).

Ashton, Rosemary, *Little Germany: Exile and Asylum in Victorian Britain* (Oxford, 1986).

Assael, Brenda, *The London Restaurant, 1840–1914* (Oxford, 2018).

Aston, Mark, *Foul Deeds and Suspicious Deaths in Hampstead, Holborn and St Pancras* (London, 2005).

Atkin, Nicolas, *The Forgotten French: Exiles in the British Isles, 1940–44* (Manchester, 2003).

Auerbach, Sascha, *Race, Law and 'The Chinese Puzzle' in Imperial Britain* (Basingstoke, 2012).

Augustyn, Heather, *Ska: The Rhythm of Liberation* (Plymouth, 2013).

Back, Les, Crabbe, Tim and Solomos, John, *The Changing Face of Football: Racism, Identity and Multiculture in the English Game* (Oxford, 2001).

Bade, Klaus J., *Migration in European History* (Oxford, 2003).

Bailey, Craig, *Irish London: Middle-Class Migration in the Global Eighteenth Century* (Liverpool, 2013).

Baines, Dudley, 'European Labour Markets, Emigration and Internal Migration', in Timothy J. Hatton and Jeffrey G. Williamson, eds, *Migration and the International Labour Market* (London, 1994).

Bains, Jas and Johal, Sanjeev, *Corner Flags and Corner Shops: The Asian Football Experience* (London, 1998).

Baldoli, Claudia, 'The Remaking of the Italian Community in London: L'Italia Nostra and the Creation of a Little Fascist Italy during the 1930s', *London Journal*, vol. 26 (2001).

Ball, Stephen, 'Whither the Small Independent Takeaway?', *International Journal of Contemporary Hospitality Management*, 8 (1996).

Ballinger, Annette, *Dead Women Walking: Executed Women in England and Wales, 1900–1955* (Aldershot, 2000).

Banerji, Sabita and Baumann, Gerd, 'Bhangra 1984–8: Fusion and Professionalization in a Genre of South Asian Dance Music', in Paul Oliver, ed., *Black Music in Britain* (Milton Keynes, 1990).

Barnes, James J. and Patience P., 'London's German Community in the Early 1930s', in Panikos Panayi, ed., *Germans in Britain since 1500* (London, 1996).

Barnes, James J. and Patience P., *Nazis in Pre-War London, 1930–1939: The Fate and Role of German Party Members and British Sympathizers* (Brighton, 2005).

Basu, Sharbani, *Curry: The Story of the Nation's Favourite Dish* (Stroud, 2003).

Bayly, C. A., *The Birth of the Modern World, 1780–1914* (Oxford, 2004).

Baum, Tom, *Migrant Workers in the International Hotel Industry* (Geneva, 2012).

Bebber, Brett, *Violence and Racism in Football* (London, 2012).

Bebber, Brett, ' "We Were Just Unwanted": Bussing, Migrant Dispersal and South Asians in London', *Journal of Social History*, vol. 48 (2015).

Beerbühl, Margrit Schulte, 'Commercial Networks, Transfer and Innovation: The Migration of German Merchants to England', in Stefan Manz, Margrit Schulte Beerbühl and John R. Davis, eds, *Migration and Transfer from Germany to Britain, 1660–1914* (Munich, 2007).

Beerbühl, Margrit Schulte, *The Forgotten Majority: German Merchants in London, Naturalization and Global Trade 1660–1815* (Oxford, 2014).

Benewick, Robert, *Political Violence and Public Order* (London, 1969).

Benton, Gregor and Gomez, Terence, *The Chinese in Britain, 1800–Present: Economy, Transnationalism and Identity* (Basingstoke, 2011).

Berghahn, Marion, *Continental Britons: German-Jewish Refugees from Nazi Germany* (Oxford, 1988).

Bermant, Chaim, *The Cousinhood: The Anglo-Jewish Gentry* (London, 1971).

Bermant, Chaim, *Point of Arrival: A Study of London's East End* (London, 1975).

Berridge, Virginia, 'East End Opium Dens and Narcotic Use in Britain', *London Journal*, vol. 4 (1978).

Besagni, Olive, *A Better Life: A History of London's Italian Immigrant Families in Clerkenwell's Little Italy in the 19th and 20th Centuries* (London, 2011).

Bhachu, Parminder, *Dangerous Designs: Asian Women Fashion the Diaspora Economies* (London, 2004).

Bhachu, Parminder, *Twice Migrants: East African Sikh Settlers in Britain* (London, 1985).

Bhogal, Vicky, *A Year of Cooking Like Mummyji* (London, 2005).

Billig, Michael, *Fascists: A Social Psychological Profile of the National Front* (London, 1978).

Birchall, Christopher, *Embassy, Emigrants and Englishmen: The Three-Hundred Year History of a Russian Orthodox Church in London* (New York, 2014).

Bird, Peter, *The First Food Empire: A History of J. Lyons & Co.* (Chichester, 2000).

Bishop Theodoritos of Nazianos, 'History of the Greek Cathedral of Saint Sophia in London', in George Kakavas, ed., *Treasured Offerings: The Legacy of the Greek Orthodox Cathedral of St. Sophia London* (London, 2002).

Black, Gerry, *Living Up West: Jewish Life in London's West End* (London, 1994).

Black, Robert, 'Buddhism', in Linda Woodhead and Rebecca Catto, *Religion and Change in Modern Britain* (Abingdon, 2012).

Blake, Andrew, *The Land without Music* (Manchester, 1977).

Bloch, Alice, *The Migration and Settlement of Refugees in Britain* (Basingstoke, 2002).

Bloch, Howard, *Earlham Grove Shul* (London, 1997).

Bloom, Clive, *Violent London: 2000 Years of Riots, Rebels and Revolts* (Basingstoke, 2010).

Boddy, Kasia, *Boxing: A Cultural History* (London, 2008).

Bodnar, John, *The Transplanted: A History of Immigrants in Urban America* (Bloomington, IN, 1985).

Bodner, Alan, *When Boxing was a Jewish Sport* (London, 1997).

Boehmer, Elleke, *Indian Arrivals, 1870–1915: Networks of British Empire* (Oxford, 2015).

Bogan, Bernard Canon, 'History of Irish Immigration to England: The Irish in Southwark', *Christus Rex*, vol. 12 (1958).

Born, Karl Erich, *International Banking in the 19th and 20th Centuries* (Leamington Spa, 1983).

Boulton, David, *Jazz in Britain* (London, 1958).

Bourke, Ann, 'The Road to Fame and Fortune: Insights on the Career Paths of Young Irish Professional Footballers in England', *Journal of Youth Studies*, vol. 5 (2002).

Bourne, Stephen, *Mother Country: Britain's Black Community on the Home Front, 1939–45* (Stroud, 2010).

Bourne, Stephen, *The Motherland Calls: Britain's Black Servicemen and Women* (Stroud, 2012).

Bourne, Stephen, *Speak of Me as I Am: The Black Presence in Southwark Since 1600* (London, 2005).

Bowden, Gregory Houston, *British Gastronomy: The Rise of the Great Restaurants* (London, 1975).

Braber, Ben, *Jews in Glasgow 1879–1939: Immigration and Integration* (London, 2007).

Bradbury, Steven, 'Institutional Racism, Whiteness and the Under-Representation of Minorities in Leadership Positions in Football in Europe', *Soccer & Society*, vol. 14 (2013).

Bradley, Lloyd, *Sounds like London: 100 Years of Black Music in the Capital* (London, 2013).

Brailsford, Dennis, *Bareknuckles: A Social History of Prize Fighting* (Cambridge, 1988).

Braunthal, Julius, *History of the International, 1864–1914* (London, 1966).

Brenner, Michael and Reuveni, Gideon, eds, *Emancipation through Muscles: Jews and Sports in Europe* (Lincoln, NE, 2006).

Brigden, Susan, *London and the Reformation* (London, 2014).

Briggs, Daniel, *The English Riots of 2011: A Summer of Discontent* (Hook, 2012).

Brinson, Charmian and Dove, Richard, *Politics by Other Means: The Free German League of Culture in London 1939–1946* (London, 2010).

Brock, Peter, 'The Polish Revolutionary Commune in London', *Slavonic and East European Review*, vol. 35 (1956).

Brotman, Adolph G., 'Jewish Communal Organization', in Julius Gould and Shaul Esh, eds, *Jewish life in Modern Britain* (London, 1964).

Brown, Linda Keller and Mussell, Kay, eds, *Ethnic and Regional Foodways in the United States: The Performance of Group Identity* (Knoxville, TN, 1985).

Brown, Mark S., 'Religion and Economic Activity in the South Asian Population', *Ethnic and Racial Studies*, vol. 23 (2000).

Bucholz, Robert O. and Ward, Joseph P., *London: A Social and Cultural History, 1550–1750* (Cambridge, 2012).

Buckman, Joseph, *Immigrants and the Class Struggle: The Jewish Immigrant in Leeds, 1880–1914* (Manchester, 1983).

Burdsey, Daniel, *British Asians and Football: Culture, Identity and Exclusion* (Abingdon, 2018).

Burdsey, Daniel, 'Obstacle Race? "Race", Racism and the Recruitment of British Asian Professional Footballers', *Patterns of Prejudice*, vol. 38 (2004).

Burnett, John, *England Eats Out: A Social History of Eating Out in England from 1830 to the Present* (London, 2004).

Burrell, Kathy, 'Introduction: Migration to the UK from Poland: Continuity and Change in East-West European Mobility', in Kathy Burrell, ed., *Polish Migration to the UK in the 'New' European Union: After 2004* (Farnham, 2009).

Burrell, Kathy, ' "The World in One City": Migrant Lives in Liverpool', *North West Geography*, vol. 17 (2017).

Burton, Antoinette M., *At the Heart of the Empire: Indians and the Colonial Encounter in Late-Victorian Britain* (London, 1998).

Bush, Julia, *Behind the Lines: East London Labour 1914–1919* (London, 1984).

Campbell, Sean, *'Irish Blood, English Heart': Second-Generation Irish Musicians in England* (Cork, 2011).

Cantle, Ted, *Community Cohesion: A New Framework for Race and Diversity* (Basingstoke, 2005).

Carpenter, Kirsty, *Refugees of the French Revolution: Émigrés in London, 1789–1802* (Basingstoke, 1999).

Carter, Trevor, *Shattering Illusions: West Indians in British Politics* (London, 1986).

Cashmore, Ernest, *Black Sportsmen* (London, 1982).

Cashmore, Ernest, *Rastaman: The Rastafarian Movement in England* (London, 1979).

Cassis, Youssef, *City Bankers, 1890–1914* (Cambridge, 1994).

Castles, Stephen, et al., *Here for Good: Western Europe's New Ethnic Minorities* (London, 1984).

Castles, Stephen and Kosack, Godula, *Immigrant Workers and Class Structure into Western Europe* (London, 1973).

Castles, Stephen, de Haas, Hein and Miller, Mark J., *The Age of Migration: International Population Movements in the Modern World*, 5th edn (Palgrave, 2013).

Castro, John Paul De, *The Gordon Riots* (London, 1926).

Catsiyannis, Timotheous, *The Greek Community of London* (London, 1993).

Cesarani, David, 'The Forgotten Port Jews of London: Court Jews who were also Port Jews', in David Cesarani, ed., *Port Jews: Jewish Communities in Cosmopolitan Trading Centres, 1550–1950* (London, 2002).

Cesarani, David, 'A Funny Thing Happened on the Way to the Suburbs: Social Change in Anglo-Jewry Between the Wars, 1914–1945', *Jewish History and Culture*, vol. 1 (1998).

Cesarani, David, ed., *The Making of Modern Anglo-Jewry* (Oxford, 1990).

Chapman, Pat, *The 1999 Good Curry Guide* (London, 1998).

Chapman, Pat, *Curry Club Bangladeshi Restaurant Curries* (London, 1996).

Chapman, Pat, *The Good Curry Guide to Indian Restaurants* (Haslemere, 1983).

Chapman, Stanley, 'Ethnicity and Money Making in Nineteenth-Century Britain', *Renaissance and Modern Studies*, vol. 38 (1995).

Chapman, Stanley, 'The International Houses: The Continental Contribution to British Commerce', *Journal of European Economic History*, vol. 6 (1977).

Chapman, Stanley, *Merchant Enterprise in Britain: From the Industrial Revolution to World War I* (Cambridge, 1992).

Chapman, Stanley, *The Rise of Merchant Banking* (London, 1984).

Chatburn, Tom, 'Trinidad All Stars: The Steel Pan Movement in Britain', in Paul Oliver, ed., *Black Music in Britain* (Milton Keynes, 1990).

Chatziioannou, Maria Christina, 'Greek Merchants in Victorian England', in Dimitris Tziovas, ed., *Greek Diaspora and Migration since 1700: Society, Politics and Culture* (Farnham, 2009).

Chatziioannou, Maria Christina and Harlaftis, Gelina, 'From the Levant to the City of London: Mercantile Credit in the Greek International Commercial Networks of the Eighteenth and Nineteenth Centuries', in Philip L. Cottrell, Evan Lange and Ulf Olsson, eds, *Centres and Peripheries in Banking: The Historical Development of Financial Markets* (Aldershot, 2007).

Chesney, Kellow, *The Victorian Underworld* (Harmondsworth, 1972).

Chitty, C. W., 'Aliens in England in the Sixteenth Century', *Race*, vol. 8 (1966).

Clark, Greg, *The Making of a World City: London 1991 to 2021* (Chichester, 2015).

Clarke, J. H., *England under the Heel of the Jew* (London, 1918).

Clavane, Anthony, *Does Your Rabbi Know You're Here? The Story of English Football's Forgotten Tribe* (London, 2012).

Cloonan, Martin and Brennan, Matt, 'Alien Invasions: The British Musicians' Union and Foreign Musicians', *Popular Music*, vol. 32 (2013).

Cohen, Norman, 'Trends in Anglo-Jewish Religious Life', in Julius Gould and Shaul Esh, eds, *Jewish Life in Modern Britain* (London, 1964).

Colley, Linda, *Britons: Forging the Nation, 1707–1837* (London, 1994).

Collingham, Lizzie, *Curry: A Biography* (London, 2005).

Collins, Hattie, *This is Grime* (London, 2016).

Collins, Marcus, 'Pride and Prejudice: West Indian Men in Mid-Twentieth Century Britain', *Journal of British Studies*, vol. 40 (2001).

Colpi, Terri, *The Italian Factor: The Italian Community in Great Britain* (Edinburgh, 1991).

Communist Party of Great Britain, *London Landmarks: A Guide with Maps to Places where Marx, Engels and Lenin Lived and Worked* (London, 1963).

Conway, Martin and Gotovich, José, eds, *Europe in Exile: European Exile Communities in Britain, 1940–45* (Oxford, 2001).

Coogan, Tim Pat, *The IRA* (New York, 2002).

Copsey, Nigel, *Contemporary British Fascism: The British National Party and the Quest for Legitimacy* (Basingstoke, 2004).

Corbally, John, 'The Jarring Irish: Postwar Immigration to the Heart of Empire', *Radical History Review*, no. 104 (2009).

Costello, Ray, *Black Liverpool: The Early History of Britain's Oldest Black Community 1730–1918* (Liverpool, 2001).

Cowley, John, 'London is the Place: Caribbean Music in the Context of Empire, 1900–60', in Paul Oliver, ed., *Black Music in Britain* (Milton Keynes, 1990).

Cowley, John, 'uBungca (Oxford Bags): Recordings in London of African and West Indian Music in the 1920s and 1930s', *Musical Traditions*, no. 12 (Summer 1994).

Cronin, Mike, ed., *The Failure of British Fascism: The Far Right and the Fight for Political Recognition* (Basingstoke, 1996).

Crowhurst, Basil, *A History of the British Ice Cream Industry* (Westerham, 2000).

Curran, Conor, 'Irish-born Players in England's Football Leagues, 1945–2010: An Historical and Geographical Assessment', *Sport in Society*, vol. 19 (2016).

Curran, Conor, *Irish Soccer Migrants: A Social and Cultural History* (Cork, 2017).

Curran, Conor, 'The Migration of Irish-Born Footballers to England, 1945–2010', *Soccer and Society*, vol. 16 (2015).

Curtis, L. P., *Anglo-Saxons and Celts* (New York, 1968).

Daunton, Martin, 'London and the World', in Celina Fox, ed., *London: World City, 1800–1840* (London, 1992).

David-Guillou, Angèle, 'Early Musicians' Unions in Britain, France, and the United States: On the Possibilities and Impossibilities of Transnational Militant Transfers in an International Industry', *Labour History Review*, vol. 74 (2009).

Davies, Norman, 'The Poles in Great Britain, 1914–1919', *Slavonic and East European Review*, vol. 50 (1972).

Davis, Christie, 'The Irish Joke as a Social Phenomenon', in John Durant and Jonathan Miller, eds, *Laughing Matters: A Serious Look at Humour* (London, 1988).

Davis, Dorothy, *A History of Shopping* (London, 1966).

Davis, Graham, *The Irish in Britain* (Dublin, 1991).

Davis, Graham, 'Little Irelands', in Roger Swift and Sheridan Gilley, eds, *The Irish in Britain, 1815–1939* (London, 1989).

Davis, John, 'Rents and Race in 1960s London: New Light on Rachmanism', *Twentieth Century British History*, vol. 12 (2001).

Davis, John R., 'Friedrich Max Müller and the Migration of German Academics to Britain in the Nineteenth Century', in Stefan Manz, Margrit Schulte Beerbühl and John R. Davis, eds, *Migration and Transfer from Germany to Britain, 1660–1914* (Munich, 2007).

Davison, R. B., *Black British Immigrants to England* (London, 1966).

Dawes, Frank V., *Not in Front of the Servants: Domestic Service in England, 1850–1939* (London, 1973).

Debrunner, Werner, *Presence and Prestige: Africans in Europe: A History of Africans in Europe Before 1918* (Basel, 1979).

Decho, Pam and Diamond, Claire, *Latin Americans in London: A Select List of Prominent Americans in London, c. 1880–1996* (London, 1998).

Dee, David, *The 'Estranged' Generation? Social and Generational Change in Interwar British Jewry* (Basingstoke, 2017).

Dee, David, *Sport and British Jewry: Integration, Ethnicity and Anti-Semitism, 1890–1970* (Manchester, 2013).

Delaney, Enda, *Demography, State and Society: Irish Migration to Britain, 1921–1971* (Liverpool, 2000).

Delaney, Enda, *The Irish in Post-War Britain* (Oxford, 2007).

Dempsey, Suzanne, 'The Italian Community in London during the Reign of Edward II', *London Journal*, vol. 18 (1993).

Derwent, Grace, *Roman London* (London, 1968).

Desai, Rashmi, *Indian Immigrants in Britain* (London, 1963).

Diner, Hasia R., *Hungering for America: Italian, Irish and Jewish Foodways in the Age of Migration* (London, 2001).

Doctor, Vikram, 'Ralli Brothers', *Economic Times*, 2 August 2015.

Dougherty, Beverly A., 'German and Italian Merchant Colonies in Early Modern England', in Victor N. Zakharov, Gelina Harlaftis and Olga Katsiardi-Hering, eds, *Merchant Colonies in the Early Modern Period* (London, 2012).

Dowling, Theodore and Fletcher, E. W., *Hellenism in England* (London, 1915).

Driver, Felix and Gilbert, David, 'Heart of Empire? Landscape, Space and Performance in Imperial London', *Environment and Planning D*, vol. 16 (1998).

du Noyer, Paul, *In the City: A Celebration of London Music* (London, 2009).

Efron, John, 'When is a Yid Not a Jew? The Strange Case of Supporter Identity at Tottenham Hotspur', in Michael Brenner and Gideon Reuveni, eds, *Emancipation through Muscles: Jews and Sports in Europe* (Lincoln, NE, 2006).

Ehrlich, Cyril, *First Philharmonic: A History of the Royal Philharmonic Society* (Oxford, 1995).

Ehrlich, Cyril, *The Music Profession in Britain since the Eighteenth Century: A Social History* (Oxford, 1985).

Ehrman, Edwina, Forsyth, Hazel, Peltz, Lucy and Ross, Cathy, *London Eats Out: 500 Years of Capital Dining* (London, 1999).

Elkin, Robert, *Royal Philharmonic: The Annals of the Royal Philharmonic Society* (London, 1946).

Elliot, Richard, 'Football's Irish Exodus: Examining the Factors Influencing Irish Player Migration to English Professional Leagues', *International Review for the Sociology of Sport*, vol. 51 (2016).

Elman, Peter, 'The Beginnings of the Jewish Trade Union Movement in England', *Transactions of the Jewish Historical Society of England*, vol. 17 (1952).

Endelman, Todd, *The Jews of Britain 1656–2000* (London, 2002).

Endelman, Todd, *The Jews of Georgian England: Tradition and Change in a Liberal Society* (Ann Arbor, MI, 1999).

Endelman, Todd, 'Native Jews and Foreign Jews in London, 1870–1914', in D. Berger, ed., *The Legacy of Jewish Emigration and its Impact* (New York, 1983).

Endelman, Todd, ' "Practices of a Low Anthropological Level": A Schechita Controversy of the 1950s', in Anne J. Kershen, ed., *Food in the Migrant Experience* (Aldershot, 2002).

Endelman, Todd, *Radical Assimilation in English Jewish History, 1656–1945* (Bloomington and Indianapolis, IN, 1990).

Englander, David, 'Booth's Jews: The Presentation of Jews and Judaism in "Life and Labour of the People of London" ', *Victorian Studies*, vol. 32 (1989).

Englander, David, 'Integrated but Insecure: A Portrait of Anglo-Jewry at the Close of the Twentieth Century', in Gerald Parsons, ed., *The Growth of Religious Diversity in Britain* (Abingdon, 1993).

Fast, Vera K., *Children's Exodus: A History of the Kindertransport* (London, 2011).

Favell, Adrian, *Eurostars and Eurocities: Free Movement and Mobility in an Integrating Europe* (Oxford, 2008).

Feldman, David, *Englishmen and Jews: Social Relations and Political Culture, 1840–1914* (London, 1994).

Ferguson, Priscilla Parkhurst, *Accounting for Taste: The Triumph of French Cuisine* (London, 2004).

Fiedler, Herma, 'German Musicians in England and their Influence to the End of the Eighteenth Century', *German Life and Letters*, vol. 4 (1939).

Finestein, Israel, *A Short History of Anglo-Jewry* (London, 1957).

Finlay, Roger, *Population and Metropolis: The Demography of London, 1580–1650* (Cambridge, 1981).

Finney, Nissa and Simpson, Ludi, *'Sleepwalking to Segregation?' Challenging Myths About Race and Immigration* (Bristol, 2009).

Fisher, Michael H., Lahiri, Shompa and Thandi, Shinder, *A South Asian History of Britain* (Oxford, 2007).

Fishman, William J., *East End 1888* (London, 1988).

Fishman, William J., *East End Jewish Radicals, 1875–1914* (London, 1975).

Fishman, William J., 'A People's Journée: The Battle of Cable Street (October 4th 1936)', in Frederick Krantz, ed., *History from Below: Studies in Popular Protest and Popular Ideology in Honour of George Rudé* (Montreal, 1985).

Fitzgerald, Martin, *Political Parties and Black People: Participation, Representation and Exploitation* (London, 1984).

Fitzpatrick, David, ' "A Particular Tramping People": The Irish in Britain, 1801–70', in W. E. Vaughan, ed., *A New History of Ireland*, vol. 5 (Oxford, 1989).

Foner, Nancy, *From Ellis Island to JFK: New York's Two Great Waves of Immigration* (London, 2000).

Foot, Paul, *Immigration and Race in British Politics* (Harmondsworth, 1965).

Fox, Celina, ed., *London: World City, 1800–1840* (London, 1992).

Fox, Pam, *The Jewish Community of Golders Green: A Social History* (Stroud, 2016).

Freitag, Sabine, ed., *Exiles from European Revolutions: Refugees in Mid-Victorian England* (Oxford, 2003).

Fryer, Peter, *Staying Power: The History of Black People in Britain* (London, 1984).

Fyvel, T. R., *The Insecure Offenders: Rebellious Youth in the Welfare State* (Harmondsworth, 1963).

Gainer, Bernard, *The Alien Invasion: The Origins of the Aliens Act of 1905* (London, 1972).

Gallagher, Tom, *The Uneasy Peace: Religious Tension in Modern Glasgow, 1819–1940* (Manchester, 1987).

Garland, Jon and Rowe, Michael, *Racism and Anti-Racism in Football* (Basingstoke, 2001).

Garrard, John A., *The English and Immigration, 1880–1910* (London, 1971).

Gartner, Lloyd P., *The Jewish Immigrant in England, 1870–1914*, 3rd edn (London, 2010).

Gay, Ignacio Ramos, ' "Black Blokes Who Spoke Like East-Enders": Nation, Race and Hooliganism in Cass Pennant's *Cass*', *Journal of Postcolonial Writing*, vol. 52 (2016).

Geiss, Immanuel, *The Pan-African Movement* (London, 1974).

George, Joan, *Merchants to Magnates, Intrigue and Survival: Armenians in London, 1900–2000* (London, 2009).

George, M. Dorothy, *London Life in the Eighteenth Century* (Harmondsworth, 1966).

Gerzina, Gretchen, *Black London: Life Before Emancipation* (New Brunswick, NJ, 1995).

Gilley, Sheridan, 'Catholic Faith of the Irish Slums: London, 1840–70', in H. J. Dyos and M. Wolff, eds, *The Victorian City: Images and Realities* (London, 1973).

Gilley, Sheridan, 'English Attitudes towards the Irish, 1789–1900', in Colin Holmes, ed., *Immigrants and Minorities in British Society* (London, 1978).

Gilley, Sheridan, 'The Garibaldi Riots of 1862', *Historical Journal*, vol. 16 (1973).

Gilley, Sheridan, 'The Roman Catholic Mission to the Irish in London, 1840–1860', *Recusant History*, vol. 10 (1969–70).

Gilliat-Ray, Sophie, *Muslims in Britain: An Introduction* (Cambridge, 2010).

Gillman, Peter and Leni, *'Collar the Lot': How Britain Interned and Expelled Its Wartime Refugees* (London, 1980).

Gilroy, Paul, *The Black Atlantic: Modernity and Double Consciousness* (London, 1993).

Gimson, Andrew, 'Backbone of England', *Spectator*, 1 June 2002.

Giulianotti, Richard and Robertson, Roland, 'The Globalization of Football: A Study in the Glocalization of the "Serious Life" ', *British Journal of Sociology*, vol. 55 (2004).

Glasman, Judy, 'London Synagogues in the Late Nineteenth Century: Design in Context', *London Journal*, vol. 13 (1988).

Glees, Anthony, *Exile Politics during the Second World War: The German Social Democrats in Britain* (Oxford, 1982).

Glynn, Sarah, *Class, Ethnicity and Religion in the Bengali East End: A Political History* (Manchester, 2015).

Godley, Andrew, *Jewish Immigrant Entrepreneurship in New York and London, 1880–1914: Enterprise and Culture* (Basingstoke, 2001).

Goldblatt, David, *The Ball is Round: A Global History of Football* (London, 2007).

Goldbolt, Jim, *A History of Jazz in Britain, 1919–50* (London, 1984).

Goldbolt, Jim, *A History of Jazz in Britain 1950–1970* (London, 1989).

Goodwin, Matthew J., 'The Extreme Right in Britain: Still an "Ugly Duckling" but for How Long?', *Political Quarterly*, vol. 78 (2007).

Goody, Jack, *Food and Love: A Cultural History of East and West* (London, 1998).

Gordon, Paul, *White Law: Racism in the Police, Courts and Prisons* (London, 1983).

Goulbourne, Harry, *Race Relations in Britain Since 1945* (Basingstoke, 1998).

Gould, Julius and Esh, Shaul, eds, *Jewish Life in Modern Britain* (London, 1964).

Goulston, Michael, 'The Status of the Anglo-Jewish Rabbinate, 1840–1914', *Jewish Journal of Sociology*, vol. 10 (1968).

Graham, David, Schmool, Marlena and Waterman, Stanley, *Jews in Britain: A Snapshot from the 2001 Census* (London, 2007).

Gray, Breda, 'From "Ethnicity" to "Diaspora": 1980s Emigration and "Multicultural" London', in Andy Bielenberg, ed., *The Irish Diaspora* (Harlow, 2000).

Green, David R., *From Artisans to Paupers: Economic Change and Poverty in London, 1790–1870* (Aldershot, 1995).

Green, David R., 'Little Italy in Victorian London: Holborn's Italian Community', *Camden History Review*, vol. 15 (1988).

Green, Jeffrey P., 'Afro-American Symphony: Popular Black Concert Hall Performers', in Paul Oliver, ed., *Black Music in Britain* (Milton Keynes, 1990).

Green, Jeffrey P., *Black Edwardians: Black People in Britain, 1901–1914* (London, 1998).

Green, Shirley, *Rachman: The Slum Landlord Whose Name Became a Byword for Evil* (London, 1979).

Greengrass, Mark, 'Protestant Exiles and their Assimilation in Early Modern England', *Immigrants and Minorities*, vol. 4 (1985).

Grove, Peter and Colleen, *Curry Culture: A Very British Love Affair* (Surbiton, 2005).

Guest, Matthew, Olson, Elizabeth and Wolfe, John, 'Christianity: Loss of Monopoly', in Linda Woodhead and Rebecca Catto, eds, *Religion and Change in Modern Britain* (Abingdon, 2012).

Guyotte, Roland L. and Posadas, Barbara M., 'Interracial Marriages and Transnational Families: Chicago's Filipinos in the Aftermath of World War II', *Journal of American Ethnic History*, vol. 9 (1990).

Gwynn, Robin D., *Huguenot Heritage: The History and Contribution of the Huguenots in Britain* (London, 1988).

Hackett, Sarah, *Foreigners, Minorities and Integration: The Muslim Immigrant Experience in Britain and Germany* (Manchester, 2013).

Hagen, Antje, *Deutsche Direktinvestitionen in Grossbritannien, 1871–1918* (Stuttgart, 1997).

Hancox, Dan, *Inner City Pressure: The Story of Grime* (London, 2018).

Handlin, Oscar, *The Uprooted: The Epic Story of the Great Migration that Made the American Peoples*, 2nd edn (Boston, MA, 1973).

Harlaftis, Gelina, *A History of Greek-owned Shipping: The Making of an International Tramp Fleet, 1830 to the Present Day* (London, 1996).

Harper, Marjory and Constantine, Stephen, *Migration and Empire* (Oxford, 2014).

Harris, Jonathan, 'London's Greek Community', in George Kakavas, ed., *Treasured Offerings: The Legacy of the Greek Orthodox Cathedral of St. Sophia London* (London, 2002).

Harrison, Molly, *People and Shopping* (London, 1975).

Haywood, Ian and Seed, John, eds, *The Gordon Riots: Politics, Culture and Insurrection in Late Eighteenth-Century Britain* (Cambridge, 2012).

Herberg, Will, *Protestant-Catholic-Jew: An Essay in American Religious Sociology* (Chicago, IL, 1983).

Hewitt, Roger, *White Talk Black Talk: Inter-Racial Friendship and Communication amongst Adolescents* (Cambridge, 1986).

Hibbert, Christopher, *King Mob: The Story of Lord George Gordon and the London Riots of 1780* (London, 1958).

Hibbert, Christopher, *London: The Biography of a City* (Harmondsworth, 1977).

Hickman, Mary J., *Religion, Class and Identity: The State, the Catholic Church, and the Education of the Irish in Britain* (Aldershot, 1995).

Hickman, Mary and Walter, Bronwen, *Discrimination and the Irish Community in Britain* (London, 1997).

Hickson, Kevin, 'The Postwar Consensus Revisited', *Political Quarterly*, vol. 75 (2004).

Higonnet, Patrice L. R., *Paris: Capital of the World* (London, 2002).

Hillaby, Joe, 'London: The Thirteenth-Century Jewry', *Transactions of the Jewish Historical Society of England*, vol. 33 (1990–2).

Hillaby, Joe, 'The London Jewry: William I to John', *Transactions of the Jewish Historical Society of England*, vol. 33 (1992–4).

Hillman, Nicholas, 'A Chorus of "Execration"? Enoch Powell's "Rivers of Blood" Forty Years On', *Patterns of Prejudice*, vol. 42 (2008).

Hiro, Dilip, *Black British, White British* (London, 1971).

Hirschfeld, Gerhard, ed., *Exile in Great Britain: Refugees from Hitler's Germany* (Leamington Spa, 1984).

Hobsbawm, Eric, *The Age of Empire, 1875–1914* (Harmondsworth, 1987).

Hobsbawm, Eric, 'The Example of the English Middle Classes', in Jürgen Kocka and Allen Mitchell, eds, *Bourgeois Society in Nineteenth-Century Europe* (Oxford, 1993).

Hobsbawm, Eric, *Industry and Empire* (London, 1969).

Holden, Mark, *Murder in Notting Hill* (Winchester, 2011).

Hollingsworth, Barry, 'The Society of Friends of Russian Freedom: English Liberals and Russian Socialists', *Oxford Slavonic Papers*, vol. 3 (1970).

Holmes, Colin, *Anti-Semitism in British Society, 1876–1939* (London, 1979).

Holmes, Colin, 'Cosmopolitan London', in Anne J. Kershen, ed., *London the Promised Land? The Migrant Experience in a Capital City* (Aldershot, 1997).

Holmes, Colin, *John Bull's Island: Immigration and British Society, 1871–1971* (Basingstoke, 1988).

Holmes, Colin, 'The Tredegar Riots of 1911: Anti-Jewish Disturbances in South Wales', *Welsh History Review*, vol. 11 (1982).

Holmes, Martin, 'Evil May-Day 1517: The Story of a Riot', *History Today*, vol. 15 (September 1965).

Holohan, Anne, *Working Lives: The Irish in Britain* (Hayes, 1995).

Holt, Richard and Mason, Tony, *Sport in Britain 1945–2000* (Oxford, 2000).

Huc-Hepher, Saskia and Drake, Helen, 'From the 16ème to South Ken? A Study of the Contemporary French Population in London', in Debra Kelly and Martyn Cornick, *A History of the French in London: Liberty, Equality, Opportunity* (London, 2013).

Huffman, Joseph P., *Family, Commerce and Religion in Cologne: Anglo-German Emigrants, c.1000–c.1300* (Cambridge, 1998).

Huggett, Frank Edward, *Life Below Stairs: Domestic Servants in England from Victorian Times* (London, 1977).

Husbands, Christopher T., 'East End Racism, 1900–1980: Geographical Continuities in Vigilantist and Extreme Right-wing Political Behaviour', *London Journal*, vol. 8 (1982).

Husbands, Christopher T., *Racial Exclusionism and the City: The Urban Support of the National Front* (London, 1983)

Hutchison, John, 'Diaspora Dilemmas and Shifting Allegiances: The Irish in London between Nationalism, Catholicism and Labourism (1900–22)', *Studies in Ethnicity and Nationalism*, vol. 10 (2010).

Hutton, Seán, 'The Irish in London', in Nick Merriman, ed., *The Peopling of London: Fifteen Thousand Years of Settlement from Overseas* (London, 1993).

Hyams, Paul, 'The Jewish Minority in Medieval England, 1066–1290', *Journal of Jewish Studies*, vol. 25 (1974).

Hyamson, A. M., *The History of the Jews in England* (London, 1908).

Hyder, Rehan, *Brimful of Asia: Negotiating Ethnicity on the UK Music Scene* (Aldershot, 2004).

Innis-Jiménez, Michael, *Steel Barrio: The Great Mexican Migration to South Chicago, 1915–1940* (New York, 2013).

Inwood, Stephen, *A History of London* (London, 1998).

Jackson, John A., 'The Irish in East London', *East London Papers*, vol. 6 (1963).

Jarvis, F. Anne M. R., 'German Musicians in London, c. 1750–1850', in Stefan Manz, Margrit Schulte Beerbühl and John R. Davis, eds, *Migration and Transfer from Germany to Britain, 1660–1914* (Munich, 2007).

Jeffcoate, Graham, *Deutsche Drucker und Buchhändler in London, 1680–1811: Strukturen und Bedeutung des Deutschen Anteils am englischen Buchhandel* (Berlin, 2015).

Jefferys, James B., *Retail Trading in Britain, 1830–1950* (Cambridge, 1954).

Jenkinson, Jacqueline, *Black 1919: Racism, Riots and Resistance in Imperial Britain* (Liverpool, 2009).

Jones, Charles A., *International Business in the Nineteenth Century: The Rise and Fall of a Cosmopolitan Bourgeoisie* (Brighton, 1987).

Jones, Douglas, 'The Chinese in Britain: The Origins and Development of a Community', *New Community*, vol. 14 (1987).

Jones, Emrys, ed., *The Welsh in London, 1500–1800* (Cardiff, 2001).

Jones, Gareth Stedman, *Outcast London: A Study in the Relationship between Classes in Victorian Society* (Harmondsworth, 1984).

Jones, Geoffrey, 'Foreign Multinationals and British Industry before 1945', *Economic History Review*, 2nd series, vol. 61 (1988).

Jones, Phillip, *Quickly to Her Fate* (Barton On Sea, 2010).

Jones, Simon, *Black Culture, White Youth: The Reggae Tradition from JA to UK* (Basingstoke, 1988).

Jones, Trevor, 'Small Asian Businesses in Retreat? The Case of the UK', *Journal of Ethnic and Migration Studies*, vol. 29 (2003).

Julius, Anthony, *Trials of the Diaspora: A History of Anti-Semitism in England* (Oxford, 2010).

Kaddish, Sharman, *A Good Jew or a Good Englishman? The Jewish Lads' and Girls' Brigade, 1895–1995* (London, 1995).

Kakavas, George, ed., *Treasured Offerings: The Legacy of the Greek Orthodox Cathedral of St. Sophia London* (London, 2002).

Kalman, R., 'The Jewish East End: Where Was It?', in Aubrey Newman, ed., *The Jewish East End* (London, 1981).

Kalra, Virinder S., *From Textile Mills to Taxi Ranks: Experiences of Migration, Labour and Social Change* (Farnham, 2000).

Karpf, Ernst, *Eine Stadt und ihre Einwanderer: 700 Jahre Migrationsgeschichte in Frankfurt am Main* (Frankfurt, 2013).

Katz, David S., *The Jews in the History of England, 1485–1850* (Oxford, 1994).

Kaufmann, Miranda, *Black Tudors: The Untold Story* (London, 2017).

Kay, Diana and Miles, Robert, *Refugees or Migrant Workers? European Volunteer Workers in Britain* (London, 1992).

Kay, George, *Food Supply and Ethnic Minorities: Its Availability and Quality* (London, 1986).

Keil, Hartmut and Jentz, John B., eds, *German Workers in Industrial Chicago, 1850–1910: A Comparative Perspective* (DeKalb, IL, 1983).

Kelly, Debra, 'A Migrant Culture on Display: The French Migrant and French Gastronomy in London (Nineteenth to Twenty-First Centuries)', *Modern Languages Open* (2016).

Kelly, Debra and Cornick, Martyn, eds, *A History of the French in London: Liberty, Equality, Opportunity* (London, 2013).

Kelly, Seamus, 'The Migration of Irish Professional Footballers: The Good, the Bad and the Ugly', in Richard Elliott and John Harris, eds, *Football and Migration: Perspectives, Places, Players* (London, 2012).

Kershen, Anne J., 'The Jewish Community in London', in Nick Merriman, ed., *The Peopling of London: 15,000 Years of Settlement from Overseas* (London, 1993).

Kershen, Anne J., 'London's Migrant Landscape in the 21st Century', in Anne J. Kershen, ed., *London the Promised Land Revisited: The Changing Face of the London Migrant Landscape in the Early 21st Century* (London, 2015).

Kershen, Anne J., *Strangers, Aliens and Asians: Huguenots, Jews and Bangladeshis in Spitalfields, 1660–2000* (London, 2005).

Kershen, Anne J., 'Time when England said "Welcome" ', *Church Times*, 12 June 2015.

Kershen, Anne J., *Uniting the Tailors: Trade Unionism among the Tailoring Workers of London and Leeds, 1870–1939* (Ilford, 1995).

Kershen, Anne J., ed., *Food in the Migrant Experience* (Aldershot, 2002).

Kershen, Anne J., ed., *London the Promised Land? The Migrant Experience in a Capital City* (Aldershot, 1997).

Kershen, Anne J., ed., *London the Promised Land Revisited: The Changing Face of the London Migrant Landscape in the Early 21st Century* (London, 2015).

Kershen, Anne J. and Romain, Jonathan A., *Tradition and Change: A History of Reform Judaism in Britain, 1840–1895* (London, 1995).

Kettenacker, Lothar, 'The Germans after 1945', in Panikos Panayi, ed., *Germans in Britain since 1500* (London, 1996).

Khabra, Gurdeep, 'Music in the Margins? Popular Music Heritage and British Bhangra Music', *International Journal of Heritage Studies*, vol. 20 (2014).

Kilvington, Daniel, 'British Asians and Football: How the "Beautiful Game" Needs to Change', *The Conversation*, 29 November 2017.

King-Dorset, Rodriguez, *Black Dance in London, 1730–1850: Innovation, Tradition and Resistance* (London, 2008).

Kirchberger, Ulrike, *Aspekte deutsch-britischer Expansion: Die Überseeinteressen der deutschen Migranten in Großbritannien in der Mitte des 19. Jahrhunderts* (Stuttgart, 1999).

Kirchberger, Ulrike, 'Deutsche Naturwissenschaftler im britischen Empire: Die Erforschung der au ereuropäischen Welt im Spannungsfeld zwischen deutschem und britischem Imperialismus', *Historische Zeitschrift*, vol. 271 (2000).

Kivisto, Peter, *Multiculturalism in a Global Society* (Oxford, 2002).

Kohn, Marek, *Dope Girls: The Birth of the British Drug Underground* (London, 1992).

Kosmin, Barry, 'Political Identity in Battersea', in Sandra Williamson, et al., *Living in South London: Perspectives on Battersea, 1871–1971* (Aldershot, 1982).

Kosmin, Barry A. and Levy, Caren, *Jewish Identity in an Anglo-Jewish Community* (London, 1983).

Kuepper, William G., Lackey, G. Lynne and Swinerton, E. Nelson, *Ugandan Asians in Great Britain: Forced Migration and Social Absorption* (London, 1975).

Kushner, Tony, 'An Alien Occupation: Jewish Refugees and Domestic Service in Britain, 1933–1948', in Werner E. Mosse, et al., eds, *Second Chance: Two Centuries of German-Speaking Jews in the United Kingdom* (Tübingen, 1991).

Kushner, Tony, 'Antisemitism and Austerity: The August 1947 Riots in Britain', in Panikos Panayi, ed., *Racial Violence in Britain in the Nineteenth and Twentieth Centuries* (London, 1996).

Kushner, Tony, 'The Fascist as "Other"? Racism and Neo-Nazism in Contemporary Britain', *Patterns of Prejudice*, vol. 28 (1994).

Kushner, Tony, 'The Impact of British Anti-Semitism, 1918–1945', in David Cesarani, ed., *The Making of Modern Anglo Jewry* (Oxford, 1990).

Kushner, Tony, *The Persistence of Prejudice: Anti-Semitism in British Society during the Second World War* (Manchester, 1989).

Kushner, Tony, *Remembering Refugees: Then and Now* (Manchester, 2006).

Kushner, Tony and Knox, Katherine, *Refugees in an Age of Genocide: Global, National and Local Perspectives During the Twentieth Century* (London, 1999).

Kushner, Tony and Valman, Nadia, eds, *Remembering Cable Street: Fascism and Anti-Fascism in British Society* (London, 2000).

Kynaston, David, *City of London* (London, 2012).

Lafitte, François, *The Internment of Aliens* (originally 1940; London, 1988).

Lahiri, Shompa, *Indians in Britain: Anglo-Indian Encounters, Race and Identity, 1880–1930* (London, 2000).

Lanfranchi, Pierre and Taylor, Matthew, *Moving with the Ball: The Migration of Professional Footballers* (Oxford, 2001).

Lattek, Christine, *Revolutionary Refugees: German Socialism in Britain, 1840–1860* (London, 2006).

Layton-Henry, Zig, 'The Electoral Participation of Black and Asian Britons: Integration or Alienation', *Parliamentary Affairs*, vol. 38 (1985).

Lebzelter, Gisela C., *Political Antisemitism in England, 1918–1939* (New York, 1978).

Lee, M. P., *Chinese Cookery* (London, 1943).

Lees, Lynn Hollen, *Exiles of Erin: Irish Immigrants in Victorian London* (Manchester, 1979).

Lees, Lynn Hollen, 'Patterns of Lower-Class Life: Irish Slum Communities in Nineteenth-Century London', in Stephan Thernstrom and Richard Sennett, eds, *Nineteenth-Century Cities: Essays in the New Urban History* (London, 1969).

Leiken, Robert S., *Europe's Angry Muslims: The Revolt of the Second Generation* (Oxford, 2015).

Levi, Erik, 'The German-Jewish Contribution to Musical Life in Britain', in Werner E. Mosse, et al., eds, *Second Chance: Two Centuries of German-Speaking Jews in the United Kingdom* (Tübingen, 1991).

Lewis, D. S., *Illusions of Grandeur: Mosley, Fascism and British Society, 1931–81* (Manchester, 1987).

Linehan, Thomas P., *East London for Mosley: The British Union of Fascists in East London and South-West Essex, 1933–40* (London, 1996).

Lipman, V. D., *A Century of Social Service* (London, 1959).

Lipman, V. D., *A History of the Jews in Britain Since 1858* (Leicester, 1990).

Lipman, V. D., 'Jewish Settlement in the East End – 1840–1940', in Aubrey Newman, ed., *The Jewish East End* (London, 1981).

Lipman, V. D., 'The Rise of Jewish Suburbia', *Transactions of the Jewish Historical Society of England*, vol. 21 (1968).

Lipman, V. D., 'The Structure of London Jewry in the Mid-Nineteenth Century', in H. J. Zimmels, J. Rabinowitz and Israel Feinstein, eds, *Essays in Honor of Chief Rabbi Israel Brodie* (London, 1967).

Lipman, V. D., 'A Survey of Anglo-Jewry in 1851', *Transactions of the Jewish Historical Society of England*, vol. 17 (1951–2).

Little, Kenneth, *Negroes in Britain* (London, 1972).

Lloyd, T. H., *Alien Merchants in England in the High Middle Ages* (Brighton, 1982).

Lloyd, T. H., *England and the German Hanse, 1157–1611: A Study in their Trade and Commercial Diplomacy* (Cambridge, 1991).

Lo, Kenneth, *Chinese Food* (Newton Abbot, 1972).

Lockwood, Allison, *Passionate Pilgrims: The American Traveller in Great Britain, 1800–1914* (London, 1981).

London, Louise, 'British Immigration Policy Control Procedures and Jewish Refugees, 1933–1939', in Werner E. Mosse, et al., eds, *Second Chance: Two Centuries of German-Speaking Jews in the United Kingdom* (Tübingen, 1991).

Lunn, Kenneth, 'Parliamentary Politics and the "Jewish Vote" in Whitechapel, 1906–1914', in Aubrey Newman, ed., *The Jewish East End, 1840–1939* (London, 1981).

Luu, Lien Bich, *Immigrants and the Industries of London* (Aldershot, 2005).

Lynch, Anne, *The Irish in Exile* (London, 1988).

Lysandrou, Sandra, *Cyprus Cooking for Friends: Traditional and Modern Recipes from Cyprus Including Taverna Meze and Sweets* (Nicosia, 1994).

Mac an Ghaill, Martin, 'The Irish in Britain: The Invisibility of Ethnicity and Anti-Irish Racism', *Journal of Ethnic and Migration Studies*, vol. 26 (2000).

MacDermott, T. P., 'Irish Workers in Tyneside in the Nineteenth Century', in Norman McCord, ed., *Essays in Tyneside Labour History* (Newcastle-upon-Tyne, 1977).

MacDonald, Roderick J., 'Dr Harold Arundel Moody and the League of Coloured Peoples, 1931–1947: A Retrospective View', *Race*, vol. 14 (1973).

MacRaild, Donald M., *Faith, Fraternity and Fighting: The Orange Order and Irish Migrants in Northern England, c. 1850–1920* (Liverpool, 2005).

MacRaild, Donald M., *Irish Migrants in Modern Britain, 1750–1922* (Basingstoke, 1999).

MacRaild, Donald M., ' "No Irish Need Apply": The Origins and Persistence of a Prejudice', *Labour History Review*, vol. 78 (2013).

Magee, Gary B. and Thompson, Andrew S., *Empire and Globalisation: Networks of People, Goods and Capital, c.1850–1914* (Cambridge, 2010).

Magee, Jonathan and Sugden, John, ' "The World at their Feet": Professional Football and International Labour Migration', *Journal of Sport and Social Issues*, vol. 26 (2002).

Makalani, Minkah, *In the Cause of Freedom: Radical Black Internationalism from Harlem to London, 1917–1939* (Chapel Hill, NC, 2011).

Malet, Marian and Grenville, Anthony, eds, *Changing Countries: The Experience and Achievement of German-Speaking Exiles from Hitler in Britain, 1933 to Today* (London, 2002).

Mandle, W. F., *Anti-Semitism and the British Union of Fascists* (London, 1968).

Manning, Patrick, *Migration in World History*, 2nd edn (London, 2013).

Manz, Stefan, *Migranten und Internierte: Deutsche in Glasgow, 1864–1918* (Stuttgart, 2003).

Manz, Stefan and Panayi, Panikos, eds, *Refugees and Cultural Transfers to Britain* (Abingdon, 2013).

Marks, Lara, 'Race, Class and Gender: The Experience of Jewish Prostitutes and other Jewish Women in the East End of London at the Turn of the Century', in Joan Grant, ed., *Women, Migration and Empire* (Stoke-on-Trent, 1996).

Marriot, John, *Beyond the Tower: A History of East London* (London, 2011).

Mars, Valerie, 'Experiencing French Cookery in Nineteenth-Century London', in Debra Kelly and Martyn Cornick, eds, *A History of the French in London: Liberty, Equality, Opportunity* (London, 2013).

Martin, Rudolf Emil, *Anarchismus und seine Träger* (Berlin, 1887).

Massil, William I., *Immigrant Furniture Workers in London, 1881–1939 and the Jewish Contribution to the Furniture Trade* (London, 1997).

Matera, Marc, *Black London: The Imperial Metropolis and Decolonization in the Twentieth Century* (Oakland, CA, 2015).

McGladdery, Gary, *The Provisional IRA in England: The Bombing Campaign, 1973–1997* (Dublin, 2006).

McGovern, Patrick, 'Globalization or Internationalization? Foreign Footballers in the English League, 1946–95', *Sociology*, vol. 36 (2002).

McGovern, Patrick, 'The Irish Brawn Drain: English League Clubs and Irish Footballers, 1946–1995', *British Journal of Sociology*, vol. 51 (2000)

McGowan, Jack, ' "Dispute", "Battle", "Siege", "Farce"? Grunwick 30 Years On', *Contemporary British History*, vol. 22 (2008).

McVeigh, Simon, *Concert Life in London from Mozart to Haydn* (Cambridge, 1993).

McVeigh, Simon, 'Italian Violinists in Eighteenth-Century London', in Reinhard Strohm, ed., *The Eighteenth-Century Diaspora of Italian Music and Musicians* (Turnhout, 2001).

Meetoo, Veena and Mirza, Heidi Safia, ' "There is Nothing 'Honourable' about Honour Killings": Gender, Violence and the Limits of Multiculturalism', *Women's Studies International Forum*, vol. 30 (2007).

Mennell, Stephen, *All Manners of Food: Eating and Taste in England and France from the Middle Ages to the Present* (Oxford, 1985).

Merrifield, Ralph, *Roman London* (London, 1969).

Merriman, Nick, 'The Invisible Settlers: From Prehistoric Times to Huguenots', in Nick Merriman, ed., *The Peopling of London: Fifteen Thousand Years of Settlement from Overseas* (London, 1993)

Metcalf, Hilary, Modood, Tariq and Virdee, Satnam, *Asian Self-Employment: The Interaction of Culture and Economics in England* (London, 1996).

Miles, Henry Downes, *Pugilistica: The History of English Boxing* (Edinburgh, 1906).

Miles, Robert, 'The Riots of 1958: The Ideological Construction of Race Relations as a Political Force in Britain', *Immigrants and Minorities*, vol. 3 (1984).

Miller, Rebecca S., 'Hucklebucking at the Tea Dances: Irish Showbands in Britain, 1959–1969', *Popular Music History*, vol. 9 (2014).

MINTeL, Leisure Intelligence, *Ethnic Restaurants*, January 1998.

M.-N. B., *History of the Russian Orthodox Church in London, 1707–1977* (London, 1978).

Model, Suzanne and Fisher, Gene, 'Unions Between Blacks and Whites: England Compared with the USA', *Ethnic and Racial Studies*, vol. 25 (2002).

Modood, Tariq, *Multiculturalism: A Civic Idea*, 2nd edn (Cambridge, 2013).

Moore, Hilary, *Inside British Jazz: Crossing Borders of Race and Class* (Abingdon, 2016).

Morris, John, *Londinium: London in the Roman Empire* (London, 1982).

Morris, Jonathan, *Coffee: A Global History* (London, 2018).

Mosse, W. E., et al., eds, *Second Chance: Two Centuries of German-Speaking Jews in the United Kingdom* (Tübingen, 1991).

Moulton, Mo, *Ireland and the Irish in Interwar England* (Cambridge, 2014).

Muhs, Rudlof, 'Jews of German Background in British Politics', in W. E. Mosse, et al., eds, *Second Chance: Two Centuries of German-Speaking Jews in the United Kingdom* (Tübingen, 1991).

Müller, Friedeborg L., *History of German Lutheran Congregations in England, 1900–1950* (Frankfurt, 1987).

Mundill, Robin R., *England's Jewish Solution: Experiment and Expulsion* (Cambridge, 1998).

Murray, Tony, *London Irish Fictions: Narrative, Diaspora and Identity* (Liverpool, 2012).

Musgrave, Michael, *The Musical Life of Crystal Palace* (Cambridge, 1995).

Musson, A. E., 'The Great Depression in Britain, 1873–1896: A Reappraisal', *Journal of Economic History*, vol. 19 (1959).

Myers, Norma, *Reconstructing the Black Past: Blacks in Britain, 1780–1830* (London, 1996).

Nagle, John, *Multiculturalism's Double Bind: Creating Inclusivity, Cosmopolitanism and Difference* (Farnham, 2009).

Nead, Lynda, *Victorian Babylon: People, Streets and Images in Nineteenth-Century London* (London, 2000).

Neal, Frank, *Sectarian Violence: The Liverpool Experience, 1819–1914* (Manchester, 1988).

Nenadic, Stena, ed., *Scots in London in the Eighteenth Century* (Lewisburg, PA, 2010).

Nettel, Reginald, *The Orchestra in England: A Social History* (London, 1946).

Newman, Aubrey, *The Board of Deputies of British Jews* (London, 1982).

Newman, Aubrey, 'The Poor Jews' Temporary Shelter: An Episode in Migration Studies', *Transactions of the Jewish Historical Society of England*, vol. 40 (2005).

Newman, Aubrey, *The United Synagogue, 1880–1970* (London, 1977).

Newman, Aubrey, ed., *The Jewish East End, 1840–1939* (London, 1981).

Newsinger, John, *Fenians in Mid-Victorian Britain* (London, 1994).

Nicolaou, Nearchos, *Cooking from Cyprus: Including Selected Recipes of Taverna Meze*, 10th edn (Nicosia, 1990).

Norman, E. R., *Anti-Catholicism in Victorian England* (London, 1968).

Norton, Brian M., *Americans in London: An Anecdotal Street Guide to the Homes and Haunts of Americans from John Adams to Fred Astaire* (London, 1988).

Nott, James J., *Music for the People: Popular Music and Dance in Interwar Britain* (Oxford, 2002).

Oakley, Robin, *Changing Patterns of Distribution of Cypriot Settlement* (Coventry, 1987).

O'Connor, Kevin, *The Irish in Britain* (Dublin, 1974).

O'Day, Alan, 'The Political Organization of the Irish in Britain, 1867–90', in Roger Swift and Sheridan Gilley, eds, *The Irish in Britain, 1815–1939* (London, 1989).

O'Day, Alan, 'Varieties of Anti-Irish Behaviour in Britain, 1846–1922', in Panikos Panayi, ed., *Racial Violence in Britain in the Nineteenth and Twentieth Centuries* (London, 1996).

Ogden, Philip E., 'Foreword', in Anne J. Kershen, ed., *London the Promised Land Revisited: The Changing Face of the London Migrant Landscape in the Early 21st Century* (London, 2015).

O'Grady, Anne, *Irish Migration to London in the 1940s and 1950s* (London, 1988).

Okokon, Susan, *Black Londoners: A History* (Stroud, 2009).

Oliver, Paul, ed., *Black Music in Britain* (Milton Keynes, 1990).

O'Neill, Kevin, *Where Have All the Irish Gone? The Sad Demise of Ireland's Once Relevant Footballers* (Worthing, 2017).

Ormond, David, *The Dutch in London: The Influence of an Immigrant Community* (London, 1973).

Osterhammel, Jürgen, *The Transformation of the World: A Global History of the Nineteenth Century* (Oxford, 2014).

Otterness, Philip, *Becoming German: The 1709 Palatine Migration to New York* (Ithaca, NY, 2004).

Pai, Hsiao-Hung, *Chinese Whispers: The True Story behind Britain's Hidden Army of Labour* (London, 2008).

Palaver, Wolfgang, Rudolph, Harriet and Regensburger, Dietmar, *The European Wars of Religion: An Interdisciplinary Reassessment of Sources, Interpretations, and Myths* (Abingdon, 2015).

Panayi, Panikos, 'The Anglicisation of East European Jewish Food in Britain', in Stefan Manz and Panikos Panayi, eds, *Refugees and Cultural Transfers to Britain* (Abingdon, 2013).

Panayi, Panikos, 'Anti-German Riots in London During the First World War', *German History*, vol. 7 (1989).

Panayi, Panikos, 'The British Empire Union in World War I', in Tony Kushner and Kenneth Lunn, eds, *The Politics of Marginality: Race, the Radical Right and Minorities in Twentieth-Century Britain* (London, 1990).

Panayi, Panikos, 'Cosmopolis: London's Ethnic Minorities', in Andrew Gibson and Joe Kerr, eds, *London from Punk to Blair* (London, 2003).

Panayi, Panikos, *The Enemy in Our Midst: Germans in Britain During the First World War* (Oxford, 1991).

Panayi, Panikos, *Fish and Chips* (London, 2014).

Panayi, Panikos, *German Immigrants in Britain during the Nineteenth Century, 1815–1914* (Oxford, 1995).

Panayi, Panikos, 'The German Poor and Working Classes in Victorian and Edwardian London', in Geoffrey Alderman and Colin Holmes, eds, *Outsiders and Outcasts* (London, 1993).

Panayi, Panikos, 'Germans in Eighteenth-Century Britain', in Panikos Panayi, ed., *Germans in Britain since 1500* (London, 1996).

Panayi, Panikos, *The Germans in India: Elite European Migrants in the British Empire* (Manchester, 2017).

Panayi, Panikos, 'Germans in London', in Nick Merriman, ed., *The Peopling of London: Fifteen Thousand Years of Settlement from Overseas* (London, 1993).

Panayi, Panikos, *Immigration, Ethnicity and Racism in Britain, 1815–1945* (Manchester, 1994).

Panayi, Panikos, *An Immigration History of Britain: Multicultural Racism Since 1800* (London, 2010).

Panayi, Panikos, *Spicing Up Britain: The Multicultural History of British Food* (London, 2008).

Panayi, Panikos, 'The Spicing Up of English Provincial Life: The History of Curry in Leicester', in Anne J. Kershen, ed., *Food in the Migrant Experience* (Aldershot, 2002).

Panayi, Panikos, ed., *Germans in Britain since 1500* (London, 1996).

Panayi, Panikos, ed., *Racial Violence in Britain in the Nineteenth and Twentieth Centuries* (London, 1996).

Panayi, Panikos and Manz, Stefan, 'The Rise and Fall of Germans in the British Hospitality Industry, c.1880–1920', *Food and History*, vol. 11 (2013).

Parker, Greg, *Probate Inventories of French Immigrants in Early Modern London* (London, 2016).

Parkes, James, 'The History of the Anglo-Jewish Community', in Maurice Freedman, ed., *A Minority in Britain: Social Studies of the Anglo-Jewish Community* (London, 1955).

Parsonage, Catherine, *The Evolution of Jazz in Britain, 1880–1935* (Aldershot, 2005).

Parsonage, Catherine, 'Fascination and Fear: Responses to Early Jazz in Britain', in Neil A. Wynn, ed., *Cross the Water Blues: African American Music in Europe* (Jackson, MI, 2007).

Paul, Kathleen, *Whitewashing Britain: Race and Citizenship in the Post-war Era* (Ithaca, NY, 1997).

Peach, Ceri, 'Does Britain Have Ghettos?', *Transactions of the Institute of British Geographers*, New Series, vol. 21 (1996).

Peach, Ceri, 'South Asian Migration and Settlement in Great Britain, 1951–2001', *Contemporary South Asia*, vol. 15 (2006).

Pearson, Geoffrey, ' "Paki-Bashing" in a North East Lancashire Cotton Town: A Case Study and its History', in Geoff Mungham and Geoffrey Pearson, eds, *Working-Class Youth Culture* (London, 1976).

Pennybacker, Susan D., *From Scottsboro to Munich: Race and Political Culture in 1930s Britain* (Princeton, NJ, 2009).

Pennybacker, Susan D., 'The Universal Races Congress, London Political Culture, and Imperial Dissent, 1900–1939', *Radical History Review*, Issue 92 (2005).

Perry, Kennetta Hammond, *London is the Place for Me: Black Britons, Citizenship, and the Politics of Race* (Oxford, 2015).

Perry, Thomas W., *Public Opinion, Propaganda and Politics in Eighteenth-Century England: A Study of the Jew Bill of 1753* (Cambridge, MA, 1962).

Pettegree, Andrew, *Foreign Protestant Communities in Sixteenth-Century London* (Oxford, 1986).

Pickering, Michael, *Blackface Minstrelsy in Britain* (Aldershot, 2008).

Pietsch, Tamson, *Empire of Scholars: Universities, Networks and the British Academic World, 1850–1939* (Manchester, 2013).

Pilkington, Edward, *Beyond the Mother Country: West Indians and the Notting Hill White Riots* (London, 1988).

Pohl, Manfred, 'Deutsche Bank London Agency Founded 100 Years Ago', in Deutsche Bank, ed., *Studies on Economic and Monetary Problems and on Banking History* (Frankfurt, 1988).

Poliakov, Léon, *The History of Anti-Semitism*, vol. 4, *Suicidal Europe, 1870–1933* (Oxford, 1985).

Pollard, Naomi, Latorre, Maria and Sriskandarajah, Dhananjayan, *Floodgates or Turnstiles? Post-EU Enlargement Migration Flows to (and from) the UK* (London, 2008).

Pollins, Harold, *Economic History of the Jews in England* (London, 1982).

Pollins, Harold, 'German Jews in British Industry', in Werner E. Mosse, et al., eds, *Second Chance: Two Centuries of German-Speaking Jews in the United Kingdom* (Tübingen, 1991).

Pollins, Harold, *Hopeful Travellers: Jewish Migrants and Settlers in Nineteenth-Century Britain* (London, 1991).

Poros, Maritsa V., *Modern Migrations: Gujarati Indian Networks in New York and London* (Stanford, CA, 2011).

Porter, Bernard, *The Refugee Question in Mid-Victorian Politics* (Cambridge, 1979).

Porter, Roy, *London: A Social History* (London, 1994).

Poulton, Emma, 'Towards Understanding: Antisemitism and the Contested Uses and Meanings of "Yid" in English Football', *Ethnic and Racial Studies*, vol. 39 (2016).

Powell, David, *Counter Revolution: The Tesco Story* (London, 1991).

Pugh, Martin, *Hurrah for the Blackshirts! Fascists and Fascism in Britain Between the Wars* (London, 2006).

Quail, John, *The Slow Burning Fuse: The Lost History of British Anarchists* (London, 1978).

Quinlivan, Patrick and Rose, Paul, *The Fenians in England, 1865–1872* (London, 1982).

Ram, Monder, Abbas, Tahir, Sanghera, Balihar and Hillin, Guy, ' "Currying Favour with the Locals": Balti Owners and Business Enclaves', *International Journal of Entrepreneurial Behaviour and Research*, 6 (2000).

Ram, Vidya, 'Britain Proposes Controversial Changes to Investor Visas', *Businessline*, 26 February 2014.

Ramdin, Ron, *The Making of the Black Working Class in Britain* (Aldershot, 1987).

Ranc, David, *Foreign Players and Football Supporters: The Old Firm, Arsenal, Paris Saint-German* (Manchester, 2012).

Randall, Elizabeth, 'A Special Case? London's French Protestants', in Debra Kelly and Martyn Cornick, eds, *A History of the French in London: Liberty, Equality, Opportunity* (London, 2013).

Rapoport, Michel, 'The London French from the Belle Epoque to the End of the Inter-War Period', in Debra Kelly and Martyn Cornick, eds, *A History of the French in London: Liberty, Equality, Opportunity* (London, 2013).

Rasmussen, Steen Eiler, *London: The Unique City* (London, 1937).

Rehin, George F., 'Blackface Street Minstrels in Victorian London and its Resorts: Popular Culture and its Racial Connotations as Revealed in Polite Opinion', *Journal of Popular Culture*, vol. 15 (1981).

Richardson, D. J., 'J. Lyons & Co. Ltd.: Caterers & Food Manufacturers, 1894 to 1939', in D. J. Oddy and Derek S. Miller, eds, *The Making of the Modern British Diet* (London, 1976).

Riello, Giorgio, 'The Taste of Italy: Italian Businesses and the Culinary Delicacies of Georgian London', *London Journal*, vol. 31 (2006).

Ritchie, J. M., *German Exiles: British Perspectives* (New York, 1997).

Ritzer, George, *The McDonaldization of Society*, New Century Edition (London, 2000).

Roberts, J. A. G., *From China to Chinatown: Chinese Food in the West* (London, 2002).

Robinson, Vaughan, *Transients, Settlers and Refugees: Asians in Britain* (Oxford, 1986).

Roderick, Martin, *The Work of Professional Football: A Labour of Love?* (Abingdon, 2006).

Rodmell, Paul, *Opera in the British Isles, 1875–1918* (Farnham, 2013).

Rogers, Colin, *The Battle of Stepney: The Sidney Street Siege* (London, 1981).

Rohr, Deborah, *The Careers of British Musicians 1750–1850: A Profession of Artisans* (Cambridge, 2001).

Rojek, Wojciech, 'The Government of the Republic of Poland in Exile, 1945–92', in Peter D. Stachura, ed., *The Poles in Britain, 1940–2000: From Betrayal to Assimilation* (London, 2004).

Rollin, Glenda and Jack, *Sky Sports Football Yearbook, 2010–11* (London, 2010).

Rosenberg, Edgar, *From Shylock to Svengali: Jewish Stereotypes in English Fiction* (Stanford, CA, 1960).

Rössler Hans, ' "Die Zuckerbäcker waren vornehmlich Hannoveraner": Zur Geschichte der Wanderung aus dem Elbe-Weser-Dreieck in die Britische Zuckerindustrie', *Jahrbuch der Männer vom Morgenstern*, vol. 81 (2003).

Roth, Cecil, *The Great Synagogue London, 1690–1940* (London, 1950).

Roth, Cecil, *A History of the Jews in England* (Oxford, 1964).

Roth, Cecil, *The Rise of Provincial Jewry: The Early History of the Jewish Communities in the English Countryside* (London, 1950).

Rowe, Michael, *The Racialization of Disorder in Twentieth-Century Britain* (Aldershot, 1998).

Royle, Tom, *Working for McDonald's in Europe: The Unequal Struggle* (London, 2000).

Rozin, Mordechai, *The Rich and the Poor: Jewish Philanthropy and Social Control in Nineteenth-Century London* (Brighton, 1999).

Rubinstein, W. D., 'Henry Page Croft and the National Party, 1917–22', *Journal of Contemporary History*, vol. 9 (1974).

Rubinstein, W. D., *A History of the Jews in the English-Speaking World: Great Britain* (Basingstoke, 1996).

Rudé, George, 'The Gordon Riots: A Study of the Rioters and their Victims', *Transactions of the Royal Historical Society*, vol. 6 (1956).

Rudé, George, *Hanoverian London* (London, 1971).

Rudé, George, 'The London Mob of the Eighteenth Century', *Historical Journal*, vol. 2 (1959).

Russell, Dave, *Popular Music in England, 1840–1914*, 2nd edn (Manchester, 1997).

Ryan, Louise, 'Passing Time: Irish Women Remembering and Re-telling Stories of Migration to Britain', in Panikos Panayi and Kathy Burrell, eds, *Histories and Memories: Migrants and their History in Britain* (London, 2006).

Rye, Howard, 'Fearsome Means of Discord: Early Encounters with Black Jazz', in Paul Oliver, ed., *Black Music in Britain* (Milton Keynes, 1990).

Salbstein, M. C. N., *The Emancipation of the Jews in Britain: The Question of the Admission of the Jews to Parliament* (London, 1982).

Saleem, Shahed, *The British Mosque: An Architectural and Social History* (Swindon, 2018).

Sandhu, Sukhdev, *London Calling: How Black and Asian Writers Imagined a City* (London, 2004).

Sassen, Saskia, *The Global City: New York, London, Tokyo*, 2nd edn (Princeton, NJ, 2001).

Schlosser, Eric, *Fast Food Nation* (London, 2002).

Schmiechen, James A., *Sweated Industries and Sweated Labour: The London Clothing Trades, 1860–1914* (London, 1984).

Schneer, Jonathan, *London 1900: The Imperial Metropolis* (London, 1999).

Schürer, K. and Day, Joe, 'Migration to London and the Development of the North-South Divide, 1851–1951', *Social History*, vol. 44 (2019).

Schwarz, Leonard, *London in the Age of Industrialisation* (Cambridge, 2004).

Schwartz, Roberta Freund, *How Britain Got the Blues: The Transmission and Reception of American Blues Style in the United Kingdom* (Aldershot, 2007).

Scobie, Edward, *Black Britannia: A History of Blacks in Britain* (Chicago, IL, 1972).

Scott, Derek B., *Sounds of the Metropolis* (Oxford, 2011).

Scouloudi, Irene, 'Alien Immigration in London, 1558–1640', *Proceedings of the Huguenot Society of London*, vol. 16 (1938).

Searle, G. R., *Corruption in British Politics, 1895–1930* (Oxford, 1987).

Searle, Townley, *Strange News from China: A First Chinese Cookbook* (London, 1932).

Seed, John, 'Limehouse Blues: Looking for Chinatown in the London Docks, 1900–40', *History Workshop Journal*, Issue 62 (2006).

Selwood, Jacob, *Diversity and Difference in Early Modern London* (Farnham, 2010).

Selwood, Jacob, 'Jewish Immigration, Anti-Semitism and the Diversity of Early Modern London', *Jewish Culture and History*, vol. 10 (2008).

Seth, Andrew and Randall, Geoffrey, *The Grocers: The Rise of the Supermarket Chains* (London, 2001).

Shang, Anthony, *The Chinese in Britain* (London, 1984).

Shang, Anthony, 'The Chinese in London', in Nick Merriman, ed., *The Peopling of London: Fifteen Thousand Years of Settlement from Overseas* (London, 1993).

Sharot, Stephen, 'Religious Change in Native Orthodoxy in London, 1870–1914: Rabbinate and Clergy', *Jewish Journal of Sociology*, vol. 15 (1973).

Sharot, Stephen, 'Religious Change in Native Orthodoxy in London, 1870–1914: The Synagogue Service', *Jewish Journal of Sociology*, vol. 15 (1973).

Sherwood, Marika, *Origins of Pan-Africanism: Henry Sylvester Williams, Africa, and the African Diaspora* (London, 2012).

Shoemaker, Robert B., *The London Mob: Violence and Disorder in Eighteenth-Century England* (London, 2004).

Shukra, Kalbir, *The Changing Face of Black Politics in Britain* (London, 1998).

Shyllon, Florian, *Black People in Britain, 1555–1833* (London, 1977).

Simons, Andrew, 'Black British Swing: The African Diaspora's Contribution to England's Own Jazz of the 1930s and 1940s', in Andy Linehan, ed., *Aural History: Essays on Recorded Sound* (London, 2001).

Simpson, Julian, *Migrant Architects of the NHS: South Asian Doctors and the Reinvention of British General Practice (1940s–1980s)* (Manchester, 2018).

Simpson, W. W., 'The Council of Citizens of East London: A Postscript', in Aubrey Newman, ed., *The Jewish East End* (London, 1981).

Singer, Steven, 'The Anglo-Jewish Ministry in Early Victorian London', *Modern Judaism*, vol. 5 (1985).

Singh, Gurharpal and Tatla, Darshan Singh, *Sikhs in Britain: The Making of a Community* (London, 2006).

Slatter, John, ed., *From the Other Shore: Russian Political Emigrants in Britain, 1880–1917* (London, 1984).

Smith, Elaine, 'Jews and Politics in the East End of London, 1918–1939', in David Cesarani, ed., *The Making of Modern Anglo-Jewry* (Oxford, 1990).

Smith, Evan and Varnava, Andrekos, 'Creating a "Suspect Community": Monitoring and Controlling the Cypriot Community in Inter-War London', *English Historical Review*, vol. 132 (2017).

Smith, Steve Alexander, *British Black Gospel: The Foundations of this Vibrant UK Sound* (Oxford, 2009).

Snowman, Daniel, *The Hitler Emigrés: The Cultural Impact on Britain of Refugees from Nazism* (London, 2003).

Sorohan, Seán, *Irish London during the Troubles* (Dublin, 2012).

Spencer, Ian R. G., *British Immigration Policy: The Making of Multi-Racial Britain* (London, 1997).

Sponza, Lucio, 'The Anti-Italian Riots, June 1940', in Panikos Panayi, ed., *Racial Violence in Britain in the Nineteenth and Twentieth Centuries* (London, 1996).

Sponza, Lucio, 'The British Government and the Internment of Italians', in David Cesarani and Tony Kushner, eds, *The Internment of Aliens in Twentieth-Century Britain* (London, 1993).

Sponza, Lucio, *Divided Loyalties: Italians in Britain during the Second World War* (Frankfurt, 2000).

Sponza, Lucio, *Italian Immigrants in Nineteenth-Century Britain* (Leicester, 1988).

Sponza, Lucio, 'Italian "Penny Ice-Men" in Victorian London', in Anne J. Kershen, ed., *Food in the Migrant Experience* (Aldershot, 2002).

Sponza, Lucio, 'Italians in London', in Nick Merriman, ed., *The Peopling of London: Fifteen Thousand Years of Settlement from Overseas* (London, 1993).

Sprang, Rebecca L., *The Invention of the Restaurant: Paris and Modern Gastronomic Culture* (London, 2000).

Srebrnik, Henry Felix, *London Jews and British Communism, 1935–1945* (Ilford, 1995).

Steinmetz, Susanne, 'The German Churches of London', in Panikos Panayi, ed., *Germans in Britain since 1500* (London, 1996).

Stent, Ronald A., *A Bespattered Page? The Internment of His Majesty's 'Most Loyal Enemy Aliens'* (London, 1980).

Stevenson, John, *Popular Disturbances in England, 1700–1870* (London, 1979).

Stratton, Jon, *When Music Migrates: Crossing British and European Racial Faultlines, 1945–2010* (London, 2016).

Stratton, Jon and Zuberi, Nabeel, eds, *Black Popular Music in Britain since 1945* (London, 2016).

Sword, Keith, 'The Poles in London', in Nick Merriman, ed., *The Peopling of London: Fifteen Thousand Years of Settlement from Overseas* (London, 1993).

Tabili, Laura, 'The Construction of Racial Difference in Twentieth-Century Britain: The Special Restriction (Coloured Alien Seamen) Order, 1925', *Journal of British Studies*, vol. 33 (1994).

Tacoma, Laurens E., *Moving Romans: Migration to Rome in the Principate* (Oxford, 2016).

Tames, Richard, *Feeding London: A Taste of History* (London, 2003).

Tananbaum, Susan L., 'Ironing out the Ghetto Bend: Sports, Character and Acculturation among Jewish Immigrants in Britain', *Journal of Sport History*, vol. 31 (2004).

Tananbaum, Susan L., *Jewish Immigrants in London, 1880–1939* (London, 2014).

Tannahill, J. A., *European Volunteer Workers in Britain* (Manchester, 1958).

Taylor, Matthew, *The Association Game: A History of British Football* (Harlow, 2008).

Taylor, Matthew, 'From Source to Subject: Sport, History, and Autobiography', *Journal of Sport History*, vol. 35 (2008).

Taylor, Matthew, 'Global Players? Football Migration and Globalization, c. 1930–2000', *Historical Social Research*, vol. 31 (2006).

Taylor, Simon, *A Land of Dreams: A Study of Jewish and Caribbean Migrant Communities in England* (London, 1993).

Taylor, Stan, *The National Front in English Politics* (London, 1982).

Temperley, Nicholas, 'Xenophilia in British Musical History', in Bennett Zon, ed., *Nineteenth-Century British Musical Studies*, vol. 1 (Aldershot, 1999).

Theodorou, Zena and Kyriacou, Sav, 'Cypriots in London', in Nick Merriman, ed., *The Peopling of London: Fifteen Thousand Years of Settlement from Overseas* (London, 1993).

Thomas, Terence, 'Hindu Dharma in Dispersion', in Gerald Parsons, ed., *The Growth of Religious Diversity in Britain* (Abingdon, 1993).

Thrupp, Sylvia L., 'Aliens in and Around London in the Fifteenth Century', in A. E. J. Hollaender and William Kelloway, eds, *Studies in London History: Presented to Philip Edmund Jones* (London, 1969).

Thurlow, Richard, 'The Authorities and the Anti-Jewish Disturbances in the 1930s', in Panikos Panayi, ed., *Racial Violence in Britain in the Nineteenth and Twentieth Centuries* (London, 1996).

Thurlow, Richard, 'The Failure of British Fascism', in Andrew Thorpe, ed., *The Failure of Political Extremism in Inter-War Britain* (Exeter, 1989).

Thurlow, Richard, *Fascism in Britain* (Oxford, 1987).

Tilles, Daniel, *British Fascist Antisemitism and Jewish Responses, 1932–40* (London, 2015).

Toczek, Nick, *Haters, Baiters and Would-Be Dictators: Anti-Semitism and the UK Far-Right* (Abingdon, 2016).

Thompson, Keith, *Under Siege: Racial Violence in Britain Today* (London, 1988).

Toynbee, Jason, Tackley, Catherine and Doffman, Mark, 'Another Place, Another Race? Thinking Through Jazz, Ethnicity and Diaspora in Britain', in Jason Toynbee, Catherine Tackley and Mark Doffman, eds, *Black British Jazz: Rules, Ownership and Performance* (Aldershot, 2014).

Turton, Jacqueline, 'Mayhew's Irish: The Irish Poor in Mid Nineteenth-Century London', in Roger Swift and Sheridan Gilley, eds, *The Irish in Victorian Britain: The Local Dimension* (Dublin, 1999).

Twine, France Winddance, *A White Side of Black Britain: Interracial Intimacy and Racial Literacy* (London, 2010).

Ugolini, Wendy, *Experiencing the War as the 'Enemy Other': Italian Scottish Experience in World War II* (Manchester, 2011).

United Synagogue Kashrut Board, *The Really Jewish Food Guide, 2005/5765* (London, 2005).

Vertovec, Steven, 'Super-Diversity and its Implications', *Ethnic and Racial Studies*, vol. 30 (2007).

Vigne, Randolph and Littleton, Charles, eds, *From Strangers to Citizens: The Integration of Immigrant Communities in Britain, Ireland and Colonial America, 1550–1750* (Brighton, 2001).

Visram, Rosina, *Asians in Britain: 400 Years of History* (London, 2002).

Wagner, Richard, *Das Judenthum in der Musik* (Leipzig, 1869).

Wainwright, A. Martin, *'The Better Class' of Indians: Social Rank, Imperial Identity and South Asians in Britain, 1858–1914* (Manchester, 2008).

Walkowitz, Judith R., *Nights Out: Life in Cosmopolitan London* (London, 2012).

Wall, Christine, Clarke, Linda, McGuire, Charles and Muñoz-Rojas, Olivia, *Building the Barbican, 1962–1982: Taking the Industry out of the Dark Ages* (London, 2014).

Wall, Christine, Clarke, Linda, McGuire, Charles and Muñoz-Rojas, Olivia, *Building the South Bank Arts Centre: The Art of Concrete* (London, 2014).

Walton, John K., *Fish and Chips and the British Working Class* (Manchester, 1992).

Walvin, James, *Black and White: The Negro and English Society, 1555–1945* (London, 1973).

Walvin, James, *The People's Game: The Social History of British Football* (London, 1975).

Ward, Andrew, *Dark Midnight When I Rise: The Story of the Jubilee Singers, Who Introduced the World to the Music of Black America* (New York, 2001).

Warde, Alan, 'Continuity and Change in British Restaurants, 1951–2001: Evidence from the *Good Food Guide*', in Marc Jacobs and Peter Scholliers, eds, *Eating Out in Europe: Picnics, Gourmet Dining and Snacks Since the Late Eighteenth Century* (Oxford, 2003).

Warde, Alan and Martens, Lydia, *Eating Out: Social Differentiation, Consumption and Pleasure* (Cambridge, 2000).

Wasserstein, Bernard, *Vanishing Diaspora: The Jews of Europe Since 1945* (London, 1996).

Watson, James L., ed., *Between Two Cultures: Migrants and Minorities in Britain* (Oxford, 1977).

Webb, Clive, 'Special Relationships: Mixed Race Couples in Post-War Britain and the United States', *Women's History Review*, vol. 26 (2017).

Webb, Simon, *Life in Roman London* (Stroud, 2011).

Weber, Max, *The Protestant Ethic and the Spirit of Capitalism* (originally 1904; London, 1976 edn).

Wemyss, Georgie, *The Invisible Empire: White Discourse, Tolerance and Belonging* (Abingdon, 2016).

Werbner, Pnina, *The Migration Process: Capital, Gifts and Offerings among British Pakistanis* (Oxford, 1990).

White, Jerry, *Campbell Bunk: The Worst Street in North London Between the Wars* (London, 1986).

White, Jerry, *London in the Eighteenth Century: A Great and Monstrous Thing* (London, 2013).

White, Jerry, *London in the Nineteenth Century: 'A Human Awful Wonder of God'* (London, 2007).

White, Jerry, *London in the Twentieth Century: A City and Its People* (London, 2008).

Whittall, Daniel, 'Creating Black Places in Imperial London: The League of Coloured Peoples and Aggrey House, 1931–1943', *London Journal*, vol. 36 (2011).

Wickenden, James, *Colour in Britain* (London, 1958).

Wicks, Margaret C. W., *The Italian Exiles in London, 1816–48* (New York, 1968 reprint).

Williams, Bill, *The Making of Manchester Jewry, 1740–1875* (Manchester, 1976).

Williamson, Jeffrey, 'The Impact of the Irish on British Labour Markets during the Industrial Revolution', in Roger Swift and Sheridan Gilley, eds, *The Irish in Britain, 1815–1939* (London, 1989).

Wills, Clair, *Lovers and Strangers: An Immigrant History of Post-War Britain* (London, 2017).

Wilson, A. N., *London: A Short History* (London, 2004).

Wilson, Francesca M., *They Came as Strangers: The Story of Refugees to Great Britain* (London, 1959).

Wilson, Patrick, *Murderess: A Study of the Women Executed in Britain since 1843* (London, 1971).

Wistrich, Robert, *Antisemitism: The Longest Hatred* (New York, 1991).

Wolffe, John, 'Fragmented Universality', in Gerald Parsons, ed., *The Growth of Religious Diversity in Britain* (Abingdon, 1993).

Woodhead, Linda and Catto, Rebecca, eds, *Religion and Change in Modern Britain* (Abingdon, 2012).

Woodhead, Lindy, *Shopping, Seduction and Mr Selfridge* (London, 2007).

Woolridge, Joyce, 'These Sporting Lives: Football Autobiographies 1945–1980', *Sport in History*, vol. 28 (2008).

Wyatt, Michael, *The Italian Encounter with Tudor England: A Cultural Politics of Translation* (Cambridge, 2005).

Wynn, Neil A, ed., *Cross the Water Blues: African American Music in Europe* (Jackson, MI, 2007).

Yungblut, Laura Hunt, *Strangers Settled Here Amongst Us: Policies, Perceptions and the Presence of Aliens in Elizabethan England* (London, 1996).

Zembe, Christopher Roy, *Zimbabwean Communities in Britain: Imperial and Post-Colonial Identities and Legacies* (Basingstoke, 2018).

Zuberi, Nabeel, *Sounds English: Transnational Popular Music* (Chicago, IL, 2001).

Zucchi, John E., *The Little Slaves of the Harp: Italian Child Street Musicians in Nineteenth-Century Paris, London and New York* (London, 1992).

UNPUBLISHED THESES

Ashgar, Mohamad Ali, 'Bangladeshi Community Organisations in East London: A Case Study Analysis' (University of Birmingham PhD, 1994).

Baxter, Susan Chui Chie, 'A Political Economy of the Ethnic Chinese Catering Industry' (Aston University PhD, 1988).

Bolam, Tabitha, 'Class and the Reception of European Street Musicians in Victorian London' (De Montfort University BA History, 2016).

Hall, Reginald Richard, 'Irish Music and Dance in London 1890–1970: A Sociocultural History' (University of Sussex PhD, 1994).

Jones, M. A., 'The Role of the United Kingdom in the Transatlantic Emigrant Trade, 1815–1875' (University of Oxford D.Phil. thesis, 1955).

Marshall, Edward Nicholas Philip, 'Ambivalent Images: A Survey of Jewish Involvement and Representation in the British Entertainment Industry, 1880–1980' (Royal Holloway, University of London PhD, 2010).

Smith, Elaine, 'East End Jews in Politics, 1918–1939: A Study in Class and Ethnicity' (Leicester University PhD, 1990).

WEBSITES

Arsenal Fan TV (AFTV), https://www.youtube.com/channel/UCBTy8j2cPy6zw68godcE7MQ

Arsenal Football Club, https://www.arsenal.com

Barry Hugman's Footballers, http://hugmansfootballers.com

BBC News, http://news.bbc.co.uk

Chelsea Football Club, https://www.chelseafc.com

Church Response for Refugees, https://www.forrefugees.uk

Cypriot Football League of England, http://www.kopaleague.com/l/fg/1_481600611.html

Electoral Commission, 'EU Referendum Results', https://www.electoralcommission.org.uk/find-information-by-subject/elections-and-referendums/past-elections-and-referendums/eu-referendum/electorate-and-count-information

Football Unites, Racism Divides, Ruth Johnson, Howard Holmes and Phil Vasili, 'South African Footballers in Britain', http://www.furd.org/default.asp?intPageID=22&intResourceID=90

Harden's London Restaurants, https://www.hardens.com

Island Lyrics, http://www.islandlyrics.com

KPMG, *Labour Migration in the Hospitality Sector: A KPMG Report for the British Hospitality Association* (2017), https://www.bha.org.uk/wordpress/wp-content/uploads/2017/05/BHA-EU-migration-final-report-170518-public-vSTC.pdf

Le Caprice, https://www.le-caprice.co.uk

'List of Ethnic Minority Politicians in the United Kingdom', https://en.wikipedia.org/wiki/List_of_ethnic_minority_politicians_in_the_United_Kingdom

London Assembly Members, https://www.london.gov.uk/people/assembly

Rasa Restaurants, http://rasarestaurants.com

BIBLIOGRAPHY

Sports People's Think Tank and Network Fare, 'Ethnic Minorities and Coaching in Elite Level Football in England: A Call to Action', 2014, http://thesptt.com/wp-content/uploads/2015/10/We-speak-with-one-voice-REPORT.pdf

Striking Women, 'The Grunwick Dispute', http://www.striking-women.org/module/striking-out/grunwick-dispute

Swadhinata Trust, https://www.swadhinata.org.uk

'This is Your Life', Jack Kid Berg, originally broadcast in 1987, https://www.youtube.com/watch?v=Ae_yky14xtI

UK Council for International Student Affairs, 'International (non-UK) Students in UK HE in 2016–17', https://ukcisa.org.uk/Research--Policy/Statistics/International-student-statistics-UK-higher-education

YOUGOV, 'Survey for Commission for Racial Equality', https://d25d2506sfb94s.cloudfront.net/today_uk_import/YG-Archives-lif-commracial-RacialEquality-040728.pdf

INDEX